EUROPEAN POLITICS TODAY

EUROPEAN POLITICS TODAY

SECOND EDITION

EDITORS

Gabriel A. Almond
Stanford University

Russell J. Dalton
University of California, Irvine

G. Bingham Powell, Jr.
University of Rochester

Longman

New York   San Francisco   Boston
London   Toronto   Sydney   Tokyo   Singapore   Madrid
Mexico City   Munich   Paris   Cape Town   Hong Kong   Montreal

Publisher: Priscilla McGeehon
Associate Editor: Anita Castro
Marketing Manager: Megan Galvin-Fak
Production Manager: Joseph Vella
Project Coordination, Text Design, and Electronic Page Makeup: Shepherd, Inc.
Senior Cover Design Manager: Nancy Danahy
Cover Designer: Kay Petronio
Senior Manufacturing Buyer: Dennis J. Para
Printer and Binder: Maple-Vail Book Manufacturing Group
Cover Printer: John P. Pow Company, Inc.

Library of Congress Cataloging-in-Publication Data
European politics today / editors Gabriel A. Almond, Russell J. Dalton,
    G. Bingham Powell.
        p.   cm.
    Includes index.
    ISBN 0-321-08612-0
    1. Europe. Western—Politics and government. 2. Europe—Politics and
government—1989- 3. Democracy—Europe.   4. Europe, Eastern—Politics and
government. 5. Democratization—Europe.   I. Almond, Gabriel Abraham, 1911-II.
Dalton, Russell J.   III. Powell, G. Bingham.

JN94.A58 E89 2001
320.94—dc21   2001029054

Please visit our website at http://www.ablongman.com

ISBN 0-321-08612-0

1 2 3 4 5 6 7 8 9 10—MA—04 03 02 01

CONTRIBUTORS

GABRIEL A. ALMOND
Stanford University

RUSSELL J. DALTON
University of California, Irvine

G. BINGHAM POWELL, JR.
University of Rochester

KATHLEEN MONTGOMERY
Illinois Wesleyan University

THOMAS F. REMINGTON
Emory University

RICHARD ROSE
University of Strathclyde, Glasgow

ALBERTA SBRAGIA
University of Pittsburgh

MARTIN A. SCHAIN
New York University

DONALD SHARE
University of Puget Sound

RAY TARAS
Tulane University

BRIEF CONTENTS

DETAILED CONTENTS

PREFACE

This new edition of *European Politics Today* brings up to date our introduction to the politics of the new Europe. Unlike most European politics textbooks, it bridges the East/West divide, celebrating the extraordinary changes of the last decade. A continent historically torn by division and conflict now encompasses 38 nations that are almost all democratic in reality or aspiration and oriented towards market, rather than command economies. Significant parts of this new Europe, including some countries of the former Soviet orbit, have begun the process of merging sovereignty in a European Union. This book recognizes the many implications of this unity, as well as the great diversity that still remains within Europe. The success of the first edition in spanning this East/West divide has led to this new edition.

Given its historical and cultural commonalities, Europe is a natural unit for an area studies approach to political science. Its nation-states have borrowed from each other and imitated each other, as well as competed against each other, for a very long time. Today, their economies and cultures are more closely interdependent than ever before. Europe's political cultures share many historical and political reference points. Its societies were all affected, in varying ways, by the Renaissance; by the Reformation and the subsequent religious wars; by the Enlightenment and the French Revolution; by the formation and later collapse of European-centered international empires; by the industrial revolution, beginning in England in mid-18th century (although most of Eastern and southern Europe came to this later); by fascism and communism; by the terrible wars of the twentieth century, and the Holocaust; and by the Cold War of the last decades. Learning about the general European setting helps us to understand the politics of each one of the particular European countries. Conversely, of course, the dynamic forces of the region cannot be understood independently of the politics of individual countries.

The Organization of This Book

As a text studying a specific geographic region, the book can be used in various ways. The simplest, of course, is to follow the chapters in consecutive order. We begin with three chapters that consider the European experience as a whole. Chapter 1 describes the geography and history of the contemporary nations, as well as the two critical features differentiating them: the sharply varying levels of economic development and the patterns of ethnic and religious division. The chapter also introduces the student to the theme of Europe's special relationship with democracy and democratization. While providing a sophisticated overview, we try to keep technical political science terms to a minimum. We suggest that all courses begin with this introductory chapter.

Chapters 2 and 3 discuss the nature, bases, and variety of democracy across the European systems. Chapter 2 examines how Europeans think and act in politics, focusing especially on the mutual expectations of citizens and policymakers in democracies. Chapter 3 offers an overview of the main features of constitutional arrangements, party systems, and policymaking processes in European democracies. These chapters assume no specific background in political science or the politics of the individual countries. They provide concepts and generalizations that can help students understand the working of politics in specific countries. Thus, it may be helpful for students to read and discuss these chapters, their concepts and generalizations, before turning to the individual countries presented in the rest of the book.

Other instructors may prefer to have students read and discuss the politics of one or more specific countries and then return to Chapter 2 and Chapter 3 to see how the detailed play of the political culture and political process in a given country fits into the broader concepts and patterns.

The country authors introduce their materials with sufficient clarity and autonomy to make it possible for the students to read them after, before, or concurrently with Chapters 2 and 3. Chapters 4 and 5 introduce the politics of two well-established democracies (Britain and France), while Chapters 6 and 7 describe the political systems in two more recently consolidated ones (Germany and Spain). The last three country chapters (Russia, Poland, and Hungary) describe political systems that began transitions to democratic politics in the 1990s, and for which the issues of democratic consolidation are paramount.

Chapter 11 describes the political system of the European Union. We think it makes the most sense to conclude with an account of this new and very complex political system, which coordinates in a confederal system the politics and policies of some fifteen European countries, with potential future members in Eastern Europe.

Finally, the book offers an appendix to help instructors coordinate the presentation of material in the introductory chapters and specific country chapters. The appendix outlines the framework of specific topics that are discussed in the introductory chapters and in each country study, indicating the pages where these topics are presented.

Europe and the Origin of Political Science

Modern political science began in the European Renaissance and Enlightenment, out of efforts to explain and interpret the political struggles of those centuries. Niccolo Machiavelli, concerned over the fate of republican Florence in the conflicts between the Vatican and the Holy Roman Empire, is viewed as the first modern political theorist. His little book, *The Prince,* was a manual for political leaders, telling them how to conduct themselves in foreign and domestic affairs, in such a way as to enhance their power. The French scholar Montesquieu applied what he had learned from the histories of Greece and Rome to the political institutions of eighteenth-century France and England and is viewed as the first great political sociologist and comparativist in modern times.

Political studies have spread in synchrony with the three democratic waves described by Samuel Huntington.[1] Modern political studies originated in the countries of the "first wave"—in England and the old Commonwealth, the United States, and Western Europe. In the nineteenth and early twentieth centuries a stellar array of European scholars—Alexis de Tocqueville, John Stuart Mill, Karl Marx, Herbert Spencer, Vilfredo Pareto, Max Weber, Emile Durkheim, Gaetano Mosca, Moissaye Ostrogorski, Otto Hintze, and many others sought to make sense of European history as it had unfolded over time. Spencer, Marx, Weber, and Durkheim were the great interpreters of industrialization, secularization, and modernization; Weber and Hintze captured the essence of the modern state and bureaucracy. Tocqueville, Mill, Marx, Pareto, Mosca, and Michels set the terms of the ideological conflict of the twentieth century among liberal and social democracy, revolutionary socialism, and fascism.

The European scholarly community eventually extended to other parts of the world, not cumulatively but in response to the ideological, political, and military perturbations of twentieth-century history. As American culture matured in the late nineteenth and early twentieth centuries, the European root stock flourished and "mutated," exploring phenomena peculiar to the American setting (the "boss and the machine," the "lobby" and "pressure groups") and bringing a participatory and populist culture to bear on the study of political institutions and processes. The ideology of technological progress in the United States gave its political science a push in the direction of empirical rigor and quantitative methodology.

The "reverse wave" of fascism and Nazism uprooted well-established scholarly traditions in such countries as France, Germany, Italy, and Poland. When rights and freedoms were suppressed in Nazi-dominated Europe in the 1930s and 1940s, Europe's scholarly tradition either went underground, or was carried away by its intellectual exiles primarily to the United States. In America this tradition contributed to the flowering of social and political science scholarship in the decades of the Cold War. From its roots in America and Europe, scholarly research on politics spread wherever peoples became free to participate in political life, to carry on research, to publish and to teach.

The second wave of democratization in the 1950s gave new impetus to political science and especially to the application of systematic analysis of politics in new areas of the world. This stimulated the comparative study of political cultures and the effects of different levels of modernization on political processes.

However, from the end of World War II through the late 1980s, the Soviet control over Eastern Europe and its imposition of authoritarian communist systems and command control economies created a fundamental division between Eastern and Western Europe. Academic scholarship reflected that division in its research and in the courses offered to students. Eastern European area studies and Western European area studies focused on different problems and used, necessarily, very different research methods. Naturally, there were correspondingly different groups of courses for students taught by the scholars from these contrasting communities.

The culmination of the "third wave" of democracy in Eastern Europe and the former Soviet Union itself has stimulated a reunification of "European" scholarship. The countries of Eastern, Central, and Western Europe and the scholars who study them have begun to recognize and reassert their common heritage and respond to their geographic proximity. The 38 nations of the new Europe aspire to political democracy. The ideas and research tools developed to study the culture, institutions, and processes of Western Europe are being rapidly assimilated and applied to countries previously inaccessible to them. Conversely, the new democratic experiences in Eastern and Central Europe can lead to richer understanding of the experience with democracy in the West. It is thus possible, after the 50 years of division imposed by Soviet control, to speak and write of a common European experience.

This book responds to the dissolving of the barriers between Eastern and Western Europe by offering teacher and student the opportunity to apply political science analysis on a truly European scale. We can appreciate the commonalities and yet take advantage of the differences across Europe. We can apply the theories of modern political science in analysis of countries sharing the common European experience, but recently differentiated by history into quite different introductions to democratic politics and its concomitants.

In Western Europe we can examine how politics functions in established democracies. Our analyses show the richness and variety of the democratic experience, enabling the comparison of the politics of consensual and conflictual cultures, majoritarian and proportional institutional rules, two-party and multiparty electoral competition, interventionist or market-dominated economic policies. We can also examine how democracy has taken root in several Western European nations, such as Germany and Spain, within the last 50 years.

In Eastern Europe a decade of experience since the collapse of Soviet domination provides remarkable opportunities to use modern political science techniques to observe the interaction between political culture and the formation of new political institutions. The new party systems of Eastern Europe provide natural experiments where we can examine processes of forming identities, organizations, and strategies. Furthermore, Eastern Europeans are experimenting with new forms of democratic institutions and new political-economic combinations. Of course, democracy itself faces severe challenges in some parts of Eastern Europe, with fundamental consequences for both democratic theory and world politics.

This book also builds upon the highly successful model of Almond, Powell, Strøm, and Dalton's introductory text, *Comparative Politics Today*.[2] We use the same basic well-tested conceptual framework in describing the cultures and structures of the political system. Four of our country chapters (England, France, Germany, and Russia) are derived from that text, although completely revised for this new volume. However, it is not necessary to understand the formal theoretical framework of *Comparative Politics Today* in order to study the European experience in this volume.

New to This Edition

- **"Current political issues"** sections at the beginning of each country chapter discuss the contemporary problems facing that nation. These issue sections help to intrigue students in the material and set them up to understand how the political systems in each country address the problems.
- **Example boxes** have been added to each chapter providing students with current and topical examples that illustrate key concepts and theories in the text, increases student interest, and adds visual appeal to the layout of the book.
- A **"Country Bio"** at the start of each chapter gives students a quick factual overview of the nation: its size, social composition, leadership, etc.
- **Internet links** have been added to the end of most chapters, enabling students to locate government agencies, news media and other online information sources for the nations discussed in the book.

Acknowledgments

The development of a book requires the support and advice of many people, and we want to acknowledge their contributions. Because this book builds on the success of *Comparative Politics Today*, we have benefited from the contributors to this global introduction to comparative politics; we have benefited indirectly from the experiences of our predecessor volume and directly by including four of its authors in this new book. As editors, we owe a special debt to the contributors to *European Politics Today*. They have produced excellent accounts of politics in their nations of specialization, linked to the larger issues of comparative political studies. We want to acknowledge our debt to their written contribution and our admiration for their tolerance of our frequent editorial requests. It has been a pleasure working with each of them.

The support of the publisher is also essential to a book's success. Eric Stano and Anita Castro, became our supportive editors at Longman and carried this book through to completion.

We also profited from the advice of many colleagues. Patrick O'Neal at the University of Puget Sound was the first to use a manuscript copy of the first edition in a class, and generously provided us with thoughtful and useful comments from his experience. In addition, the following colleagues read all or portions of the first edition manuscript and offered their advice: Paul Pierson, Harvard University; Thomas Lancaster, Emory University; Minton F. Goldman, Northeastern University; Larry Elowitz, George College and State University; Neil J. Mitchell, University of New Mexico; Gunther Mega, Western Michigan University; Pauletta Otis, University of Northern Colorado; Michael Baum, Valdosta State; Oliver Woshinsky, University of Southern Maine; Susan Scarrow, University of Houston; Lawrence Sullivan, Adelphi University; and Lyndelle Fairlie, San Diego State University.

The second edition benefited from the comments of our own students at UC Irvine and the University of Rochester who used this book. We also received scholarly reviews from John G. Francis, University of Utah and Bob Switky, Suny-Brockport. Gail McElroy provided valuable research assistance for the editors. Andrew Drummond carefully assembled the index and the analytic appendix. The book is much improved because of all of these contributions.

Supplements

- Microsoft® Encarta® Interactive World Atlas CD-ROM. Available at a significant discount when ordered packaged with the text. Contact your local Allyn & Bacon/Longman representative for more information.

European Politics Today marks a new era in Europe's history: a continent comprised of free, democratic and market-oriented societies. We also hope that this new edition will continue the progress toward a new era in the study of European politics, where a comprehensive study of the European political experience replaces a curriculum dividing Europe in half. *European Politics Today* will help students and scholars understand the new Europe and the contribution this region continues to make to the development of political science.

✑ NOTES ✑

1. Samuel Huntington, *The Third Wave: Democratization in the Late Twentieth Century* (Norman, OK: University of Oklahoma Press, 1981).
2. Gabriel A. Almond, G. Bingham Powell, Kaare Strom, and Russell Dalton, eds., *Comparative Politics Today: A World View*, 7th ed. (New York: Addison Wesley Longman, 2000).
3. For those wanting to learn more about this general introductory framework, see Gabriel A. Almond, G. Bingham Powell, Kaare Strom, and Russell Dalton, *Comparative Politics: A Theoretical Framework*, 3rd ed. (New York: Addison Wesley Longman, 2001).

Gabriel A. Almond

Russell J. Dalton

G. Bingham Powell, Jr.

CHAPTER 1

THE EUROPEAN CONTEXT

Enlightened Europeans for centuries have dreamed of a prosperous continent leading the world in the pursuit of the arts of peace. One of the most fateful expressions of this aspiration came from Mikhail Gorbachev, the last General Secretary of the Soviet Union, in his book *Perestroika (Opening)* which appeared in 1987, early in his tenure. To a then divided and unbelieving world, Gorbachev wrote the first words promising an end to the "Cold War" that had divided Europe into two nuclear armed camps for the better part of half a century. "Europe from the Atlantic to the Urals is a cultural-historical entity united by the common heritage of the Renaissance and Enlightenment. . . . Europe's historic chance and its future lie in peaceful cooperation between the states of that continent."[1]

This image of a cooperative and peaceful Europe moves us because it contrasts so sharply with the reality of Europe's past—not only the tensions and brutalities of the Cold War, but the two great wars and the barbarisms and holocausts of this century, the unremitting smaller wars and imperialist conquests of preceding centuries. Historic Europe has been an ambivalent force—destructive and creative at the same time.

On the creative side, the dominant forms of political and economic organization in the world today—the bureaucratic state, the industrial market economy, and representative democracy—had their origins in Europe. They were created in a tempestuous half millennium marked by intense divisions and conflict. The modern state was shaped in a series of costly wars stretching from the seventeenth century to the twentieth, culminating in the tragic and bloody devastations of World Wars I and II. The industrial *market economy* emerged in Protestant Europe and America, transforming the social and class structure of societies, and creating the tensions out of which came the democratic impulses of the nineteenth and twentieth centuries. Representative democracy traces its modern origins to the struggle during the seventeenth to nineteenth centuries in Britain to reform and democratize parliament, and to the American and French Revolutions of 1776 and 1789. The first wave of democratization in the modern world was confined to Europe and a few of Europe's former colonies.

Europe's influence on the contemporary world has been far out of proportion to its size and was not foreshadowed in its earlier history. In the Middle Ages and early Renaissance, Christian Europe was relatively backward and defensive, divided into a number of decentralized kingdoms, hundreds of principalities, dukedoms, baronies, and "free

1

cities," and in the thrall of a hierarchical and corrupt Roman Catholic Church establishment. The dynamic forces of Islam reached into Spain from North Africa and into southern Europe from Asia Minor.

In the subsequent three centuries, the Renaissance, the Reformation, the Enlightenment, and the Industrial Revolution transformed Europe in fundamental ways—in its aspirations and ideas, its technology, its social structure, and in its political organization. Europe became concentrated into a small number of expansive, bureaucratically centralized states, drawing upon a growing industry and commercial agriculture, with professional and technologically sophisticated armies and navies. By the end of the nineteenth century, Europe was the proactive continent, with the rest of the world reactive. In the twentieth century, and especially since the end of World War II, Europe (now joined with its North American offspring) has relaxed its hold, but not without leaving its values and institutions implanted in the rest of the world, where they have combined and interacted with indigenous forms.

The Purpose and Organization of This Book

This book celebrates a new Europe. Europe has historically been a continent torn by division and conflict. The development of European integration in postwar Western Europe and the end of the East/West Cold War division have, we hope, altered this historic pattern. Democratic in reality or in aspiration, oriented toward market rather than command control economies, the 38 nations of this new Europe are no longer divided ideologically or pitted against each other in unremitting war. Significant parts of this new Europe, including some countries of the former Soviet orbit, have begun the process of merging sovereignties in a European Union.

European Politics Today differs from nearly all other European politics textbooks by bridging the East/West divide. This is a book about Europe, not just Western Europe or Eastern Europe. Our first goal is to provide students and scholars with an introduction to the politics of Europe as a cultural and political region. The nations of Europe have varied histories, but they share common experiences in the social, economic, and political developments that shaped contemporary Europe. As we have already suggested, they were all affected in differing degrees by the Renaissance, the Reformation, the *Enlightenment,* and the Industrial Revolution. They shared actively or passively in the historical experience of the rising nationalism of the nineteenth century, and in the Communism, Fascism, and the terrible wars of the twentieth century. The European experience is also relevant to Americans who live in a modern democracy that originated as a transplanted European fragment, which could not avoid involvement in Europe's politics and wars, and which hosted successive generations of exiles fleeing Europe's turmoils.

Our second goal is to introduce many of the concepts and theories of modern political science by showing how the institutions and processes of democracy work in the nations of contemporary Europe. Modern political science was formed in trying to grasp and explain the workings of the political and economic structures that originated in Europe and have spread to the rest of the world: the bureaucratic state, the industrial market economy, and representative democratic government. Thus the unique European experience is relevant to anyone trying to understand and utilize modern political science. We use the concepts and tools of political science to examine the richness and variety of the democratic experience, its values, institutions, and processes, as they work in many well-established democratic systems and as they are being initiated in some new democracies.

European Politics Today contains three introductory chapters, eight chapters presenting individual European political systems, and two appendices for documentation and comparison. The three introductory chapters set the stage for understanding the political systems of Europe today. This first chapter seeks to place the European nations geographically and in the context of European history, recalling the emergence of contemporary nations through centuries of conflict and consolidation. Relations between European nations continue to be an important part of the politics of each nation, given new possibilities by the end of Soviet domination of Eastern Europe and new forms, especially by the organizations of the European Union. This chapter also discusses two critical features of each country's domestic environment that help create different problems and possibilities for its politics: national economic conditions and ethnic division or unity. In conclusion, the chapter introduces a continuing theme of this book: Europe's special relationship with democracy and democratization.

Concerns about the nature, bases, and varieties of democracy in Europe also help shape the subsequent chapters. Chapter 2 provides an overview of how Europeans think and act politically. It focuses especially on what democracy expects of its citizens and what citizens in old and new democracies expect of their governments. Chapter 3 offers a similar overview of the main features of European democratic constitutional arrangements, party systems, and policymaking processes. Appendix A provides data describing some features of the environment and the constitution in each of the 38 individual nations of Europe.

Chapters 4–10 apply the general themes and concepts introduced in Chapters 1–3 to specific European political systems, including some well-established democracies (England and France), some more recently consolidated ones (Germany and Spain), and some grappling with the early stages of transition to democratic politics (Russia, Poland, and Hungary). The chapters on specific political systems conclude in Chapter 11 with analysis of the arrangements and political processes of the European Community, taking shape as an increasingly important and complex political system in its own right and one which influences all the other European systems.

Appendix B outlines the framework of specific topics that are discussed in the introductory chapters and in each country study, indicating the pages where these topics are treated. This appendix makes it possible to pursue and compare general topics from the introductory chapters across the political systems treated in the book and to return easily from the country discussions to the introductory presentation.

The Emergence of Today's Europe

Europe is a large peninsula (with subpeninsulas and associated islands) extending out of the Eurasian landmass, with its eastern border in the Ural Mountains and its western border on the Atlantic. It ranges from the Arctic Ocean in the north, to the Mediterranean Sea on the south, almost touching Africa at the Straits of Gibraltar. It is the next to smallest of the seven continents, larger than Australia, but smaller than Antarctica—roughly four million square miles in extent, with some three-quarters of a billion inhabitants.

The major changes in the political map of Europe, up until the most recent ones, have been formalized in a series of treaties following major European wars in the last several centuries. The *Peace of Westphalia* terminated the "Thirty Years Wars" of religion (1618–1648), triggered by the *Protestant Reformation*. Figure 1.1 presents Europe in 1648 as it was organized following the Peace of Westphalia. The whole of southeastern Europe with its Hungarians, Romanians, Bulgarians, Greeks, and other nationalities lived behind the veil of the Ottoman Empire, the domain of the Turkish sultanate. Central Europe was just beginning to take shape out of the mist of the Holy Roman Empire, in the form of Austria, Prussia, Switzerland, and Poland. Northern Europe was dominated by a huge Sweden swollen from its victories in the religious wars. The Europe that was to come was foreshadowed in a tier of countries bordering on the Atlantic and hence with maritime access to the rest of the world—Spain, Portugal, England, the Netherlands, and France—whose early achievement of coherence as states enabled them to become the architects of world imperialism from the seventeenth to the nineteenth centuries.

The *Treaty of Vienna* terminated the Napoleonic Wars following the French Revolution (1796–1815). The Europe that emerged after the French Revolution and the Napoleonic Wars reflected the dissolution of the Holy Roman Empire and the retreat of the Ottoman Empire toward its Asia Minor roots. Prussia, later to be Germany, had taken major steps to powerful statehood. Poland and Finland were gobbled up by Russia, as that enormous empire moved westward into the "Holy Alliance" of post-Napoleonic Europe. Much of the politics of nineteenth-century Europe was concerned with accommodating an increasingly powerful and expansive

FIGURE 1.1   Europe in 1648

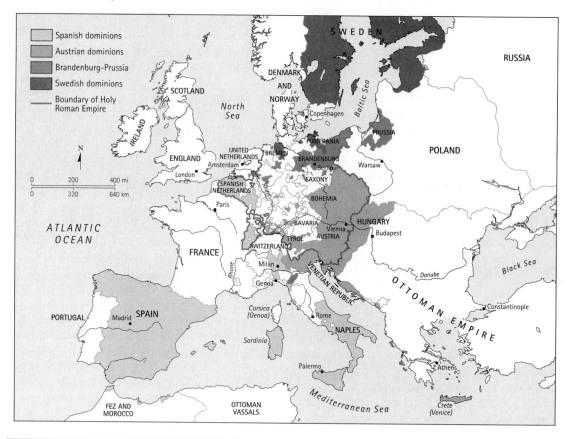

Prussian-dominated Germany, and an Italian state uniting the kingdoms and principalities of the Italian peninsula. The Ottoman Empire earned its reputation as the "sick man of Europe" losing a part of Greece in the early nineteenth century, and Bulgaria in the early twentieth.

The *Treaty of Versailles* terminated World War I (1914–1918), following on the great power competition of the late nineteenth and early twentieth centuries. World War I was hard on empires; the defeated Ottoman Empire was driven back to its Turkish base and the multi-ethnic Austro-Hungarian Empire was split into Austria, Hungary, Yugoslavia, and Czechoslovakia. The defeated Russian Empire—now Bolshevik Russia—was pressed back from its

control of Finland, Estonia, Latvia, Lithuania, and Poland. Europe during the "between the wars" decades was much like contemporary Europe in national membership, with the exception that Ukraine, Belarus, and Moldavia were still integral parts of Russia.

World War II was brought on by the aggressions of the *Axis* (Nazi Germany, Fascist Italy, and authoritarian Japan). Almost all of Western Europe, with the notable exception of the United Kingdom, was overpowered, brutalized, and "coordinated" by Nazi armies in the first years of World War II. With great slaughter and destruction the hold of Nazi Germany on Europe was broken and pressed back in 1942–1945, by the bloodied troops of the Soviet

FIGURE 1.2 Europe in the Cold War

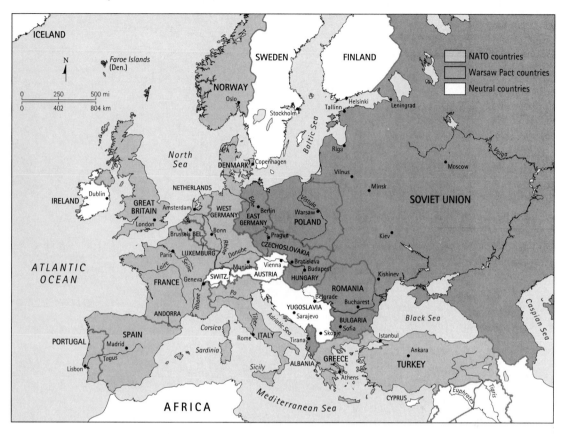

Union from the east, and the armed forces of the United States, Britain, and their allies from the west. The line demarcating the junction of the Soviet and the Anglo-American forces in the middle of Germany in 1945 became the *Iron Curtain* of the second half of the twentieth century. World War II did not culminate in a single set of settlements as in the earlier cases, but in individual treaties among the combatants.

Figure 1.2 depicts the Europe of the *Cold War*—a sharply divided continent with its eastern part under political control and military occupation by a powerful, nuclear-armed Soviet Union, and with a nuclear-tipped western part tightly drawn together under American leadership in the NATO alliance.

Europe was frozen in what seemed like a permanent confrontation.

The most recent remaking of the European map resulted from a series of independent and relatively nonviolent acts of individual countries in the former Soviet orbit. Figure 1.3 presents a map of contemporary Europe after the end of the Cold War, when the Soviet Union withdrew from Eastern Europe and split into 15 independent political entities. Four European nations (Russia, Belarus, Ukraine, and Moldova) formed from the dissolution of the Soviet Union itself in 1991. The Baltic countries that had been independent between the two World Wars—Estonia, Latvia, and Lithuania—reasserted their independence after the collapse of

FIGURE 1.3   Europe Today

the Soviet bloc. Five countries emerged from the dissolution of Yugoslavia in 1991–1992: Slovenia, Croatia, Macedonia, Bosnia-Herzegovina, and a rump Yugoslavia containing Serbia, Montenegro, and a predominately Albanian Kosovo. Two nations emerged from the former Czechoslovakia in 1993: the Czech Republic and Slovakia. With patience you should be able to count 38 countries in Figure 1.3.

We still think of Europe as divided into Western and Eastern parts, a view surviving from the Cold War and Winston Churchill's dramatic image of the "iron curtain," stretching across the middle of the continent. From this perspective, 19 of the 38 countries of contemporary Europe are the East European successors to the old Soviet Communist bloc. The remainder, what we think of as Western

Europe, includes considerable parts that are not geographically "western." It includes a southern tier of countries extending from Portugal to Greece and Cyprus. In longitudinal terms Greece is more "eastern" than Poland and the Czech Republic. Similarly, the northern European countries of Finland, Sweden, Norway, and Denmark are as far to the East as Hungary and Croatia. In a geographical sense, "western" Europe includes Iceland, Ireland, the United Kingdom, France, the Netherlands, Belgium, and Luxembourg, while Germany, Austria, and Switzerland are Central European countries. In this book, however, we most frequently refer to "Eastern" versus "Western" Europe, because of the important legacies of economic conditions (discussed in this chapter), public opinion (Chapter 2), and democratic institutions (Chapter 3) that were bequeathed by the very different twentieth-century experiences of the countries identified by this "geographic" division.

European Integration

The state- and nation-building history of Europe would not be complete without introducing recent important trends toward integration. Europe in the last decades has been not only disaggregating, but combining and uniting for general as well as specific purposes. The industrialized countries of Western Europe, after centuries of costly and destructive wars, found that the peaceful and free exchange of ideas, products, and persons across national boundaries greatly enhances productivity. Step by step in recent decades Western Europeans created a common *market economy*, and they are currently poised at the threshold of even greater integration.

The *European Economic Community (EEC)* was formed in 1957 and originally consisted of six countries: France, Germany, Italy, Belgium, the Netherlands, and Luxembourg.[2] The European Community expanded in the 1970s and 1980s to include Britain, Ireland, Denmark, Greece, Spain, and Portugal. The membership expanded again in 1995 to include Austria, Finland, and Sweden, and the reformed organization renamed itself the *European Union (EU)*.[3] In 1997 the EU recommended beginning detailed negotiations about membership with a number of Eastern European countries that had applied for consideration. In this process of integration the Europeans have been creating regional institutions with limited policymaking power and with resources to address common projects as the provision of development aid to poorer countries and regions. The European Union might be called a "confederate state" in which the governing institutions have policymaking authority, but they must rely on the member governments for enforcement, implementation, and revenue. (See Chapter 11 for a more complete account of the European Union's origin and functioning.)

Another change in the international structure involves security policy. The international security arrangements put in place on the Soviet and Western sides during the Cold War no longer fit the contemporary ideological and geopolitical situation. The *North Atlantic Treaty Organization (NATO 1949)* was formed early in the Cold War under American leadership in order to mobilize Western European countries against the communist threat. The Soviet bloc formed the *Warsaw Pact* (1955) to counter NATO; the *Council for Mutual Economic Assistance (COMECON 1959)* coordinated the eastern economies in response to the European Union. Both the Warsaw Pact and COMECON dissolved with the end of the Cold War. The Soviet Union itself has been dissolved and replaced by 15 independent republics associated in the *Commonwealth of Independent States (CIS)* that includes all of the former Soviet republics with the exception of Lithuania, Latvia, Estonia, and Georgia. The functions and scope of the Russia-sponsored CIS are still unspecified.

The Western international organizations of the EU and NATO are still in operation, but they are searching for new equilibria in scope and function. The European Union has invited Poland, Hungary, the Czech Republic, Estonia, and Slovenia to begin the accession process; others are on the waiting list. While NATO is currently playing an important role in the Bosnian and Kosovan crises, it is not clear what that organization's security functions will be in the new Europe. The close Cold War security relationship of the United States to Europe is no longer justified by a "Soviet" threat. At the same time, three of the former members of the Soviet bloc—Poland, Hungary, and the Czech Republic—have been included in the NATO security system. Russia opposes these trends, viewing them as a threat to isolate it internationally. Thus Eastern Europe is a region of internal and international instability as these formerly authoritarian and dominated countries remodel their political and economic arrangements and reach out for international security.

Describing Europe: Large and Small Countries

The range of variation in the size of European countries is enormous. Figure 1.4 provides a spatial image of the differences in population for twelve Western and Eastern European countries, from largest to

FIGURE 1.4   Population of Selected Western and Eastern European Countries in 1998

FIGURE 1.4   Population of Selected Western and Eastern European Countries in 1998

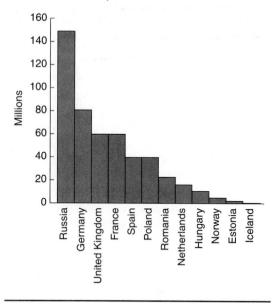

Source: World Bank, *World Development Indicators 2000;* retrieved May 31, 2000 from http://www.worldbank.org/data/wdi2000/pdfs/tab2_1.pdf

smallest.[4] Russia with nearly 150 million inhabitants is represented by the tall column on the left. Some 32 million inhabitants of Russia live east of the Urals, in the Asian part of the country. Even if we deduct these eastern residents, European Russia is still the giant of Europe with a population 50 percent larger than that of Germany, which is the second most populous European country. Iceland with fewer than 300,000 inhabitants is practically invisible on the extreme right of the figure. The population of European Russia is four hundred times that of Iceland. The United Kingdom is the third highest column with about 59 million residents. France is fourth in population size; Spain and Poland are fifth and sixth. Hungary is a relatively small nation, with around 10 million inhabitants.

Grouping our 38 countries according to population, we have nine large European countries with populations of 20 million and over. Among the Western European countries, Germany is the giant, followed by France, the United Kingdom, and Italy,

with Spain not far behind. On the Eastern side the large countries are Russia, Ukraine, Poland, and Romania. There are 15 medium-sized countries ranging from 5 million to about 15 million, 9 of these in Western Europe and the remaining 6 in Eastern Europe. The 14 smallest European countries have populations that range from fewer than 5 million inhabitants to under 1 million each for tiny Cyprus, Luxembourg, and Iceland. (All 38 countries and their populations are enumerated in Appendix A.)[5]

When we compare European countries according to their geographic area, we get a somewhat different pattern. European Russia comes out on top in both population and geographic size; the ratio of its area to the second largest nation is even greater than that of its population. European Russia is only half again as populous as Germany; it has eight times the area of France, its nearest area competitor on the European continent. The larger West European countries with areas exceeding 100,000 square miles include France, Spain, Sweden, Norway, Germany, Finland, and Italy. The United Kingdom is slightly under the hundred thousand mark. The Eastern giants are European Russia, Ukraine, and Poland. Romania is just below the hundred thousand mark.

These two magnitudes of population and area do not in themselves explain much about the politics and policies of these European states. Size, of course, makes a difference in warfare, as Napoleon and Hitler discovered on the wintry steppes of Russia. It also makes a difference in the availability of resources, in problems of governmental centralization, and the like. Similarly, the relation between area and population is important. America had a frontier for growth and expansion. Asian Russia has been a frontier for that country. The economic development choices of the Netherlands and other densely populated countries were powerfully constrained by their population patterns.

One of the most important population questions is the rate of increase, a fact that has important implications for economic growth. The most recent data show that Europe has the smallest population growth rate of all the world regions. Between 1965 and 1998, Europe had only a 0.4 percent average annual increase, in comparison with the Middle

East and North Africa (2.8), Sub-Saharan Africa (2.7), South Asia (2.2), and Latin America and the Caribbean (2.1).[6] This bodes well for continued economic growth in Europe, since gains in economic productivity will increase per capita income, rather than being spread among an ever-increasing population.

The sheer magnitude of a country's economy can also be important, since it tells us about a country's size in terms of international trade and its status in the international community. Germany is at the top among the European countries with a $2,200 billion economy as of the late 1990s, contrasted with an Albanian economy of around $3 billion. The other large Western European economies—France, the United Kingdom, and Italy—generate over $1,200 billion each year, while the larger Eastern European economies range from the $330 billion mark for Russia, $151 billion for Poland, to around $50 billion for the Czech Republic, Ukraine, and Hungary. Thus we can think of large and small countries in terms of economic size as well as population size. By this measure Germany is over six times the size of Russia, despite having half the population.

Describing Europe: Rich and Poor Countries

The economic measures most vital to internal politics are expressed in relationship to population size: what occupations divide the citizens in the labor force; how productive are their efforts; how is their collective income to be divided? Table 1.1 presents a comparison of the economic performance of those Western and Eastern European countries that are treated in depth in this book (plus Romania for purposes of comparison). Additional data on all European countries are contained in Appendix A.

As a starting point, the last column in the table underscores the fact that the economies of Eastern Europe still have substantial agricultural sectors in comparison with the heavily industrialized and urbanized societies of Western Europe. In Germany, France, and the United Kingdom, the agricultural percentage of the labor force is 5 percent or less. Even in Spain slightly less than 10 percent of the labor force is now employed in agriculture, a figure matched only by the most developed Eastern European economies, such as Hungary. In contrast, more than a fifth of Poland's labor force is employed in agriculture, while Romania, like many other Eastern European nations, retains an even larger percentage. Even Russia still has a substantial agricultural labor force. The relative size of the agricultural labor force is significant for two reasons. On the one hand, a larger agricultural labor force is usually an indicator of lower economic development and productivity. Highly productive modern economies manage their agricultural needs with quite small farm populations, even if the nature of their land and skills make this sector valuable. On the other hand, large agricultural sectors usually are interested in promoting and protecting agricultural products, and these interests find expression in political organizations likely to resist economic modernization policies.

There are two measures of income and productivity in Table 1.1: per capita *Gross National Product (GNP)* and *Purchasing Power Parity (PPP)*. Both of these measures take national currency statistics and recalculate them to allow for international comparisons. Per capita GNP measures the aggregate size of the economy; the international recalculations are based on financial exchange rates. Conversion rates are not necessarily accurate representations of what can be purchased by a given currency in food, shelter, clothing, and other amenities in a nation. PPP attempts to measure the same size of the economy per capita, based on the purchasing power of the currency, its capacity to buy goods and services in the domestic market. Most economists consider PPP to be a more appropriate estimate of personal income, although it is more difficult to measure.[7]

If we use the exchange rate version of GNP to measure personal income, the ratio between Germany at the top and Romania at the bottom is 20 to 1. If we use the PPP, the contrast between the richest and poorest of these eight nations is "only" 4 to 1. The PPP figure is closer to the reality of economic welfare in Europe today. The PPP statistics indicate that the economic contrasts between Eastern and Western Europe are striking, although less formidable than implied by per-capita GNP statistics. The

TABLE 1.1   Aspects of Economic Development for Selected European Countries

	Population (millions)	Average Inflation (%) 1990–1998	Per Capita GNP 1994	GDP Growth (%) 1990–1998	Per Capita PPP 1998	Percent of Labor Force in Agriculture (%)
Germany	82.1	2.6	$26,570	1.5	$22,026	4
France	58.8	1.9	24,210	1.5	21,214	5
United Kingdom	59.1	3.0	21,410	2.2	20,314	2
Spain	39.3	4.2	14,100	1.9	15,960	9
Russia	146.9	137.0	2,260	−7.0	6,180	14
Hungary	10.1	22.7	4,510	0.5	9,832	8
Poland	38.7	30.8	3,910	4.6	7,543	20
Romania	22.5	118.5	1,360	−0.7	5,572	39

Source: World Bank, *World Development Indicators 2000;* retrieved May 31, 2000 from http://www.worldbank.org/data/wdi2000/pdfs/tab1_1.pdf, tab4_16.pdf, 4_1.pdf, 1_3.pdf, 2_4.pdf. The inflation measure is the change in the consumer price index (CPI).

average PPP among the nations of Western Europe in 1998 was about $22,000, while in Eastern Europe it was about $6,000. Hungary's average personal income is a little less than one-half that of Germany and France, and roughly two-thirds of Spain. Russia and Poland have economies yielding about one-third of those of Germany and France. These differences, while large, are within the range of what can be overcome in time through human effort, political organization and will, and the disciplined power of constructive policies. Japan, the East Asian "Tiger" countries (Taiwan, South Korea, Singapore), are examples of successful development that has overcome handicaps of this magnitude, although the crises in East Asia in the late 1990s brought out vulnerabilities of their rapidly growing economies.

Table 1.1 also shows that in terms of economic growth the gap between Western and most Eastern European economies was growing, not diminishing, in the 1990–1998 period.[8] All the Western European countries had positive economic growth rates for the 1990s; the average country grew annually at about 2 percent. In contrast, most Eastern European countries struggled with the very difficult problems of transition from communist "command control" economies to market economies. The average country declined nearly 2½ percent a year. The

Eastern European average conceals great differences, moreover, in success in managing the economic transition. Poland (Chapter 9) is by far the most successful Eastern European economy; its average gain of 4.5 percent per year was larger than the gains of most Western European countries. By the end of the decade seven Eastern European countries were showing positive average growth numbers for the decade, with strong gains in recent years after a difficult beginning. As we see in Table 1.1, Hungary (Chapter 10) was among these, with an average gain of .5 percent a year.

While a few other Eastern European countries, like Romania, are close to attaining positive growth in the decade, most lag badly. Bulgaria, Belarus, and the three Baltic states lost 2–6 percent yearly in the 1990s. Russia (Chapter 8,) whose sheer size and military power inevitably imply great influence in the region, lost an average of 7 percent a year in its GDP; the figures for Moldova and Ukraine are even worse. In much of Eastern Europe citizens are not as well off today in purely economic terms as they were under communism (a topic further discussed in Chapter 2). If we add inflationary statistics to the economic growth picture, they increase our sense of concern.[9] Table 1.1 indicates that for the period from 1990–1998 Russia averaged an *annual* rate of inflation of 137 percent; Romania's average was

118 percent; Poland's, about 30 percent; and Hungary's, 23 percent. The bulk of these price increases directly followed from the economic transitions of the late 1980s and early 1990s, and in many countries they have come down in recent years. But western inflation rates are uniformly much lower; the worst inflation rate in the West (Spain at 4.2 percent) is still half of the lowest rate among the Eastern European cases. The data for Eastern Europe are troubling. We would anticipate that governments in poor or middle income countries confronted with growth problems of this kind would encounter serious discontent, and that some of the new democratic institutions of these countries would be running into rough waters.

Democratic Policies and Welfare in Europe

Economic conditions and public policies work together in shaping the welfare of citizens and, in turn, their satisfactions or frustrations with democratic politics. In general, the public policies that have emerged in the wealthy democratic societies of Western Europe have responded to the desires of their citizens for extensive social "safety nets"; substantial public sectors that include, for example, government-run public transit systems; and relative economic equality. (For evidence on Europeans' expectations about policy, see Chapter 2.) Governments have also been concerned with the economic problems of unemployment, inflation, and growth, which tend to worry voters in all modern societies. In recent years governments have also been responding to pressure from citizens and Green parties to pay more attention to the environment.

Various social safety net factors, such as unemployment benefits, social security, and medical care, tend to be much more extensive and more thoroughly publicly financed in most European countries than in the United States. Historically, the European societies developed these systems earlier and in many countries they were markedly extended by the reconstruction efforts required after the two world wars. Massive public involvement in housing was also stimulated by postwar reconstruction and today remains a prominent feature in many Euro-

pean nations. Education, on the other hand, was an earlier focus in the United States and only in recent years have Western European countries begun to offer higher education to more than a small elite.

The extensive social services are largely responsible for the greater size of government in proportion to the private sectors of the society in most of Western Europe. In the early 1990s the median current government expenditure in Western Europe was around 45 percent of the gross national product (compared with around 35 percent in the United States). However, there is a substantial variation in Western Europe, with government spending in Switzerland similar to that of the United States but approaching 60 percent of GNP in Denmark and Sweden. The size of the welfare effort is shaped by partisan ideology and party control of government, as well as by the interest group systems, bureaucratic traditions, and state capacity.[10] In the 1990s budgetary pressures resulted in some cutbacks in the size of the public sectors.

Substantial differences in the size of the public sector are also shaped by the degree of a government's direct operation of economic enterprises, a factor that is driven to some extent by past and present party control of government. For example, in the early 1980s conservative governments sold off substantial government enterprises in Britain and Germany (privatization), while a socialist government was acquiring them in France. More recently, market-dominated economies and competition have seemed to yield superior economic performance, increasing privatization trends in many countries.

The Eastern European countries began their democratic experience in the early 1990s with controlled economies that guaranteed some kind of employment for all able-bodied citizens of working age, fixed prices for goods and services, ensured relative income equality, and provided welfare systems that promised security for the young, the old, and those unable to work. Most of these countries also had great shortages of consumer goods, poor economic productivity, and a standard of living far behind their Western European counterparts. Economic dissatisfaction was a large factor in disillusionment with the communist governments.

Box 1.1   Varieties of Capitalism?

A group of scholars engaged in cross-national studies of "political economy" distinguish between varieties of capitalism—on the one hand Organized Market Economies (OME), and on the other, Liberal Market Economies (LME). The Liberal Market Economies stress the value of market competition in setting labor costs, prices, and the quantity and quality of output, while the Organized Market Economies tend to supplement market pressures by institutional coordination of one kind or another, through trades unions, trade associations, and the intervention of government agencies. Among the economically advanced countries, the United States, Britain, Ireland, Canada, Australia, and New Zealand are Liberal Market Economies. Another ten, including Germany, Switzerland, Austria, the Scandinavian, and the Low countries, fall into the Organized Market category. Another six are considered mixed (France, Italy, Spain, Portugal, Greece, and Turkey).

As the pace of globalization has increased and the Liberal Market Economies have outperformed the Organized Market Economies in innovation, employment growth, and productivity, some observers foresee an impending triumph of the Liberal Model and disappearance of the organized one. But a longer view of economic performance suggests that it is likely that in response to global pressures, the Organized Market Economies will modify their internal controls, improve their productivity and job creation, and continue to provide an alternative to the Liberal Market model. Thus, despite the considerable pressures for liberalization, a leading authority concludes that there will " . . remain at least two viable models for economic success, whose fate will turn as much on politics as on the economics of adjustment."

Source: Peter Hall, "Organized Market Economies and Unemployment in Europe: Is It Finally Time to Accept Liberal Orthodoxy?", forthcoming in Nancy Bermeo, ed., *Context and Consequence: The Effects of Unemployment in the New Europe* (New York: Cambridge University Press, forthcoming). Also see Peter Hall and David Soskice, *Varieties of Capitalism: The Institutional Foundations of Comparative Advantage* (Harvard University and Wissenschaftzentrum Berlin, forthcoming).

Eastern Europeans hoped to attain the higher living standards of the West without paying the costs of unemployment, inflation, and inequality. They began by freeing prices, encouraging free competition and investment, and withdrawing government control of industry through varying degrees of "privatization." Unfortunately, it has proved difficult to move from a controlled economy to a competitive one. In some countries it has been hard even to dismantle the old system, let alone to build a new one. (See the discussion of economic change in Russia in Chapter 8.) Even where this has been achieved most rapidly and successfully, as in Poland, it was at the cost of further short-term drops in living standards and a great deal of confusion as citizens learn to live with uncertainties in prices, employment, and so forth (see Chapter 9). Debates over the speed of transition, the protection needed for the less fortunate, and the possibility of achieving both change and protection have been bitter and divisive. In several countries the desire to soften the harsh costs of transition brought formerly communist parties back into power. This policy issue continues to dominate the politics of most of the countries of Eastern Europe. The region also faces a huge task of cleaning up vast environmental damage created by the Communist governments' ruthless pursuit of industrialization, but this is lower in the list of priorities.

Table 1.2 presents four measures of welfare and public policy results in Western and Eastern European countries: education, television ownership, income distribution, and infant mortality. These measures reflect past public policy decisions, and thus the performance of governments, but also problems and potential policy problems for the future. The proportion of an age cohort enrolled in education is one measure of governmental performance. As shown in the first column of the table, most European countries, East and West, are successful in keeping their young people in school; there also seems to be gender equality in access to secondary education in both the Western and Eastern areas.

TABLE 1.2   Aspects of Social Development for Selected European Countries

	Percentage in School as Percentage of Age Group (secondary) (college)		TV sets per 1000 1998	Percentage of Income to Lower 20%	Percentage of Income to Upper 20%	Infant Mortality per 1000 births
Germany	104	47	580	13.3	38.5	5
France	111	51	601	14.2	35.8	5
United Kingdom	129	52	645	11.5	43.0	6
Spain	120	53	506	12.6	40.3	5
Russia	na	41	420	8.6	53.7	17
Hungary	98	25	437	12.5	39.9	10
Poland	98	24	413	12.6	40.9	10
Romania	78	23	233	13.6	37.3	21

Source: World Bank, *World Development Indicators 2000,* retrieved May 31, 2000 from
http://www.worldbank.org/data/wdi2000/pdfspdfs/tab2_10.pdf,tab5_11.pdf,tab2_8.pdf,tab1_2.pdf.

High levels of literacy in these countries are consistent with these education figures. The percentage of young people enrolled in colleges and universities, as shown in column 2, is another story. Hungary, Poland, and Romania sent about a quarter of their young people into universities and technical colleges in 1997. This is far more than the 6 percent figure of the world's low income countries, but it is only half the rate of the Western European nations, and a quarter that of the United States.

If we consider public expenditures on education as a measure of public effort, the differences in the percentage of GNP spent on education are relatively small across these eight nations. That is, these countries are making proportionately equal efforts to educate their children. In 1997 West Germany spent 4.8 percent of its GNP on education, the United Kingdom, 5.3 percent, compared with Russia's 3.5 percent and Poland's 7.5 percent. If, however, we consider that the GNP of the Western countries was several times larger than that of the Eastern countries, the same percentage of effort converts into substantially larger inputs into Western European spending on such things as construction and maintenance of schools, teacher salaries, pupil/teacher ratios, educational equipment, and the like.

Table 1.2 also shows television set ownership, as an indicator of exposure to mass media. In this respect, most Eastern Europeans do not lag too far behind their Western European counterparts. They have about four hundred TV sets per thousand citizens, compared to around six hundred for Germany, France, and Britain. Their television ownership is well above the 172 average for the world's low and middle income countries generally and, like the high literacy levels, underscores the openness of these societies to information. However, state control of television continues to be an important political issue in a substantial number of countries.

In the field of public health the only datum we have for all of our selected countries is infant mortality per thousand live births in 1994. To the extent that this indicator reflects general health standards in these countries, the differences are quite substantial. Romania reports 21 infant deaths per thousand during the first year of life; Russia is next with 17. In contrast, Germany, France, and Spain had only 5 infant deaths per 1,000 births.

The distribution of income reported in Table 1.2 for Western and Eastern countries reflects an ironic situation: After only a few years following the introduction of a market economy, Russia has the most unequal distribution of income among all the countries listed in the table, Western and Eastern. More than half of Russia's total income goes to the top 20 percent of income recipients, and only

8.6 percent goes to the bottom fifth. Although not as severe as the discrepancies in some South American countries and South Africa, it is among the world's less equitable distributions, which contributes to its political tensions (see Chapter 8). In contrast, Hungary and Poland do much better jobs of equalizing income with around 40 percent to the top fifth and 13 percent going to the bottom fifth. Distributions in Western Europe are fairly similar to these.

Development, Modernization, and Democracy

Statistical comparisons of Western and Eastern Europe thus yield substantial differences in economic levels and welfare provisions. If we take purchasing power parity as a measure of economic productivity, the Eastern European economies are less than a third of the per-capita level of the richer Western European economies. The Eastern countries have larger rural, agricultural sectors, and there are significant differences in the provision of higher education and health services. By these purely economic and social measures, most of our Eastern European countries fall into the World Bank classification of "middle income countries," ranging from "lower middle income" (e.g., Ukraine, Bulgaria, Russia, and Poland) to "upper middle income" (e.g., Hungary, the Czech Republic, Slovenia).[11] Statistical measures (see previous discussion and Appendix A) also suggest that most Eastern Europeans are educated and literate people, exposed to the "world culture." They have the makings of "civil societies"; although long stultified by Communist control, interest groups, voluntary associations, and competitive media of communication are growing.

On the troubling side, high rates of inflation and negative rates of growth in many Eastern Europe and the former Soviet states show that they are experiencing serious developmental difficulties. They are involved in "dual transitions"—simultaneous efforts to replace collectivist with market economies, and to replace centralized, authoritarian regimes with pluralistic, democratic ones.[12] By comparison, the most recently democratized nations of the West—Spain and Portugal—grew economically at extremely rapid rates (around 5 percent per year)

in the decade before they began to democratize, and continued to do so after their authoritarian regimes were set aside. Similarly, Taiwan and South Korea succeeded in developing productive economies and more or less stable democratic institutions by separating these processes. During their several decade-long efforts at economic development, these two nations were dominated by authoritarian regimes. Democratization came after productive market economies had already been established.

Students of democratization have long debated the relationship between economic development and democratization. Indeed, the great ideological struggles of the nineteenth and twentieth centuries turned on these issues. Karl Marx anticipated that the development of the capitalist economy and the rise of the *"bourgeoisie"* would signal the decline of feudalism, and the introduction of bourgeois democracy, which would in turn be supplanted by socialist democracy after the working class ousts the bourgeoisie.

The realistic studies of modern political science replaced the Marxist view of the relationship between economics and politics with more limited observations and forecasts. In the 1950s and 1960s many leading political scientists drew attention to a strong statistical association between economic development, social and political mobilization, and democracy.[13] These "social mobilization" studies of the 1950s and 1960s pointed out that economic growth and industrialization were associated with urbanization, the spread of education and literacy, and exposure to the mass media of communication. They argued that these conditions would result in greater political awareness and activity ("mobilization"), the formation of voluntary associations and competitive political parties, and the attainment of what came to be called *civil society*. These elements of a civil society would both demand and support more democratic political systems.

Contrary to early hopes, many of the democracies that were established in Asia and Africa in the immediate post–World War II years soon collapsed into dictatorships of one kind or another. Moreover, all of the Eastern European countries were forcefully assimilated into the Communist orbit at the onset of the postwar period; efforts to break free in

Hungary in 1956 (see Chapter 10) and Czechoslovakia in 1968 were repressed by Soviet troops. Spain and Portugal came through World War II as authoritarian regimes; Greece and Turkey fell under military control in the 1960s and 1970s. At about the same time, well-established democracies in Latin America were overthrown even in such relatively developed countries as Chile and Uruguay. It became evident that the road to economic development could be long and hard—and that at least in the short run, economic development could be politically destabilizing. The theory of development, modernization, and democracy came under sharp attack.[14]

However, development theory seemed to "kick in," so to speak, in the late 1970s and 1980s; rapid and sustained economic growth in authoritarian Spain (see Chapter 7), Portugal, Greece, Chile, South Korea, Taiwan, and other nations weakened the legitimacy of authoritarian regimes and created "civil societies" demanding democratic freedoms and amenities. The culmination of these events came with the dramatic collapse of the Soviet Union and the establishment of new democracies in the newly free countries of Eastern Europe. (The collapse of the Soviet Union is discussed more fully in Chapter 8.) The dominant political ideas of the 1990s were democracy and the market economy.

After a substantial period in remission, then, *modernization* theory once again is among the leading themes that we use in speculating about prospects for democracy in the modern world. In view of the experiences of the last decades, as well as the European historical experience, we have a better understanding of the complexity of the interaction of economic, social, and political institutions and forces.[15] There is no doubt that stable or "consolidated" democracy is strongly associated statistically with economic development. But the relationship has to be understood as holding true over the long run. It is shaped by the more dispersed resources for power and coercion in a complex economy,[16] by the more participatory values, perceptions, and demands of an educated and organized citizenry,[17] and by the presence of greater resources to meet human needs. There is a whole set of connecting relationships—structural discontinuities,

breakdowns and synergies, interventions of chance, and failures and triumphs of leaders—that weaken or strengthen the connection between a growing economy and a democratic polity.

From this perspective as we write of Europe at the opening of the third millennium, there seems to be a serious division of realities and prospects. There is a set of Western European countries—economically developed, democratically consolidated, and largely organized in a confederation—whose democracies are well established. There is also a small group of Eastern European countries that have nearly joined them. But there is a large set of Eastern European nations that are far less economically productive, often plagued by inflation and economic stagnation, and struggling with democratic ways of coping with change and conflict. With such a short experience of political independence and such limited and fragile socioeconomic bases, we would expect substantial difficulty in sustaining stable democratic government in parts of Eastern Europe. The literature we have cited on modernization and democracy would lead us to expect as much.

Sadly enough, these forecasts seem to be accurate, with democratic freedoms under pressure in about half of Eastern Europe, especially in the countries with lower levels of economic development. We can see this situation visually in Figure 1.5, a scattergram that depicts the relationship between economic development and political freedom for the nations of Europe. The *Freedom Scores* in the figure are taken from the 1999–2000 report of Freedom House, a New York–based nonprofit organization that provides annual ratings by expert observers of political rights and civil liberties in each country. The economic development measure—expressed as purchasing power parity (PPP)—is taken from the World Bank's *World Development Report* of 2000.[18] Each circle or square dot in the figure represents a single country, with circles representing countries in Eastern Europe and squares countries in Western Europe.

Toward the top right of Figure 1.5, indicated by the small squares, we see the Western European countries. All except one receive the top or next to top Freedom Score and have economic productivity levels higher than even the most developed Eastern

FIGURE 1.5   Economic Development and Freedom in Europe

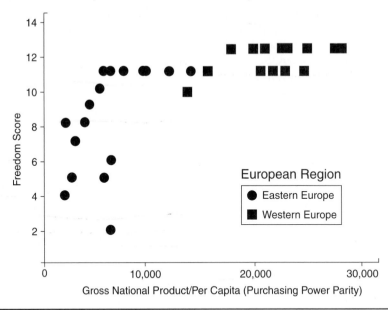

Note: Freedom is combined civil rights and political liberties, from Freedom House (possible range 0–12).

European countries. The poorest Western European country, Greece, has a PPP level slightly below the richest Eastern European country (Slovenia) and a Freedom score that was slightly lower than the top Eastern European countries. Spain is slightly better off than Slovenia and notably more economically developed than the Czech Republic and Hungary, the next most developed Eastern countries, with whom it shares a similarly high freedom score. Freedom House considers any country with a score of 9 or more to be "Free." All six Eastern European countries with a PPP/capita over $7,500 achieve that designation (including Poland and Hungary, discussed in Chapters 9 and 10), as do a few poorer countries.

In the lower left of the figure are five dually troubled Eastern European countries—Yugoslavia, Bosnia, Albania, Ukraine, and Moldova—which have PPP/capitas under $3,500 and all of which are rated only "Partly Free" (Freedom Scores ranging from 4 through 8) by Freedom House. While each country has its own story, Freedom House's observers reported various pressures and constraints on the mass media, limited rights for minorities, and problems in establishing the rule of law as frequent themes.[19] Many of these problems also plague the seven somewhat more prosperous Eastern European countries in the $4,000–$7,000 range. Their political freedom scores run the full range from authoritarian Belarus through partially free Russia, Croatia, and Macedonia, to fully free Latvia, Lithuania, and Romania, showing the importance of leadership, ethnic division, international tensions, and other factors. (See the discussion of the difficulties in establishing the rule of law in Russia in Chapter 8.) Belarus, dominated by an increasingly powerful president, was the only European country scored as completely not free.

The lower levels of economic development among some Eastern European nations makes it difficult for these countries to sustain democracy. Another way of looking at Figure 1.5 is to observe that of the 16 Eastern European countries whose PPP per capita had been less than, say, Hungary's $9,832 in 1998, slightly less than half of them were fully free democracies on January 1, 2000. The rest were, at best, only "partly free." In a statistical sense, this suggests that some of these nations will succeed in sustaining democracy, but that others may falter or fail. In a human sense it means that good leadership may play a particularly critical role in these poorer nations. It also means that it is important that the lagging Eastern European countries begin to overcome the difficulties of economic transition and move toward growth and economic development, as Poland seems to have done (see Chapter 9).

Of course, in considering the prospects for democracy, economic development and modernization are not the only considerations. On the one hand, today's international trends, values, and institutions may help support democracy as a political system. On the other, religious and ethnic cleavages are added to economic development problems in many of the newly independent Eastern European countries. Democracy can arouse new expectations from suppressed minorities, and the absence of resources in the poorer nations can make accommodation of these particularly difficult. This consideration brings us to the troubling prospects of religious and ethnic conflict in Europe.

Ethnic and Religious Conflict in Europe

In the long course of European prehistory and history, through the forces of population growth and decline, migration, warfare, famine, and disease, an ethno-religious distribution of great complexity has taken shape. If we explore the strata and outcroppings of these movements of peoples, we see evidence of a Celtic past, still surviving on the European periphery and in remote mountain valleys. Traces of a long Roman domination can still be seen. There is evidence of great migrations of Goths, Vandals, and Huns from the Asian steppes; Moors, Berbers, and Ottoman Turks from the Middle East; and Vikings and Norsemen from the North. These peoples brought their languages and religions with them. Over time these languages and beliefs combined and differentiated, partly through long-term processes of intermittent fighting, trading, and in-

termarrying, and partly through the deliberate actions of political and military elites seeking effective ways of extracting resources and recruiting military forces. Populations sharing the same beliefs and speaking in the same tongue could be reached, mobilized, and exploited more effectively.

Religion provided one central basis of differentiation. The great religions of the world offer coherent systems of values and standards of behavior beyond local customs and memories to their adherents. Periodically, they have swept across tribes and peoples to create, by force or example, more unified cultural systems. Before the Reformation, the Catholic Church had provided much of the cultural unity for the extremely fragmented political systems in Christian Europe. Its legacy of magnificent cathedrals and splendid works of art inspires the viewer even today. The birth of modern Europe in the *Renaissance* and the *Reformation* was associated with the shattering of religious unity. The religious wars of the sixteenth and seventeenth centuries created, at the cost of dreadful suffering, lines of religious cleavage that shaped the formation of the European nation-states and continues to influence their politics today.[20]

When the struggle between Catholicism and the forces of Protestant dissent in the Reformation and Counterreformation had stabilized, dissenting religious minorities within each state had largely been expelled or converted. This produced relatively homogeneous religious groupings in most countries. National governments dominated Protestant churches in northwest Europe, usually without much internal religious conflict. In much of Eastern Europe, too, secular governments established dominance over and collaboration with the Eastern Orthodox Church.

In southwestern Europe, the Catholic Church prevailed. The Counterreformation regained France and some German states from Protestantism, held Italy and the Austro-Hungarian empire (including Belgium and Spain), and reclaimed some ground from Islam to the East. The French Revolution of 1789 then unleashed a secular rebellion against the Catholic Church that left its mark on politics and party systems, as a "secular-clerical" divide, for two centuries. The emergence of democracy and the development of mass education resulted in intense internal conflict over the role of the Church in politics and public policy.

Thus along the fault line between North and South lay a series of states with both Catholic and Protestant populations—the United Kingdom, the Netherlands, Germany, Switzerland, Czechoslovakia. In these states political conflict between Catholics and Protestants, as well as between clericalism and secularism, has been a fact of European political life that has endured through today, with a new focus on education, abortion, and the rights of women—areas in which religious identities and values have been particularly divisive. Apart from the religious issues as such, the followers of the faiths have been historically organized into separate communities with distinct social and political organizations.

A decline in church attendance and other religious practices throughout most of Western Europe since World War II has shifted the political balance in secular directions and decreased the sense of communal conflict associated with religious division. Nonetheless, at least until very recently a voter's frequency of church attendance was usually the best single predictor of his or her vote choice in most Western European nations with substantial Catholic populations. (See the discussions of the role of religion in voter's choices in France, Germany, and Spain in Chapters 5, 6, and 7; the lesser, but still significant, role of religion in party voting in Poland and Hungary is discussed in Chapters 9 and 10.)

Ethnicity may sometimes be associated with religion, but in the modern world it is additionally or even primarily associated with language, custom, and historical memories. Max Weber, in his (classic) introduction to sociological theory *Economy and Society,* defined ethnic groups as "those human groups that entertain a subjective belief in their common descent because of similarities of physical type or of customs or both, or because of memories of colonization and migration. . . . (I)t does not matter whether or not an objective blood relationship exists."[21]

Ethnicity can be a powerful force in politics. It provides an important basis for mobilization of common interests and deeply felt personal identities. It can be especially potent where allied with *nationalism,* a belief that a common ethnic group should be the basis of a geographically defined independent state. The formation of large nation-states between the sixteenth to the nineteenth centuries suppressed many of the lessor particularisms of custom and dialect in favor of a few relatively dominant ones. The spread of printing and literacy replaced both Latin as the international language of the educated and the myriad local dialects with intermediate linguistic groupings, linked to larger independent states. The rise of mass education and mass media in the nineteenth and twentieth centuries tended further to obscure and devalue the surviving parochialisms. People came to identify themselves with some larger "nationality," and according to their social conditions and new ideological beliefs. They were the French, the Spaniards, the English, and the Germans; they were members of the working class or the bourgeoisie; they were conservatives, liberals, or socialists of one kind or another. Nation-states became both the foci of local political activity and, with enormous human costs, the actors in catastrophic international conflict. In the aftermath of World War II under the ideological pressure of the Cold War, ethnic particularisms within the nation-states were even further subordinated.

As international tensions diminished, however, and the penetration of mass media and education became even more widespread, the ethnic minorities of Western Europe again became a basis for political mobilization. The rise of ethnic issues was facilitated by the collapse of domestic communism and the decline of socialism. Revolutionary, even Marxist, socialism hardly exists any more. The *bureaucratic state*—centralized, regulative, extractive, and distributive—is under attack. The collapse of the Soviet bloc and Marxist-Leninist beliefs in the last decade created further incentives and opportunities for political mobilization along ethnic lines.

In Eastern Europe the implications of the withdrawal of Soviet control were, of course, even more dramatic. As a matter of ideology and policy, any political aspirations of ethnic minorities as such had been ruthlessly repressed. Yet, the bureaucratic

BOX 1.2   Ethnicity Defined

The point that ethnicity is based on subjective belief in common descent, rather than a necessary physical reality, is stressed by Donald Horowitz, the leading contemporary authority on ethnicity and politics. Horowitz points out that the concept of ethnicity has to be elastic, since groups physically quite similar but differing in language, religion, customs, marriage patterns, and historical memories may consider themselves to be "ethnically" different. For example, the Serbs, Croats, and Muslim Bosnians (of the same physical stock) may believe themselves to be descended from different ancestors. Here, following Gurr and his associates, we use the term "ethnicity" even more generally to refer to all groups "whose core members share a distinctive and enduring collective identity based on cultural traits and lifeways that matter to them and to others with whom they interact."

Sources: Donald Horowitz, *Ethnic Groups and Conflict* (Berkeley: University of California Press, 1985), pp. 52–53. T. Robert Gurr, *Minorities at Risk: A Global View of Ethnopolitical Conflicts* (Washington: U.S. Institute of Peace Press, 1993), p. 3. We draw particularly on Monty G. Marshall, "States at Risk: Ethnopolitics in the Multinational States of Eastern Europe," in Gurr.

and even party organizations in the Soviet Union, Czechoslovakia, and Yugoslavia were constructed to recognize and even encourage local ethnic cultures based on language and history, even while religion was generally suppressed. Regional leaders in both bureaucracy and party were often members of the locally dominant minority. This duality in Soviet policy, dating back to Lenin's initial understanding of the problems created by ethnic nationalism, greatly facilitated the breakup of the Soviet Union, Yugoslavia, and later Czechoslovakia, when central controls were removed. The overthrow of most of these authoritarian political systems and the introduction of free discussion and mass media, especially in the absence of well-entrenched democratic party systems, created political space for ethnic and religious particularisms to maneuver within the newly independent political systems.

Of our thirty-eight European countries, less than half are relatively free of ethnic conflict. These include the five Scandinavian countries, Austria, Greece, and Portugal in Western Europe and Albania, Hungary, Poland, the Czech Republic, Slovakia, and Slovenia in Eastern Europe. While these countries are largely homogeneous in language and religion, even among them there are small ethnic minorities that might become politically mobilized (Swedes in Finland, non-Muslims in Albania), or

larger groups that have been conflictual in the past (religion in Catholic and mixed Western Europe or the Socialist-Catholic civil war in Austria in the early 1930s). The remaining countries manifest more substantial ethno-religious conflict in one form or another.

Tables 1.3 to 1.5 provide a sense of the diversity, dangers, and promises of ethno-religious conflicts in Europe. Table 1.3 emphasizes the dangers by showing the seven "hot spots," where conflict has taken the most violent form in recent years. These confrontations all involve efforts by one or more ethnic or religious groups to change the boundaries of existing states or to form new ones. Disputes over nation-state boundaries find no simple solution through democratic procedures. If the conflict comes to violence, the struggle can quickly degenerate into "ethnic cleansing," the forcible eviction or destruction of local minorities. Ethnic differences and historic grievances have this capacity to justify dehumanization of the "ethnically" different and cruelties of unimaginable proportions. Casualties in Bosnia, Cyprus, Chechnya, and Kosovo have numbered in the tens of thousands. While less deadly than all-out civil war, terrorism in Northern Ireland in the United Kingdom, in Basque Spain, and French Corsica has taken many lives and shattered the peace of these countries for many decades.

TABLE 1.3 Violent Ethno-Religious Conflict in Contemporary Europe

	Groups	Bases of Conflict	Geographic Distribution	Solutions
Bosnia-Herzegovina	Serbs v. Muslims	R,C,L[a]	Mosaic, Interface, Diaspora	UN, NATO Peacekeeping
Yugoslavia-Kosovo	Serbs v. Albanians	R,C,L	Interface, Mosaic, Diaspora	UN, NATO Peacekeeping
Cyprus	Turks v. Greeks	R,L,C,H	Interface, Diaspora	Diplomacy, UN Negotiation
France	Corsicana v. French	L,C,H	Interface	Terrorism
Russia	Chechens v. Russians	R,L,C,H	Interface/Enclave	Russian army, Guerrilla action
Spain	Basques v. Spanish	L,C,H	Interface/Enclave	Terrorism
United Kingdom	Catholic v. Protestant Irish	R,C,H	Interface, Diaspora	Devolution, Power-sharing

[a]Abbreviations indicate religion (R), culture (C), language (L), and history (H).

While ethnic conflict can inflict terrible costs, it need not. Table 1.4 shows examples of ethno-religious conflicts that at one time were the cause of or had the potential for serious violence. These conflicts still retain sharp communal awareness, but there seems to be a stable and constitutionally protected status for group relations. Three such "solutions" for ethnic conflict are shown in the last column: consociationalism, federalism, and secession. *Consociationalism* involves the systematic sharing of political power among the different groups, giving each group control over its own life.[22] This system allows each group to veto collective policies that it believes will affect it adversely, and it provides for proportionate sharing of national offices and resources. Austria, Belgium (in its religious dispute), the Netherlands, and Switzerland have been the classic users of this approach, which offers security to communal groups at the cost of the efficiency and redistributive possibilities of majority rule. Austria, for example, used elaborate arrangements for sharing power between the Socialists and the Catholics in the 1950s and 1960s to prevent recurrence of the community conflicts that led to civil war in the early 1930s. The Netherlands and Bel-gium handled explosive religious conflicts in the same fashion. At a regional level, this was the successful Italian approach to relations with its German-speaking minority in South Tyrol.

The other two solutions that recognize special status for communal relations are geographic. *Federalism* involves geographic decentralization and the sharing of power between the central government and the regions. *Secession* involves redefining the state boundaries, allowing an ethnic group either to form a new nation-state or to join with a neighboring one. The possibilities for federalism and secession involve, of course, the geographic distribution of the members of the ethnic groups themselves. These geographic distributions are shown in the fourth column of Table 1.3 and subsequent tables. We use the classification scheme appearing in Ian Budge, Kenneth Newton, et al., *The Politics of the New Europe.*[23] They distinguish among four geostrategic ethnic situations: (1) *interface*, where a minority is concentrated at a national boundary; (2) *enclave*, where a minority is concentrated and wholly surrounded by host territory; (3) *mosaic*, where a minority is widely distributed; (4) *diaspora*, where a minority originated from a foreign country

TABLE 1.4   Constitutional Solutions to Ethno-Religious Conflict in Contemporary Europe: Consociational, Federal, and Secessionist

	Groups	Bases of Conflict	Geographic Distribution	Solutions
Austria	Catholics v. Socialists	R,H[a]	Mosaic	Consociation
Belgium	Flemings v. Walloons,	L,C	Interface	Federation, Consociation
	Catholics v. Secular	R,H	Mosaic	Consociation
Czechoslovakia	Czechs v. Slovaks	L,R	Interface	Secession
United Kingdom	Irish v. British	R,C,L,H	Interface	Secession
Italy	Germans v. Italians	L,C	Interface	Consociation
Netherlands	Catholics v. Protestant v. Secular; Socialist v. Liberal	R,H	Interface, Mosaic	Consociation
Russia	Tatars v. Russians	L,R	Enclave, Mosaic	Federation
Spain	Catalans v. Spanish	L,C	Interface	Federation
Sweden	Norwegians v. Swedes	L	Interface	Secession
Switzerland	Germans v. French v. Italians	L	Interface	Federation, Consociation
	Catholics v. Protestants	R	Interface	Federation, Consociation

[a]Abbreviations indicate religion (R), culture (C), language (L), and history (H).

and retains these prior loyalties. Needless to say, a minority group may fit into more than one of these circumstances.

Generally speaking, secession is a realistic solution only in interface situations, as in Sweden/Norway and the Czech Republic/Slovakia. The presence of some mosaic in part of the territory can create long-term difficulties. For example, the secession of the Irish Republic from the United Kingdom in 1922 left an enduring problem in the northern six counties with mixed Protestant-Catholic populations (Northern Ireland). Federalism may be a solution for either interfaces or enclaves, as in Switzerland and the Tatar Republic in Russia. Minorities that are dispersed in a mosaic situation cannot easily be accommodated through either of the geographic approaches; consociationalism remains as an alternative or additional possibility. Belgium has created substantial federalism in response to conflicts between its French and Flemish language communities; the presence of Brussels, with a mixed, but majority French, population inside Flanders has been a continuing difficulty with the federal approach.

While these more or less successful "solutions" to ethnic conflict indicate the possibilities for containing violence, they are each bought at substantial cost and require some tolerance from leaders and followers on all sides. Russia seems to have created a more or less successful federal relationship with the Tatars. The Russian suspension of Chechnyan federal autonomy and the continuance of Chechnyan terrorism and guerrilla warfare illustrates failure, however. The more militant Chechnyans have been unwilling to lay down arms in a situation short of secession and the Russian central government has refused to allow this (see Chapter 8).

Most of the successor countries in the territory of the former Soviet bloc (the exceptions being Poland, Hungary, Romania, and Slovenia) may be viewed as potentially conflictual (even to the point of violence), as shown in Table 1.5. The breakup of the Soviet Union, Czechoslovakia, and Yugoslavia still left mixed ethnic populations in many states. Moreover, although religion was sharply suppressed under communist control, Eastern Europe is distinctive for the extent to which religion and language simultaneously divide many of the same

TABLE 1.5   Potential for Serious Conflict in Former Soviet Bloc Countries

Countries	Minority Groups	Bases of Conflict	Geographic Distribution
Belarus	Russians (13%)	R[a]	Mosaic, Diaspora
Croatia	Serbs (12%)	L,R	Interface, Mosaic, Diaspora
Estonia	Russians (30%)	L,R	Mosaic, Diaspora
Latvia	Russians (33%)	L,R	Mosaic, Diaspora
Lithuania	Russians (9%)	L,R	Mosaic, Diaspora
Macedonia	Albanians (20%)	L,R	Interface, Diaspora
Moldova	Russians, Ukrainians (25%)	L,C	Mosaic, Diaspora
Russia	Muslims in Caucasus, Asia	L,R,C	Interface, Diaspora
Ukraine	Russians (22%)	R	Mosaic, Interface, Diaspora
Yugoslavia	Albanians (17%)	L,R	Interface, Diaspora

[a]Abbreviations indicate religion (R), culture (C), language (L), and history (H).

groups. A glance at the geographic distribution column in Table 1.5 also shows how many of the ethnic situations in Eastern Europe involve diasporas—that is, relations between an internal minority group and a neighboring country. The substantial Russian populations left in most of the countries bordering the new Russian Federation after the breakup of the Soviet Union are involved in both mosaic relationships with the host ethnic majority and a diaspora relationship with Russia. For example, Russian minorities constitute around a third of the population of Estonia and Latvia. This situation has already created severe tensions, both domestic and "international." The states of the former Yugoslavia, with the exception of Slovenia, face a variety of complex ethnic pulls. Two countries not shown in the table, the Czech Republic and Slovakia, have mixed Catholic-Protestant populations, but at the moment this division does not seem a serious cause of tension.

Another source of ethnic conflict is the presence of recent immigrants and foreign workers, primarily in Western Europe. During previous periods of economic boom, a number of Western European countries invited foreign workers to fill vacancies in the labor force. Many came, and their families often followed. Germany has almost 2 million Turks and Kurds; in Switzerland, nonresidents account for over 10 percent of the population. Although usually denied formal citizenship, these workers and their families have become long-term residents. With the economic difficulties and political conflict in many parts of Eastern Europe since the breakdown of Soviet control, there have been new waves of immigrants, legal and illegal, to all Western European countries that would accept them. Moreover, Western European countries whose former colonial empires created special relationships with now independent nations in Africa, Asia, and the Caribbean have had substantial numbers of immigrants from those areas. For instance, 3 million Algerian Muslims now reside in France.

The presence of these groups, especially when coupled with high unemployment and other economic tensions, has stimulated expressions of ethnic nationalism by majority groups. The minorities have been the target of rising, though still sporadic, ethnic violence in a number of countries. There were numerous attacks and several foreigners were killed in Germany in the early 1990s, although the situation has quieted as the economy has improved, national leaders have taken firmer antiviolence stands, and immigration has been curtailed. Immigrant groups have become a rallying point for disruptive nationalist parties calling for strong limits on immigration (adopted in many countries), the immediate expulsion of the groups, or worse (see Chapter 3).

Ethno-religious politics can be merged into the normal political processes of democratic competition. This can occur either through routine acceptance of originally intractable differences or through gradual assimilation of the groups into a common culture. The best example of such routinization is probably relations between Protestants and Catholics, or clericals and seculars, in most of Western (and thus far Eastern) Europe. Northern Ireland is an outstanding exception, as is the extreme religious right in the United States where the "right to life" movement verges toward intermittent violence. Elsewhere, issues associated with Catholicism, Protestantism, and secularism seem manageable through ordinary party or interest-group politics.

As communal differences have narrowed in the Netherlands and Austria, consociational patterns have also gradually weakened. Similarly, smaller linguistic and/or historically distinctive groups have gradually lost their distinctiveness and identity in many regions of the world. At the level of complete assimilation, the English are no longer able to distinguish between Normans and Saxons. But such merging remains only a long-term possibility and political activists sometimes have remarkable success in reviving ethnic differences and demands in apparently highly assimilated areas, such as the revival of nationalism in Scotland since the 1970s. Similarly, the long-smoldering North-South regional and cultural differences in Italy have recently given rise to a separatist party in the North, which has been making increasingly vocal demands for secession. Finally, new historical experiences can be the basis for new "ethnic" identities based on a common sense of shared suffering, such as the East-West regional differences in the reunited Germany (see Chapter 6). These are operating within a federal system, but not one designed for these regional differences. It is, of course, too early to say whether these currently routinized processes of dealing with new communal identities will continue to succeed.

Samuel Huntington argues in his recent book, *"The Clash of Civilizations,"* that the political map of the future will be dominated by clashing ethno-religious civilizations: the Judeo-Christian, the Eastern Orthodox Christian, the Islamic, the Chinese, the Japanese, the Hindu, and others.[24] He challenges the optimistic belief in the emergence of a unified, rational-secular *world culture.* Just a few years ago another imaginative historian, Francis Fukuyama, in the euphoria of the collapse of Communism and the Soviet Union, forecast "the end of history" and the world triumph of the secular democratic enlightenment and the market economy.[25] These two historical projections capture the conflict between an emerging democratic-market civilization, with its base in science, technology, secular education, and communication, and the market, and a persisting and mobilizing world of religious and ethnic parochialisms. Huntington's vision of this encounter obscures the unifying trends with their powerful material and spiritual incentives of productivity, welfare, and participation. Fukuyama's vision obscures the persistence and importance of the sense of safety and identity deriving from familiar beliefs, tongues, and historical experiences. Only taken together can their powerful messages about the future of development, ethnicity, and democracy be interpreted.

Democracy and Democratization

Modern *democracy,* as Samuel Huntington points out, has emerged in *"three waves."*[26] The first began in the aftermath of the American and French revolutions and continued for more than a century through World War I, the "war to make the world safe for democracy." In this first wave successful democracy was largely a phenomenon of Europe and its colonial offspring, but it was to founder on the Depression of the 1930s and then recede to form the "reverse wave" of *fascist* and *communist* authoritarianism. These disasters, above all the terrible replacement of Germany's democratic Weimar Republic by Hitler's brutal and aggressive Nazi dictatorship, are also a critical part of the European experience.

The second wave, which Huntington calls the "short wave," lasted from the defeat of fascism in World War II and the breakup of the European colonial empires afterward, until approximately the mid-1960s. While a large number of countries in Europe, East Asia, Africa, and Latin America became formally democratic in these post–World War II years, most of them collapsed quickly into authoritarian regimes of one kind or another. The interwar democracies of Eastern Europe, like their authoritarian counterparts, were repressed by Soviet military force and replaced with Communist authoritarianism. The overthrow of democracy in Greece by military coup in 1967 represents Western Europe's contributions to the reversal of the second wave.

The third wave began in southern Europe in the mid-1970s, with democratic transformations in Portugal, Spain (see Chapter 7), and Greece, and then quickly spread into Latin America, East Asia, and Africa. In the late 1980s, to the surprise of the rest of the world, it engulfed the Eastern European satellites of the Soviet Union. Then in the early 1990s the Soviet Union itself collapsed into its ethno-national components. Without warning from the worlds of scholarship and the media, democracy, now the formal regime in more than three-quarters of the independent countries in the world, had become the "only game in town." It had no expansive, ideological rivals, with the possible exception of the theocratic Islamic regimes of the Middle East. The surviving communist regimes—China, North Korea, Vietnam, and Cuba—have remained defensive.

Given this history, Europe has been a primary laboratory of natural experiments with politics. The modern bureaucratic state, representative parliamentary institutions, various electoral systems, political parties and party systems, interest groups, specialized media of communication—the whole modern political apparatus—emerged first in Europe and its colonies. They emerged at different times, in different parts of the continent, in differing degrees and sequences, and as a consequence of different conditions and events. Most of the rest of the planet has now assimilated these institutions and practices and is in the process of combining them (sometimes more and sometimes less successfully) with indigenous cultures and institutions. Hence, when we study Europe we are observing the origins of modern politics and describing most of the political models for political institutions and theories in the rest of the world. We are also observing some of the greatest triumphs and greatest disasters of democratic politics.

In their book on democratic transitions, Juan Linz and Alfred Stepan draw our attention to the fact that though we are currently in an era of democracy and democratization, we should avoid what they call "democratic triumphalism."[27] The assumption that the ideological battle has been finally won, and that all of the countries of the world are now moving toward a stable *democratic consolidation*, is dangerously misleading. Linz and Stepan remind us that, though not in "style" at this time, there are still totalitarian, and "post-totalitarian" regimes in the world, and several varieties and large numbers of authoritarian ones. Many of the formally democratic regimes in many parts of the world are teetering at the point of economic, social, and political breakdown.[28]

In addition, regimes that seem to be in *democratic transition* may not be moving ahead on some inevitable course toward "completing" the process but may instead be pausing in "halfway houses." A recent study of these processes in Singapore, Malaysia, and Thailand provides examples of these halfway houses—democratic-authoritarian mixes—which seem to have attained a stable equilibrium likely to persist for some time into the future.[29]

At the present time, as the third wave of democracy seems to be reaching its peak, and showing signs of reversal in some parts of the world, the 19 Eastern European countries, free now to shape their own futures after more than half a century of suppression, are a crucial battleground in the long human struggle for freedom and welfare. Nothing would affect the balance of this struggle more than rapid economic growth and consolidated democratization in such countries as the Russian Federation, Ukraine, Belarus, and Romania, to say nothing of the Czech Republic, Poland, and Hungary, where successful economic and political transitions seem to be underway. Moreover, the consolidated democracies of Western Europe can still go much further to achieve a more fully realized democratization that bases responsive public policies on a participating and confident citizenry.

These then are some of the major challenges of European political studies to which this book is an introduction. How can scholars draw effectively from the great fund of experience and knowledge, most richly based on Western European political and economic studies, in order to illuminate, interpret, and forecast the issues and prospects of democratic Eastern Europe?

∽ KEY TERMS ∽

Axis
bourgeoisie
bureaucratic state
civil society
Cold War
Commonwealth of
    Independent States
    (CIS)
communism
consociationalism
Council for Mutual
    Economic
    Assistance
    (COMECON)
democracy, three
    waves of

democratic
    consolidation
democratic transition
diaspora
enclave
Enlightenment
ethnicity, ethnic conflict
European Economic
    Community (EEC)
European Union (EU)
fascist authoritarianism
federalism
Freedom Score

gross national product
    (GNP)/ gross
    domestic product
    (GDP)
industrialization
interface
Iron Curtain
market economy
modernization
mosaic
nationalism
Nazism-National
    Socialism—Nazi
    Dictatorship

North Atlantic Treaty
    Organization
    (NATO)
Peace of Westphalia
perestroika
Protestant Reformation
Purchasing Power Parity
    (PPP)
Reformation
Renaissance
secession
Treaty of Versailles
Treaty of Vienna
Warsaw Pact
world culture

∽ SUGGESTED READINGS ∽

Budge, Ian, and Kenneth Newton, et al. *The Politics of the New Europe.* New York: Addison Wesley Longman, 1997.

Dahl, Robert A. *Democracy and Its Critics.* New Haven: Yale University Press, 1989.

———. *Polyarchy: Participation and Opposition.* New Haven: Yale University Press, 1971.

Diamond, Larry. *Developing Democracy: Toward Consolidation.* Baltimore: Johns Hopkins University Press, 1999.

Fukuyama, Francis. *The End of History and the Last Man.* New York: Avon Books, 1992.

Horowitz, Donald. *Ethnic Groups and Conflict.* Berkeley: University of California Press, 1985.

Huntington, Samuel. *The Clash of Civilizations and the Remaking of the World Order.* New York: Simon and Schuster, 1996.

———. *The Third Wave: Democratization in the Late Twentieth Century.* Norman, OK: University of Oklahoma University Press, 1991.

Linz, Juan, and Alfred Stepan. *Problems of Democratic Transition and Consolidation.* Baltimore: Johns Hopkins University Press, 1996.

Lipset, Seymour Martin, and Stein Rokkan. *Party Systems and Voter Alignments.* New York: Free Press, 1967.

Sbragia, Alberta, ed. *Europolitics, Institutions, and Policy Making in the New European Community.* Washington: Brookings Institution, 1992.

ENDNOTES

1. Mikhail Gorbachev, *Perestroika: New Thinking for Our Country and the World* (New York: Harper and Row, 1987), pp. 190, 197.

2. See Chapter 11; also see Leon Lindberg, *The Political Dynamics of European Economic Integration* (Stanford: Stanford University Press, 1963).

3. See Chapter 11; see also Alberta Sbragia, *Europolitics: Institutions and Policymaking in the "New" European Community* (Washington: Brookings, 1992); Desmond Dian, *Ever Closer Union? An Introduction to the European Community* (Boulder: Lynne Rienner, 1994).

4. See also Appendix A for population size and other statistics for all 38 European nations.

5. We have consistently excluded from our analysis the interesting "micro-states" of Andorra, Liechtenstein, Monaco, San Marino, and Vatican City, all of them with populations of less than 50,000 permanent residents, and sustained by varying complex treaties and agreements with their surrounding nation-states.

6. World Bank, *World Development Indicators 2000;* retrieved May 3, 2000 from http://www.worldbank.org/data/wdi2000/pdfs/tab1_4.pdf

7. Goods generally cost less in agricultural societies than in urbanized, industrial societies; thus the PPP adjustments in Eastern Europe are greater because living costs are lower in these societies. At the same time, agricultural societies are also likely to generate lower living standards, as seen in Table 1.1.

8. Economic growth figures are based on Gross Domestic Product (GDP), which is similar to GNP, but (roughly speaking) excludes income sent home from nonresidents. Because of the great disruptions in the Eastern European economies, especially in the early years of conversion to freer markets, all the statistics from the early 1990s, and thus change analyses based on those years, must be viewed with caution.

9. We have to treat the statistics for inflation in Eastern European countries with particular care. Many of these countries experienced "shock" market conversion therapies during the early 1990s, as parts of the state-controlled economies were privatized and as price subsidies were reduced or eliminated.

10. See, for example, David Cameron, "The Expansion of the Public Economy," *American Political Science Review* 72 (1978): 1243–61; Peter Flora and Arnold Heidenheimer, eds., *The Development of the Welfare States in Europe and America* (New Brunswick: Transaction Press, 1981); Douglas Hibbs, *The Political Economy of Industrial Democracies* (Cambridge: Harvard University Press, 1987); Alexander Hicks and Duane Swank, "Politics, Institutions, and Welfare Spending in Industrialized Democracies 1960–82," *American Political Science Review* 86 (1992): 658–74.

11. Albania is clearly the poorest nation in Eastern Europe, falling into an international "lower income" category. Moldova and some parts of the former Yugoslavia, such as Macedonia and Bosnia, also seem to be substantially less economically developed than the rest of Eastern Europe.

12. Omar G. Encarnacion, "The Politics of Dual Transitions," *Comparative Politics* 28 (July 1996): 477–92.

13. Daniel Lerner, *The Passing of Traditional Society* (New York: Free Press, 1958); Karl Deutsch, "Social Mobilization and Political Development," *American Political Science Review* (September 1961): 493 ff.; Seymour Martin Lipset, "Some Social Requisites of Democracy," *American Political Science Review* (September 1959); James Coleman, "Conclusion: The Political Systems of the Developing Areas" in Almond and Coleman, *The Politics of the Developing Areas* (Princeton, NJ: the Princeton University Press, 1960, pp. 532–77); Robert Dahl, *Polyarchy: Participation and Opposition* (New Haven: Yale University Press, 1971); Samuel Huntington, *Political Order in Changing Societies* (New Haven: Yale University Press, 1968).

14. A "dependency" school of political theory gained substantial headway among American, European, Latin American, African, and Asian intellectuals. The dependency movement argued that "developmentalism" was a sham, a new version of the ideology of capitalism that concealed the essential exploitiveness of the capitalist world economy. The political reality in the world was control of the third world periphery by American and European "multinational" capitalist corporations, backed up by first world military force, and their indigenous henchmen. The authoritarian regimes instituted in these years were believed intended to enforce this systematic exploitation of peripheral economies.

15. For a careful review and updating of development theory, see Larry Diamond, "Economic Development and Democracy Reconsidered," in G. Marks and L. Diamond, eds., *Reexamining Democracy* (Newbury Park, CA: Sage, 1992); see also Seymour Martin Lipset, "Second Thoughts and Recent Findings," in Lipset, *Political Man*, rev. ed. (Baltimore: Johns Hopkins University Press, 1981).

16. On the theme of the dispersion of potential political resources in modernized societies, see especially Tatu Vanhanen, *Prospects of Democracy: A Study of 172 Countries* (New York: Routledge, 1997) and Robert E. Dahl, *Democracy and Its Critics* (New Haven: Yale University Press, 1989), pp. 251–54. Also, from a different but not unrelated point of view, see the "class" analyses of Dietrich Reuschemeyer, Evelyne Huber Stephens, and John D. Stephens, *Capitalist Development and Democracy* (Chicago: University of Chicago Press, 1992), pp. 75–78 ff.

17. On the connections between modernization, citizen attitudes of trust and participation, and democracy, see especially Gabriel A. Almond and Sidney Verba, *The Civic Culture: Political Attitudes and Democracy in Five Nations* (Princeton: Princeton University Press, 1963) and Ronald Inglehart, *Modernization and Postmodernization: Cultural, Economic and Political Change in 43 Societies* (Princeton: Princeton University Press, 1997), Ch. 6.

18. Freedom House ratings are taken from their website, http://www.freedomhouse.org/ratings, retrieved May 31, 2000. Ratings are as of January 1, 2000; World Bank, *World Development Indicators 2000*; retrieved May 31, 2000 from http://www.worldbank.org/data/wdi2000/pdfs/tab1_1.pdf.

19. Brief, but very useful, summaries of the situation of political rights and civil liberties in each country in the late 1990s can be found in Freedom House, *Freedom in the World 1998–1999*, at their website, http://www.freedomhouse.org/survey99, examined May 31, 2000. Also see the report on press freedom in each country, "Press Survey 2000," at http://freedomhouse.org/pfs2000 and Box 3.2 in Ch. 3.

20. Seymour Martin Lipset and Stein Rokkan, "Cleavage Structures, Party Systems and Voter Alignments: An Introduction," in Lipset and Rokkan, eds., *Party Systems and Voter Alignments* (New York: Free Press, 1967); the authors present a detailed analysis of the impact of religion on European nation-building and party formation.

21. Max Weber, *Economy and Society: An Outline of Interpretive Sociology*, edited by Guenther Roth and Claus Wittich (Berkeley: University of California Press, 1978), p. 389.

22. Arend Lijphart, *The Politics of Accomodation: Pluralism and Democracy in the Netherlands* (Berkeley: University of California Press, 1968); Arend Lijphart, *Democracy in Plural Societies* (New Haven: Yale University Press, 1977).

23. Ian Budge, Kenneth Newton, et al., *The Politics of the New Europe* (New York: Addison Wesley Longman, 1997), Ch. 4.

24. Samuel Huntington, *The Clash of Civilizations and the Remaking of the World Order* (New York: Simon and Schuster, 1996).

25. Francis Fukuyama, *The End of History and the Last Man* (New York: Avon Books, 1992).

26. Samuel Huntington, *The Third Wave: Democratization in the Late Twentieth Century* (Norman, OK: University of Oklahoma Press, 1991).

27. Juan Linz and Alfred Stepan, *Problems of Democratic Transition and Consolidation: Southern Europe, South America, and Post-Communist Europe* (Baltimore: Johns Hopkins University Press, 1996).

28. Ibid. For a generally sober account of democratic prospects in the contemporary world, see Larry Diamond, *Is the Third Wave of Democratization Over?* (Baltimore: Johns Hopkins University Press, 1998). For accounts of earlier overthrows of democracies, see Juan Linz and Alfred Stepan, *The Breakdown of Democratic Regimes* (Baltimore: Johns Hopkins University Press, 1978). Linz is also the author of an important typology of authoritarian regimes, "Totalitarian and Authoritarian Regimes," in F. Greenstein and N. Polsby, eds., *Handbook of Political Science*, vol. 3 (Reading, MA: Addison-Wesley, 1975).

29. William Case, "Can the 'Halfway House' Stand? Semi-democracy and Elite Theory in Three Southeast Asian Countries," *Comparative Politics* 28 (July 1996): 437–64.

CHAPTER 2

DEMOCRATIC POLITICAL CULTURE
AND POLITICAL ACTION

Virtually all the nations of today's Europe—east and west, north and south—have converged on a single political destiny: They are all democratic or claim to be. This is a radical change from Europe's modern history. In 1917 when the United States entered World War I on the side of the Allies, Woodrow Wilson mistakenly claimed that the goal of the war was to make the world "safe for democracy." A little more than two decades later, Nazism, Fascism, and Japanese militarism plunged the world into a second and even larger world war. At the end of World War II, an "Iron Curtain" divided Europe into a democratic western part and a communist eastern part—in a "cold war" lasting for almost half a century. Now at the start of the twenty-first century, the cold war has ended with the collapse of communism, and at least the formal democratization of the nineteen independent European nations carved out of the territories of the former Soviet Union and the bloc of European nations which it dominated.

There is wide variation in the practice of democracy by the many European nations (see Chapter 3). For instance, Britain has had organized and competitive political parties for well over a century and a half, while Bulgaria is still learning how to organize democratic political parties and elections. West Europeans are more likely to turn out to vote and to be engaged in other electoral activities. Western European nations tend to have complex civil societies where individuals join and form organizations and participate in social affairs and politics. These institutions and behaviors are just beginning to develop in the East.

These differences among nations illustrate the natural variation that can occur within the democratic mold, variation produced by the structure of political institutions, historical experiences, and the values of the citizenry. The Germans have a Constitutional Court, for example, which acts as an ombudsman for individuals who feel their rights have been violated; the British lack a written constitution or such a tradition of judicial constitutional review. The Swiss make heavy use of referendums because the constitution provides for their use, while other European democracies lack this constitutional ability to hold national votes on significant issues.

Beyond institutional structures, political systems also differ because their citizens vary in how they think and act politically. Citizens in the West have a long experience with democratic elections and autonomous social groups to represent their interests. These experiences have nurtured attachments to democratic values and an understanding of how the democratic process functions. Even within Western Europe, moreover, people differ in their emphasis on different aspects of the democratic model: the French are more likely to engage in protest because of their revolutionary historical traditions; the British favor more conventional politics. Differences in the proportion of the public who vote is partially a function of legal institutions such as registration laws, but voter turnout also depends on the sense of obligation to participate among the public. Such variations in political norms shape the nature of politics in a nation.

The question of political norms has special relevance to the study of Eastern Europe. To what extent have democratic values and norms become consolidated in the new democracies of the East? Furthermore, East Europeans may have different expectations for how democracy should function and their role as individuals within this new political system. What has been the legacy of their communist histories? Democracy requires that its citizens share its fundamental values, and the development of such values in the East remains one of the important questions in the study of European politics.

By examining citizen attitudes and behavior, this chapter should help us understand what democracy expects of its citizens, what citizens expect of their government, and the variations in how democratic citizens can participate in the political process in the various parts of Europe.

The Cultural Foundations of Democracy

As the democratization wave swept across Eastern Europe in the early 1990s, the key questions were whether, where, and how it might succeed. The answer would not only determine the political fate of the East; it held immediate implications for the peace and stability of Western Europe. In the 1970s,

political analysts were similarly concerned about the viability of new democracies in southern Europe—Spain, Portugal, and Greece. In the 1950s political experts asked about the democratic potential of postwar Germany and Italy.

Democratic progress in Eastern Europe over the past decade has been quite remarkable. Despite severe economic downturn, struggles with new democratic procedures, and a host of social problems, most of these nations have maintained their democratic course. But beyond the institutional changes, there is a deeper question of whether East Europeans have accepted democratic principles and learned their rights and responsibilities under a democratic system. The futures of these new democracies partially will depend on the values and beliefs of their citizens. If people share the values of the political system, then it is more likely that they and the system can function more effectively. If the public rejects the system or does not agree with its principles, it can lead to the type of revolts that swept across Eastern Europe in the early 1990s, when one authoritarian communist regime after another fell in a largely bloodless series of revolutions.

We refer to these shared attitudes as the *political culture* of a nation.[1] The political culture summarizes what the people think and feel about politics, attitudes that have evolved from history and traditions. During times of regime change, the agreement between the public's political norms and the institutions and procedures of the new political system is especially important. For example, most scholars believe that the Weimar Republic collapsed in the 1930s because many German citizens and elites did not really believe in democracy. Prior experiences had taught Germans to accept authoritarian and ethnocentric values, attitudes that would make them susceptible to the demagogic appeals of Hitler and the Third Reich. Thus post–World War II West Germany once again faced the question of whether the new institutions of democracy could succeed if Germans lacked democratic values and attachments to the new democratic system. Fortunately, military defeat and a postwar economic growth led to a transformation of the West German political culture (see Chapter 6). The Spanish transition to democracy generated similar questions, and fortunately a similarly positive answer (see Chapter 7).

Now we face the same question for the citizens in Eastern Europe. What are the enduring historical, political, and cultural legacies of communism and the pre-communist regimes of Eastern Europe? Do Poles, Czechs, Russians, and the other nationalities of Eastern European adhere to a set of political values that support the democratic process, or has prior communist rule created undemocratic and authoritarian values that may produce a fragile new political order. For example, today we are asking again whether Germans accept the democratic process that has emerged since the fall of the Berlin Wall—only now the question involves the Federal Republic's new citizens in the East.

Political culture is not only important for predicting the viability of a new political system, it also influences the style of politics within a given institutional framework. The style of Italian politics, for example, differs from Dutch politics, although both are democracies with multiparty systems, parliamentary structures, and coalition governments. When Czechoslovakia divided in 1993 into the Czech and Slovak Republics, it was immediately apparent that political expectations varied in these two new nations despite their common political heritage. Institutional structures can explain a portion of these cross-national differences, but a substantial part of the explanation is how the public and the elites envision the political process.

Social Trust and Democracy

What does it take to become a democratic polity? One of the recurring themes in political theory and observation is that a political culture develops from the pattern of social relations in a nation. Tocqueville, for instance, wrote that democracy should develop as a habit of the heart reflecting basic values and patterns of social relations: "The manners of the people may be considered as one of the great general causes to which the maintenance of a democratic republic in the United States is attributable."[2] The first president of Czechoslovakia, Tomas Masaryk, similarly argued that democracy is not only a form of government, it is not only what is written in constitutions; democracy is a view of life, rests on faith in man, in humanity, and in human nature.

Research on modern democracies similarly shows that tolerance and patterns of cooperative social relationships are the wellsprings of the democratic process.[3] A society such as Norway, with its tolerance and social trust, provides a fertile ground for developing a democratic political culture and a democratic polity.[4] Other analysts have suggested that social trust and cooperative social relations improve one's health, lower crime rates, improve child welfare, lessen social inequality, and generally improve the quality of life—a seeming panacea for societal needs.[5] Authoritarian political systems, such as Nazi Germany or Spain under Franco, often built upon and fostered societies in which interpersonal trust and cooperation were absent, and therefore democratic discourse was difficult to maintain.

This theory about the cultural basis of democracy has led to much speculation about the potential social base for democracy in Eastern Europe.[6] On the one hand, the collectivist nature of communism was designed to develop a feeling of mutual solidarity among the citizenry. Communist systems spawned aspects of a civil society that might have provided a training ground for democratic social norms to develop. Worker collectives addressed employment-related problems, neighborhood collectives handled residential issues, and joint action was encouraged by the state. On the other hand, communist systems sustained themselves through force and coercion. The public was told to be obedient to the state, and security police ensured conformity to the regime's directives. Collective action was allowed, but only under direction of the monopolistic Communist Party and the state; the type of spontaneous and autonomous social life that Tocqueville admired in America could not flourish in the East.

Evidence of the link between social relations and democratic politics—and a first view of the values of East Europeans—can be seen in a recent survey in which citizens in twenty European nations were asked whether they trust their fellow citizens. Figure 2.1 illustrates how the levels of interpersonal trust varies across nations in 1995–1998—after several years of democratic experience.[7] For comparative purposes we include data for the United States as well. The nations with continuous democratic

FIGURE 2.1 Personal Trust and Democracy

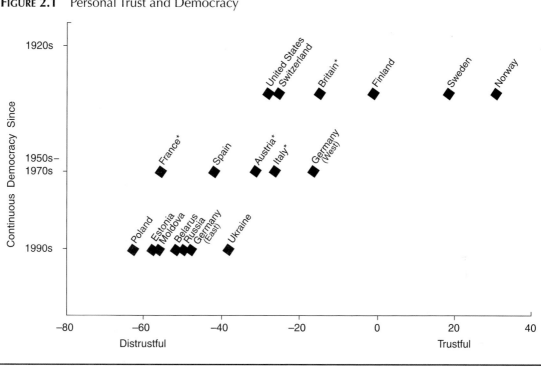

Source: Personal trust from *1995–1998 World Values Survey.*

histories during this century display relatively high levels of interpersonal trust; the two nations (Germany and Spain) that experienced authoritarian disruption in mid-century have publics which are slightly less trustful.

The evidence from Eastern Europe is ambiguous on the potential democratic culture in these nations. Levels of interpersonal trust are generally lower for Eastern Europe and the former states of the Soviet Union (Russia, Belarus, and the Baltic states) than for the established Western democracies. Communism did not create a trusting and tolerant citizenry and these patterns have carried over to the present. At the same time, the levels of social trust in Eastern Europe are not markedly different from the situation in the postwar transitional democracies in the West (Germany and Spain). Moreover, these are the public sentiments that exist near the beginning of the democratic transition; subsequent experiences may encourage (or discourage) social trust.

We may ask whether democracies create a trustful and tolerant society, or whether a trustful society leads to a democratic political system. Obviously it works both ways. For example, West Germans were more trustful than East Germans in 1990 and this continues in 1996; this may have been a result of Westerners living in a democratic system as well as democracy encouraging this aspect of the culture. The important conclusion is that there is a relationship between social and political life. It is difficult for democracy to endure when people lack trust and respect for each other. When these values exist, a democratic government must reinforce them; when they are lacking, an aspiring democracy must create them. The legacy of communism's impact on social trust has persisted during the 1990s, and the hope is that democratization will gradually change these norms.

The political culture begins with social relations, but it develops into more specific political attitudes. These elements of the political culture determine the viability of a democratic political system and the style of politics within the existing institutional structure.

The Levels of a Political Culture

Beyond social norms, the political culture embodies citizen orientations toward three levels: (1) the political system, (2) the political and policymaking process, and (3) policy outputs (Table 2.1). The *system* level involves the citizens' and leaders' views of the political community and the values and organizations that hold the political system together. Does the public identify with the nation and accept the general system of government? The *process* level encompasses expectations of how politics should function and individuals' relationship to the political process. For instance, public attitudes toward the procedures of government and political institutions, such as the principles of pluralist democracy and support for parliamentary government, are important in defining how politics actually functions. The *policy* level deals with citizens' and leaders' expectations from the government. What are the government's policy goals and how are they to be achieved?

TABLE 2.1 The Aspects of Political Culture

Aspects of Political Culture	Examples
System	Pride in nation
	National identity
	Legitimacy of government
Process	Role of citizens
	Perceptions of political rights
	Norms of political process
Policy	Role of government
	Governmental policy priorities

The System Level

Public attitudes toward the nation and the political system are an important component of a nation's political culture. These sentiments are often acquired early in life through the influence of parents and the educational system. Therefore, these are fairly stable beliefs that are relatively independent of attitudes on more specific political matters.

Public acceptance of the legitimacy of the political system provides a foundation for a successful, or at least enduring, political system. When citizens believe that they ought to obey the laws, then legitimacy is high. If they question the authority of the state, or if they comply only from fear, then legitimacy is low. A major problem in building support for a new political system is to convince the citizenry that the new government is legitimate, and thus its directives should be followed voluntarily.

A strong emotional tie to the nation also can provide a basis of support that reinforces the public's acceptance of the polity and can maintain a political system through temporary periods of political stress. Supportive attitudes toward the nation can be one basis of legitimacy for the government and its actions. The deep sense of national pride and national destiny voiced by Winston Churchill during World War II struck a responsive chord with the British public, thus enabling Britain to endure in the face of a major challenge to its existence. In contrast, in Weimar Germany most of the people did not identify with its democratic institutions and thus when they faced political and economic crisis, their loyalties shifted toward a new system.

A similar question now faces many of the nations of Eastern Europe. Some nations, such as Poland, have a strong national identity, but many others are relatively new political constructs that lack public identifications. Virtually all East European nations have new constitutions written during the 1990s, and many have existed as independent nations for only a few years. The past few decades have also seen considerable tumult and political debate in many Western European states. Thus we might ask whether European publics—in West and East—have a strong sense of national identity.

Feelings of pride in one's nation are a revealing example of this aspect of the political culture, as shown in Figure 2.2. By the mid–1990s, the worst upheavals of the political transition were past in most of Eastern Europe, and it was more likely that enduring national traits were beginning to appear. Most nations enjoy widespread feelings of pride among their citizens. Americans are noted for their expressions of national pride, but equal enthusiasm is displayed by the Poles, the Portuguese, the Span-

Figure 2.2 Feelings of National Pride (percent "Very Proud" and "Proud")

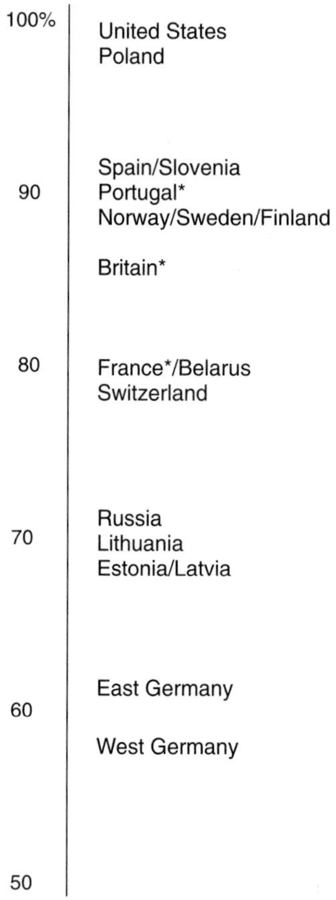

100%	United States Poland
90	Spain/Slovenia Portugal* Norway/Sweden/Finland Britain*
80	France*/Belarus Switzerland
70	Russia Lithuania Estonia/Latvia
60	East Germany West Germany
50	

Source: *1995–98 World Values Survey;* nations marked by an asterisk are from the *1990–1991 World Values Survey.*

ish, and other nationalities around the world. Strong feelings about the nation exist in both Western and Eastern Europe. National pride is not a function of the longevity or past political form of the nation.

More problematic are the cases where the populace does not identify with the nation; this raises warning signals for the polity and the system. For example, national pride was relatively low in Czechoslovakia in an earlier survey conducted in 1990—within three years the nation had split in two. In the German case, many political leaders have consciously worked to avoid the nationalism of the past, and it shows. The German publics in both the eastern and western regions are reserved in their feelings of national pride. National pride is also relatively restrained in Russia, most likely a reflection of the struggles Russia has faced over the decade: the collapse of the Soviet Union, the loss of superpower status, and the failures of the economy. Most Europeans, however, express pride in their nation virtually regardless of its historical traditions or national status. Like pride in a sports team, true fans are supportive regardless of what occurs on the field.

The Process Level

The second level of the political culture involves what the public expects of the political process. What do Hungarians think is expected of them as citizens, and what do they expect of their government? Are their views different from those of British or Spanish citizens?

Political theorists generally stress three norms as the basis of the Western democratic process. The first is the Lockean emphasis on popular sovereignty as the basis of governmental authority and the final arbiter of politics. Democracy must, above all, be based on the rule of the people. The second is a commitment to the equality of citizens based on the arguments of Jefferson, Bentham, and Paine. The third is the principle of majoritarian decision making, with adequate protection of minority rights. These principles lead to specific procedures by which democratic processes are ensured, such as formulated in Robert Dahl's "conditions of polyarchy."[8]

Research on Western European countries generally finds broad public support for *democratic values.*[9] The publics and political elites accept the principle of organizing political institutions based on popular control through regular elections, as well as the principles of party competition and the turnover of leadership through elections. Most Western Europeans recognize the legitimacy of conflict over political means and ends, while opposing violence as means of political settlement. These citizens also broadly endorse the right of individual participation and majority rule, paired with the protection of minority rights.

At the same time, we cannot become complacent about public support for democracy in the

Box 2.1   A Persistent Political Culture

Although Britain follows democratic procedures, it remains a constitutional monarchy and its traditions underscore the importance attached to the Crown. For example, the Queen of England presides over the opening of the new Parliament following the general elections. The Lords and Ladies assemble in the House of Lords, along with the Bishops of the Church, foreign ambassadors, members of the royal family, and other dignitaries. When the Queen arrives from the palace, the members of the House of Commons are summoned by Blackrod following a centuries old tradition. When both houses of parliament are assembled, the Queen delivers an address outlining the policies of "her" government during the next legislative session.

(The opening of Parliament, as well as weekly Question Hour in the House of Commons, are broadcast on C-SPAN by many U.S. cable television systems).

West. Often there is a gap between public support for these democratic norms in principle and their application in specific cases. Many people say they support free speech, but they are less willing to actually grant this right to political groups that challenge or attack their values. Still, most citizens in the established democracies of the West accept the principles upon which their democratic system was founded and functions today.

Prior European transitions from authoritarianism to democracy show how a prior authoritarian state could leave a negative cultural heritage. Postwar Italy began with a cultural legacy of fascist attitudes that was not conducive to the workings of democracy, but the Italian culture was transformed and democratic values became the norm.[10] The postwar German public held broadly undemocratic views, and the remaking of the West German political culture over the next generation was quite remarkable. Postwar Austria struggled to overcome a similar cultural inheritance from fascism. The more recent democratic transitions in Spain and Portugal reflected this same pattern. The Francoist regime was born as an antidemocratic movement and was based on authoritarian norms. With Franco's failing health and Spain's efforts to integrate itself into Western Europe, the Spanish process of cultural transformation created new public values that were more conducive to democracy (see Chapter 7).

In short in several Western European nations the hostility of a prior right-wing authoritarian state toward pluralism and democratic procedures created an undemocratic (or antidemocratic) political culture among its citizenry. The subsequent democratic regime inherited a public that was critical of its institutions and unsupportive of its norms. The new regime's task was to remold citizen beliefs into a culture compatible with democratic processes.

The cultural legacy of communism raises a similar question for the nations of Eastern Europe. At the outset of the democratization process, it was difficult to know whether these nations would face the same cultural problems as the previous authoritarian/democratic transitions in Western Europe. Democracy illustrated the internal contradictions of the communist system. Although the Soviet Union and other Eastern European states suppressed dissent and prohibited meaningful forms of representative democracy, the official rhetoric of these regimes often endorsed democratic principles. Elections were regularly held, and turnout routinely topped 90 percent of the eligible electorate. Many of these governments also mobilized their citizenry into an array of political organizations, ranging from labor unions to women's federations and state-sanctioned environmental groups. While some communist regimes were openly authoritarian, others displayed examples of a nascent form of democracy. Gorbachev's reforms of *perestroika* and *glasnost* built upon these tendencies, and stronger reform movements existed within Eastern Europe.[11]

Almost as soon as the Berlin Wall fell, survey researchers moved eastward, quickly assembling a wealth of findings on the attitudes of Russians and East Europeans toward democratic institutions and procedures. Several observers have found surpris-

FIGURE 2.3   Democratic Values in Western and Eastern Europe, 1996

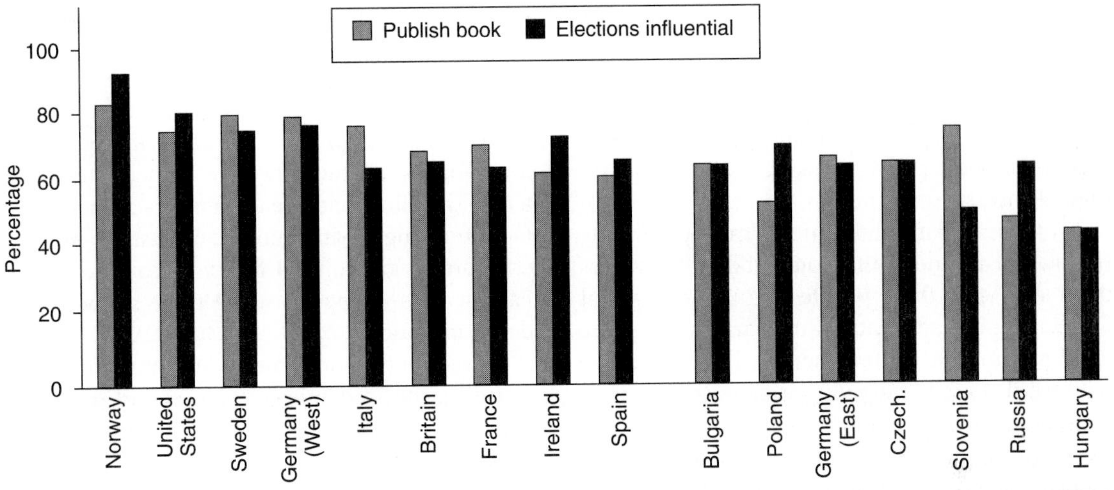

Note: Percentages indicate agreement with the statements "revolutionaries should be allowed to publish books expressing their views" and "elections are a good way of making governments pay attention to the important political issues facing our country." Missing data are excluded from the calculations of percentages.

Source: International Social Survey Program, 1996.

ingly high levels of support for basic democratic principles in the former Soviet Union and other East European nations.[12] Figure 2.3 compares the opinions of Westerners and Easterners on two basic examples of democratic values: willingness to allow a revolutionary to publish a book and belief that elections make government responsive. Almost two-thirds of the public in Western Europe are willing to allow even a revolutionary the opportunity to publish a book, and East Europeans average only a few percentage points lower. Similarly, most Westerners believe that elections make government pay attention to the people, and these opinions are only slightly lower in the East. Indeed, since the earliest surveys after the collapse of communism, East Europeans have displayed surprising support for democratic values. One should also note that democratic sentiments are among the lowest in Russia, a likely reflection of the economic and social tumult that has accompanied the transition toward democracy.

The support for democratic principles in Eastern Europe is somewhat surprising given the attempts of the prior regimes to instill communist values among the citizenry. To many Eastern Euro-

peans, however, these democratic rights represent a new reality for which they had fought the old regime. The Solidarity demonstrations in Poland, the protests in central Prague, the candlelight marches in Leipzig, and the public response to the August 1991 Russian coup demonstrate this commitment. Having newly won these freedoms, Eastern Europeans apparently openly endorse them.

After half a century or more of communism, how did these publics come to express such support for democratic norms? There is no single answer, and researchers point to several factors. The limited empirical evidence suggests that support for the prior communist system eroded sharply during the 1980s. Eastern Europeans saw their living standards decline during the decade, and the government seemed unwilling or unable to respond. This eroded popular support for the communist system and its values. And, ironically, the old regimes had voiced support for democratic principles, even if the reality of the communist system was much different. These democratic sentiments were further encouraged by *perestroika* and *glasnost* reforms—albeit with different consequences than Gorbachev had envisioned. The positive model of the West also appealed to many Easterners, as seen in the mass exodus from East Germany in 1989. Furthermore, the euphoria of the democratization wave in 1989–1991 undoubtedly boosted support for the new political creed. Even with these explanations, the extensive support for democratic principles in Eastern Europe is still a surprising starting point for these democratic transitions.

Although democratic principles appear fairly similar in East and West, more striking differences often appear in how people evaluate the actual functioning of democracy in their nation. In some Eastern European nations there is a widening gap between the public's support for democratic principles and their views of the present political process. For instance, a recent poll commissioned by the European Union found that the majority of the public in sixteen of nineteen Eastern European and former-Soviet nations was dissatisfied with the way democracy was developing in their nation.[13] There are increasing frustrations with the ability of the new political institutions to deal with the economic and social problems existing in Eastern Europe, which may eventually carry over to public support for the democratic process itself.[14] Furthermore, events such as the Bosnian and Kosovo conflicts, the rise of an authoritarian government in Belarus, and the internal political struggles in Russia constantly remind us that the prospects for democracy remain uncertain in many Eastern European states.

In the end, we should be cautious in reaching conclusions from Eastern European public opinion surveys as democracy is still developing in these nations. It is difficult to evaluate the depth of Easterners' feelings about democracy, whether these are enduring cultural norms or the temporary response to traumatic political events. Still, even if public expressions of democratic values lack the permanence to be described as an enduring political culture, the widespread expression of such values is a positive signal for democratic prospects in the East. The citizens in most post-communist states began their experience with democracy by espousing strong support for democratic principles, which facilitates the democratization process. As two of the nations in this volume demonstrate, Poland and Hungary

have made impressive progress in developing competitive elections, ensuring the rule of law, and protecting democratic liberties. Democratic development in Russia is less certain—but still we have to be impressed by the survival of even fragile democracy in Russia. Most Russians value democracy and freedom—although a significant minority still longs for a less democratic state. Rather than the apathy or hostility that greeted democracy after transitions from right-wing authoritarian states in Western Europe, the cultural legacy of communism in Eastern Europe appears to be more supportive of democratization.

By comparison, most Western Europeans broadly endorse democratic values and principles. However, dissatisfaction with the incumbents of office and the current governing parties is growing in the West.[15] For instance, the French political system recently has experienced a series of political scandals reaching up to the highest political officials. Criticisms of the political parties have become commonplace in many other Western party systems, and public identification with political parties has generally eroded. Up to this point, the dissatisfaction with the holders of democratic office has not generalized into disaffection with the democratic process. Indeed, the goal of democratic politics is to give the public an institutionalized way to express their dissatisfaction by electing new public officials and changing the policies of government.

The Policy Expectations Level

A third level of the political culture is the public's expectations of what government should achieve. In one sense, these expectations involve specific policy demands. When Soviet mineworkers protest the government's privatization programs or British farmers lobby the European Union on agricultural policy, they are testing the democratic process. More broadly, public views about policy—the legitimate scope of government, the needs and wants that government should address, and the areas that should remain in the private sphere—define the parameters for government action.

The history of Western democracies records great conflict over just these questions. Industrialization raised issues about the government's role in providing the infrastructure for modern commerce. The labor and social democratic movements of the nineteenth century focused debate on the government's rightful role in the provision of basic social needs and the management of the economy. The urbanization process within Europe created new demands on municipal governments, and new questions of urban development and redevelopment. More recently, the environmental movement has demanded that governments address the environmental costs of economic activity and ensure environmental quality. Other social interests have pressed the government to become active in everything from training rock bands to preserving the nation's historic sites.

Indeed, nearly all Western European democracies have seen government activity grow during the latter half the twentieth century (see Chapter 1). The various branches of government in the United States spend roughly a third of the GNP, but many European governments account for half (or more!) of the GNP. Governments are now responsible for a variety of social and personal conditions that were once outside the domain of government activity. Analysts attribute at least a portion of this growth to the expanding expectations of the public.[16] People expect and demand more of their government and they are promised more by politicians; thus government has expanded to meet these expectations. As Anthony King has written: "Once upon a time, man looked to God to order the world. Then he looked to the market. Now he looks to government."[17]

These public expectations have several important implications for contemporary European politics. Although most Western Europeans expect more of their government, there are still sharp cross-national and domestic differences in exactly what is expected. Labor unions want government to expand the benefits given to workers; businesses want government to provide tax incentives and subsidies to spur economic growth. Environmentalists want the government to spend more on protecting the environment; commuters want the government to build more roads and expand public transportation. The essence of democratic politics is to find the balance between these competing interests.

As Western European governments grew over the past generation, some people began to complain against high taxation and the excess of government action. Some political analysts claimed that government was overloaded by the excessive demands it faced.[18] They argued that too many demands for too many policies were more than what democratic government could provide in an effective and efficient way. Others maintained that government was usurping individual freedom and private initiative. Public opinion surveys showed a renewed skepticism of government action as many Europeans began to question the government's appropriate role in society. Margaret Thatcher rode these sentiments to power in Britain; she championed a neoconservative campaign in the 1980s that scaled back government by privatizing government-owned businesses and reducing the government's responsibility in other policy areas. Conservative governments in the Netherlands, Scandinavia, Germany, and the United States have echoed these statements and policies. Thus, during the past decade, many Western European societies have renewed the debate about the appropriate role of government.

GOVERNMENT AND THE ECONOMY   Just as Western Europeans began questioning the appropriate role of government in the 1980s, the political changes in Eastern Europe and the Soviet Union added a new theme to this discussion. State corporations and government agencies almost exclusively controlled the command economies of Eastern Europe. The government set both wages and prices as well as directing the economy. It was also responsible for providing for individual needs, ranging from guaranteed employment to the provision of housing and health care. "Cradle to grave socialism" was more than just a slogan in Eastern Europe.

The collapse of these systems has created new questions. The lack of popular support for the communist political system also weakened support for the socialist economic system. This clearly occurred in Eastern Europe, as non-communist governments and their citizens rushed to privatize their economies. This partially reflected the economic failures of the old regime. The Eastern European economies could provide the basic needs of their citizens, but they were uncompetitive on the world market and fell steadily behind the economic progress of the West.

The democratization of Eastern European political systems was paralleled by a privatization of their economies. To what extent do Eastern Europeans carry forward their expectations for government activities from the experiences of the prior regimes? Do Poles and Hungarians expect the new governments to guarantee employment despite the economic principles of their new market economies? Similarly, do Germans in the West and East have similar expectations about what services government should provide, or has unification created a public with sharply contrasting views of the government's appropriate role? The collapse of communism does not necessarily mean that Eastern Europeans have rejected the socialist principles of their former systems—principles that could often conflict with their new market economies.

We can describe the present policy norms of Europeans by comparing opinions in several areas. At the heart of the debate on the government's role is the question of government management of the economy. This separates both conservatives and liberals in the West, as well as forms a potential East-West divide. Comparative research shows that levels of economic development are one influence on these opinions; the citizens of less-affluent nations are generally more in favor of government action as a strategy for economic development.[19] In addition, we want to compare the nations with established market economies in the West with the new market economies in Eastern Europe.

Figure 2.4 shows how various groups of nations differ in their support for government control of wages and prices as examples of government management of the economy. The more-affluent countries of northern Europe (for example, Germany, France, Britain, Sweden, and Denmark) are less likely to favor government management of the economy. Resistance to government management has grown in these nations, paralleling the privatization of government-owned businesses and the sell-off of some government monopolies. The less-affluent nations of Western Europe (Ireland, Spain,

and Italy) are somewhat more supportive of government management of the economy.

Equally interesting are the results for Eastern Europe. The dismantling of the socialist economies in the East was accompanied by the public's endorsement of a greater role for a market economy. But East Europeans are still more likely to favor a greater role for government in the economy, especially in Russia. A full 90 percent of the Russian public felt the government should control prices—partially a reaction to the runaway inflation that plagued Russia in the 1990s—and 68 percent of Russians also believe the government should control wages. More generally, Russians remain relatively supportive of a socialist economy because the experience with capitalism has fallen far short of the experience in the West.[20]

It is illuminating to compare support for a government managed economy in the various social strata in Eastern Europe. The better educated are the "carriers of the creed" in most societies.[21] These are the individuals who normally occupy positions of status and influence; they are the operators of the existing economic and political systems. In addition, adherence to the norms of the regime was often a criterion for gaining access to higher education in Eastern Europe. One could not attend the university without being a member in the correct communist youth groups, and without a good family record of support for the regime. Thus we would expect the better educated to espouse the values of the communist and socialist systems of pre-1989. In fact, just the opposite occurs. When the old regimes were just ending in the early 1990s, the better-educated Eastern Europeans showed little affection for socialism.[22] Instead of adhering to the values of the old regime, as is normally the case, the better educated were the strongest advocates for a privatized economy. In some ways this is not surprising; the intelligentsia of the communist society led the protests in East Berlin or Prague, and the faces of young university students were prominent in these crowds. Perhaps communism fell as rapidly as it did because it had lost the support of the operators and technicians of the old regime.

The communist regimes were better able to socialize the less educated into believing in govern-

FIGURE 2.4   Support for Government Management of the Economy

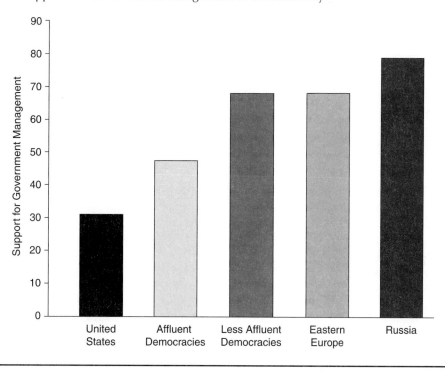

Source: International Social Survey Program, 1996. The figure averages support for government control of wages and control of prices.

ment management of the economy. This pattern holds in most of the nations in Eastern Europe. Think of the irony: these regimes claimed to represent workers and peasants, and the less educated actually adhered to these socialist principles. The true beneficiaries of these regimes—the better educated—doubted their value. This may be attributed to the fact that the better educated were more aware of the superior productivity of the market systems of the West.

In contrast to the generally steady political progress that has been made over the past decade, Eastern Europeans have had a tumultuous economic experience (see Chapter 1). Living standards declined precipitously in many nations after the collapse of communism, and the economic shocks of capitalist market forces were unsettling to many. Yet support for market principles still exists. A 1996 survey by the European Union found that market

reforms received majority support among Eastern Europeans, although 65 percent of Russians said it was wrong for their nation.[23]

The juxtaposition of economic and political images can be seen clearly in results from the 1998 *New Democracies Barometer*.[24] Residents in Central and Eastern Europe were asked to judge the past, present, and future economic and political systems. Figure 2.5 shows that most Eastern Europeans, even in 1998, expressed greater approval for the pre-1989 socialist economy than for the contemporary economic system. Russian images show an even greater contrast: in 1996, 83 percent of Russians approved of the former economic system, versus only 18 percent for the present system.[25] This is a clear signal of the disaffection that has resulted from the drop in living standards and the economic insecurities that have accompanied the restructuring of these economies.

FIGURE 2.5   Public Approval of the Economic and Political Systems in Central and Eastern Europe, 1998

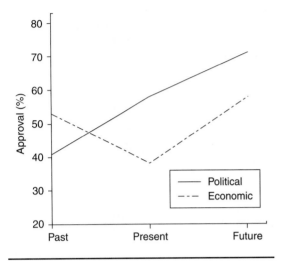

Source: Richard Rose and Christian Haerfer, *New Democracies Barometer V* (Strathclyde: Center for the Study of Public Policy, 1998): 17, 25; combined results from representative surveys in Bulgaria, the Czech Republic, Hungary, Poland, Romania, Slovakia, and Slovenia.

At the same time, there are several positive indicators in these opinion surveys. Approval of the present economic system has improved between 1991 and 1998. Furthermore, Eastern Europeans remain optimistic that the economic system in five years time will be much better. In addition, there is a significant juxtaposition of economic and political images. The citizens of Eastern Europe are more positive about their present political system than the pre-1989 system, and these impressions have improved since 1991. Political expectations for the future are very optimistic, even though most Eastern Europeans expect that it will require several more years to deal with the problems inherited from the communists.

THE GOVERNMENT'S POLICY RESPONSIBILITIES   Government management of the economy is one of the most basic forms of its policy activities. Governments are also involved in a great many other social activities, from deterring crime to protecting the quality of the environment. Recent public opinion surveys show that many people believe the government is responsible for promoting individual well-being and guaranteeing the quality of life for its citizens—and both Westerners and Easterners share these expectations.

Table 2.2 displays the percentage of the public in several European nations (and the United States) who think the government is "definitely responsible" for dealing with specific social problems. East Europeans, who were conditioned by their former regimes to expect big government, have high expectations of their democratic governments. Most citizens in East Germany, Hungary, Poland, and Russia believe the government is definitely responsible for providing for health care, providing a decent standard of living for the elderly, protecting the environment, and lessening unemployment. Expectations of the state are especially high among Russians.

At the same time, many West Europeans share these high expectations of government. The British, Spaniards, Italians, and Norwegians also have high expectations of their governments. Thus support for government action to resolve social needs is a core element of the European political culture, even if there are significant cross-national differences in exactly what is expected.

In comparison to most Europeans, Americans are more reserved in accepting government action. Even in areas where the government is a primary actor, such as care of the elderly and unemployment, only a minority of Americans view these problems as definite government responsibilities. The United States is a major exception among Western democracies in its limited support for activist government. Analysts often explain the conservative socioeconomic attitudes of Americans by the individualist nature of American political culture and the absence of a socialist working-class party.

Some political scientists cite these opinions as the reason that the scope of government has grown so large in Europe over the past generation. Others claim that these opinions result from the growth of government activism, which has conditioned the public to expect even more from government.[26] In either case, these expectations are another example of how political culture and political outcomes tend to converge. Governments can grow more easily

TABLE 2.2 Government Responsibility for Dealing with Social Issues (in %)

	United States	Britain	France	Spain	Italy	Sweden	Norway	West Germany	East Germany	Hungary	Poland	Russia
Provide health care for sick	39	82	53	81	81	71	87	51	66	71	69	82
Provide decent living standard for the elderly	38	73	51	80	76	69	86	48	64	63	68	87
Strict environmental laws	46	63	67	69	69	58	56	58	72	56	60	71
Give aid to needy college students	35	38	59	75	59	36	34	27	43	37	48	63
Keep prices under control	25	44	42	59	59	45	53	23	43	38	41	68
Provide job for everyone who wants one	14	29	40	61	41	35	48	28	57	47	58	71
Reduce income differences between rich and poor	17	36	49	57	41	43	41	25	48	41	48	49
Provide housing for those who need it	20	37	44	70	45	27	22	20	38	22	39	52
Provide a decent living standard for the unemployed	13	29	34	59	30	39	41	17	38	16	31	39
Provide industry with help	17	41	36	64	28	33	23	16	27	35	39	51
Average	26	47	48	68	53	46	49	31	50	43	50	63

Source: 1996 International Social Survey Program. Table entries are the percentage who say that each area should definitely be the government's responsibility. Missing data were excluded in the calculation of percentages.

when the public accepts (and expects) that they will grow. Governments are more likely to shrink when public support for government activism wanes. Thus it is more than a coincidence that the expansion of the welfare state in Scandinavian countries coincided with broad public support for social programs, while Margaret Thatcher's program of privatizing government-owned industries in Britain coincided with decreasing public support for nationalized industry.

Debates about the proper role of government will be a continuing feature of contemporary politics. But it is clear that most Europeans expect their government to protect social welfare, help the economy, and guarantee the quality of life. The question is not whether government should act, but how it should manage the diverse demands the public makes upon it.

Participation and Democracy

Democracy empowers its citizens with the ability to affect the course of government and to influence policy. Participation is one source of the legitimacy of a democratic system. The history of modern democracies is marked by the slow and often conflictual expansion of the public's participation in the political process. The growth of democracy can be measured by the public's broadening access to politics and the government's responsiveness to public demands.

Modern democracy is *representative democracy*; it enshrines elections as the main institution of democracy and the primary vehicle for public participation and democratic governance. Through elections, the public controls the selection of political leaders, which determines the formation of government and the policies the government will likely implement.

Although *election turnout* is now a standard part of contemporary democracy, the expansion of the franchise in Western Europe occurred only during the past century. At the start of the twentieth century most European democracies severely restricted the voting franchise. Britain, for instance, limited election rolls by placing significant residency and finan-

cial restrictions on voting and by allowing multiple votes for business owners and university graduates. In 1900 only 14 percent of the British adult population was eligible to vote. Similarly, Prussia used a weighted voting rule that gave a triple vote to the landed aristocracy and a single vote to laborers. Almost without exception, women were denied the right to vote.

During the twentieth century, suffrage rights were gradually extended to the adult population in Western Europe. Property restrictions were steadily rolled back. Most nations acknowledged the right of women to vote early in the century, but some countries delayed—most notably France until 1944 and Switzerland until 1970. During the 1970s, most nations also reduced the minimum voting age to eighteen. By the later half of this century, voting rights were essentially universal among the adult populations in Western Europe.

Even though the communist parties of Eastern Europe did not permit open competition, these nations also held regular elections, sometimes with multiple parties or a unified slate of candidates. Voting turnout routinely exceeded 90 percent of the eligible electorate; the last Soviet-era election of 1984 had an official turnout rate of 99.9 percent. Elections were not a method of popular influence, however; they were a means for the government to mobilize and indoctrinate the populace. Communist Party officials used elections as a way of propagandizing people, it reminded them that nonvoting signified opposition to the regime, which might jeopardize the nonvoter (and local officials who were responsible for ensuring a large turnout). Thus voting levels were consistently high even if some ballots had to be cast by election officials themselves. Nevertheless, elections were held and the public learned the mechanics of campaigns and the voting process.

Today, most eligible citizens participate in national elections in European democracies. Moreover, voting is a significant method of citizen influence because it selects political elites and determines the composition of the government. Elections also provide an opportunity for political

FIGURE 2.6   Levels of Election Turnout in Western and Eastern Europe

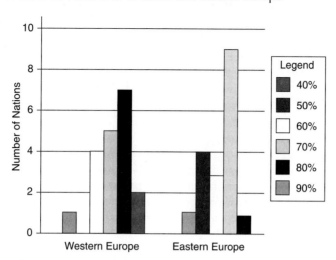

activists to participate in the selection of party candidates and to try to influence the political views of others. In some countries as many as a tenth to a fifth of the electorate attend a campaign meeting, work for a party, or participate in other campaign activities. Elections are national civics lessons in which voters learn about the past and future programs of the parties, participate in the democratic process, and decide about the issues facing their nation.

Figure 2.6 displays the distribution of election turnout in Western and Eastern Europe in the most recent national election for which data are available. What is most striking is the large range in voting turnout across these nations. The lowest level of involvement is in a well-established democracy, Switzerland, where less than half of the eligible electorate (43 percent) actually voted in 1999. Voting rates are consistently higher in most other European nations; in two nations where voting is still compulsory, turnout tops 90 percent (Belgium and Cyprus). Turnout rates in Eastern Europe were often quite high in the first elections after the democratic transition; now turnout in the East is a bit lower than the average levels of the established democracies in the West.

Cross-national differences in voting turnout illustrate how comparative analysis can identify the underlying nature of the democratic process.[27] Research finds that laws and institutions, such as the type of electoral system or registration regulations, directly affect participation rates. In addition, political competition and the structure of party choices strongly influence turnout levels. We know, for example, that turnout in American elections is significantly below the norm for European democracies, and this can largely be explained by such uniquely American characteristics as complicated registration requirements and the frequency of elections.[28]

Voting is the most common form of political action and the basis of representative democracy. Thus it is somewhat worrisome that electoral participation has gradually declined over the last few decades.[29] Turnout rates have decreased in most of Western Europe, especially in the early 1990s. Furthermore, participation in campaign activities beyond voting is also declining. Fewer citizens, even in established democracies, attend a campaign rally or display their partisan support during a campaign. Similarly, high turnout levels in the first democratic elections in Eastern Europe often have been followed by a drop-off in later elections. If elections

BOX 2.2 Protest in Action

Coal miners in several Eastern European nations have been active in organizing protests against the communist regimes during the democratic transitions, and have become one of the more assertive participants under the new democratic system. In Russia, for example, miners organized a series of strikes in the mid-1990s to protest their unpaid back wages and government plans to close down several mines. The unions claimed that up to a fourth of their members went without a paycheck each week. In the spring of 1998, Siberian coal miners went on strike and blockaded the Trans-Siberian railway for more than a week. There were sporadic actions of violence, and some spouses went on a hunger strike. Hundreds of union members set up a camp outside of Moscow for the summer to continue their protests. The government eventually persuaded the miners to return to work by taking emergency measures to pay off wage arrears and promising to investigate the reasons that wages were chronically going unpaid. Coal miners had been the first group of workers to mobilize independently under the Soviet regime when they launched a massive strike under Gorbachev in 1989, and they continue to demonstrate their political influence in the post-communist period.

are the celebration of democratic politics, fewer individuals seem to be joining in these celebrations.

The decrease of electoral participation is even more surprising when compared with the socioeconomic development of Europe described in the previous chapter. Contemporary electorates are better educated, better informed, and more interested in politics than their predecessors. Europeans are also more democratic in their values than was the public a generation ago. Nevertheless, electoral participation has decreased. Richard Brody refers to this as "the puzzle of political participation."[30] Why is electoral participation limited and decreasing, if the public's political skills and resources are increasing?

At the core of this question is a concern with the vitality of the democratic process. This view holds that higher levels of voting turnout are a positive feature for democracy. In general this is correct; democratic nations with high levels of turnout in elections are more successful in involving their citizens in the political process. Consequently, the decrease in turnout is often attributed to growing alienation from politics or a more general decline in civic life.

Another explanation for reduced levels of electoral participation is the development of a new style of *participatory democracy* among Western European publics. Instead of relying on indirect influence through elected officials, a growing share of contemporary publics now tries to influence politics directly. Referendums and initiatives are one way the public can directly decide public policy. More generally, citizen-action groups and public interest groups are pressing for greater consultative procedures for citizen input in policy formation and administration.[31]

Many citizen groups champion new styles of *unconventional political action*. Environmentalists climb polluting smokestacks, dye the effluents of polluters, stage mock die-ins, and risk their own lives to save whales and harp seals. Protest has become the extension of conventional politics used by the full range of societal interests (see Box 2.2). In addition, citizen groups press for the reform of policy formation and administrative procedures to provide greater direct citizen input in the policy process. Furthermore, newly formed Green parties have championed these calls for a more participatory democracy in Western Europe. Public interest groups ranging from the women's movement to local amenity societies support these reforms.

These developments may permanently change the style of political participation in advanced industrial democracies. New social movements have created an infrastructure for continued citizen involvement in the policy process. For instance, in Germany administrative law now gives the public more say in policy administration; in Italy new legislation gives the public legal standing in defending the environment in court, and the use of initiatives and referendums is generally increasing. Citizen groups such as these have legitimated direct-action methods of participation for other citizen groups. Today, Gray Panthers protest for senior citizen rights, consumers are active monitors of industry, and citizen groups of all kinds are proliferating.

The situation, of course, was different in communist Eastern Europe. These regimes involved the public in mass membership groups and state-sponsored political organizations.[32] In East Germany, for example, there were millions of members in the labor unions, the women's federation, and the German-Soviet Friendship Society. The number of citizens involved in political activity was possibly greater than in the West, but it was controlled by the Communist Party and state agencies.

This situation changed with the democratic revolutions of the 1990s. The political demonstrations of Solidarity, the mass protests in Leipzig and East Berlin, and the public demonstrations in the streets of Prague toppled communist regimes across Eastern Europe. These were "people power" revolutions where public pressures brought down the old regimes and created democracies in their place. The Eastern Europeans very quickly became involved in democratic politics.

The extent of participatory democracy among Europeans can be estimated by the public's involvement in protest and other forms of direct action. As Table 2.3 shows, most Western Europeans have signed a petition, the mildest form of participatory democracy. One can hardly enter a Marks & Spencer in Britain or a Kaufhof in Germany without being asked to sign a petition. In some nations, this form of direct action is more common than voting in

TABLE 2.3 Cross-National Levels of Unconventional Political Action (in %)

Signed a Petition		Participated in a Challenging Act[a]	
Britain°	75	Sweden	46
Sweden	72	Italy°	37
United States	71	France°	36
Switzerland	68	Norway	34
Germany (West)	66	Germany (West)	33
Norway	65	Netherlands°	27
Germany (East)	57	Germany (East)	27
France°	51	United States	25
Netherlands°	49	Britain°	25
Italy°	42	Latvia	23
Finland	39	Russia	22
Latvia	31	Finland	22
Lithuania	31	Estonia	22
Spain	22	Spain	22
Poland	20	Belarus	22
Slovenia	19	Lithuania	17
Ukraine	14	Slovenia	13
Russia	11	Poland	12
Belarus	10	Switzerland	12
Moldova	10	Moldova	9

[a]Respondents have engaged in at least one of the following acts: lawful demonstration, boycott, unofficial strike, or occupation of a building.
Source: 1995–98 *World Values Survey;* nations marked by an asterisk are from the *1990–1991 World Values Survey.*

elections. Signing petitions is less common among Eastern Europeans, especially in the successor states of the Soviet Union (Russia, Ukraine, Belarus, and Moldova). Even a decade after the democratic transitions, it appears that unconventional politics is more widely used and more easily tolerated in the established democracies of the West.

Political protest is an even stronger measure of direct political action. The second column in Table 2.3 shows that participation in a demonstration, a boycott, or other elite-challenging forms of protest is fairly common. Such unconventional action now often matches or exceeds normal involvement in campaign activities among Western Europeans.[33] Average Swedish, French, or Italian citizens are as likely to have engaged in protest activities as they are to have attended a campaign rally or worked for a candidate. The pattern of protest activity is more varied across Eastern Europe, although in almost all of these nations protest has declined as the tumultuous events of 1990–1991 have passed into history. The highest level of protest occurred in the former East Germany, where large-scale and widespread mass protests brought down the regime. Protest levels are quite low in Moldova, Poland, and Slovenia, which might signal that formerly communist nations hesitate to accept protest, except that Switzerland also ranks low. Protest reflects, at least in part, cultural norms supporting the use of challenging activities.

The nature of protest politics also differs between Western and Eastern Europe. The expansion of protest activities in Western Europe came as an extension of democratic rights to include new direct forms of participatory democracy. Protest in Eastern Europe arose to challenge the old political order and was often used by those without other sources of political power. Because protest politics was so successful, these participatory methods will likely continue even as the institutions of representative democracy, such as political parties and pressure groups, develop in Eastern Europe.

We thus need to speak of two significant developments in European political participation in the last two decades. First, there has been a quantitative growth in the public's involvement and interest in political matters. Many Europeans turn out at the polls, others work on political campaigns, a sizable number of individuals contact their representative directly to discuss political issues, many people belong to local community organizations, and large numbers are members of public interest groups.[34] Therefore some analysts describe the last two decades as a *participatory revolution*, during which public involvement in the democratic process grew. Now, the expansion of democracy to Eastern Europe gives additional meaning to this term.

Second, there has been a qualitative change in the patterns of political participation. The methods of representative democracy—voting and campaign work—are important activities because they determine the control of government. However, these are relatively blunt democratic tools since the typical election involves many issues and candidates. Some theorists even criticize representative democracy as a mechanism designed to limit the public's influence over government. Participatory democracy produces a qualitatively different form of citizen input. Involvement in a citizen action group or direct contact with policymakers allows the public to focus attention on a specific policy concern. The voice of the public is also louder when the citizens express their views themselves. Direct action gives citizens greater control over the timing and methods of participation, compared with the institutionalized framework of elections. Therefore the growing use of citizen-initiated participation increases popular control of political elites. Citizen participation is becoming more closely linked to citizen influence.

Recognizing that there are alternative methods of political action, researchers have found that different kinds of people engage in the various forms of participation.[35] Because voting places the least demands upon its participants, it is the most common form of political action and involves a diverse mix of people. By comparison, direct action methods require greater personal initiative and more sophisticated political skills. It is much more demanding to organize a letter-writing campaign or participate in a demonstration than to cast a ballot at the next election. Consequently, participation in direct forms of action often varies considerably by social status. While voting is spread across the electorate, direct action is now disproportionately used by the affluent and better educated. Similarly, only those with strong political beliefs are likely to become active in single-issue groups. This situation increases the participation gap between lower-status and higher-status individuals. As the better educated expand their political influence through direct action methods, less-educated citizens might be unable to compete on the same terms. Ironically, overall increases in political involvement may mask growing inequalities in citizen participation and influence, which run counter to democratic ideals.

The strength of the democratic process is its ability to adapt, evolve, and become more democratic. In recent years the political systems in most Western European states have adopted forms of participatory democracy and given their citizenry new methods to participate in the decisions affecting their lives. The nations of Western Europe vary in their emphasis on representative and participatory democracy, but nearly all are now characterized by a mix of these styles.

As they are learning about democracy, many Eastern Europeans have ambivalent feelings toward both of these styles of democratic participation. They recognize elections and representative democracy as essential elements of the modern democratic process. At the same time, many Easterners are disillusioned by the competitive style of electoral politics as practiced in the West. Many people are drawn to the principles of participatory democracy, albeit with a plebiscitarian emphasis. The conditions of affluence and civil society that nurture participatory democracy in the West are underdeveloped in the East; therefore participation in citizen action groups and direct action methods are relatively low in Eastern Europe. Ray Taras's discussion of Polish participation patterns illustrates their ambivalence to both representative and participatory styles of action (Chapter 9). Many Eastern Europeans still seem unsure about how best to participate in democratic politics, even if they support the principles of democracy.

The challenge for established and emerging democracies is to expand the opportunities for citizens to participate in the political process. To meet this challenge also means ensuring an equality of political rights and opportunities that will be even more difficult to guarantee with these new participation forms.

The Role of Interest Groups

A more institutionalized form of expressing citizen interests occurs through the activities of social or political groups that represent the interests of their members. In contrast to individual political action, interest groups normally have an established organizational base and often have professional staffs that provide expertise and leadership. In addition, interest groups often participate in the policymaking process, serving on government advisory bodies and testifying at parliamentary hearings.

Interest groups may take many forms. *Anomic interest groups* are generally spontaneous groups that form suddenly when many individuals respond to frustration, disappointment, or other strongly emotional events. They are flash affairs, rising and subsiding suddenly. Spontaneous student protest or an impromptu demonstration by frustrated soccer fans are examples of anomic groups. They normally act, and then dissipate. Like anomic groups, *nonassociational groups* rarely are well organized, and their activity is episodic. They differ from anomic groups because they are based on common interests of ethnicity, region, religion, occupation, or perhaps kinship. Because of these continuing economic or cultural ties, nonassociational groups have more continuity than anomic groups. *Institutional groups* have a formal structure and have other political or social functions besides interest articulation, such as political parties, business corporations, legislatures, armies, bureaucracies, and churches. Either as corporate bodies or as smaller groups within these bodies (legislative blocs, officer cliques, groups in the clergy, or ideological cliques in bureaucracies), such groups express their own interests or represent the interest of other groups in the society. The influence of institutional interest groups is usually derived from the strength of their primary organizational base, for instance, their union members or their affiliated businesses.

Political scientists often focus on *associational groups*. These groups form explicitly to represent the interests of a particular group. This includes trade unions, chambers of commerce and manufacturers' associations, ethnic associations, and religious associations. A special subset of associational groups includes civic groups, voluntary associations, and other groups formed to represent a policy interest or political perspective. These organizations have orderly procedures for formulating interests and demands, and they usually employ a full-time professional staff. Associational groups are often very active in representing the interests of their members in the policy process. For instance, in recent debates about health care in the United States there has been an enormous mobilization of pressure groups and lobbyists, representatives of doctors, health insurance organizations, and consumer groups, in efforts to influence legislation.

Thus, social interests can manifest themselves in many different ways. To highlight the different types of interest groups, we can describe various groups that involve members of the working class:

Anomic group: a spontaneous group of working class
individuals living in the same neighborhood
Nonassociational group: the working class as a
collective
Institutional group: the labor department within the
government
Associational group: a labor union

One of the distinctive features of West European democracies is the richness of the organizational life—all of these different types of groups exist. Moreover, in recent decades there has been a flowering of new groups to protect the environment, ensure equal rights for women, and advocate other public interests. Analysts often describe this organizational activity as comprising the *civil society* and maintain that a vibrant civil society is an essential base for a vibrant democracy.[36] Participation in associational and institutional groups socializes individuals into the types of political skills and cooperative relations that are part of a well-functioning society. Group activity also can help citizens to develop their own policy preferences, provide important information about politics, and help them articulate their interests to policymakers. Thus, an active public involved in a diversity of interest groups provides a fertile

ground for democracy, and one of the questions facing democracy in Eastern Europe is whether such a civil society can develop.

Associational interest groups are often directly involved in policymaking. Their organizational base gives them an advantage over nonassociational groups, and their tactics and goals are often recognized as legitimate in society. Labor unions, for example, are often central political actors because they represent the mass of the working class; in the same way, business associations often speak for the corporate interests of the nation. Farmers associations and religious groups are also major actors in the politics of most European nations. Indeed, in most European capitals the list of formal associational groups registered as lobbyists numbers into the thousands. By formally representing social interests, associational groups may limit the influence of anomic, nonassociational, and institutional groups.

Another type of associational group is composed of citizens who are united not by a common economic or individual self-interest, but by a common belief in a political ideology or a policy goal.[37] The environmental movement, women's groups, and other civic groups are examples of an associational group. These are pseudo-groups, in the sense that members may seldom interact directly and do not share common social characteristics (such as employment or ethnicity) but are bound together by their support of a political organization, such as Greenpeace or Amnesty International.

Many of the chapters on East Europe in this book discuss the problems faced by these newly democratized nations in building a rich associational group life in societies where organized groups have long been suppressed or controlled.[38] The Communist Party and the government bureaucracy dominated these nations for over 40 years, and the government controlled associational life in order to pursue its own goals. The process of building new, independent associational groups to articulate the specialized interests of different citizens is already underway and will be important to the democratic process.

While Eastern Europe faces questions of how to develop a rich associational life, there are also new questions about whether existing civil society is declining in the West. Memberships in labor unions and religious associations are down in most West European nations, as are memberships in some professional associations. Robert Putnam has written extensively on a similar pattern in the United States and implicitly suggests that a general pattern of social disengagement is possible in other contemporary democracies.[39] Instead of getting together with other citizens to solve community problems, as Tocqueville described the democratic ethos, Putnam claims that too many of us sit in front of our television screens and computer monitors experiencing a virtual reality. The evidence from Western Europe suggests that organizational involvement is increasing but that new styles of engagement are replacing the declining membership in some traditional associational groups.[40] This debate is still unresolved, but it underscores the importance attached to organizational life as a foundation of democracy.

The Public and Democracy

In many ways, the citizenry defines the essence of democratic politics. In its practice, democracy is a German at the polls casting a vote for her preferred party, a French farmer driving his tractor to Paris to demand changes in government agricultural policy, a Hungarian writing a letter to the Budapest *People's Freedom* to criticize government policy, or Russian mine workers protesting a cut in government benefits.

Public wants and needs set the priorities that democratic governments strive to address; citizen expectations of the political process influence the ways in which that process works and the kinds of policies it produces. Citizen participation in the political process presses a democracy to match its lofty ideals.

At the same time, we know that politics is a complex process. Interest groups, government officials, and others lobby their representatives about pending legislation. The priorities of government are the result of the complex interactions among these political actors. Through the various elements of the democratic process, it is obvious that public values and political institutions interact and influence each other, defining how politics really functions.

Our emphasis on the citizenry in this chapter does not presume that political culture and citizen action have a deterministic impact on the political process. Other parts of the process—interest groups, political parties, and political leaders—act as intermediaries between the public and policy outcomes, and their direct impact is often greater in the short term. Similarly, if we want to predict the success of democracy in Eastern Europe, it is much more important in the short term to study the actions and values of elites and the role of institutions.

Thus, the importance of citizen politics is not in explaining the daily outcomes of politics but in determining the broad boundaries of the political system. One political scientist described public opinion as a set of dikes, channeling the course of democratic politics and defining its boundaries. Research shows that the public's policy preferences influence policy outcomes in a democratic system—but this is through a complex and sometimes circuitous route.[41] In the same way, the public's expectations of politics and support for the political system determine the long-term functioning of the system. The immediate success of Eastern European democracies may depend on elite actions, but their long-term success depends on creating a democratic political culture among both the public and the elites. Democracy cannot endure in a nation without democrats.

Given this role for citizen values and behavior, our findings offer valuable insights into the democratic process in Europe. There are nearly two dozen established democracies in the West and nearly an equal number of new democracies in the East. The citizens in these nations generally share a common democratic creed, and these political systems are built upon common principles. Most Europeans express support for their political system and a sense of national identity, expectations about an activist government are also common.

Where these publics differ is in their conceptions about *how* the democratic process should function. The citizens of some nations display a more participatory style of democracy, with high levels of conventional and unconventional political action. The Dutch and the Danes, for example, are activist publics with institutional structures that encourage the representation of diverse political interests. Other Europeans, such as the British, accept a more representative style of democracy, placing greater reliance on the actions and judgments of elites and the role of elections as instruments of popular control. Other nationalities, such as the French or Italians, seem to follow a more conflictual style of politics, where protest and political strife are almost routine. Democracy follows a single set of principles, but it takes life in many forms.

The nations of Eastern Europe are now making choices about whether to become democratic and how to practice democracy. The transition to democracy will not be easy. These nations have a half-century of communist rule and they must surmount the legacy of this authoritarian rule. Many nations in Eastern Europe have suffered from violence and political corruption. Chapter 1 showed that several Eastern European nations still merit a poor score for political rights and their low civil liberties records. Some political experts argue that another form of authoritarian state lies in the future of these nations.

We do not overlook these difficulties, but we also note that these democratic transitions generally began with a majority of the citizenry and elites supporting democratic principles. Moreover, the international community is actively working to encourage freedom and political liberties in Eastern Europe. If democracy successfully takes root, we would expect that Eastern Europeans would also search for democratic forms that meet their particular histories and their expectations. Political debates over representative and participatory democracy, and over various institutional choices for democratic politics, are especially real in Eastern Europe as these systems are now taking shape. Thus the evolution of democracy continues with new trends among the consolidated democracies in the West and still unclear trends developing among the traditional democracies in Eastern Europe. How these two democratization processes develop will define the political fate of Europe in the next century.

✑ KEY TERMS ✑

anomic interest group	election turnout	participatory democracy	representative
associational group	institutional group	participatory revolution	democracy
civil society	new social movements	political culture	unconventional
democratic values	nonassociational group		political action

✑ SUGGESTED READINGS ✑

Almond, Gabriel, and Sidney Verba. *The Civic Culture.* Princeton: Princeton University Press, 1963.

———, eds. *The Civic Culture Revisited.* Boston: Little Brown, 1980.

Borre, Ole, and Elinor Scarbrough, eds. *The Scope of Government.* Oxford: Oxford University Press, 1995.

Brown, Archie, and Jack Gray. *Political Culture and Political Change in Communist States,* 2nd ed. New York: Holmes and Meier, 1979.

Dalton, Russell. *Citizen Politics: Public Opinion and Political Parties in Advanced Industrial Democracies,* 2nd ed. Chatham, NJ: Chatham House, 1996.

Eckstein, Harry, Frederic Fleron, Erik Hoffman, and William Reisinger, eds. *Can Democracy Take Root in Post-Soviet Russia? Explorations in State-Society Relations.* Latham, MD: Rowman & Littlefield, 1998.

Inglehart, Ronald. *Culture Shift in Advanced Industrial Society.* Princeton: Princeton University Press, 1990.

———. *Modernization and Postmodernization.* Princeton: Princeton University Press, 1997.

Jennings, M. Kent, and Jan van Deth, eds. *Continuities in Political Action.* Berlin: deGruyter, 1990.

Kaase, Max, and Ken Newton, eds. *Beliefs in Government.* Oxford: Oxford University Press, 1995.

Klingemann, Hans-Dieter, and Dieter Fuchs, eds. *Citizens and the State.* Oxford: Oxford University Press, 1995.

LeDuc, Lawrence, Richard Niemi, and Pippa Norris, eds. *Comparing Democracies: Global Elections and Parties.* Newbury Park, CA: Sage, 1996.

Norris, Pippa, ed. *Critical Citizens: Global Support for Democratic Governance.* Oxford: Oxford University Press, 1999.

Petro, Nicholai. *The Rebirth of Russian Democracy: An Interpretation of Political Culture.* Cambridge: Harvard University Press, 1995.

Pharr, Susan, and Robert Putnam, eds. *Discontented Democracies: What's Troubling the Trilateral Countries?* Princeton, Princeton University Press, 2000.

Putnam, Robert. *Bowling Alone: The Collapse and Revival of American Community.* New York: Simon and Schuster, 2000.

Putnam, Robert. *Making Democracy Work.* Cambridge: Harvard University Press, 1995.

Richardson, Jeremy, ed. *Pressure Groups.* New York: Oxford University Press, 1993.

Rose, Richard, William Mishler, and Christian Haerpfer. *Democracy and Its Alternatives: Understanding Post-Communist Societies.* Johns Hopkins University Press, 1998.

Verba, Sidney, Norman Nie, and Jae-on Kim. *Participation and Political Equality.* Cambridge: Cambridge University Press, 1978.

Verba, Sidney, Kay Schlozman, and Henry Brady. 1995. *Voice and Equality: Civic Volunteerism in American Politics.* Cambridge: Harvard University Press.

White, Stephen, Richard Rose, and Ian McAllister. *How Russia Votes.* Chatham, NJ: Chatham House Publishers, 1996.

✑ ENDNOTES ✑

1. Gabriel Almond and Sidney Verba, *The Civic Culture* (Princeton: Princeton University Press, 1963); Almond and Verba, eds., *The Civic Culture Revisited* (Boston: Little Brown, 1980).

2. Alexis de Tocqueville, *Democracy in America* (New York: Knopf, 1945), p. 299.

3. Almond and Verba, *The Civic Culture,* Ch. 10; Harry Eckstein, "Authority Relations and Government Performance," *Comparative Political Studies* 2 (1969): 269–325; Robert Putnam, *Making Democracy Work* (Cambridge: Harvard University Press, 1993).

4. Harry Eckstein, *Division and Cohesion in Democracy* (Princeton: Princeton University Press, 1966).

5. Robert Putnam, *Bowling Alone: The Collapse and Revival of American Community* (New York: Simon and Schuster, 2000).

6. Archie Brown and Jack Gray, eds., *Political Culture and Political Change in Communist States,* 2nd ed. (New York: Holmes and Meier, 1979); Robert Tucker, *Political Culture and Leadership in Soviet Russia* (New York: Norton, 1987).

7. For an interesting comparison, the first edition of *European Politics Today* included the same figure based on 1990–1991 survey data. Figure 2.1 is from the 1995–1998 *World Values Survey.* The survey asks this question: "Can most people be trusted, or can't you be too careful when dealing with people?" The horizontal axis plots the difference between the percentage giving trustful and distrustful responses. Also see Ronald Inglehart, *Culture Shift in Advanced Industrial Society* (Princeton: Princeton University Press, 1990), Ch. 1; Ronald Inglehart, *Modernism and Postmodernism* (Princeton: Princeton University Press, 1997).

8. Robert Dahl, *Polyarchy* (New Haven: Yale University Press, 1971).

9. Russell Dalton, "Political Support in Advanced Industrial Democracies," in P. Norris, ed. *Critical Citizens* (Oxford: Oxford University Press, 1999); Hans-Dieter Klingemann and Dieter Fuchs, eds., *Citizens and the State* (Oxford: Oxford University Press, 1995).

10. Giacamo Sani, "The Political Culture of Italy," in Almond and Verba, eds., *The Civic Culture Revisited.*

11. Nicholai Petro provocatively argues that there are strong currents of democracy and civil society that predate the communist era, in *The Rebirth of Russian Democracy: An Interpretation of Political Culture* (Cambridge: Harvard University Press, 1995); for a counter view see Harry Eckstein et al., *Can Democracy Take Root in Post-Soviet Russia?* (Lanham, MD: Rowman & Littlefield, 1998).

12. Richard Rose, William Mishler, and Christian Haerpfer, *Democracy and Its Alternatives: Understanding Post-Communist Societies* (Johns Hopkins University Press, 1998); William Reisinger, Arthur Miller, and Vicki Hesli, "Political Values in Russia, Ukraine, and Lithuania," *British Journal of Political Science* 24 (1994): 183–223; James Gibson et al., "Emerging Democratic Values in Soviet Political Culture," in A. Miller, W. Reisinger, and V. Hesli, eds., *Public Opinion and Regime Change* (Boulder, CO: Westview Press, 1993); Russell Dalton, "Communists and Democrats: Attitudes Toward Democracy in the Two Germanies," *British Journal of Political Science* 24 (1994): 469–93. Compare with Robert Rohrschneider, *Learning Democracy: Democratic and Economic Values in Unified Germany* (New York: Oxford University Press, 1999).

13. *Central and East European Eurobarometer 6* (Brussels: Commission of the European Communities, 1996).

14. G. Evans and S. Whitefield, "The Politics and Economics of Democratic Commitment," *British Journal of Political Science* 25 (1995): 485–514; Arthur Miller, Vicki Hesli, and William Reisinger, "Reassessing Mass Support for Political and Economic Change in the Former USSR," *American Political Science Review* 88 (1994): 399–411; Stephen White, Richard Rose, and Ian McAllister, *How Russia Votes* (Chatham, NJ: Chatham House, 1996).

15. Norris, ed., *Critical Citizens;* Susan Pharr and Robert Putnam, eds., *Discontented Democracies* (Princeton: Princeton University Press, 2000).

16. Ole Borre and Elinor Scarbrough, eds., *The Scope of Government* (Oxford: Oxford University Press, 1995).

17. Anthony King, "Overload: Problems of Governing in the 1970s," *Political Studies* 23 (1975): 166.

18. Richard Rose and Guy Peters, *Can Government Go Bankrupt?* (New York: Basic Books, 1978); Crozier, Huntington, and Watanuki, *The Crisis of Democracy*; Samuel Brittan, "The Economic Contradictions of Democracy," *British Journal of Political Science* 5 (1975): 129–59; Claus Offe, *The Contradictions of the Welfare State* (London: Hutchinson, 1984).

19. Inglehart, *Culture Shift*, Ch. 8; Ole Borre and Jose Manuel Viega, "Government Intervention in the Economy," in Borre and Scarborough, *The Scope of Government*.

20. See also Raymond Duch, "Tolerating Economic Reform," *American Political Science Review* 87 (1993): 590–608; Richard Rose, *New Democracies Barometer V: A Twelve Nation Survey* (Glasgow: University of Strathclyde, 1998).

21. For instance, the better educated are more likely to espouse democratic values if they live in a democratic system, and German public opinion surveys immediately after the collapse of the Third Reich found that the better educated were more likely to support the tenets of fascism. This point is, however, debated for post-communist societies. See Ada Finifter, "Attitudes Toward Individual Responsibility and Political Reform in the Former Soviet Union," *American Political Science Review* 90 (1996): 138–52; Arthur Miller, William Reisinger, and Vicki Hesli, "Understanding Political Change in Post-Soviet Societies," *American Political Science Review* 90 (1996): 153–66.

22. See, for example, Figure 2.6 in the first edition of *European Politics Today*, p. 45.

23. *Central and East European Eurobarometer 6.*

24. Rose and Haerpfer, *New Democracies Barometer V*; for another less sanguine view see Raymond Duch, "Economic Chaos and the Fragility of Democratic Transition in the Former Communist Regimes," *Journal of Politics* 57 (1995): 121–58.

25. Stephen White, Richard Rose, and Ian McAllister, *How Russia Votes* (Chatham, NJ: Chatham House, 1996), p. 12.

26. Ole Borre, "Beliefs and the Scope of Government," in Borre and Scarbrough, *The Scope of Government*.

27. G. Bingham Powell, "Voting Turnout in Thirty Democracies," in R. Rose, ed., *Electoral Participation* (Beverly Hills: Sage, 1980); Robert Jackman, "Political Institutions and Turnout in the Industrialized Democracies," *American Political Science Review* 81 (1987): 405–24.

28. G. Bingham Powell, "American Turnout in Comparative Perspective," *American Political Science Review* 80 (1986): 17–44; Ray Wolfinger and Steve Rosenstone, *Who Votes?* (New Haven: Yale University Press, 1980).

29. Miki Caul and Mark Gray, "The Decline of Election Turnout in Advanced Industrial Democracies," *Comparative Political Studies* 33 (2000).

30. Richard Brody, "The Puzzle of Participation in America," in A. King, ed., *The New American Political System* (Washington: American Enterprise Institute, 1978).

31. M. Kent Jennings and Jan van Deth, eds., *Continuities in Political Action* (Berlin: deGruyter, 1990); Richard Topf, "Beyond Electoral Participation," in Klingemann and Fuchs, *Citizens and the State*.

32. Donald Schulz and Jan Adams, eds., *Political Participation in Communist Systems* (New York: Pergamon Press, 1981).

33. Dalton, *Citizen Politics*, Chs. 3, 4; Geraint Parry, George Moyser, and Neil Day, *Political Participation and Democracy in Britain* (Cambridge: Cambridge University Press, 1992).

34. Klingemann and Fuchs, *Citizens and the State*, Chs. 2, 3; Parry, Moyser, and Day, *Political Participation and Democracy in Britain*.

35. Sidney Verba, Norman Nie, and Jae-on Kim, *Participation and Political Equality* (Cambridge: Cambridge University Press, 1978); Dalton, *Citizen Politics*, Chs. 3, 4.

36. Putnam, *Bowling Alone*; Grzegorz Ekiert and Jan Kubik, *Rebellious Civil Society: Popular Protest and Democratic Consolidation in Poland, 1989–1993* (Ann Arbor: University of Michigan Press, 1999); Jean Cohen and A. Arato, *Civil Society and Political Theory* (Cambridge, MA: MIT Press, 1992).

37. David Meyer and Sidney Tarrow, eds., *The Social Movement Society: Contentious Politics for a New Century* (Lanham, MD: Rowman & Littlefield 1998); Russell Dalton, *The Green Rainbow: Environmental Interest Groups in Western Europe* (New Haven, CT: Yale University Press, 1994); Amrita Basu, ed., *The Challenge of Local Feminisms: Women's Movement in Global Perspective* (Boulder, CO: Westview Press, 1995); Valerie Sperling, *Organizing Women in Contemporary Russia* (New York: Cambridge University Press, 1999).

38. Anna Seleny, "Old Political Rationalities and New Democracies: Compromise and Confrontation in Hungary and Poland Title" *World Politics* 51 (1999): 484–519; Walter Connor, *Tattered Banners: Labor, Conflict, and Corporatism in Postcommunist Russia* (Boulder, CO: Westview Press, 1996).

39. Putnam, *Bowling Alone*; Robert Putnam, "Bowling Alone," *Journal of Democracy* (1995) 6: 65–78.

40. Peter Hall, "Social Capital in Britain," *British Journal of Political Science* 29: 417–61; Bernard Weßels, "Organizing Capacity of Societies and Modernity," in J. van Deth, ed., *Private Groups and Public Life: Social Participation, Voluntary Associations, and Political Involvement in Representative Democracies* (London: Routledge, 1997).

41. Benjamin Page and Robert Shapiro, *The Rational Public* (Chicago: University of Chicago Press, 1992); James Stimson, Michael McKuen, and Robert Erikson, "Dynamic Representation," *American Political Science Review* 89 (1995): 546–65.

CHAPTER 3

DEMOCRATIC GOVERNMENT IN EUROPE

Most European governments are liberal democracies in practice, claim, or aspiration. That is, the leaders claim to be doing what their citizens want them to do and to be subject to citizens' control through competitive elections. The term "liberal" in "liberal democracy" reminds us that it is the wishes of citizens, not some image of their true interests, that should shape policy. Citizens must be free to organize and express these desires. The term also implies respect for the rights of minorities.

In Western Europe *liberal democracy* has been established as the working form of government. By the early 1980s, the remaining authoritarian governments (in Greece, Portugal, and Spain) had made successful transitions to democracy. The last serious challenge to a national democratic government in Western Europe was the 1981 attempted coup in Spain.[1] Some Western European nations have been challenged by serious conflict; some have constrained democratic freedoms in a limited way or in local areas. At least one, Italy, has failed to win citizen support for its political performance and made a massive attempt in the 1990s to replace its politicians and restructure its politics. But all the Western European political systems are now working primarily within a framework of competitive elections, representative assemblies, and civil rights.[2]

The nations of Central and Eastern Europe present a more varied picture (see Figure 1.5 in Chapter 1). The practice of government in Eastern Europe in the 1990s covered a wide range—from working democracy to authoritarian domination. In the successor countries of Yugoslavia—Croatia, Bosnia-Herzogovina, and Serbia—there was civil war. Most of Eastern Europe had been dominated and penetrated by the Soviet Union until 1989 or 1991. Its citizens had endured authoritarian rule from above, not the exchange of electoral choice and policymaker response. While the citizens strongly supported the introduction of the new democratic freedoms and, usually, market economies (see Chapter 2), it has not always been easy to sustain them. Not only the lack of experience with democratic institutions, but the social and economic conditions work against easy stabilization of democracy in much of Eastern Europe. Some countries, such as Poland and Hungary (Chapter 9 and Chapter 10), seem to have established consolidated democracies. But answers to the fundamental questions of government remain provisional in others, including Russia (Chapter 8), while authoritarian leaders and movements dominate a few such as Belarus and Yugoslavia (until Fall 2000).

TABLE 3.1   Distinguishing Features of Parliamentary and Presidential Democracies

Distinguishing Features[a]	Parliamentary Democracies	Presidential Democracies
Title of chief executive	Prime minister (head of government)	President (head of state and government)
Selection of assembly	By citizens in competitive election	By citizens in competitive election
Selection of chief executive	By assembly after election or removal	By citizens in competitive election
Removal of chief executive before fixed term?	By assembly: (No) confidence vote	Fixed terms
Dismissal of assembly before fixed term?	Prime minister may call for early election[b]	Fixed terms
Authority to legislate	Assembly only	Assembly plus president (e.g., veto)
Implications for party relations in assembly and executive	Same parties control both; cohesive party voting	Different party control possible; less cohesive party voting

[a]These define the pure parliamentary and presidential types; as discussed in the text, many constitutional systems, especially in Eastern Europe, "mix" the features of the two types.
[b]Some constitutional systems that are parliamentary in all other ways do not allow for early legislative elections. All parliamentary democracies provide for legislative elections after some maximum time (from three to five years) since the last election.

This chapter describes how Europeans govern themselves, how these nations vary in their approaches to democratic government. We shall see that there are many different ways to run a democracy and better understand how the different institutions and practices fit together, with distinct advantages and disadvantages. The nations of Eastern Europe offer additional variations and experience in democratic institutions and practices. Moreover, they offer new tests of our ideas about new democracies—why some survive and others fail.

Constitutional Organization: Rules for Making Rules

General agreement on a constitution that specifies how the laws must be made and how the decision makers are chosen stabilizes a political system. Working out such agreement is a critical task for a new democracy. A "constitution" in this sense may be a single written document, a set of statutes and practices, or some combination of these. Because the constitutional rules are so fundamental in determining political advantage in a society, changes in these rules typically follow massive and disruptive upheavals. The choice of constitutional arrangements may shape subsequent politics for generations.

Parliamentary or Presidential Democracies

Constitution makers and scholars begin, perhaps, by debating whether to choose some variation of a presidential or a parliamentary democracy. These alternatives specify the relationship between the *assembly*,[3] which represents the people and has primary authority to make the laws, and the *executive*, which has authority to carry out the laws. In both parliamentary and presidential democracies the assembly is directly elected by the citizens and has significant legislative authority. In a *parliamentary democracy* the assembly and the executive are closely tied in their origin and their survival. The people elect the assembly (parliament) and the assembly chooses and can dismiss the executive (prime minister and cabinet). All the authority to make and execute laws derives from the elected assembly. Some of these features are shown in column 1 of Table 3.1.

In a *presidential democracy*, such as that in the United States, the people elect the assembly and the president separately. The president is both head of state and chief executive. He or she appoints a government (cabinet), which serves the president. Both president and assembly have fixed terms; neither can dismiss the other before the next election. (If there are provisions for impeaching the president or members of the cabinet, they specify extraordinary conditions and require an extraordinary vote.) While primary legislative authority, at least over critical items such as raising and spending money, usually remains with the assembly, the president is also given some role, typically the right to veto legislation. In the United States, legislation can become law over the president's veto only by passing it again (in both Houses of the Congress) with a two-thirds majority. Various presidential systems confer different legislative powers on their chief executives.[4] The distinguishing features of presidential systems are shown in the third column of Table 3.1.

In Western Europe the typical arrangement for democratic policymaking is some version of a parliamentary system. The national parliament "makes the laws" and also chooses—and can replace—the prime minister and his or her cabinet, which are referred to as the "government." The *cabinet* is composed primarily of the heads of the executive agencies. If the government is defeated in a vote of confidence in the legislature, it must resign, which means either a new government (as in Germany in 1982; see Chapter 6) or a general election, or both (as in Britain in 1979; see Chapter 4).

The *confidence vote*, and its mirror image the "vote of no confidence," or "vote of censure," is a critical feature of parliamentary (and mixed) political systems. Whatever the name, the government must win the vote or resign from office.[5] If it resigns, a new election may be called or the parties in the assembly may try to bargain to form a new government. The outcome depends on the constitutional rules, customs, and political situation. A vote of no confidence or censure is usually called by the opposition to try to evict a government, or at least embarrass it, if its majority is thin. But a confidence vote may be called by the prime minister to force the assembly, especially members of the parties sharing the govern-

ment, to choose between passing the government's legislation or evicting the government. It is typically attached to a bill (a policy proposal) that is favored by the prime minister, but not by the parliamentary majority. By attaching a confidence motion to the bill, the prime minister forces the members of parliament to choose between the bill and the fall of the cabinet. This can be a particularly painful choice for dissident members of the prime minister's own party. If they don't vote for the bill, they may bring down their own government, and perhaps immediately have to face the voters to boot (see Box 3.1).

Relations between the parliament and the government vary with specific constitutional arrangements and with different balances of partisan power. In almost all parliamentary systems, the government—the cabinet and its related agencies—is the major policymaker, while the parliament provides an arena for debate, consent, and final authorization. In Western Europe the most important single individual is usually the *prime minister*, who is the head of government and who can attach specific legislation to the fate of that government.[6] The office of prime minister goes by different names in different countries (prime minister in Britain, premier in France, and chancellor in Germany, for example) but functions in a similar fashion. The formal head of state may be a president or monarch, but usually these figures are not directly elected by the citizens and have limited political influence.[7]

One lesson of the Western European experience with parliamentary systems is that the government, which controls policy, depends on regular and disciplined party support to survive. An important practical consequence of such dependence is that in experienced parliamentary systems the members of the political party in government tend to become extremely cohesive in their voting in the legislature (see the last line in Table 3.1). Strong and regular support by the party members is necessary to keep their government from being replaced. This party voting cohesion is further encouraged by the dependence of individual members of parliament on the goodwill of the party leadership if they are to advance to influential and prestigious positions in the cabinet. The tendency of Western Europeans to vote for parties, not individual representatives, has come

in(entive

Box 3.1   The Confidence Vote in Parliamentary Democracies

British prime ministers have often resorted to the confidence motion in order to bring rebellious party members into line. Usually, the threat alone is enough to ensure party discipline and pass important legislation. However, in 1993, Conservative Prime Minister John Major faced a parliamentary crisis over the ratification of the Maastricht Treaty, which expanded the powers of the European Union. Major had only a slim majority in the House of Commons, and many "Euro-skeptics" in his own party were opposed to the Maastricht Treaty. About twenty of these Conservative dissidents voted with the opposition and helped defeat the Maastricht Treaty in the House

of Commons. Immediately after this embarrassing defeat, however, Major introduced a confidence motion on his Maastricht policy and announced that if he lost this vote, he would dissolve the House of Commons and hold new elections. Many of the Conservative dissidents feared that their party would do poorly in such an election and that they might personally lose their seats. Major's confidence motion passed by a vote of 339 to 299, and the House of Commons approved the Maastricht Treaty. Thus, the confidence vote actually helps explain why party discipline tends to be stronger in parliamentary than in presidential systems.

both to reflect and to encourage party cohesion of the representatives.

The strong *party cohesion* (often called "discipline") in Western European parliaments is frequently in marked contrast to the U.S. Congress, where party affiliation is only one of several features shaping congressional voting choices. Party cohesion varies greatly on different issues and at different times. On the average "party" vote on substantive issues in the U.S. Congress in the 1990s, a little more than 80 percent of the party members voted together.[8] On the average vote, about 15 percent of the party members voted with the opposite party, while others would fail to vote. The votes of members of the U.S. Congress are influenced by their constituents, supporting interest groups, and their personal opinions, as well as by party affiliation (which is, of course, often related to these). In the Western European parliamentary systems, when the parties disagree, over 95 percent of the party members vote together on the average vote. Most of the time the major parties enjoy nearly perfect internal cohesion.[9]

A second lesson of parliamentary arrangements in Western Europe has been that the degree of concentration or fragmentation of parties in the parliament immediately affects the selection and retention of the executive. For this reason the rules for

assembly representation are especially important in parliamentary systems (as discussed in this chapter). Where party competition and parliamentary representation create a majority for a single party, this party will control the executive and be able to carry out election promises in a stable and powerful way. This concentrated political power may, however, ignore and even threaten the preferences of minorities.

When elections result in a parliament divided between many parties, at least some of them must negotiate with each other to choose and sustain a government. If legislative negotiations are difficult, governments may frequently be dismissed or resign (as in Italy, where the average prime minister and cabinet have lasted less than a year). However, different groups and factions in the country have the opportunity to participate in the bargaining over the governments and their policies.

Figure 3.1 displays the patterns of constitutional structures in Western and Eastern Europe.[10] There are no purely presidential systems. Most Western European nations have parliamentary systems (see the left bars in Figure 3.1). A handful of Western European countries, including France (Chapter 5), have "mixed" systems that combine parliamentary and presidential elements. In such *mixed presidential-parliamentary systems* the assembly

FIGURE 3.1   Number of Parliamentary and Mixed Executive Systems in Western and Eastern Europe in 2000

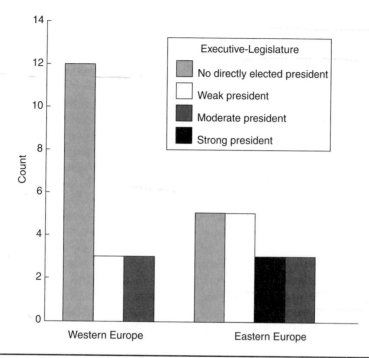

Source: The classifications of presidential powers are based on Shugart and Carey 1992, updated where necessary, and Hellman and Tucker.

and the executive institutions are neither completely separate from each other in their election and survival, as in a (pure) presidential system, nor completely fused, as in a (pure) parliamentary system. At least one of the elements of separation is compromised. In mixed systems with "weak" presidencies, the directly elected president has exercised largely ceremonial powers, as in Austria, Iceland, and Ireland; these countries are usually discussed as if they were ordinary parliamentary systems. In countries with at least moderately powerful presidencies, such as France, the directly elected president appoints the "government" (prime minister and cabinet), whose installation or continuation is, however, dependent on sustaining support in the legislature. The president is usually able to dissolve the legislature and call for new elections; he or she may also have some direct policymaking powers.

As shown in Figure 3.1, the Eastern European constitution makers have been much influenced by the experience of the mixed systems, especially that of France, whose constitution has been partly imitated in several countries (such as Poland, Romania, and Russia). About a third of the Eastern European constitutions are purely parliamentary. (See the discussion of Hungary in Chapter 10.) A similar number are predominately parliamentary, having directly elected, but fairly weak and ceremonial presidents. However, the presidents in Lithuania, Poland, and Romania seem to have powers at least equal to those of the French president, and should therefore be considered mixed systems.[1] Their presidents are directly elected and appoint prime ministers and cabinets which can, entirely or in part, be removed by the assembly. As shown in the far right column of Figure 3.1, the democratic presidents in

Croatia, and, especially, Russia (see Chapter 8) and Ukraine, have even stronger policymaking powers of their own. These may come close to being predominantly presidential systems, despite the presence of prime ministers whose tenure is subject to assembly approval.

While we are still learning about the possibilities of mixed systems from the many new Eastern European cases, thus far the basic lessons from France seem to apply:[12] (1) a president heading a party that controls the assembly can control politics; (2) even without such control a clever president with substantial support can dominate policymaking if the opposition is divided; (3) if the legislature is controlled by a united opposition, however, the president's influence will be much less and the center of policymaking may shift to the parties controlling the assembly and their prime minister. (Compare the French experience with such "cohabitation" in 1986–1988, 1993–1995, and 1997– in Chapter 5 to that of Poland in 1993–1996 in Chapter 9.) The fragmented party systems and internal divisions within the parties themselves have facilitated presidential influence in much of Eastern Europe.

Debate over the advantages of parliamentary and presidential approaches has been heated. Scholarly opinion, based largely on the favorable Western European experience (and unfavorable Latin American experience), has tended to favor the parliamentary systems.[13] Parliamentary systems, their proponents argue, can represent a wide range of public opinion in the assembly and see that it bears directly on the executive, which must be sustained continuously by the parliament. If the elected representatives of the people disapprove of the actions of the executive, they can change governments.

In presidential systems there is always the possibility of a confrontation between a strong president who controls the executive—which is usually a primary source of new legislation as well as its implementation—and the assembly that must provide the legal basis for policy and, critically, vote the funding for it. Such confrontation is particularly likely when these two key institutions are controlled by different political parties. In the United States such "divided government" has often been associated with deadlock and policy "immobilism,"

such as the conflict between the Republican Congress and Democratic president that briefly shut down many government programs in the winter of 1995–1996. When the conflict is very severe, as in Chile in the early 1970s, for example, the strife between these two legitimately chosen representatives of the people can tear the political system apart. Or, a strong president can use executive powers to repress democratic competition.

On the other hand, advocates of presidential systems, and the constitution makers in many new democracies in recent years, point to the advantages of fixed presidential terms and direct election for efficiency and accountability.[14] These loom especially large when the legislature is divided into multiple parties and factions that cannot consistently support the same government. Moreover, the president is chosen directly by the people, not through a process of political "wheeling and dealing," as in parliamentary systems. Independent of a legislative majority for daily survival and elected by the whole nation, the president should be able to take a larger view of national interest than can individual legislators or the prime ministers they choose.

Unfortunately, the negative arguments on both sides of the presidential/parliamentary debate can find support in the Eastern European experience. Conflict over the relative powers of president and legislature has been characteristic of the mixed systems;[15] government stability has been a problem in a number of parliamentary governments and in some mixed systems with moderately strong presidents as well. Over the last eight years, serious limitations of democracy, as indicated by Freedom Scores below seven in multiple years, have appeared at least temporarily in all of the three mixed systems with strong presidential powers (Croatia, Russia, and Ukraine). In each of the other constitutional types, only about a third of the countries has experienced such severe problems with the transition to democracy. The Freedom House Report of Press Freedom in 1999 has a very similar tale to tell. (See Box 3.2.) From the opposite point of view, the most consistently democratic and free systems include every constitutional type except mixed-strong presidential. An easier transition is perhaps most associated with higher levels of economic development and success in avoiding ethno-nationalist entanglements. Yet, despite the many problems, clear failures of transitions to democracy have emerged only in Yugoslavia (a parliamentary system at the federal level, but presidential in the key region of Serbia), Belarus, a strong presidential system, and Bosnia, which was plunged quickly into a civil war from which it has not yet fully recovered.[16] With so few cases and so many problems, the question of relative constitutional advantage remains open to dispute, with an edge at this point to those suspicious of strong presidential powers.

Limiting and Dispersing Policymaking Power

The basic parliamentary or mixed parliamentary/presidential democracies in Europe are embedded in varied and complex constitutional arrangements. Many of these can be usefully understood as requiring the policymakers to secure the consent of the representatives of more than a simple majority of citizens. The British political system is in many ways the simplest system, because a government in control of the lower house of parliament, the House of Commons, need not share power with other institutions or political opponents.

Four different kinds of institutional arrangements are widely used, individually or in combination, to limit the power of government policymakers in Western Europe: strong legislative committees, bicameralism, judicial review, and federalism. The first approach requires *power-sharing* with opposition parties within the parliamentary arena itself. *Strong committee systems* that give committees power in drafting laws and require proportional sharing of the committee chairmanships with opposition parties are found in such countries as Austria, Belgium, Denmark, Germany, Hungary, and Norway. Such requirements usually make it necessary for government majorities to take greater account of minority oppositions.

Another approach is *bicameralism*—a system in which power is shared between two houses of the national legislature. If different parties control different institutions, then wider bargaining is necessary if policies are to be made. Constitutions in Germany, Russia, and Switzerland, for example,

provide (as in the United States) for a second legislative house with significant power and a different basis of election. In some countries, such as Germany, the upper house may directly represent regional governments, which may be controlled by different parties than the national government.

In many Western European nations, actions by legislative majorities may also be constrained in a third way, by provisions for *judicial review* by special constitutional courts or councils, which is a third approach to limiting majority power. Although such courts have not usually been as active as the U.S. Supreme Court, they have become more assertive in recent years, and often successful in restraining government majorities who press constitutional boundaries too hard.[17] The constitutions of newly free Eastern European nations generally provide for constitutional courts, and in a number of countries these have played influential roles in constraining government policies and even defining the new constitutional powers themselves. However, their powers and legitimacy are not everywhere accepted. In some countries, as in Russia, Belarus, and Albania, they have been subjects of severe dispute.

A fourth important approach to dispersing power involves *federalism*, in which policymaking power is shared between a national government representing the citizens as a whole and representatives of geographic subunits. Germany and Switzerland, for example, have provided for a full sharing of power in some policy areas between the national government and regional governments (called *Laender* in Germany and *Cantons* in Switzerland). Recent developments in Western Europe have emphasized further decentralization or even power-sharing between the national government and geographic regions, most extensively in Belgium, but also in such traditionally centralized countries as France, Italy, and Spain. Moreover, the increasingly important institutions of the European Union mean that some policymaking power is dispersed "upward" to this international body (see Chapter 11).

Federalism can be a valuable approach to accommodating the concerns of distinctive ethnic groups; yet national governments often fear that the

[handwritten margin note: reason to be wary]

regional governments will be a springboard to a breakup of the country, as happened in Yugoslavia. Russia's war in Chechnya, in contrast to the bargained autonomy within the Russian Federation for a number of other regions, illustrates the disaster that can accompany failed accommodation. A federal system in Czechoslovakia came to an end when the two components broke up, peacefully, into the separate states of the Czech Republic and Slovakia.

Constitutional Organization: Electoral Rules

European democracies operate primarily as representative democracies. Direct voting on policy through referenda is rare except in Switzerland. (However, directly consulting the voters on major constitutional changes, including joining the European Union, is a fairly common practice.) Therefore the rules for electing the representatives are also a critical part of the constitutional arrangements. Although these rules are often established only as ordinary legislation, they play a fundamental part in shaping the ongoing political process and once established are only rarely modified in a substantial way.[18]

Proportional Representation

[handwritten margin note: Key: certain percentages]

Most of the democracies of Western Europe have long favored some version of *proportional representation (PR)* in electing representatives to parliament. PR provides for multimember legislative districts with parties represented in proportion to their voter support in the district. The larger the number of representatives from a district, the easier for small parties to gain seats. For example, it may take 33 percent of the district vote to gain a representative in a small (three representative) Irish district, but only 5 percent to gain a representative in a large (twenty representative) Italian district. Sometimes the districts are further supplemented with additional legislators elected from the nation as a whole.[19] Or, as in the Netherlands, the entire (150 seat) legislature may be elected from the nation at large, permitting the electoral success of very small parties.

Proportional representation rules make possible a very accurate conversion of voter support into legislative representation, but they make it difficult for single parties to gain legislative majorities.[20] In order to limit the number of parties in the legislature many countries have some minimum "threshold" of votes that must be won in order to enter parliament. Figure 3.2 shows some features of the election laws in Western and Eastern Europe. The first three bars in each region show countries with PR but different thresholds for representation.

As we see in Figure 3.2, only three Western European countries, and only two in Eastern Europe, now have thresholds as low as 3 percent. Most commonly, as shown in the second column, the European proportional representation electoral systems require parties to win 4 to 9 percent of the vote to enter the national parliament. Even though such thresholds seem low, even 4- or 5-percent thresholds can eliminate representation of many voters (but also help constrain fragmentation in the legislature) if the party system is extremely splintered. Nonetheless, it is hard for individual parties to win legislative majorities under these rules. As shown in the third column, in Western Europe a few countries with proportional representation have small districts or other special rules that raise the effective threshold even higher, making it harder for small parties to enter the legislature and easier for large parties to win majorities.[21] There are no election rules of this type in Eastern Europe.

Single-Member District Plurality Systems

The best-known alternative to proportional representation is the "first-past-the-post" system, in which a country is divided into single-member districts and in each district the candidate with the most votes (plurality) wins. This is, of course, the system used in legislative elections in Britain, the United States, and Canada. Such plurality systems tend to distort political representation, especially in multiparty situations, both because of the short-term "mechanical" effects in the simple aggregation of votes and winners across districts and, to a lesser

FIGURE 3.2   Legislative Election Rules in Western and Eastern Europe in 2000

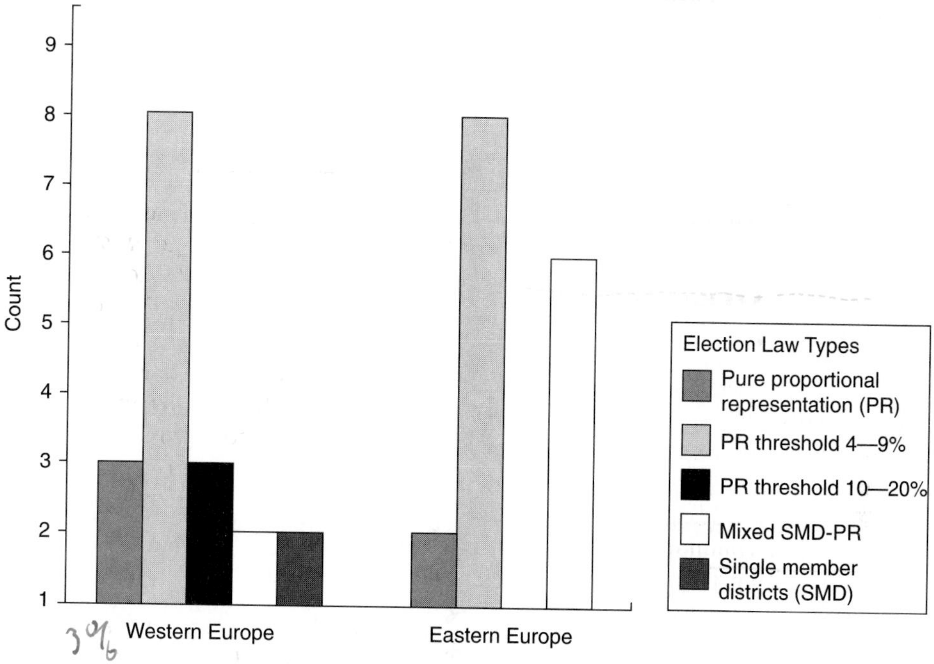

Election Law Types
- Pure proportional representation (PR)
- PR threshold 4—9%
- PR threshold 10—20%
- Mixed SMD-PR
- Single member districts (SMD)

Source: Estimates of "Effective Thresholds" from Lijphart, 1994, updated where necessary.

degree, because of effects on voters and politicians anticipating the mechanical effects. Small parties are shut out unless their votes are concentrated in a few districts. Even medium-sized parties (25 percent or so) whose votes are spread evenly across many districts can come in second nearly everywhere and win few seats. In Britain in 1997, for example, the Liberal Democratic Party won 17 percent of the national vote, but carried only about 7 percent of the parliamentary seats. In the same election the Labour Party gained a commanding parliamentary majority while carrying only 44 percent of the vote (see Chapter 4). The tendency of these election rules to create "two-party" systems in the legislatures is known as "Duverger's Law," after the distinguished French political scientist who gave it a clear and dramatic statement.[22]

Only Britain uses simple first-past-the-post voting in national parliamentary elections in Europe.

However, single-member districts with provisions for a second-round runoff between leading candidates, used in France and for part of the legislature in a number of countries, as discussed in this chapter, can still sharply affect and distort representation and create legislative majorities. Britain and France, the two European countries with only single-member district representation, appear in the last bar of Figure 3.2.

Mixed Electoral Systems

The designers of the German "Basic Law" after World War II pioneered an approach that combines proportional representation and single-member districts (white bar within each region of Figure 3.2). In the German system the country is divided into single-member districts whose representatives make up half of the legislature; the other half is elected with proportional representation rules from party lists (with a 5-percent minimum threshold). Each voter casts two votes: one for an individual candidate from his or her district and one for a list of candidates provided by a political party. In this way each voter has a representative from his or her geographic district to whom to turn for help on local problems, but the party list deputies are explicitly allocated to help ensure a more equitable party representation. (See Chapter 6 for a more complete discussion of the German electoral rules and their consequences.)

In the new democracies of Eastern Europe, constitution writers have opted for a variety of electoral systems, as we see in the right side of Figure 3.2. Concerned about too many small parties in the legislature, but also with fair representation, almost all of the Eastern European countries using proportional representation electoral systems have favored thresholds in the 4- to 9-percent range, usually at the lower end. _Mixed electoral rules_, inspired by the German election system, have also found wide favor, as shown in the white bar on the right side of the figure. However, many of these systems lack the degree of compensation for distortion found in the German election rules.[23] Without such compensation, where half or more of the seats are single-member districts, as in Albania, Hungary, Lithuania, Macedonia, and Russia, the results can over- or underrepresent parties to a very substantial degree. (See also Figure 3.3 and the associated discussion of political parties that follows.)

In the systems with strong presidents the rules for electing the president are also important. In Europe the most common approach requires a second round if no candidate wins a majority of votes on the first round (which is very common). Usually only the two leading candidates go on to the second round, which is held a week or two after the first (as happened in France and Poland in 1995, as discussed in Chapters 5 and 9; and in Russia in 1996, as discussed in Chapter 8). The timing of legislative and presidential elections is also important. If the two elections are held at the same time, or nearly so, it is much more likely that the same party or coalition will control both presidency and legislature.[24]

The Joint Effect of Policymaking Rules and Election Rules

In most of Western Europe the rules for electing policymakers and the rules for policymaking work together to encourage the representation of many different groups of citizens through multiple political parties and the involvement of those parties in policymaking in diverse ways. Probably only Britain, France, and Greece could be characterized as having rules that typically give unshared political power to directly elected majority governments. The other Western European nations provide examples of a variety of institutional arrangements to enhance representation and disperse political influence within and/ or beyond the national government.

The makers of the new Eastern European constitutions have been torn between the fear of strong government and the sense of need for it. They are also torn between the desire to involve as many citizens as possible and the concern that too dispersed representation will create deadlock. Different groups and parties, needless to say, have tried to negotiate constitutions that favor their particular circumstances. The emergent constitutions frequently combine diverse elements, such as mixed presidential-parliamentary systems and mixed election rules. Experience with these policy rules in France and these election rules in Germany and, recently, Italy suggests that specific conditions and specific party strategies can make quite a difference in their impact. For this reason, it can take a number of elections before their full implications are fully understood and political leaders and citizens anticipate them in their behavior. This can be clearly seen in Eastern Europe in the struggles between legislatures and executives and in the confusions of party competition in the first few elections.

Parties and Party Competition

Building Party Systems

In liberal democracies political parties provide a critical link between citizens and policymakers, structuring and organizing the vote on one side and the organization of governments and policymaking on the other. The party systems of Western Europe are highly developed. In most countries there are many continuities in organization and alignments of voters between the party systems that emerged 75 years ago and those competing in Western Europe today.[25] Party leaders and organizers have had many elections to build organizations, form alliances, and refine their strategies. Although each new election brings new challenges, new voters, and sometimes new parties, many lessons of the past are encoded in the surviving organizations as well as in the memories of party leaders.

In Eastern Europe, on the other hand, the Soviet-backed communist parties permitted no competition, and only selected allies, at most, were permitted to offer candidates. Moreover, the communist parties attempted to penetrate the entire society and pull all those interested in public life into their networks. Even in nations with a democratic history, such as Czechoslovakia and Hungary (see Chapter 10), few parties from the pre-communist era have returned as significant factors.[26] Not only have most pre-authoritarian parties failed to reemerge, but the former communist parties themselves have survived and often prospered. They have nearly everywhere benefitted from their organizational bases, often the only significant organizational structures in the societies outside the state bureaucracy.

It has been very difficult to build new party organizations in the few, tumult-filled years since 1989 in Eastern Europe or since 1991 in the countries of the former Soviet Union. The sudden expansion of democratic opportunity initially overwhelmed the potential organizers of opposition parties, who had no experience with competitive politics. The absence of independent social and economic organizations, especially the trade unions and churches that were historically the focus of much initial party organization in Western Europe, has made building new party organizations far more difficult.[27] Naturally, party building has been especially difficult in a huge, geographically diverse nation such as Russia. Democratic elections in Eastern Europe since 1989 have often been charac-

terized by many new parties, small parties, and independent candidates. After the elections, the assemblies have frequently experienced lack of coherence within parties and break-offs of new party groups, as well as difficulties in forming governments based on stable coalitions between parties. (See the discussions in Chapters 9 and 10 on Poland and Hungary.)

Political sociologists Lipset and Rokkan inferred from the early Western European experience that the first decade of mass suffrage is critical for the future organization of party politics.[28] They observed that voter preferences based on social class and religion (called "cleavages") characterized most Western European party systems from the 1920s to the 1960s. In the Catholic societies of Mediterranean Western Europe, for example, voters' frequency of church attendance was a strong predictor of their party attachments. In central Western Europe, religious affiliation as Protestant or Catholic often predicted party support, while in northern Europe a voter's occupation most powerfully shaped his or her partisanship. These voter attachments were anchored by the alignments of social organizations (labor unions and voluntary groups) and party organizations.

Although somewhat diminished by decline in religiosity or trade union strength, as well by increased geographic mobility and the provision of welfare safety nets, the historic cleavages continue to organize many Western European party systems today.[29] Religious, ethnic, and economic cleavages may yet crystalize in Eastern Europe, too. Analyses of voting in the Polish election of 1993, for example, showed some of the effects of church attendance that we might expect in a Catholic nation, as well as a relationship between agricultural employment and vote for the Peasant Party.[30] But the nature of local communist rule in each country, including the levels of coercion and corruption, and the mode of transition from communism have also shaped post-communist party competition.[31] The process of creating stable alignments between society and party seems slower and more difficult than many would have anticipated.[32]

The Number of Parties

Political scientists have emphasized two major distinctions in analyzing the performance of Western European party systems: (1) number of parties and (2) extremist parties. The first distinguishes *multiparty systems* from two-party, or at least *majority-electing party systems*. Multiparty systems seem to offer a wider range of choices to voters (see Figure 3.4), explicit representation of social and political groups, and more inclusiveness in policymaking. Majority-electing systems seem to offer clearer political responsibility, more stable governments, and the direct implementation of campaign promises.

Most Western European party systems fall clearly into the multiparty category. In the average Western European election, six or seven parties win at least 1 percent of the vote, with as many as twelve such parties in the Netherlands in the 1970s and Belgium in the 1980s. These numbers pale, however, when compared with the numbers of parties competing in the new electoral landscapes in Eastern Europe: about forty in Russia in 1995, for example, plus many independent candidates. Such figures can be somewhat misleading if there are a few large parties together with many very small ones. It is more revealing to compare the relative numbers of parties through a weighting approach that calculates the "effective number" of parties in the election and in the legislature. This number tells us roughly how many parties of equal size would be the equivalent of the current distribution.[33]

If we take this approach, we find that the average "effective" number of parties winning *votes* in Western Europe in the late 1990s was a little under five. Britain, Greece, Portugal, and Spain were at the low end with effectively about three parties, while Belgium was at the high end with over ten, followed by France and Italy with about seven. The average in Eastern Europe was somewhat higher. Estonia and Latvia had effectively about six parties winning votes; Russia had nearly seven (see Chapter 8), while Ukraine had over eleven. The effective number of competing parties had declined from the previous election in a number of Eastern Europe countries, indicating some consolidation of the new party systems. In many cases this decline reflects the formation of election alliances, rather than fully unified parties (as in Poland in 1997; see Chapter 9). These numbers decline further, if we look at the legislature, because the election laws prevent many smaller parties from winning seats in parliament. The average number is a little over four effective parties in the legislatures in both East and West. The reductions are greater in Eastern Europe because even low barriers shut out very small parties.

These averages themselves hide quite wide variation, as is clearly illustrated in Figure 3.3, which groups the countries by the effective number of parties in the *legislatures*. In Western Europe, there are effectively two-party systems in the legislatures in Britain, Greece, and Spain. We see that most countries have effectively three (Germany) to five (France) parties in the legislature. At the more fragmented end, Italy and Belgium have over six. In Eastern Europe, the mode is also three in the legislature (as in Poland and Hungary). There is an effectively two-party system and quite a few around three, but also a number with six or more (including Russia). Despite the general similarity in the distribution, the figure overstates somewhat the comparability to Western Europe, because many of the larger "parties" are really electoral coalitions of several parties and are less cohesive in their behavior in the legislature. Figure 3.3, like the voting averages, should also remind Americans how very unusual is their truly two-party system.

Western and Eastern Europe illustrate how election laws and party competition interact to shape the number of parties in the legislature. In Western Europe there is not much difference in the effects of the election laws in the two lower-threshold categories from Figure 3.2; both reduce the effective number of parties by about half a party, as does the mixed German system. With thresholds of 10 percent or more, as in Greece and Ireland, we start to find substantial reductions in the numbers of parties that make it into the legislature. In the two single-member district systems of Britain and France these reductions are quite striking: the number of effective parties in the legislature is often half of what it would be under proportional representation.

FIGURE 3.3   Effective Number of Parties in the Legislature in Western and Eastern Europe in 2000

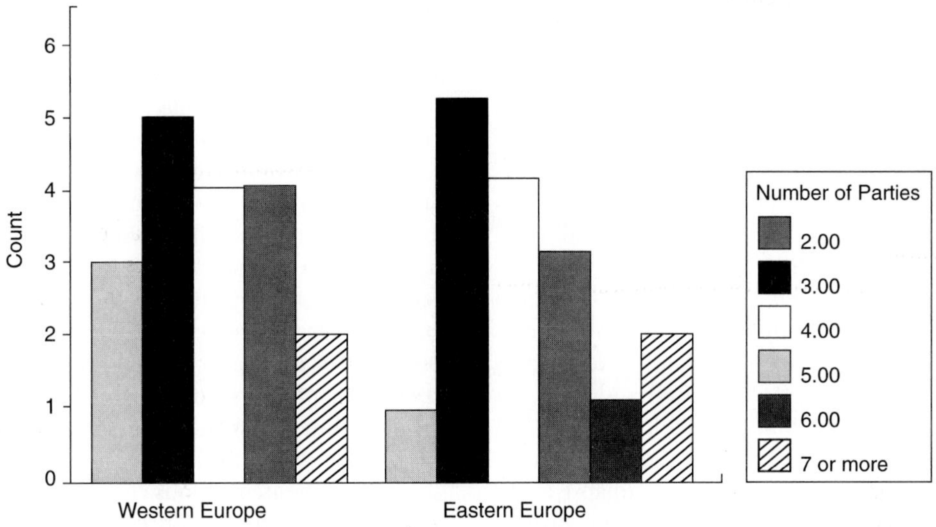

Source: See the discussion of the "Effective Number" of parties in this chapter and in Lijphart, 1994, Ch. 7.

Eastern Europe is different in two notable ways. First, in a number of countries even rather low thresholds have made very large difference. This is because political party leaders (and followers) in the many new party systems are only gradually learning enough about the electorate and the rules to coalesce into a smaller number of parties. We would expect that eventually the party leaders and organizers in these new democracies would be able to build larger and more coherent parties, at least large enough to surmount a barrier of 4 or 5 percent. This learning seems to have taken place in Poland: in 1993 too many parties competed, especially on the political right, splitting the votes and missing the threshold, leaving about a third of the voters unrepresented in the legislature. In the 1997 elections the leaders coordinated a more limited set of party offerings and most of these parties attained legislative representation (see Chapter 9). Several other countries, including Russia, have also made substantial progress in consolidating parties to overcome electoral thresholds.

The second difference in Eastern Europe is the very scattered representation associated with some of the single-member district elections, notably in Ukraine, but also in the single-member districts of the Russian legislative elections.[34] To a degree unfamiliar in modern Western Europe, many representatives campaigned as independents, representing local leaders, not national (or even local) political parties. This was in part a consequence of somewhat dubious constraints on democratic freedoms. To an even greater extent, it was probably the consequence of difficulties in forming national political parties without having developed local district organizations. This difficulty has added to legislative weakness (and, in fact, presidential dominance) in those countries. However, in the smaller countries of Albania, Hungary, Lithuania, and Macedonia, the single-member district parts of the legislature have contributed to fewer legislative parties, as expected.

Extremist Parties

A second distinction in the literature on political parties focuses on "extremism" (or "polarization") in the party system. Many theorists suggest that the continued performance of democracy is threatened by *extremist parties*—major groups espousing dramatically different policy packages (ideologies) or challenging the basic ground rules of the society.[35] Italian political scientist Giovanni Sartori argued that the polarized systems enhance the ideological intensity of the policy debate, encouraging a pattern of irresponsible "outbidding" by extremist parties. Extremism also discourages turnovers of power that could keep incumbent parties responsible to citizens.[36] Sartori thus attributed the instability of postwar Italy, Weimar Germany, and Third and Fourth Republic France to such polarization.

Substantial research, based largely on Western Europe, suggests that support for extremist parties is associated with less durable governments, probably with mass turmoil as well, although not necessarily with instability of democracy itself. A significant presence of extremist parties makes parliamentary governments more likely to collapse in the face of economic adversity, more internally diverse, and more characterized by the return of many of the same (non-extreme) parties in successive governments.[37]

Data from the late 1970s and early 1980s showed parties that could be classified as "extremists"—in terms of either the extreme policy self-placements or the alienation of their supporters—had the support of over 20 percent of the electorate in Belgium, Denmark, Finland, France, and Italy,[38] but substantially less in the rest of Western Europe. A comparison in the early 1990s finds these percentages somewhat reduced, as the collapse of international communism has moderated the position of some left parties. Classification of parties based on expert assessments and somewhat limited survey data suggest support for such parties was still at the 20–percent level in Italy and France, about 10 to 15 percent in Austria and Belgium, and 5 to 10 percent in Denmark, Greece, the Netherlands, Norway, and Sweden.[39]

The rise of new, populist, rightist parties, often appealing to concerns about immigrants and/or relations with the European Union contributed notably to extremism in the 1990s. The National Front in France, for example, rose from a small percentage of the vote in the early 1970s to 12 to 15 percent in recent elections. The National Front's controversial leader Jean-Marie Le Pen called for expulsion of ille-

gal immigrants and all immigrants after a maximum stay of a year or two, a ban on even tourist visas for Africans and Arabs from North Africa, preferential treatment of French citizens in jobs and public housing, and very tight citizenship requirements.[40] Such parties pose and reflect the familiar potential for unstable government and citizen turmoil.

In Eastern Europe a number of countries have substantial support for parties that could well be considered extremist. Zhirinovsky's (ill-named) Liberal Democratic Party in Russia, which promises personal dictatorship at home and wildly aggressive foreign policy abroad, would be a serious threat to democracy if its leader should come to power. A number of parties in the former Yugoslavia have stressed ethnic domination or ethnic expansionism in ways that bode ill for democratic accommodation. Given the tremendous changes in Eastern Europe and the legitimate concerns of their citizens, it is difficult to adopt a single criteria for an extremist "protest" party. But analysis of a survey in 1994 suggested that parties over a third of whose supporters felt that democracy was not working "at all" in their countries won over 15 percent of the vote in such countries as Albania, Belarus, Bulgaria, Romania, Russia, and Ukraine (and boycotted the election in Macedonia); patterns of alienation and support seemed somewhat less threatening in the Czech Republic, Estonia, Hungary, Latvia, Lithuania, Poland, Slovenia, and Slovakia,[41] but there were unsettling indicators in some of these as well. As suggested by their subsequent Freedom Scores and the 1999 Survey of Freedom of the Press (Box 3.2), some of these concerns have been born out.

A critical question in most of Eastern Europe concerns the parties that are direct descendants of the authoritarian communist parties that so long dominated the region. These for the most part call themselves "socialist" or "social democrat" (except in Russia) and claim to be democratic. (Many are required by the law or even the constitution to make this claim in order to compete in elections.) Some of them have undergone great changes in organization, people, and policies, while others are still largely unreconstructed in organization and personnel from their communist predecessors. Some of them continue to adapt as circumstances change. The *formerly communist parties* and their potential "extremism" must be evaluated individually in each country. Compare, for example, the very different stances toward democracy and toward market economic policies of the Communists in Russia, the Alliance of the Democratic Left (SLD) in Poland, and the Hungarian Socialist Party, as discussed in Chapters 8 through 10.[42]

The Content of Party Competition

People often discuss party competition in the multiparty systems of Western Europe by relating the parties to different positions on a *left-right continuum*.[43] Economic or even "class" differences have long been the primary focus of party competition in Western Europe. Almost every party system has had one or more parties claiming to be on the "left" in the sense of representing the interests of the "working class." In most Western European nations socialist or *social democratic parties* have been the predominant parties of the left with smaller communist or New Left challengers. Economic issues continue to define the main differences between "left" and "right" parties in Western Europe. However, the substance of difference has changed substantially in recent years, anticipating, but also encouraged by, the collapse of international communism.

Most "left" parties in Western Europe have now abandoned the idea of full government ownership of the economy, which was a major element of classic socialism. The combination of support for a large welfare system, redistribution of income from the better-off to the less fortunate through taxes and transfer payments, and a mixed (but predominately market) economy is often called a "social democratic" approach. It contrasts to varying degrees with a *"rightist" party* approach that stresses economic competition, less personal reliance on the government, and less government involvement of all kinds.

Figure 3.4 shows the parties on the "left-right" scale in the Western European democracies of Britain, France, Germany, and Spain, and the Eastern European democracy of Poland. The United States is shown for purposes of comparison. The position of the parties is based on the self-placement of citizens who voted for the party.[44] The height of the bars on the graph shows the voting support that each party received in the election year shown at the left of each line. Only parties getting about 5 percent of the vote or more are shown in the figure. The United States has only two parties, of course, with the Democrats somewhat to the left and the Republicans somewhat to the right. In most democracies the two main parties are further apart on the left-right scale. The graph shows clearly the communist or formerly communist parties well on the left in France, Germany, Spain, and Poland, with more moderate social democratic or labor parties closer to the center. Britain and Germany have small centrist parties in the Liberal Democrats and FDP. Each country has one or more large parties of the moderate right. France stands out in Western Europe with 13 percent of the vote going to the right-extremist National Front Party (Chapter 5).

Figure 3.4 also shows why in some multiparty systems, such as France, the number of parties and their dispersion across the left-right spectrum make this language helpful for voters. Without something like a single dimension to organize politics, it is difficult for voters in any democracy to compare their wishes with the promises and actions of policymakers.[45] With many smaller parties offering a variety of alternatives, voters find it especially helpful to characterize debate in terms of something like "left" and "right." In time the left-right language, which originated in the physical placement of the new members of the Assembly at the time of the French Revolution 200 years ago, has become a shorthand summary of a number of the issues that are important to Western Europeans.[46] Despite many changes in political alternatives, most Western European party systems still present their voters with a fairly wide range of choices between left, center, and right parties. As shown at the bottom of the figure, the "left-right" language also comfortably describes a wide party range in Poland, with the former communists (SLD) rather far to the left and the AWL (itself a coalition of smaller parties) well to the right, with other parties between them. Both religious and economic issues shape the left-right dialogue in Poland (Chapter 9).

Economic issues have been important in Eastern Europe, but they have often focused on the

FIGURE 3.4 Placement of Parties on the Left-Right Scale and Their Voter Support in Election

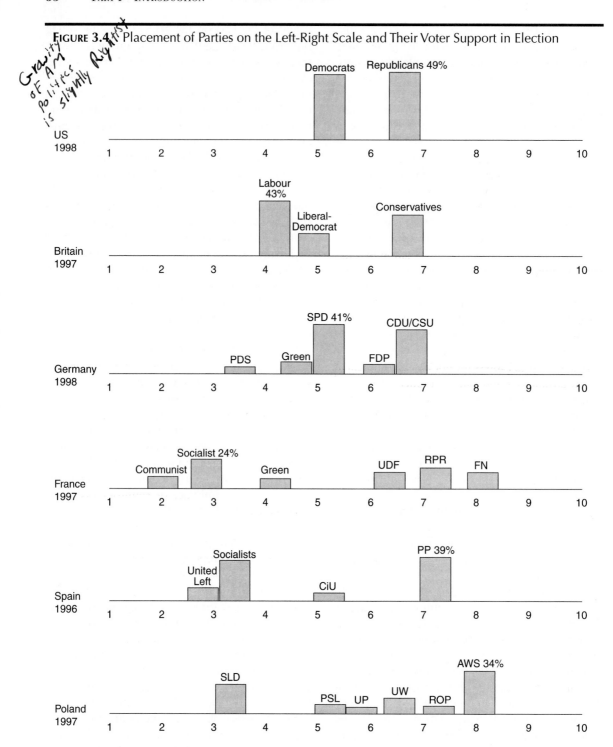

Gravity of American politics is slightly Rightist

Source: Party positions from the self-placements of party voters. The height of the bar is the percent of vote won by the party in the election shown on the left.

difficult transition from the old communist "command control" systems—in which the government owned the economy and directly decided wages, prices, investment, and so forth—to a system in which the market determines prices and government plays a lesser role. While most contemporary parties favor the transition in general terms, they often disagree sharply on the pace and extent of this economic transition. For a variety of reasons, economic conditions have been difficult and quite painful to many groups in these societies. Not only did absolute living standards decline throughout Eastern Europe in the early 1990s, but groups accustomed to guaranteed jobs have had to face unemployment (real and potential), inflation that has made saving difficult, and increased income disparities. As mentioned in Chapter 1, income inequalities in Russia are now greater than in Western Europe. A few individuals—often "insiders" from the old system—have become very rich, while others have become poorer. Naturally, political parties have appeared to express the grievances and fears of the disadvantaged and call for moderation in the process or protection of the vulnerable. Other parties have stressed the ultimate benefits to be won if the short-term pain can be borne.

In a survey in 1993, political scientists John Huber and Ronald Inglehart asked experts to describe the major content of the left-right dimension of party competition and to propose additional dimensions if they wished.[47] Economic or class issues were mentioned by more experts than any other kind of issue in most of the European countries they surveyed. In Western Europe economic issues constituted 60 pecent of all mentions, while in Eastern Europe it was about 40 percent. Not surprisingly, in Eastern Europe the problems of economic "transition" and "class" advantage became entangled in many ways with the issue of political democracy itself. The experts on the Eastern European countries offered "authoritarian or democratic government" as defining the left-right party competition in about 20 percent of all mentions. This dimension of party competition included issues of government control of the media, civil liberties, and political rights, as well as freedom, authoritarianism, and democracy explicitly. In four of their ten Eastern European

countries, including Russia, as many or more of the experts defined the left-right spectrum in these terms as in economic terms. In another three, "authoritarian or democratic" issues were the second most frequently mentioned. In Western Europe these issues received some mention in five countries, but the average for all of Western Europe was only about 5 percent.

Of course, other issues are also involved in party competition, in both West and East. Clashes between parties representing "new" and "traditional" values, including religious values, continue to be prominent in several countries, especially those with Catholic populations. In the last two decades, *Green parties* challenged the industrialization and pollution associated with economic growth policies. They have often forced older and larger parties to adopt at least some pro-environment programs, even at some cost to jobs and profits. In Germany in 1998 the Green Party joined with the SPD to form the governing coalition (Chapter 6.) Because of the serious pollution inherited from Soviet rule, Eastern Europe may offer great potential for Green parties, but these issues have so far been largely overshadowed by those of the economy and democracy. Another recent issue is the focus on the fear of "foreigners" or minority ethnic groups. Far-right parties focusing on fears and issues of this type have obtained 6 to 10 percent, or more, of the vote in a number of countries (as previously noted).

The relationship with the emerging European Union has also been an important and divisive issue in some countries. As the European Union has expanded its power over the trade, monetary, and social policies of the member nations, the consequences of those policies have inevitably helped some groups and hurt others. Whether or not to join the Union, or to participate in each new expansion of its powers, has been very controversial in Britain and Denmark. In Norway, debate over the European Union reshaped party competition. In Eastern Europe, many of the newly independent democracies want rapid incorporation into the European Union to protect their political independence and encourage their economies, but others fear the loss of their autonomy (see Chapter 11).

FIGURE 3.5 Types of Government Formed After Elections in Western and Eastern Europe

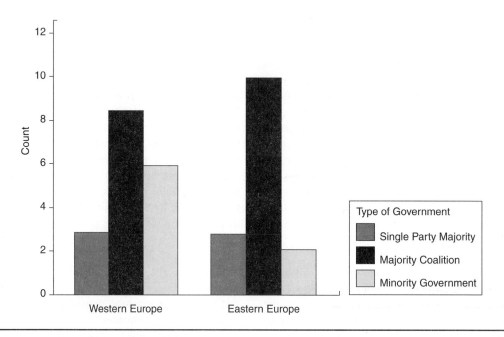

Sources: Keesing's Contemporary Archives, Electoral Studies. Note that "single party majority" refers to governments containing one party whose representatives constitute a majority in the legislature, even if additional parties also share cabinet seats.

Government Formation and Policymaking

Forming Governments

In parliamentary and mixed parliamentary-presidential systems the election is followed by *forming governments*. In some situations this process is obvious, rapid, and nearly automatic. When a single political party wins a majority of seats in the parliament, it almost always forms a government with the party head as prime minister and seldom shares cabinet posts with other parties. As shown in Figure 3.5, after recent elections only three Western European countries have had single-party governments commanding legislative majorities; these were elected in Britain, Greece, and Spain. In Eastern Europe in the late 1990s single parties or elec-

toral alliances won majorities in Albania, Bulgaria, and Lithuania, although they added additional parties to several of the governments.

Government formation is also relatively simple when a collective legislative majority is won by several parties that had formed a pre-election coalition. Such coalitions may take a variety of forms, including jointly announced policy promises, loose statements of similar objectives, or measures of electoral cooperation. Parties currently in government together may simply announce that they will extend their government if they win the election collectively. Such pre-election agreements were the rule in Germany from the early 1970s until the 1998 election (as discussed in Chapter 6) and characterize most elections in France, as well as a number of elections in Ireland, Denmark, Sweden, and Norway, and an occasional election elsewhere. Such coalitions may be encouraged by provisions in the election rules. For example, after Italy adopted new election laws with 75 percent single-member districts in 1993, the two subsequent elections saw pre-election coalitions that led directly to the formation of *coalition governments*. About 20 percent of the Western European governments were the product of majorities won by such a pre-election party coalition (not shown separately in the figure).

When no single party or preannounced coalition of parties wins a legislative majority, the process of forming a government is less straightforward and may be prolonged and difficult. In Figure 3.5 the tall middle bar shows that a multi-party majority coalition, either announced before or negotiated after the election, is the most common type of government in both regions. The process of building a government is shaped by various constitutional rules and procedures, as well as by the presence or absence of pre-election commitments. Typically, the head of state asks the leader of the largest political party to attempt to negotiate a government; if he or she fails, another party leader will be asked. In another variation, the head of state asks an "informateur" to sound out possible coalitions first. Postelection bargaining is the basis of virtually all government formation in Belgium, Finland, and the Netherlands, as well as pre-1994 Italy. It is a frequent event in many nations throughout Europe, both immediately after the election and after the breakup of a coalition government. (See the discussions of coalition formation after recent elections in Germany in Chapter 6, Poland in Chapter 9, and Hungary in Chapter 10).

In Western Europe about a third of all governments are *"minority" governments*, shown by the last bar in Figure 3.5. In such cases the government's continuing existence is dependent on support from a party, or shifting set of parties, not included in the cabinet. Minority governments can be a stopgap to the next election if elections usually provide majorities (as in Britain in 1974), an alternative to majorities where the rules in any case provide for a great deal of influence from nongoverning parties (as in Norway), or a sign of deadlock in the legislature (as has frequently happened in Italy).[48] As we see in Figure 3.5, such minority governments have appeared in Eastern Europe as well, but they have been less common there. (See the discussion of minority governments in Poland in Chapter 9.)

After the formation of a multiparty government, the cabinet positions are shared among the parties in the government. The parties in coalition governments usually receive such "portfolios" in proportion to their relative strength in the legislature. They also tend to demand and receive ministries reflecting their particular constituency interests, such as the Ministry of Agriculture going to parties with strong rural support. In the mixed presidential-parliamentary systems the president may be able to exert some influence over the composition of the cabinet, even if his or her party does not control the legislature. The president is often designated by the constitution as having special responsibility in areas of defense, security, and foreign policy, which may enhance his or her influence in these areas.

Single-party majority governments usually endure without change until the next election, at least in mature party systems such as Britain. In parliamentary systems, coalition governments that command a majority in the legislature and that are "minimal winning," in the sense that dropping even one party will cost the coalition its majority control of parliament, are also usually quite durable (see the discussion of German coalitions in Chapter 6). Such governments have lasted two and a half to three years in Western Europe on average. However, governments whose parties control only a minority of seats in parliament frequently fail before the next regularly scheduled election, lasting only about a year and a half on average and less in some countries.[49] When governments fall between elections—either because they lose a vote of (no) confidence or because they resign in anticipation of this—the bargaining process must begin again. In mixed presidential systems the president may be able to use the threat of dissolving the assembly and other policy-making powers to sustain a minority government, as in France (1988–1993) and in Russia (until the president acquired majority support in the 1999 election).

Policymaking by Cabinet Governments

During the period between elections, the policymaking process in parliamentary systems is heavily, but not exclusively, shaped by the composition of the cabinet government. In systems with concentrated political power, such as Britain and France, a single party or coalition winning the election expects and is expected to carry out its campaign promises. If the competing parties or coalitions offer contrasting choices, changing party governments usually makes a notable policy difference. When the new coalition government of socialists and communists came to power in France after the 1981 elections, it made many dramatic policy changes, such as nationalizing private banks and the five largest industrial corporations, as well as raising both the minimum wage and social security payments.

In countries that offer more influence to parties outside of government (through sharing committee chairs, strong upper houses of the legislature, federal decentralization, minority governments, etc.), the composition of governments usually makes less dramatic difference to public policy. Frequent changes in governments can also limit the impact of elections and parties on policy, as it takes time for new executives to shape policy.[50]

In mixed presidential-parliamentary systems the president may be able to play an important role in policymaking. The president may be able to shape the government (prime minister and cabinet) through his powers of appointment and the influence of his party in the legislature. The president may also have executive powers directly conferred by the constitutional rules. As a directly elected head of state, the president often receives special powers in the area of foreign or defense policy. Some, like the presidents of the United States and Russia, have the power to veto legislation, so that it does not become law unless passed again by a larger legislative margin. Some presidents have the power to issue "decrees" that have the force of law for limited periods or even (as in the Russian case) until replaced by appropriate legislative action. Where the president's powers are largely dependent on his or her ability to name the government, as in France,

influence over policy will largely depend on the balance in the legislature (see Chapter 5). Where the president has powers of veto and decree, as in Russia, the president and his or her own staff will independently be more important in policymaking. (See the discussion of the Russian president's dominating role in the policy process in Chapter 8.)

Of course, all governments face various constraints from international conditions and/or from the economies and societies in which they operate. A government may come to power committed to economic expansion yet be forced to change policies because of the international monetary situation, as was true of the French Socialists in the early 1980s. Governments in most Western European countries were frustrated by the difficulties in reducing unemployment in the 1990s.

Interest Groups and Policymaking

As we discussed in Chapter 2, associational interest groups are formed to express the interests of particular groups of citizens in policymaking in a systematic and organized way. In all modern societies such groups play a major role in shaping and implementing public policy. However, research in comparative politics has shown that democratic nations differ significantly in how interest groups are structured and how they are connected to government policymaking institutions. The differences in the types of connections allow us to talk of different interest group systems in modern societies. Across the Western European democracies, interest group systems vary between two contrasting models: pluralist and democratic corporatist.[51]

Pluralist interest group systems are characterized by several features that involve both how interests are organized and how they participate in the political process:

- Multiple groups may represent a single societal interest.
- Non-compulsory, limited membership in associational groups.
- Groups often have a loose, or decentralized organizational structure.
- A clear separation between interest groups and the government.

FIGURE 3.6   Interest Group Systems of Labor Unions

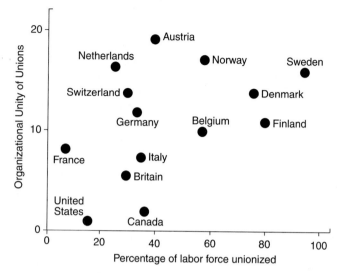

Source: Data for the percentage of the labor force unionized is from Organization for Economic Cooperation and Development, *Employment Outlook, July 1997* (Paris: OECD 1997): 71; the unity of unions is from Arend Lijphart and Marcus Crepaz, "Corporatism and Consensus Democracy in Eighteen Countries," *British Journal of Political Science* 21 (1991): 235–56.

For instance, not only are there different groups for different social sectors, such as labor unions, business associations, and professional groups, but there may be many multiple labor unions or business associations within each sector. These groups compete among themselves for membership and influence, and all simultaneously press their demands on policymakers and the bureaucracies. The United States is the best-known example of a strongly pluralist interest group system. Because of the fragmentation of interests in France (Chapter 5), this nation also is sometimes cited as having pluralist tendencies.

Corporatist interest group systems are more commonly found in the West European democracies. The corporatist systems are characterized by much more organized representation of interests:

- A single peak association normally represents each societal interest.
- Membership in the peak association is often compulsory and nearly universal.
- Umbrella groups are centrally organized and direct the actions of their members.

- Groups are often systematically involved in making and implementing policy.

For instance, in a corporatist system there may be a single peak association that represents all the major business or industrial interests. The Federation of German Industry (BDI) or the Confederation of British Industry (CBI) are examples of corporatist business associations; these are matched by corporatist labor movements: the German Federation of Trade Unions (DGB) or Britain's Trade Union Congress (TUC). A pluralist system may have a wide diversity of business groups that act separately. The most thoroughly corporatist interest group systems are in Austria, the Netherlands, and the Scandinavian nations of Norway and Sweden. Substantial democratic corporatist tendencies are also found in Germany and Denmark.

Because different sectors of a society may vary in their organized interest groups and in their government relations, we must be cautious about generalizing too much about interest group systems. However, Figure 3.6 shows the striking differences in organization of the labor movements in some industrialized societies. The countries are arrayed along the horizontal axis in terms of the percentage of the total labor force that belongs to a labor union. The vertical axis displays the degree or organizational unity within the labor union movement. In Sweden, for example, about 90 percent of the nonagricultural workforce is organized into unions, and the movement is highly centralized and united on most labor-related issues.

In Britain approximately a third of the labor force is unionized and these unions are not as highly coordinated as those of the corporatist countries. The member unions in the British Trade Union Congress have strong traditions of individual autonomy and are themselves relatively decentralized. Moreover, the influence of the labor unions on government policymakers has waned over the past two decades. The Thatcher government moved away from direct negotiation with labor, and thus away from corporatism in the 1980s, and even the Labour Party distanced itself from the labor unions in the 1990s. Germany has a similar level of union membership, but the German unions are relatively well coordinated and negotiate national wage policies with representatives of business and government.

Figure 3.6 also shows that union membership in France is quite low, with only about one worker in six or fewer belonging to a union. Moreover, the union movements themselves are relatively fragmented and decentralized. The United States is the polar opposite to Sweden; only about a sixth of the labor force is unionized, and the unions maintain a great deal of independence. In these countries there are few traditions of "social partnership" between government, unions, and employer associations. In the area of labor policy, at least, these are highly pluralist, not corporatist, interest group systems.

In some democratic systems, for example France and Italy, some interest groups such as trade unions and peasant associations have been controlled by the Communist Party or the Roman Catholic Church. Usually, these groups mobilized support for the political parties or social institutions that dominated them. This lack of autonomy had serious consequences for politics. Denial of independent expression to interest groups may lead to outbreaks of violence, and the subordination of in-terest groups may limit the adaptability of the political process. However, these restrictive structures seem to be breaking down, particularly with the reorganization and weakening of the formerly communist parties.

The best-studied democratic corporatist arrangements have been in the area of economic problems. Some statistics indicate that countries with corporatist economic systems have better records than more pluralist countries in sustaining employment, restraining inflation, and increasing social spending.[52] This might occur because groups learn to negotiate with each other and find common ground, rather than follow the competitive style of pluralist systems that may lead to more labor strikes and preemptive actions by business. In other words, the structure of interests can affect their methods of action and their likely success within the democratic process.

In Eastern Europe, communist parties (governments) penetrated and contolled virtually all organized groups until the collapse of Soviet control in 1989. Since then there has been an explosion of new groups and splintering and division of the ones previously dominated by the authoritarian governments. (See the discussions of interest groups in Russia, Poland, and Hungary in Chapters 8 to 10.) One of the many problems of these societies has been to bring some order into this chaotic situation, while at the same time encouraging freedom in group formation and the representation of many varieties of interests. Another problem has been to prevent the remaining institutional groups of the old systems, especially in the government bureaucracy and the government-run industries and businesses—often now formally "privatized" but practically run by the same people—from dominating policymaking. (See especially Russia, Chapter 8.)

Corruption, the Rule of Law, and Democracy

Democracy is a complicated system of government. It depends on competitive elections to link the actions of government to the desires of citizens.[53] It also requires the rule of law to see that those actions are implemented fairly. The rule of law can fail in many ways. When the president decides to continue past the end of his term of office or ignore the rulings of a constitutional court (as in Belarus), democracy may end. When the ruling parties demand kickbacks of public money from construction firms seeking public works contracts or bribes from interest groups asking for special legislation, the democratic process is subverted. When tax officials and border authorities are open to cash payments to overlook tax deficiencies and customs violations, democratic lawmaking is undermined. Corruption of all kinds and at all levels can also open the way to organized and violent criminal penetration of policymaking.

No democracy is immune to these threats to the rule of law. But some countries suffer much more grievously than others from corrupt practices in making and implementing public policies. In such countries citizens who must interact with the government find that they are forced into participation in corruption to gain even basic benefits, a situation that weakens their confidence in the meaningfulness of democracy. In Western Europe the most blatant examples of public corruption emerged in Italy in the early 1990s, when the judicial investigation called "Operation Clean Hands" revealed that the incumbent political parties had demanded and received billions of lira in bribes from business organizations and used them to finance both party organizational activity and lavish lifestyles for their leaders. At the same time other investigations were uncovering the depth of the penetration of organized crime into Italian politics, particularly in the South, using both bribery and violence. These revelations destroyed most of the political parties and leaders that had dominated Italian politics, sparking constitutional change and a new party system.[54]

In Eastern Europe establishing the rule of law has been one of the most difficult parts of the transition to democracy.[55] The communist dictatorships had in many Eastern European countries coexisted with large amounts of corruption, sometimes even encouraged it as a means of overcoming the inefficiencies of the vast bureaucracies. The abuse of power to gain personal benefits was common at all levels, especially in countries in which communist regimes had been imposed upon traditional, economically undeveloped societies.[56] Such habits were not easily overcome, especially at the lower levels of

government. They were sustained by the generally low levels of economic development and exacerbated in the short run by the slumping economies and lagging salary payments that made life desperate for many government employees. The privatization of the economies that had so long been run as part of the government also created unusual, nearly irresistable, opportunities for insiders to abuse their positions and acquire some of the new wealth. (See the discussion of the rule of law in Russia, Chapter 8.)

While corruption and criminal activity are by their nature difficult to study systematically, interesting comparisons are offered by The Internet Center for Corruption Research, which uses surveys of businesses to estimate levels of corruption in different countries. Their "Corruption Perceptions Index" rates about one hundred countries in the world each year on a scale from 0 (most corrupt) to 10 (most clean). In 1999 a majority of Western European countries, including Britain and Germany, rated 8 or higher, although only Denmark was awarded a perfect 10. The Western European average of 7.8 was just above the United States. France and Spain were rated somewhat less "clean," but of the Western European nations only Italy was ranked (just) below the scale midpoint of 5.0.[57]

Unfortunately, but not surprisingly, all the Eastern European nations fell well below the Western European average. Slovenia, Estonia, and Hungary (Chapter 10) were rated above Italy, while the Czech Republic and Poland (Chapter 9) were just below it. The average score in Eastern Europe was only 3.6. Russia (Chapter 8) was a very discouraging 2.4, ahead of only Albania and Yugoslavia on the European continent. Statistical analysis suggests that in Europe and across the world the level of economic development (as measured by Purchasing Power Parity scores) is a very powerful predictor of cleaner politics. However, presumably because of the problems of overcoming its communist heritage and managing an economic transition, the Eastern European region scores somewhat more poorly than its economic development level would lead us to expect.[58] Corruption is recognized as a serious problem within most of these countries, but is easier to raise as an election issue than to overcome through improved government.

Box 3.2 Democratic Failure: An Unfree Press

One of the surest threats to democracy is failure to sustain free broadcast and print media. Freedom House's *Press Freedom Survey 2000* evaluates constraints on these freedoms in many countries in 1999. All the countries of Western Europe and about half of the countries in Eastern Europe, including Poland and Hungary (Chapters 9 and 10), were generally classified as having a "free" press.

Seven Eastern European countries, including Russia (Chapter 8), experienced sufficient problems that they were classified as having an only "partly free" press in 1999. For example, the report noted that in Russia:

- "Year-long in Moscow government operatives harassed or physically abused journalists."

Moreover, to defend the military campaign in Chechnya, the new Russian minister for the media "stressed the need 'to protect the state from the press.' He implied that a free press threatened the security of the nation."

In three countries, Belarus, Croatia, and Yugoslavia, the attack on press freedoms went much further:

- Not only are the national broadcase media in Belarus state monopolies, but "Libel and defamation laws carry penalties of up to four years' imprisonment or two years in a labor camp for insulting President Lukashenka."
- In Croatia, "journalists received death threats, were interrogated by police, and were indicted for publishing reports considered offensive to the government."
- The government in Yugoslavia adopted a new Law on Public Information that "introduced the supposition of guilt of any media charged with ill-defined 'misdemeanors'; bans the rebroadcast of foreign transmissions in Serbian and minority languages; requires prior permission of any person whose voice, name, or image is used in a report; (and) introduces exorbitant fines against media convicted of misdemeanors."

The Freedom House analysis classified Belarus, Croatia, and Yugoslavia as having media that were "not free." It is clear that these three countries had far to go on the journey toward effective democracy.

Source: Freedom House, *Press Freedom Survey 2000*, as downloaded July 20, 2000, from www.freedomhouse. org/pfs2000/.

Introducing and Sustaining Democracy

Historically, most of the world's democracies have been located in Europe. Europe has thus been the source of much of our knowledge of the practical alternatives for introducing and running democratic governments. It has also been the site of some of the most famous failures of democracy, most notably the collapse of Germany's Weimar Republic into Nazi dictatorship, with terrible consequences for the entire world. While a smaller percentage of the world's democracies in the 1990s may be located in Europe, there is little doubt that the democratization experiences of Eastern Europe will add greatly to our understanding of the process.

The general approach to managing democratic conflict in Western Europe, as we have already explained, has tended to involve power-sharing through a variety of constitutional and electoral devices, encouraging multiple political parties and multiple paths to influence policymaking. In some countries the efforts to overcome deep conflicts gave rise to an even more distinctive form of guaranteed power- and policy-sharing called the "consociational" approach.[59] (See Chapter 1.) The Netherlands, Austria, Belgium, and Switzerland offer prominent examples of elite-negotiated agreements between segments of deeply divided societies. Agreements to share political power and guarantee both influence and shares of benefits to all segments (whether defined by religious, linguistic, or occupational criteria) were buttressed by formal organizational arrangements. Although some of these arrangements have been dismantled as social segments have become less distinctive and conflicts less intense, their successes demonstrate a valuable approach to conflict management in seriously divided societies.

Statistical analyses of conflict and turmoil based largely, but not entirely, on the Western European experience suggest that various representational power-sharing processes can have some success in diminishing "street" turmoil of riots and protests.[60] Such turmoil is likely to be more intense under the limited routes to influence in majoritarian democracies. On the other hand, the proportional representation and power-sharing strategies may bring turmoil "inside" the institutions, putting extremist parties in the legislature and making stable cabinet government more difficult. Moreover, once the process of violent conflict is underway, achievement of elite agreements can be insufficient. Northern Ireland has demonstrated repeatedly that power-sharing agreements cannot really be sustained in a democracy without the assent of the majority of citizens, who will simply replace leaders they view as betraying their interests.

Western Europe offers substantial experience with threats to democracy by violence and military intervention. A common thread in these experiences has been the need for those whose political positions depend on citizen support—the organized political parties—to rally behind democracy in crises. In the 1930s the bitterly suspicious socialist and middle-class parties failed to unite against the Nazis in Germany and careened into civil war in Austria. In Greece conservative fears of a new Socialist government encouraged the military to overthrow democracy in 1967. In contrast, the backing of all political parties for (limited) government antiterrorist measures in Italy in the 1970s helped sustain democracy against intensive bombing and assassination campaigns. Democratic heads of state with backing of all major parties were able to defeat attempted coups in France in 1961 and Spain in 1981 by rallying citizens as well as loyalist groups in the military.

Battles against terrorism and violence (especially violence against immigrant groups) continue in a number of Western European countries. Democratic governments must maintain the critical balance between upholding the security of all their residents while avoiding too great infringements on their freedoms. This is, of course, easier where citizens share common values and positive economic conditions as well as experience with responsive democratic government. In Eastern Europe the conditions are generally much worse, as the reconstruction of the economies has been intensely painful even where it has gone relatively quickly. In most areas it has been slow and hesitant. In many countries citizens do not share either common values or, at this point, much confidence in democratic government.

Yet, in most of Eastern Europe, it should be emphasized, the revolution that has occurred since 1989 has been remarkable in managing vast change with little violence. Democracy is shaky in some nations. (See Box 3.2 on problems in sustaining freedom of the press in parts of Eastern Europe.) But it seems to be building a firm foundation in others, perhaps more successfully than we originally expected. Parties are learning to develop internal cohesion and accommodate differences with political opponents. Governments are learning to deal with dissent without suppressing dissenters or the press, to manage economies without taking them over, to provide safety nets for citizens without destroying their incentives. Citizens are demanding a rule of law. The current decade is a critical time for the region formerly dominated by the Soviet Union; there is great potential, but also great risk. The devastating wars in Chechnya and in the former Yugoslavia—especially in Bosnia where the horrors of "ethnic cleansing" were added to the destruction and displacement of modern warfare—show the potential cost of failure.

No one has yet found perfect institutions for making public policy. European democratic institutions are no exception; they are far from perfect in either West or East. It is easy to find flaws in constitutional arrangements, competitive party systems, and democratic policymaking processes. It is even easier to criticize the policies of a current government; good leadership and wise policies are not guaranteed by democratic institutions. Yet bitter experience in Europe and in nations everywhere shows that democracy is more likely than any other form of government to sustain personal freedoms, encourage equal treatment under the law, and protect the rights of minorities. Moreover, democracies seldom go to war against each other. Democratic government is the best security for the hard-won personal freedoms of the citizens of Eastern Europe and the newfound peace that has replaced Europe's destructive wars. Building democracy has thus had profound consequences for all Europeans. There is no doubt that the European experiences will continue to teach the world about the limits and potentials of democratic government.

✌ KEY TERMS ✌

assembly
bicameralism
cabinet
coalition government
communist
     parties/formerly
     communist parties
confidence vote
executive
extremist parties
federalism

forming a government
freedom of the press
Green parties
judicial review
left-right continuum
liberal democracy
minority government
mixed electoral rules
mixed presidential-
     parliamentary
     systems

multiparty
     system/majority-
     electing party
     system
parliamentary
     democracy
party cohesion
power-sharing
presidential democracy

prime minister
proportional
     representation (PR)
rightist parties
single-member districts
social democratic
     parties
strong committee
     systems

✌ SUGGESTED READINGS ✌

Bartolini, Stefano, and Peter Mair. *Identity, Competition and Electoral Availability: The Stabilization of European Electorates.* New York: Cambridge University Press, 1990.

Bowler, Shaun, David M. Farrell, and Richard W. Katz. *Party Cohesion, Party Discipline and the Organization of Parliaments.* Columbus: Ohio State University Press, 1999.

Cox, Gary. *Making Votes Count: Strategic Coordination in the World's Electoral Systems.* New York: Cambridge University Press, 1997.

Doering, Herbert, ed. *Parliaments and Majority Rule in Western Europe.* New York: St. Martin's, 1995.

Franklin, Mark, Thomas Mackie, and Henry Valen, et al. *Electoral Change: Responses to Evolving Social and Attitudinal Structures in Western Countries.* New York: Cambridge University Press, 1992.

Geddes, Barbara. "A Comparative Perspective on the Leninist Legacy in Eastern Europe." *Comparative Political Studies* 28 (July 1995): 239–74.

Hellman, Joel. "Constitutional and Economic Reform in Post-Communist Transitions." *Eastern European Constitutional Review* (Winter 1996): 46–56.

Jones, G. W., ed. "West European Prime Ministers." *West European Politics* (Special Issue) 14, No. 2 (April 1991).

Katzenstein, Peter. *Small States in World Markets: Industrial Policy in Europe.* Ithaca, NY: Cornell University Press, 1985.

Kitschelt, Herbert. *The Transformation of European Social Democracy.* New York: Cambridge University Press, 1994.

———, Zdenka Mansfedlova, Radoslaw Markowski, and Gabor Toka. *Post-Communist Party Systems: Competition, Representation and Inter-Party Cooperation.* New York: Cambridge University Press, 1999.

Laver, Michael, and Norman Schofield. *Multiparty Government: The Politics of Coalition in Europe.* New York: Oxford University Press, 1990.

Laver, Michael, and Kenneth A. Shepsle, eds. *Cabinet Ministers and Parliamentary Government.* New York: Cambridge University Press, 1994.

LeDuc, Lawrence, Richard G. Niemi, and Pippa Norris, eds. *Comparing Democracies: Elections and Voting in Global Perspective.* Thousand Oaks, CA: Sage, 1996.

Lijphart, Arend. *Democracy in Plural Societies.* New Haven: Yale University Press, 1977.

———. *Electoral Systems and Party Systems: A Study of Twenty-Seven Democracies, 1945–1990.* New York: Oxford University, 1994.

———. *Patterns of Democracy: Government Forms and Performance in Thirty-Six Countries..* New Haven: Yale University Press, 1999.

Lipset, Seymour M., and Stein Rokkan. *Party Systems and Voter Alignments.* New York: Free Press, 1967.

Norton, Philip, ed. "Parliaments in Western Europe." *West European Politics* (Special Issue) 13, No. 3 (July 1990).

Powell, G. Bingham. *Contemporary Democracies: Participation, Stability and Violence.* Cambridge: Harvard University Press, 1982.

———. *Elections as Instruments of Democracy: Majoritarian and Proportional Visions.* New Haven: Yale University Press, 2000.

Rose, Richard. *Do Parties Make a Difference?* 2nd ed. Chatham, NJ: Chatham House, 1984.

Sartori, Giovanni. *Comparative Constitutional Engineering.* New York: NYU Press, 1997.

———. *Parties and Party Systems: A Framework for Analysis.* New York: Cambridge University Press, 1976.

Shugart, Matthew Soberg, and John Carey. *Presidents and Assemblies: Constitutional Design and Electoral Dynamics.* New York: Cambridge University Press, 1992.

Strom, Kaare. *Minority Government and Majority Rule.* New York: Cambridge University Press, 1990.

Volcansek, Mary L., ed. "Judicial Politics and Policymaking in Western Europe." *West European Politics* (Special Issue) 15, No. 3 (July 1992).

ENDNOTES

1. This does not mean, of course, that there will be no challenges in the future. The last few years have seen the collapse and replacement of the party system in Italy and continuing serious challenges at the regional level in Northern Ireland and in Spain.

2. One can find, of course, various flaws in contemporary Western European democracies, particularly in violence directed against immigrants and some other minorities; in the rise of antidemocratic extremist groups and parties, especially on the political right in the 1990s; in constraints on civil rights when confronting terrorist activities; in slow responsiveness to citizen concerns about environmental issues and so forth.

3. We use the term "assembly" here, rather than legislature, to emphasize that the authority for and practice of legislation—making laws—vary in different constitutional systems. The assembly may not have the sole authority, as in presidential and federal systems, for example, and seldom is the most important source of legislation.

4. For general analysis and comparison of presidential powers, see Matthew S. Shugart and John M. Carey, *Presidents and Assemblies* (New York: Cambridge University Press, 1992), especially Ch. 8. Also valuable is Scott Mainwaring and Matthew Shugart, *Presidentialism and Democracy in Latin America* (New York: Cambridge University Press, 1997) and see the references in Note 11.

5. In Germany, Hungary, and Spain the constitutions specify "constructive" votes of no confidence, which can force the government to resign only if an alternative government is explicitly designated and supported.

6. For an analysis of the power of the prime minister, who can attach the fate of a particular policy to a vote on government survival, see John D. Huber, "The Vote of Confidence in Parliamentary Democracies," *American Political Science Review* 90 (June 1966): 269–82. See also the essays in Michael Laver and Kenneth A. Shepsle, *Cabinet Ministers and Parliamentary Government* (New York: Cambridge University Press, 1994).

7. It is important to avoid confusion between the formal titles, and their various translations, of government officials and the source of their selection and bases of their powers—which determine the type of political system. Thus Germany and Italy are considered parliamentary systems, even though each has an official head of state, whose official title is "president." Spain is considered a parliamentary system (whose head of state is the monarch), even though the chief executive's official title is "President of the Government," or "President of the Council of Ministers." We generally refer to the head of the executives in Germany and Spain as "prime ministers," although their official titles are, respectively, "Chancellor" and "President of the Government."

8. *Congressional Quarterly*, December 21, 1996, p. 3461; this analysis considers only votes in which the two major parties oppose each other and does not include voting for official House leadership positions (on which voting tends to be strictly along party lines).

9. In the British House of Commons in the 1987–1992 session of Parliament, both parties were perfectly cohesive on 80 percent of the votes where parties took official stands. (Philip Norton, "Parliamentary Behavior Since 1945," *Talking Politics*, VIII (1995–96), p. 112.) For evidence of similar cohesion in Germany in the 1970s and 1980s, see Thomas Saalfield, "The West German Bundestag after Forty Years," *West European Politics* 13, No. 3 (July 1990): 74. For evidence of over 90 percent party voting in the French Fifth Republic, see Philip E. Converse and Roy Pierce, *Political Representation in France* (Cambridge: Harvard University Press, 1986), pp. 552–61. However, for a discussion of lack of party cohesion in the early years of Spanish democracy (1979–1982), see Chapter 7. On party cohesion generally, see Shawn Bowler, David M. Farrell, and Richard W. Katz, *Party Cohesion, Party Discipline and the Organization of Parliaments* (Columbus: Ohio State University Press, 1999).

10. Figures 3.1 through 3.3 are based on eighteen countries in Western Europe and sixteen countries in Eastern Europe.

Three Eastern European countries are not included: Bosnia, still recovering from civil war, and Belarus and Yugoslavia, which were predominately authoritarian systems, not democracies at this time.

11. The classification in Figure 3.1 and the associated analysis is based on an updated analysis of formal presidential powers by Joel Helman and Richard Tucker, based conceptually on Shugart and Carey's *Presidents and Assemblies*, 1992. Also see Joel Hellman, "Constitutional and Economic Reform in Postcommunist Transitions," *Eastern European Constitutional Review* (Winter 1996): 46–56; Christian Lucky, "A Comparative Chart of Presidential Powers in Eastern Europe," *EECR* (Fall 93/Winter 94): 81–94; Matthew Shugart "Of Presidents and Parliaments," *EECR* (Winter 1993): 30–32; and Lee Kendall Metcalf, "Measuring Presidential Power," *Comparative Political Studies* (June 2000): 660–85.

12. See Chapter 5; Roy Pierce, "The Executive Divided Against Itself: Cohabitation in France 1986–1988" *Governance* 4, No. 3 (July 1991): 270–94; and John D. Huber, *Rationalizing Parliament: Legislative Institutions and Party Politics in France* (New York: Cambridge University Press, 1996).

13. See Arend Lijphart, ed., *Parliamentary versus Presidential Government* (Oxford: Oxford University Press, 1992); Juan Linz and Arturo Valenzuela, eds., *The Failure of Presidential Government* (Baltimore: Johns Hopkins University Press, 1994); G. Bingham Powell, Jr., *Contemporary Democracies: Participation, Stability and Violence* (Cambridge, MA: Harvard University Press, 1982), Chs. 6, 10; Alfred Stepan and Cindy Skach, "Constitutional Frameworks and Democratic Consolidation: Parliamentarism versus Presidentialism," *World Politics* 46 (October 1993): 1–22.

14. See Shugart and Carey, *Presidents and Assemblies.*

15. See Thomas A. Baylis, "Presidents Versus Prime Ministers: Shaping Executive Authority in Eastern Europe," *World Politics* (April 1996): 297–323, and the discussion of Poland in Chapter 9.

16. These three countries were classified as definitely "not free" for half of more of the decade. Yugoslavia failed to make the initial transition even to a partly free democracy, at least until the overthrow of Milosovic in Fall 2000, which may limit its relevance to the constitutional debate. Bosnia's collective presidency is also unique in the European setting.

17. See the essays in Mary L. Volcansek, ed., "Judicial Politics and Policymaking in Western Europe," a special issue of *West European Politics* 15, No. 3 (July 1992); and in Martin Shapiro and Alec Stone, "The New Constitutional Politics of Europe," a special issue of *Comparative Political Studies* 26, No. 4 (January 1994).

18. However, in the French Fourth Republic (1947–1958) governments frequently tinkered with the election laws to seek electoral advantage. In France in 1986 and in Greece in 1989 governments introduced proportional representation with low thresholds to try to limit expected losses; these partly successful changes were eventually reversed by their successors. Several of the new Eastern European democracies, including Bulgaria, Macedonia, and Ukraine, have also modified their election rules.

19. For a detailed analysis, see Arend Lijphart, *Electoral Systems and Party Systems: A Study of Twenty-Seven Democracies, 1945–1990* (New York: Oxford University Press, 1994).

20. Accurate representation under PR also requires that the districts (if any) have numbers of representatives proportional to their (adult) population. This requirement is met in most Western European nations except Spain, which has substantial underrepresentation of some districts and overrepresentation of others.

21. These countries are Greece, Ireland, and Spain. For a general discussion of the concept of "effective threshold" for party representation, taking account of many special features of the election laws, not just the formal threshold, see Lijphart, *Electoral Systems and Party Systems*, Ch. 2; later in the book Lijphart estimates the effective threshold in each electoral system.

22. Maurice Duverger, *Political Parties: Their Organization and Activity in the Modern State* [1954], trans. Barbara and Robert North (New York: Wiley, 1963). For more recent discussions of electoral systems and their consequences, see Rein Taagepera and Matthew Shugart, *Seats and Votes* (New Haven: Yale University Press, 1989); Gary Cox, *Making Votes Count* (New York: Cambridge University Press, 1997).

23. As explained in Chapter 6, in the German version of a "mixed" system the party-list seats are distributed among the parties after the election so as to make the overall legislative representation (combined single-member district representatives and party-list representatives) correspond as closely as possible to the party vote percentages. A party like the Free Democrats, which rarely carries any single-member districts, gets an extra helping of party-list seats to bring its overall proportion into balance with its vote. As discussed in Chapter 8, in the Russian version (also used in Japan and some other mixed systems) the party-list seats are not used to compensate for party underrepresentation in the single-member district outcomes. Other European systems use various degrees of compensation. The complicated mixed Hungarian system is discussed in Chapter 10.

24. See Matthew Soberg Shugart, "The Electoral Cycle and Institutional Sources of Divided Presidential Government," *American Political Science Review* 89 (June 1995): 327–43.

25. See especially Seymour Martin Lipset and Stein Rokkan, eds., *Party Systems and Voter Alignments* (New York: Free Press, 1967), Ch. 1.

26. Barbara Geddes, "A Comparative Perspective on the Leninist Legacy in Eastern Europe," *Comparative Political Studies* 28 (July 1995): 239–74. See especially the table on p. 244, showing the vote for "historic" parties in Latin America and Eastern Europe.

27. Geddes, "A Comparative Perspective," pp. 255–56. Poland is exceptional among Eastern European countries in having had a relatively strong Catholic church and independent (though repressed) trade union movement (see Chapter 9).

28. Lipset and Rokkan, *Party Systems and Voter Alignments.*

29. See the recent summary by Russell J. Dalton, "Political Cleavages, Issues, and Electoral Change," in Lawrence LeDuc, Richard G. Niemi, and Pippa Norris, eds., *Comparing Democracies: Elections and Voting in Global Perspective* (Thousand Oaks, CA: Sage, 1996), pp. 319–42.

30. See Krzysztof Jasiewicz, "Polish Politics on the Eve of the 1993 Elections: Towards Fragmentation or Pluralism," *Communist and Post Communist Studies* (December 26, 1993): 387–411. Also see Herbet Kitschelt, Zdenka Mansfelova, Radoslaw Markowski, and Gabor Toka, *Post Communist Party Systems: Competition, Representation and Inter-Party Competition* (New York: Cambridge University Press, 1999), Ch. 8.

31. See especially Kitschelt, et al., *Post Communist Party Systems,* Ch. 1.

32. In addition to Kitschelt, et al., *Post Communist Party Systems,* see Attila Aagh, "The End of the Beginning: The Partial Consolidation of East Central European Parties and Party Systems, in Paul Pennings and Jan-Erik Lane, eds., *Comparing Party System Change* (New York: Routledge, 1998), pp. 202–15; and the essays in Kay Lawson, Andrea Rommele, and Georgi Karasimeonov, eds., *Cleavages, Parties and Voters: Studies from Bulgaria, the Czech Republic, Hungary, Poland and Romania* (Westport CT: Praeger, 1999).

33. From Markku Laakso and Rein Taagepera, " 'Effective' Number of Parties: A Measure with Application to West Europe," *Comparative Political Studies* 12 (April 1979): 3–27. See also Arend Lijphart, *Democracies* (New Haven: Yale University Press, 1984), Ch. 7. Mathematically, the number is

$$\frac{1}{\sum_{i}^{n} P_i^2}$$

P_i is the proportion of votes or seats of the *i*th party.

34. See Robert G. Moser, "The Impact of the Electoral System on Post-Communist Party Development: The Case of the 1993 Russian Parliamentary Elections," *Electoral Studies* 14 (December 1995): 377–98.

35. For example, Duverger, *Political Parties,* 1954, pp. 419–20; see also the discussion in Powell, *Contemporary Democracies,* Ch. 5.

36. Giovanni Sartori, *Parties and Party Systems,* (New York: Cambridge University Press, 1976), Ch. 6; and see G. Bingham Powell, Jr., "The Competitive Consequences of Polarized Pluralism," in Manfred Holler, ed., *The Logic of Multiparty Systems* (Dordrecht, Netherlands: Martinus Nijhoff, 1987), pp. 173–90.

37. Paul Warwick, "Economic Trends and Government Survival in West European Parliamentary Democracies," *American Political Science Review* 86 (December 1992): 875–87. A very large body of research exists on this topic, beginning especially with Michael Taylor and Valentine Herman, "Party Systems and Government Stability," *American Political Science Review* 65 (March 1971): 28–37; see the reviews in Powell, *Contemporary Democracies,* Ch. 7 and in Warwick.

38. See G. Bingham Powell, Jr., "Extremist Parties, Electoral Polarization, and Citizen Turmoil," *American Journal of Political Science* 30 (1986): 357–78. Alternatively, we could use the 1982 survey of experts conducted by Francis Castles and Peter Mair, "Left-Right Political Scales: Some Expert Judgments," *European Journal of Political Research* 12 (1984): 73–88. Using their experts' classification of parties, if we count parties under 2 on their 0–10 scale as left extremists and parties over 8 as right extremists, we find that support for such parties in elections of the late 1970s or early 1980s is 24% in Denmark, 18% in Finland, 4% in Belgium, 38% in Italy, and 17% in France (38% if we count the Guallists who get 8.2).

39. Expert party ratings from a 1993 survey by John Huber and Ronald Inglehart, "Expert Interpretations of Party Space and Party Locations in 42 Societies," *Party Politics* 1 (1995): 73–111. We classified parties rated under 2.5 or over 8.5 on their 1–10 scale as left or right "extremists" on left-right. We used survey data from *Euro-Barometer 41,* March–June 1994, to classify a party as extremist if the percentage saying democracy not working "at all" was over 25 percent and at least 10 percent above its country's average. Extremist parties by one or both of these measures included the Communists and National Front in France; Refounded Communists, PDS and MSI in Italy; FPOe in Austria; Volksunie and Vlamms Bloc in Belgium; Progress and Red-Green List in Denmark; KKE in Greece; RV and Progress in Norway; New Democracy in Sweden; CDS in Portugal; PDS and Republikans in Germany. For an "expert assessment" approach listing "extreme right" parties in Western Europe, see Cas Mudde, "Defining the Extreme Right Party Family," *West European Politics* 19, No. 2 (April 1996): 235.

40. See discussion in *The Economist,* November 23, 1991, pp. 56–57.

41. Calculated from *Central and Eastern Euro-Barometer 5: Political and Economic Change, November 1994,* Ann Arbor, MI: ICPSR, 1995, with parties classified as extremists if the percentage of their supporters saying "democracy does not work at all" is over 33 percent and at least 10 percent beyond the national average.

42. For an analysis that attempts to explain differences in the role of formerly communist parties in terms of the way the older communist systems were governed and the nature of the transition to democracy, see the discussion in Kitschelt, *Post-Communist Party Systems.*

43. Americans use the terms "liberal" and "conservative" in roughly this sense; "liberal" means something quite different in Europe, so it is safer, as well as regionally correct, to stay with "left."

44. The citizen placements in France are from the *Euro-Barometer 47, Spring 1997,* survey. Those in Britain, Spain, and Poland are from the *Comparative Election Study* surveys in 1996 and 1997, with the eleven point scale converted to a

ten point scale for comparability. For Germany, see Chapter 6. The United States placements are from the *1998 U.S. National Election Study*, converting the seven point scale to a ten point. Roughly similar results derive from a survey of experts in 1993, reported in Huber and Inglehart, "Expert Interpretations," although using the average voter self-placment (as done here) tends to pull placement of the more extreme parties somewhat toward the center.

45. On this idea and the issues involved, see also G. Bingham Powell, Jr., *Elections as Instruments of Democracy: Majoritarian and Proportional Visions* (New Haven: Yale University Press, 2000), esp. Ch. 7 and references.

46. See Ronald Inglehart, "The Changing Structure of Political Cleavages in Western Society," in Russell J. Dalton, Scott C. Flanagan, and Paul Allen Beck, *Electoral Change in Advanced Industrial Societies* (Princeton: Princeton University Press, 1984), pp. 25–69.

47. Huber and Inglehart, "Expert Interpretations."

48. See the fine discussion in Kaare Strom, *Minority Government and Majority Rule* (New York: Cambridge University Press, 1990).

49. Governments built on an "excessive" number of parties are also frequently unstable, prone to additional bargaining and to being reduced to the minimum number needed for parliamentary control.

50. See classic analyses of France in the Fourth Republic by Philip Williams, *Crisis and Compromise: Politics in the Fourth Republic* (Hamden, CT: Archon Press, 1964), esp. p. 405. But the issue is controversial; see the discussion and one of the few empirical comparative studies in John Huber, "How Does Cabinet Instability Affect Political Performance? Portfolio Volatility and Health Care Cost Containment in Parliamentary Democracies," *American Political Science Review* 92 (1996): 577–91.

51. Philippe Schmitter, "Interest Intermediation and Regime Governability," in Suzanne Berger, ed., *Organizing Interests in Western Europe* (New York: Cambridge University Press, 1981), Ch. 12; Arend Lijphart and Markus Crepaz, "Corporatism and Consensus Democracy in 18 Countries," *British Journal of Political Science*, 21:2 (April 1991): 235–46; Wyn Grant, ed., *The Political Economy of Corporatism.* (New York: St. Martin's Press, 1985).

52. On the relative success of the corporatist systems in economic performance see Miriam Golden, "The Dynamics of Trade Unionism and National Economic Performance," *American Political Science Review*, 87:2 (June 1993): 439–54; Arend Lijphart, Ronald Rogowski, and R. Kent Weaver, "Separation of Powers and Cleavage Management," in R. Kent Weaver and Bert A. Rockman, *Do Institutions Matter? Government Capabilities in the United States and Abroad* (Washington, D.C.: The Brookings Institution, 1993), pp. 302–44.

53. See Powell, *Elections as Instruments of Democracy*, 2000.

54. For a readable account of "Operation Clean Hands," see Mark Gilbert, *The Italian Revolution: The End of Politics Italian Style?* (Boulder, CO: Westview Press, 1995), Ch. 8. Mafia violence is discussed in Chapter 3.

55. See, for example, the essays by Stephen Holmes, et al., "Crime and Corruption after Communism," in *East European Constitutional Review* 6 (Fall 1997): 69–98.

56. See Kitschelt, et al., *Post-Communist Systems*, pp. 21–28 and 36–37 and the references therein.

57. All scores were obtained from the website of the Internet Center for Corruption Research (a joint project of Goettingen University and Transperancy International), downloaded from gwdu19.gwdg.de/~uwvw/ on July 24, 2000. The site contains an explanation of the methodology as well as scores for 99 countries in 1999.

58. Also see Daniel Treisman, "The Causes of Corruption: A Cross-National Study," *Journal of Public Economics*, 76 (June 2000): 399–457, who suggests less developed economies, a shorter exposure to democracy, and federalism among the factors encouraging more corruption cross nationally. The first two explain poor performance of the East European region in his analysis.

59. The critical contributor to analysis of this approach has been Arend Lijphart; see especially *Democracy in Plural Societies* (New Haven: Yale University Press, 1977). See also our discussion in Chapter 1.

60. Powell, *Contemporary Democracies*, Chs. 4, 5, 10.

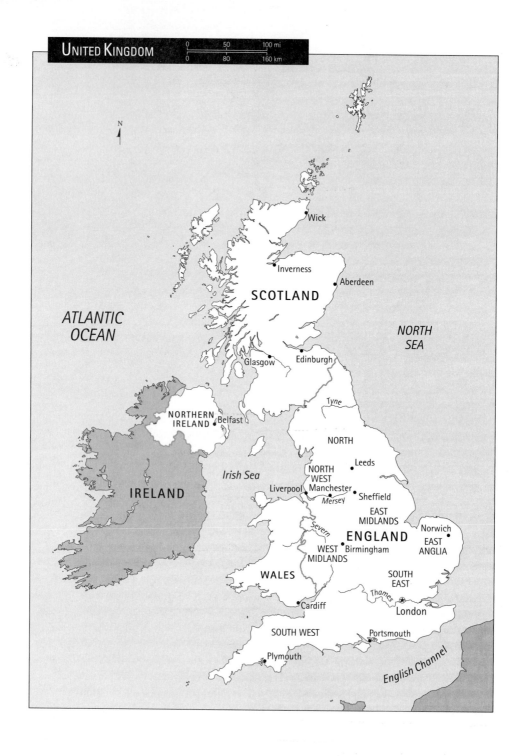

UNITED KINGDOM

0   50   100 mi
0   80   160 km

N

ATLANTIC
OCEAN

NORTH
SEA

Wick

Inverness

Aberdeen

SCOTLAND

Glasgow   Edinburgh

Tyne

NORTHERN
IRELAND   Belfast

IRELAND

Irish Sea

NORTH

NORTH   Leeds
WEST
Liverpool   Manchester   Sheffield
Mersey
EAST
MIDLANDS
Severn   ENGLAND   Norwich
WEST   Birmingham   EAST
MIDLANDS   ANGLIA

WALES   SOUTH
EAST

Cardiff   Thames   London

SOUTH WEST   Portsmouth

Plymouth   English Channel

CHAPTER 4

POLITICS IN ENGLAND

RICHARD ROSE

Country Bio–United Kingdom

POPULATION   58.6 Million

TERRITORY   94,525 sq. mi

YEAR OF INDEPENDENCE   from twelfth century

YEAR OF CURRENT CONSTITUTION   unwritten; partly statutes, partly common law and practice

HEAD OF STATE   Queen Elizabeth II

HEAD OF GOVERNMENT   Prime Minister Tony Blair

LANGUAGE(S)   English, Welsh (about 600,000), Scottish form of Gaelic (about 60,000)

RELIGION   Anglican 26.1 million, Roman Catholic 5.7 million, Presbyterian 2.6 million, Methodist 1.3 million, Other Christian 2.6 million, Muslim 1.2 million, Sikh 600,000, Hindu 400,000, Jewish 300,000. The remainder have no religious identification.

In a world of new democracies, England is different, because it is an old democracy. Unlike new democracies in Eastern Europe, Latin America, and Asia, England did not become a democracy overnight due to the collapse of a dictatorship. It became a democracy by evolution rather than revolution. Democratization was a slow process that occurred over the centuries. The rule of law was established in the seventeenth century; the accountability of the executive became clear in the eighteenth century; political parties organized in the nineteenth century; and, even though competitive elections had been held for more than a century, the right of every adult man and woman to vote was not recognized until the twentieth century.

The evolution of democracy in England also stands in contrast to the dominant European practice of countries switching between democratic and undemocratic regimes. Whereas the oldest English person has lived under the same constitution all his or her life, the oldest Germans have lived under four or five constitutions, two democratic and two or three undemocratic.[1]

The gradual evolution of political institutions means that at no point in history did representatives of the English people meet together to decide what kind of government they would like to have, as happened in the American constitutional convention of the 1780s, and in dozens of new democracies in the past two decades. Politicians have been socialized to accept institutions as a legacy from their predecessors; these are the rules of the game by which they compete for office. Ordinary citizens have been socialized to accept established institutions too.

The influence of British democracy can be found in places as far-flung as Australia, Canada, India, and the United States. Just as Alexis de Tocqueville traveled to America in 1831 to seek the secrets of democracy, so might we journey to England to seek the secrets of stable representative government. Yet its limitations as a model are shown by the failure of attempts to transplant its institutions to countries gaining independence from the British Empire, and even more by the failure of its institutions to bring political stability in Northern Ireland.

Current Policy Challenges

At the start of the millennium, Prime Minister Tony Blair wants to create a New Britain, a "cool Britannia" that has more in common with the world of pop stars than the world of Winston Churchill, and makes the Beatles and Princess Diana central figures in its heritage. Yet rebranding a country is not as easy as rebranding pop groups or designer fashions.

Blair entered office in 1997 promising a fresh look at political institutions and policies. In personal political terms, he had no commitment to the policies of his predecessors, Conservative or Labour. To win the election he had to get rid of "old Labour" commitments to socialist economic measures and to create a *New Labour Party* promoting a vague Third Way philosophy modeled on the strategy of President Bill Clinton. Blair committed the New Labour Party to accept many of the free market economic policies of the previous Thatcher government. In setting out Labour's manifesto, Blair proclaimed, "We are proud now to be the party of modern, dynamic business, proud now to be the

party of law and order, proud now to be the party of the family, and proud now to be the party pledged not to increase income tax."[2]

In his first term of office, the big achievement of Tony Blair has been to demonstrate that the Labour Party is no longer tied to its past tradition of representing industrial workers, trade unions, and the poor, and to demonstrate by his lifestyle and frequently repeated exhortations, that he believes in opportunity for all, and especially for aspiring Britons whose votes are critical for his reelection. Blair's government has benefited from an abnormally lengthy economic boom, providing additional public revenue without raising taxes. This is important, as an aging population requires more health care, an educated population demands better education for their children, and a more prosperous society wants a better environment to match improved housing. The New Labour government has sought to improve public services by achieving greater efficiency. It is trying to do so by centralized controls and inspection. From the right, the Conservatives attack the government for not being radical enough in promoting private initiatives. The *Liberal Democrats* criticize the government for not raising taxes a little in order to raise health and education standards higher by spending more money. Tony Blair is content to be attacked from both sides, believing that by staying in the middle he will have majority support and be assured a long period in office.

Constitutional reforms have been a major priority for the New Labour government. Hereditary members of the House of Lords have lost their guaranteed right to sit in the upper house of Parliament. Devolution legislation has established a separate Parliament in Scotland, and a less powerful representative assembly in Wales. London has elected a mayor for the first time. While the Blair administration is promoting decentralization, its critics charge that its "control freak" mentality is creating central control through the prime minister's dual role as leader of the governing party and head of British government.

Democracy provides a set of procedures for deciding who governs; the winner of an election must spend his or her term of office dealing with problems that cannot be gotten rid of by marking a ballot. Nor does a modern prime minister have as much freedom of choice as he or she would wish. Like it or not, the problems that face the prime minister today are the same problems that have faced his predecessors. Even though crime in the streets is not nearly so high as in American cities, it has increased enough to worry British people of all parties. The New Labour government has responded to such anxieties by promising to be both tough on crime and tough on the causes of crime. Measures it has introduced have been criticized by civil liberties groups as being unfairly tough.

In a changing world, the big question is: Where does England belong? Politically, it is central to the state of the United Kingdom, which consists of a union of the territories of England, Scotland, Wales, and Northern Ireland under a Parliament in London. As the nation contributing five-sixths of the population of the United Kingdom, England is preeminent within the United Kingdom.

Geographically, England is a part of Europe, but its island character has made *insularity* one of the country's most striking cultural characteristics. Even though there is no other continent to which the island could be assigned, English people do not usually think of themselves as part of Europe. The United Kingdom is a member of the European Union but its commitment is limited. For example, Britain did not participate in the launch of the new European currency. Tony Blair has pledged to put British interests "first, second, and last" in negotiations about the European Union. However, any attempt by the prime minister to cooperate with the other 14 member states of the European Union results in compromises that British critics of ties with the European Union denounce as "giving away" Britain's sovereignty.

The Constraints of History

The Making of Modern England

Every country is constrained by its history: the legacy of the past limits current choices. For most of its history, England was governed by the rule of law but the government was not democratic in the modern sense. However, the establishment of procedures that lawfully checked the arbitrary authority of the King greatly eased gradual evolution into a democratic political system.

Compared with its European neighbors, England has been fortunate in solving many of the fundamental problems of governance early. The Crown was established as the central political authority in medieval times. The supremacy of the state's secular power over the church was settled in the sixteenth century when Henry VIII broke with the Roman Catholic Church to establish the Church of England. The power struggle between Crown and Parliament was resolved by a civil war in which Parliament triumphed and a weakened monarch was restored in 1660. Parliament was able to hold the Crown accountable, but Parliament represented only a small portion of the population.

There is no agreement among political scientists about when England developed a modern system of government.[3] A constitutional historian might date the change at 1485, the start of the centralizing Tudor monarchy; an economic historian from the beginning of the Industrial Revolution at about 1760; and a frustrated reformer might proclaim that it has not happened yet. The most reasonable judgment is that modern government developed during the very long reign of Queen Victoria from 1837 to 1901, when government institutions were created to cope with the problems of a society that was increasingly urban, literate, industrial, and critical of unchanged traditions.

The 1832 Reform Act started a gradual process of enfranchising the masses. A majority of English males got the right to vote by 1885. Concurrently, *Conservative* and Liberal party organizations began to contest elections nationwide. In 1911 the government of the Crown became fully accountable to the elected House of Commons. The right to vote was extended to all adult men and women in 1918.

The Industrial Revolution created a demand for government to make cities safe and healthy. In the mid-nineteenth century institutions of governance were transformed from an aristocratic appendage of the royal household to a system that could enact and implement laws on public health, education, and safety in the workplace and collect the taxes needed to pay for new public services. The 1906 Liberal government introduced old-age pensions and unemployment insurance. The *Labour Party,* founded in 1900 to secure the representation of manual workers in Parliament, first briefly formed a minority government in 1924, following splits in the Liberal Party. Interwar governments expanded welfare services. The gross national product (GNP) increased greatly, and the share claimed by government increased even more. In 1890 public spending was equal to 8 percent of GNP; in 1910 the share had risen to 12 percent and by 1920 to 26 percent. Since the end of World War II, public spending has fluctuated between a third and a half of the gross national product.

The creation of a modern system of government does not make the problems of governing disappear. England emerged on the winning side in two world wars, but its political influence was reduced. Political developments since World War II can be divided into five stages.

First, during World War II an all-party coalition government led by Winston Churchill laid the foundations for a *mixed economy Keynesian welfare state.* The government created full employment to fight the war and rationed food to ensure "fair shares for all." From this coalition emerged the Beveridge Report on social welfare, John Maynard Keynes's Full Employment White Paper of 1944, and the Butler Education Act of 1944. These three measures—the first two named after Liberals and the third after a Conservative—were landmarks in the development of the British welfare state. The fair shares policy was continued by the Labour government of Clement Attlee elected in 1945. The National Health Service was established in 1948, providing medical care for all without charge. Coal mines, gas and electricity, railways, and the steel industries were nationalized (that is, taken into government ownership). By 1951 the Labour government had exhausted its catalog of agreed changes, but its economic policies had yet to produce prosperity.

In the second stage, the Conservatives retained power from 1951 to 1964, maintaining a period of social consensus. Administrations under Winston Churchill, Anthony Eden, and Harold Macmillan were anxious to assure the electorate that they could be trusted to conserve a widely popular welfare state. Keynesian techniques for promoting economic growth, full employment, and low inflation showed evidence of success. Rationing was ended and living standards rose as consumer goods such as automobiles and refrigerators, once thought the privilege of a few, became widely distributed.

The third stage commenced in the early 1960s with a flood of books on the theme "What's wrong with Britain?" Continuities with the past were attacked as the dead hand of tradition. Politicians promoted managerial activism. The Labour Party won the 1964 election under Harold Wilson campaigning with the vague but activist slogan, "Let's go with Labour." New titles were given government department offices, symbolizing a desire to change for its own sake. Behind the entrance of these restyled offices, the same people went through the same routines as before. The economy did not grow as predicted, and in 1967 the Wilson government was forced to devalue the pound and seek a loan from the International Monetary Fund. Labour lost the 1970 election.

The 1970–1974 Conservative government under Edward Heath showed that the defects of managerial activism were not confined to one leader or party. Plans laid out by teams of advisers in opposition failed to work. The major achievement of the Heath administration—joining the European Community—divided his own party and also the opposition. In trying to limit unprecedented inflation by controlling wages, Heath risked his authority in a confrontation with the National Union of Mineworkers. The result was a stalemate, and industry working a three-day week because of a shortage of coal. The prime minister called an election—its theme exemplified by a single question: Who governs?

The "Who Governs?" election of February 28, 1974, showed many voters rejecting both major parties. The Conservative share of the vote dropped to 38 percent and Labour's to 37 percent, while the Liberal vote more than doubled to 19 percent. Due to anomalies in the electoral system, Labour won the most seats in the House of Commons, but no party had an absolute majority there. Labour formed a minority government, with Harold Wilson again prime minister. A second election in October 1974 gave Labour a bare majority. The Labour government proclaimed a social contract limiting wage increases in return for increased public spending on social welfare benefits. Inflation, rising unemployment, and a contraction in the economy caused this policy to collapse. James Callaghan succeeded Wilson as prime minister in 1976. Keynesian policies were abandoned in 1977 when Labour relied on another loan from the International Monetary Fund to stabilize its currency.

The 1979 general election won by Margaret Thatcher ushered in the fourth stage. Thatcher—the first woman to serve as prime minister of a major European country—sought a radical break with the past. She regarded the economic failures of previous governments as arising from too much consensual compromise and too little conviction. "The Old Testament prophets did not say 'Brothers, I want a consensus.' They said: 'This is my faith. This is what I passionately believe. If you believe it too, then come with me.' "[4] Above all, she believed that the market rather than government should make the most important decisions in society (see Box 4.1).

Divisions among opponents enabled Thatcher to lead her party to three successive election victories without ever winning as much as 44 percent of the total vote. Militant left-wing activists seized control of the Labour Party; its 1983 election manifesto was described by a Labour MP as the longest suicide note in history. In protest, four former Labour Cabinet ministers formed a centrist Social Democratic Party (SDP) in 1981 and made an alliance with the Liberal Party. Neil Kinnock succeeded Michael Foot as Labour leader and sought to steer the party back toward the center-left, but the journey took a long time. After Thatcher's third successive election victory in 1987, the SDP leadership joined with the Liberals in a newly merged party, the Liberal Democrats, under Liberal MP Paddy Ashdown.

While preaching against big government, Thatcher did not court electoral defeat by imposing radical cuts on the biggest spending and most popular programs of the government. In consequence,

---

Box 4.1   The Meaning of Thatcherism

Among British prime ministers, Margaret Thatcher was unique in giving her name to the political ideology, *Thatcherism*. She believed in strong government—as long as it was in her hands. In foreign policy she was a formidable proponent of what she saw as Britain's national interest in dealings with the European Union and in alliance with President Ronald Reagan. The 1982 Argentine invasion of the sparsely populated Falkland Islands, a remote British colony in the South Atlantic, led to a brief, virtually bloodless and victorious war against Argentina. Thatcher was also quick to assert her personal authority against colleagues in the Cabinet and against civil servants.* The autonomy of local government was curbed by central government and the residential property tax replaced by a poll tax on each adult.

Thatcher's central conviction was that the market offered a cure for the country's economic difficulties. As Milton Friedman, the Nobel Prize–winning monetary economist, noted: "Mrs. Thatcher represents a different tradition. She represents a tradition of the nineteenth-century Liberal, of Manchester Liberalism, of free market free trade."† In economic policy the Thatcher administration experienced both successes and frustrations. Her anti-inflation policies succeeded but unemployment doubled. Industrial relations acts gave members the right to elect their union's leaders and vote on whether to hold a strike. It introduced what were described as "businesslike" methods for managing everything from hospitals and universities to museums, hoping to reduce public spending and taxation.

*Cf. Hugo Young, *One of Us* (London: Macmillan, 1989); Dennis Kavanagh, *Thatcherism and British Politics* (Oxford, England: Oxford University Press, 1990); and Margaret Thatcher, *The Downing Street Years* (New York: HarperCollins, 1993).
†"Thatcher Praised by Her Guru," *The Guardian* (London), March 12, 1983; cf. Ivor Crewe and Donald Searing, "Ideological Change in the British Conservative Party," *American Political Science Review* 62, No. 2 (1988): 361–84.

British government continued to grow in the Thatcher era. In the year before Thatcher took office, government spending was 39 percent of the national product; by 1984 that figure had risen to almost 44 percent, before falling to 40 percent in her last full year in office. While the Conservative majority in Parliament endorsed Thatcher's policies, it did not win the hearts and minds of the electorate. When voters were asked on the tenth anniversary of Thatcher's period in office whether or not they approved of "the Thatcher revolution," less than one-third responded yes.[5]

Within the Conservative Party, Thatcher's increasingly autocratic treatment of Cabinet colleagues created resentment, and during her third term of office this was reinforced by opinion polls and defeats in by-elections for seats that unexpectedly fell vacant in the House of Commons. In autumn 1990, disgruntled Conservative members of Parliament (MPs) forced a ballot for the party leadership. In the first round, the prime minister won just over half the votes of Conservative MPs. But under the party's complicated rules for electing a leader, this was not enough to confirm Thatcher in office; she resigned rather than risk a humiliating defeat on a second ballot. Conservative MPs elected a relatively unknown John Major as party leader.

In his first electoral test in 1992, John Major won an unprecedented fourth consecutive term for the Conservative government. Shortly after the 1992 election his economic policy of a strong British pound crashed under pressure from foreign speculators. He was criticized by Thatcherites in the Conservative Party for being soft on Europe, agreeing to the Maastricht Treaty on expanding the powers of the European Union. However, he presided over the *privatization* of the coal industry and the railways. Although personally above suspicion, Major's administration was plagued by the exposure of Conservative MPs' sleazy behavior, involving sex, money, or both. By 1993 Major reached the lowest popularity rating in the history of the Gallup Poll. In June 1995 he took the unprecedented step of calling and winning reelection to the party leadership, but his authority was not restored.   Why not

A fifth stage in postwar British politics opened after Tony Blair became Labour leader in 1994. Blair was elected leader because he did *not* talk or look like an ordinary Labour Party member. Instead of being from a poor background, he was educated at boarding school and went on to study law at Oxford. Instead of having grown up in the Labour movement, his parents were Conservatives, and he joined the Labour Party with the encouragement of a girlfriend, Cheri Booth (now his wife and a very successful lawyer). His qualities appealed to middle-class voters whose support Labour needed to move from opposition to government (see Box 4.2). New Labour won a landslide majority in the House of Commons at the May 1, 1997, general election, even though it received a smaller share of the popular vote than Margaret Thatcher in 1979. It gained a big majority in the House of Commons because the Conservative vote fell to its lowest share since 1832.

The continuity of England's political institutions is remarkable. Prince Charles, the heir to an ancient Crown, pilots jet airplanes, and a medieval-named Chancellor of the Exchequer pilots the British pound through the deep waters of the international economy. Yet symbols of continuity often mask great changes in English life. Parliament was once a supporter of royal authority. Today Parliament is primarily an electoral college deciding which party leader controls the government.

The Environment of Politics

One Crown but Five Nations

The Queen of England is the best known monarch in the world, yet there is no such entity as an English state. In international law, the state is the United Kingdom of Great Britain and Northern Ireland. The *United Kingdom* was created in 1801 as the climax of a process of expansion begun in the twelfth century. Great Britain, the principal part of the United Kingdom, is divided into three parts: England, Scotland, and Wales. The other part of the United Kingdom, Northern Ireland, consists of six counties of Ulster. The remainder of Ireland broke away to form a separate state in 1921, as the culmination of a rebellion against the Crown launched in Dublin in 1916.

The United Kingdom is a multinational state. In England, many people think of themselves as both

---

Box 4.2   New Labour—Left, Right and Centre

New Labour is a party of ideas and ideals, but not of outdated ideology. What counts is what works. The objectives are radical. The means will be modern.

I want to renew faith in politics by being honest about the last 18 years. Some things the Conservatives got right. We will not change them. It is where they got things wrong that we will make change.

I want a Britain which we all feel part of, in whose future we all have a stake, in which what I want for my own children I want for yours.

We want to put behind us the bitter political struggles of left and right that have torn our country apart for too many decades. Many of these conflicts have no relevance whatsoever to the modern world—public versus private, bosses versus workers, middle class versus working class. It is time to move on and move forward. We are proud of our history, proud of what we have achieved—but we must learn from our history, not be chained to it.*

*Rt. Hon. Tony Blair, foreword to the 1997 Labour Party Election Manifesto.
Source: House of Commons Library.

English and British, or confuse the two terms. In Scotland, a big majority see themselves as exclusive Scots or Scottish and British. In Wales, where a substantial portion of the resident population was born in England, identities are divided more equally between Welsh, British, or both. In Northern Ireland, people divide themselves into two nations. Most Catholics see themselves as Irish while the great majority of Protestants see themselves as British.

Wales was joined with England in the sixteenth century and administered thereafter as if it were a part of England. Its most distinctive feature is the ancient Welsh language. Industrialization drew most Welsh people close to England. The proportion of Welsh-speakers has declined from more than half at the beginning of this century to below a quarter. Within Wales there are very sharp contrasts between the more populous industrial, and English-speaking south, and the less populous, rural, Welsh-speaking northwest. In 1964 a separate Welsh Office was established for administrative purposes, and its head was made a Cabinet minister.

Scotland was once an independent kingdom; since the 1707 Act of Union, there has been a common Parliament for the whole of Great Britain. However, the Scots have retained separate legal, religious, and educational institutions, and there has been a separate Scottish Office responsible for administration. The head of the Scottish Office has been a Cabinet minister bound to the collective decisions of a British Cabinet.[6]

Northern Ireland is the most un-English part of the United Kingdom. Formally, it is a secular polity, but differences between Protestants and Catholics about national identity dominate its politics. Protestants, comprising more than three-fifths of the population, want to remain part of the United Kingdom. Until 1972 the Protestant majority governed through a home-rule Parliament at Stormont, a suburb of Belfast. Many of the Catholic minority did not support this regime, wanting to leave the United Kingdom and join the Republic of Ireland, which claimed the territory of Northern Ireland in its constitution.

Since the start of demonstrations by Catholics against discrimination in Northern Ireland in 1968, the land has been in turmoil. Demonstrations turned to street violence in August 1969, and the British Army intervened. The illegal *Irish Republican Army (IRA)* was revived and in 1971 began a military campaign to remove Northern Ireland from the United Kingdom. In retaliation, Protestants organized illegal forces, too. Since August 1969, more than 3,200 people have been killed in political violence. After adjusting for population differences, the deaths from political violence are equivalent to 110,000 political deaths in Britain or more than 500,000 deaths in America.

British policy in Northern Ireland has been erratic. In 1969 the British Army went into action to protect Catholics. In 1971 it helped intern hundreds of Catholics without trial in an unsuccessful attempt to break the IRA. In 1972 the British government abolished the Stormont Parliament, placing government in the hands of a Northern Ireland Office under a British Cabinet minister.

A stable agreement about Northern Ireland requires the support of paramilitary organizations involved in violence on each side of the religious divide, as well as of parties solely committed to parliamentary politics. In 1994 the IRA announced a cessation of its military activity, and Sinn Fein, the party political wing of the Irish Republican Movement, agreed to talks. Protestant paramilitary forces also ceased activities. Former U.S. Senator George Mitchell chaired a series of negotiating sessions as a non-Irish, non-British outsider. On Good Friday, 1998, an agreement for a power-sharing elected executive and cross-border institutions involving both Dublin and Belfast was reached and put to a referendum in Northern Ireland. It was endorsed by a very large majority of Catholics and a small majority of Protestants. An election to a representative Northern Ireland Assembly followed in June, 1998. Protestant representation divided between parties for and against the agreement, and Catholic representation divided between the nonviolent Social Democratic and Labour Party (SDLP) and Sinn Fein.

A new Northern Ireland Executive has been formed on principles the opposite of British government. The government is a coalition of representatives of Protestants and Catholics, and not just of the majority group in the Commons (which is Protestant and Unionist). Moreover, the Executive incorporates political groups such as Sinn Fein, which has been linked with the IRA, as well as parties seeking power through the ballot box. The Executive's first priority is to end violence: this requires decommissioning of substantial arms held by paramilitary forces and the creation of a system of policing acceptable both to Unionists and Republicans.

Party politics differs in each nation of the United Kingdom (see Table 4.1). Northern Ireland is extreme, for British parties do not contest seats there. In Scotland, four parties compete. In the 1997 general election the Labour Party won a plurality of the vote, and the Scottish National Party, which wants an independent Scotland, came second in votes. The Conservatives failed to win a single Scottish seat. In Wales, the nationalist party, *Plaid Cymru*, polls less than one-tenth of the Welsh vote. The most distinctive feature of Welsh politics is the disproportionately high Labour vote.

A sustained campaign by proponents of devolution led to devolution of legislative powers to Scotland and major administrative responsibilities to Wales. Referendums on devolution were held in September 1997. In Scotland, 74 percent voted in

TABLE 4.1   Division of the Vote by Nation

	Percentage Share of Vote in 1997				
	England	**Scotland**	**Wales**	**Northern Ireland**	**United Kingdom**
New Labour	43.5	45.6	54.7	0	43.2
Conservatives	33.7	17.5	19.6	1.2	30.7
Liberal Democrats	18.0	13.0	12.4	0	16.8
Nationalists	0	22.1	9.9	89.5[a]	4.6
Other	4.8	1.8	3.4	9.3	4.7
Population (in millions)	48.9	5.1	2.9	1.6	58.6

[a]Of which, 49.3 percent cast for pro-British Unionist parties supported by Protestants, and 40.2 percent cast for Irish Nationalist parties, such as the SDLP and Sinn Fein, supported by Catholics.
Source: House of Commons Library.

favor of a Scottish Parliament, and 63 percent voted in favor of it having a limited power to raise or reduce taxes. In Wales, a Welsh Assembly was endorsed by 50.3 percent on a low turnout. The Welsh endorsement of an Assembly was lower because Plaid Cymru wants to promote use of the Welsh language, creating fears among the four-fifths who do not speak Welsh that they will be penalized because they are not bilingual as Welsh-speakers are.

The first election of a Parliament in Scotland with powers to legislate, tax, and spend, and of a nonlegislative Assembly for Wales was held on May 6, 1999, under a system of proportional representation. With 34 percent of the proportional representation vote, the Labour Party won 56 seats; this was not enough to give it a majority in the 129–seat Parliament. With 28 percent of the vote, the Scottish National Party came in second with 35 seats. The Conservative Party won 14 percent of the vote and 18 seats, and the Liberal Democrats 13 percent of the vote and 17 seats. As the party with the most seats, Labour provided the First Minister in the Parliament, but to achieve a majority in the Scottish Parliament it formed a coalition government with the Liberal Democrats.

In Wales, the proportional representation electoral system gave Labour, with 36 percent of the vote, 28 seats, just short of a majority in the 60-seat Assembly. In second place was the Welsh Nationalist Party (Plaid Cymru), with 17 seats and 31 percent of the vote. The Conservatives gained 9 seats with 16 percent of the vote. The Liberal Democrats won 6 seats with 12 percent of the vote. Initially, Labour led the Welsh Assembly as a minority government; a coalition executive of Labour and Liberal Democrats was formed in the year 2000. Powers over Welsh legislation and total public expenditure remain in the hands of a British Cabinet minister.

The United Kingdom is a union—that is, a political system having only one source of authority, the British Parliament. It thus differs from a federal system such as the United States or Germany. However, institutions governing the United Kingdom are not uniform. Special administrative institutions exist in Scotland and Wales, and devolution increases their political legitimacy by creating the popularly elected assemblies. Northern Ireland has always been the subject of exceptional legislation. Yet the doctrine of territorial justice means that pensions, unemployment benefits, health care, and education are meant to be equally provided to everyone wherever they live in the United Kingdom.

Politics in England is the focus of this chapter because England dominates the United Kingdom. Its population constitutes five-sixths of the total of the United Kingdom, and the remainder is divided among three different nations (see again Table 4.1). No United Kingdom government will ever overlook what is central to England, and politicians who wish to advance in British government must accept the norms of English society. Tony, Blair has reminded Scottish voters, "Sovereignty rests with me, as an English MP, and that's the way it will stay."[7]

A Multiracial England

Through the centuries England has received a small but noteworthy number of immigrants from other parts of Europe. The Queen herself is descended from royalty who came from Hanover, Germany, to assume the English throne in 1714. Until the outbreak of anti-German sentiment in World War I, the surname of the royal family was Saxe-Coburg-Gotha. By royal proclamation in 1917, George V changed the family name to Windsor.

Most post–World War II immigrants have been attracted to England by jobs, and by the late 1950s job seekers began to arrive in England from the West Indies, Pakistan, India, Hong Kong, and other parts of the multiracial British Commonwealth. Estimates of the nonwhite population of the United Kingdom have risen from 74,000 in 1951 to 3.7 million today, 6.5 percent of the population. Public opinion has opposed the immigration of nonwhites—as reflected by Conservative and Labour governments passing laws limiting the number of nonwhite immigrants.

The new Commonwealth immigrants have only one characteristic in common: they are not white. Beyond that, immigrants share neither culture nor religion. West Indians speak English as their native language and have a Christian tradition; immigrants from India and Pakistan are Hindus,

Muslims, or Sikhs, and most speak English as a second language. The small number of African immigrants are divided by nationality. Chinese from Hong Kong have a distinctive culture too. Altogether, more than half of immigrants come from the Indian subcontinent, a quarter are black people from the Caribbean or Africa, under a tenth are Asian, and the remainder include mixed races and peoples from other parts of the world.

Today, the important issues of race relations are about the position of nonwhite British-born offspring of immigrants. Whatever their country of origin, they differ in how they see themselves: 64 percent of Caribbean origin identify as British, as do more than three-fifths of Pakistanis, Indians, and Bangladeshis, and two-fifths of Chinese. Laws to encourage better race relations and antidiscrimination measures have been enacted. However, provisions for enforcement by the courts are very weak in comparison with American legislation. In combating discrimination, the government-sponsored Commission for Racial Equality relies primarily on investigation and conciliation rather than prosecution through the courts.

Immigrants and their offspring are gradually becoming integrated into electoral politics, as residential concentration makes local politicians aware of their potential impact as a voting bloc. There are now hundreds of elected nonwhite councillors in local government; a disproportionate number are Labour, the party favored by immigrant voters. At the 1997 general election, the nine nonwhite MPs elected reflected a broad diversity of immigrant backgrounds: India, Pakistan, Guyana, Aden, Ghana, and the American state of Georgia.

Insularity and Involvement

For centuries the English Channel has represented a literal as well as a symbolic gulf between England and continental Europe. The opening in 1994 of the Channel Tunnel linking England and France has not closed the gap. Half of Britons say they do not feel at all European, and only 23 percent say that they feel strongly or somewhat European. Depending on circumstances, politicians claim that England is close to the United States, or to the Commonwealth countries scattered around the globe, or to Europe.[8]

Insularity is not to be confused with isolation. Britain is a member of more than 125 different international bodies, including the United Nations, the European Union, and NATO. The British Empire has been replaced by a free association of 50 sovereign states—the Commonwealth—with members on every continent. The independent status of its chief members is shown by the absence of the word "British" from the name of the Commonwealth. Commonwealth countries differ from each other greatly in wealth, language, culture, and religion, and in their commitment to democracy.

British foreign policy since 1945 is a story of contracting military and diplomatic commitments. Britain retains one of the five permanent places in the Security Council of the United Nations, but Britain's military power is now limited. Victory in the 1982 Falklands War did not demonstrate front-rank military power, for the Argentine military force that seized this small, isolated British colony was badly organized. When a Gallup Poll asked whether people would rather Britain were a leading world power or a small neutral country like Sweden or Switzerland, 49 percent chose being a small power as against 34 percent wanting their country to be a world power.[9]

Whereas military force is rarely used, economic transactions are continuous. England depends on world trade, importing much food and many raw materials. To pay for imports, England exports a wide range of manufactured goods, as well as such "invisible" services as the financial institutions of the city of London. The value of the British pound in exchange for the dollar has fluctuated in the past 20 years from above $2.50 to less than $1.25. Speeches and votes in Parliament could not maintain government policy to support a "strong" pound against the flight of speculative capital from London into currencies of other countries. At the start of 2001, the value of a pound fluctuated between $1.40 and $1.60.

As England's world position has declined, the government has increasingly looked to Europe. In a jet age, the English Channel is no longer a barrier to travel to the European continent. Television and the Internet carry news, sports, and entertainment across national boundaries. Economic ties have grown. For example, the Ford Motor Company links its manufacturing plants in England with factories across Western Europe, just as it links Ford factories between American states.

When the European Community was established in 1957, Britain did not join, because its leaders considered the country aloof from the problems of continental neighbors ravaged by war. When it joined in 1973 under the leadership of Edward Heath, political controversy cut across party lines. A 1975 national referendum on membership voted 67 to 33 percent in favor of remaining in Europe. But public opinion and politicians have remained divided about what role Britain can or should play in Europe. Before the Maastricht Treaty enhancing the powers of the European Union was confirmed by Parliament, rebellions by Conservative MPs inflicted defeats on the Major government.

Meanwhile, European politics has grown in significance, symbolized by the Community changing its name to the European Union. Enhanced powers to promote a Single European Market impose limitations on what can be decided in London. British ministers spend an increasing amount of their time negotiating with their opposite numbers in fourteen other countries of Europe on matters ranging from the fundamentals of the economy to whether British beer should be served in metric units or by the traditional measure of a British pint.

The British government cannot insulate the country from changes in the world. English people cannot choose to be a small, rich country like Switzerland or Sweden. The effective choice today is between England being a big, rich country or a big, relatively poor European country. Exchanging nominal sovereignty to participate in the European Union presents no problems to governments in small countries, which have always recognized the influence of bigger neighbors. However, it is a shock to many British politicians who pride themselves on Britain's independence, its ability to prevent invasion in World War II, and its ties with countries on many continents, including a dated "special relationship" with the United States. Moreover, a majority of British people are against cooperating with other countries if it means giving up some independence.

The diversity of political outlooks within the European Union is so great that representatives of British government can normally find allies for any British cause. But to do so the government must act like a major player in the politics of the European Union. The central European issue of Tony Blair's first term of office was the creation of the European Monetary Union. On domestic political grounds as well as economic grounds, Blair announced that Britain would stand aside, at least until he had won another general election. Moreover, he pledged a referendum would be held before Britain entered an economic arrangement that would lead to the abolition of the British pound, a highly contentious domestic issue, and its replacement by the euro, the new currency in most countries of the European Union.

A generation ago the American diplomat Dean Acheson declared: "Great Britain has lost an empire and has not yet found a role." An American ambassador to Britain has subsequently reenforced the point by arguing, "If Britain's voice is less influential in Paris or Bonn, it is likely to be less influential in Washington."[10]

The Structure of Government

As well as understanding what government does, we must understand what government is. Descriptions of a government often start with its constitution. However, England has no written constitution. At no time in the past was there a break with tradition that forced politicians to write down how the country should be governed, as happened after the American Revolution.

The *unwritten constitution* of England is a jumble of acts of Parliament, judicial pronouncements, customs, and conventions about the rules of the political game. The vagueness of the constitution makes it flexible, a point that political leaders such as Margaret Thatcher and Tony Blair have been ready to exploit. Instead of giving written guarantees to citizens, as the American Bill of Rights does, the rights of English people are meant to be secured by trustworthy governors. In the words of a constitutional lawyer, J. A. G. Griffith, "The Constitution is what happens."[11]

Comparing the written American and the unwritten English constitution emphasizes how few are the constraints of an unwritten constitution (see Table 4.2). The U.S. Constitution gives the Supreme Court the final power to decide what the government may or may not do. In England, by contrast, the final authority is Parliament, where the government of the day commands a majority of votes. The Bill of Rights in the U.S. Constitution allows anyone to seek redress in the courts for infringement of personal rights, whereas in England an individual who believes his or her personal rights are infringed by an act of Parliament has no redress through the courts. Whereas amendments to the U.S. Constitution must receive the endorsement of well over half the states and members of Congress, the unwritten constitution can be changed by a majority vote in Parliament, or by the government of the day choosing to act in an unprecedented manner.

English courts claim no power to declare an act of Parliament unconstitutional. Courts ask whether the executive acts within its statutory powers. Many statutes delegate broad discretion to a Cabinet minister or public authority; the courts do not question how the executive exercises its delegated discretion. Even if the courts rule that the government has improperly exercised its authority, the effect of such a judgment can be annulled by a subsequent act of Parliament retroactively authorizing an action.

People who believe the British government abuses its powers have called for a written constitution with an effective Bill of Rights to protect individuals against abuses of authority. Unhappy with the way in which the Conservative government wielded power for 18 years, the New Labour government has incorporated the European Convention on Human Rights into English law. Insofar as this novel arrangement encourages people who believe their rights aggrieved to turn to the courts and judges to uphold their claims, this will be a major innovation in English constitutional practice.

The _Crown_ rather than a constitution symbolizes the authority of government. However, the monarch is only a ceremonial head of state; the public reaction to the accidental death of Princess Diana was a media event equal to the assassination of President Kennedy. But it was not a political event, for neither her ex-husband nor her son, Prince William, each an heir to the throne, can expect to wield any political power. Queen Elizabeth II does not affect the actions of what is described as Her Majesty's Government. While the queen gives formal assent to laws passed by Parliament, she may not publicly state an opinion about legislation. The queen is expected to respect the will of Parliament, as communicated to her by the leader of the majority party in Parliament, the prime minister.

What constitutes the Crown? No simple answer can be given. The Crown is a symbol to which people are asked to give loyalty. It is a concept of indefinite territory; it does not refer to a particular com-

TABLE 4.2   Comparing an Unwritten and a Written Constitution

	England (unwritten)	United States (written)
Origins	Medieval customs	1787 Constitutional Convention
Form	Unwritten, indefinite	Written, precise
Final power	Majority in Parliament	Supreme Court
Bill of individual rights	No	Yes
Amendment	Ordinary vote in Parliament; unprecedented action by government	More than majority vote in Congress, states
Centrality in political debate	Low	High

munity of people. The idea of the Crown combines the dignified parts of the constitution, which sanctify authority by tradition and myth, with the efficient parts, which carry out the work of government.

In everyday political conversation, English people talk about government, not the constitution. The term *government* is used in many senses (see Figure 4.1). People may speak of the Queen's government, to emphasize enduring and nonpartisan features, or they may refer to the government by the name of the current prime minister to stress its personal and transitory features, or refer to a Labour or Conservative government to emphasize partisanship. The term *government officials* usually refers to civil servants. Collectively, the executive agencies of government are often referred to as *Whitehall*, after the London street in which many major government offices are located. *Downing Street*, where the prime minister's residence is located, is a short and narrow street off Whitehall. The *Palace of Westminster*, which houses *Parliament*—that is, the popularly elected House of Commons and the nonelected

House of Lords—is at the bottom end of the street called Whitehall.

What the Prime Minister Says and Does

Within the Cabinet, the *prime minister* occupies a unique position, sometimes referred to as *primus inter pares* (first among equals). But as Winston Churchill once wrote, "There can be no comparison between the positions of number one, and numbers two, three or four."[12]

The preeminence of the prime minister is ambiguous. A politician at the apex of government is remote from what is happening on the ground. The more responsibilities attributed to the prime minister, the less time there is to devote to any one task. Like a president, a prime minister is the prisoner of the political law of first things first. The imperatives of the prime minister are as follows.

1. *Party management through patronage.* A prime minister may be self-interested but he or she is

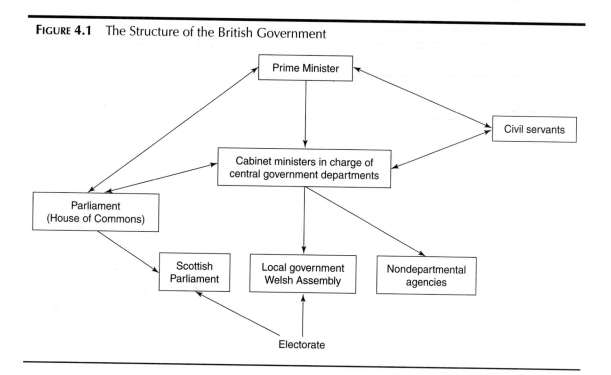

FIGURE 4.1   The Structure of the British Government

not self-employed. To become prime minister, a politician must first be elected leader of his or her party. To remain prime minister, a politician must retain the confidence of the parliamentary party as well as that of the electorate. The prime minister has formidable powers of patronage. He or she appoints about a quarter of MPs in the governing party to jobs in the government as ministers or junior ministers; they sit on front bench seats in the House of Commons. MPs not appointed to a post are backbenchers; many ingratiate themselves with the party leader in hopes of becoming a government minister.

In making ministerial appointments, a prime minister can use any of four different criteria: (a) personal loyalty (rewarding friends); (b) co-option (silencing critics by giving them an office so that they are committed to support the government); (c) representativeness (for example, appointing a woman or someone from Scotland or Wales); and (d) competence in giving direction to a government department.

2. *Parliamentary performance.* The prime minister appears in the House of Commons weekly for half an hour of questions from MPs, engaging in rapid-fire repartee with a highly partisan audience. Unprotected by a speechwriter's script, the prime minister must show that he or she is a good advocate of the government's policies or suffer loss of support. He or she occasionally makes statements to the House or participates in debates on major issues.

3. *Media performance.* The publicity that is thrust on the incumbent of Downing Street constantly bears the marks of partisan controversy. Television enables a prime minister to speak directly to the electorate, and the media will always focus attention on news from or about Downing Street. Tony Blair has gone further than any of his predecessors, creating a team of "spin doctors" in Downing Street doing what it can to project the best image of the prime minister by influencing media coverage on an around-the-clock basis. Media eminence is a double-edged sword. When the news is bad,

such as widespread popular protests at taxes that make gasoline cost more than anywhere else in Europe, the prime minister appears in an unfavorable light.

4. *Winning elections.* The only election a prime minister must win is that as party leader. Six of the eleven prime ministers since 1945—Winston Churchill, Anthony Eden, Harold Macmillan, Alec Douglas-Home, James Callaghan, and John Major—first entered Downing Street during the middle of a Parliament rather than by winning a national election. Once in office, a prime minister must pay attention to frequent and well-publicized opinion polls. While the personality of a prime minister remains relatively static, his or her popularity can fluctuate by as much as 30 or 40 percentage points in public opinion polls.[13] In the 15 elections since 1945, the prime minister of the day has eight times led the governing party to victory and seven times to defeat.

5. *Making and balancing policies.* Leading government is a political rather than a managerial task. While the prime minister is responsible for the overall direction of government policy, he or she does not have time to deal with all the issues facing more than 15 ministries. Economic policy and foreign affairs are the primary policy concerns of a prime minister. The prime minister must deal with heads of foreign governments around the world. He or she must also keep a watchful eye on Treasury policy concerning the economy, since what happens in the economy often influences the government's popularity with the electorate. When there are conflicts between international and domestic policy priorities, the prime minister is the one person who can strike a balance between pressures from the world "out there" and pressures from the domestic electorate. The number of "intermestic" policies (that is, problems combining both an international and domestic element) is increasing.

A prime minister can initiate new policies and stimulate departments into action. When departmental proposals are brought forward that are politically contentious, he or she may question or defer them. When a prime minister asks an awkward question or gives advice, no Cabinet minister can ignore it. While the directives that a prime minister can issue are limited by a lack of staff and time, Tony Blair has strengthened his influence in Whitehall by giving authority to personal assistants over civil servants and using his Policy Unit to track the activities of ministers.

While the formal powers of the office remain constant, individual prime ministers have differed in how they view their job, and in their political circumstances (see Figure 4.2). Clement Attlee, Labour prime minister from 1945 to 1951, was a nonassertive spokesperson for the lowest common denominator of views within the Cabinet. When an aging Winston Churchill succeeded in 1951, he concentrated on foreign affairs, exerting little influence in domestic policy, and the same was true of his successor, Anthony Eden. Harold Macmillan intervened strategically on a limited number of domestic and international issues, while giving ministers great scope on everyday matters. Alec Douglas-Home was weak because he lacked knowledge of economic affairs, the chief problem during his administration.

Both Edward Heath and Harold Wilson were initially committed to an activist definition of the prime minister's job. But Wilson often showed more interest in public relations than in policies. Heath pursued major domestic and foreign policy objectives. However, in 1974, the electorate rejected Heath's aggressive direction of the economy, and Wilson won office promising to replace confrontation between management and unions with political conciliation. James Callaghan, who succeeded Wilson in 1976, also emphasized consensus.

Margaret Thatcher reacted against her predecessors. She had strong views about many major policies and was ready to assert them, even if they contradicted her Cabinet colleagues. Associates gave her the nickname TINA

FIGURE 4.2 Prime Minister and Governments Since 1940

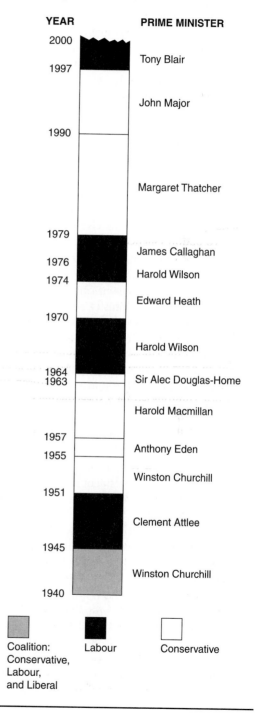

because of her motto: There Is No Alternative. Thatcher was no respecter of protocol, being prepared to push her views against the wishes of Cabinet colleagues and civil service advisers by any means necessary. In the end, her "bossiness" caused a revolt of Cabinet colleagues that helped bring about her downfall, and made colleagues welcome John Major in place of a hectoring leader. However, his conciliatory manner was often interpreted as a sign of weakness, and disputes between colleagues created friction within the Cabinet. At one point, the prime minister referred to his Cabinet colleagues as "bastards."

Tony Blair has emphasized "going public," appealing to the people through the media rather than through the House of Commons or Cabinet. This has led to charges of government by cronies. While many of Blair's changes had precedents, altogether they appear to be an effort to create a permanent campaign team on behalf of the prime minister, somewhat analogous to the White House. However, as successive American presidents have found, the skills needed to influence large government bureaucracies are different from campaign skills.

As an individual, a British prime minister has less formal authority than an American president. The president is directly elected for a fixed four-year term. A prime minister is chosen by colleagues for an indefinite term—no longer than the life of a Parliament—thus being less secure in office. The president is the undoubted leader of the federal executive and can dismiss Cabinet appointees with little fear of the consequences; by contrast, senior colleagues of a prime minister are potential rivals for leadership. Yet collectively, the British government is more powerful. Armed with the authority of the Cabinet and support from the majority party in the Commons, a prime minister can be certain that virtually all legislation introduced will be enacted into law. By contrast, Congress defeats many legislative proposals of a president. The prime minister is at the apex of a unitary government, with powers not limited by the courts or by a written constitution. Al-

though the president is the leading person in the executive branch of the federal government, the White House is without authority over Congress, state and local government, and the judiciary.

The Cabinet and the Cabinet Ministers

The *Cabinet* consists of senior ministers, members of either the House of Commons or House of Lords and appointed by the prime minister. Its members are thus the heads of Whitehall departments and leading figures in the majority party in Parliament. Walter Bagehot aptly described the Cabinet as securing "the close union, the nearly complete fusion of the executive and legislative powers."[14]

The convention of Cabinet responsibility requires that all ministers, including dozens too junior to sit in the Cabinet, give public support to a Cabinet decision—or at least refrain from making public criticism. Such is the political pain of giving up office that it is rare for a minister to resign from the government because of disagreements on issues. The prime minister seeks to keep any one Cabinet colleague from becoming strong enough to be a potential rival for his or her office.

Each Cabinet minister is responsible for a particular government department, and his or her political reputation depends on the skill with which its cause is advanced in Whitehall, in Parliament, with pressure groups, and in the media. Each minister is inclined to see issues from a departmental perspective. Cabinet ministers prefer to go along silently with their colleagues' proposals in exchange for endorsement of their own measures.

Ministers often compete for scarce resources, and conflicts inevitably arise between departments. For example, the health minister may press for increased spending while treasury ministers oppose such moves—regardless of the party in power. Cabinet ministers prefer to resolve their differences in a committee or by informal negotiations with the prime minister or with affected colleagues, so that the full Cabinet is presented with a recommendation that is difficult to challenge. The typical Cabinet committee includes the ministers whose departments are most affected by an issue, and a chair who has the confidence of the prime minister.

If the Cabinet is the keystone in the arch of central government, Whitehall departments are the building blocks (see Box 4.3). Most decisions of government are taken within departments. Every Cabinet decision must be administered or supervised by a department or by cooperation between departments. Some departments are organized primarily in terms of clients and others by services.

Major Whitehall departments differ greatly from each other. For example, the Home Office has a staff approximately ten times larger than the Treasury. Because of the importance of the economy, however, the Treasury has more senior civil servants. The Home Office has more staff at lower levels because of the scale of its routine tasks involving supervision of police, fire, prison, drugs, cruelty to animals, control of obscene publications, race relations, and so on. The Treasury concentrates on one big task, the management of the economy. The varied tasks of the Home Secretary also make him or her much more vulnerable to adverse publicity if, for example, a convicted murderer escapes from prison. But the job of the Chancellor of the Exchequer, the minister in charge of the Treasury, is more important politically, insofar as economic performance affects the governing party's electoral fate.

A minister has many roles—from policymaker who may initiate policies, select among alternatives brought forward from within the department, or avoid making any decision to chief executive of a large bureaucracy, formally responsible for all that is done by thousands of civil servants and having vague oversight responsibility for activities undertaken by agencies to whom Whitehall is increasingly contracting out responsibility for delivering public services. In addition, a minister is a department's ambassador to the world outside, its representative in the Cabinet and the Commons, in discussions with pressure groups, and in the mass media. Not least, Cabinet ministers are individuals with ambitions to rise in politics. The typical minister is not an expert in a subject but an expert in parliamentary politics, willing to deal with any department that offers opportunities to further his or her political career.

Tony Blair's attitude has been to dispense with Cabinet coordination of policy, preferring to call into Downing Street responsibility for issues affecting his popularity or those that cut across two or

---

Box 4.3   Departmental Organization and Reorganization

Departments are usually multipurpose institutions with a variety of tasks; each combines administrative units brought together as a result of government expansion and reorganizations adopted on grounds of efficiency, policy, fashion, or political expediency.* For example, since 1964 responsibilities for trade, industry, and technology have been placed in departments labeled Technology, then Trade and Industry, then separated into separate departments for Trade and for Industry, and once again reunited as a single Trade and Industry department. Each time that the title on the front door of the department was changed, most officials and programs continued as before.

The Cabinet created by Tony Blair upon becoming prime minister in 1997 had the following departments:

1. *Economic affairs:* treasury; trade and industry; transport; agriculture

2. *External affairs:* foreign and commonwealth office; defense; international development
3. *Social services:* education and employment; health; social security; culture, media, and sport
4. *Territorial:* environment (including English local government, the regions and housing); the Scottish Office; the Welsh Office; the Northern Ireland Office
5. *Law:* Lord Chancellor's office; home office
6. *Managing government business:* Leader of the House of Commons; Chief Whip in the House of Commons; Leader of the House of Lords; Chancellor of the Duchy of Lancaster

*See Richard Rose, *Ministers and Ministries: A Functional Analysis* (Oxford, England: Clarendon Press, 1987).

more departments. Because of his concern with continuous campaigning, Blair has given his personal staff at Downing Street greater influence over what ministers say and do—insofar as it attracts media attention. The effect of all this is to personalize the appearance of British government. Although Blair is more prominent than any of his predecessors, he does not have any more time during the week to investigate policies.[15]

The Civil Service

Although government could continue for months without new legislation, it would collapse overnight if hundreds of thousands of civil servants stopped administering laws and delivering public services. The largest number of civil servants are clerical staff with little discretion; they undertake the routine activities of a large bureaucracy. Only if these duties are executed satisfactorily can ministers have the time and opportunity to make new policies.

The most important group of civil servants is the smallest: the few hundred higher civil servants who advise ministers and oversee work of the departments. Civil servants, rather than ministers, are the most important coordinating personnel in Whitehall. Every Cabinet committee is shadowed by a committee of civil servants from the same departments. Because civil servants are more numerous, they can devote more time to interdepartmental negotiations. As permanent officials, civil servants are prone to seek agreement, and they deal with most issues without troubling the prime minister or a full meeting of Cabinet.

Top British civil servants deny they are politicians because of the partisan connotations of the term. However, their work is political because they are concerned with what government ought to do, formulating, reviewing, and advising on broad policies. A briefing seeking to recruit bright graduates for the higher civil service declares: "You will be involved from the outset in matters of major policy or resource allocation and, under the guidance of experienced administrators, encouraged to put forward your own constructive ideas and to take responsible decisions." Top civil servants are not apolitical; they are bipartisan, ready to work for whichever party is the winner of an election. Their

style is not that of the professional American athlete for whom winning is all-important. English civil servants have grown up playing cricket; its motto is that winning is less important than how one plays the game.

The relationship between ministers and higher civil servants is critical in government, for a Cabinet minister spends more time with civil servants than with partisan colleagues. Cabinet ministers first of all expect higher civil servants to be responsive to their political views and to formulate policies in keeping with the governing party's overall objectives, those of the ministers and such objectives as Downing Street may emphasize. A busy politician does not have time to go into details about the problems facing a department; he or she wants a "brief"—that is, a politically astute analysis of a problem. Civil servants prefer to work for a minister who has clear views on policy, who will make decisions and stick to them, who will listen to advice from his or her staff before making a decision, including warnings of difficulties in enacting party policy.

Second, a minister wants officials to promote his or her department's policies to other Whitehall departments, pressure groups, and the media, thus projecting the minister's own reputation as a mover and shaker in government. Civil servants prefer working for a political heavyweight who can carry the department's cause to victory in interdepartmental battles.

In the traditional Whitehall model, both ministers and civil servants concentrated on political management rather than administrative concerns. Civil servants were expected to think like politicians, anticipating what their minister would want and objections that Parliament, pressure groups, and the media would raise. Ministers were also expected to think like civil servants, recognizing all the obstacles to achieving politically desirable goals, and scaling down their ambitions when ways could not be found to overcome these obstacles.

The Thatcher government introduced a new phenomenon in Whitehall: a prime minister who believed civil servants were inferior to businesspeople because they did not have to "earn" their living—that is, make a profit. Management was made the buzzword in Whitehall, and departments were supposed to be run in a businesslike fashion, with cost-cutting substituted for the entrepreneur's goal of increasing the profits of an organization. The policy has continued since. Parts of government departments have been thus "hived off" to form separate public agencies, with their own accounts and performance targets. If the task at hand is noncontroversial, such as the issuing of car licenses, it is possible to apply efficiency criteria without political controversy. But if the task is politically sensitive, such as running prisons, ministers cannot avoid blame if a child murderer escapes from an independently managed prison.

The Blair government has endorsed management as a means to secure "value for money," a necessary part of its political strategy of containing public expenditure and taxation. It is also welcome because the job of a company's chief executive officer (CEO), the undisputed decision maker in a profit-making firm, is equated with the office of prime minister. Cabinet ministers can then be treated as if they were divisional chiefs in a company, responsible for delivering what the CEO wants or risking loss of their jobs. However, the business school model is inconsistent with the British constitution, and Blair does not yet have enough staff, enough formal authority, or enough knowledge of British government to impose his views. In his first term of office, Blair has given greatest priority to announcing policies that are sure to make headlines, whether or not they affect the work of departmental ministers.

The Role of Parliament

The principal division in Parliament is between the party with a majority of seats in the House of Commons and the opposition party. The Cabinet gets its way because its members are the leading politicians in the party with a majority in the Commons. If a bill or a motion is identified as a vote of confidence in the government, the government will fall if it is defeated. MPs in the majority party almost invariably vote as the party leadership instructs, because only by voting as a bloc can their party maintain control of government.

In nine out of ten votes in the Commons, voting is 100 percent along party lines. If a handful of MPs votes against the party whip or abstains, this is head-

lined as a rebellion. The government's state of mind is summed up in the words of a Labour Cabinet minister who declared, "It's carrying democracy too far if you don't know the result of the vote before the meeting."[16] The government rather than Parliament has the power of the purse. Whitehall departments draft bills presented to Parliament. Only a very small percentage of amendments to legislation are carried without government backing. This presents an interesting contrast with the U.S. Congress, where each house controls its own proceedings independent of the White House and can be at loggerheads when different parties control each branch. An American president may ask Congress to enact a bill but cannot compel a favorable vote.

Within the governing party, backbench MPs have opportunities to influence government, individually and collectively. The whip is expected to listen to the views of dissatisfied backbench MPs and to convey their concerns to ministers. In the corridors, dining rooms, and committees of the Commons, backbenchers can tell ministers what they think is wrong with government policy. Rebellions within the governing party are usually directed toward extreme positions rather than the political center, thus failing to attract support across the parties. The opposition cannot expect to alter major government decisions because it lacks a majority of votes in the Commons. The opposition accepts the frustrations going with its minority status for the life of a Parliament, because it hopes to win a majority at the next election.

The first function of the Commons is to weigh political reputations. MPs continually assess their colleagues as ministers and potential ministers. A minister may win a formal vote of confidence but lose status if his or her arguments are demolished in debate.

Talking about legislation—not the actual writing of laws—is a second function of the House of Commons. Backbench MPs, especially in the governing party, can demand that the government do something about an issue or voice opposition to a proposed government action. Ministers decide the general principles of bills, which are written by specialist lawyers acting on instructions from civil servants spelling out a minister's intentions. The procedures of the Commons force a minister to explain and defend a bill in detail. In theory a government bill can be substantially amended or even withdrawn as a consequence of criticism in Parliament—but such incidents are rare. Laws are described as acts of Parliament, but it would be more accurate if they were stamped "Made in Whitehall."

The third function of MPs is to scrutinize how Whitehall departments administer public policies. An MP may write to a minister, questioning a departmental decision called to his or her attention by a constituent or pressure group. MPs can request the parliamentary commissioner for administration (also known as the ombudsman, after the Scandinavian prototype) to investigate complaints about maladministration. Committees of a small number of MPs scrutinize administration and policy, interviewing civil servants and ministers. However, as a committee moves from discussing details to questions of political principle, it raises the question of confidence in the government. Party loyalty usually guarantees that the government will not lose a committee vote.

Publicizing issues is a fourth function of Parliament. An MP has much more access to the mass media than an ordinary citizen. However, only the quality newspapers read by one-tenth of the electorate report speeches made in the Commons. Television has access to Parliament, but news programs usually show only sound bites. The public's lack of interest in debate is matched by that of MPs. Only one-sixth of backbenchers regularly listen to their colleagues' speeches in the House of Commons.

A newly elected MP contemplating his or her role as one among 659 members of the House of Commons is faced with many alternatives. An MP may decide to be a party loyalist, voting as the leadership decides, without participating in deliberations about policy. The MP who wishes more attention can make a mark by brilliance in debate, by acting as an acknowledged representative of a pressure group, or in a nonpartisan way—for example, as a wit. An MP is expected to speak for constituency interests, but constituents accept that their MP will not vote against party policy if it is in conflict with local interests. The only role that an MP rarely undertakes is that of lawmaker.

Among modern Parliaments, the House of Lords is unique because a number of the members of this second chamber have inherited their seats from an ancestor given a peerage generations or centuries ago. There are also Church of England bishops and law lords. Since 1958, membership has been much altered by the appointment of life peers by the prime minister. Many peers are retired members of the House of Commons; they find the more relaxed pace of the Lords suited to their advancing years. Some are distinguished in other fields. The government often introduces relatively noncontroversial legislation in the Lords if it deals with technical matters, and it uses the Lords as a revising chamber to amend bills. In addition, the Lords can discuss public issues on matters of partisan controversy or on such cross-party topics as pornography or the future of hill farming. The Lords' power to reject bills passed by the Commons was formidable until the Parliament Act of 1911 abolished its right of veto, substituting the power to delay the enactment of legislation. Occasionally, the Lords delays the passage of a major government bill or forces the government to accept amendments against its wishes.

Because the Lords is not elected it cannot claim to represent the nation. Nor can it claim to be impartial because Conservative peers have always greatly outnumbered Labour peers. In 1999 the New Labour government abolished the right of all hereditary peers to sit in the House of Lords. While all parties accept the need for some kind of second chamber to revise legislation and provide some specialist ministers who are not MPs, the next step in changing the upper house of Parliament is less clear. The last thing the government of the day wants is a reform that gives the upper chamber enough legitimacy to challenge a House of Commons that invariably endorses the legislation of the government of the day.

The limited influence of both houses of Parliament encourages proposals for reform. Backbench MPs perennially demand changes to make their jobs more interesting and to give them more influence. New Labour MPs, especially women elected in 1997 have criticized procedures inherited from past centuries as inappropriate for the new millennium.

However, the power to make changes rests with the Cabinet rather than the House of Commons. Whatever criticisms MPs made of Parliament while in opposition, once in Cabinet party leaders have an interest in existing arrangements that greatly limit the power of Parliament to influence or stop what ministers do.

Government as a Network

The ship of state has only one tiller—but two pairs of hands give it direction. Policies are the joint product of the actions of Cabinet ministers and civil servants. Anything that affects one part affects the whole system. If the caliber of the civil service deteriorates, this reduces the performance of the Cabinet. If a prime minister or Cabinet ministers are unrealistic or uncertain in setting policy objectives, civil servants are handicapped in what they do.

In an era of big government, power does not rest in a single individual or office; it is manifest in a network of relations within and between institutions. Policymaking involves the interaction between prime minister, ministers, and leading civil servants, all of whom share in what has been described as the "village life" of Whitehall—and this English village is far smaller and more intimate than the city full of politicians found within the Washington beltway.[17]

The prime minister is the single most important person in government but not all-important. R. H. S. Crossman, a Labour minister, has advanced the circular argument that important decisions are made by the prime minister, and the decisions made by individual ministers and Cabinet collectively are thereby treated as "not at all important."[18] But to say that the prime minister makes the most important decisions and departmental ministers the secondary decisions begs the question: What is an important decision? The decisions in which the prime minister is not involved, such as routine spending on social security and health, are more numerous, involve more money, and affect more lives than most decisions taken in Downing Street. Moreover, the issues immediately concerning the prime minister, such as foreign affairs and the international dimension of the economy, are issues where the power of British government has declined

in the postwar era. Yet the prime minister must concentrate on these issues because they involve relations between heads of government, even though he or she is often negotiating from weakness.

Scarcity of prime ministerial time is a second major limitation on the influence of the prime minister. The more attention given to international affairs and the economy, the less time there is for all the other concerns of Cabinet ministers. One Downing Street official has described policymaking in this way: "It's like skating over an enormous globe of thin ice. You have to keep moving fast all the time."[19] Trying to do everything risks imposing self-inflicted wounds.

The third limitation is that a small staff restricts prime ministerial interventions. Only a few dozen civil servants and political appointees work for the prime minister in Downing Street. There are less than one hundred political appointees serving the whole of the Blair government, a far cry from the thousands of appointees of the U.S. president.

Within the Whitehall network, a core set of ministers are especially important in determining policies. The Chancellor of the Exchequer is responsible for promoting economic growth, taxing, and spending, each an important political issue. The Foreign Secretary deals every day with foreign governments, seeking to define and advance British interests, and faces constraints from abroad that cannot be ignored. The government chief whip, the link with MPs outside the Cabinet, advises the prime minister about issues that are likely to be particularly sensitive to the party's MPs or even threaten rebellion.

A small number of higher civil servants are also central in the network. The secretary of the Cabinet writes the minutes of Cabinet meetings and sees that appropriate follow-up measures are taken. He or she is in daily contact with the prime minister about what is happening within Whitehall and disseminates requests from the prime minister to departments. The Cabinet Office staff serves all Cabinet committees, tracking developments throughout government. Within a department, the permanent secretary, its highest-ranking civil servant, usually has much more knowledge of a department's problems than a transitory Cabinet minister and the few political appointees advising the minister.

The Whitehall policy network connects people in different formal institutions of government, but its operations are determined by the widespread acceptance of informal customs and traditions. Since there is no written constitution, a determined prime minister can challenge the network and seek to change it to his or her ends. In the past two decades, Margaret Thatcher and Tony Blair have each sought to stamp their own authority on British government and to change the rules of the game from village cricket to hard ball. By trebling the number of special policy advisers attached to Downing Street and ministers, Tony Blair has increased the number of partisans in the policymaking network. But this has also increased the people whose primary concern is with promoting personal as well as political interests. The result has been more friction and more embarrassing leaks about personalities and policies.

Political Culture and Legitimacy

The government can claim full legitimacy only if fundamental "rules of the game," such as the accountability of governors to the electorate and the rule of law, are adhered to by governors. Criticism of the government and demands to change some rules, such as the electoral system, is consistent with legitimacy—as long as changes are within a democratic framework. English people simultaneously value their form of government while making many specific criticisms about how it works. In the phrase of the English writer E. M. Forster, they give "two cheers for democracy."

How Should Political Authority Be Exercised?

The *trusteeship theory of government* assumes that leaders act in the public interest, and should take the initiative in determining what government does. It is summed up in the epigram, "The government's job is to govern." MPs and the Cabinet are not expected to ask what people want, but to use their own judgment to do what they believe is in the best interests of society. In the words of a Conservative Cabinet minister, government is "for the people,

with, but not by, the people."[20] Margaret Thatcher, confident in her political beliefs, saw herself as a trustee of the national interest, rather than simply responding to reports of the latest focus group exploring public opinion. Tony Blair talks like a trustee when he claims to lead a government for all the people.

The trusteeship doctrine is popular with the party in office because it provides a justification for doing whatever the government wishes. Civil servants find the doctrine congenial because they serve the governing party, and see themselves as permanent (albeit nonelected) trustees of the public interest. The opposition party rejects this theory because it lacks the power of government.

The *collectivist theory* sees government as balancing competing interests of major socioeconomic groups. From a collectivist perspective, parties and pressure groups advocating group or class interests are more authoritative than individual voters. Aggregating preferences is inevitable in a country with more than 50 million people.[21] Traditional Conservatives emphasize harmony between different classes in society. Those better off were expected to help those who are less well off by supporting public services and voluntary activities; those with little education were expected to defer to their betters. The socialist vision of group politics emphasized class divisions, with trade unions and business as important as government in determining national policy, and working-class citizens using their votes to redress their lack of economic capital. But gradually party leaders have distanced themselves from organized interests as they realize that votes are cast by individuals rather than business association or trade unions.

The *individualist theory* of representation emphasizes the importance of each citizen in the political process. Liberal Democrats argue that political parties should represent individuals, not organized group interests. However, individuals are rarely offered a referendum giving them the opportunity to vote directly on what government does—and when they are it is the government of the day that determines the question. In the 1980s Margaret Thatcher was an outspoken advocate of economic individualism, regarding each person as responsible for his or her achievement of welfare through activity in the marketplace. This absolved government of the responsibility of promoting collective interests. She even went so far as to declare, "There is no such thing as society." As part of his radical centrist approach, Tony Blair has rejected collectivist doctrines and distanced himself from ties with unions. He emphasizes that government should adopt policies enabling individuals to make the most of their individual abilities through education, job training, and other public policies.

Legitimacy of the System

However authority is justified, the great majority of English people find it inconceivable that there should be a fundamental change in the way the country is governed, as has happened in countries such as Germany and France within recent memory. Even Nationalist parties in Scotland and Wales do not reject parliamentary institutions; what they want is an independent Parliament for Scotland and for Wales.

The legitimacy of government is evidenced by the readiness of the English people to comply with basic political laws. Law enforcement does not require large numbers of armed police. In proportion to its population, England's police force is one-third smaller than that of America, Germany, or France. The crimes that occur in England are antisocial actions such as street violence, rather than political crimes against the state, such as assassinations. The one notable exception is Northern Ireland, where many major crimes, from murder to bank robbery, are political crimes carried out as part of a campaign to overturn the elected government.

Political theorists offer conflicting explanations about the causes of political legitimacy in England. The legitimacy accorded to the government is not the result of economic calculations about whether the British form of parliamentary democracy "pays" best, as rational choice theories propound. British government has been less successful in promoting economic growth than most European countries. Yet during the depression of the 1930s, British Communist and Fascist parties received only derisory votes, while their support was great in France,

Germany, and Italy. Likewise, inflation and unemployment in the 1970s and 1980s failed to stimulate extremist politics.

The symbols of a common past, such as the monarchy, are sometimes cited as major determinants of legitimacy. But surveys of public opinion show that the Queen has little political significance; her popularity derives from the fact that she is nonpolitical. The popularity of a monarch is a consequence, not a cause, of political legitimacy. In Northern Ireland, where the minority denies the legitimacy of British government, the Queen is a symbol of divisions between Unionists and Irish Republicans who reject the Crown.

Habit and tradition appear to be the chief explanations for the persisting legitimacy of authority. A survey asking people why they support the government found that the most popular reason was "It's the best form of government we know." Authority is not perfect or even trouble free: It is valued on the basis of experience. As Winston Churchill told the House of Commons:

> No one pretends that democracy is perfect or all wise. Indeed, it has been said that democracy is the worst form of government, except all those other forms that have been tried from time to time.[22]

Abuses of Power

The theory of the British constitution is that a popularly elected Parliament is the only institution with the authority to check abuses of power by the executive. The courts are supposed to confine their role to interpreting laws that Parliament enacts. In practice, Parliament is not an effective check on executive power, because the potential abusers in Cabinet also lead the majority party in Parliament. When a member of the government is under attack, the tendency is to close ranks in defense of a colleague rather than admit a mistake or willful wrongdoing. A vote of censure against a leading Cabinet minister tends to be treated in the House of Commons as a vote of confidence in the government of the day.

The power of the government to "get away" with mistakes is supported by official secrecy. The

Whitehall view is that information is a scarce commodity that should not be given out freely; publicity about policymaking is not in the "public" (sic) interest, for it can make government appear uncertain or divided about what should be done. Politicians often hide their deliberations behind the veil of collective Cabinet responsibility. The Whitehall view is restrictive: "The need to know still dominates the right to know."[23] Senior public officials can be very selective in what they do and do not say. Government documents are usually shown to the press only when a politician wants to influence events by leaking them. Secrecy remains strong because it serves the interests of the most important people in government, Cabinet ministers and civil servants. The 1999 Official Secrets Act reduced but did not end the executive's power to keep secret the exchange of views within the Whitehall network (see Box 4.4). In the name of "bringing the people in," the Blair government has greatly increased the number and political role of publicity staff in Downing Street and ministries. The flow of information being communicated has increased substantially—but the communication is a one-way street, from Whitehall to the media and its audiences.

If criticized, officials sometimes mislead public bodies. When accused in court of telling a lie about the British government's efforts in 1987 to suppress an embarrassing memoir by a retired intelligence officer, the then head of the civil service and secretary to the Cabinet, Robert Armstrong, described the government's statements as "a misleading impression, not a lie. It was being economical with the truth." In 1994 William Waldegrave, the Conservative minister nominally responsible for open government, told a Commons select committee that "in exceptional cases it is necessary to say something that is untrue in the House of Commons." In the Churchill Matrix trial, the government used national security as the justification for withholding information from the courts affecting the trial of five business executives being prosecuted for shipping arms to Iraq, when government ministers had in fact encouraged this. The prosecution collapsed when the truth leaked out.[24]

Terrorist activities causing disruption, destruction, and death have put law enforcement under great pressure. In Northern Ireland, violence by the illegal IRA and by armed Protestant groups has been met by Crown forces "bending" the law. On Bloody Sunday, 1971, British soldiers shot and killed Irish protesters peacefully demonstrating in Londonderry. In England the police sometimes extract confessions or plant evidence on terrorist suspects. While the initial result is conviction and imprisonment, this is often followed up by a long

---

Box 4.4   Conflicting Loyalties Among Civil Servants

The inability of Parliament to hold the government of the day accountable for palpable misdeeds disturbs senior civil servants who know what is going on and risk becoming accessories before the fact if they assist ministers in producing statements that mislead Parliament. Some even challenge the doctrine that a civil servant must support a minister, whatever the official's personal opinion. In one well-publicized case, a Ministry of Defense official, Clive Ponting, leaked to the House of Commons evidence that questioned the accuracy of government statements about the conduct of the Falklands War. He was indicted and tried for violating the Official Secrets Act. The judge asked the jury to think about the issue this way: "Can it then be in the interests of the state to go against the policy of the government of the day?" The jury concluded that it could be; Ponting was acquitted. However, most senior civil servants are unwilling to become whistle-blowers challenging actions of ministers, thereby jeopardizing their own careers. They hope that "the system" will find a way to stop or expose political malfeasance.*

*Graham Wilson and Anthony Barker, "Whitehall's Disobedient Servants? Senior Officials' Potential Resistance to Ministers in British Government Departments," *British Journal of Political Science* 27, No. 2 (1997): 223–46.

campaign about a miscarriage of justice that eventually rights whatever wrongs have been committed by the police.

In the 1990s, newspapers featured a series of reports of "sleazy" behavior by Members of Parliament who were using their public office to advance their private interests. In response, the government set up a Committee of Inquiry on Standards in Public Life. A Parliamentary Commissioner of Standards has since been established to investigate complaints against individual MPs independently of a partisan House of Commons. In the 1997 election constituents took direct action against two MPs accused of taking cash for asking questions in Parliament; they were defeated at the polls.

The unresponsiveness of government to Parliament has encouraged popular protest—but the legitimacy of government means that protest is usually kept within lawful bounds (see Figure 4.3). Ninety-two percent of British people say they are prepared to express dissatisfaction with a policy by putting their name on a petition and almost half would participate in a lawful protest demonstration. But the majority reject activities that may break the law: 29 percent might join an unofficial strike, and 12 percent occupy a building or factory to protest about an issue. The English protest potential tends to be lower than that of the French and similar to Germans, and English people are ready to support the government if it decides to take strong measures against illegal protest groups.

Culture as a Constraint on Policy

The powers of British government are limited by cultural norms concerning what government should and should not do. In the words of one High Court judge: "In the constitution of this country, there are no guaranteed or absolute rights. The safeguard of British liberty is in the good sense of the people and in the system of representative and responsible government which has been evolved."[25]

The values of the political culture impose limitations on the scope of public policy. Cultural norms about freedom of speech prevent political censorship. They have also made it difficult for gov-

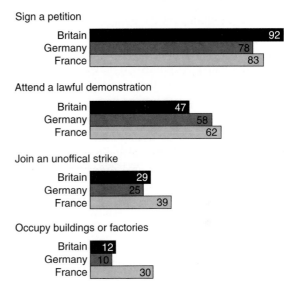

FIGURE 4.3 Differentiating Between Lawful and Unlawful Protests

Percent of those who have or might:

Sign a petition
Britain 92
Germany 78
France 83

Attend a lawful demonstration
Britain 47
Germany 58
France 62

Join an unofficial strike
Britain 29
Germany 25
France 39

Occupy buildings or factories
Britain 12
Germany 10
France 30

Source: *World Values Survey, 1990,* as reported in Sheena Ashford and Noel Timms, *What Europe Thinks: A Study of West European Values* (Brookfield, VT: Dartmouth, 1992), pp. 100–101. German data are for West Germany only.

ernment to enact laws to protect the privacy of the Royal Family against intrusion by aggressive journalists and photographers. This had fatal consequences when Princess Diana's car crashed while being pursued at high speed by photographers. In the "swinging 1960s," laws against homosexual relations were repealed and abortion legalized. AIDS is regarded as a disease rather than as a cause of shame or moralizing. Cultural expectations also influence what politicians must do. Regardless of party preference, the great majority of British people believe that government ought to provide education, health services, and social security.

Today, the most significant limits on the scope of public policy are practical and political. Public expenditure on popular policies such as the health service is limited by the extent to which the economy grows and the reluctance of both Conservative and New Labour governments to raise more money to spend on popular social policies by increasing unpopular taxes.

Political Socialization

Socialization influences the political division of labor. At an early age children learn about social differences relevant to politics; a small proportion become interested in politics, a larger proportion become apathetic and the median person takes some but not too much interest in politics. The predispositions that a young person forms by the time she or he is old enough to vote are modified by adult experience. A middle-aged English person has voted in five or six general elections and is likely to evaluate subsequent political events in the light of what has already been learned.

Family and Gender

The family's influence comes first chronologically; political attitudes learned within the family become intertwined with primary family loyalties. A child may not know what the Labour or Conservative party stands for, but if it is the party of Mom and Dad this can be enough to create identification with a party.

The influence of family on voting is limited; 36 percent do not know how one or both of their parents usually voted, or their parents voted for opposing parties. Among those who report knowing which party both parents supported, just over half vote as their parents have done. In the electorate as a whole, only 35 percent say that they know how both parents voted and voted for the same party.[26] Children also acquire a religious identification from their parents. Except in Northern Ireland, religion no longer has a substantial influence on voting, and there are no groups comparable to the American religious right.

Children learn different social roles according to gender, yet as adult citizens men and women have the same legal right to vote and participate in politics. Bipartisan interest in appealing to women is illustrated by the 1976 Sex Discrimination Act, prohibiting discrimination in employment. It was enacted by a Labour government following a report by a Conservative government.

Today all political parties seek the votes of women, since women are a majority of the electorate. However, parties do not want to offend men, for even though they are a minority, they constitute 48 percent of the electorate. Whether politicians are talking about economic, social, or international issues, they usually try to stress common concerns of both men and women. At each general election, women divide between parties in much the same way as men.

Men and women tend to have similar political attitudes. On most political issues women divide into two contrasting groups, and so do men. For example, more than half of women and half of men favor capital punishment and a substantial minority in each group oppose it. Even on the issue of the display of sex and nudity in the media, which registers a substantial difference of 20 percentage points, both women and men differ among themselves. Gender differences are less important than class or education as influences on party loyalties.

Gender differences do, however, lead to differences in political participation. Even though women constitute more than half the electorate, men are almost twice as likely as women to be local government councillors. Women constitute almost half the employees in the civil service, but they are heavily concentrated at lower-level clerical jobs; women hold less than 10 percent of the top jobs in the civil service. A record number of women stood as major party candidates for the Commons in 1997, but male candidates still outnumbered women by a margin of more than four to one. A record number of women—119—was elected to the House of Commons, but the Commons remains more than four-fifths male. Five women became members of the first Blair Cabinet, another record, but women remain a minority among Cabinet ministers.[27]

Education

Even though individuals have different IQs, each vote counts equally in the ballot box. Yet education has traditionally assumed inequality. The majority of the population was once considered fit for only a minimum of education; in today's electorate the oldest voters left school at the age of fourteen and the median voter by the age of seventeen. The highly educated are a small fraction of the population; they expect and are expected to play a leading role in politics.

Within the state system, the great majority of pupils attend comprehensive secondary schools, which recruit students of all levels of ability. Within the school, pupils are often divided into an academic stream headed for university, a stream heading for examinations at an advanced level superior to the average American high school education, and many who leave with only a basic education. English "public" schools are actually what Americans call private schools. They accept pupils with a wide range of intellectual abilities—as long as their parents can pay high tuition fees. Approximately 6 percent of young persons attend public schools. Whereas at one time graduates of Eton, Harrow, and other leading public schools predominated in Cabinet, today less than a third of all MPs have attended public schools.

Top jobs in politics often go to those who have a common touch, as indicated by attendance at a state secondary school. John Major attended state secondary schools, and so did his immediate Conservative and Labour predecessors. The current Conservative leader, William Hague, went to a comprehensive school where most pupils were not expected to go to university. By contrast, the Labour prime minister Tony Blair went to Scotland's major public school.

Up to one-third of young persons are now in some form of post-secondary education. Tuition was free until 1998 when an annual charge of £1000 (about $1,500) was introduced by the New Labour government. In the 1960s many new universities were created, and in the 1990s many polytechnics, offering a mixture of academic and vocational courses like American state colleges, were relabeled as universities. Today, the great majority of institutions called universities have little special social prestige, and many lack any tradition of promoting research.

The stratification of English education used to imply that the more education a person had, the more likely a person was to be Conservative. This is no longer the case. People with a university degree or its equivalent are currently less likely to vote Conservative than people with a minimum of education. The minority who are most educated now divide their vote between all three big parties, with the Liberal Democrats doing relatively well. The most pro-Conservative groups are those with an intermediate education and a middle-class job.

Education is strongly related to active participation in politics. The more education a person has, the greater the possibility of climbing the political ladder. People with a minimum of education constitute more than half the electorate but less than half of all local government councillors and less than 2 percent of all MPs. The relatively small percentage of university graduates in the country constitutes 70 percent of all MPs. The expansion of universities has broken the dominance of Oxford and Cambridge. The concentration in top political jobs of graduates of many different British universities is a sign of a meritocracy—that is, governors qualified by education replacing an aristocracy based on birth and family.

Class

The concept of *class* can refer to occupational status or serve as a shorthand term for income, education, status, and lifestyle. Occupation is the most commonly used indicator of class in England. Manual workers are usually described as the working class and nonmanual workers as the middle class.

Party competition has traditionally been interpreted in class terms; the Conservative Party has been described as a middle-class party, and Labour as a working-class party. The upper class of aristocrats with inherited titles, land, and, sometimes, money, are too few in number to influence elections—and today their popular influence is likely to be less than celebrities such as film stars or rock musicians. One reason why class appears relatively important in England is that there are no big divisions on race, religion, or language, as in the United States, Canada, or Northern Ireland.

The relationship between class and party is limited. At the 1997 election, no party won as much as half the vote of middle-class electors, and Labour won just half the vote of skilled manual workers (see Table 4.3). Only two-fifths of voters were middle-class Conservatives or working-class Labour voters, due to the cross-class appeal of both parties. The

TABLE 4.3   Social Differences and Voting

	(percentage of voters in 1997)			
	Labour	**Conservative**	**Liberal/Democratic**	**Other**
Gender				
Women	44	32	18	6
Men	45	31	17	7
Difference, men/women	1	1	1	1
Age				
18–24	49	27	16	8
25–34	49	28	16	7
35–44	48	28	17	7
45–54	41	31	20	8
55–64	39	36	17	8
65 plus	41	36	17	6
Difference, young/old	8	9	1	2
Class				
Solid middle	31	41	22	6
Lower middle	37	37	18	8
Skilled manual	50	27	16	7
Unskilled manual	59	21	13	7
Difference, top/bottom	28	20	9	1

Source: MORI, results of 13,544 interviews with the electorate conducted during the 1997 election campaign between March 21–April 29, 1997. For details, see *British Public Opinion*, 20, Nos. 3/4, p. 2. The four classes are AB, C1, C2, and DE.

Liberal Democrats and other smaller parties draw a fifth or more of the vote in every class. Less than one in seven voters conforms to the stereotype of a middle-class person (nonmanual occupation, above-average education, homeowner, no trade union membership, and subjective identification with the middle class), or its counterpart working-class stereotype. Most Britons have a mixture of middle-class and working-class attributes. The mixed class group has been increasing, as changes in the economy have led to a reduction in manual jobs and an increase in middle-class jobs. Many occupations such as technicians and office workers now have an indeterminate status and voting behavior.

Socioeconomic experiences other than occupation also influence voting. At each level of the class structure, people who belong to trade unions are more likely to vote Labour than Conservative. Housing creates neighborhoods with political relevance. About one-sixth of voters live in local government-owned houses clustered together on a housing estate specifically identified as such. Labour wins more than three-fifths of the vote of council tenants, while, regardless of class, Conservatives do relatively well among home-owners.

Mass Media

The mass media tends to reenforce differences arising from class and education. The British press is sharply divided into a few quality papers that carry news and comment at an intellectual level higher than American newspapers, and mass circulation tabloids that carry trivia and trash. Most papers tend to lean toward one party but not uncritically so. When the Conservatives became unpopular with the electorate in the 1990s, some newspapers that were previously pro-Conservative sought to follow their voters in admiring Tony Blair, and Blair has actively courted the support of right-wing newspapers in an attempt to broaden his electoral appeal.

Historically, radio and television were a monopoly of the British Broadcasting Corporation

(BBC). Seeking to educate and to elevate, the BBC was also very respectful of all forms of authority, including government. The introduction of commercial television in the 1950s and commercial radio in the following decade has made all broadcasting channels populist in competing for audiences. There are now five channels plus cable TV and a great variety of radio stations. Today current affairs programs often seek audiences by exposing alleged failings of government, and TV personalities make their names by the tough cross-examination of politicians of all parties.

There remain strict controls on the political output of television and radio stations. The law forbids selling advertising to politicians, parties, or political causes. The government of the day controls the renewal of licenses and, in the case of the BBC, the annual fee of about $150 that every viewer must pay for noncommercial BBC programs. Hence, broadcasters try to avoid favoring one party, recognizing that over a period of years control of government and decisions about licenses and fees are likely to change hands between parties.

Since political socialization is a lifetime learning process, the loyalties of voters are shaped by an accumulation of influences. In the course of a lifetime, an individual develops values expressing what government ought to do. These political values are independent of family and socioeconomic interests. Economic values concerned with trade unions, the welfare state, business, and privatization influence choices between parties. "New" noneconomic values such as protecting the environment and morality account for little variation in the vote, because parties usually lack a distinctive and well-established position.

How the government handles current issues affects the economy and public expenditure, but the judgments that people make about government performance reflect their preexisting values, and this is particularly true of popular evaluations of party and leader images. The influence of such current issues and ephemeral personalities is often overrated, for those who focus on today's events forget that voters have had a lifetime to learn which party they prefer.

Party identification adds little to the way in which people vote. In part, this is because the primary identifications of voters are with family, socioeconomic interests, and political values. It is also due to changes in the party system. In the lifetime of the oldest voters, the Labour Party has split twice, the Liberals have virtually collapsed and then partially recovered, the Conservatives have twice fundamentally reoriented their policies, and the Nationalists have gained ground in Scotland and Wales. Tony Blair's political strategy has further eroded the significance of party identification, for he explicitly rejects any identification of his New Labour Party with socialism or with the working class, integral parts of the old Labour Party.

Political Participation and Recruitment

Participation

If political participation is defined as paying taxes and drawing benefits from public programs, then everyone is involved, for public policies provide benefits at every stage of life, from maternity allowance to mothers through education, employment and unemployment benefits, health care, and pensions in old age.[28]

An election is the one opportunity people have to influence government directly. Every citizen aged 18 or over is eligible to vote. Local government officials register voters, and the list is revised annually, ensuring that nearly everyone eligible to vote is actually registered. Turnout at general elections has averaged 77 percent since 1950; it was 71.5 percent at the 1997 election. Turnout figures are much higher than for American presidential elections.

Casting a vote and signing a petition are the only political activities of the majority of British people (see Figure 4.4). Five-sixths or more do not attend political meetings, do not contact their Member of Parliament, do not have a high interest in politics, and do not belong to a political party.[29] Depending on the measure used, from 3 percent to 14 percent can be described as regularly participating in politics. If elected office is the measure of political involvement, the proportion drops below 1 percent.

The wider the definition of political participation, the greater the number who can be said to be

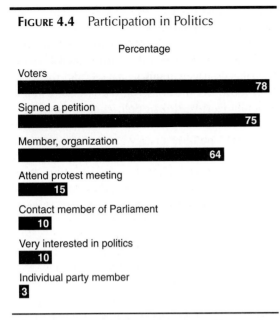

FIGURE 4.4   Participation in Politics

Percentage

Voters
78

Signed a petition
75

Member, organization
64

Attend protest meeting
15

Contact member of Parliament
10

Very interested in politics
10

Individual party member
3

Source: Official statistics and Geraint Parry, George Moyser, and Neil Day, *Political Participation and Democracy in Britain* (New York: Cambridge University Press, 1992), counting any involvement in the past five years as participation.

involved in politics, at least indirectly. An estimated 64 percent of the population belongs to at least one organization that can act as an interest group, such as an anglers' club concerned about the pollution of a local stream or the Automobile Association, which represents motorists. But most people join organizations such as sports or gardening clubs for nonpolitical purposes. For example, only a limited minority of trade union members take an interest in the political activities of their union, and half vote against Labour, the party that unions support. Many ad hoc groups reflect local concern about a single issue—for example, the need for a stop sign when there has been an accident in a neighborhood. The concentration of politics and media in London makes it possible for a London-based protest meeting with a few thousand people to get press coverage, even though those participating are only one–one-hundredth of 1 percent of the electorate.

Political Recruitment

We can view recruitment into politics deductively or inductively. The deductive approach defines the job

to be done and individuals are recruited with skills appropriate to the task; this is the route favored by management consultants. Alternatively, we can inductively examine the influences that lead people into politics and ask: Given their skills and motives, what can such people do? The constraints of history and institutions make the inductive approach more realistic.

The most important political roles in Britain are those of Cabinet minister, higher civil servant, and *intermittent public person*, analogous to informal advisers to presidents. Each group has its own recruitment pattern. To become a Cabinet minister, an individual must first be elected to Parliament and spend years attracting positive attention there. Individuals enter the civil service shortly after leaving university by passing a highly competitive entrance examination; promotion is based on achievement and approval by seniors. Intermittent public persons gain access to ministers and civil servants because of their expertise or position in organizations outside politics, or because they are personally trusted by leading politicians.

In all political roles, experience is positively valued. Starting early on a political career is usually a precondition of success. But aspiring Cabinet ministers are not expected to begin in local politics and work their way gradually to the top at Westminster. Instead, at an early age an individual becomes a "cadet" recruit to a junior position such as a parliamentary assistant to an MP or a "gofer" for a Cabinet minister. This can lead to a central political role after gaining skill and seniority.

Geography is a second major influence on recruitment. Ministers, higher civil servants, and other public persons spend their working lives in London. A change at Downing Street does not bring in policymakers from a different part of the country, as can happen in the White House when a president from Texas succeeds a president from Arkansas or California. Since London is atypical of the cities and towns in which most British people live, there is a gap between the everyday lives of policymakers and the majority on whose behalf they act.

Cabinet Ministers

For a person ambitious to be a Cabinet minister, becoming an MP is the necessary first step. Nomination for a winnable or safe seat in the House of Commons is in the hands of local party selection committees. There are no American-style primaries in which all electors can vote. A candidate does not have to be resident in the constituency in which he or she is nominated. Hence, it is possible for a young person to go straight from university to a job in the House of Commons or party headquarters, and then look around the country for a nomination for a winneable seat. Once selected for a constituency in which his or her party has a big majority, the MP can then expect to be reelected routinely for a decade or more.

After entering the House of Commons, an MP seeks to get noticed there. Some ways of doing so—for example, grabbing headlines by questioning the wisdom of the party leadership—make it difficult to gain promotion to ministerial rank. Other approaches assist promotion, such as successfully attacking opposition leaders in debate or being well informed about a politically important topic. So too does gaining the personal friendship of leading politicians.

Experience in the Commons does not prepare an individual for the work of a minister. An MP's chief concerns are dealing with people and talking about what government ought to do. A minister must also be able to handle paperwork, relate political generalities to specific technical problems facing a ministry, and take hard decisions when no alternative is popular.

The restriction of ministerial appointments to experienced MPs prevents a nationwide canvass for appointees. A prime minister must distribute about 100 jobs among approximately 200 MPs in the governing party who have had experience in Parliament and not ruled themselves out of consideration for office on grounds of parliamentary inexperience, old age, political extremism, personal unreliability, or lack of interest in office. An MP has a better than even chance of a junior ministerial appointment if he or she serves three terms in Parliament.

A minister learns on the job. Usually, an MP is first given a junior post as an Under Secretary and then promoted to Minister of State before becoming a full member of the Cabinet. In the process, an individual is usually shuffled from one department to another, having to learn new subject matter with each shift of departments.

The average minister can expect to stay in a particular job for only two years. The rate of ministerial turnover in Britain is one of the highest in Europe. The minister who gets a new job as the result of a reshuffle usually arrives at a department with no previous experience of its problems. It takes time to learn how to deal with the particular problems of a department. Anthony Crosland, an able Labour minister, reckoned: "It takes you six months to get your head properly above water, a year to get the general drift of most of the field, and two years really to master the whole of a department."[30] A minister's lack of substantial expertise in his or her department has produced criticism of the recruitment system. Defenders of the current system argue that such criticisms ignore the first requirement of being a successful minister—expertise in managing the politics of the House of Commons.

Higher Civil Servants

Whereas MPs come and go from ministerial office with great frequency, civil servants have a job in Whitehall for the whole of their working lives. Higher civil servants are recruited without specific professional qualifications or training. They are meant to be the "best and the brightest"—a requirement that has usually meant getting a prestigious degree in history, literature, or languages. The Fulton Committee on the Civil Service recommended that recruits should have "relevant" specialist knowledge, but members could not decide what kind of knowledge was relevant to the work of government.[31] The Civil Service Commission tests candidates for ability to summarize lengthy prose papers, to resolve a problem by fitting specific facts to general regulations, to draw inferences from a simple table of social statistics, and to perform well in group discussions of problems of government.

Because bright civil service entrants lack specialized skills and need decades to reach the highest posts, role socialization into Whitehall by senior civil servants is especially important. The process makes for continuity, since the head of the civil service usually starts there as a young official under a head who had himself entered the civil service many decades before.

In the course of a career, civil servants become specialists in the difficult task of managing political ministers and government business. As the television series, *Yes, Minister* shows, they are adept at saying "yes" to a Cabinet minister when they mean "perhaps" and saying "up to a point" when they really mean "no." Increasingly, ministers have tended to discourage civil service advisers from pointing out obstacles to what the government wants to do; they are looking for "can do" advisers from outside the civil service as well as inside.

Most leaders of institutions such as the universities, banks, churches and trade unions do not think of themselves as politicians and have not stood for public office. They are principally concerned with their own organization. But when government actions impinge on their work, they become involved in politics, offering ministers advice and sometimes criticisms. When an organization is publicly funded, as is the case of the universities or the British Broadcasting Corporation, political pressures are continuous.

Expert advisers are sought by government departments and ministers lacking specialist knowledge about such problems as environmental pollution or experimental medical procedures such as cloning. Government departments have many advisory committees with academic experts and interest group representatives. Economists are particularly prominent in offering advice to government. In Britain the supply of economists of diverse views is so great that each party leader can shop around and choose economists whose policy prescriptions endorse their own political inclinations. Margaret Thatcher had no difficulty in finding Nobel laureates and professors to endorse her views; the same is true of Tony Blair.

Selective Recruitment

Nothing could be more selective than a parliamentary election that results in one person becoming prime minister of a country with 58 million people. Yet nothing is more representative, because an election is the one occasion when every adult can participate in politics with equal effect.

Traditionally, leaders in English society had high social status and wealth before gaining political office. However, since the 1960s England has experienced the rise of the fulltime professional politician. Aristocrats, business people, or trade union leaders can no longer expect to translate their high standing in other fields into an important political position.

As careers become more specialized, a professional politician gains increased expertise in his or her own sphere but becomes increasingly remote from other spheres. After years of interviewing persons in leading positions in many areas of English life, Anthony Sampson concluded: "My own fear is not that the Establishment in Britain is too close, but that it is not close enough, that the circles are overlapping less and less and that one-half of the ring has very little contact with the other half."[32]

Yet the greater the scope of activities defined as political, the greater the number of people actively involved in government. Government influence has forced company directors, television executives, and university heads to become involved in politics and public policy. Leadership in organizations outside Whitehall gives such individuals freedom to act independently of government, but the interdependence of public and private institutions, whether profitmaking or nonprofit, is now so great that sooner or later they meet in discussions about what constitutes the public interest.

Organizing Group Interests

Civil society—that is, institutions independent of government—has flourished in Britain for centuries. So confident are leaders of civil society in their position that they readily discuss public affairs with government officials in expectation that they can exert pressure on behalf of interests they represent.

The Confederation of British Industries is the chief representative organization of British business. As its name implies, its membership is large and varied. The biggest firms or industries, such as automobiles, usually make direct representations to ministries, especially the Board of Trade and the Department of Education and Employment. The Institute of Directors represents the highest-paid individuals at the top of large and small businesses.

Banks and financial institutions in the City of London have their own channels of representation through the Bank of England, the central Bank, and directly to the Treasury.

The comparable organization of labour is the Trades Union Congress (TUC); its members are trade unions that sometimes have conflicting interests when it comes to bargaining about wage differentials. Most member unions of the TUC are affiliated with the Labour Party, and some leading trade unionists have even been Communists or Maoists. None has ever been a supporter of the Conservative Party. The membership of trade unions has shifted from industrial workers in coal and railways to white collar workers in the public sector, such as teachers and health service workers. Changes in employment patterns have eroded union membership; about one-third of the labor force belongs to unions. Tony Blair has consciously sought to keep unions at a distance in order to project a New Labour image.

Unlike political parties, interest groups do not seek influence by contesting elections; they want to influence policies regardless of which party wins. Nonetheless, there do remain ties between interest groups and political parties. Trade unions have been institutionally part of the Labour Party since its foundation in 1900. The connection between business associations and the Conservatives is not a formal one, but the private enterprise philosophy of the Conservative Party is congenial to business. Notwithstanding common interests, both trade unions and business groups demonstrate their autonomy by criticizing partisan allies when they are thought to be acting against the group's interest.

Party politicians similarly seek to distance themselves from pressure groups. Tony Blair has sought to distance the New Labour Party from trade unions, turning to new rich millionaires for money to finance expensive New Labour public relations activities. The Conservatives seek votes by claiming that their policies can raise the living standards of ordinary workers better than can those of trade unions.

To lobby successfully, interest groups must be able to identify those officials most important in making public policy. They concentrate attention on Whitehall. When pressure groups were asked to rank the most influential offices and institutions, they named the prime minister first by a length, Cabinet ministers second, the media third, and senior civil servants fourth (see Figure 4.5). Less than 1 percent thought MPs outside the ministerial ranks were of primary importance. However, pressure groups do not expect to spend a lot of time in Downing Street. Most pressure group contacts are with divisions of government departments concerned with issues of little public concern but of immediate interest to the group. Groups that concentrate on confrontational media publicity make it difficult to gain a sympathetic private hearing from government departments.[33]

What Interest Groups Want

The scope of group demands varies enormously—from the narrow concerns of an association for

FIGURE 4.5   Pressure Group View of Who Holds Most Power

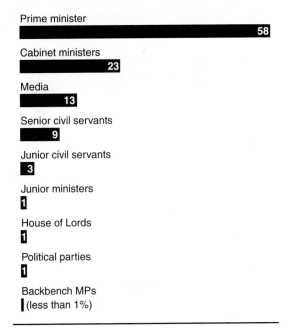

Percentage naming first

Prime minister — 58
Cabinet ministers — 23
Media — 13
Senior civil servants — 9
Junior civil servants — 3
Junior ministers — 1
House of Lords — 1
Political parties — 1
Backbench MPs (less than 1%)

Source: Survey of officials of business, labor, and campaign groups, as reported in Rob Baggott, "The Measurement of Change in Pressure Group Politics," *Talking Politics 5*, No. 1 (1992): 19.

wounded ex-servicemen to the encompassing economic policies of organizations such as the Confederation of British Industries and the Trades Union Congress. Groups also differ in the nature of their interests; some are concerned with material objectives, whereas others deal with single causes such as violence in the media or race relations. Most interest groups pursue four goals:

1. Information about government policies and changes in policies
2. Sympathetic administration of established policies
3. Influence on policymaking
4. Symbolic status, such as being given the prefix "Royal" in their title

Whitehall departments are happy to consult with interest groups insofar as they can provide government officials with reciprocal benefits:

1. Cooperation in the administration of existing policies
2. Information about what is happening in their field
3. Evaluation of the consequences of policies under consideration
4. Assistance in implementing new policies

When the needs of Whitehall and interest groups are complementary, they can bargain as professionals sharing common concerns. When each needs the other, bargaining operates on the principle of exchange. Both sides seek a negotiated agreement, because this avoids decisions being made by politicians who know less and care less about details than interest group officials and civil servants involved in departmental administration.

Organizing for Political Action in Civil Society

Interest groups vary greatly in their capacity to organize potential supporters. Workers in a one-industry town are easily organized in a trade union, because they are in frequent contact with each other away from work as well as on the job; they are a social group as well as a political group. By contrast, consumers are more difficult to organize because they are interested only in goods and services, not in

their relations with other customers; they are a category rather than a social group.

The more committed members are to a pressure group's goals, the more confidently leaders can speak for a united membership. In the absence of commitment, a group can be ineffective. For example, when the leader of the National Union of Mineworkers (NUM), Arthur Scargill, called a yearlong strike against the government-owned National Coal Board in 1984, he refused to allow union members to vote on the action. Denied a strike ballot, many members felt no commitment to obey the strike order. As a result, the NUM lost its strike and its membership split into two separate unions.

Whitehall civil servants find it administratively convenient to deal with united interest groups that can implement agreements. But decades of attempts to plan the British economy demonstrate that business and union leaders cannot guarantee that their nominal followers will carry out bargains that leaders make. Group members who care about an issue may also disagree about what their leaders ought to do. Individuals usually have a multiplicity of identities that are often in conflict—for example, as workers desiring higher wages and as consumers wanting lower prices. The spread of mass consumption and decline in trade union memberships has altered the balance between these priorities.

Even if a pressure group is internally united, its demands may be counteracted by opposing demands from other groups. This is normally the case in economic policy, where interests are well defined, well organized, and competing. Ministers can play off producers against consumers or business against unions to increase their own scope for choice and present their policies as "something for everybody" compromises.

The more a group's values are consistent with the cultural norms of society as a whole, the easier it is to equate its interest with the public interest. But in an open society such as England the claims of one group to speak for the public interest can easily be challenged by competing groups.

The centralization of authority in British government means that interest groups must accept as given the political values and priorities of the governing party. Trade unions expect to see their influence increase when a Labour government is in office and business groups have similar expectations when the Conservatives are in power. However, a prime minister seeking to broaden the government's base of support can try to build bridges with nominal allies of the opposition—thereby strengthening the government. Tony Blair's New Labour government has conspicuously solicited support from business leaders. It has also kept the party's traditional allies in the trade unions at a distance, reckoning they have no other party to support.

Insider pressure groups usually have values in harmony with every party. These groups are often noncontroversial, such as the Royal National Institute for the Blind. The primary concern of permanent insiders is to negotiate on details of administration and finance, and to press for the expansion of programs benefiting the group. They advance their case in quiet negotiations with Whitehall departments. Demands tend to be restricted to what is politically possible in the short term, given the values and commitments of the government of the day.[34]

Outsider pressure groups are unable to negotiate because their demands are inconsistent with the party in power. If they are inconsistent with the views of the opposition as well, then outsider groups are completely marginalized. Excluded from influence in Whitehall, outsider groups often campaign through the media. To television viewers and readers of serious newspapers, their demonstrations appear as evidence of their importance; in fact, they are often signs of a lack of political influence.

Complete outsiders are excluded from Whitehall, whatever the government of the day, because their demands go against prevailing cultural norms. For example, the Ministry of Defense does not consult pacifist groups, for there is nothing to negotiate when principles are mutually exclusive. Green pressure groups face the dilemma of campaigning for fundamental change in hopes that eventually Whitehall departments will turn their way, or working within the system in order to improve the environment to some extent but not as much as ecologists would like.

Keeping Pressure Groups at a Distance

For a generation after World War II ministers endorsed the corporatist philosophy of bringing together business, trade union, and political representatives in tripartite institutions to discuss such controversial issues as dealing with inflation and unemployment, and the restructuring of declining industries. Corporatist bargaining assumed a consensus on political priorities and goals; its critics alleged that such a consensus was "taking the politics out of politics." It also assumed that the leaders of each group could deliver the cooperation of those they claimed to represent. In practice, neither Labour nor Conservative governments were able to maintain a consensus. Nor were interest group leaders able to deliver their nominal followers. By 1979, unemployment and inflation were both out of control.

The Thatcher administration demonstrated that a government firmly committed to distinctive values can ignore group demands and lay down its own pattern of policy. It did so by dealing at arm's-length with both trade unions and business groups. Instead of consulting and negotiating with interest groups, it practiced *state-distancing*, keeping the government out of the everyday activities of the marketplace such as wage bargaining and deciding prices and investment.

A state-distancing strategy concentrates on policies that government can carry out without the agreement of interest groups. It emphasizes the use of legislation to achieve goals, since no interest group can defy an act of Parliament. Laws have reduced the capacity of trade unions to frustrate government policies through industrial action. The sale of state-owned industries has removed government from immediate responsibility for the operation of major industries. One of the first measures of the New Labour government was to transfer to the Bank of England responsibility for monetary policy, while keeping in the government's hands the right to set policy goals for which the Bank is responsible.

State-distancing places less reliance on negotiations with interest groups and more on the independent authority of the Crown. Business and labor are free to carry on as they like—but only within the pattern imposed by the government's policy and legislation. Most unions and some business leaders do not like being "outside the loop" when government makes decisions. Education and health service pressure groups like it even less, because they depend upon government appropriations to fund their activities and cannot effectively turn to the market as an alternative source of revenue.

While in opposition, Tony Blair often spoke about the need to achieve "the reinvention of community,"[35] implying endorsement of corporatist institutions of cooperation between representatives of different groups in society. However, since becoming prime minister. Blair has made sure that meetings with groups are on terms laid down by Downing Street, and when conflicts are apparent between groups he prefers to lecture both on the need to pursue an ill-defined public interest rather than take sides or broker agreement between conflicting parties.

Party System and Electoral Choice

British government is party government. It is the political parties that organize the selection of candidates, place policies on the political agenda, and elect the leader who will become prime minister or the alternative prime minister. An election gives voters the choice of deciding between parties competing for the right to govern.

Because of the multiplicity of competing parties, what happens to one party affects what happens to others. When the Labour Party became unpopular in the 1980s, this enabled the Conservatives to win four successive elections with well under half the popular vote. When the Conservative government became very unpopular after winning the 1992 election, Tony Blair's New Labour Party won a landslide victory with a lower percentage of the vote than Gerald Ford or Michael Dukakis took when losing their presidential contests. When both the largest parties are discredited, this gives an opportunity for a third party to gain support, such as the Liberal Democrats in England or the Scottish National Party.

A Multiplicity of Choices

A general election must occur at least once every five years; within that period, the prime minister is free to call an election at any time. Although every prime minister tries to pick a date when victory is very likely, often this does not happen.

A general election offers a voter a very simple choice: only one office is at stake, that of MP for the constituency, and an elector endorses one among a handful of candidates to represent the constituency in the House of Commons. Because people see elections as national contests, they will usually vote for their party, even if dissatisfied with their local candidate or ignorant of the candidate's name and character. The party leader's name is not on the ballot.

Within each constituency, the winner is the candidate with the largest number of votes, even though this can be less than half. The winner of the election nationally is the party that wins the most constituency seats. In 1951 and again in February 1974, the party winning the most votes did not win the most seats and thus did not form the government.

Between 1945 and 1970, the British system was a two-party system, as the Conservative and Labour parties together took an average of 91 percent of the popular vote and in 1951 as much as 97 percent (see Figure 4.6). The Liberals had difficulty finding candidates to contest most seats and even more difficulty winning votes. Support for the two largest parties was evenly balanced; Labour won four elections and the Conservatives won four.

A *multiparty system* emerged in 1974. The Liberals won nearly one-fifth of the vote, and the Nationalists did well in Scotland, Wales, and Northern Ireland in both contests that year. Together, the Conservative and Labour parties took only 75 percent of the vote. The 1980s saw the Labour Party vote plummet as the Alliance of Liberals and Social Democrats won up to a quarter of the popular vote, and nearly surpassed Labour's reduced support. The Alliance broke up after the 1987 election, with most Social Democrats joining an enlarged Liberal Democratic Party. The fragmentation of voters and parties has continued since.[36]

FIGURE 4.6   Votes Cast in General Elections Since 1945

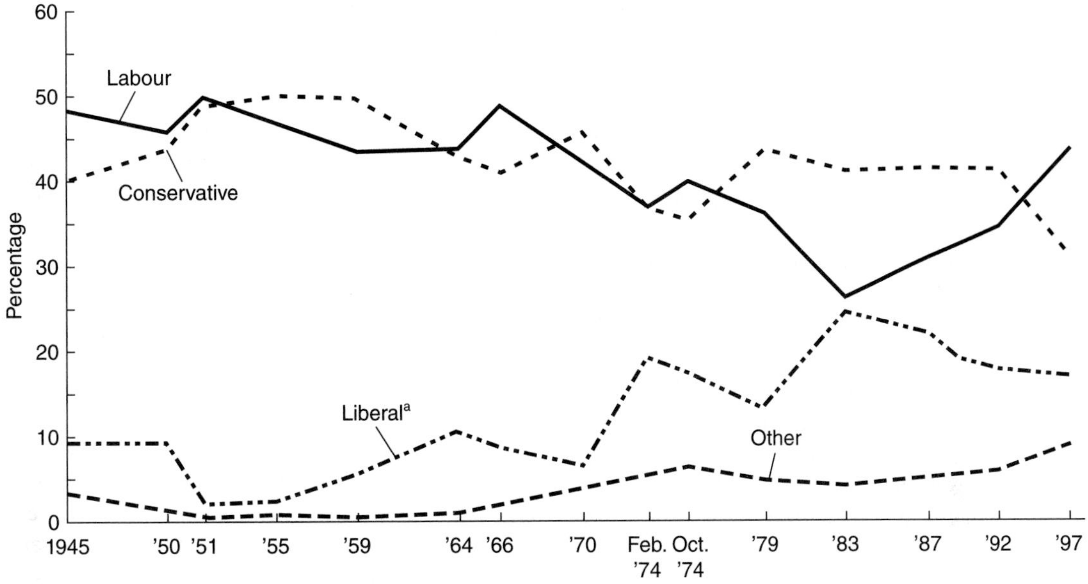

[a]1945–1979 Liberal Party; 1983–1987 Alliance of Liberals and Social Democratic Party; since then known as Liberal Democrats.

1. In England, three parties—New Labour, Conservatives, and Liberal Democrats—compete for votes. In 1997 a Referendum party fought an anti-European Union campaign in the great majority of seats too. In Scotland and Wales there are normally four parties, for the Scottish National and Plaid Cymru (Welsh Nationalist) parties win seats too. In Northern Ireland, at least five parties normally contest seats.

2. The two largest parties do not monopolize the vote. Since 1974, the Conservative and Labour parties together have won an average of just under three-quarters of the vote. In 1997 the two largest parties took 74 percent, leaving more than a quarter of the total vote to be divided among a multiplicity of other parties.

3. The two largest parties nationally are often not the two front-running parties at the constituency level. In the 1997 election, the first and second parties in England were New Labour and the Conservatives; in Scotland, New Labour and the

Scottish Nationalists; in Wales, New Labour and the Conservatives, and in Northern Ireland, the Ulster Unionists and the pro-Irish Social Democratic and Labour Party. The Conservatives won no parliamentary seats in Scotland or Wales. In Northern Ireland all 18 seats were won by parties that did not contest seats in Great Britain.

4. More than half a dozen parties consistently win seats in the House of Commons. In 1997 there were ten "third parties" represented in the Commons, holding a total of 75 seats.

5. Significant shifts in voting usually do not involve individuals moving between the Conservative and New Labour parties but in and out of the ranks of abstainers or in between the Liberal Democrats and the two largest parties.

Since 1945 control of British government has alternated between the Conservative and Labour parties. One or the other party has monopolized Cabinet posts during its term of office. Yet no party with a majority in Parliament has won as much as half the popular vote since 1935.

British parliamentary elections use a *first-past-the-post electoral system*. It is a system of disproportional representation that manufactures a House of Commons majority for one party, even though the party has a minority of the popular vote. If only two parties contest a constituency, the candidate with the most votes will have an absolute majority. But when three or more candidates do so, a candidate with less than half the vote can win the seat thanks to the division of the vote among a multiplicity of competitors. In the hard-fought 1992 contest between four parties in Inverness, the Liberal Democrats won the seat with only 26 percent of the vote there. At the 1997 election, voters had a choice between at least four candidates in virtually every seat.

To win a substantial number of seats in the House of Commons, a party must either win at least one-third of the popular vote nationwide or concentrate its votes in a limited number of constituencies. Nationalist parties in Scotland, Wales, and Northern Ireland win seats because they concentrate their candidates in one part of the United Kingdom. Although the Liberal Democrats win more than a sixth of the popular vote, because their support is spread relatively evenly across the country, their candidates are far more likely to finish second or third rather than first.

In 1997 New Labour won almost two-thirds of the seats in the House of Commons even though it took well under half the vote (see Figure 4.7). The Conservative Party won almost a third of the vote but took only a quarter of the seats. The Liberal Democrats were specially disadvantaged by the electoral system. In a totally proportional system of representation, the party's vote share would have secured 111 seats; in fact, it gained less than half this number. Even more important, in a proportional representation system New Labour's vote would not have given it a majority of seats in the Commons, and it would have had to govern in coalition with the Liberal Democrats.

Defenders of the British electoral system argue that proportionality is not a goal in itself. If it were, then the United States could not have a president chosen through an electoral process that sometimes awards the White House to a candidate with less than half the popular vote. The first-past-the-post system is justified because it clearly places responsibility for government in the hands of a single party rather than diffusing it in a coalition, as happens in continental European countries where Parliaments

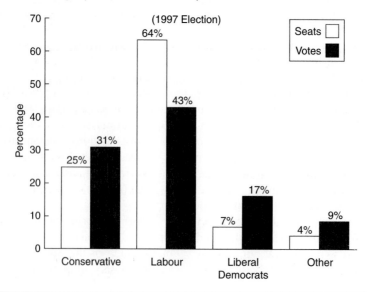

FIGURE 4.7   Effects of a Disproportional Electoral System

(1997 Election)

Seats ☐
Votes ■

Conservative: Seats 25%, Votes 31%
Labour: Seats 64%, Votes 43%
Liberal Democrats: Seats 7%, Votes 17%
Other: Seats 4%, Votes 9%

are elected by proportional representation. Critics say it is wrong to give the party coming third in the popular vote the power to determine who governs by choosing whether to ally itself with the party second or first in the popular vote in order to produce a majority coalition.

The strongest advocates of proportional representation are the Liberal Democrats, the party that would benefit most from a change in the electoral system. A change is also supported by those who believe that a coalition government is a better government because it encourages a broader interparty consensus.

Successive British governments have altered the electoral system for votes that do not affect the composition of the Westminster Parliament. Northern Ireland voters have used a form of proportional representation for almost two decades. The Scottish Parliament and Welsh Assembly are elected by a mixed system in which some representatives are returned from single-member districts and others are elected by proportional representation. In the election of the Mayor of Greater London in 2000, the alternative vote was used to make sure that the Mayor was the first or second choice of more than half the voters. In ballots for British Members of the European Parliament, proportional representation is used.

In his first term of office, Tony Blair encouraged talk about electoral reform, and alternative proposals were put forward by a government-appointed Commission. But this has produced a counter-mobilization against changing the system. Many MPs elected by first-past-the-post are satisfied with what they benefit from, and traditional Labour MPs fear that a coalition government in which Labour Party views were constrained by a coalition would be less sympathetic to labour interests.

Control of Party Organization

Political parties are often referred to as machines, but this description is very misleading, for parties cannot manufacture votes. Nor can a political party be commanded as an army can be commanded. Parties are like universities; they are inherently *decentralized*, and people belong to them for a variety of motives.[37]

Much of the effort devoted to party organization is concerned with keeping together three disparate parts of the party: those who vote for it, the small minority who are active in its constituency associations, and the party in Parliament. If the party has a majority in Parliament, the prime minister must make sure that the other parts of the party support government policy, even if the majority of party members or MPs do not like what the leadership is doing.

Constituency parties are nationally significant because each selects its parliamentary candidate. The decentralization of the selection process allows the choice of parliamentary candidates with a wide variety of political outlooks and abilities.[38] The Thatcher era introduced an ideological litmus test, and the hard left used constituency pressure to push Labour MPs to the left. Under Tony Blair the Labour Party has introduced more central direction in choosing candidates. One argument for doing so is that it would promote the adoption of more women candidates in winnable seats; the number of Labour women MPs rose from 37 in 1992 to 101 in 1997. Left-wing Labour activists argued that central direction has been used to purge old style socialists and put in Blair loyalists.

The London headquarters of each party provides more or less routine organizational and publicity services to constituency parties and to the party in Parliament. Each party has an annual conference to debate policy and to vote on some policy resolutions. The Labour Party leader is elected by an electoral college composed of Labour MPs, constituency party members, and trade unions. As part of a drive to prevent criticism of the leadership and public disunity, Tony Blair has created a New Labour Party organization that increases his control of the party and reduces the influence of party activists and trade unions.

The Liberal Democrats have a small central organization, in keeping with their relatively few MPs. Liberal Democrats have sought to build up the party's strength by winning council seats at local government elections and at parliamentary elections, targeting seats where the party is strong locally. In 1997 this strategy paid off, as its share of the national vote fell, while the number of its MPs doubled.

The Conservative Party in Parliament has been separate from the campaigning arm of the party, Conservative Central Office, and local constituency associations. Until 1965, the party leader was not elected but "emerged" as the result of consultation among senior MPs and peers. Following the party's dismal showing in the 1997 election, John Major immediately resigned as party leader. William Hague, a 36-year-old with a precocious political career, was elected by MPs. Hague, a onetime management consultant, cited the party's defeat and the success of New Labour as arguments for introducing a major reorganization of the Conservative Party, giving the leader more power.

The party leader is strongest when he or she is also prime minister. Constitutional principles and Cabinet patronage strengthen a prime minister's hand. Moreover, an open attack on a prime minister threatens electoral defeat as a result of conflict within the party. Blair bluntly told the 1998 party conference that their choice was not between a socialist or a New Labour government, but between his New Labour government or a Conservative government.

Party Images and Appeals

Differences of ideology are often simplified as a left-right scale, with the left representing socialist values and the right the values of Conservatives. While the terminology of left and right is part of the language of elite politicians, it is rejected by the great majority of British voters. When asked to place themselves on a left-right scale, the median voter chooses the central position, and only a tenth place themselves on the far left or far right. Consequently, parties that veer far to one or another extreme risk losing votes.

When public opinion is examined across a variety of issues, such as inflation, protecting the environment, spending money on the health service, and trade union legislation, a majority of Conservative, Labour, and Liberal Democratic voters agree on most issues. Tony Blair has proclaimed the goal of making New Labour a party that is "the political arm of none other than the British people as a whole." In articulating this view, Blair is denying the existence of politics, that is, debate about what the government of the day ought to do. William Hague was elected Conservative leader to make the party appealing to more voters, but his efforts to unite the party by conciliating pro-market and nationalist Conservatives risk losing votes from the more moderate (and larger) section of the electorate. Big divi-

sions in contemporary British politics often cut across party lines, for example, attitudes toward the European Union. On some issues, individuals in all parties are of two minds; for example, people would like more spending on popular social programs such as health and education but without any increase in taxes.

Any attempt to impute a coherent ideology to a political party is doomed to failure, for institutions cannot think, and parties are not organized to debate philosophy but to fight elections. Instead of campaigning in ideological terms or by appealing to collective economic interests in left versus right terms, British parties increasingly stress consensual goals, such as promoting peace and prosperity. They compete in terms of which party or which party leader can best be trusted to do what people want. The titles of election manifestos are virtually interchangeable between the Conservative and Labour parties—and so too is much of their content (see Table 4.4). Parties can appeal in positive terms, promising "the best future for Britain" or "Let's go" or concentrate on dangers posed by their opponents.

In office, the governing party has the votes to enact any parliamentary legislation it wishes, regardless of protests by the opposition. However, most of the legislation introduced by the government is noncontroversial or so popular that the opposition does not dare vote against the bill's principle. For every government bill that the opposition votes against on principle in the House of Commons, three are adopted with interparty agreement.[39] Prior to the 1997 general election, the Labour Party even pledged that it would not immediately alter the spending limits in the budget of the Conservative government. In office, New Labour actually cut income taxes. When traditional Labour supporters complained that New Labour has sacrificed the party's heart in order to win office and administer Thatcherite policies, Blair's government began to boost spending on popular programmes.

The freedom of action of the governing party is also limited by constraints embedded in the obligations of office. Once in office, ministers find that all the laws enacted by their predecessors must be enforced, even if the government of the day would not have enacted them. Civil servants point out that any

TABLE 4.4   Consensual Title of Party Election Manifestos

Year	Conservatives	Labour
1964	Prosperity with a Purpose	Let's Go with Labour
1966	Action, not Words	Time for Decision
1970	A Better Tomorrow	Now Britain's Strong—Let's Make It Great to Live In
1974	Firm Action for a Fair Britain	Let Us Work Together
1974	Putting Britain First	Britain Will Win with Labour
1979	The Conservative Manifesto	The Labour Way Is the Better Way
1983	The Challenge of Our Times	The New Hope for Britain
1987	The Next Moves Forward	Britain Will Win
1992	The Best Future for Britain	Time to Get Britain Working Again
1997	You Can Only Be Sure with the	Because Britain Deserves Better
2001	Time For Common Sense	Ambition For Britain

big change in policy is likely to face big difficulties. A newly elected government also inherits many commitments to foreign countries and to the European Union. As a former Conservative minister said of his Labour successors, "They inherited our problems and our remedies."[40]

Making and Delivering Government Policies

In a unitary state, decisions made by central government are of fundamental importance, for they are binding on all types of public agencies. But for ordinary individuals, the actions of government are tangible only when services are delivered to them in local schools, a doctor's office, or in their community.

Whitehall normally delivers public policies indirectly, adopting laws, laying down standards, and providing money, while responsibility for delivering services is in the hands of a variety of other institutions. The relations between Whitehall and other agencies involve *intra*governmental politics, since non-Whitehall institutions lack the resources and legal powers of state and local government in a federal system such as the United States. The new public administration model is that Whitehall should contract for the delivery of services with local government, the health service, and public or private enterprises. In this model, Whitehall pays for services and the agencies receiving its funds are accountable for delivering services.

Centralization and Its Limits

Most of the policies for which a Cabinet minister answers to the House of Commons are not of his or her choice but are inherited from predecessors of the same or a different party. When the Thatcher administration entered office in 1979, it inherited hundreds of programs and thousands of laws enacted by preceding governments, including some on the statute books since 1760 or earlier. The median law was more than half a century old.[41] In more than a decade, the Thatcher administration introduced dozens of new programs and repealed some inherited from its predecessors and some of its own. Yet when Margaret Thatcher left office, two-thirds of the programs for which the government was responsible were programs such as the national health service, that it had inherited from previous administrations (see Figure 4.8). When expenditure is analyzed, the influence of the "dead hand" of the past is greater still. Only 11 percent of public expenditure was devoted to programs that Thatcher started and almost three-quarters went to programs based on laws enacted before the end of World War II.

Tony Blair's government gives priority to headline-catching statements of intention that attract

FIGURE 4.8   Inheritance of Past Programs and the Scope for Choice

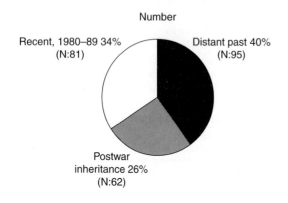

INHERITED PROGRAMS

Number

Recent, 1980–89 34%
(N:81)

Distant past 40%
(N:95)

Postwar
inheritance 26%
(N:62)

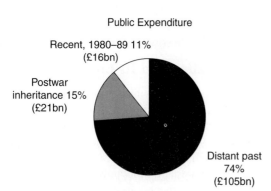

Public Expenditure

Recent, 1980–89 11%
(£16bn)

Postwar
inheritance 15%
(£21bn)

Distant past
74%
(£105bn)

immediate and positive media attention. Its public relations agenda is set a week ahead. But turning such statements of popular intentions into acts of government can take years. To introduce a new policy, it is necessary to run "the Whitehall obstacle race."[42] This takes time, and time is always the scarcest commodity in Ten Downing Street.

To make a headline statement of good intentions a binding government policy, a minister needs to ensure that the prime minister sees a departmental initiative as fitting into the government's overall political strategy. If money is required to finance a new program or boast of increased expenditure on an existing program, the Treasury must authorize this before a bill can be put to Parliament. No Chancellor of the Exchequer wants the political blame for introducing higher taxes to pay for programs that bring popularity to other ministers. Ministers in charge of spending departments dislike constant Treasury reminders that there are strict cash limits on what they can spend and can try to mobilize support from the prime minister, party activists, and the media. However, a veteran Treasury official has argued that no prime minister can ignore the Treasury "because the Treasury stands for reality."[43]

In addition to securing the political support of the prime minister and the Treasury, a minister must negotiate agreement with Whitehall ministers whose programs are affected by proposed changes, with public agencies outside Whitehall, and with affected interest groups. After these negotiations, a minister must pilot a bill through Parliament. While the votes needed to secure passage are assured, if a matter is controversial a minister will face attacks from the Opposition and a host of amendments designed to test the minister's understanding of a policy.

The limit of *centralization* is set by Whitehall's unwillingness to be responsible for delivering major services of the welfare state. The Whitehall tradition is to avoid dirtying its hands with the "low politics" of collecting rubbish or delivering education. Westminster likes to focus upon the glamorous "high" politics of foreign affairs and economic management. To this, Tony Blair has added a desire to "associate" himself with popular concerns, whether about inner city issues or schooling—but to leave the task of delivering policies to agencies at a distance from Downing Street. Most central government expenditure pays for goods and services produced and delivered by public agencies outside Whitehall ministries, and five-sixths of public employees work for non-Whitehall agencies.[44]

Decentralization and Its Limits

There are many reasons why ministers do not want to be in charge of delivering services. Ministers may wish to avoid charges of political interference (for example, tax collection by the Board of Inland Revenue). They may also want to allow flexibility in the market (the Bank of England), lend an aura of im-

Box 4.5 Delivering Public Services on the Doorstep

The growth of government has caused a shift from government in Westminster to delivering public services on the doorstep. Government on the scale that we know it today could not exist if all its activities were concentrated in London, for five-sixths of the country's population lives elsewhere. As the demand for public services has increased, government has grown chiefly through pluralization—that is, the multiplication of familiar institutions delivering such services as primary education and health care.*

Education is an example of the combination of central authority and localized service delivery. It is authorized by an act of Parliament, financed principally by central government, and the minister in charge of education is a Member of Parliament and Cabinet. However, the delivery of primary and secondary education is the responsibility of local government and in-

creasingly of a board of governors of a school. Control of day-to-day activities within the school is in the hands of members of the teaching profession. Central government is increasingly seeking to monitor the performance of schools in nationwide examinations in an effort to get value for money or, its critics say, squeezing expenditure on schools. But since the Department of Education employs only 1 percent of the people working in education, success depends on actions taken by others.

*See Richard Rose, "From Government at the Centre to Government Nationwide," in Y. Meny and V. Wright, eds., *Centre-Periphery Relations in Western Europe* (London: George Allen and Unwin, 1985), pp. 13–32; and Richard Rose, "The Growth of Government Organizations," in C. Campbell and B. G. Peters, eds., *Organizing Government, Governing Organizations* (Pittsburgh: University of Pittsburgh Press, 1988), pp. 99–128.

---

partiality to quasi-judicial activities (the Monopolies Commission), show respect for the extragovernmental origins of an institution (Oxford and Cambridge universities), allow qualified professionals to regulate technical matters (the Royal College of Physicians and Surgeons), or remove controversial matters from Whitehall (the Family Planning Association). Nondepartmental organizations include (1) local and devolved government, (2) executive authorities, (3) administrative tribunals, and (4) advisory committees.

Local government delivers services such as education, police protection, refuse collection, housing, and cemeteries. Collectively, local government accounts for about a fifth of total public expenditure. Elected councils are responsible for these services.[45] Local council elections are fought on party lines. In the days of the two-party system, many cities were solidly Labour for a generation or more, while leafy suburbs and agricultural counties were overwhelmingly Conservative. The Liberal Democrats now win many seats in local elections and can sometimes hold the balance of power, introducing coalition government into town halls. Being a councillor is

usually a part-time job and some payment is made for time spent on local government work.

Within local government, the critical political relationship is between part-time councillors who chair the committees responsible for specific services, such as education or housing, and the full-time professionals who actually undertake the day-to-day administration of local services. Unlike higher civil servants in Whitehall, the chief local government officials are specialists appointed on grounds of expertise, and this is reflected in advice given councillors, whatever their party (see Box 4.5).

The government of the day has the power to rewrite the laws that determine what local government does. In 1972, 1985, and 1996, major Acts of Parliament altered the boundaries of local authorities in a vain search to find a balance between efficiency (assumed to correlate with fewer councils covering more people and more square miles) and responsiveness (assumed to require more councils with a smaller territory and fewer people). The New Labour government assumed that elected mayors are a good way of holding government accountable, and a mayor was elected for Greater London in spring 2000. It claims that elected mayors can strengthen local decision making. Cities such as New York and Chicago are cited as positive examples of elected mayors—but no British government would give local authorities the independence in taxing and spending that American local government enjoys.[46]

Frequent reforms have produced a jumble of institutions. Much of local government is divided into two tiers of county and district councils; there are also some single-tier authorities responsible for all local services. Both Conservative and Labour parties are centralist. The statement—"Local councillors are not necessarily political animals; we could manage without them"—was made by a left-wing law professor.[47]

Central government has great influence on local expenditure. Acts of Parliament make councils responsible for delivering major services, and central government grants and subsidies are the largest source of local government revenue. The Thatcher government replaced the local property tax with a poll tax on every adult living in a local authority; it believed that this would make voters more aware of the costs of local government and keep spending down. In practice, the tax was difficult to implement and produced a political backlash. The Major government was quick to replace the poll tax with a community charge that once again related local taxation to the value of the house as well as to the number of people living there.[48] There is no local income tax, since the central government does not want to give local authorities the degree of fiscal independence that American local government has.

The 1997 New Labour manifesto stated as its general intention, "Local decision-making should be less constrained by central government." But it also stated that the government would "reserve powers to control excessive council tax rises" and its overall expenditure plans left little room for an increase in central government grant. It also made clear its desire to hold local authorities to strict targets of performance. The manifesto expressed a willingness to consider the introduction of a regional tier of government in England—but local councillors, including Labour councillors, oppose

this on the grounds that any powers given regional government would be taken from local authorities, and a regional tier of government would increase bureaucracy.

Devolution has given a degree of autonomy to the delivery of public services in Scotland, Wales, and Northern Ireland. The new Scottish Parliament has the right to enact legislation affecting a large range of social and public services of direct concern to individuals and communities, such as education, health, and roads. It also is responsible for determining spending priorities, but the money spent is allocated by the Treasury. The Welsh Assembly has more administrative discretion, but no legislative or taxing powers. Northern Ireland is exceptional, in that the key service is police and security—and this is kept under the control of British ministers, with the Army and intelligence services in the background.

Both Conservative and Labour politicians justify centralization in terms of *territorial justice*—that is, the same standards of public policy ought to apply everywhere in the country. For example, schools in inner cities and rural areas should have the same standards as those in the suburbs. This can be achieved only if central government tax revenues are redistributed from richer to poorer parts of England. Ministers emphasize that they are accountable to a national electorate of tens of millions of people, whereas local councillors are only accountable to an electorate ranging from tens of thousands to no more than a few hundred thousand. Instead of small being beautiful, bigger electorates are assumed to be better.

Because central government depends on local authorities to deliver programs and local authorities depend on the center for their legal authority and money, the two groups cannot ignore each other. However, when they negotiate, they are unequally matched. The center's control of legislation and finance gives it the power to impose its way.

Executive authorities are responsible for the delivery of many public services outside the framework of ministries or elected local councils. The National Health Service (NHS) is the biggest. Most families contact a doctor at least once a year, and NHS hospitals provide major services from birth to death. The NHS is not one organization but a multiplicity of institutions, of which the most important are hospitals and the doctors and dentists who operate as self-employed professionals, albeit nearly all their income is derived from the NHS and they must work to its guidelines. Access to the national health service is provided without charge to every citizen—a costly undertaking for the government. Because of this, government has sought to hold down costs for treatment. But public spending on health service continues to rise because of the needs of an ageing population, new forms of medical treatment, and the public demand for better health care.

British government also sponsors more than a thousand *Quasi-Autonomous Non-Governmental Organizations (quangos)*. The purposes of quangos differ greatly; some are purely advisers on policy and others deliver public services. All are created by an Act of Parliament or by an executive decision; their heads are appointed by a Cabinet minister; public money can be appropriated to finance their activities; and, when things go wrong, Parliament has difficulty in assigning responsibility for decisions.

Administrative tribunals are quasi-judicial bodies that make expert judgments in such fields as medical negligence or become involved in handling a large number of small claims, such as disputes about whether the rent for a flat is or is not fair. Ministers may use them to avoid involvement in politically controversial issues, such as decisions about deporting immigrants. Tribunals normally work much more quickly and cheaply than the courts. However, the quasi-judicial role of tribunals has created a demand for independent auditing of their procedures, to ensure that they are fair to all sides. The work of supervising some 70 tribunals is in the hands of a quango, the Council on Tribunals.

Advisory committees draw on the expertise of individuals and organizations involved in activities for which Whitehall departments are responsible. Ministry of Agriculture officials can turn to advisory committees for detailed information about farming practices; the Department of Trade and Industry can turn to business associations on general matters of trade and to particular industrial associations and related trade unions for information about the problems of a particular industry. Because they have no executive powers, advisory committees usually cost very little to run. Often their members are unpaid, because attendance at meetings requires little time. Representatives of interest groups are glad to serve because this gives them privileged information about Whitehall and an opportunity to influence government in matters in which they are directly interested.

Turning to the Market

The 1945–1951 Labour government turned away from the market because its Socialist leaders believed that government planning was better able than private enterprise to promote economic growth and full employment. Moreover, trade unions wanted ownership of major industries in the hands of government. The Attlee government nationalized many basic industries, such as electricity, gas, coal, the railways, and airlines. State ownership meant that industries did not have to run at a profit; some consistently made money while others consistently lost money and required big subsidies. Government ownership politicized wage negotiations and investment decisions.

Confronted by soaring financial costs and tired of second-guessing management, the Thatcher government adopted the radical plan of *privatization*, selling shares of nationalized industries on the stock market. Profitmaking industries such as telephones, oil, and gas were sold without difficulty. Selling council houses to tenants at prices well below the market price was popular with tenants. Industries that were losing money, such as British Airways, British Steel, British Rail, and the coal mines had to be reorganized, and unprofitable activities shed to make them attractive to buyers. Industries needing large public subsidies to maintain public services, such as the railways, have continued to receive subsidies after privatization.

Privatization has been justified on grounds of economic efficiency (the market is better than civil servants in determining investment, production, and prices); political ideology (the power of government is reduced); service (private enterprise is more consumer-oriented than are civil servants); and short-term financial gain (revenue from the sale of public assets can provide billions in revenue for government). Although the Labour Party initially opposed privatization, it soon abandoned the idea of spending billions to repurchase privatized industries and realized it would be electorally disastrous to take back from private owners council houses and shares bought at bargain prices.

Government has established new agencies to regulate privatized industries deemed to operate in the public interest. New regulatory agencies supervise privatized firms in telephones, gas, electricity, broadcasting, and water. Regulation is particularly important when there is a substantial element of monopoly in an industry. In such cases the government regulatory agency seeks to promote competition and often has the power to fix price increases at a lower rate than inflation. This forces companies to become more efficient by cutting costs or investing in the development of new services, if they want to increase their profits.

From Trust to Contract

Historically, the British civil service has relied on trust in delivering policies. British civil servants are much more rulebound than their German counterparts and less worried about being dragged into court to justify their actions than are American officials. Intragovernmental relations between Whitehall departments and nationalized industries or representatives of local authorities have been regarded as a process of discussion in which consensual understandings would be arrived at and upheld by all sides without the force of law, or debate and division in Parliament.

However, the Thatcher government considered lengthy deliberations to be inefficient, serving as obstructions to its political goals. It sought to make public administration more "businesslike" in spending public money. Thatcher's *financial management initiative* recommended savings that seemed large in cash terms, totalling billions of pounds over the years—but they constituted far less than 1 percent of the trillions that British government spends in a decade.

The "next steps" initiative has made contracts with independent agencies to undertake the day-to-day delivery of such central government services as automobile licenses, patents, and social security benefits from policymaking agencies. The theory is

that government can obtain the greatest value for money by buying services from the private sector, ranging from cleaning the floors or operating staff canteens in government offices to prison services. In addition, the government has sought to save money on capital expenditure and reduce the size of the public deficit through the private finance initiative, inviting banks and profitmaking companies to loan money for some or all of the costs of investment in public services such as toll bridges that have a capacity to generate revenue.[49]

Government by contract faces political limits because the departmental minister must answer to Parliament when something goes wrong with a service delivered by a contracted agency. The Prison Service is a textbook example. It was established as an executive agency separate from the Home Office in 1993 to bring in private management to reduce unit costs in the face of a rising "demand" for prison services due to changes in crime rates and sentencing policies. However, when prisoners escape and other problems erupt, the Home Secretary has sought to blame the business executive brought in to head the Prison Service. The Prison Service head replies by attacking the minister's refusal to live up to the terms of the contract agreed between them.

The proliferation of many agencies, each with a distinctive and narrow responsibility for a limited number of policies, tends to fragment government. For example, a single parent may have to deal with half a dozen different agencies to secure all the public services to which she or he is entitled. The Blair government has reacted by endorsing the idea of "joined up" government, linking the provision of related services so that they can more effectively and easily be received by citizens. In order to achieve this goal, Whitehall must centralize powers that it has previously contracted out.

The Contingency of Influence

The theory of British government is centralist: All roads lead to Downing Street, the place where the Cabinet meets and where the homes of the prime minister, the Chancellor of the Exchequer, and the chief whip of the parliamentary party are located. The Treasury and the Foreign Office buildings are only a few steps away. In practice, policymaking is multidimensional, for those involved can be divided horizontally between ministries, executive agencies, and other forms of quangos, and vertically between central government and local authorities and other nondepartmental public bodies that deliver services.

Influence is contingent: it varies with the problem at hand. Decisions about war and peace tend to be taken at the very center by the highest-ranking political and military officials. By contrast, decisions about whether a particular piece of land should be used for housing are normally made by local authorities. Most political decisions involve two or more government agencies, and therefore require discussion and bargaining before a decision can be implemented. The making of policy is constrained by disputes within government much more than by differences between the governing party and its opponents. Many tentacles of the octopus of government work against each other, as each public agency claims to represent a significant but conflicting definition of the public interest.

While the center of central government has been pressing harder on other parts of British government, Whitehall itself has been losing influence because of treaty obligations with the European Union. The Single Europe Act promotes British exports, but it also increases the scope for European Union regulation of the British economy. Whitehall has adopted a variety of strategies in its European Union negotiations, including noncooperation and public dispute. Ironically, it is just these tactics that local government and British executive agencies use when they disagree with Whitehall.

Why Public Policy Matters

However she or he votes, an ordinary citizen does not need to look far to see the outputs of government: if there is a school-age child or a pensioner in the house, the benefits to the family are continuous and visible. If a person is ill, the care provided by doctors and hospitals is an important output of public policy; so too are police protection and tight controls of land use that maintain greenery even in urban landscapes. Today the average household annually receives two significant welfare state benefits, such as education, health care, or a pension.

The biggest spending program of British government—social security—is also the most popular, for it transfers money from government to more than 10 million pensioners, plus millions of invalids, the unemployed, women on maternity leave, and poor people needing to supplement their limited resources. The Thatcher government decided that the great bulk of spending could not be cut, for that would mean committing political suicide. The New Labour government of Tony Blair has decided it is seeking to emulate the "Welfare to Work" program of President Clinton and limit the growth of spending on social security. Spending on health and education are its major priorities, and these two programs are second and third in their claim on the public purse. Together, social security, health, and education account for more than half of total public expenditure (see Figure 4.9). Payments on debt interest rank fourth in size. Almost all objects of public expenditure are for programs that cannot easily be

FIGURE 4.9   Tax and Spending, 1995

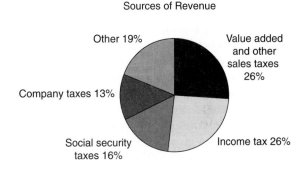

Sources of Revenue

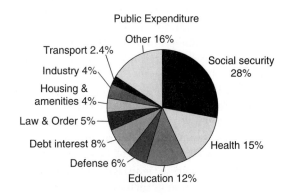

Public Expenditure

Source: *The Government's Annual Report, 99/00.* London: Stationery Office, 2000. p. 58.

TABLE 4.5   Public Preference for More Taxing and Spending Rather Than Less

(in percentages)	1979	1983	1987	1992	1997
Taxing should be cut even if it means some reduction in government services, such as health, education, and welfare.	34	23	12	10	7
Things should be left as they are.	25	22	21	20	18
Government services such as health, education, and welfare should be extended even if it means some increases in taxes.	34	49	61	66	72
Don't know	7	6	5	4	3

Source: Nationwide Gallup Poll surveys, as reported in the *Gallup Political and Economic Index,* No. 441 (May 1997): p. 30.

cut. Defense spending has been falling in relative terms through the years, thus leaving little scope for further cuts. Spending on police and prisons, classic responsibilities of government, is rising. Housing expenditure has been cut but a greater priority is being given to promoting the environment and recreation.

Since there is no item in the public budget labeled as "waste," any government wanting to reduce public spending must squeeze existing programs—and big savings can be made only by squeezing popular programs such as health and education or pensions—and this would risk a big political backlash (see Table 4.5). When Margaret Thatcher entered office in 1979, the public divided almost equally into three groups: (1) those wanting to spend more and tax more, (2) those wanting to cut taxes even if it meant a reduction in public services, and (3) those wanting to leave things as they are. Thatcher's campaign to cut taxes and public spending produced a reaction in favor of public expenditure, so that a majority soon favored taxing and spending more on social programs. By the time Tony Blair became prime minister, 72 percent said they would pay more taxes in order to improve popular government services.

To produce the benefits of public policy, government relies on three major resources: (1) laws, (2) money, and (3) personnel. Most policies involve a combination of these resources, but they do not do so equally. Policies regulating individual behavior, such as marriage and divorce, are law-intensive; measures such as social security, that pay benefits to millions of people, are money-intensive; and the delivery of services such as health care are labor-intensive.

Laws are the unique resource of government, for private enterprises cannot enact laws and the contracts only operate if the laws of the land are respected. The executive of British government is exceptional in its capacity to draft laws and regulations that will be approved without substantial amendment by Parliament. Moreover, many laws give ministers significant discretion in administration. For example, an employer may be required to provide "reasonable" toilet facilities rather than having all features of lavatories specified, down to the size and height of a toilet seat.

Public employees are needed to administer laws and deliver major services. Privatizing public services has reduced the number of people counted as civil servants or public employees, but it has not reduced to the same extent the number who depend on public spending for their job. In total, more than a fifth of the entire British labor force depends on government for their job.

To meet the costs of public policy, British government collects almost 38 percent of the national product in taxation and does so with little tax evasion (see Figure 4.9). Taxes on consumption are important, accounting for more than a quarter of tax revenue. There is a value-added tax of 17.5 percent on the sale of almost all goods and services. Income tax accounts for more than a quarter of taxation. The top rate of taxation is 40 percent; since there are no state or local income taxes, a well-to-do person can be taxed at a lower total rate than a well off person living in New York City. Social security taxes are paid by deductions from wages and additional contributions of employers; these account for an additional sixth of tax revenue. Taxes on the profits of corporations claim an eighth of tax revenue. Since profits fluctuate from year to year, the government prefers to make businesses contribute to social security taxes and act as a collection agency for sales taxes, both larger and more reliable sources of income. Additional revenue is generated by the National Lottery, launched in 1993. While more people play the lottery than vote in a general election, it adds little more than 1 percent to the government's revenue.

Policy Outcomes and Changes in Society

Although living conditions reflect public policy, only a totalitarian regime claims responsibility for everything that happens in society. In an open society such as England, social conditions are a consequence of the interaction of public policies, the national and international economy, the not-for-profit institutions of civil society, and individual and household activities free of state control. The term welfare state is misleading. Total welfare in society is the sum of a "welfare mix," combining actions of government, the market, and the nonmonetized production of welfare in the household.[50]

Defense against threats to security at home and abroad is a unique responsibility of government. In an interdependent world, British government seeks to guarantee national security by participating in international alliances. Britain was a founder member of NATO, and it has sent troops to fight alongside American forces in the Gulf War in 1991 and in Kosovo in 1999. Maintaining order at home also requires the cooperation of others. This is clearest in Northern Ireland, where Whitehall negotiates with leaders of armed paramilitary organizations as well as with elected representatives. Crime prevention depends not only on policing and courts but also on the disposition of people to act illegally. Over the decades the crime rate has been rising, but it remains much lower than in the United States.

Both Conservative and Labour governments accept responsibility for the economy. Most firms are profitmaking, consumers can spend money as they like, and wages and prices are principally decided in the market. Increasingly, what happens to the British economy is also influenced by what happens in other countries of the European Union and on other continents too. Government influences the market through taxing and spending policies, interest rates, and policies for growth and unemployment. However, it cannot isolate the country from what happens elsewhere in the global economy.

In each decade since World War II, the British economy has grown significantly. Compounding a small annual rate of economic growth over many decades cumulatively results in a big rise in living standards. Per capita national income has more than tripled since 1945. Many consumer goods that were once thought of as luxuries, such as owning a car or one's own home, are now mass consumption goods. Things unknown in 1945, such as air travel abroad or VCRs, are now commonplace. Between 1989 and 1999, the 1.9 percent annual rate of growth in the real gross domestic product placed Britain below the median point among 15 member states of the European Union, and well below the American growth rate.

Poverty can be found in Britain; the extent depends on the definition used. If poverty is defined in relative terms such as having less than half the average wage, this is consistent with a rising standard of living in absolute terms. If poverty is defined as being trapped at a low income level for many years, then only 4 percent are long-term poor.

On all the major indicators of social well-being, the British people enjoy a higher standard of living today than a generation ago. Infant mortality has declined by more than four-fifths since 1951. Life expectancy for men and women has risen by 12 years. A gender gap remains, as women on average live four years longer than men. The postwar expansion of schools has significantly raised the quantity of education available. Classes are smaller in size, and upwards of a third of British youths go on to further education, usually in institutions that did not exist in 1950. Two-thirds of families are now home-owners; millions of substandard pre–1914 houses without an indoor toilet or bath have been razed, and nine-tenths report satisfaction with their housing.

The outputs of public policy play a significant part in the everyday life of British people. Everyone makes major use of health and education programs. Children at school or patients seeing a doctor do not think of themselves as participating in politics. Yet the services received are designed and paid for by government. Welfare state benefits—free education, health care, or the guarantee of an income in old age or unemployment—are so taken for granted today that most people see them as nonpolitical. They do not want a change in government after an election to cause radical changes in major social policies.

Popular Expectations

For more than a century, commentators on English society have often bemoaned the relative decline in the country's achievements compared with America, European countries, or now Japan. But ordinary people do not compare their lives with other countries; the most important comparison is with their own past. Evaluating change across time shows great improvements in the living conditions of most English people compared with their parents or grandparents. The longer the time span, the greater the improvements. British government remains an international leader in terms of such basic political goods as freedom of the individual, the absence of corruption, and administrative efficiency and honesty. The great majority of people are proud of the achievements of Britain and would not want to be a citizen of any other country.

Frustration with government shortcomings arises only if people expect a very high level of achievement. In fact, most English people usually do not expect government to succeed, especially in its efforts to manage the economy. This view is supported by experience of past decades. Paradoxically, a government presiding over high unemployment and a slow growth economy would be living up to pessimistic expectations rather than creating political frustrations. When there are low or falling expectations, any time in which the economy does not get worse can be considered a reprieve from expected bad news.

English people do not hold government responsible for what is most important in their lives; they evaluate their personal circumstances differently from public policy. When people are asked each year whether they think next year will be better or worse personally than the preceding year, on nine-tenths of the occasions a majority say they expect the coming year to be all right for themselves, even though many expect economic difficulties for the country as a whole. National prosperity is desirable but not a necessary condition for personal well-being. When people are asked to evaluate their lives, they are most satisfied with their family, friends, home, and job, and least satisfied with major political institutions of society.[51]

Satisfaction with the present goes along with a recognition of change. Most people expect government to make changes; they differ principally about whether changes have gone too far, are about right, or have not gone far enough (see Table 4.6). Tony Blair entered office in 1997 proclaiming a desire to make Britain "new," promoting the Millennium Dome in London as a symbol of a new era but the Dome failed to attract many millions of visitors and became a money-losing embarrassment to the government.

The British people accept change, but not too much. Before New Labour entered government, public opinion surveys asked people what they thought of the tempo of change on major issues: the median person usually replied that it was about right. This is the case for issues as different as modern methods for teaching children and steps to promote equality for women and minorities. The only issue where there is a popular demand for greater change is in the provision of welfare benefits. The average Briton thinks things have gone too far in lowering respect for authority, reducing military force, and sex in the media.

Consistent with his desire to identify with the wishes of all the people. Tony Blair endorses both continuity and change. The New Labour election manifesto opened with a statement that combined pride in the past with the expectation that government should actively promote improvements.

I believe in Britain. It is a great country with a great history. The British people are a great people. But I believe Britain can and must be better.

TABLE 4.6   Evaluation of the Tempo of Change in British Life

	(percentage answering)		
	Gone too far	About right	Not enough
Lowering of respect for authority	62	10	23
Reduction in Britain's military force	55	25	9
Nudity and sex in films, magazines	48	35	10
Going easy on lawbreakers	45	8	44
Modern methods of teaching children	42	22	22
Promotion of equality for minorities	28	32	29
Abortion available national health service	21	42	11
Steps to ensure equality for women	12	39	43
Welfare benefits	21	19	53

Note: Rows do not total to 100 percent because the table does not show those replying "don't know."
Source: Gallup Political and Economic Index, No. 405 (May 1994): pp. 36–37.

✎ KEY TERMS ✎

Cabinet
centralization
class
collectivist theory of government
Conservative Party
Crown
decentralization
devolution
Downing Street
financial management initiative

first-past-the-post electoral system
government
individualist theory
insider and outsider pressure groups
insularity
intermittent public persons
Irish Republican Army (IRA)
Labour Party

Liberal Democrats
mixed economy
Keynesian welfare state
multiparty system
New Labour Party
Northern Ireland
Palace of Westminster
Parliament
prime minister
privatization
Quasi-Autonomous Non-Governmental

Organizations (quangos)
Scotland
state-distancing
territorial justice
Thatcherism
trusteeship theory of government
United Kingdom
unwritten constitution
Wales
Whitehall

✎ SUGGESTED READINGS ✎

Barberis, Peter, ed. *The Whitehall Reader.* Philadelphia: Open University Press, 1996.

Bogdanor, Vernon. *The Monarchy and the Constitution.* Oxford, England: Clarendon Press, 1995.

Butler, D. E., and Geraint Butler. *Twentieth Century British Political Facts, 1900–2000,* 8th ed. London: Macmillan, 2000.

Butler, D. E., and Dennis Kavanagh. *The British General Election of 1997.* Basingstoke, England: Macmillan, 1997.

Evans, Geoffrey, and Pippa Norris, eds. *Critical Elections: British Parties and Voters in Long-Term Perspective.* London: Sage Publications, 1999.

George, Stephen. *An Awkward Partner: Britain in the European Community,* 3rd ed. Oxford, England: Oxford University Press, 1998.

Grant, Wyn. *Pressure Groups and British Politics.* New York: St. Martin's Press, 2000.

Hayward, Jack, B. Barry, and A. Brown, eds. *The British Study of Politics in the Twentieth Century.* Oxford: Oxford University Press, 1999.

Hazell, Robert, ed. *Constitutional Futures: A History of the Next Ten Years.* New York: Oxford University Press, 1999.

James, Simon. *British Cabinet Government,* 2nd ed. New York: Routledge, 1999.

Jordan, Grant, ed. "Protest Politics: Cause Groups and Campaigns," a special issue of *Parliamentary Affairs* 51, No. 3 (1998): 309–485.

Jowell, J., and D. Oliver, eds. *The Changing Constitution*, 3rd ed. Oxford, England: Clarendon Press, 1994.

McLean, Ian. *The Concise Oxford Dictionary of Politics*. New York: Oxford University Press, 1996.

Norris, Pippa. *Electoral Change Since 1945*. Cambridge, MA: Blackwell, 1997.

Norris, Pippa, and Joni Lovenduski. *Political Recruitment: Gender, Race, and Class in the British Parliament*. New York: Cambridge University Press, 1995.

Ridley, F. F., and Michael Rush, eds. *British Government and Politics since 1945*. Oxford, England: Oxford University Press, 1995.

Rose, Richard. *Do Parties Make a Difference?* 2nd ed. Chatham, NJ: Chatham House, 1984.

———. *Ordinary People in Public Policy*. Newbury Park, CA: Sage, 1989.

———. *The Prime Minister in a Shrinking World*. Boston: Polity Press, 2001.

Rose, Richard, and Phillip L. Davies. *Inheritance in Public Policy: Change Without Choice in Britain*. New Haven, CT: Yale University Press, 1994.

Saggar, Shamit, ed. *Race and British Electoral Politics*. London: UCL Press, 1998.

Smith, Martin J. 1999. *The Core Executive in Britain*. London: Macmillan, 1999.

Social Trends. London: Stationery Office, annual.

Whitaker's Almanack. London: J. Whitaker, annual.

Wilson, David, and Chris Game. *Local Government in the United Kingdom*, 2nd ed. Basingstoke: Macmillan, 1998.

www.open.gov.uk

www.parliament.uk/commons

www.pm.gov.uk

www.mori.com (public opinion polls)

✑ Endnotes ✑

1. See Richard Rose, *What Is Europe? A Dynamic Perspective* (New York: Addison Wesley Longman, 1996), Ch. 3.

2. John Kampfner and David Wighton, "Blair Seals Labour's Switch to Low Tax Party." *Financial Times*, March 27, 1997.

3. See Richard Rose, "England: A Traditionally Modern Political Culture," in Lucian W. Pye and Sidney Verba, eds., *Political Culture and Political Development* (Princeton, NJ: Princeton University Press), 1965, pp. 83–129.

4. Quoted in Richard Rose, *Do Parties Make a Difference?* 2nd ed. (Chatham, NJ: Chatham House, 1984).

5. Cf. Andrew Dilnot and Paul Johnson, eds., *Election Briefing 1997* (London: Institute for Fiscal Studies, Commentary 60, 1997), p. 2.

6. Alice Brown, David McCrone, and Lindsay Paterson, *Politics and Society in Scotland*, 2nd ed. (London: Macmillan, 1998).

7. John Kampfner and David Wighton, "Reeling in Scotland to Bring England in Step," *Financial Times*, April 5, 1997.

8. *NOP Social and Political Research*, a nationwide survey of 1,921 respondents, March 17–23, 1995.

9. *Gallup Political and Economic Index*, London No. 390 (February 1993): 42.

10. U.S. Ambassador Raymond Seitz, quoted in Timothy Garton Ash, "Britain? Where's Britain?" *The Independent* (London), June 9, 1994. See also Dean Acheson, "Britain's Independent Role About Played Out," *The Times* (London), December 6, 1962.

11. Quoted in Peter Hennessy, "Raw Politics Decide Procedure in Whitehall," *New Statesman and Nation* (London), October 24, 1986, p. 10.

12. Winston Churchill, *Their Finest Hour* (London: Cassell, 1949), p. 14.

13. See Richard Rose, "A Crisis of Confidence in the Party System or in Individual Leaders." *Contemporary Record* 9, No. 2 (1995): 273–93.

14. Walter Bagehot, *The English Constitution* (London: World's Classics, 1955), p. 9.

15. See Richard Rose, *The Prime Minister in a Shrinking World* (Boston: Polity Press, 2001).

16. Eric Varley, quoted in A. Michie and S. Hoggart, *The Pact* (London: Quartet Books, 1978), p. 13.

17. Hugh Heclo and Aaron Wildavsky, *The Private Government of Public Money* (London: Macmillan, 1974).

18. R. H. S. Crossman, "Introduction to Walter Bagehot," *The English Constitution* (London: Fontana, 1963 edition), pp. 51ff.

19. Bernard Ingham, press secretary to Margaret Thatcher, quoted in Rose, "British Government: The Job at the Top," in R. Rose and E. Suleiman, eds., *Presidents and Prime Ministers* (Washington DC: American Enterprise Institute, 1980), p. 43.

20. L. S. Amery, *Thoughts on the Constitution* (London: Oxford University Press, 1953), p. 21. See also Anthony H. Birch, *Representatives and Responsible Government* (London: George Allen and Unwin, 1964).

21. See Samuel H. Beer, *Modern British Politics*, 3rd ed. (London: Faber and Faber, 1982).

22. House of Commons, *Hansard* (London: Her Majesty's Stationery Office), November 11, 1947, col. 206.

23. Cf. Colin Bennett, "From the Dark to the Light: The Open Government Debate in Britain," *Journal of Public Policy* 5, No. 2 (1985): 209; italics in the original.

24. On the arms for Iraq case and the subsequent independent investigation chaired by Sir Richard Scott, see "Under the Scott-Light," a special issue of *Parliamentary Affairs* 50, No. 1 (1997).

25. Lord Wright, in *Liversidge v. Sir John Anderson and Another*, 1941, quoted in G. Le May, *British Government, 1914–1953* (London: Methuen, 1955), p. 332.

26. See Richard Rose and Ian McAllister, *The Loyalties of Voters* (Newbury Park, CA: 1990), Ch. 3.

27. See Joni Lovenduski and Pippa Norris, eds., "Women in Politics," a special issue of *Parliamentary Affairs*, 49, No. 1 (1996).

28. Rose, *Ordinary People in Public Policy*, Ch. 1.

29. For full discussion, see Geraint Parry, George Moyser, and Neil Day, *Political Participation and Democracy in Britain* (New York: Cambridge University Press, 1992), p. 48ff, and Peter Hall, "Social Capital in Britain," *British Journal of Political Science*, 29, 3, 1999, 417–462.

30. Quoted in Maurice Kogan, *The Politics of Education* (Harmondsworth, England: Penguin, 1971), p. 135.

31. See the Fulton Committee, *Report*, vol. 1, pp. 27ff., and Appendix E, especially p. 162.

32. Anthony Sampson, *Anatomy of Britain* (London: Hodder and Stoughton, 1962), pp. 222–23. See also Peter Riddell, *Honest Opportunism: the Rise of the Career Politician* (London: Hamish Hamilton, 1993).

33. See Rob Baggott, "The Measurement of Change in Pressure Groups," *Talking Politics* 5, No. 1 (1992): 18–22.

34. See W. A. Maloney, G. Jordan, and A. M. McLaughlin, "Interest Groups and Public Policy: The Insider/Outsider Model Revisited," *Journal of Public Policy* 14, No. 1 (1994): 17–38.

35. Tony Blair, *New Britain: My Vision of a Young Country* (London: Fourth Estate, 1996), p. 299.

36. For voting in the era of classic two-party competition, see David Butler and Donald Stokes, *Political Change in Britain*, 2nd ed. (London: Macmillan, 1974).

37. On the internal politics of parties, see Eric Shaw, *The Labour Party Since 1945* (Oxford, England: Blackwell, 1997) and Steve Ludlam and Martin J. Smith, eds., *Contemporary British Conservatism* (Basingstoke, England: Macmillan, 1996).

38. See Patrick Seyd and Paul F. Whiteley, *Labour's Grass Roots: The Politics of Party Membership* (Oxford, England: Clarendon Press, 1992) and Paul Whiteley, Patrick Seyd, and Jeremy Richardson, *True Blues: The Politics of Conservative Party Membership* (Oxford: Clarendon Press, 1994).

39. For details, see Denis Van Mechelen and Richard Rose, *Patterns of Parliamentary Legislation* (Aldershot, England: Gower, 1986), Table 5.2, and more generally, Rose, *Do Parties Make a Difference?*

40. Reginald Maudling, quoted in David Butler and Michael Pinto-Duschinsky, *The British General Election of 1970* (London: Macmillan, 1971), p. 62.

41. Rose and Davies, *Inheritance in Public Policy*, p. 28.

42. Hugh Dalton, *Call Back Yesterday* (London: Muller, 1953), p. 237.

43. Sir Leo Pliatzky, quoted in Peter Hennessy, "The Guilt of the Treasury 1000," *New Statesman*, January 23, 1987.

44. See J. G. Bulpitt, *Territory and Power in the United Kingdom* (Manchester, England: Manchester University Press, 1983) and, for empirical details, Rose, *Ministers and Ministries*, Oxford: Clarendon Press, 1987, Ch. 3.

45. Colin Rallings and Michael Thrasher, *Local Elections in Britain* (Boston: Routledge, 1997).

46. See Paul Peterson, "The American Mayor: Elections and Institutions," *Parliamentary Affairs*, 53, 4, 2000, 667–79.

47. J. A. G. Griffith, *Central Departments and Local Authorities* (London: George Allen and Unwin, 1966), p. 542. Cf. Simon Jenkins, *Accountable to None: The Tory Nationalization of Britain* (Harmondsworth, England: Penguin, 1996).

48. David Butler, Andrew Adonis, and Tony Travers, *Failure in British Government: The Politics of the Poll Tax* (Oxford, England: Oxford University Press, 1994).

49. Cf. David Farnham and Sylvia Horton, eds., *Managing the New Public Services*, 2nd ed. (Basingstoke, England: Macmillan, 1996); and Kieran Walsh, *Public Services and Market Mechanisms* (Basingstoke, England: Macmillan, 1995).

50. See Richard Rose, "The Dynamics of the Welfare Mix in Britain," in Richard Rose and Rei Shiratori, eds., *The Welfare State East and West* (New York: Oxford University Press, 1986), pp. 80–106.

51. Rose, *Ordinary People on Public Policy*, pp. 175ff.

FRANCE

| 0 | 75 | 150 mi |
| 0 | 120 | 240 km |

NORTH SEA

UNITED KINGDOM

NETHER-LANDS

GERMANY

Rhine

LUXEMBOURG

BELGIUM

Lille •
NORD

Paris
RÉGION
PARISIENNE

HAUTE

PICARDIE

LORRAINE

ALSACE

LIECHTENSTEIN

English Channel

Seine

CHAMPAGNE

BASSE

BRETAGNE

PAYS DE'
LA LOIRE

Loire

CENTRE

BOURGOGNE

FRANCHE-
COMTE

SWITZERLAND

Nantes

POITOU-
CHARENTE

Clermont-
Ferrand

Lyon

Grenoble

ITALY

LIMOUSIN

Bay of Biscay

AUVERGNE

RHÔNE-
ALPES

Bordeaux •

Garonne

AQUITAINE

MIDI-
PYRÉNÉES

Rhone

Toulouse

LANGUEDOC

PROVENCE-
ALPES-CÔTE
D' AZUR

Nice

MONACO

Marseille

Toulon

N

CORSE

Corsica

ANDORRA

MEDITERRANEAN
SEA

SPAIN

Sardinia

CHAPTER 5

POLITICS IN FRANCE

MARTIN A. SCHAIN

Country Bio–France

POPULATION   59 Million

TERRITORY   211,208 sq. mi

YEAR OF INDEPENDENCE   486

YEAR OF CURRENT CONSTITUTION   1958

HEAD OF STATE   President Jacques Chirac

HEAD OF GOVERNMENT   Prime Minister Lionel Jospin

LANGUAGE(S) FRENCH   100%, rapidly declining regional dialects and languages (Provencal, Breton, Alsatian, Corsican, Catalan, Basque, Flemish)

RELIGION   Roman Catholic 90%, Protestant 2%, Jewish 1%, Muslim 1%, unaffiliated 6%

On May 7, 1995, Jacques Chirac was elected the fifth president of France's Fifth Republic, marking the end of François Mitterrand's presidency, the longest in the history of the five French republics. The Chirac era, however, proved to be short-lived. After a tumultuous two years, marked by only partially successful attempts to cut back on public spending (despite an 80 percent majority in the National Assembly) and some of the largest strike movements since 1968, the president decided to call surprise legislative elections in May 1997. Chirac's gamble proved to be ill-conceived, and by June a coalition of the left led by Socialist Lionel Jospin (who had lost to Chirac in 1995) took power. Although Jacques Chirac remains president until 2002, Lionel Jospin will likely run the country as prime minister for the same period.

This was the third change of government coalition since 1993. Nevertheless, French citizens now appear to have more confidence in the key institutions of the Republic than they have had at any time in French history, although increasingly they have little confidence in the politicians who are running them. The stability of the Republic has surprised many of the French as well as the outside world. By combining two models of democratic government, the presidential and the parliamentary, the *Fifth*

Republic has succeeded in a constitutional experiment that now serves France well. For the first time since the French Revolution, there is no important political party or sector of public opinion that challenges the legitimacy of the regime.

Does this mean No reason to revolt?

Current Policy Challenges

At a time in American history when political parties have been deeply divided and the party system highly polarized, and when national government often seems to be immobilized by divided government, French politics seem almost tranquil by comparison. The French have lived with divided government ("cohabitation") for most of the period since 1986 without impeding decision-making effectiveness and without undermining institutional legitimacy. At the same time, the French electorate is clearly concerned about many of the same issues that have concerned Americans during the past decade. French voters are most worried about high unemployment rates that are more than twice U.S. rates. Anxiety about unemployment is related to deep concern in France about the consequences of European monetary union, a concern that was only exacerbated by the falling value of the Euro during the year after its establishment. In every national election since 1981, voters have demonstrated their dissatisfaction by rejecting the government in power. They are also concerned about political corruption at every level. Hardly a month passes without a politician being accused of corrupt practices, or another being tried or jailed.

Increasingly, French voters and governments are disturbed by rising crime levels and the problems of urban violence. In France, these problems are frequently referred to as problems of the "suburbs," since impoverished neighborhoods, frequently with large immigrant populations, are often found in the old working-class suburbs that surround large cities. These concerns were related to the rise of an extreme right party, and its increasing importance between 1983 and 1999. Until the party split in early 1999, the electoral importance of the National Front—an anti-immigrant party that advocated strong nationalism—tended to undermined the stability of the parties of the center-right

French Rev

and support anti-immigrant and racist sentiments among the electorate as a whole. Although the party never held power at the national level, it maintained strong and growing influence over the political agenda until conflict among its leaders resulted in the division of the party.

We should emphasize, however, that many of the issues that are at the heart of American politics today are of little concern to the French electorate. French voters are not at all interested in the private lives of their political leaders. Nor is there much concern among voters about the size of the state. There have been considerable efforts in the past decade to reduce the level of public spending, but there is no support for massive cuts in welfare state programs, which have always been more extensive in France than in the United States. In fact, recent surveys indicate that French voters are willing to sacrifice a great deal to maintain these programs as well as high levels of state-subsidized social security and long vacations. On the other hand, unlike their American counterparts, French voters have been deeply concerned about the environmental and health consequences of genetically modified organisms.

A Historical Perspective

France is one of the oldest nation-states of Europe. The period of unstable revolutionary regimes that followed the storming of the Bastille in 1789 ended in the seizure of power by *Napoléon Bonaparte* a decade later. The French Revolution began with the establishment of a constitutional monarchy in 1791 (the First Republic), but the monarchy was overthrown the following year, and three more constitutions preceded Napoleon's seizure of power on the eighteenth day of the revolutionary month of Brumaire (November 10, 1799) and the establishment of the First Empire three years later. The other European powers formed an alliance and forced Napoleon's surrender as well as the restoration of the Bourbon monarchy. Another revolution in 1830 drove the last Bourbon from the French throne and replaced him with Louis Philippe of the House of Orléans, who promised a more moderate rule bounded by a new constitution.

Growing dissatisfaction among the rising bourgeoisie and the urban population produced still another Paris revolution in 1848. With it came the proclamation of the Second Republic (1848–1852) and universal male suffrage. Conflict between its middle-class and lower-class components, however, kept the republican government ineffective, and out of the disorder rose another Napoléon, nephew of the first emperor. Louis Napoléon, crowned Napoléon III in 1852, brought stability to France for more than a decade, but his last years were marked by growing indecision and ill-conceived foreign ventures. His defeat and capture in the Franco-Prussian War (1870) began another turbulent period: France was occupied and forced into a humiliating armistice; radicals in Paris proclaimed the Paris Commune, which held out for two months in 1871, until crushed by the conservative French government forces. In the commune's aftermath, the struggle between republicans and monarchists led to the establishment of a conservative Third Republic in 1871 and to a new constitution in 1875. The Third Republic proved to be the longest regime in modern France, surviving World War I and lasting until France's defeat and occupation by Nazi Germany in 1940.

World War II deeply divided France. A defeated France was divided into a zone occupied by the Germans, while a French government sympathetic to the Germans, lead by Marshall Pétain, governed a "free" zone in the southern half of the country from Vichy. From July 1940 until August 1944 the government of France was a dictatorship. Slowly, a resistance movement that rejected the new order began to emerge under the leadership of General *Charles de Gaulle* and gained greater strength and support after the Allied invasion of North Africa and the German occupation of the "free" zone at the end of 1942. When German forces were driven from occupied Paris in 1944, de Gaulle entered the city with the hope that sweeping reforms would give France the viable democracy it had long sought. After less than two years, he resigned as head of the Provisional Government, impatient as he was with the country's return to traditional party politics.

In fact, the *Fourth Republic* (1946–1958) disappointed earlier hopes. Governments fell with disturbing regularity—24 governments in 12 years. At the same time, because of the narrowness of government coalitions, the same parties and the same leaders tended to participate in most of these governments. Weak leadership had great difficulty coping with the tensions created first by the Cold War, then the French war in Indochina, and finally the anticolonialist uprising in Algeria. When a threat of civil war arose over Algeria in 1958, a group of party leaders invited General de Gaulle to return to power and help the country establish stronger and more stable institutions. Since then France has lived under the constitution of the Fifth Republic, enacted by a referendum in 1958. De Gaulle was the last prime minister of the Fourth Republic, then the first president of the newly established Fifth Republic.

Economy and Society

Geographically, France is at once Atlantic, Continental, and Mediterranean; hence, it occupies a unique place in Europe. In 1999 a total of 58.9 million people, about one-fourth as many as the population of the United States, lived in an area one-fifteenth the size of the United States. It is estimated that more than 3.6 million foreigners (noncitizens) live in France, more than half of whom come from outside of Europe, mostly from North Africa and Africa. In addition, 1.8 million French citizens are foreign-born. Thus 9.2 percent of the French population is foreign-born, about the same proportion as in the United States.

Urbanization has come slowly to France, in contrast to its neighbors, but it is now highly urbanized. In 1936 only 16 French cities had a population of more than 100,000; they now number 36. Five cities have a population of more than 300,000. Compared with European countries with similar population (Britain and Germany), France has relatively few large cities; only Paris has more than a million people. Yet in 1999, 44 million people (three-quarters of the population) lived in urban areas, compared with half that number in 1936.

More than one-fifth of the urban population—more than one-sixth of the entire nation and growing—lives in the metropolitan region of Paris. This concentration of people creates staggering problems.

In a country with centuries-old traditions of administrative, economic, and cultural centralization, it has produced a dramatic gap in human and material resources between Paris and the rest of the country. The Paris region supports a per capita income about 45 percent higher and unemployment 15 to 17 percent lower than the national average. But the Paris region also has the highest concentration of foreigners in the country (twice the national percentage), and there are deep divisions between the wealthier and poorer towns that comprise the region.

Overall, French economic development, compared with other advanced industrial countries, has been respectable in the recent past. In per capita gross domestic product (GDP), France ranks among the wealthiest nations of the world, behind the Scandinavian countries, only slightly behind the United States and Germany and well ahead of Britain and Italy (see Chapter 1). During the 1980s, the French economy grew at about the European average but with an inflation rate at half the European average. During this same period, unemployment hovered around 10 percent, slightly above the European average. The unemployment rate declined between 1987 and 1990, but then began to increase rapidly after 1990. After the legislative elections in 1997, unemployment dipped again, as the French economy succeeded in creating new jobs once again. Nevertheless, in 1999, with an unemployment rate of 11.8 percent (about 1 percent higher than the average for the European Union), France was experiencing some of the same problems as some of the poorer countries of Europe: long-term youth unemployment, homelessness, and a drain on social services. Most troubling was the level of long-term unemployment (more than one year), almost 40 percent of those unemployed, and its concentration among young people (19 percent) attempting to enter the labor market.

The labor force has changed drastically since the end of World War II, in ways that have made France similar to other industrialized countries. During the decade of the 1990s, the labor force grew by more than 1.6 million, continuing a growth trend that was greater than in most European countries. Most of these new arrivals were young people, and an increasing proportion of them were women.

For over a century, the proportion of employed women—mostly in agriculture, artisan shops, and factories—was higher in France than in most European countries. Today, most women work in offices in the service sector of the economy. In 1954 women comprised 35 percent of the labor force; today, they make up 45 percent of a much larger labor force. The proportion of French women working (48 percent) is slightly lower than that of the United States but one of the highest in Western Europe.

In 1938, 37 percent of French labor was employed in agriculture; this proportion was down to 4.7 percent in 1998, and it is still declining. The percentage of the labor force employed in industry was down to about 24 percent in 1998, while employment in the service sector rose from 33 percent in 1938 to 71 percent today, somewhat smaller than the United States, and slightly above the average for Western Europe.

By comparison with other highly developed industrial countries, the agricultural sector of France remains important both economically and politically. France has more cultivated acreage than any other country in the European Union. In spite of the sharp decline in the proportion of the population engaged in agriculture, agricultural production has increased massively during the past quarter century. Throughout the 1990s, France has been a top producer and exporter of key agricultural products in Europe (meat, milk, and cereals for example), and earnings from agricultural exports have continued to grow during the past decade. But this impressive performance hides the fact that, although the income of farmers is, on the average, about equal to that of a middle-level executive, the disparity of income between the smallest and largest farms is greater than in any other country in the European Union. Nevertheless, French farm incomes have been generally higher and more stable than in most EU countries.

Because the political stability of the Third Republic depended on a large and stable peasantry, French agriculture was supported with protective tariffs that helped French farmers (and small businesses) cling to their established routines. Since 1945 there have been serious efforts to modernize agriculture. More attention was paid to the possible advantages of farm cooperatives; marginal farms were consolidated; technical education has been vastly improved; and further mechanization and experimentation are being used as avenues for long-range structural reforms. Particularly after the development of the Common Agriculture Policy (CAP) in the European Community between 1962 and 1968, consolidation of farmland proceeded rapidly. By 1985 the mean size of a French farm was larger than that of any country in Europe except Britain, Denmark, and Luxembourg.

A large proportion of the bill for agricultural modernization has been paid by subsidies from the European Union, and subsidies have increased steadily since 1967. As a result, there have been pressures (particularly from the British) to reduce CAP expenditures and to deal with the factors that increase them. With the prospect of the enlargement, and the incorporation of more countries in Eastern Europe with large agricultural sectors, these pressures have been augmented during the past few years. In addition to requiring the withdrawal of more land from production, major reforms in 1992, 1994, and 1999 at the European level have gradually moved subsidies away from price supports (that encourage greater production) and toward direct support of farm income. Nevertheless, subsidies to French farmers increased substantially in the 1990s.

French business has been both highly dispersed and highly concentrated. Even after three decades of structural reorganization of business, about half of the 2.4 million industrial and commercial enterprises in France belong to individuals. In 1999, 54 percent of the salaried workers in the country worked in small enterprises with fewer than 50 workers, and, as in other advanced industrial societies, this proportion has been slowly increasing, primarily because of the movement of labor into the service sector.

Nevertheless, from the perspective of production, some of the most advanced French industries are highly concentrated, and the few firms at the top account for most of the employment and business turnover. Even in some of the older sectors (such as automobile manufacture, ship construction, and rubber), half or more of the employment and busi-

ness turnover is concentrated in the top four firms. Among the 200 largest industrial groups in the world in 1997, 21 were located in France, about the same as in Germany.

The organization of industry and commerce in France changed significantly during the decade of the 1990s. In 1997, among the top 20 enterprises in France, only 4 were public, compared with 13 ten years before. During this decade, the process of privatization had reduced the number of public enterprises by 24 percent and the number of those working in those enterprises by 31 percent. To the managerial elite trained in the "grandes écoles" were added a more diverse group of entrepreneurs who had ascended during the period of Socialist governments. Nevertheless, despite a continuing process of privatization, relations between industry and the state have remained close.

Constitution and Governmental Structure

The *Constitution of 1958* is the sixteenth since the fall of the Bastille in 1789. Past republican regimes, known less for their achievements than for their instability, were invariably based on the principle that Parliament could overturn a government no longer backed by a majority of the elected representatives. Such an arrangement can work satisfactorily, as it does in most of Western Europe, when the country (and Parliament) embrace two—or a few—well-organized parties. The party or the coalition that gains a majority at the polls forms the government and can count on the almost unconditional support of its members in Parliament until the next elections. At that time, it is either kept in power or replaced by an equally disciplined party or coalition of parties.

The Executive

Why France never had the disciplined parties necessary for such a system will be explained in this chapter. The point for now is that the constitution that General de Gaulle submitted for popular approval in 1958 offered to remedy previous failings. In preceding republics the president was little more than a figurehead. According to the new constitution, the *president of the Republic* was to become a visible head of state. He was to be placed "above the parties" to represent the unity of the national community. As guardian of the constitution, he was to be an arbiter who would rely on other powers—Parliament, the Cabinet, or the people—for the full weight of government action. He would have the option of appealing to the people in two ways. With the agreement of the government or Parliament, he could submit certain important pieces of legislation to the electorate as a referendum, and, after consulting with the prime minister and the parliamentary leaders, he could dissolve Parliament and call for new elections. In case of grave threat "to the institutions of the Republic," the president also had the option of invoking emergency powers.

Virtually all of the most powerful constitutional powers of the president—those that give the president formal power—have been used sparingly. Emergency powers were used only once (by General de Gaulle in 1961), when the rebellion of the generals in Algiers clearly justified such use. The mutiny collapsed after a few days, not because a constitutional provision provided residual powers but because de Gaulle's authority was unimpaired and hence left the rebels isolated and impotent. President de Gaulle dissolved Parliament twice (in 1962 and 1968), each time to exploit a political opportunity to strengthen the majority supporting presidential policies (see Figure 5.1).

Upon his election to the presidency in 1981, the Socialist François Mitterrand dissolved the National Assembly, and did so again after his reelection seven years later, in order to open the way for parliamentary elections. Because of the political momentum of Mitterrand's victories as a presidential candidate, he expected that early parliamentary elections would provide him with reliable majorities in the National Assembly. Finally, President Jacques Chirac dissolved the National Assembly in April 1997 in an attempt to extend the conservative majority into the next century and to gain political support for the reduction of public spending. The president lost his gamble.

The legitimacy and political authority of the president have been greatly augmented by popular elections. According to the 1958 constitution, the president was to be elected indirectly by a college comprised mostly of local government officials. In

FIGURE 5.1   French Presidents and Prime Ministers since 1958

PRIME MINISTER	YEAR	PRESIDENT
Lionel Jospin	1997	
Alain Juppé	1995	Jacques Chirac
Edouard Balladur	1993	
Pierre Bérégovoy	1992	
Edith Cresson	1991	
Michel Rocard	1988	
Jacques Chirac	1986	
Laurent Fabius	1984	
Pierre Mauroy	1981	François Mitterrand
Raymond Barre	1976	
Jacques Chirac	1974	Valéry Giscard d'Estaing
Pierre Messmer	1972	
Jacques Chaban-Delmas	1969	Georges Pompidou
Maurice Couve de Murville	1968	
Georges Pompidou	1962	
Michel Debré	1958	Charles De Gaulle

1962, however, a constitutional amendment by referendum replaced the original design with a system of popular election of the president for a renewable term of seven years; in September 2000, the presidential term was reduced to five years—once again by constitutional amendment—a term that would coincide with the normal legislative mandate beginning in 2002. At present, France is one of six countries in Western Europe to select its president by direct popular vote; the others are Portugal, Ireland, Austria, Iceland, and Finland.

President de Gaulle outlined his view of the office when he said that power "emanates directly from the people, which implies that the Head of State, elected by the nation, is the source and holder of this power." Every president who has succeeded de Gaulle has maintained the general's basic interpretation of the office, but there have been some changes in the way the presidency has functioned (for details, see pages 000–000).

The *prime minister*, appointed by the president, has been responsible for the day-to-day running of the government, but the division of responsibility between the president and his prime minister varies not only with the personalities of those who hold each of the executive offices but also with the conditions under which the prime minister serves.

The Legislature

The legislature is composed of two houses: the *National Assembly* and the *Senate* (see Figure 5.2). The National Assembly is elected directly for five years by all citizens over 18; it may be dissolved at any

FIGURE 5.2 Structure of the French Government

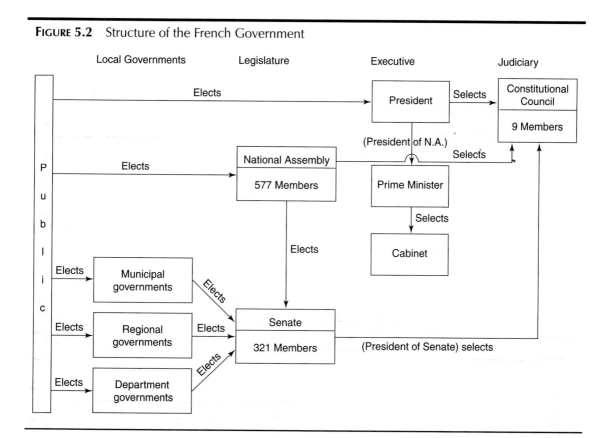

time, though not twice within one year. The instability of previous regimes had been attributed mostly to the constant meddling of Parliament with the activities of the executive. The Constitution of 1958 strove to put an end to the subordination of government to Parliament. It imposed strict rules of behavior on each deputy and on Parliament as a body. These requirements, it was hoped, would ensure the needed equilibrium.

Now the government, rather than the legislature, is in control of proceedings in both houses and can require priority for bills it wishes to promote. The president rather than the prime minister generally chooses the Cabinet members. Parliament still enacts laws, but the domain of such laws is strictly defined. Many areas of modern life that in other democracies are regulated by laws debated and approved by Parliament are turned over to rule making by the executive in France.

The 19 standing committees of the National Assembly under the Fourth Republic were reduced to six and the committees were enlarged to about 73 to 145 members to prevent interaction among highly specialized deputies who could become effective rivals of the ministers. Each deputy is restricted to one committee, and party groups are represented in each committee in proportion to their size in the National Assembly.

It is not surprising that the new constitution spelled out in detail the conditions under which the National Assembly could overthrow a government. An explicit motion of censure must be formulated and passed by more than one-half of the members of the house. Even after a motion of censure is passed, the government may resist the pressure to resign: The president can dissolve the Assembly and call for new elections. During the first year after these elections, a new dissolution of Parliament is prohibited by the constitution. The vote of censure is the only way Parliament can condemn the conduct of government, but no government has been censured since 1962. Since that time every government has had a working (if not always friendly) majority in the National Assembly.

The National Assembly, whose 577 members are elected for five years, shares legislative functions with the Senate. Not only in France, but in all countries without a federal structure, the problem of how to organize a bicameral legislature is complex. How should the membership of the second chamber be defined if there are no territorial units to be represented? The 321 members of the Senate (the "upper house") are elected indirectly for a term of nine years (one-third every three years) by an electoral college of less than 50,000 representatives from municipal, departmental, and regional councils in which rural constituencies are overrepresented. The upper house has the right to initiate legislation and must consider all bills adopted by the National Assembly. If the two houses disagree on pending legislation, the government can appoint a joint committee. If the views of the two houses are not reconciled, the government may resubmit the bill (either the original bill or as amended by the Senate) to the National Assembly for a definitive vote (Article 45). Therefore, unlike the United States, the two houses are not equal in either power or influence (see again Figure 5.2).

The Judiciary

Until the Fifth Republic, France had no judicial check on the constitutionality of the actions of its political authorities. The *Constitutional Council* was originally conceived primarily as a safeguard against any legislative erosion of the constraints that the constitution has placed on the prerogatives of Parliament.[1] In part because of a constitutional amendment in 1974, however, the council has played an increasingly important role in the legislative process (see pp. 000–000).

Political Culture

Themes of Political Culture

THE BURDEN OF HISTORY Historical thinking can prove both a bond and—as the American Civil War demonstrates—a hindrance to consensus. The French are so fascinated by their own history that feuds of the past are constantly superimposed on the conflicts of the present. This passionate use of historical memories, resulting in seemingly inflexible ambitions, warnings, and taboos, complicates political decision making. In de Gaulle's words, France is "weighed down by history."

ABSTRACTION AND SYMBOLISM   In the Age of Enlightenment the monarchy left the educated classes free to voice their views on many topics, provided the discussion remained general and abstract. The urge to discuss a wide range of problems, even trivial ones, in broad philosophical terms has hardly diminished. The exaltation of the abstract is reflected in the significance attributed to symbols and rituals. Rural communities that fought on opposite sides in the French Revolution still pay homage to different heroes, two centuries later. They seem to have no real quarrel with each other, but inherited symbols and their political and religious habits have kept them apart.[2] This tradition helps explain why a nation united by almost universal admiration for a common historical experience holds to conflicting interpretations of its meaning.

DISTRUST OF GOVERNMENT AND POLITICS   The French have long shared in the widespread ambivalence of modern times that combines distrust of government with high expectations from it. The French citizens' simultaneous distrust of authority and craving for it fed on both individualism and a passion for equality. This attitude has produced a self-reliant individual convinced that he was responsible to himself, and perhaps to his family, for what he was and might become. Obstacles were created by the outside world, the "they" who operate beyond the circle of the family, the family firm, the village. Most of the time, however, "they" were identified with the government.

Memories reaching back to the eighteenth century justified a state of mind that was potentially, if seldom overtly, insubordinate. A strong government was considered to be reactionary by nature, even if it pretended to be progressive. When citizens participated in public life, they hoped to weaken governmental authority rather than encourage change, even when change was overdue. At times this individualism was tainted with anarchism. Yet the French also accommodated themselves rather easily to bureaucratic rule. Since administrative rulings supposedly treat all situations with the same yard-

stick, they satisfy the sharp sense of equality possessed by a people who have felt forever short-changed by the government and by the privileges those in power bestow on others.

Even though the Revolution of 1789 did not break with the past as completely as is commonly believed, it conditioned the general outlook on crisis and compromise, continuity and change. Sudden change rather than gradual mutation, dramatic conflicts couched in the language of mutually exclusive, radical ideologies—these are the experiences that have excited the French at historical moments when their minds were particularly malleable. In fact, what appears to the outsider as permanent instability is a fairly regular alternation between brief violent crises and prolonged periods of routine. The French are accustomed to thinking that no thorough change can ever be brought about except by a major upheaval. Since the great revolution, every French adult has experienced—usually more than once—occasions of political excitement followed by disappointment. This process has led at times to moral exhaustion and widespread skepticism about any possibility of change.

Whether they originated within the country or were brought about by international conflict, most of France's political crises have resulted in a constitutional crisis. Each time, the triumphant forces have codified their norms and philosophy, usually in a comprehensive document. This history explains why constitutions have never played the role of fundamental charters. Prior to the Fifth Republic, their norms were satisfactory to only one segment of the polity and hotly contested by others.

In the years immediately following 1958, the reaction to the constitution of the Fifth Republic resembled that to other constitutions in France. Support for its institutions was generally limited to voters who supported the governments of the day. This began to change after 1962, with the popular election of the president. The election of Mitterrand to the presidency in 1981, and the peaceful transfer of power from a right to a left majority in the National Assembly, laid to rest the 200-year-old constitutional debate among French elites, and proved to be the capstone of acceptance of the institutions of the Fifth Republic among the masses of French citizens.

Confidence in institutions, which has been relatively strong, has tended to vary with the perceived closeness of institutions to the daily lives of people. When French people are asked in which institutions they have the most confidence, they invariably give the highest ratings to local officials, rather than to political parties or national representatives (see Figure 5.3). In recent years distrust in government officials has been high, but expectations of government remain high as well.

Religious and Antireligious Traditions

France is at once a Catholic country—73 percent of the French population identified themselves as Catholic in 1997 (87 percent in 1974)—and a country that the Church itself considers as "dechristianized." Of those who describe themselves as Catholic, only 12 percent attend mass regularly (down from 21 percent in 1974), and 83 percent either never go to church at all or go only occasionally, for such ceremonies as baptism or marriage.[3]

Until well into the present century, the mutual hostility between believers and nonbelievers was one of the main features of the political culture. Since the Revolution, it has divided society and political life at all levels. Even now, there are important differences between the political behavior of practicing Catholics and nonbelievers.

French Catholics viewed the Revolution of 1789 as the work of satanic men, and enemies of the Church became militant in their opposition to Catholic forms and symbols. This division continued through the nineteenth century. With the establishment of the Third Republic in 1875, differences between the political subcultures of Catholicism and anticlericalism deepened further. After a few years, militant anti-clericalism took firm control of the Republic. Parliament rescinded the centuries-old

FIGURE 5.3   Feelings of Confidence in Various Political Institutions

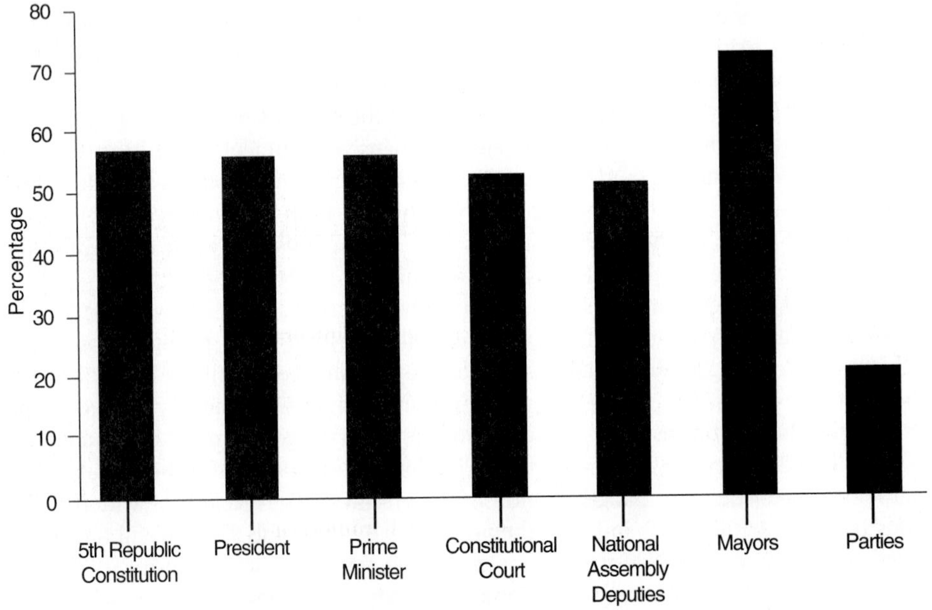

Source: Sofres, *L'etat de l'opinion 1994* (Paris: Editions du Seuil, 1994), p. 235.

compact with the Vatican, expelled most Catholic orders, and severed all ties between church and state, so that "the moral unity of the country could be reestablished." The militancy of the Republican regime was matched by the Pope, who excommunicated every deputy who voted for the separation laws in 1905. Faithful Catholics were driven to the view that only the overthrow of the regime could overcome their isolation. As in other European Catholic countries, the difference between the political right and left was largely determined by attitudes toward the Catholic Church. Nonetheless, for a total of 60 years (1879–1939), with rare exceptions, no practicing Catholic obtained Cabinet rank in any of the numerous ministries, even those dominated by the right.

The gap began to narrow during the inter-war period and after Catholics and agnostics found themselves side by side, and sometimes joined together, in the resistance movement during World War II. Leftist movements and, more recently, the Socialist Party have attracted a large number of young Catholics, even though the depth of religious practice continues to be the best predictor—with remarkable stability—of whether a voter will support an established party of the right.

Religious practice has been declining in all industrialized countries since the 1950s, and, in France, the space of the Catholic world has been shrinking, in some ways quite dramatically, since the 1960s. Religious practice has declined among all social groups in France, but it has declined the most among those groups that were the most observant. Farmers have been, by far, the most observant group in France, but their church attendance in 1997 was only 23 percent. Blue-collar workers, for most of this century, have been the least observant: Now only 4 percent admit to attending church regularly. The estrangement between the working class and the Church, which occurred in France as in other countries of Continental Europe during the early stages of industrialization, contributed to the class consciousness of the workers and to making a majority of them into followers of radical rather than conservative parties. The legacy of this estrangement remains a central fact of French reli-

gious, cultural, and, to a considerable extent, political life.

What we have presented so far does not convey the important changes that have taken place within the Catholic subculture. Today, the vast majority of those who identify themselves as Catholics reject some of the most important teachings of the Church, including its positions on abortion, premarital sex, and marriage of priests. Even among regularly practicing Catholics, there is considerable opposition to the positions of the Church. Only 16 percent of identified Catholics perceive the role of the Church as important in political life, and Catholicism no longer functions as a well-integrated community, with a common view of the world and common social values. In the 1990s, the Catholic Church has been ordaining only 20 percent of the number of priests it ordained in the early 1960s. There are now fewer than 30,000 priests in France, an insufficient number to serve many dioceses.

Most private schools in France are Catholic parochial schools, which have been subsidized by the state since the Fourth Republic. The status of these schools (in a country in which state support for Catholic schools, attended by 17 percent of French students, coexists with the separation of church and state) has never been fully settled. In 1998, 10 percent of primary schools, but 32 percent of secondary schools, were private. Although church attendance continues to decline, events during the 1980s indicate that there remains considerable support for parochial education.

French Jews (numbering about 700,000 or 1.3 percent of the population since the exodus that followed Algerian independence in 1962) have been sufficiently well integrated into French society so that it is not possible to speak of a Jewish vote. One recent study demonstrates that, like other French voters, Jews tend to vote left or right, according to degree of religious practice. Nevertheless, Jews have consistently supported the Republic. Protestants (just under 1 million or 1.7 percent of the population and growing) have, at least until recently, lived somewhat apart, with heavy concentrations in Alsace, in the Paris metropolitan area, and in some regions of central and southeastern France. About two-thirds of Protestants belong to the upper bourgeoisie. The proportion of Protestants in high public positions has been very large. Until recently, they usually voted more leftist than others in their socioeconomic position or in the same region. Although many Protestants have been prominent in the Socialist Party, since the 1950s their electoral behavior, like their activities in cultural and economic associations, has been determined by factors other than religion.

Islam is now France's second religion. One scholar has estimated that there are now as many as 3 million *Muslims* in France, two-thirds of whom are immigrants from Muslim countries. The emergence and growth of Islamic institutions in France has been part of a larger phenomenon of the integration of the new immigration into France. In the last decade the affirmation of religious identification coincided with (and to some extent was a part of) the social and political mobilization and organization of immigrants from Muslim countries. There are now over a thousand mosques in France, as well as another thousand rooms set aside for prayer.

The emergence of Islam has challenged the traditional French view of the separation of church and state. Unlike Catholics, who have insisted on the right to maintain their own schools, or Protestants, who have supported the principle of secular state schools, some Muslim groups have insisted both on the right to attend state schools and, while attending them, to conserve practices (especially with regard to dress and similar matters) considered contrary to the French tradition of secularism by state education authorities. The patterns of affirmation of religious practice, however, are generally similar to those of Catholics and Jews in France. Only 27 percent of Muslims claimed to be practicing in 1994, 30 percent fewer than five years before.

Class and Status

Feelings about class differences shape a society's authority pattern and the style in which authority is exercised. The French, like the English, are very conscious of living in a society divided into classes. But since equality is valued more highly in France than in England, deference toward the upper classes is far less developed, and resentful antagonism is widespread.

The number of those who are conscious of belonging to a class has been relatively strong in France, particularly among workers. One important study, for example, found a far greater intensity of spontaneous class consciousness among French workers in the 1970s than among comparable groups of British workers.[4] Yet, spontaneous class identity has been declining since the 1970s. In 1994, 61 percent of respondents felt that they belonged to a class, compared with 68 percent 18 years earlier. The decline of class commitments has been greatest among blue-collar workers (down to 47 percent) and least among white-collar employees and executives. One survey in 1997 revealed that a majority of workers identified as middle class. Among middle managers, feelings of class identity had actually increased. By the 1990s French workers identified themselves as belonging to a class less frequently than any other major salaried group (see Box 5.1).

Box 5.1   Class and Identity

With which class do respondents identify? In general, there has been a decline in working-class identification (among all groups) of more than 40 percent since 1966 and an increase in middle-class identification of over 80 percent. While the declining number of blue-collar workers, as well as executives and businesspeople, are generally clear about their class identification, white-collar workers and middle management are more divided. About 25 percent of white-collar workers think of themselves as working class, compared with 41 percent who identify themselves as middle class.

—Laurent Chanussy

Existing evidence indicates that economic and social transformations have reduced the level of class identification but have not eradicated subjective feelings about class differences and class antagonism. Indeed, the strike movements during the past four years seem to have intensified class feelings. In addition, as the number of immigrant workers among the least qualified workers has grown, traditional class differences have been reinforced by a growing sense of racial and ethnic differences.

Political Socialization

The attitudinal patterns that we have analyzed here have been shaped through experience with the political system, as well as through some key institutions and agents. Some agents, such as political associations, act to socialize political values quite directly, while others, such as the family and the media, tend to act in a more indirect manner.

In an old country like France, agents of political socialization change slowly, even when regimes change rapidly. Socializing agents are carriers of a broader cultural tradition. Like any other teaching process, political socialization passes on from one generation to the next "a mixture of attitudes developed in a mixture of historical periods." But "traditions, everyone agrees, do not form a constituted and fixed set of values, of knowledge and of representations; socialization never functions as a simple mechanism of identical reproduction. . . . [but rather as] an important instrument for the reorganization and the reinvention of tradition."[5]

Family

For those French who view their neighbors and fellow citizens with distrust, and the institutions around them with cynicism, the family is a safe haven. Concern for stability, steady income, property, and continuity were common to bourgeois and peasant families, though not to urban or agricultural workers. The training of children in bourgeois and peasant families was marked by close supervision, incessant correction, and strict sanctions.

Particularly during the last 20 years, the life of the French family, the role of its members, and its relationship to outsiders have all undergone fundamental, and sometimes contradictory, changes. Very few people condemn the idea of couples living together without being married. In 1997, 40 percent of all births were outside of marriage (compared with 6.4 percent in 1968), a percentage only slightly lower than in the United States, and higher than any other country in the EU except Denmark and Sweden. The proportion of births outside of marriage is highest among women outside of the labor force and working-class women (with the notable exception of immigrant women). Almost none of these children are in one-parent families, however, in the sense that in virtually all cases they are legally recognized by both parents before their first birthday. Nevertheless, 15 percent of children below the age of 19 live with only one of their natural parents, mostly due to divorce. The number of divorces was more than 43 percent the number of marriages in 1997, and it has almost doubled since 1976, when new and more flexible divorce legislation came into effect.

Legislative changes have only gradually modified the legal incapacities of married women that existed in the Napoleonic legal codes. Not until 1970 did the law proclaim the absolute equality of the two parents in the exercise of parental authority and for the moral and material management of the family. Because women have insisted on labor-saving devices for house and farm, they have been described as the "secret agents of modernity" in the countryside.[6] Almost half of all women over the age of 15 are now employed, and 80 percent of French women between the ages of 25 and 49 are now working continuously during their adult years.

The employment of a greater number of married women has affected the role of the family as a vehicle of socialization. Working women differ from those who are not employed in regard to moral concepts, religious practice, political interest, electoral participation, party alignment, and so on. In their general orientations, employed women are far closer to the men of the milieu, the class, or the age group to which they belong, than to women who are not employed.[7]

Although family structure, values, and behavior have changed, the family remains an important structure through which political values broadly conceived are transmitted from generation to generation.

Several studies have demonstrated a significant influence of parents over the religious socialization and the left-right political choices made by their children.[8]

There is perhaps no greater tribute to the continuing effectiveness of the French family than the results of a survey of French youth taken by the French government in 1994. With 25 percent of 18- to 24-year-olds unemployed, it was hardly surprising that the survey revealed that 78 percent of young people had little confidence in the schools to prepare them for the future. What was more surprising was how much confidence young people had in their families. More than 75 percent felt that their parents had confidence in them, that they were loved at home, and that their families had prepared them well for the future. In a survey taken in 1999, the family was ranked second only to school as a source of deep and durable friendship.

The effectiveness of the family as an agent of socialization for general religious and ideological orientations does not mean that succeeding generations do not have formative experiences of their own or that there are no significant differences in the political commitments of different age cohorts. Therefore, political socialization is a product not only of the family experience but also of childhood experiences with peers, education, and the changing larger world. Thus young people of Algerian origin, born in France, are somewhat more likely than their counterparts of French origin to practice religion but are far less likely to practice than their counterparts born in Algeria.[9]

Associations and Socialization

The French bias against authority might have encouraged association if the egalitarian thrust and the competition between individuals did not work in the opposite direction. The ambivalence about participation in group life was not merely negativistic apathy but was related to a lack of belief in the value of cooperation. On the one hand, this cultural ambivalence is reinforced by legal restrictions on associational life, as well as by a strong republican tradition hostile to groups serving as intermediaries between the people and the state. On the other hand, the state and local governments traditionally subsidize numerous associations (including trade unions) and give some associations (not always the same ones that were subsidized) privileged access to decision-making power.

After World War II, *overall* membership in associations in France was comparable to other European countries, but lower than in the United States. However, group membership in France was concentrated in politicized associations that reinforced existing social divisions and was less common for independent social and fraternal groups. Membership in key professional organizations, especially trade unions, was much lower in France than in other European countries.

During the past two decades there has been a sharp increase in the number of associations, while the overall percentage of membership among the adult population remains relatively constant. The pattern of association, however, changed considerably. The more traditional advocacy and political groups, politicized unions, and professional associations suffered sharp declines in absolute (and proportional) membership; sports associations, self-help groups, and newly established ethnic associations now attract larger numbers of people. As more middle-class people have joined associations, working-class people have dropped out.[10]

To some extent these changes reflect shifting attitudes about political commitment in France. Although associational life remains strong, *militantisme* (with its implication of deep and abiding commitment) seems to have diminished. Older advocacy and professional associations that were built on this kind of commitment have declined, while newer groups have been built on different and often more limited commitment.

New legislation has also produced changes. A law passed in 1981 made it possible for immigrant groups to form their own organizations; this encouraged the emergence of thousands of associations that mobilize on the basis of ethnic origins. Decentralization legislation passed a few years later encouraged municipalities to support the creation of local associations to perform municipal services.

Even with these changing patterns, there remain uncertainties about the role of associations, old and new, in the socialization process of individuals. Some observers seem to confirm that membership in French organizations involves less actual participation than in American or British organizations and hence has less impact on social and political attitudes. The cultural distrust noted previously is manifest less in lower overall membership than in the inability of organizational leaders to relate to their members and to mobilize them for action.

Education

The most important way a community preserves and transmits its cultural and political values is through education. Napoléon Bonaparte recognized the significance of education, and well into the second half of the twentieth century the French educational system remained an imposing historical monument, in the unmistakable style of the First Empire. The edifice Napoléon erected combined education at all levels, from primary school to postgraduate professional training, into one centralized corporation: the imperial university. Its job was to teach the national doctrine through uniform programs at various levels.

As the strict military discipline of the Napoleonic model has been loosened by succeeding regimes, each has discovered that the machinery created by Napoléon was a convenient and coherent instrument for transmitting the values—both changing and permanent—of French civilization. The centralized imperial university has therefore never been truly dismantled. The Minister of Education, who presides over a ministry that employs almost a million people, continues to control curriculum and teaching methods, the criteria for selection and advancement of pupils and teachers, and the content of examinations.

Making advancement at every step depend on passing an examination is not peculiar to France (it is also a pattern in Japan, as well as other countries). What is distinctly French is an obsessive and quite unrealistic belief that everybody is equal before an examination. The idea that education is an effective weapon for emancipation and social betterment has had popular as well as official recognition. Farmers and workers regard the instruction of their children, a better instruction than they had, as an important weapon in the fight against the others in an oppressive world. The *baccalauréat*—the certificate of completion of the academic secondary school, the lycée—has remained almost the sole means of access to higher education. But such a system suits and profits best those self-motivated middle-class children for whom it was designed.

During the Fifth Republic, the structure of the French educational system at every level has undergone significant change. The secondary schools, which trained only 700,000 students as late as 1945, now provide instruction for almost 6 million. Between 1958 and 1998, the number of students in higher education rose from 170,000 to 2.1 million. By 1998 the proportion of 20- to 24-year-olds in higher education (40 percent) was as high as that of any other European country.[11]

The introduction of a comprehensive middle school with a common core curriculum in 1963 basically altered the system of early academic selection, and other reforms eliminated rigid ability tracking. However, implementation of reforms, whether passed by governments of the right or the left, has often been difficult because of the opposition from middle-class parents and from teachers' unions of the left.[12] Although 62 percent of the relevant generation passed the *baccalauréat* in 1998 (double the proportion of 1980), education reforms have altered only slightly the vast differences in the success of children from different social backgrounds.

Because of the principle of open admission, every holder of the *baccalauréat* can gain entrance to a university. But there is, as in some American state universities, a rather ruthless elimination at the end of the first year and sometimes later. Here again students of lower-class background fare worse than the others. In addition, the number of students from such backgrounds is disproportionately great in fields in which diplomas have the lowest value in the professional market and where unemployment is greatest.

The most ambitious attempt ever made to reform the university system at one stroke came in the wake of the student rebellion of 1968, followed by other reforms in the 1970s and 1980s. They strove, by different means, to encourage the autonomy of each university; the participation of teachers, students, and staff in the running of the university; and the collaboration among different disciplines. Some of the reforms, though duly enacted, were withdrawn by the government because of massive protest demonstrations in the streets. Others failed to be implemented because of the widespread resistance by those concerned. Administrative autonomy has remained fragmentary as the ministry has held the financial purse strings as well as the right to grant degrees. Today the widely lamented crisis of the university system has hardly been alleviated, while the size of the student population has continued to increase (though more modestly than in earlier years).

An additional characteristic of the French system of higher education is the parallel system of *grandes écoles,* a sector of higher education that functions outside of the network of universities under rules that permit a high degree of selectivity. As university enrollment has multiplied (by more than 500 percent since 1960), the more prestigious *grandes écoles* have hardly increased the number of students admitted upon strict entrance examinations.[13] For more than a century the best of the *grandes écoles* have been the training ground of highly specialized elites. The schools prepare students for careers in engineering, business management, and the top ranks of the civil service. Their different recruitment of students and of teaching staffs as well as their teaching methods have an impact on the outlook and even on the temperament of many of their graduates. In contrast to university graduates, virtually all graduates of the *grandes écoles* are immediately placed and often assume positions of great responsibility (see pp. 161–162).

Socialization and Communication

In a country such as France, the political effectiveness of the mass media is often determined by the way in which people appraise the integrity of the instrument and whether they believe that it serves or disturbs the functioning of the political system. In the past, business firms, tycoons, political parties, and governments (both French and foreign) often backed major newspapers. Today, the press operates under the same conditions as it does in other Western democracies, except that daily press revenue from advertising remains lower than elsewhere. Most newspapers and magazines are owned

by business enterprises, many of them conglomerates that extend into fields other than periodical publications.

In spite of a growth in population, the circulation of daily newspapers and their number has been declining since the war. The decline in readership, a common phenomenon in most Western democracies, is due, among other factors, to competition from other media such as television, radio, and the Internet. It has been accompanied by a decline in the number of newspapers.

Television has replaced all other media as a primary source of political information in France, and to a greater extent than in Germany, Britain, or the United States.[14] Television has increasingly become the primary mediator between political forces and individual citizens, and, as in other countries, it has had an impact on the organization and substance of politics. First, a personality that plays well on television (not just a unique personality such as Charles de Gaulle) has become an essential ingredient of politics. As in other countries, image and spectacle have become important elements of politics. Second, television has helped set the agenda of political issues, by choosing among the great variety of themes, problems, and issues dealt with by political and social forces, and by magnifying them for mass publics. Finally, television has become the arena within which national electoral campaigns take place, largely displacing mass rallies and meetings. Nevertheless, confidence in various sources of political information varies among different groups. Young people and shopkeepers are most confident in radio information, while managers are more confident in the written press than television for political information.

Until 1982, all broadcasting and television stations that originated programs on French territory were owned by the state and operated by personnel whom the state appointed and remunerated. Since then, in successive steps, the basic system of state monopoly has been dismantled. As a first and quite important step, the (Socialist!) government introduced legislation in 1982 authorizing private radio stations to operate in France. The move attempted to regularize and regulate more than a thousand pirate radio stations already in existence. Inevitably, this vast network of 1,600 stations is becoming increasingly consolidated—not by the state but by private entrepreneurs who provide programming services, and who in some instances are effectively buying control of a large number of local stations.

The 1982 legislation also reorganized the public television system. It granted new rights of reply to government communications and allotted free time to all political parties during electoral campaigns. During the following years, however, these changes were dwarfed by a process of gradual privatization, begun under the Socialists and continued by the conservatives after 1986, and by the globalization of television broadcasting. In 1998, more than 130 television channels were available to French viewers, compared with 30 in 1990 and 3 in 1980.

Mass and Elite Recruitment

Political Participation and Voting

In most democracies, no form of political participation is as extensive as voting. Although France is a unitary state, elections are held with considerable frequency at every territorial level. Councilors are elected for each of the more than 36,000 communes in France, for each of the 100 departments (counties), and for each of the 22 regions. Deputies to the National Assembly are elected at least once every five years, and the president of the Republic is elected (or reelected) at least once every seven years (every five years after 2002). In addition, elections for representatives to the European Parliament have been held in France, as well as every other country in the European Community, every five years since 1979.

France was the first European country to enfranchise a mass electorate, and France was also the first European country to demonstrate that a mass electorate did not preclude the possibility of authoritarian government. The electoral law of 1848 enfranchised all male citizens over the age of 21, but within five years this same mass electorate had ratified Louis Napoléon's coup d'état and his establishment of the Second Empire. Rather than restrict the electorate, Napoléon perfected new modern techniques for manipulating a mass electorate by gerrymandering districts, skillfully using public works as

patronage for official candidates, and exerting pressure through the administrative hierarchy.

From the Second Empire to the end of World War II, the size of the electorate remained more or less stable, but it suddenly more than doubled when women 21 years of age and older were granted the vote in 1944. After the voting age was lowered to 18 in 1974, 2.5 million voters were added to the rolls, and by 1997, there were about 40 million voters in France.

Electoral Participation and Abstention

Surprisingly, in both the Third and the Fourth Republics general disenchantment with parliamentary institutions never prevented a high turnout at national elections. Since the consolidation of republican institutions in 1885 (and with the one exception of the somewhat abnormal post–World War I election of 1919), electoral participation never fell to less than 71 percent of registered voters, and in most elections participation was much higher.[15]

Voting participation in elections of the Fifth Republic has undergone a significant change and fluctuates far more than during previous republics. Abstention tends to be highest in referendums and European elections, and lowest in presidential contests, with other elections falling somewhere in between (see Table 5.1).

During the 1980s, the normal level of abstention increased substantially. In the 1988 legislative election, an abstention rate of 34.3 percent set a record for legislative elections for any of the French republics. The elections for the European Parliament had always attracted relatively few voters, but in 1994 almost half the registered voters stayed home (slightly fewer than in 1989). A new record was set in 1988: almost 63 percent of the registered voters chose not to vote on a referendum on a new government for New Caledonia.

These high and growing levels of abstention, which are such a striking departure from what had come to be regarded as the norm, are not equally distributed among the electorate. They have been growing faster among voters of the left than among voters of the right, and faster in working-class constituencies than in more middle-class constituencies. Rising abstention seems to be linked to a larger

TABLE 5.1 French Referendums (R) and Second Ballots of Presidential Elections (P), 1958–2000 (Voting in Metropolitan France)

Date	Registered Voters (millions)	Abstentions (percentage registered)	"Yes" Votes† for Winning Candidate (percentage registered)	(percentage cast)	Winner	"No" Votes† for Losing Candidate (percentage registered)	(percentage registered)	Loser
9/28/58(R)	26.6	15.1	66.4	79.2		17.4	20.7	
1/8/61(R)	27.2	23.5	55.9	75.3		18.4	24.7	
4/8/62(R)	27.0	24.4	64.9	90.7		6.6	9.3	
10/28/62(R)	27.6	22.7	46.4	61.7		28.8	38.2	
12/19/65(P)	28.2	15.4	44.8	54.5	De Gaulle	37.4	45.5	Mitterrand
4/18/69(R)	28.7	19.4	36.7	46.7		41.6	53.2	
6/15/69(P)	28.8	30.9	37.2	57.5	Pompidou	27.4	42.4	Poher
4/23/72(R)	29.1	39.5	36.1	67.7		17.2	32.3	
5/19/74(P)	29.8	12.1	43.9	50.7	Giscard d'Estaing	42.8	49.3	Mitterrand
5/10/81(P)	35.5	13.6	43.8	52.2	Mitterrand	40.1	47.8	Giscard d'Estaing
5/8/88(P)	38.2	15.9	43.8	54.0	Mitterrand	37.3	46.0	Chirac
11/6/88(R)	37.8	63.0	26.1	80.0		6.5	20.0	
9/20/92(R)	37.1	28.9	34.9	50.8		33.8	49.2	
5/7/95(P)	39.9	20.1	39.5	52.6	Chirac	35.6	47.4	Jospin
9/24/00(R)	39.6	69.7	18.6	73.2		6.8	26.8	

phenomenon of change in the party system. Since the late 1970s, there has been a trend of declining confidence by voters in all political parties, some of which is expressed through growing abstention rates among voters who formerly voted for both right and left. Abstention from voting is one aspect of the major structural change that the French party system is undergoing. Even when the abstention level declined to around 30 percent during the electoral cycle of 1992–1997, it never reverted to the average of about 15 percent of the pre-1981 period. Nevertheless, in contrast with the United States, among the 90 percent of the electorate that is registered to vote, individual abstention appears to be cyclical and there are almost no permanent abstainers.[16]

As in other countries, age, social class, and education were and remain important factors in determining the degree of electoral participation, both registration and voting. The least educated, the lowest income groups, and the youngest and oldest age groups vote less frequently.

Voting in Parliamentary Elections

Since the early days of the Third Republic, France has experimented with a great number of electoral systems and devices without obtaining more satisfactory results in terms of government coherence. The stability of the Fifth Republic cannot be attributed to the method of electing National Assembly deputies, for the system is essentially the same one used during the most troubled years of the Third Republic. As in the United States, a rather small number of electoral districts (577) are represented by a single deputy. On the first election day only those candidates who obtain a majority of all votes cast are elected; this is a relatively rare occurrence because of the abundance of candidates. Candidates who obtain support of less than 12.5 percent of the registered voters are dropped for the "second round" a week later. Others voluntarily withdraw in favor of a better-placed candidate close to their party on the political spectrum. Pre-election agreements between Communists and Socialists have usually led to the weaker candidate withdrawing after the first round, if both survive. Similar arrangements usually exist between the Rally for the Republic (RPR) and the Union for French Democracy

(UDF), although more often they agree not to compete in the same district even on the first round. As a result, generally three (or at most four) candidates face each other in the second round, in which a plurality of votes ensures election.

This means that the first round is somewhat similar to American primary elections, except that in the French case the primary is among candidates of parties allied in coalitions of the left or center-right. In the end, bipolarity generally results. There is considerable pressure on political parties to develop electoral alliances, since those that do not are placed at a strong disadvantage in terms of representation.

More recently, the National Front has been more or less isolated from coalition arrangements with the parties of the center-right in national elections (though less and less at the subnational level). Consequently, in 1997, with electoral support of 15 percent, only one of their candidates was finally elected. In comparison, the Communist Party benefited from an electoral agreement with the Socialists: With 10 percent of the vote, 37 of their candidates were elected. Not surprisingly, the leading party (or coalition of parties) generally ends up with a considerably larger number of seats than is justified by its share in the popular vote.

Voting in Referendums

As we have seen, French traditions of representative government frowned on any direct appeals to the electorate, mainly because the two Napoléons had used the referendum to establish or extend their powers. The 1958 constitution of the Fifth Republic made only modest departures from the classic representative model. Although the constitution was submitted to the electorate for approval, the direct appeal to the voters that it permitted under carefully prescribed conditions was hedged by parliamentary controls.

Between 1958 and 1969 the French electorate voted five times on referendums (see again Table 5.1). In 1958 a vote against the new constitution might have involved the country in a civil war, which it had narrowly escaped a few months earlier. The two referendums that followed endorsed the peace settlement in the Algerian War. In 1962, hardly four years after he had enacted by referendum his "own" constitution, General de Gaulle asked the electorate to endorse a constitutional amendment of great significance: to elect the president of the Republic by direct popular suffrage. Since then public opinion polls have revealed that both popular election of the president and consultation of the electorate by referendum on important issues are widely approved.

Favorable attitudes toward the referendum and the popular election of the president, however, did not prevent the electorate from voting down another proposal submitted by de Gaulle in 1969, thereby causing his resignation. Nothing in the constitution compelled de Gaulle to resign, but his highly personal concept of his role, no longer accepted by a majority of the electorate, made his resignation inevitable.

Since 1969 there have been only four referendums. De Gaulle's successor Georges Pompidou called a referendum for the admission of Britain to the Common Market. (For the results of referendums and presidential elections between 1958 and 2000, see Table 5.1.) The first referendum during the Mitterrand period, in 1988, dealt with approval for an accord between warring parties on the future of New Caledonia; the referendum was a condition of the agreement. Sixty-three percent of the voters stayed home, but the accord was approved. The electorate was far more extensively mobilized when the question of ratifying the so-called *Maastricht Treaty* on the European Union was submitted to referendum in September 1992, and the results were far more significant for the future of French political life (see Box 5.2). The last referendum—on reduction of the presidential term from seven to five years—was in September 2000. Although the amendment to the constitution was overwhelmingly approved (by 73 percent of those who voted), the referendum was most notable for the record number of abstentions—almost 70 percent.

Public opinion polls indicate, nevertheless, that the referendum as a form of public participation is still regarded favorably by the electorate. It ranked just behind the popularly elected presidency and the Constitutional Council, among the most highly

---

Box 5.2 French Parities and the Maastricht Referendum of 1992

With the support of the President of the Republic, the leaders of the Socialist Party, most (but not all) of the leaders of the conservative opposition as well as two-thirds of the electorate before the summer, the proposition approving of the treaty to establish a European Union, with European citizenship and (eventually) a single European currency, was expected to achieve an impressive majority in the September referendum. It was also expected to give a boost of support for the Socialist president and government in anticipation of the 1993 legislative elections. The results were far different. The proposed treaty split the electorates of each of the major political parties in unanticipated ways and the summer campaign proved to be particularly bitter. The Gaullist opposition to the treaty was partly a revolt against the leadership of *Jacques Chirac*, and it was supported by a clear majority of RPR deputies and voters. The campaign of the Centrist opponents was also an attack against their leader, former president Giscard d'Estaing, but it did not gain widespread support. Within the left, the Communists proved to be weak but bitter opponents to the approval of the treaty, and Socialist leaders less than enthusiastic proponents. The National Front was united in its opposition.

In the end, the treaty was approved on September 20 by a slim majority of the voters, but the results were a political disaster for those who won. For each of the major parties, their "natural" electorates split badly, and the results—in which opposition to the treaty was concentrated among the less privileged voters and in the poorest regions of the country—were widely viewed as a broad rejection of established political leadership.*

*On the referendum, see Andrew Appleton, "The Maastricht Referendum and the Party System," in Keeler and Schain, eds., *Chirac's Challenge*.

approved institutional innovations of the Fifth Republic. In one of its first moves, the new government under President Jacques Chirac in 1995 passed a constitutional amendment that expanded the use of the referendum in the areas of social and economic policy.

Voting in Presidential Elections

Presidential elections by direct popular suffrage are for French voters the most important expressions of the general will. After the presidential elections of 1965, it had become evident that French voters derived great satisfaction from knowing that, unlike past parliamentary elections, national and not parochial alignments were at stake, and that they were invited to pronounce themselves effectively on such issues. The traditional and once deeply rooted attitude that the only useful vote was against the government no longer made sense when almost everybody knew that the task was to elect an executive endowed with strong powers for seven years. Accordingly, turnout in presidential elections, with one exception, has been the highest of all elections.

The nomination procedures for presidential candidates make it very easy to put a candidate on the first ballot, far easier than in presidential primaries in the United States. So far, however, no presidential candidate, not even de Gaulle in 1965, has obtained the absolute majority needed to ensure election on the first ballot. In runoffs, held two weeks after the first ballot, only the two most successful candidates face each other. All serious candidates have been backed by a party or a coalition of parties, the provisions of the law notwithstanding. The French understood soon what the citizens of the United States learned during the seedtime of their republic: It is impossible to mount a successful national political campaign without the support, skill, and experience of a political party.

If all the presidential campaigns have fascinated French voters and foreign observers, it is not only due to the novelty of a nationwide competition in a country accustomed to small constituencies and local contests. Style and content of campaign oratory have generally been of high quality. Because the formal campaigns are short and concentrated, radio, television, and newspapers are able to grant candidates, commentators, and forecasters considerable time and space. The televised duels between the presidential candidates in the last three elections, patterned after debates between presidential candidates in the United States, but longer and of far higher quality, were viewed by at least half of the population.

Informal campaigns, however, are long and arduous. The fixed term of the French presidency means that, unless the president dies or resigns, there are no snap elections for the chief executive as there are from time to time in Britain and Germany. As a result, even in the absence of primaries, the informal campaign begins to get quite intense years before the election. In many ways, the presidential campaign of 2002 began well before the new millenium.

Just as in the United States, electoral coalitions that elect a president are different from those that secure a legislative majority for a government. This means that any candidate for the presidency who owes his nomination to his position as party leader must appeal to an audience broader than a single party. Once elected, the candidate seeks to establish political distance from his party origins. Although at the time of his first election he was more closely identified as a party leader than his predecessors in the presidency, Mitterrand successfully established the necessary distance between party and office, which explains a great deal about his political success in 1988. François Mitterrand was the first and only president in the history of the Fifth Republic to have been elected twice in popular elections.

Although the 1995 presidential election deeply divided each of the major parties of the right, the process of coalition building around presidential elections has probably been the key element in political party consolidation and in the development of party coalitions since 1968. The prize of the presidency has become so significant, as we shall see, that it has preoccupied the parties of both the right and the left since the 1960s and has influenced their organization, their tactics, and their relations with one another.

Recruitment and Style of Elites

Until the Fifth Republic, Parliament provided the nucleus of French decision makers. Besides members of

Parliament, elected officers of municipalities or departments, some local party leaders, and a few journalists of national renown were counted among what is known in France as the *political class,* altogether comprising not more than 15,000 or 20,000 persons. All gravitated toward the halls of the National Assembly or the Senate.

Compared with the British House of Commons, the membership of the lower house of the French Parliament has always been of more modest social origin. From about 1879 on, professionals (lawyers, doctors, and journalists) increasingly dominated the Chamber of Deputies, now called the National Assembly; the vast majority were local notables, trained in law and experienced in local administration.

A substantial change in political recruitment occurred during the Fourth Republic, when for the first time the percentage of self-employed became a minority. The professional background of today's deputies, and the changes that have taken place since the war, generally reflect both the waxing and waning strength of the parties at a given election, as well as more general trends to be observed in the parliaments of other democracies. The steady decline in the number of farmers is, of course, in part the consequence of the general decline of the farming population. The steadily diminishing share of blue- and white-collar workers is at least in part to be explained by the professionalization of parliamentary personnel, as well as by the decline of the Communist Party that began in the 1980s.

What is most striking about the professional background of deputies under the Fifth Republic is the number who have come from the public sector: almost half the deputies in the 1980s, and 44 percent after the victory of the left in 1997. The number of top civil servants in the National Assembly has risen constantly since 1958, and the left landslide of 1981 only accentuated this process. Although the majority of high civil servants lean toward parties of the right, more than a third of those who sat in the Assembly elected in 1997 were part of the Socialist group. Even more important than their number is the political weight that these deputy-bureaucrats carry in Parliament. Some of the civil servants who run for election to Parliament have previously held positions in the political executive, either as members of the ministerial staffs or as junior ministers. Not surprisingly, in Parliament they are frequently candidates for a post in the Cabinet.

More than in any other Western democracy, the highest ranks of the civil service are the training and recruitment grounds for top positions in both politics and industry. Among the high civil servants, about 2,300 are members of the most important administrative agencies, the *grands corps,* from which the vast majority of the roughly 500 administrators engaged in political decision making are drawn.[17] The recruitment base of the highest levels of the civil service remains extremely narrow. The knowledge and capability required to pass the various examinations gives clear advantages to the children of senior civil servants. As a result, the ranking bureaucracy forms something approaching a hereditary class. There have been several important attempts to develop a system of more open recruitment into the higher civil service, but all of them have been only marginally successful.

The *Ecole Nationale d'Administration (ENA)* and the *Ecole Polytechnique,* together with the other *grandes écoles,* play an essential role in the recruitment of administrative, political, and business elites. Virtually all the members of the most prestigious *grands corps* are recruited directly from the graduating classes of the ENA and the Polytechnique (most of whose graduates have also attended other *grandes écoles*). What differentiates the members of the *grands corps* from other ranking administrators is their general competence and mobility. At any one time as many as two-thirds of the members of one of these corps might be on leave or on special missions to other administrative agencies or special assignments to positions of influence.

They might also be, and frequently are, engaged in politics either as members of Parliament (46 in the National Assembly elected in 1997) and of local government, or as members of the executive: 11 of the 16 prime ministers who have served since 1959 have been members of a *grand corps* who attended a *grande école,* and the percentage of ministers in any given government who are members of one of the *grand corps* has varied between 10 and 60 percent. A recent study calculates that 40 percent of those who graduated from ENA between 1960 and

1990 served as ministerial advisors. Thus the *grandes écoles—grands corps* group, though small in membership, has produced, and continues to produce, a remarkable proportion of the country's political elite.

The same system is also becoming increasingly important recruiting high business executives. Movement from the public sector to the private sector is facilitated because members of the *grands corps* can go on leave for years, while they retain their seniority and pension rights, as well as the right to return to their job.[18] (Few who leave do in fact return.) In 1993, 47 percent of the directors of the 200 largest companies in France were from the civil service (up from 41 percent in 1985). In the early 1990s, 17 percent of all ENA graduates were working in French industry. Moreover, though the number of ENA graduates is small (about 170 a year), it is three times larger now than in the early 1960s.

Thus the relationship between the *grandes écoles* and the *grands corps,* on the one hand, and politics and business, on the other hand, provides structure for an influential elite and survives changes in the political orientation of governments. While this system is not politically monolithic, the narrowness of its recruitment contributes to a persistent similarity of style and operation, and to the fairly stable—at times rigid—value system of its operators.

For outsiders, this tight network has been difficult to penetrate. Even during the 1980s—the period when industrial restructuring and privatization of state-run enterprises encouraged a new breed of freewheeling businesspeople in the United States under Reagan and in Britain under Thatcher—a similar process had a very limited impact on the recruitment of new elites in France.

The Importance of Gender

The representation of women among French political elites is close to the lowest in Western Europe. While women comprise well over half the electorate, barely 11 percent of the deputies in the National Assembly and only 6 percent of the members of the Senate are women. Women fare better at the local level, where they comprised 22 percent of the municipal councilors elected in 1995.

Political parties structure access to political representation far more in France than in the United States, and the left has generally made a greater effort to recruit women than has the right. Thus, when the Socialists and Communists gained a substantial number of seats in the 1997 legislative elections, the proportion of women in the National Assembly almost doubled. In contrast to the United States, political advancement in France has generally required a deep involvement in political parties, with a bias in favor of professional politicians and administrators. However, relatively few women have made this kind of long-term commitment to political life.

Periodically, this dearth of representation has been recognized by governments and parties of the right and the left, but little has been done, either because the remedies have been rejected by the Constitutional Council, or because they have challenged accepted institutional norms. In 1982, the Constitutional Council overturned legislation that restricted party lists for municipal council elections to no more than 75 percent candidates of one gender. By the 1990s there was a growing consensus among leaders of all political parties in favor of amending the Constitution to permit positive discrimination in favor of greater parity of gender representation in representative institutions. Thus, with support of both the president of the Republic and the prime minister and without dissent, the National Assembly passed an amendment in December 1998 that stipulated that ". . . the law [and not the constitution] determines the conditions for the organization of equal access of men and women to electoral mandates and elective functions." The amendment was finalized in June 1999, and during the following year enforcement legislation was passed to require greater gender parity at least in the selection of candidates. This is a significant departure for the French political system, which has resisted the use of quotas in the name of republican equality.

Perhaps the most important change in the political behavior of French women has been in their voting patterns. During the Fourth Republic, a majority of women consistently voted for parties of the right. However, as church attendance among women has declined, their political orientation moved from right to left. In every national election since the 1980s, a clear majority of women have voted for the left.[19]

Interest Groups

The Expression of Interests

Political participation in France has been generally structured by organized groups and political parties, and, as in many other European countries, the organization of political life has been largely defined within the historical cleavages of class and religious traditions that we analyzed previously. Interest groups have therefore frequently shared ideological roots and commitments with the political parties with which they have occasionally had organizational connections.

Actual memberships in almost all groups engaged in production have varied considerably over time by sector, but they are generally much smaller than comparable groups in other industrialized countries. In the 1990s no more than 11 percent of workers belonged to trade unions (a decline of half over 25 years); about 50 percent of French farmers and 75 percent of large industrial enterprises belonged to their respective organizations (see following discussion).[20] Historically, many of the important production groups have experienced a surge of new members at dramatic moments in the country's social or political history but a decline as conditions have become normal, leaving some associations with too small a membership to justify their claims of representativeness.

The treasuries of groups are often so depleted that they are unable to employ a competent staff, or they are dependent on direct and indirect forms of state support. The modern interest group official is a fairly recent phenomenon to be found only in certain sectors of the group system, such as business associations.

Interest groups have also been weakened by ideological division. Separate groups that defend the interests of workers, farmers, veterans, schoolchildren, and consumers are divided in France by ideological preferences. The ideological division of representation forces each organization to compete

for the same clientele in order to establish their representativeness. The result is that even established French interest groups exhibit a radicalism in action and announced objectives that is rare in countries of similar levels of development and is more generally found in an early industrial era. For groups that lack the means of using the information media, such tactics also become a way to put their case before the public at large. In such a setting, even the defense of purely economic, social, or cultural interests takes on a political color.

The Labor Movement

The French labor movement is divided into national confederations of differing political sympathies, although historical experiences have driven French labor, unlike other European trade unions, to avoid direct organizational ties with political parties.[21] Membership has declined steeply since 1975, but there are indications that the decline has at least leveled off since 1994. Nevertheless, although union membership is declining in every industrialized country (except Sweden), it is now the lowest by far in France. Surveys show that the youngest group of salaried workers has virtually deserted the trade union movement, and that after 1990 candidates supported by nonunion groups in various plant-level elections have attracted more votes than any of the established union organizations.[22] In fact unions have been losing members and (electoral) support at the very time when the trade union movement has become better institutionalized at the workplace and better protected by legislation than at any other time in its history.

Despite these clear weaknesses, French workers still maintain considerable (and increasing) confidence in unions to defend their interests during periods of labor conflict. Since 1994, as strike levels and support for collective action have risen, confidence in unions and their leadership of strike movements has also risen. Indeed, during the massive strikes of public service workers in the fall of 1995, truckers in the fall of 1996, and truckers and taxi drivers (protesting against the rising price of oil) in the fall of 2000, public support for the strikers remained far higher than confidence in the government against which the strikes were directed.[23]

French labor has been the sector that has had the most difficulty dealing with ideological fragmentation. Indeed, the decline in membership has not encouraged consolidation, but it has resulted in more fragmentation (see following discussion). Unlike the United States, workers in France may be represented by several union federations in the same plant, store, or school. As a result, there is constant competition among unions at every level for membership and support. Even during periods when the national unions have agreed to act together, animosities at the plant level have sometimes prevented cooperation. Moreover, the weakness of union organization at the plant level—which is where most lengthy strikes are called—means that unions are difficult bargaining partners.

Unions at this level maintain only weak control over the strike weapon. Although union militants are quite adept at sensitizing workers, and in this sense at engendering many of the preconditions for strike action as well as channeling strike movements once they begin, they have considerable difficulty in effectively calling strikes and ending them. Thus unions are highly dependent on the general environment, what they call the social climate, in order to support their positions at the bargaining table. Because their ability to mobilize workers at any given moment is an essential criterion of their representativeness, union ability to represent workers is frequently in question.

Legislation passed by the government of the left in 1982–1983 (the Auroux laws) was meant to strengthen the union's position at the plant level. By creating an "obligation to negotiate" for management and by protecting the right of expression for workers, the government hoped to stimulate collective negotiations. In fact, this type of Wagner Act (the basic law of U.S. industrial relations) of French labor has brought about some important changes in industrial relations and has stimulated collective negotiations. However, given their increasing weakness, unions have been poorly placed to take advantage of the potential benefits of the legislation, which has refocused French industrial relations on the plant level, without necessarily increasing the effectiveness of unions. The small number of union representatives, increasingly involved in committees

and discussions, appears to have lost much contact with workers on the shop floor.

The oldest and, by some measures, the largest of the union confederations is the *Confédération Générale du Travail* (CGT, General Confederation of Labor). Since WWII, the CGT has been identified closely with the Communist Party, with which it maintains a considerable overlap of leadership. Yet by tradition, and by its relative effectiveness as the largest labor organization, it has enrolled many non-Communists among its members. Its domination has been diminishing in the 1990s, however, mostly because the CGT has lost more membership and support than have other unions.

The second strongest labor organization is the *Confédération Française Democratique du Travail* (CFDT, French Democratic Confederation of Labor). In many ways the CFDT is the most original and the most interesting of all labor movements in Western Europe. An offshoot of a Catholic trade union movement, its earlier calls for worker self-management (*autogestion*) were integrated into the Auroux laws. The leaders of the CFDT see the policy of the confederation as an alternative to the oppositional stance of the CGT. The CFDT now offers itself as a potential partner to modern capitalist management. This movement to the right has resulted in splits in several of the CFDT public service unions, and the establishment of a new national rival, the Solidaire Unitaire et Democratique (SUD, Solidarity United and Democratic) in 1988. The split was further accentuated by the opposition of CFDT leadership to the massive public service strike of 1995.

The third major labor confederation, *Force Ouvrière* (FO, Workers' Force), was formed at the beginning of the Cold War in 1948 in reaction to the Communist domination of the CGT. It is the only major trade union organization that claims to have gained membership and has clearly gained more support than any other union organization in recent years. This relative success is certainly connected with the steady decline of the Communist Party. The FO adheres to a position that is close to the traditions of American trade unionism and has focused on collective bargaining as a counterweight to employers and the state. Nevertheless, during the strike movements of 1995 and 1996, FO leadership strongly supported the more radical elements of striking workers.

One of the most important and influential of the "autonomous" unions is the *Fédération de l'Education Nationale* (FEN, Federation of National Education), the teachers' union. At the end of 1992, as a result of growing internal conflict and declining membership, FEN split. The rump of FEN has joined with other independent unions to form the *Union Nationale des Syndicats Autonomes* (UNSA, National Union of Autonomous Unions), and in October 1994, was officially recognized by the government, which in legal terms meant that the government placed it on the same level as the other national confederations. Nevertheless, by 1996, FEN and UNSA was substantially weakened, when the rival *La Fédération Syndicale Unitaire* (FSU, United Union Federation)—which is close to the Communist Party—gained greater support in social elections, support that was reaffirmed in 1999.

In addition to the fragmentation that resulted from differences within existing organizations, there are also challenges from the outside. In 1995 the National Front took the initiative to organize several new unions, and when the government and the courts blocked these initiatives, the extreme-right party began to penetrate existing unions.

Thus, at a time when strong opposition to government action and growing support for strike mobilization seems to give union organizations an opportunity to increase both their organizational strength and their support, the trade union movement is more fragmented than it has ever been before. As in the past, massive strike movements have accentuated divisions and rivalries rather than provoke unity.

Business Interests

Since the end of World War II, French business has kept most trade associations and employers' organizations within one dominant and exceptionally well-staffed confederation, renamed in 1998 the *Mouvement des Entreprises de France* (MEDEF, The Movement of French Business). However, divergent interests, differing economic concepts, and indeed conflicting ideologies have frequently prevented the national organization from acting forcefully and at times have hampered its representativeness in nego-

tiations with government or trade unions. Nevertheless, the MEDEF (formerly called CNPF—the National Confederation of French Business) weathered the difficult years of the nationalization introduced by the Socialists, and the restructuring of social legislation and industrial relations, without lessening its status as an influential interest group.

Since the MEDEF is dominated primarily by big business, shopkeepers and the owners of many small firms feel that they are better defended by more movement-oriented groups than by the streamlined modern lobby of the MEDEF.[24] As a result there has been a succession of small business and shopkeeper movements that have at times challenged the established organization and that have evolved into organized associations in their own right.

Agricultural Interests

The defense of agricultural interests has a long record of internal strife. However, under the Fifth Republic, the *Fédération Nationale des Syndicats Agricoles* (FNSEA, National Federation of Agricultural Unions), though one of several representative farm organizations, has dominated this sector and has served as an effective instrument for modernizing French agriculture. The rural reform legislation of the 1960s provided for the "collaboration of the professional agricultural organizations," and from the outset, real collaboration was offered only to the FNSEA. From this privileged position the federation gained both patronage and control over key institutions that were transforming agriculture, and it used these instruments to organize a large proportion of French farmers. Thus, having established its domination over the farming sector with the support of a succession of governments, it then periodically demonstrated opposition to government policy with the support of the vast majority of a declining number of farmers.[25]

The principal challenges to the FNSEA in recent years have been external rather than internal, as the agricultural sector has continued to suffer from the fruits of its own productive success. Under pressure from the *European Union (EU)*, France agreed in 1992 to major reforms of the Common Agricultural Policy that took substantial amounts of land out of production and replaced some price supports with direct payments to farmers. That same year, the European Union reached an agreement with the United States that reduced subsidized grain exports and cut back cultivation of oilseed products. Although France is the largest exporter of these products, FNSEA protests (some of them violent) were joined by farm unions from throughout the EU, which ultimately resulted in a face-saving GATT accord in 1994. Pressures to further reduce the budget of CAP have only increased with the process of expansion of the EU toward the east, and the substantial opposition in France (and other parts of Europe) to the importation of genetically modified agricultural products has increased the tensions with GATT (now WTO).

If organized interests are expressed through an impressive range of different kinds of organizations, from the weak and fragmented trade union movement to the well-organized FNSEA that strongly influences the development and implementation of agriculture policy, what seems to differentiate French groups from those of other industrial countries is their style of expression and their forms of activity.

Means of Access and Styles of Action

In preceding regimes, organized interests found Parliament the most convenient means of access to political power. During the Third and Fourth Republics, the highly specialized and powerful committees of both houses of Parliament often seemed to be little more than institutional facades for interest groups which frequently substituted bills of their own design for those submitted by the government.

Among the reasons given in 1958 for reforming and rationalizing Parliament was the desire to reduce the role of organized interests in the legislative process. By and large this has been accomplished, but interest groups have not lost all influence on rule making and policy formation. To be effective, groups now use the channels that the best equipped have long found most rewarding, channels that give them direct access to the administration. The indispensable collaboration between organized private interests and the state is institutionalized in advisory committees that are attached to most administrative agencies and composed mainly of civil servants and group representatives. Nonetheless, tendencies toward privileged access, sometimes called *neocorporatism*, have, with the exception of agriculture and big business, remained weak in France. The weak organization of the labor and small business sectors means that organizations in these sectors are often regarded as unreliable partners.

Organized interests also attempt to bring pressure to bear on the political executive. For a long time the ministerial staffs—the circle of personal collaborators who support every French minister—are an important target. Inasmuch as the present regime has strengthened the position of the political executive, it has also enabled both the prime minister and the president to function more effectively as arbiters between competing claims and to exercise stricter control over many agencies and ministries.

It is not surprising that some interests have easier access to governmental bureaus than others. An affinity of views between group representatives and public administrators might be based on common outlook, common social origin, or education. The official of an important trade association or of their well-organized peak association, the MENEF, who already sorted out the raw demands of constituents and submits them in rational fashion, easily gets a more sympathetic hearing in the bureaus than an organization that seeks to defend atomistic interests by mobilizing latent resentment.

High civil servants tend to distinguish between "professional organizations," which they consider serious or dynamic enough to listen to, and "interest groups," which should be kept at a distance. The perspectives of interest representatives tend to reflect their own strength as well as their experience in collaborating with different parts of the state and government. Trade union representatives acknowledge their reliance on the social climate (the level of strike activity) to determine their ability to bargain effectively with the state. Representatives of business claim to rely more on contacts with civil servants, compared with those of agriculture who say that they rely more on contacts at the ministerial level.[26]

Central to the kind of state interest group collaboration described as neocorporatism is the notion that the state plays a key role in both shaping and defining the legitimacy of the interest group universe, and in establishing the rules by which the collaboration takes place. The French state, at various levels, has strongly influenced the relationship among groups and even their existence in key areas through official recognition and subsidization. Although representative organizations may exist with or without official recognition, this designation gives them access to consultative bodies, the right to sign collective agreements (especially important in the case of trade unions), and the right to certain forms of subsidies. Therefore recognition is an important tool that both conservative and Socialist governments have used to influence the group universe.

The French state subsidizes interest groups, both indirectly and directly. By favoring some groups over others through recognition and subsidization, the role of the state seems to conform to neocorporatist criteria. However, in other ways the neocorporatist model is less applicable in France than in other Euro-pean countries. Neocorporatist policymaking presumes close collaboration between the state administration and a dominant interest group (or coalition of groups) in major socioeconomic sectors (agriculture, labor, and employers). Yet, what stands out in the French case, as noted previously, is the unevenness of this pattern of collaboration.[27]

If in the neocorporatist pattern organizational action is controlled by interest group leaders and coordinated with bargaining, for French interest groups mass action such as street demonstrations, wildcat strikes, and attacks on government property are often poorly controlled by group leadership. Indeed, it can be argued that group protest is more effective in France (at least negatively) than in other industrialized countries because it is part of a pattern of group-state relations, in which protests remain limited in scope and intensity, but government recognizes them as a valid expression of interest. Only in this way can we understand why quite frequently governments backed by a majority in parliament were ready to make concessions to weakly organized interest groups[28] (see Box 5.3).

Box 5.3　Protest in France

During the early years of Socialist governments, more and more people—farmers, artisans, small businesspeople, truckers, doctors, medical students, all of them organized either by old-established or newly formed interest groups—took to the streets to protest impending legislation or just out of fear for their status. In quite a few cases, the demonstrations led to violence and near riots. The same scenario took place under later conservative governments. Demonstrations by college and high school students forced the withdrawal of a planned university reform under the Chirac government in 1987, and a planned imposition of a "youth" minimum wage by the Balladur government in 1994 (with an 80 percent majority in the National Assembly), ostensibly to encourage greater employment of young people, was dropped when high school students opposed it in the streets of Paris and other large cities. After a month of public service strikes, and massive demonstrations in November and December 1995, the new Chirac government abandoned a plan to reorganize the nationalized railway system and revised a plan to reorganize the civil service. A year later, striking truckers won major concessions from a still weakened government. In the autumn of 2000, a protest lead by truckers and taxi drivers (that spread to England) against the rising price of oil and gasoline forced the Jospin government to lower consumer taxes on fuel. Until the summer of 2000, the government benefited from unprecedented support in public opinion.

Sources: 1986—*Les Elections législatives du mars 1986* (Paris: *Le Monde*/Supplément aux dossiers et documents du Monde, 1986); 1988—*Les Elections législative du 5 juin et 12 juin 1988* (Paris: *Le Monde*/Supplément aux dossiers et documents du Monde, 1988). *Les Elections législatives du mars 1993* (Paris: Le Monde/Supplément aux dossiers du Monde, 1993). CSA, "Les elections legislatives du 25 mai 1997," p. 18. *Le Monde* May 27 and June 3, 1997. *The Economist* September 16, 2000.

Political Parties

The Traditional Party System

Some analysts of election data see a chronic and seemingly unalterable division of the French into two large political families, each motivated by a different mood or temperament and usually classified as the right and the left. If we view elections from this perspective, political alignments have remained surprisingly stable over long periods of history. As late as 1962, the opposition to de Gaulle was strongest in departments (see p. 168) where for more than a century republican traditions had a solid foundation. The alignments in the presidential contest of 1974 and the parliamentary elections of 1978 mirrored the same divisions. Soon thereafter, however, the left's inroads into formerly conservative strongholds had changed the traditional geographic distribution of votes. Majorities have changed at each legislative election since 1981, and few departments now remain solid bastions for either the right or the left.

The electoral systems of both the Third and Fifth Republics seemed to favor a simplification of political alignments. In most constituencies runoff elections result in the confrontation of two candidates, each more or less representing one of the two camps. A simple and stable division could have resulted long ago in a pattern of two parties or coalitions alternating in having power and being in opposition, and hence giving valid expression to the voters' opinions. Why has this not occurred?

Except for the Socialists and the Communists, and more recently the RPR, French party organizations have mostly remained as skeletal as the parties were in other countries at the time of their nineteenth-century beginnings. French parties developed in a mainly preindustrial and preurban environment, catering at first to upper-middle-class and later to middle-class elements. Their foremost and sometimes only function was to provide an organizational framework for selecting and electing candidates for local, departmental, and national offices. Even among the better-organized parties, party organization tends to be both fragmentary at the national level, and local in orientation, with only modest linkage between the two levels.

This form of representation and party organization survives largely because voters support it. An electorate that distrusts authority and wants representation to protect it against arbitrary government is likely to be suspicious of parties organized for political reform. For all their antagonism, the republican and anti-republican traditions have one thing in common: their aversion to well-established and strongly organized parties. Party membership has always been low, except during short and dramatic situations. As late as the 1960s no more than 2 percent of registered voters were party members; in other European democracies, particularly Britain and Germany, some parties have a following of more than a million members, a membership level never achieved by any French political party. Organizational weakness contributes to the endurance of a multiparty system, and a weak multiparty system feeds into the abstract and ideological style of French politics. To avoid the suggestion that they represent no more than limited interests or personalities, these weak parties phrase even the narrowest political issues in lofty ideological terms.

During the Third and Fourth Republics, neither the right nor the left could govern by itself for any length of time, because both lacked a majority and both included extreme parties that contested the legitimacy of the political order. As a normal consequence of this party system, an unstable center coalition was in control of the government most of the time, no matter what the outcome of the preceding elections. Between 1789 and the advent of the Fifth Republic, republican France was ruled by governments of the center for all but 30 years. In a two- or three-party system, major parties normally move toward the political center in order to gain stability and cohesion. But where extreme party plurality prevails, the center is unable to become a political force. In France, centrist coalitions were an effective, if limited, means of maintaining a regime, but an ineffective means of developing coherent policy.

The Fifth Republic created a new political framework that had a major, if gradual and mostly unforeseen, influence on all parties and on their relationships to each other. The emerging party system, in turn, had an important impact on the way that the institutions of the system actually worked.[29] The strengthening of parliamentary party discipline in the 1970s gave meaning to strong executive leadership of president and prime minister (who were leaders of the reconstructed parties) and served to stabilize the political process. The main political parties also became the principal arenas within which alternative policies were developed and debated. However, as the national political system became more competitive in the 1980s, the locus of policy debate shifted political leaders, on one hand, and marginal political organizations, on the other. The main political parties continue to dominate the organization of parliamentary work and the selection of candidates but became far less important as mass membership organizations. Thus in 1997, at least 48 parties presented 6,360 candidates for 577 seats in the National Assembly, a record for the Fifth Republic. The four main parties were supported by 67 percent of the electorate, with the National Front attracting an additional 15 percent. Thus, even if we include the National Front, almost 20 percent of the electorate supported an array of issue-based and personality-based parties. However, only eight parties are represented in the National Assembly in six parliamentary groups, three allied in the left majority, three in the right opposition.

The Main Parties: The Right and Center

RALLY FOR THE REPUBLIC The Rally for the Republic (RPR) is a direct lineal descendant of the Gaullist party, thrown hastily together after de Gaulle's return to power in 1958. Only weeks after its birth, it won more than 20 percent of the vote and almost 40 percent of the seats in the first Parliament of the new republic (see Table 5.2).

De Gaulle himself, preferring the methods of direct democracy, had little use for any party including his own. But his advisers, foremost among them Georges Pompidou, one of his prime ministers and later his successor, saw the need for a better organized party if future elections were to be won and an orderly succession of the charismatic leader was to ensure a Gaullism *sans* de Gaulle. In several respects the new party was different from the tradi-

tional conservative parties of the right. It appealed directly to a broad coalition of groups and classes, including a part of the working class. The party's leadership successfully built a membership that, according to claims, at one time reached several hundred thousand. Yet the membership's role was generally limited to appearances at mass meetings and assisting in propaganda efforts at election time. An important novelty was that the party's representatives in Parliament followed strict discipline in voting on policy. Electoral success increased with each contest until the landslide election, held after the *events of 1968*—the massive strikes and student demonstrations of May and June—enabled the Gaullists to hold a majority of seats in the National Assembly, a record never before attained under a republican regime in France.

For 16 years (from 1958 to 1974) both the presidency and the premiership were in Gaullist hands. But in 1974, after the death of both Charles de Gaulle and Georges Pompidou, with the election of Valéry Giscard-d'Estaing—a prominent conservative who was not a Gaullist—to the presidency (with the help of part of the Gaullist leadership), the party's status deteriorated and electoral support declined.

For a time, the decline of the party was turned around by the energy of Jacques Chirac, whose career was typical of the young generation of French political leaders. A graduate of the ENA, he entered on a political rather than a bureaucratic career. He was elected to Parliament at 34 years of age and had occupied important Cabinet posts under Pompidou. After the elections of 1974, he transformed the old Gaullist party into the Rally for the Republic.

The RPR was quite different from its Gaullist predecessors. Although Chirac frequently invoked Gaullism as his inspiration, he avoided the populist language that had served the movement at its beginnings. The RPR's appeal was now directed quite clearly to a more restricted, well-defined constituency of the right, similar to the classic conservative clientele. Its electorate overrepresented older, wealthier voters, as well as farmers (see Table 5.3); its voters were most likely to define themselves as being on the right, were most anti-left, were most positive toward business and parochial schools,

TABLE 5.2 First Ballot of French Parliamentary Elections in the Fifth Republic and Seats Won in the National Assembly in Both Ballots[a] (VOTING IN METROPOLITAN FRANCE)

Party	1958 %*	1958 S**	1962 %	1962 S	1967 %	1967 S	1968 %	1968 S	1973 %	1973 S	1978 %	1978 S	1981 %	1981 S	1986[a] %	1986[a] S	1988 %	1988 S	1993 %	1993 S	1997 %	1997 S
Registered Voters (in millions)	27.24		27.53		28.3		28.3		29.9		34.4		35.54		36.61		37.95		37		39.2	
Abstentions (%)	22.9		31.3		19.1		19.9		18.7		16.6		29.13		21.5		34.3		31.0		32	
Communists (PCF)	19.1	10	21.8	41	22.5	73	20.0	34	21.2	73	20.5	86	16.2	44	9.7	35	11.3	27	9.1	24	10	37
Socialists (PS)	15.5	47	12.5	66	19.0	121	16.5	41	18.9	89	22.6	107	37.6	267	31.6	208	34.8	274	19.2	61	23.7	245
Left Radicals	—	—	—	—	—	—	—	8	1.5	12	2.1	10	—	14	3	2	1.1	2	—	8	1.5	13
Radicals	7.3	33	7.8	—	—		—		—		—		—		—		—		—		—	
Center Outside Government			7.8	39	12.6	41	10.3	33	12.4	31	—	—	—	—	—	—	—	—	—	—	—	—
Majority	22.1	118	9.6		—		—		—		—		—		—		—		—		—	
MRP	11.6	64	9.1	55	—	—	—		—		—		—		—		—		—		—	
UDF (RI and other centrists in government majority)	—	—	4.4	36	—	—	—	—	10.6	77	21.4	119	19.2	63	42.0	129	18.5	130	18.8	207	14.8	109
Gaullists (RPR)	17.6	212	32.0	233	37.7	200	43.65	293	23.9	184	22.5	155	20.8	85		145	19.2	128	19.7	242	16.8	140
National Front (FN)	—		—		—		—		—		—		—		9.9	35	9.8	1	12.7	0	15.1	1
Others	6.8	0	2.8	0	8.2	10	9.5	16	11.5	24	10.9	14	6.2	16	6.6	23	5.3	15	20.5[b]	37[c]	18.7[d]	32[e]

aThe 1986 election was by proportional representation.
bIncludes the three Green parties which received 10.9 percent of the vote.
cIncludes 36 unaffiliated deputies of the right.
dIncludes the Green parties vote of 6.3 percent, as well as votes for smaller movements of the right and the left.
eIncludes eight ecologists, seven dissident Socialists, and other unaffiliated deputies.
*Votes cast (%).
**Seats in Parliament.

TABLE 5.3   Sociological Analysis of the Electorate in the First Ballot Legislative Elections of 1997 (percentage of category voting)

	(Abst)[a]	PCF	X-Left	PS/Other left	Greens	UDF/RPR/ Other right	FN	Other
Sex								
Men	(33)	10	3	27	6	35	18	1
Women	(37)	9	2	28	8	38	13	2
Age								
18–24	(40)	7	6	28	10	33	14	2
25–34	(43)	9	2	27	10	32	18	2
35–49	(34)	10	3	28	9	32	16	2
50–64	(30)	12	2	29	4	38	15	—
65+	(33)	10	1	25	2	50	12	—
Shopkeepers, craftsmen, and business		4	1	20	8	49	17	1
Executives, professionals, and intellectuals		8	3	35	8	39	7	2
Middle management		7	3	35	17	32	14	1
White collar		12	4	29	9	29	16	1
Workers		12	3	28	6	24	25	2
Inactive/retired		11	2	24	4	44	13	2
Maastricht vote								
Yes		7	1	35	8	40	8	1
No		16	3	13	5	32	30	1
Total		10	2.5	27.7	6.9	36.5	15.1	1.3

[a]Abstention and blank ballots, average of both ballots, from *Le Monde,* June 5, 1997.

were most likely to vote for personality rather than ideas, and were least supportive of a woman's right to abortion.

Neither as party leader, nor as unsuccessful presidential candidate running against Mitterrand in 1981 and 1988, nor as prime minister between 1986 and 1988 did Chirac show any of the earlier concerns of Gaullism for the role of the state in modernizing the economy and society. Instead, after presiding over a government that dubbed itself neoliberal and that engaged in a round of privatization of previously nationalized industries between 1986 and 1988, he set out to assure those who feared change.

Nevertheless, the party's electoral level slumped after 1973, and in the 1980s its vote remained more or less stagnant. Even in the massive electoral vic-

tory for the right in 1993, when the conservative coalition gained 80 percent of the parliamentary seats, the RPR just edged out their conservative rivals with less than 20 percent of the vote in the first round of the elections. In 1997, its vote declined to 16.8 percent, less than two points more than the National Front. Nevertheless, with an estimated 100,000 members in 1997 (relatively low by European standards), the RPR was the largest party in France (see Figure 5.4).[30]

Thus the RPR is a long way from the party once dominated with a firm hand by Gaullist "barons". The organizing discourse of Gaullism is long gone, and the party has not been able to replace it with an ideologically based unity. The victory of Jacques Chirac in the 1995 presidential elections should have given the new president an opportunity to

FIGURE 5.4 Political Representation in the National Assembly After the Elections of 1993 and 1997

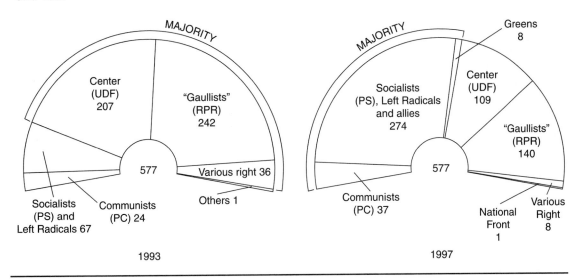

rebuild the RPR as a party of government. However, the seeming unending series of political crises after the summer of 1995, and the disastrous losses in the June 1997 legislative elections, only encouraged and intensified the divisions within the party, and between the RPR and its (now) opposition partners. In 1999, Chirac lost control over the party, when his chosen candidate was defeated in an election for party president. Then, in the fall of 2000, Chirac's presumed candidacy for reelection in 2002 was apparently undermined by dramatic new evidence of massive corruption in the Paris party machine that directly implicated the president (and former mayor of Paris).

THE UNION FOR FRENCH DEMOCRACY (UDF) To prevent the center's exclusion from power in the Gaullist republic had been the foremost concern of Valéry Giscard d'Estaing. His small party, the Parti républicain, the Republican Party (PR), had been the typical party, or rather non-party, of French conservatism. It came into existence in 1962, when Giscard and a few other conservative deputies opposed de Gaulle's strictures against European unity and his referendum on direct elections for the presi-

dency. From that time on the group provided a small complement for the majority in Parliament. Giscard himself, a scion of families long prominent in business, banking, and public service, had been Finance Minister under both de Gaulle and Pompidou before his election to the presidency in 1974. His party never aspired to be a mass party but rather derived its political strength from its representatives in Parliament, many of whom moved in and out of Cabinet posts, and from local leaders who occupied fairly important posts in municipal and departmental councils.

In order to increase the weight of the PR at the time when Chirac had given a new elan to Gaullism, Giscard, as President of the Republic, chose the way that parties of the right and center have always found opportune: a heterogeneous alliance among groups and personalities organized to support the president in anticipation of the 1978 legislative elections. The result was the *Union for French Democracy (UDF)*, which included, in addition to Giscard's Republicans, remnants of a Catholic party (CDS), the once militant anti-Catholic Radicals, and some former Socialists. The ideological battles of the past within the center had become meaningless, but the parties that formed the UDF found it inopportune to abandon their own weak organizational structures. It is estimated that all of the parties of the UDF combined had no more than 38,000 members in 1995. UDF remains a federated party of notables, a vehicle and arena of contention for its leaders.

The centrist federation was reasonably successful in determining at election time who would be the best placed conservative candidate and in providing, wherever possible, a counterweight to the better organized RPR. Since 1981, the UDF and the RPR have generally cooperated in elections at all levels. However, as the National Front gained in electoral support after 1983, RPR and UDF were compelled to present more and more joint candidates in the first round of parliamentary elections to avoid being defeated by the FN. Nevertheless, even combined, they have been incapable of increasing the percentage of their vote beyond 45 percent, even though they won majorities in Parliament in 1986 and 1993. The two governments organized after the election of Jacques Chirac (in 1995) under Prime Minister *Alain Juppé* were double coalitions: first coalitions of factions within the RPR and the UDF, then coalitions between RPR and UDF. Thus the representatives of the UDF exercised considerable influence over the policymaking process, both as members of the cabinet and as chairs of three of the six permanent committees of the National Assembly.

The deep divisions within the UDF were exacerbated after both the 1997 legislative elections, when the UDF became the third party of the right in terms of electoral support (just behind the National Front), and the 1998 regional elections, when five (UDF) regional parties accepted the support of the National Front, and the party split two months later. The liberal (conservative in U.S. terms) minority of the deputies formed a new parliamentary group: Démocratie Libérale (DL, Liberal Democracy). At the same time, the RPR, UDF and DL joined in a loose intergroup in the National Assembly, which they called *L'Alliance*, the Alliance. However, in opposition there has been little incentive for the fragmented parties of the right to cooperate fully. It is possible, however, that they will cobble

together a firmer alliance in anticipation of a new cycle of elections, beginning in 2001.

THE NATIONAL FRONT   Divisions within the right have resulted in part from different reactions to the rise of the National Front (FN) during the Mitterrand presidency. Until the 1980s, the FN, founded by *Jean-Marie Le Pen* in 1972, was one of a number of relatively obscure parties of the far right. In none of the elections prior to 1983 did FN attract more than 1 percent of the national vote. In the 1984 elections for the European Parliament, the National Front built on support in local elections the year before and attracted almost 10 percent of the vote, to the consternation of the established parties of the right and the left.

In the parliamentary elections of 1986 the FN again won almost 10 percent (about 2.7 million votes) of the total vote (and in metropolitan France, more votes than the Communists) and established itself as a substantial political force. Two-thirds of these votes came from voters who had previously supported established parties of the right, but the remainder came from some former left voters (mostly Socialists) or from new voters and former abstainers. Profiting from the change to proportional representation in 1986, which Mitterrand had introduced partly in order to divide the right, 35 FN deputies entered Parliament. In the 1993 legislative elections, National Front candidates attracted almost 13 percent of the vote in the first round, but because the electoral system had reverted back to single-member districts, the party elected no deputies. In the 1997 legislative elections, with over 15 percent of the vote, FN became the second conservative party in France and sent a record number of candidates into the second round. However, only one of these candidates was elected.

In 1992, the right depended on the party for its majority in 14 out of 22 regions. In 1998 this dependency was translated into a political breakthrough for the National Front when five UDF regional leaders formally accepted FN support to maintain their regional presidencies. In 1995, for the first time FN won municipal elections in three cities and gained representation in almost half of the larger towns in France. It gained one additional city in a special election in 1997. However this major breakthrough brought to a head a growing rivalry between party leader Le Pen and the architect of the party organization, Bruno Mégret, whose coalition strategy had been successful in the 1998 regional elections. By the end of 1998, Mégret and his supporters were expelled from the party. In 1999, the two factions became two separate parties, reducing the influence and electoral strength of both.

The National Front has often been compared to a shopkeeper movement that attracted 2.5 million votes in the legislative elections of 1956 (the Poujadist movement) and then faded from the scene.[31] But the FN draws its electoral and organizational support from big-city, rather than small-town, France, and its supporters come more from transfers from the right than had those of Pierre Poujade. In addition, the National Front has been far more successful than the Poujadist movement in building a strong organizational network. Because of changes in the electoral system, FN never had more than one deputy in the National Assembly after 1988, but there are still altogether hundreds of elected representatives on the regional, departmental, and local levels (as well as in the European Parliament). In 1992 it was estimated that the National Front had 50,000 members (compared with 10,000 in 1985).

The influence of the divided FN has certainly waned since 1998, but the process of party emergence and construction over a 15-year period had an impact on voters of all parties, especially on those who would normally vote for the right and on young workers who had formerly been mobilized by the now weakened French Communist Party (see following discussion). Approval of the ideas favored by the FN increased dramatically among *all* voters in the 1980s, and in the 1990s averaged around 35 percent. Through the dynamics of party competition, the National Front systematically forced other political parties to place these issues high on their political agenda.

The Left

THE SOCIALIST PARTY In comparison with the solid social-democratic parties in other European countries, le Parti Socialist, the French *Socialist Party*

(PS), lacked muscle almost since its beginnings in 1905. Slow and uneven industrialization and reluctance to organize have not only blocked the development of labor unions but also deprived the PS of the base of working-class strength that accrued to other labor parties from their affiliation with a trade union movement.

Unlike the British Labour Party, the early manifestations of the PS also failed to absorb middle-class radicals, the equivalent of the Liberals in England. The Socialist program, formulated in terms of doctrinaire Marxism, prevented inroads into the electorate of the left-of-center middle-class parties for a long time. The pre-Fifth Republic party was never strong enough to assume control of the government by itself. Its weakness reduced it to being at best one of several partners in the unstable coalition governments of the Third and Fourth Republics.

The emergence of the French Communist Party in 1920 effectively deprived the Socialists of core working class support. Most of the Socialists' working-class following was concentrated in a few regions of traditional strength, such as the industrial north and urban agglomeration in the center. However, the party had some strongholds elsewhere—among the wine-growers of the south, devotees of republican ideals, of anticlericalism, and of producers' cooperatives. The proportion of civil servants, especially teachers, and of people living on fixed income has at all times been far higher among Socialist voters than in the population at large. This support made for a stable but not particularly dynamic following.

The party encountered considerable difficulties under the changed conditions in the Fifth Republic. After several false starts, the old party dissolved and a new Socialist Party was organized in the summer of 1969, which had considerable success in attracting new members and in reversing its electoral decline. Incipient public disenchantment with conservative governments and new conservative leadership combined with the strong leadership of François Mitterrand to bring about this reversal in Socialist fortunes (see Box 5.4).

Compared with the past, the party membership reached respectable heights in the 1980s (about 180,000 by 1983), though it was still not comparable

Box 5.4 François Mitterrand and the Rise of the New Socialist Party

Though *François Mitterrand* was a politician since the Fourth Republic (he had also served briefly as a government official under the Vichy Regime), he was a new recruit to socialism. He had run for the presidency in 1965 with Socialist and Communist support but joined the Socialist Party only shortly before he imposed himself as its General Secretary in 1971. Ten years later, he led the party to victory in the presidential and legislative elections. Mitterrand's own anticapitalism was often strident, yet concern for social justice clearly outweighed his interest in economic blueprints for a socialist future. Nevertheless, the preamble of his party's program stated: "Because socialists are convinced democrats, they believe that no genuine democracy can exist in a capitalist society. In that sense the Socialist Party is a revolutionary party."

If Mitterrand strove for a common program with the Communists, he did so because he believed that only a coalition of the parties on the left offered a credible alternative to the right and center-right governments that had ruled since 1958. But such an alternative was suspect to the voters as long as the Communists were stronger and better organized than the PS. Hence, Mitterrand pledged that he would win for the Socialists millions of voters who had traditionally voted Communist. Such frankness promoted the very goals that it announced: the growing organizational and electoral strength of the PS.

to the large labor parties of Britain and the continent. In terms of social origin the new membership came predominantly from the salaried middle classes, the professions, the civil service, and especially the teaching profession. Workers rallied to the PS in large numbers in the 1970s, but they were still represented rather sparsely in the party's leadership. But the PS did in the 1970s what other European socialist parties were unable to do: It attracted leaders of some of the new social movements that emerged out of the activism of the late 1960s, among them ecologists and regionalists, as well as leaders of small parties of the non-Communist left.[32]

Mitterrand reaped the benefits of the elections of 1981. With the party's leader as president of the Republic and a Socialist majority in Parliament (but also supported by the Communists), the PS found itself in a situation it had never known—and for which it was ill-prepared. The following years of undivided power were bound to affect the party's image and outlook. The years in office between 1981 and 1986 were an intensive, and painful, learning experience for the PS at all its levels. Under pressure from Mitterrand and a succession of socialist governments, the classical socialist ideology, which had become rather empty sloganeering even before

1981, was dismantled. What the German Social Democrats had done by adopting a new program at Bad Godesberg in 1959, the French PS did in the early 1980s by its daily practice. An at least implicit belief that a more just society can and must be achieved by reforms, and the management and modernization of the capitalist system, rather than by revolutionary action is now the party's credo.

Indeed, by most measures, the Socialist Party became in the 1980s what the Gaullists had been in the 1960s, a party of government with broad support among most social groups throughout the country (see again Table 5.3). When reelected for a second seven-year term in 1988, Mitterrand carried 77 of the 96 departments of metropolitan France. The Socialists remained strong in most of their areas of traditional geographic strength, and they made some of their strongest gains in traditionally conservative areas in the west and east of the country. One consequence of this nationalization of Socialist electoral strength, however, was that the party's legislative majority depended on constituencies in which voter support was far more conditional than it was in its areas of traditional strength. In the legislative elections of 1993 the PS lost a third of its electorate compared with 1988, but far more than that in areas outside of its traditional bastions.

Social trends favored the left for a time. The decline of religious observance, urbanization, the growth of the salaried middle classes (technicians, middle management, etc.) and of the tertiary sector of the economy, and the massive entry of women into the labor market were all developments that weakened the groups that provided the right's stable strength: farmers, small businesspeople, the traditional bourgeoisie, and the nonemployed housewives. A strong and organized Socialist Party emerged just in time to take advantage of the moment when these trends formed the basis for a shift in voter loyalties, and (as we will see) to take advantage of the decline of the legitimacy of the Communist Party.

On the other hand, recent studies reveal that, as in other countries, the *basis* of loyalty of large numbers of voters, especially younger voters, was evolving during the 1980s, and became more related to individual attitudes toward specific issues than to collective loyalties based on group or class. Thus the rise of unemployment rates after 1990, the growing sense among even Socialist voters that party leadership was worn out, and the mobilization of large numbers of traditional Socialist voters against the government during the campaign for the Maastricht referendum of 1992, especially among workers, all undermined Socialist support between 1992 and 1994.

The *referendum* campaign in 1992, the massive losses of parliamentary seats in 1993, and then the confirmation of these losses in the 1994 European elections, intensified internal party rivalries and heightened the sense of crisis within the party. During ten years as a governing party (broken by two years of opposition from 1986 to 1988), leadership cohesion came to depend on the prerogatives of power. If the Fifth Republic had become normalized during the 1980s, in the sense that left and right alternated in government with each legislative election, the PS became like other governing parties in France in its dependence on governing power. One index of this normalization was the increased instance of political corruption within the party. Accusations, investigations, and convictions for corruption swept all

parties beginning in the late 1980s. For the Socialists, however, this aspect of normalization undermined the party's image and seems to have contributed to the voters' desertion of the party. Estimated membership dropped to about 100,000 in 1995, and in the runup to the 1995 presidential elections, the party had difficulty finding a viable candidate.

Under these circumstances, PS leader *Lionel Jospin* proved to be a remarkably effective presidential candidate, winning the first round before being defeated in the second round by Chirac. Indeed, this was a turning point in the PS electoral fortunes. During the period after the elections, the PS gained in the municipal elections, performed well in by-elections, and made significant gains in the (indirect) Senate elections in September 1995. But the real test for Socialist leadership came when President Chirac called surprise legislative elections in April 1997.

Although party leader Jospin and his colleagues were clearly unprepared for the short campaign, they benefited from the rapidly deteriorating popularity and the lack of efficacy of Chirac's majority. After electoral agreements with the Communists and the Greens for the second round, Jospin put together a 31-seat majority (called the *plural left*), was named prime minister, and formed the first cohabitation government of the left in June 1997. This surprise victory—the first Socialist triumph in the post-Mitterrand era—provided the party with another opportunity to build its strength as a party of government.

In fact, until the fall of 2000, the left performed remarkably well. The government benefited from declining unemployment and passed a set of important but controversial reforms, including a 35-hour work-week, domestic partnership legislation, and a constitutional amendment requiring parity for women candidacies for elective office. Under pressure from the European Union, the government also passed legislation establishing a presumption of innocence for those accused in criminal cases, and further limited the French practice of multiple office-holding (*cumul des mandats*). Finally, there were major structural reforms: the presidential term was reduced to five years (with the agreement of the president), and a process was initiated to radically alter the relationship between Corsica and the French state.

Then, with breathtaking rapidity in September 2000, the government lost what appeared to be unusually secure footing. As a result of widespread demonstrations in the streets against rising oil prices, dramatic corruption charges against the RPR that spread to the Socialist and Communist Parties, and a referendum on the reduction of the presidential mandate that was passed, but boycotted by 70 percent of the electorate (and widely perceived as unnecessary), the popularity of Jospin fell to an historic low for the Fifth Republic.

THE COMMUNISTS Until the late 1970s le Parti Communist Français, the *French Communist Party (PCF)*, was a major force in French politics, despite the fact that, except for a short interlude after the war (1944–1947), the party had been excluded since its beginning in 1920 from any participation in the national government. During most of the Fourth Republic, it received more electoral support than any other single party (with an average of just over 25 percent of the electorate). During the Fifth Republic, the party remained, until 1978, electorally dominant on the left, although it trailed the Gaullists on the right (see again Table 5.2). In addition to its successes in national elections, the party commanded significant strength at the local level until the early 1980s. Between 1977 and 1983, Communist mayors governed in about 1,500 towns in France, with a total population of about 10 million people.

Over several decades, the party's very existence constantly impinged nationally as well as locally on the rules of the political game and thereby on the system itself. The Communists defined (more or less) what left meant, while the Socialists debated the acceptability of that definition. For the parties of the right, the hegemony of the PCF provided an issue (anti-Communism) around which they could unite and on which they could attack both the Socialists and the Communists.

The seemingly impressive edifice of the Communists and of its numerous organizations of sympathizers was badly shaken, first by the rejuvenation of the PS under Mitterrand's leadership in the 1970s, and then by the collapse of international communism and the Soviet Union in the 1980s. The association of the French Communist Party with the international communist movement dominated by the Soviet Union had sharply divided Communists from Socialists in France since 1920, and was the basis of distrust and antagonism between the two "brother-enemies" of the left. Nevertheless, this association with the international movement also provided an important part of the revolutionary identity of the party, especially for its most devoted militants, an identity that endured long after the PCF ceased to be a revolutionary party in terms of its day-to-day actions. It also provided considerable financial support for the party organization and its activities, support that disappeared after 1989.

The PCF fielded its leader *Georges Marchais* as a candidate in the first ballot of the presidential election of 1981 with disastrous results: With only 15 percent of the vote, the PCF lost one-fourth of its electorate. In the parliamentary elections that followed, the number of its deputies was cut in half.

It turned out that the defeats that the party had suffered in 1981 were only the beginning of a tailspin of electoral decline.[33] The voters who left the party in 1981 never came back. Far more troubling, every subsequent election demonstrated the decline in stability of its core electorate. In the working-class suburbs of Paris, where the PCF was attracting huge majorities as late as the 1970s, its electorate had declined to less than 20 percent for its presidential candidate in 1988.

By 1997, with less than 10 percent of the vote nationally, the PCF attracted only 12 percent of the working-class vote and less than 7 percent of the vote of those under 24 years of age. To win elections, it has grown increasingly dependent on continued (and often difficult) cooperation with the Socialists, as well as on the personal popularity of some of its long-established mayors. Twenty-one of the 37 Communist deputies elected in 1997 were mayors and many others were municipal council members. These significant local roots contribute mightily to the sustenance of the concentrated geographic support in the suburbs of Paris and a few other areas that enable the PCF to maintain its representation in the National Assembly.

Loss of party membership parallels electoral decline. Between 1979 and 1987 the party lost at least 40 percent of its membership. Although claimed membership remains large by French standards, 275,000 according to 1996 party documents—but probably closer to 200,000—the PCF remains the largest mass membership party in the country. However, its organization is increasingly divided, ineffective, and challenged by successive waves of dissidence from within. By 1986, surveys revealed that dissident factions within the party were supported by two-thirds of the Communist electorate and that there was support for their case in at least 15 departmental federations of the party.

Since the legislative elections of 1993, the party has responded to these pressures. In 1994 the PCF revised its statutes to eliminate the principle of democratic centralism and to accept the presence of dissenting factions within the party. Georges Marchais, party leader since 1972, stepped down in favor of Robert Hue. Younger, and seemingly more open, Hue apologized to those who were forced out of the party in the past and promoted dialogue and discussion. Nevertheless, the dissidents have not returned and have in fact joined, in the fall of 1994, with other left factions in a loose movement called the Convention for a Progressive Alternative (CAP).

What does the marginalization of the PCF mean for the French party system? It has healed the division that had enfeebled the left since the split of the Socialist Party in 1920, in the wake of the Bolshevik seizure of power in Russia. But a price has been paid: The political representation of the French working class has been weakened. Although the fortunes of the PCF have fallen in inverse relation to the rise of the electoral strength of the PS, the proportion of workers actually voting for both parties combined has declined by 30 percent since the 1970s; perhaps most important, it appears that many young workers, who previously would have been mobilized by Communist militants, are now being mobilized to vote for the National Front.

Since the decline of the PCF has coincided with a shift of the PS toward the political center, the options of French politics have, in general, moved further to the right. Altogether, the fate of the French Communist Party in the 1990s, in the smaller arena of French politics, is an event that is no less momentous than the collapse of Communism in Eastern Europe.

The Communist Party will not disappear in the near future, however. It has held its political support at about 10 percent of the vote and sustained its local roots. In the legislative elections of 1997 the party made gains among older voters but made little progress in attracting new and younger voters, especially young workers. Nevertheless, because of its electoral agreement with the PS, the PCF increased its number of deputies in the National Assembly from 23 to 37, and once again has three ministerial positions.

Policy Processes

The Executive

As we have seen, the French constitution has a two-headed executive: As in other parliamentary regimes, the prime minister presides over the government but unlike other parliamentary regimes, the president is far from being a figurehead. It was widely predicted that such an arrangement would necessarily lead to frequent political crises. During the first 28 years of the Fifth Republic, four presidents, for all their differences in outlook and style, and each of the prime ministers who have served under them, left no doubt that the executive had only one head, the president (see again Figure 5.1).

The exercise of presidential powers in all their fullness was made possible not so much by the constitutional text as by a political fact: Between 1958 and 1986 the president and prime minister derived their legitimacy from the same majority in the electorate: the president by direct popular elections, the prime minister by the support of a majority of deputies in the National Assembly. In 1981 the electorate shifted its allegiance from the right to the left, yet for the ensuing five years president and Parliament were still on the same side of the political divide. The long years of political affinity between the holders of the two offices solidified and amplified presidential powers and shaped constitutional practices in ways that appear to have had a lasting impact even after political conditions changed. From the very beginning of the Fifth Republic, the president not only *formally* appointed the prime minister proposed by him to Parliament (as the presidents of the previous republics had also done, and as the queen of England does), but he also *chose* the prime minister and the other Cabinet ministers. In some cases the president has also dismissed a prime minister who was clearly enjoying the continuing confidence of a majority in Parliament.

Hence, the rather frequent reshuffling of Cabinet posts and personnel in the Fifth Republic was different from similar happenings in the Third and Fourth Republics. In those systems the changes occurred in response to shifts in parliamentary support and frequently in order to forestall, at least for a short time, the government's fall from power. In the present system, the president or the prime minister—depending on the circumstances—may decide to appoint, move, or dismiss a Cabinet officer on the basis of his own appreciation of the worth (or lack of it) of the individual member. This does not mean that considerations of the executive have been merely technical. They may have been highly political, but they have been exclusively those of the executive.

Since all powers proceeded from the president, the government headed by the prime minister became essentially an administrative body until 1986, despite constitutional stipulations to the contrary. The chief function of the prime minister was to provide whatever direction or resources were needed to implement the policies conceived by the chief of state. This meant primarily that the task of the government was to develop legislative proposals and present an executive budget. In many respects the government's position resembled that of the Cabinet in a presidential regime such as the United States, rather than that of a government in a parliamentary system such as Britain and the earlier French republics.

Regardless of the political circumstances (see following discussion), weekly meetings of the Cabinet always are chaired by the president and are officially called the *Council of Ministers*. They are sometimes a forum for deliberation and confrontation of different points of view, and Cabinet decisions and decrees officially emanate from the council, but in fact real decisions are made elsewhere.

The prime minister, in relation to Cabinet colleagues, is more than first among equals. Among his many functions have been the harnessing of a parliamentary majority for presidential policies, since according to the constitution the government must resign when a majority in Parliament adopts a motion of censure or rejects the governmental program. This provision distinguishes France from a truly presidential regime such as the United States or Mexico.

The relationship between president and prime minister, however, has operated quite differently during the periods of so-called cohabitation: from 1986 to 1988; then again between 1993 and 1995 when a conservative majority controlled parliament and the president was a Socialist; and since 1997, when the left holds a parliamentary majority and the president is from a conservative party. Without claiming any domain exclusively as his own, the president (Mitterrand in the first two cases, and Chirac since 1997) continued to occupy the foreground in foreign and military affairs, in accordance with his interpretation of his mandate under the constitution. The prime minister became the effective leader of the executive and pursued government objectives, but avoided interfering with presidential prerogatives.

In part as a result of the experiences of cohabitation, the role of the presidency is now less imposing than it had been before 1986. Even during the interlude of Socialist government between 1988 and 1993, the Socialist prime minister was largely responsible for the main options that were slowly developed for governmental action, with the president setting the limits and the tone. Thus, by the 1990s, the relationship between president and prime minister was more complicated than during the earlier period of the Fifth Republic, and it has varied according to the political circumstances in which each has assumed office.

Since the early days of the de Gaulle administration, the office of the chief of state is organized to maximize the ability of the president to initiate, elaborate, and frequently execute policy. In terms of function, the staff at the Elysée Palace, the French White House, composed of a general secretariat and the presidential staff, has become somewhat similar to the Executive Office of the U.S. president. Yet it is much smaller, comprising only 40 to 50 persons, with an additional support staff of several hundred people.

As the president's eyes and ears, his staff members are indispensable for the exercise of presidential powers. They are in constant contact not only with the prime minister's collaborators but also directly with individual ministries. Through these contacts the president can initiate, impede, interfere, and assure himself that presidential policies are followed.

The prime minister has a parallel network for developing and implementing policy decisions, the most important of which are the so-called interministerial meetings, regularly held gatherings of high civil servants attached to various ministries. The frequency of these sessions, chaired by a member of the prime minister's personal staff, reflects the growing centralization of administrative and decision-making authority within the office of the prime minister, and the growing importance of the prime minister's policy network in everyday policymaking within the executive.

As we have seen, two different patterns have developed for the sharing of executive power. When the presidential and parliamentary majorities are identical (as was the case between 1962 and 1986, 1988 and 1993, and 1995 and 1997) the prime minister is clearly subordinate to the president.[34] Even in this case, however, the president's power is always limited by the fact that he does not control the administrative machinery directly and must work through the prime minister's office and the ministries; cooperation between the two is thus essential for effective government. Between 1974 and 1981, and again from 1988 to 1993, the prime minister's power was further enhanced by a very narrow majority in the National Assembly, giving him the opportunity to act as a legislative coalition-builder for the executive. Under conditions of cohabitation, the prime minister clearly gains dominant authority at the expense of the president. The power to set the political agenda and to command within the executive is largely transferred to the prime minister. But the president retains the power to bargain, based on his prerogatives to make appointments, to sign or-

dinances, and to participate in decisions on defense and foreign policy.

Parliament

The constitution has severely and intentionally curtailed the powers of Parliament both as a source of legislation and as an organ of control over the executive. The fact that both houses of Parliament were confined to sessions of no more than six months in a calendar year until 1995 severely reduced effectiveness. In 1995, maximum sessions were increased to nine months, opening new possibilities for parliamentary leadership to exercise initiative and control.

Despite restrictions on parliamentary activity, the legislative output of the parliaments in the Fifth Republic is quite respectable. The average of only 98 laws per year enacted during the first 35 years of the Fifth Republic (125 per year during the reform period between 1981 and 1986) was much lower than that during the Fourth Republic. However, it is double the British average for the first 35 years after World War II.

Although either the government or Parliament may propose bills, almost all legislation is in fact proposed by the government. The government is effectively in control of proceedings in both houses and can require priority for those bills that it wishes to see adopted (see Figure 5.5). Article 44 of the constitution empowers the government to force Parliament by the so-called *blocked vote* to accept a bill in its entirety with only the amendments agreed to by the government. In recent years the blocked vote has been generally used to maintain discipline within the majority, rather than to impose the will of the executive over a chaotic Parliament. Its use has become an index of conflict within the governing party or coalition.[35] After 1986, the conservative government of Jacques Chirac and the Socialist governments of Cresson, Rocard, and Bérégovoy were all tempted to use the blocked vote more often and for the same reason: to make up for their slim majority, and hence their weak support in the National Assembly. For the Jospin government, the blocked voted is a useful tool to maintain a sometimes raucous plural coalition.

Article 38 invites Parliament to abandon "for a limited time" its legislative function to the government

Figure 5.5   How a Bill Becomes a Law

I. Legislative initiative

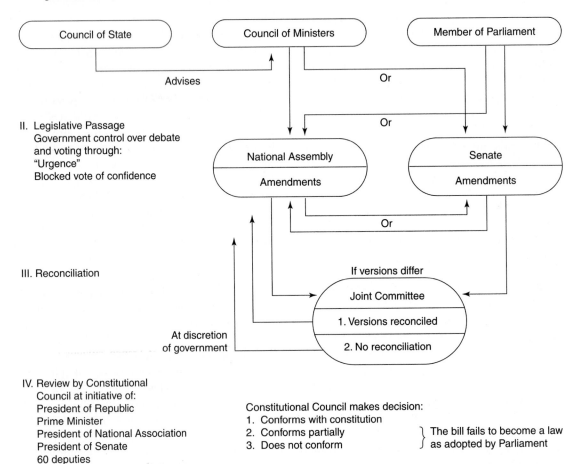

II. Legislative Passage
Government control over debate
and voting through:
"Urgence"
Blocked vote of confidence

III. Reconciliation

At discretion
of government

IV. Review by Constitutional
Council at initiative of:
President of Republic
Prime Minister
President of National Association
President of Senate
60 deputies
60 senators

Constitutional Council makes decision:
1. Conforms with constitution
2. Conforms partially
3. Does not conform   } The bill fails to become a law
                                   as adopted by Parliament

if the government wishes to act as legislator "for the implementation of its program." Once Parliament votes a broad enabling law, the government enacts legislation by way of so-called *ordinances*. Governments of the Fifth Republic made use of this possibility of executive lawmaking 22 times between 1958 and 1986, and often for important legislation, sometimes simply to expedite the legislative process. But its use is now limited by decisions of the Constitutional Council, which requires that the enabling act spell out the lim-

its of executive lawmaking with some precision. During the first period of cohabitation, Mitterrand refused to permit the government to promulgate ordinances that would have permitted it to avoid parliamentary debate.

Another constitutional provision gives the government a unique tool to ensure parliamentary support for any bill that it introduces. According to Article 49, Section 3, the prime minister may pledge the "government's responsibility" on any bill (or section of a bill) submitted to the National Assembly. In such a case, the bill is automatically "considered as adopted," without further vote, unless the deputies succeed in a *motion of censure* against the government according to the strict requirements discussed earlier. The success of this motion would likely result in new elections, but so far the threat of having to face new elections has always put sufficient pressure on the incumbent deputies not to support a motion of censure. As a consequence, whenever the government pledged its responsibility to a bill it introduced, the bill has become law without any parliamentary vote.

For many years, little use was made of this provision. Since 1979 various governments have resorted to it with some frequency. Between 1981 and 1986, the governments of the left used it for various reasons of expediency; it permitted them to enact important legislation quickly, without laying bare conflicts within the ranks of the governing majority. After 1986, governments of both the right and left resorted to this procedure with considerable frequency when they needed to overcome the precariousness of their majorities in Parliament. During the five years between 1988 and 1993, prime ministers engaged the responsibility of their governments 39 times, nine times each year in 1990 and 1991 alone.

Since June 1997 this procedure has not been used; it appears that this method of virtually excluding Parliament from meaningful participation in the legislative process is a permanent, though variable, fixture of governance. It was used for adopting some of the most important pieces of legislation: France's nuclear strike force, nationalization under the Socialists, and privatization under the conservatives, as well as annual budgets, military planning laws, social security legislation, economic plans— all have become law in this manner.

Some devices for enhancing the role of Parliament, however, have become somewhat more effective over the years. In the 1970s, the National Assembly made room for a weekly session devoted to a new kind of question period that is similar to the British (and German) version. Two days a week, the party groups select and submit a dozen or more written questions an hour in advance, in rough proportion to membership of each group, and then the relevant minister answers them. Added interest is provided by the presence of television cameras in the chamber (since 1974), which record the dialogue between the government representatives and the deputies.

By using its power to amend, Parliament has vastly expanded its role in the legislative process during the past decades. During the 1980s, amendments proposed averaged almost 5,000 a year; since 1990, however, this average has more than doubled, which has coincided with the doubling of hours devoted to legislative debate each year. About two-thirds of the amendments that are eventually adopted (27 percent of those proposed in 1998–1999) are proposed by parliamentary committees working with the government. Thus committees help shape legislation, and governments have all but abandoned their constitutionally guaranteed prerogative to declare amendments out of order.[36] The long parliamentary session introduced in 1995 has enhanced the role of committee leaders in the legislative process, and will probably increase the bargaining power of the president of the National Assembly.

Finally, the role of Parliament is enhanced by the general support that French citizens give their elected deputies. Better-organized parties both add to the deputy's role as part of a group and somewhat diminish his or her role as an independent actor, capable of influencing the legislative process merely for narrow parochial interests. Nevertheless, individual deputies still command a considerable following within their constituencies that is enhanced by the fact that 56 percent of the deputies in the National Assembly elected in 1997 were also mayors, while others held other local offices. In 1993, when confidence in political parties was at 21 percent, confidence in deputies had risen to 51 percent, and in mayors to 73 percent (see again Figure 5.3).

Because the electoral college that elects the members of the Senate is composed almost entirely of people selected by small-town mayors, the parties of the center, which are most influential in small towns, are best represented in the Upper House. At a time when the Gaullists held the absolute majority of seats in the National Assembly, their representation in the Senate amounted to not more than 12.7 percent of the total. In 1998, the parties of the center (UDF and DL) still had a few more seats than their RPR rivals, but were displaced by the Socialists as the largest single group within the Senate, a result of the strong roots that the PS has developed at the local level, as well as the initiation of limited proportional representation in senatorial elections. Although the right remains dominant in the Upper House, the Senate has not always been found on the right of the political spectrum. Its hostility to social and economic change is balanced by a forthright defense of traditional republican liberties and by a stand against demagogic appeals to latent anti-parliamentary feelings.

The Senate, in the normal legislative process, can do little more than delay legislation approved by the government and passed by the National Assembly. There is, however, one constitutional situation in which a majority in the Upper House cannot be overruled: Any constitutional amendment needs the approval of either a simple or a three-fifths majority of senators (Article 89). In the year 2000, lack of support in the Senate forced the president (and prime minister) to withdraw an amendment to create an independent judiciary and to modify significantly the amendment on parity for women (that was passed).

Some legislation of great importance, such as the atomic strike force, the organization of military tribunals in cases involving high treason, and the reorganization of local government in Corsica and the change in the system of departmental representation (in 1991), was enacted in spite of senatorial dissent. Nonetheless, until 1981 relations between the Senate and the National Assembly were relatively harmonious. The real clash with the Senate over legislation came during the years of Socialist government between 1981 and 1986, when many key bills were passed over the objections of the Senate. However, bills proposed by the government of the left that dismantled some of the "law and order" measures enacted under de Gaulle, Pompidou, and Giscard were supported by the Senate, and the Upper House played an active role when it modified the comprehensive decentralization statute passed by the Socialist majority in the Assembly. Most of the changes were accepted in joint committee.

Criticism of the Senate as an unrepresentative body, and proposals for its thorough reform, have come from Gaullists and Socialists alike (most recently in 1998). All of these proposals for reforming the Senate have failed, though some minor modifications in its composition were passed in 1976 and 1983.

Checks and Balances

France has no tradition of judicial review. As in other countries with civil law systems, and in Britain as well, the sovereignty of Parliament has meant that the legislature has the last word and that a law enacted in constitutionally prescribed forms is not subject to further scrutiny. This principle seemed to be infringed upon when the Constitution of 1958 brought forth an institutional novelty, the *Constitutional Council.* The council in certain cases must, and in other cases may upon request, examine legislation and decide whether it conforms to the constitution. A legal provision declared unconstitutional may not be promulgated.

Each of the presidents of the two houses of Parliament chooses three of the council's members, and the president of the Republic chooses another three for a (nonrenewable) nine-year term. Those who nominate the council's members were until 1974, together with the prime minister, the only ones entitled to apply to the council for constitutional scrutiny. In 1974 an amendment to Article 61 of the constitution made it possible for 60 deputies or 60 senators also to submit cases to the Constitutional Council. Since then, appeals to the council by the opposition, and at times by members of the majority, are a regular feature of the French legislative process.

Whichever side is in opposition, conservative or Socialist, routinely refers all major (sometimes minor as well) pieces of legislation to the council. In a given year, as many as 28 percent of laws passed by parliament have been submitted for review. A surprisingly high percentage of appeals lead to a declaration of unconstitutionality (see following discussion). Few decisions declare entire statutes unconstitutional, and those that declare parts of legislation unconstitutional (sometimes trivial parts) effectively invite Parliament to rewrite the text in an acceptable way.

The impact of the Constitutional Council's decisions is considerable and has sometimes modified short-term, and occasionally long-term, objectives of governments. The council assumes in its practice the role of a constitutional court. By doing so, it places itself at the juncture of law and politics, in a way similar to the U.S. Supreme Court when it reviews the constitutionality of legislation.

In a landmark decision, rendered in 1971, the council declared unconstitutional a statute, adopted by a large majority in Parliament, authorizing the prefects to refuse authorization (needed under the Law on Associations of 1901) to any association which in their opinion was likely to engage in illegal activities. To require any advance authorization violated, according to the decision, the freedom of association, one of "the fundamental principles recognized by the laws of the Republic and solemnly reaffirmed in the preamble of the Constitution." The invocation of the preamble greatly expanded the scope of constitutional law, since the preamble incorporated in its wording broad "principles of national sovereignty" as well as the "attachment to the The Declaration of Rights of Man," and an extensive Bill of Rights from the Fourth Republic constitution. For introducing a broad view of judicial review into French constitutional law, the decision was greeted as the French equivalent of the U.S. Supreme Court decision in *Marbury v. Madison*.

Some of the Constitutional Council's most important decisions, such as those on the nationalization of private enterprises (under the Socialists), on the privatization of parts of the public sector (under the conservatives), or on government control over the media (under both), conform by and large to an attitude which in the United States is called judicial restraint. A few can be qualified as activist, since they directly alter the intent of the law. But as a non-elected body, the council generally avoids interference with the major political choices of the governmental majority. In recent years, the council has nevertheless reviewed about 10 percent of legislation that is passed each year and has found that, on average, 50 percent of this legislation at least in part violates the constitution (61 percent in 1998–1999). In a period in which alternation of governments has often resulted in sharp policy changes, the council decisions have helped define an emerging consensus. By smoothing out the raw edges of new legislation in judicial language, it often makes changes ultimately more acceptable (see Box 5.5).

The approval of the council's activities by a large sector of public opinion (72 percent in 1992, slightly below the popular election of the president and the popular referendum) encourages efforts to enlarge its powers. The proposals aimed at facilitating citizens' direct access to its jurisdiction, greater openness of its procedures, and a strengthening of the Council's role in the defense of civil liberties have never succeeded in overcoming opposition to them in the Senate.

The judicial check on policymaking enhances the role of the much older *Council of State*, which in its present form dates back to 1799. The government now consults this council more extensively on all bills before they are submitted to Parliament,

Box 5.5 Judicial Review in France and the United States

Judicial review has become part of the French legislative process, but in a way that is still quite different from that of the United States.* Access remains limited, since citizens have no right to bring complaints before the council. The Constitutional Council, unlike the Supreme Court, considers legislation before it is promulgated. Since 1981, virtually all constitutional challenges have been initiated by legislative petition, a process that does not exist in the United States. A time element precludes the possibility of extensive deliberation: Rulings must be made within a month, and in emergency situations, within eight days. This is surely speedy justice, but the verdicts cannot be as explanatory as those rendered by constitutional courts in other countries. Dissenting opinions are never made public.

*Alec Stone, *The Birth of Judicial Politics in France* (New York: Oxford University Press, 1992).

and, as it has always done, on all government decrees and regulations before they are enacted. The council also gives advice on the interpretation of constitutional texts. While its advice is never binding, its prestige is so high that its recommendations are seldom ignored.

Unlike the Constitutional Council, the Council of State provides recourse to individual citizens who have claims against the administration. The judicial section of the Council of State, acting either as a court of appeal or, in more important cases, as the court of first instance, is the apex of a hierarchy of administrative tribunals. Whenever official acts are found to be devoid of a legal basis, whether those of a Cabinet minister or a village mayor, the council will annul them and grant damages to the aggrieved plaintiff.

The State and Territorial Relations

Since the time of the First Republic in the eighteenth century, when the Jacobins controlled the revolutionary National Assembly, the French state has been characterized by a high degree of centralized political and administrative authority. Although there have always been forces that have advocated *decentralization* (of political authority), as well as deconcentration (of administrative authority), the French unitary state remained (formally) "one and indivisible."[37] Essentially, this meant that subnational territorial units (communes, departments, and regions) had little formal decision-making autonomy, and were dominated by political and administrative decisions made in Paris. Both state action and territorial organization in France depended on a well-structured administration, which during long periods of political instability and unrest were relied on to keep the machinery of the state functioning.

Since the Revolution, France has been divided into 100 *departments* (four of them overseas departments), each about the size of an American county, each under the administrative responsibility of a *prefect,* and (since the Third Republic) with a directly elected general council. Since 1955, departments have been grouped into 22 *regions,* each with its own appointed prefect and, since 1986, with an elected assembly and president (see Figure 5.6).

Centralization has always been more impressive in its formal and legal aspects than it has been in practice, and the practical and political reality has

---

FIGURE 5.6   Subnational Governments in France

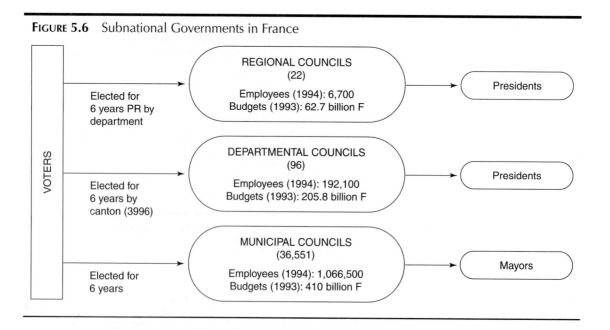

Box 5.6   The Political Durability of Local Governments

One manifestation of the political importance of local government in France has been the ability of local units to endure. It is no accident that even after recent consolidations there are still 36,551 *communes* (the basic area of local administration), each with a mayor and council, or about as many as in the original five Common Market countries and Britain together. Almost 33,000 French communes have fewer than 2,000 inhabitants, and of these more than 22,000 have fewer than 500. What is most remarkable, however, is that since 1851 the number of communes in France has been reduced by only 400. Thus, unlike every other industrialized country, the consolidation of population in urban areas has resulted in virtually no consolidation of towns and villages.

always been more complex. Although France is renowned for its centralized state, what is often ignored is that political localism dilutes centralized decision making (see Box 5.6).

The process of decentralization initiated by the government of the left between 1982 and 1986 was undoubtedly the most important and effective reform passed during that period. The strength of the reform was that it reaffirmed, reinforced, and built on the long-established system of interlocking relationships, between central and local authorities, as well as on the patterns of change during the past 25 years. To be sure, the formal roles of all the local actors were altered, but the greatest change was that the previously informal power of these actors was formalized.[38]

These powers are based on a system of mutual dependency between them and the prefects, as well as field services of the national ministries, which has existed since the Third Republic. Although the administrators of the national ministries had the formal power to implement laws, rules, and regulations at the local level, they needed the cooperation of local officials, who had the confidence of their constituents, to facilitate the acceptance of the authority of the central state and to provide information that enabled the administration to operate effectively at the local level. Local officials, in turn, needed the resources and aid of the administration to help their constituents and keep their political promises.[39] As in any relationship based on permanent interaction and on cross-functioning controls, it was not always clear who controlled whom.

Both the autonomy and the relational power of municipalities were conditioned by the extent of the mayor's contacts within the political and administrative network. These contacts were certainly reinforced by the linkage to national decision making that mayors had established through *cumul des mandats*—the ability to hold several electoral offices at the same time (limited in 1985 to two major offices, and then in 2000 to prohibit a deputy from holding a local executive office, including mayor). The change in 2000 was particularly important, since traditionally, the combining of the functions of a deputy or senator with those of a mayor or of a member of a departmental council (or both) was important for a political career. Similarly, a government minister may be, and usually is, a local official as well. Before 2000, this sometimes meant that a mayor's influence in Paris was greater than that of the prefect who held formal administrative authority over him. There was a consistent growth in the percentage of mayors of larger towns serving in Parliament. In 1997, almost 60 percent of the deputies in the National Assembly were also mayors, and perhaps two-thirds or more (and 95 percent of senators) were local officeholders at various levels.

The decentralization legislation transferred most of the formal powers of the departmental and regional prefects to the elected presidents of the departmental and regional councils. In March 1986 regional councils were elected for the first time (by a system of proportional representation). In one stroke, the remnants of formal prior administrative authorization of the decisions by local government were abandoned in favor of subsequential review by the courts of the actions of local officials. The department presidents, elected by their department councils, are now the chief departmental executive officers, and they, rather than the prefects, control the department bureaucracy.[40] This has accentuated the power of mayors of small and middle-sized towns, who control the departmental councils, to continue to protect the interests of diverse French communes. The representation of the interests of larger French cities is also enhanced by the establishment of elected regional councils, within which big-city mayors have considerable influence. More broadly, decentralization sets in motion changes that seem to be replacing the old dependency, which often amounted to complicity, between prefects and mayors, with a new interdependency—this time among elected officials. But interdependence also grows because there is almost no policy area over which one level of government has complete control.

What then is left of the role of the central bureaucracy in controlling the periphery? The greatest loss of authority has probably been that of the prefects. Their role now seems to be limited to security (law and order) matters, to the promotion of the government's industrial policies, and to the coordination of the state bureaucracy at the departmental level.

In matters of financing, the principal mechanisms through which the state has kept its hand in local government decisions (financial dependency and standards) have weakened but have not been abandoned. There is still overall financial dependence of subnational governments on the state. Particularly at the commune level, only 40 percent of the annual budget is provided for by local taxes (collected by the state). The price that is paid for financial assistance from above is enforced compliance with standards set by the state. In areas in which the state retains decision-making power—police, education, a large area of welfare, and social security, as well as a great deal of construction—administrative discretion and central control remain important.

There is now a consensus in France that the great project of decentralization has indeed been a success. The changes legislated and decreed between 1982 and 1986 have been accepted across the political spectrum, notwithstanding the fact that they have altered some of the elements of relations between center and periphery in ways that also have political consequences. Despite overlap, the efficiency of services at the communal, departmental, and regional levels appears to have increased, and the health of local economies has been strengthened by local initiatives.

This success is marred, however, by financial scandals that emerged in the 1980s and exploded in the 1990s. By the fall of 1994, one government minister was in jail, another was on the same path, and 29 members of Parliament had either been convicted or indicted. This total does not include an additional local politicians and businesspeople who were in the same predicament. Although each case is somewhat different, the common thread that linked most of them is the corrupt link between public and private complicity at the local level, and the financing of elections and political parties at the local and national levels. Indeed, this corruption is a natural outgrowth of what one scholar terms "the ignorance of conflict of interest, the will, more or less disguised, not to raise problems with regard to situations that are in themselves incompatible."[41]

Decentralization in the 1980s, combined with the system of *cumul des mandats,* gave a new impetus to local officials to do on a larger scale what they previously had done in a more limited way: to trade influence for private money, to direct kickbacks into party funding operations, and to use their public office for private advantage. The pressures that led to corruption are also linked to more expensive political campaigns and an often poorly demarcated frontier between the public and private arenas in a country in which people who emerge from the *grandes écoles-grands corps* system move easily between the two.

It is hardly surprising that, confronted with this crisis of corrupt practices, increasingly revealed by a more independent judiciary, there were widespread proposals to limit *cumul des mandats* (passed in March 2000, after a long struggle), to open the books on party finance, and to impose better controls over public spending and finance at all levels. However, scholars seem to agree that the emphasis must be on major reforms (that seem unlikely) that would better separate private from public interests.

Performance and Prospects

A Welfare State

The overall performance of Western democracies can be measured by their commitment and ability to distribute the benefits of economic growth. France has a mediocre record for spreading the benefits of the postwar boom and prosperity among all its citizens. In terms of income and of wealth, discrepancies between the rich and the poor remain somewhat greater in France than in other countries of equal development. The income gap narrowed significantly between 1976 and 1981, and then even more during the first year of Socialist government. Yet subsequent austerity measures, especially the government's successful effort to hold down wages, have widened the gap once again. The emergence of long-term unemployment has resulted in an increase in the number of the new poor, who are concentrated among those who are poorly trained for a rapidly evolving employment market. As opposed to the past, the majority of the lowest income group are no longer the elderly and retired, and heads of households with marginal jobs, but increasingly (particularly since 1990) younger people, many of them long-term unemployed, especially younger single parents.

Since large incomes permit the accumulation of wealth, the concentration of wealth is even more conspicuous than the steepness of the income pyramid. In the 1970s it was estimated that the richest 10 percent controlled between 35 and 50 percent of all wealth; the poorest 10 percent owned not more than 5 percent. In the 1990s it is estimated that the richest 10 percent of the families in the country owned 50 percent of the wealth, while the richest 20 percent owned 67 percent.

In spite of some assertions to the contrary, it is not true that the French economy as a whole is burdened with higher taxes than other countries of similar development; overall tax rates are higher than those in Germany and Britain, but lower than Denmark and Sweden. What is special about France is the distribution of its taxes: The share of indirect taxes remains far higher in France than in other industrialized countries. Indirect taxes not only drive up prices but also weigh most heavily on the poor. The percentage of revenue collected through regressive indirect taxation was the same in 1986, after five years of Socialist government, as it had been in 1980, and remains about the same now (63 percent in 1997).

The French welfare state is most effective in the area of social transfers. Their total amount has risen from 18 percent of GDP in 1970 to 29 percent in 1993, which puts France at about the same level as Germany and Denmark, but ahead of Sweden, Britain, and most other European democracies, and far ahead of the United States. A comprehensive health and social security system, established in its present form after World War II but extended since then, and a variety of programs assisting the aged, large families, the handicapped, and other such groups, disburse substantial benefits. When unemployment benefits, the cost of job-training programs, and housing subsidies are added, total costs are as high as the remainder of the public budget, with three-fourths of them borne by employers and employees.

In contrast to the United States, there have been few cutbacks in welfare state programs in France in recent years, but financing for these programs has been at the heart of government concerns since 1995 (see Table 5.4). Although, as a percentage of GDP, spending on social programs has remained stable since 1984, the government cut public spending to reduce its budget deficit in a successful effort to conform to criteria for the common European currency. Nevertheless, some important gaps remain. For example, full health benefits depend on supplementary insurance coverage generally provided to most (but not all) in the active workforce. In 1994, however, only 59 percent of unemployed workers, and 58 percent of foreign workers had this additional but necessary coverage.

High levels of unemployment and poverty, and problems of homelessness create pressures to expand social programs while diminishing the revenue base that finances them. Thus since 1998 the French government has confronted many of the

TABLE 5.4 State Spending and Welfare State Spending

	Government Expenditure as Percentage of GDP (1997)	Government Employment as Percentage of Total Employment (1994)	State Contributions to Protection Programs as Percentage of Total Spending (1994)	State Contributions to Protection Programs as Percentage of GDP (1993–95)	State Health Expenses as Percentage of GDP	
					(1984)	(1995)
Britain	35.3	19.3	28	23.7	5.2	6.6
France	**46.1**	**24.3**	**48**	**29.2**	**6.6**	**8.5**
Germany	37.5	14.9	39	29.8	6.3	8.6
Italy	44.9	—	47	24.5	5.3	6.6
Spain	35.3	—	50	22.4	4.7	6.9
Sweden	53.3	—	—	38.5	—	11.4

Source: OECD, 2000; Eurostat; *Le Monde,* May 13, 1997.

same problems facing the United States in recent years, but resistance to the American solution is widespread. The French government has had only limited success in finding ways to reduce public spending and maintain welfare state services at acceptable levels.

Nationalization and Regulation

Government-operated business enterprises have long existed in France in fields that are under private ownership in other countries of Western Europe. After several waves of nationalization in the 1930s and after the end of World War II, the government owned and operated all or part of the following: railroads; almost all energy production (mining, electricity, nuclear energy) and much of telecommunication (radio and television); most air and maritime transport; most of the aeronautic industry; 85 percent of bank deposits; 40 percent of insurance premiums; one-third of the automobile industry; one-third of the housing industry—in addition to the old state monopolies of mail services, telephone, telegraph, tobacco, and match manufacture, and sundry less important activities.

By the 1970s public concerns accounted for about 11 percent of the gross national product. Fifteen percent of the total active population, or 27 percent of all salary and wage earners (excluding agricultural labor), were paid directly by the state either as civil servants as salaried workers or on a contractual basis. Their income came close to one-third of the total sum of wages and salaries.

To enlarge the public sector in both industry and banking had been the core of the Common Program of the left. Further *nationalizations* were considered a vehicle for modernizing a country with uneven development, as well as for effective planning. The legislation enacted in 1981 and 1982 completed the nationalization of the banking sector, expanded state ownership to 13 of the 20 largest firms in France, and controlling interest to many others in such fields as machine tools, chemistry (including pharmaceutical products), glass, metals, and electrical power. In addition, the government obtained majority control of two important armaments firms and several ailing steel companies. About 22 percent of all salary and wage earners received their checks directly or indirectly from the French state in 1997. While this was high compared with the U.S. percentage, it was not out of line from other European countries. If one out of four French citizens depended on the state for their paychecks in 1994, so did one out of five Britons and one out of six Germans (see again Table 5.4).

The conservative government that held power between March 1986 and May 1988 substantially altered the structure of the nationalized sector in France. But its ambitious plans for *privatization* were halted (40 percent completed) only a year after their implementation began, in part because of the collapse of the stock market in 1987.[42] Thus some, but not all, of the companies that were nationalized by the Socialist government in 1982 were returned to private stockholders, and the conservative government privatized some companies that had long been controlled by the state. However, both the companies that were returned to private hands and those that remained in the hands of the state were quite different from what they had been a few years before. Recapitalized, restructured, and modernized, for the most part they were, in 1988, the leading edge of the French industrial machine.[43]

For the actual operation of French business, the move begun by the Socialists and continued by the conservative government toward deregulation of the economy was probably more important than privatization. The deregulation of the stock market, the banking system, telecommunications, and prices has fundamentally changed the way business is conducted in both the private and public sectors.[44] The combination of budgetary rigor and state disengagement meant a real reduction of aid to industry. Sectors in difficulty, including steel, chemicals, shipbuilding, and automobile manufacturing, were therefore forced to accelerate their rationalization plans and their cutbacks in workers.

The Socialist parliamentary victory in June 1988 effectively halted further privatization. The conservative government elected in 1993 continued to diminish state holdings in some companies and privatize others, without, however, altering the main lines of industrial and economic policy. As a result, the interventionist and regulatory weight of the state in industry is less important now than it was before the Socialists came to power. Today, all of the major remaining nationalized industries are either in the process of, or being proposed for, at least partial privatization. In addition, shares have been sold in Air France, and it has been forced to compete with other airlines within the French and European markets. The old issue of nationalization and ownership has now been bypassed, and replaced by more subtle issues of control and regulation in the context of global competition.

In other areas, the regulatory weight of the state has not diminished but has changed during the past 25 years. During the 1970s France expanded individual rights by fully establishing the rights to divorce and abortion. Under the Socialist governments of the 1980s, capital punishment was abolished, the rights of those accused of crimes were strengthened, and detention without trial was checked by new procedures. After much wrangling in Parliament, the obsolete Criminal Code dating from the time of Napoléon was replaced in 1994 when an increase in crime rates had heightened concerns for security. The new code is generally hailed as expressing a consensus across the political spectrum on questions of crime and punishment. Moreover, individual rights in France must now conform to the decisions of the European Court under the general umbrella of the European Union. Finally, in conformity with the Maastricht Treaty, citizenship rights of EU residents in France have increased during the 1990s; a right to the presumption of innocence in criminal cases has now been established.

In still other areas, the regulatory weight of the state has increased. One of the most obvious is environmental controls, which began to grow in the 1970s. In the 1990s the French state was making its first significant efforts to regulate individual behavior that has an impact on the environment: The first limitations on smoking, for example, came into effect in the late 1980s and expanded after that. In an effort to deal with the politics of immigration, particularly after 1993, the state increased the regulation of all residents of foreign origin in ways that have diminished individual rights.

Outlook: France and the New Architecture of Europe

The main concerns that dominated French politics two decades ago have changed dramatically. Nineteen years ago, a coalition of Socialists and Communists was promising a "rupture" with capitalism, and the ideological distance between left and right appeared to be enormous. Today, none of the major parties is presenting any proposal for dramatic change, and, like U.S. political parties, all the parties are making their commitments as vague and as flexible as possible. After five years of socialism and two of conservative neoliberalism, political parties appeared to be out of fresh ideas on how to deal with the major problems of the French economy and society. The transition away from a smokestack economy has been difficult and painful, and the resulting unemployment continues to dominate public concerns.

Political cleavages based on new conflicts are emerging, even if their outlines are still unclear. Indeed, the issues of the first decade of the twenty-first century may very well be more profound and untenable than those of the past. The political stakes have moved away from questioning the nature of the regime, but they have become focused much more intensely on the nature of the political community. Between 1986 and the present, this has become evident in a variety of ways.

Immigration has given way to ethnic consciousness, particularly among the children of immigrants from North Africa. Unlike most of the immigrant communities in the past, those of today have been more reluctant to assume French cultural values as their own. This in turn has led to questioning the rules of naturalization for citizenship, integration into French society, and (in the end) what it means to be French.[45] During the 1980s growing ethnic tensions were given a political voice by the National Front, which mobilized voters and solidified support on the basis of racist appeals. In part because of the growing role of the FN, ethnic consciousness and diversity have grown in France and altered the context of French politics.

A bit more than a decade ago, the Cold War and the division of Europe was a fact of life and was the basis for much of French foreign, defense, and, to some extent, domestic policy. The Cold War is long over. As a result, Eastern European ethnic consciousness and conflicts previously held in check by Soviet power, and in any case insulated from Western Europe by the Iron Curtain, now have been suddenly liberated. The disintegration of the Soviet Communist experiment (and the Soviet Union) has also had the broader impact of undermining the legitimacy of classic socialism and has thus removed from French (and European) politics many of the issues that have separated left from right for over a hundred years. Parties of the right have lost the anti-Communist glue that has contributed to their cohesiveness, but parties of the left have lost much of their purpose.

Coincidentally, this process of Eastern European disintegration has accelerated at the same time that the countries of the European Union have attempted to reinvigorate the process of Western European integration, with France in the lead. Membership in the European Union shapes almost every aspect of policy and policy planning and provides the context for the expansion and restructuring of the economy during the Fifth Republic (also see Chapter 11).[46]

At the beginning of his presidency in the early 1980s, François Mitterrand expressed his satisfaction with the existing structures of the Common Market. But, having experienced their weakness, he increasingly felt that some form of federalism—a federalist finality—would be necessary to enable Western Europe to use its considerable resources more effectively. Thus, during the Mitterrand presidency, France moved in the direction of supporting a larger and a more tightly integrated Europe, including efforts to increase the powers of European institutions and the establishment of a European monetary and political union as outlined in the Maastricht Treaty, approved somewhat reluctantly in 1992. However, what is a firm French commitment to a common European currency is generating most of the plans to cut public spending plans that have been sometimes ferociously resisted. Nevertheless, in 1998 France met all key requirements for European monetary union, and is now firmly part of the Euro group within the European Union.

The opening of French borders, not only to the products of other countries but increasingly to their people and values (all citizens of the European Union have the right to vote and run for office in the French local elections in 2001), has fed into the more general uneasiness about French national identity. The integration of French economic and social institutions with those of its neighbors will continue progressively to remove key decisions from the French government acting alone. In the past, the French economy reacted to joint decisions made in Brussels. In the future, a broader range of institutions will be forced to do the same. It is now clear that rumblings of resistance are not limited to the fringe parties (the parties of the extreme right and the Communists), but that opposition exists within all of the major political parties, especially the RPR. Here, too, there is considerable potential for new political divisions.

This chapter, written at the beginning of the twentieth-first century, during the waning days of the presidency of Jacques Chirac, presents a story of a strong and stable political system, in which political divisions have narrowed during the past ten years. However, what we may be witnessing is a reordering of political divisions that will dominate in the new century.

✍ KEY TERMS ✍

baccalauréat
blocked vote
Edouard Balladur
Napoleon Bonaparte
Cabinet (government)
Jacques Chirac
communes
Communist Party (PCF)
Confédération Française Democratique du Travail (CFDT)
Confédération Générale du Travail (CGT)
Confédération Générale du Travail-Force Ouvrière (FO)
Conseil National du Patronat Français (CNPF)

Constitution of 1958
Constitutional Council
Council of Ministers
Council of State
cumul des mandats (accumulation of electoral offices)
decentralization
Charles de Gaulle
departments
Ecole National d' Administration (ENA)
Ecole Polytechnique
European Union (European Community before 1992)
events of 1968

Fédération de d'education nationale (FEN)
Fédération National des Syndicats Agricoles (FNSEA)
Fifth Republic
Fourth Republic
grandes écoles
grands corps
Lionel Jospin
Alain Juppé
Jean-Marie Le Pen
Maastricht Treaty
Georges Marchais
François Mitterrand
Muslims
motion of censure
National Assembly (deputy)
National Front (FN)

nationalization
neocorporatism
"new" immigration
ordinances
political class
prefects
president of the Republic
prime minister
privatization
Rally for the Republic (RPR)
referendum
regions
Senate
Socialist Party (PS)
Union for French Democracy (UDF)

✍ SUGGESTED READINGS ✍

Ambler, John, ed. *The Welfare State in France.* New York: New York University Press, 1991.

Baumgartner, Frank R. *Conflict and Rhetoric in French Policymaking.* Pittsburgh, PA: University of Pittsburgh Press, 1989.

Bell, D. S., and Byron Criddle. *The French Socialist Party: The Emergence of a Party of Government,* 2nd ed. Oxford, England: Clarendon Press/Oxford, 1988.

Converse, Philip, and Roy Pierce. *Political Representation in France.* Cambridge, MA: Harvard University Press, 1986.

Gallie, Duncan. *Social Inequality and Class Radicalism in France and Britain.* London: Cambridge University Press, 1983.

Hall, Peter. *Governing the Economy: The Politics of State Intervention in Britain and France.* New York: Oxford University Press, 1986.

Hall, Peter, Jack Hayward, and Howard Machin, eds. *Developments in French Politics,* rev. ed. London: Macmillan, 1994.

Hayward, Jack. *The State and the Market Economy: Industrial Patriotism and Economic Intervention in France.* New York: New York University Press, 1986.

Hollifield, James. *Immigrants, Markets, and States: The Political Economy of Postwar Europe.* Cambridge, MA: Harvard University Press, 1992.

Hollifield, James, and George Ross, eds. *In Search of the New France.* New York: Routledge, 1991.

Howell, Chris. *Regulating Labor: The State and Industrial Relations in Postwar France.* Princeton, NJ: Princeton University Press, 1992.

Ireland, Patrick. *The Policy Challenge of Ethnic Diversity: Immigrant Politics in France and Switzerland.* Cambridge, MA: Harvard University Press, 1994.

Johnson, R. W. *The Long March of the French Left.* New York: St. Martins, 1981.

Keeler, John T. S. *The Politics of Neocorporatism in France.* New York: Oxford University Press, 1987.

Keeler, John T. S., and Martin A. Schain. *Chirac's Challenge: Liberation, Europeanization, and Malaise in France.* New York: St. Martin's, 1996.

Lewis-Beck, Michael. *How France Votes.* New York: Chatham House, 2000.

Mazur, Amy. *Gender Bias and the State: Feminist Policy at Work in France.* Pittsburgh, PA: University of Pittsburgh Press, 1995.

Schain, Martin. *French Communism and Local Power.* New York: St. Martin's, 1985.

Schmidt, Vivien A. *Democratizing France.* New York: Cambridge University Press, 1990.

———. *From State to Market: The Transformation of Business and Government.* New York: Cambridge University Press, 1996.

Smith, Rand W. *Crisis in the French Labor Movement: A Grassroots Perspective.* New York: St. Martin's, 1988.

Stone, Alec. *The Birth of Judicial Politics in France: The Constitutional Council in Comparative Perspective.* New York: Oxford University Press, 1992.

Suleiman, Ezra. *Elites in French Society.* Princeton, NJ: Princeton University Press, 1978.

———. *Private Power and Centralization in France.* Princeton, NJ: Princeton University Press, 1987.

Wilsford, David. *Doctors and the State: The Politics of Health Care in France and the United States.* Durham, NC: Duke University Press, 1991.

Wilson, Frank L. *Interest Group Politics in France.* New York: Cambridge University Press, 1987.

ENDNOTES

1. The best recent book in English, on the Constitutional Council is Alec Stone, *The Birth of Judicial Politics in France* (New York: Oxford University Press, 1992).

2. Laurence Wylie, "Social Change at the Grass Roots," in Stanley Hoffmann, Charles P. Kindleberger, Jesse R. Pitts, et al., *In Search of France* (Cambridge, MA: Harvard University Press, 1963), p. 230.

3. Interesting data on religious practice can be found in extensive opinion polls published in Sofres, *L'Etat de l'opinion 1994* (Paris: Editions du Seuil, 1994), pp. 179–99. These data are taken from an unpublished exit poll dated May 26, 1997.

4. Duncan Gallie, *Social Inequality and Class Radicalism in France and Britain* (London: Cambridge University Press, 1983), p. 34.

5. Annick Percheron, "Socialization et tradition: transmission et invention du politique," *Pouvoirs* 42 (1988): 43.

6. Edgar Morin, *The Red and the White* (New York: Pantheon Books, 1970), Ch. 8, discusses the noisy revolution of the teenagers and the silent one of women.

7. This is the amply documented thesis of Janine Mossuz-Lavau and Mariette Sineau, *Les Femmes françaises en 1978: Insertion sociale, Insertion politique* (Paris: Centre de Documentation Sciences Humaine de CNRS, 1980). The authors also found that women who were no longer working but had been employed previously were likely to express opinions closer to those of working than of nonworking women.

8. Annick Percheron and M. Kent Jennings, "Political Continuities in French Families: A New Perspective on an Old Controversy," *Comparative Politics* 13, No. 4 (July 1981).

9. Ronald Inglehart, *Culture Shift* (Princeton, NJ: Princeton University Press, 1990), Chs. 1–3 and Table 2.4, and Tribalat, *Faire France* (Paris: La Découverte, 1995), pp. 93–98.

10. The best summary of the evolution of group membership in France is found in Laurence Haeusler, "Le monde associatif de 1978 1986," in INSEE, *Données sociales 1990* (Paris: INSEE, 1990), pp. 369–70. See also Henry Ehrmann and Martin Schain, *Politics in France*, 5th ed. (New York: HarperCollins, 1992), Table 3.6, p. 103.

11. Data on education are taken from *Données Sociales 1996* (Paris: INSEE, 1996), pp. 40–47; *L'Etat de la France 97–98* (Paris: Editions la Décourerte, 1997), p. 113; *The Economist*, September 18, 1993, p. 52; *Le Monde*, October 16, 1994, p. 16; and Tableaux de—l'conomie française, 1999–2000 (Paris: INSEE, 2000), pp. 52–57.

12. John Ambler, "Constraints on Policy Innovation in Education: Thatcher's Britain and Mitterrand's France," *Comparative Politics* 20, No. 1 (October 1987). See also John Ambler, "Conflict and Consensus in French Education," in John T. S. Keeler and Martin A. Schain, eds., *Chirac's Challenge: Liberalization, Europeanization and Malaise in France* (New York: St. Martins, 1996).

13. The restrictive recruitment of the *grandes écoles* is confirmed by a recent study: "Le recruitment social de l élite scholaire depuis quarante ans," *Education et Formations*, No. 41, June 1995. Which institutions qualify as *grandes écoles* is controversial. But among the 140 or so designated as such in some estimates, only 15 or 20, with an enrollment of 2,000 to 2,500, are considered important, prestige schools. The number of engineering and business schools that are

generally considered to be *grandes écoles* has increased in recent years. Therefore the total enrollment of all these schools has increased significantly to well over 100,000.

14. These results are taken from various sources and have been compiled by Russell J. Dalton in *Citizen Politics in Western Democracies* (Chatham, NJ: Chatham House Press, 1988), p. 21. See Sofres, *L'Etat de l'opinion 1994* (Paris: Seuil, 1994), p. 232.

15. It must be noted—and this is true for all figures on electoral participation throughout this chapter—that French statistics calculate electoral participation on the basis of registered voters, while American statistics take as a basis the total number of people of voting age. About 9 percent of French citizens entitled to vote are not registered. This percentage must therefore be added to the published figures when one wishes to estimate the true rate of abstention and to compare it with the American record.

16. On abstention, see Françoise Subileau and Marie-France Toinet, *Les chemins de l'abstention* (Editions de la découverte, 1993), and Marie-France Toinet, "The Limits of Malaise in France," in Keeler and Schain, *Chirac's Challenge*, pp. 289–91.

17. There is no legal definition for any of these terms (nor is there any legal definition for a *grande école*), although they are widely used by citizens, journalists, and scholars. Thus the figures given here for the early 1980s are approximations, based on positional and reputational definitions given by J-T Bodiguel and J-L Quermonne in *La Haute fonction publique sous la Ve République* (Paris: PUF, 1983), pp. 12–25, 83–94.

18. This system has now been called into question by the *Conseil d'Etat*, the highest French administrative court. In a decision rendered in December 1996, the court annulled the appointment of a high civil servant as the assistant director of a semipublic bank on the grounds of conflict of interest. Indeed the law that was being interpreted dated back to 1919(!), amended in 1994. If broadly applied, this decision would undermine part of the basis of overlap of public and private elites; see "Pantouflage: l'onde de choc," *L'Express*, December 19, 1996, pp. 50–52.

19. Nancy J. Walker, "What We Know About Voters in Britain, France and West Germany," *Public Opinion* (May–June 1988).

20. These percentages are only approximations, since interest groups in France either refuse to publish membership figures or publish figures that are universally viewed as highly questionable. For estimates of interest group memberships, see Peter Hall, "Pluralism and Pressure Politics," in Peter Hall, Jack Hayward, and Howard Machin, *Developments in French Politics*, rev. ed. (London: Macmillan, 1994). For the most recent estimates of trade union membership, see Antoine Bevort, "Les effectifs syndiqués à la CGT et à la CFDT 1945–1990," *Communisme*, No. 35–37, 1994. Data indicate that membership decline is continuing. See also the recent study by Dominique Labbé, *La Syndicalisation en France depuis 1945* (Grenoble, France: CERAP, 1995).

21. Herrick Chapman, Mark Kesselman, and Martin Schain, *A Century of Organized Labor in France* (New York: St. Martins, 1998).

22. The most recent studies are reported in *Communisme*, 35–37, 1994, p. 77, and Sofres, *L'Etat de l'opinion 1994*, pp. 264–65. See also Mark Kesselman, "Does the French Labor Movement Have a Future?" in Keeler and Schain, *Chirac's Challenge*.

23. Sofres, *L'Etat de l'opinion 1996*, p. 246; *The Economist*, September 16, 2000; and Roland Cayrol "Unions and French Public Opinion" in Chapman, Kesselman, and Schain, *A Century of Organized Labor.*

24. The most recent serious study of the CNPF and its affiliates by Henri Weber, *Le Parti des patrons: Le CNPF 184–86* (Paris: Editions du Seuil, 1986), analyzes various trends within the patronat and is based on much detailed inside information. One of the earliest studies of the CNPF was written by Henry W. Ehrmann. *Organized Business in France* (Princeton, NJ: Princeton University Press, 1957) presents case studies about the contacts between the administration and the employers organizations, but it is now dated of course.

25. John Keeler, *The Politics of Neocorporatism in France* (New York: Oxford University Press, 1987).

26. Frank Wilson, *Interest-Group Politics in France* (New York: Cambridge University Press, 1987), pp. 151, 153, 162, 164.

27. John T. S. Keeler, "Situating France on the Pluralism-Corporatism Continuum," *Comparative Politics* 17 (January 1985): 229–49.

28. See the articles by John Ambler, Frank Baumgartner, Martin Schain, and Frank Wilson in *French Politics and Society* 12, (Spring/Summer 1994).

29. For a good survey of party developments between 1958 and 1981, see Frank L. Wilson, *French Political Parties Under the Fifth Republic* (New York: Praeger, 1982).

30. For good estimates of party membership, see Colette Ysmal, Transformations du militantisme et déclin des partis, in Pascal Perrineau, *L'Engagement Politique, déclin ou mutation?* (Paris: Presses de la FNSP, 1994), p. 48. Also see l'Etat de la France (Paris: La D—couverte, 1997), pp. 521–26.

31. Stanley Hoffmann, *Le Mouvement Poujode* (Paris: A. Colin. 1956).

32. Suzanne Berger, "From the Mouvement Poujade to the Front National," in Linda B. Miller and Michael Joseph Smith, eds. *Essays on Politics in Honor of Stanley Hoffmann* (Boulder, CO: Westview Press, 1993).

33. D. S. Bell and Byron Criddle, *The French Socialist Party: The Emergence of a Party of Government*, 2nd ed. (Oxford, England: Clarendon, 1988).

34. For an analysis of the decline of the Communist vote, see Martin Schain, "The French Communist Party: The Seeds of Its Own Decline," in Peter Katzenstein, Theodore Lowi, and Sidney Tarrow, *Comparative Theory and Political Experience* (Ithaca, NY: Cornell University Press, 1990). For additional insights into the decline of the PCF electorate, see Jane Jenson and George Ross, *View from the Inside: A French Communist Cell in Crisis* (Berkeley: University of California Press, 1984), part 5.

35. This analysis is taken from John T. S. Keeler and Maritn A. Schain, "Presidents, Premiers and Models of Democracy in France," in Keeler and Schain, eds., *Chirac's Challenge.*

36. One of the very few analyses of the use of the blocked vote, as well as the use by the government of Article 49.3, can be found in John Huber, "Restrictive Legislative Procedures in France and the United States," *American Political Science Review* 86, No. 3 (September 1992); 675–87. Huber's article is also the only attempt to compare such tools with similar procedures in the U.S. Congress.

37. Didier Maus, "Parliament in the Fifth Republic: 1958–1988," in Paul Godt, *Policy-Making in France* (New York: Pinter, 1989), p. 17; and Didier Maus, *Les grands textes de la pratique institutionelle de la Ve République* (Paris: La Documentation Française, 1992).

38. This phrase refers to the first article of the constitution of 1793, which proclaims that "The French Republic is one and indivisible." The constitution of the Fifth Republic repeats it.

39. Vivien A. Schmidt, *Democratizing France* (New York: Cambridge University Press, 1990).

40. The now classic statement of this relationship was written by Jean-Pierre Worms, who years later had major responsibilities for developing the decentralization reforms for the government of the left. See "Le Préfet et ses notables," *Sociologie du Travail* 8, No. 3 (1966): 249–75.

41. Mark Kesselman, "The Tranquil Revolution at Clochemerle: Socialist Decentralization in France," in Philip G. Cerny and Martin A. Schain, *Socialism, the State, and Public Policy in France* (New York: St. Martin's, 1985), p. 176.

42. Yves Mény, "Les formes discrètes de la corruption," in *French Politics and Society* 11, No. 4 (Fall 1993), special issue on "Etats de la corruption." Mény has also written *La Corruption et la République* (Paris: Fayard, 1992), where he develops many of these ideas on systemic contributions to corruption. In the same issue of *French Politics and Society*, Dominique Lorrain writes about the contribution of local finance to corruption, and Jean-Pierre Worms, the architect of the decentralization legislation comments on the relationship between corruption and decentralization. See also Ezra N. Suleiman, "The Politics of Corruption and the Corruption of Politics," *French Politics and Society* 9, No. 1 (Winter 1991).

43. As a result, the number of workers paid indirectly by the state declined. Nevertheless, the proportion of the workforce paid directly by the state (government employment) remained stable at about 23 percent; about a third higher than the United States, Germany, and Italy, but lower than the Scandinavian countries. See Vincent Wright, "Reshaping the State: The Implications for Public Administration," *West European Politics* 17, No. 3 (July 1994).

44. They were also controlled by the same people as when they were nationalized. None of the newly privatized firms changed managing directors. See Michel Bauer, "The Politics of State-Directed Privatization: The Case of France 1986–8," *West European Politics* 11, No. 4 (October 1988): 59.

45. Philip G. Cerny, "The 'Little Big Bang' in Paris," *European Journal of Political Research* 17, No. 2 (1989).

46. Martin Baldwin Edwards and Martin A. Schain, eds., *The Politics of Immigration in Western Europe* (London: Frank Cass, 1994).

47. See "The State in Western Europe: Retreat or Redefinition," *West European Politics* 17, No. 2 (1994).

CHAPTER 6

POLITICS IN GERMANY

RUSSELL J. DALTON

Country Bio–Germany

POPULATION   82.8 Million

TERRITORY   137,803 sq. mi

YEAR OF INDEPENDENCE   1871

YEAR OF CURRENT CONSTITUTION   1949

HEAD OF STATE   President Johannes Rau

HEAD OF GOVERNMENT   Chancellor Gerhard Schröder

LANGUAGE(S)   German

RELIGION   Protestant 38%, Roman Catholic 34%, Muslim 1.7%, unaffiliated or other 26.3%

Free elections are celebrations of the democratic process, and the Germans celebrated in an unprecedented way on September 27, 1998. After 16 years of Christian Democratic rule, the public used their democratic power to change the government. Indeed, for the first time in the history of the *Federal Republic of Germany (FRG)*, voters rejected a sitting chancellor and intentionally chose a new government through the ballot box.

There is reason to celebrate this election—not primarily because of its outcome, but because of what the election says about Germany's democratic development. This was grassroots democracy at work: citizens freely coming together, talking about politics, and making a choice they thought would benefit their nation. Voting turnout was up in 1998, running counter to the downward trend in most of Europe. Perhaps more so than any other FRG election, this election showed German democracy at its best—and that elections do matter.

The elections also reflected the lingering consequences of an even more revolutionary event: with the opening of the Berlin Wall on November 9, 1989, East and West Germany began an amazing process leading toward unification. The 1989 revolution in the East was rooted in "people power" protests against the communist regime. The East Germans' willingness to take a stand against the state, and the state's unwillingness to suppress its people with force, brought the communist system to its end. The once formidable East German government collapsed almost overnight and all eyes turned West, toward the Federal Republic of Germany as a source of stability and political reform. German unification suddenly appeared a real possibility. Protesters who had chanted "we are the people" when opposing the communist government in October took up the call for unification with a new refrain: "we are one people." In less than a year, the unimaginable was a reality. Two German states—one democratic and one communist, one with a market economy and one with a socialist planned economy—were united.

German unification has reshaped the map of Europe and it has reshaped how we think about Germany and the lessons of German history. In one sense, this change repeats the pattern of Germany's discontinuous political development that has vacillated between authoritarian states and democratic ones. Germany is building a new nation uniting East and West, and this nation has strong democratic roots. But many of the problems wrought by unification remain unresolved, and this prompted the electorate to seek a new government in 1998. The question is how well the SPD-Green government can address these issues. If they are successful, a free, democratic, and economically strong Germany can be a source of economic and political stability within the West, as well as fostering political reform throughout Eastern Europe.

Current Policy Challenges

What political problems do Germans typically read about when they open the daily newspaper or watch their favorite TV newscast—and what political problems preoccupy policymakers in Bonn and Berlin? Often the answer is the same as in most other industrial democracies. News reports analyze the state of the economy, report on crime, and generally track the social and economic health of the nation.

The most visible recent political controversy has evolved from a party finance scandal. During his tenure as chancellor, Kohl accepted illegal contributions to support his party; when this became known, Kohl refused to divulge the sources of these funds or what was promised in return. This has tarnished Kohl's personal image and may lead to criminal charges against him. As this drama unfolds, many other CDU leaders have been swept from power because of their involvement. But even more significant, this episode has raised new public doubts about the honesty of politicians and the functioning of the democratic process. Increased public skepticism of politicians and parties will be part of Kohl's political legacy and influence political opinions and political reporting for years to come.

Overshadowing any specific event has been continued concern about the problems arising from German unification. Unification achieved an important national goal for Germany, brought freedom to the residents of the former German Democratic Republic (GDR) and ended the Cold War conflict.

Unification also reflects that old proverbial punishment: "may you get what you wish." Because the economic infrastructure of the East lags far behind that of the West, news reports frequently focus on the economic problems resulting from German unification. Government agencies and the European Union have invested more than a trillion deutsche marks (DM) in the East since unification—raising taxes for all Germans in the process. And still, the nightly news routinely chronicles high unemployment levels in the East, insufficient development of the Eastern economy, and the continued financial costs of unification. In between the lines, the attentive citizen sees that other policy needs are not being met because of limited government resources. This has generated ongoing policy debates and media analyses about whether the government can continue to provide the range of benefits that traditionally have characterized the nation's social services, especially as Germany competes in a global marketplace.

The challenges of unification involve more than economics, however. Different life experiences and different values continue to divide Westerners and Easterners. Indeed, in some ways the psychological gap between the regions has grown since unification. There are growing signs of the "wall in the mind" that separates residents in both halves of the country—even in Berlin, Westerners and Easterners read separate newspapers and live separate lives, although they now reside next door to one another.

Unification has also accentuated the issue of ethnicity in Germany. Evening news broadcasts showing skinheads demonstrating, or the firebombing of a foreigner's house, evoke very negative images from Germany's past. Other news reports detail the extensive efforts the government and most Germans have made to deal with the new problems of an increasingly multicultural Germany. Today Germany has the largest foreign-born population within Europe. The new government elected in 1998 has promised to change citizenship laws and to implement other reforms to address this issue, but Germans remain divided on the appropriate responses.

Finally, the more sophisticated news programs often look ahead to Germany's new foreign policy challenges. The European Union (EU) is an increasingly visible part of political reporting, and Germans are trying to determine their desired role in a changing Europe. For example, debates about the expansion of EU membership raise questions about Germany's relationship with Eastern Europe. EU policies such as monetary union and the development of a European currency are creating internal divisions about Germany's relationship to the Union.

Despite these ongoing issues, the Federal Republic is one of the most successful and vibrant democracies in the world today. Its political system is ready to address these challenges, even while it debates the appropriate response to the political transformations in Eastern Europe and increasing unification in Western Europe. Indeed, these themes echoed through the debates of the 1998 parliamentary elections, and the new government is dedicated to trying new ways to address these policy challenges.

The Historical Legacy

The German historical experience differs considerably from that of most other European democracies. The social and political forces that modernized the rest of Europe came much later in Germany and had a less certain effect. By the nineteenth century when most nations had defined their borders, German territory was still divided among dozens of political units. Although a dominant national culture had evolved in most European states, Germany was torn by sharp religious, regional, and economic divisions. Industrialization generally was the driving force behind the modernization of Europe, but German industrialization came late and did not overturn the old feudal and aristocratic order. German history, even to the present, represents a difficult and protracted process of nation building.

The Second German Empire

Through a combination of military and diplomatic victories, Otto von Bismarck, the Prussian chancellor, enlarged the territory of Prussia and established a unified Second German Empire in 1871.[1] The empire was an authoritarian state, with only the superficial trappings of a democracy. Political power flowed from the monarch—the *Kaiser*—and the government at times bitterly suppressed potential opposition groups—especially the Roman Catholic Church and the Social Democrats. The government expected little of its citizens: They were to pay their taxes, serve in the army, and keep their mouths shut.

The strong central government pushed ahead national development during this period. Industrialization finally moved ahead, and German influence in international affairs grew steadily. The force of industrialization was not sufficient to modernize and liberalize society and the political system, however. Economic and political power remained concentrated in the hands of the bureaucracy and aristocratic traditional elites. Democratic reforms were thwarted by an authoritarian state strong enough to resist the political demands of a weak middle class. The state was supreme: its needs took precedence over those of individuals and society.

Failures of government leadership, coupled with a blindly obedient public, led Germany into World War I (1914–1918). The war devastated the nation. Almost 3 million German soldiers and civilians lost their lives, the economy was strained beyond the breaking point, and the government of the empire collapsed under the weight of its own incapacity to govern. The war ended with Germany a defeated and exhausted nation.

The Weimar Republic

First experience of democracy.

In 1919 a popularly elected constitutional assembly established the new democratic system of the *Weimar Republic*. The constitution granted all citizens the right to vote and guaranteed basic human rights. The constitution vested political power in a directly elected parliament and president, and political parties became legitimate political actors. Belatedly, the Germans had their first real experience with democracy.

From the outset, however, the Weimar government was plagued by severe problems. In the peace treaty following World War I, Germany lost all its overseas colonies and a large amount of its European territory. It was further burdened with the moral guilt for the war and large reparation payments owed to the victorious Allies. A series of radical uprisings threatened the political system. Wartime destruction and the reparations produced continuing economic problems, finally leading to an economic catastrophe in 1923. In less than a year the inflation rate was an unimaginable 26 billion percent! Ironically, the Kaiser's government that created the conditions that produced these problems was not blamed for these developments. Instead, many people criticized the empire's democratic successor—the Weimar Republic.

The fatal blow came with the Great Depression in 1929. Almost a third of the labor force became unemployed, and the public was frustrated by the government's inability to deal with the crisis. Political tensions increased, and parliamentary democracy began to fail. *Adolf Hitler* and his *National Socialist German Workers' Party (the Nazis)* were the major beneficiaries; their vote increased from a mere 2 percent in 1928 to 18 percent in 1930 and 33 percent in November 1932. Increasingly, the machinery of the democratic system malfunctioned or was bypassed. In a final attempt to restore political order, President Paul von Hindenburg appointed Hitler chancellor of the Weimar Republic in January 1933. This was democracy's death knell.

Weimar's failure resulted from a mix of factors.[2] The republic's lack of support from political elites and the public was a basic weakness. Democracy depended on an administrative and military elite that often longed for the old authoritarian political system. Elite criticism of Weimar encouraged similar sentiments among the public. Many Germans were not committed to democratic principles that could unite and guide the nation. The fledgling state then faced a series of severe economic and political crises. Such strains might have overloaded the ability of any system to govern effectively. These crises further eroded public support for the republic and opened the door to Hitler's authoritarian and nationalistic appeals. The institutional weaknesses of the political system contributed to Weimar's political vulnerability. Finally, most Germans drastically underestimated Hitler's ambitions, intentions, and political abilities. This underestimation, perhaps, was Weimar's greatest failure. *Because it gave in*

The Third Reich

The Nazis' rise to power reflected a bizarre mixture of ruthless behavior and concern for legal procedures. Hitler called for a new election in March 1933 and then suppressed the opposition parties. Although the Nazis failed to capture an absolute majority of the votes, they used their domination of the parliament to enact legislation granting Hitler dictatorial powers. Democracy was replaced by the new authoritarian "leader state" of the *Third Reich*.

Once entrenched in power, Hitler pursued extremist policies. Social and political groups that might challenge the government were destroyed, taken over by Nazi agents, or coopted into accepting the Nazi regime. The arbitrary powers of the police state grew and choked off opposition. Attacks on Jews and other minorities steadily became more violent. Massive public works projects lessened unemployment, but also built the infrastructure for a wartime economy. The government expanded and rearmed the military in violation of World War I treaties; the Reich's expansionist foreign policy challenged the international peace.

Hitler's unrestrained political ambitions finally plunged Europe into World War II in 1939. After initial victories, a series of military defeats from 1942 on led to the total collapse of the Third Reich in May 1945. A total of 60 million lives were lost worldwide in the war, including 6 million European Jews who were murdered in a Nazi campaign of systematic genocide.[3] Germany lay in ruins: Its industry and transportation systems were destroyed, its cities were rubble, millions were homeless, and even food was scarce. Hitler's grand design for a new German Reich had instead destroyed the nation in a Wagnerian Götterdämmerung.

The Occupation Period

The political division of postwar Germany began as foreign troops advanced onto German soil. At the end of the war, the Western Allies—the United States, Britain, and France—controlled Germany's Western zone and the Soviet Union occupied the Eastern zone. This was to be an interim division, but growing frictions between Western and Soviet leaders increased tensions between the regions.

In the West, the Allied military government began a denazification program to remove Nazi officials and sympathizers from the economic, military, and political systems. Under the supervision of the occupation authorities, new political parties were licensed and democratic political institutions began to develop. The economic system was reorganized along capitalist lines. Currency and market economy reforms in 1948 revitalized the economic system of the Western zone but also deepened East-West divisions.

Political change followed a much different course in the Eastern zone. The new *Socialist Unity Party (SED)* was a mechanism for the Communists to control the political process. Since the Soviets saw the capitalist system as responsible for the Third Reich, they sought to destroy the capitalist structure and construct a new socialist order in its place. By 1948 the Eastern zone was essentially a copy of the Soviet political and economic systems.

As the political distance between occupation zones widened, the Western allies favored creation of a separate German state in the West. In Bonn, a small university town along the banks of the Rhine, the Germans began their second attempt at democracy. In 1948 a Parliamentary Council drafted an interim constitution that was to last until the entire nation was reunited. In May 1949 the state governments in the West agreed on a *Basic Law (Grundgesetz)* that created the *Federal Republic of Germany (FRG)*, or West Germany.

The Soviets were greatly concerned by these developments. The Soviet blockade of Berlin in 1948, for example, was partially an attempt to halt the formation of a separate German state in the West—though it actually strengthened Western resolve. Once it became apparent that the West would follow its own course, preparations began for a separate German state in the East. A week after the formation of the Federal Republic, the People's Congress in the East approved a draft constitution. On October 7, 1949, the *German Democratic Republic (GDR)*, or East Germany, was formed. As in earlier periods of German history, a divided nation was following different paths (see Figure 6.1). It would be more than 40 years before these paths would converge.

Following Two Paths

Although they had chosen different paths (or had them chosen for them), the two German states faced many of the same challenges in their initial years. Despite the progress made by the late 1940s, the economic picture was bleak on both sides of the border. Unemployment remained high in the West and the average wage earner received less than $60 a month. In 1950 almost two-thirds of the West German public felt they had been better off before the war, and severe economic hardships were still common. The situation was even worse in the East.

West Germany had phenomenal success in meeting this economic challenge.[4] Relying on a free enterprise system championed by the *Christian Democratic Union (COU)*, the country experienced sustained and unprecedented economic growth. By the early 1950s incomes had reached the prewar level, and growth had just begun. Over the next two decades, per capita wealth nearly tripled, average hourly industrial wages increased nearly fivefold, and average incomes grew nearly sevenfold. By most economic indicators, the West German public in 1970 was several times more affluent than at any previous time in its history. This phenomenal economic growth came to be known as West Germany's *Economic Miracle (Wirtschaftswunder)*.

FIGURE 6.1   The Two Paths of Postwar Germany

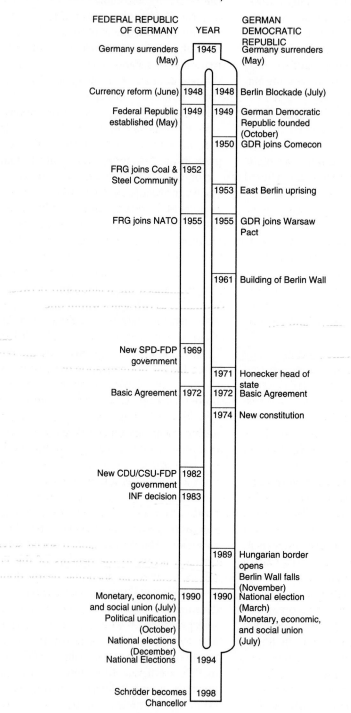

East Germany experienced its own economic miracle that was almost as impressive. Economic reform in the East was based on a system of collectivized agriculture, nationalized industry, and centralized planning.[5] In the two decades after the formation of the GDR, industrial production increased nearly fivefold and per capita national income grew by nearly equal measure. Although still lagging behind its more affluent relative in the West, the GDR became the model of prosperity among socialist states.

The problem of nation building posed another challenge. The FRG initially was viewed as a provisional state until both Germanies could be reunited. The GDR struggled to develop its own identity in the shadow of the West, as well as retaining a commitment to eventual reunification. In addition to the problems of division, the occupation authorities retained the right to intervene in the two Germanies even after 1949. Thus both states faced the challenge of defining their identity—as separate states or as parts of a larger Germany—and regaining national sovereignty.

West Germany's first chancellor, *Konrad Adenauer*, steered the nation on a course toward gaining its national sovereignty by integrating the Federal Republic into the Western alliance. The Western powers would grant greater autonomy to West Germany if it was exercised within the framework of an international body. For example, economic redevelopment was channeled through the European Coal and Steel Community and through the European Economic Community. West Germany's military rearmament occurred within the North Atlantic Treaty Organization (NATO).

The communist regime in the East countered the Federal Republic's integration into the Western alliance with calls for German unification. And yet, the GDR went about establishing itself as a separate German state. In 1952 the GDR transformed the demarcation line between East and West Germany into a fortified border and restricted access to the East. The GDR integrated its economy into the Soviet bloc through membership in the Council for Mutual Economic Assistance (COMECON), and it was a charter member of the Warsaw Pact. The Soviet Union recognized the sovereignty of the German Democratic Republic in 1954. The practical and symbolic division of Germany became official with the GDR's construction of the Berlin Wall in August 1961. More than a physical barrier between East and West, it marked the formal existence of two separate German states.

Intra-German relations took a dramatically different course once the *Social Democratic Party (SPD)* won control of West Germany's government after the 1969 elections. The new SPD chancellor, Willy Brandt, proposed a policy toward the East (*Ostpolitik*) that accepted the postwar political situation and sought reconciliation with the nations of Eastern Europe, including the GDR. West Germany signed treaties with the Soviet Union and Poland to resolve disagreements dating back to World War II and to establish new economic and political ties. In 1971 Brandt received the Nobel Peace Prize for his actions. The following year a Basic Agreement with the GDR formalized the relationship between the two Germanies as two states within one German nation.

To the East German regime, *Ostpolitik* was a mixed blessing. On the positive side, it legitimized the GDR through its recognition by the Federal Republic and the normalization of East-West relations. On the negative side, economic and social exchanges increased East Germans' exposure to Western values and ideas, which many GDR politicians worried would undermine their closed system. The revolution of 1989 seemingly confirmed their fears were correct.

After reconciliation between the two German states, both spent most of the next two decades addressing their internal needs. In the West, the SPD-led government initiated domestic policy reforms in the early 1970s that expanded social services and equalized access to the benefits of the Economic Miracle. Total social spending nearly doubled between 1969 and 1975. The momentum for political reform in the FRG slackened in the mid-1970s mainly because of global economic problems. In 1974 Helmut Schmidt became chancellor and directed a retrenchment on domestic policy reforms.

The problems of unrealized reforms and renewed economic difficulties continued into the 1980s. In 1982 the Christian Democrats enticed the *Free Democratic Party (FDP)* to form a new

---

Box 6.1   The Inefficiencies of Socialism

Because of the inefficiencies of its socialist economy, the GDR faced growing difficulties during the 1980s in competing economically with the West. For instance, to meet the consumer tastes of young East Germans, the state enterprises developed their own "Walkman" radios. However, the cost of a radio was 399 East German Marks, or about $400 in U.S. dollars. Moreover, some of the parts could not be produced in the GDR and had to be imported from Japan; it cost more to import these parts than it would have been to purchase complete Walkmans from Japan.

Source: Charles Maier, *Dissolution* (Princeton, N.J: Princeton University Press, 1997), p. 76.

---

government under the leadership of Helmut Kohl, head of the Christian Democratic Union. The new government wanted to restore the Federal Republic's economy while still providing for social needs. Kohl presided over a dramatic improvement in economic conditions: public spending was held in check, the annual federal deficit decreased, and the economy grew. The government also demonstrated its strong commitment to the Western defense alliance by accepting the deployment of new NATO nuclear missiles. The public returned Kohl's coalition to office after the January 1987 elections.

During the 1970s, the GDR also adapted to its new international status.[6] The GDR established new diplomatic ties with other nations and expanded its international presence through activities ranging from the Olympics to its new membership in the United Nations. Simultaneously, the GDR tried to insulate itself from the Western influences that accompanied *Ostpolitik* through a policy of demarcation (*Abgrenzung*) from the West. A 1974 revision of the constitution strengthened the emphasis on a separate, socialist East German state that was no longer tied to the ideal of a unified Germany. Socialism and the fraternal ties to the Soviet Union became the basis of the GDR's national identity.

Worldwide economic recession also buffeted the GDR's economy in the late 1970s. The cost competitiveness of East German products diminished in international markets, and trade deficits with the West grew steadily during the 1980s. Moreover, the consequences of long-delayed investment in the economic infrastructure began to show in a deteriorating highway system, an aging housing stock, and an outdated communications system (see Box 6.1). Although the East Germans heard frequent government reports about the successes of the economy, their living standards displayed a widening gap between official pronouncements and reality.

As East German government officials grappled with their own problems, they were also disturbed by the winds of change rising in the East. The GDR had been unquestioningly loyal to the Soviet Union, but Soviet President Mikhail Gorbachev's reformist policies of *perestroika* and *glasnost* seemed to undermine the pillars on which the East German system was built (see Chapter 8). At one point, an official GDR newspaper even censored news reports from the Soviet Union in order to downplay Gorbachev's reforms. Indeed, the stimulus for political change in East Germany came not from within but from the events sweeping across the rest of Eastern Europe.

In early 1989 the first cracks in the communist system appeared. The communist government of Poland accepted a series of democratic reforms; the Hungarian Communist Party soon endorsed the idea of free democratic elections and introduced market forces into the economy. When Hungary opened its border with neutral Austria, a steady stream of East Germans vacationing in Hungary started leaving for the West. East Germans were voting, with their feet. Almost 2 percent of the East German population emigrated to the Federal Republic over the next six months. The exodus also stimulated public demonstrations within East Germany against the regime.

As the East German government struggled with this problem, Gorbachev played a crucial role in directing the flow of events. He first signaled the Soviets' willingness to see Erich Honecker replaced as the GDR head of state by Egon Krenz. He encouraged the East German leadership to undertake a process of internal reform with the cautious advice that "life itself punishes those who delay."

Without Soviet support, the end of the old GDR system was inevitable. Rapidly growing public protests increased the pressure on the government, and the continuing exodus to the West brought the East's economy to a near standstill. The government did not govern; it barely existed, struggling from crisis to crisis. In early November the government and the SED Politburo resigned. On the evening of November 9, 1989, a GDR official announced the opening of the border between East and West Berlin. In the former no-man's land of the Berlin Wall, Berliners from East and West joyously celebrated together.

Once the euphoria of the opening of the Berlin Wall had passed, East Germany had to address the question of "what next?" The GDR government initially followed a strategy of damage control, appointing new leaders and attempting to court public support. But the power of the state and the vitality of the economy had already suffered mortal wounds. The only apparent source of stability was a policy of unification with the Federal Republic, and the rush toward German unity began.

In March 1990 the GDR had its first truly free elections since 1932. The Alliance for Germany, which included the eastern branch of the Christian Democrats, won control of the government. Helmut Kohl and Lothar de Maiziere, the new GDR leader, both forcefully moved toward unification. An intra-German treaty on July 1 gave the two nations one currency and essentially one economy. The road to complete unification opened when Kohl won Soviet concessions on the terms of unification. On October 3, 1990, after a generation of separation, the two German paths again converged.

Unification has largely occurred on Western terms. In fact, Easterners sarcastically point out that the only trace of the old regime is the one law kept from the GDR: automobiles can turn right on a red light in the East. Otherwise, the Western political structures, Western interest groups, Western political parties, and Western economic and social systems were simply exported to the East.

Unification was supposed to be the answer to a dream, but during the years that followed it must have occasionally seemed like a nightmare. The Eastern economy collapsed with the end of the GDR; at times unemployment rates in the East exceeded the worst years of the Great Depression. The burden of unification led to inflation and tax increases in the West, and the Western gross domestic product declined in 1993. The social strains of unification stimulated violent attacks against foreigners in both halves of Germany, and increasing worries about the vitality of German democracy. At the end of 1994, Kohl's coalition won a razor-thin majority in national elections and continued its attempt to resolve these issues.

Tremendous progress had been made by 1998, but many major problems remained. The economy still struggled, and more than 4 million Germans were unemployed. Needed reforms in tax laws and social programs had not been implemented. When the Germans went to the polls in 1998 they voted for a change and elected a new government headed by Gerhard Schröder. The new coalition government faces many of the same challenges: a stagnant economy, excessive government budget deficits, and growing East-West polarization. Willy Brandt's dream that the two parts of the divided nation can begin to grow together remains a dream for the future.

Social Forces

Popular accounts of unification sometimes refer to the new Germany as the fourth and richest Reich. The new Germany has about 82 million people, 68 million in the West and 14 million in the East, located in Europe's heartland. The total German economy is the largest in Europe. The combined territory of the new Germany is also large by European standards, although it is small in comparison to the United States—about the size of Montana.

The merger of two nations is more complex than the simple addition of two columns of numbers on a balance sheet, however. Unification has created new strengths, but it has also redefined and potentially strained the social system that underlies

German society and politics. The merger of East and West holds the potential for reviving some of Germany's traditional social divisions.

Economics

East and West Germany had experienced their own postwar economic miracles, but they followed different courses. Both societies experienced a sharp decline in the size of the agricultural sector after World War II; the percentage of workers employed in agriculture decreased to 4 percent in West Germany and 11 percent in the GDR. The size of the industrial sector held fairly constant in the West, accounting for about 40 percent of the workforce. Economic expansion in West Germany came in the service and technology sectors, and government employment more than doubled. In contrast, economic expansion in the GDR was concentrated in heavy industry and manufacturing. In the mid-1980s about half of the Eastern economy was in these two areas, and the service-technology sector represented a small share of the economy.

By most economic measures, both societies made dramatic economic advances across the postwar decades. But these economic advances also occurred at different rates in the West and East. In the mid-1980s the West German standard of living ranked among the highest in the world. By comparison, the purchasing power of the average East German's salary amounted to barely half the income of a Westerner. Basic staples were inexpensively priced in the East, but most consumer goods were more expensive and so-called luxury items (color televisions, washing machines, and automobiles) were beyond the reach of normal families. In 1985 about a third of the dwellings in East Germany still lacked their own baths and toilets. GDR residents lived a comfortable life by East European standards, although far short of Western standards.

German unification has meant the merger of these two different economies and social systems: the affluent West Germans and their poor cousins from the East; the sophisticated and technologically advanced industries of the West and the aging rust-belt factories of the GDR. At least in the short run, unification worsened the economic problems of the East. By some accounts, industrial production fell by two-thirds between 1989 and 1992—worse than the decline during the Great Depression. The government sold off Eastern firms, and often the first response by the new owners was to reduce the labor force. Even by early-2001, a sixth of the Eastern labor force remained unemployed.

Citizens on each side of the former border expected that some short-term economic problems would accompany unification. However, during the unification process politicians claimed that the East would enjoy a modern economic miracle in a few years. This proved overly optimistic. Only massive social payments by the FRG have maintained the living standards in the East. The government also assumed a major role in rebuilding the East's economic infrastructure and encouraging investment in the East. While the personal situation of many Easterners had improved by the early 2000s, many remain pessimistic about economic conditions in the East.[7] The persisting economic gap between East and West creates a basis for social and political division in the new Germany.

Religion

Religious differences have also divided Germans ever since the Reformation. The postwar Federal Republic saw the gradual decline of religious polarization, partially because there were equal numbers of Catholics and Protestants, and partly because of a conscious attempt to avoid the religious conflicts of the past. Secularization also gradually eroded the public's involvement in the churches. In the East, the communist government sharply limited the political and social roles of the churches.

German unification has unsettled the delicate religious balance in the new Federal Republic. Catholics comprise 42 percent of the Western public but only 7 percent of the East. Thus unification significantly changes the religious composition of the unified nation; Protestants now outnumber Catholics by nearly 5 million people. Religious parity in the West had encouraged a harmony that the new religious imbalance will test. Even more dramatic, most Easterners claim to be nonreligious, which may lead to new challenges to FRG policies that benefit religious interests. A more Protestant and secular electorate should also change the policy preferences of the German public on religiously based issues such as abortion and may potentially reshape electoral alliances.

Gender

Gender roles are another source of social differentiation. In the past, the three K's—*Kinder* (children), *Kirche* (church), and *Küche* (kitchen)—defined the woman's role, while politics and work were male matters. Attempts to lessen role differences have met with mixed success. The FRG's Basic Law guarantees the equality of the sexes, but the specific legislation to support this guarantee was often lacking. Cultural norms have changed only slowly; cross-national surveys show that West German males are more chauvinist than the average European, and West German women feel less liberated than other Europeans.[8]

The GDR constitution also guaranteed the equality of the sexes, and the government aggressively protected this guarantee. For instance, women's share of seats in the East German People's Congress was nearly twice the proportion of women in the FRG parliament. A larger percentage of Eastern women were employed, although they were underrepresented in careers with high status or authority. Maternity benefits were more generous in the East, and women had the unlimited right to abortion.

East German women were one of the first groups to suffer from the unification process. The proportion of women deputies decreased under democratic elections. Eastern women lost rights and benefits that they had held under East German law. For instance, conflicting versions of the FRG and GDR abortion laws were resolved only in 1993 by a decision of the Constitutional Court. The Court essentially adopted the FRG's prior standards, by which abortion is illegal unless one of several conditions are met. The greater expectations of Eastern women moved gender issues higher on the political agenda, and new legislation on job discrimination and women's rights was passed in 1994. Yet progress lags behind many other Western democracies.

Foreign Workers

Another new social cleavage involves Germany's growing minority of foreign workers.[9] When the Economic Miracle produced a severe labor shortage in the 1960s, West Germany recruited millions of workers from Turkey, Yugoslavia, Italy, Spain, Greece, and other less developed countries. German politicians and the public considered this a temporary situation, and the foreigners were called *guest workers (Gastarbeiter)*. Most of these guest workers worked long enough to acquire skills and some personal savings, and then returned home.

A strange thing happened, however. Germany asked only for workers, but they got human beings. Cultural centers for foreign workers emerged in many cities. Some foreign workers chose to remain in West Germany, and they naturally brought their families to join them. Foreigners brought new ways of life, as well as new hands for factory assembly lines.

From the beginning, the foreign worker population has faced several potential problems. They remain concentrated at the low end of the economic ladder, often doing work that native Germans do not want to do. Guest workers are culturally, socially, and linguistically isolated from mainstream society. The problems of social and cultural isolation are especially difficult for the children of foreigners. Foreigners have also become a target for reactionary violence as Westerners and Easterners react to the strains of unification. The nation has struggled with these problems, but the solutions are still uncertain. In 1999 the Schröder government changed the citizenship laws to better integrate foreign-born residents into German society. Addressing the issues associated with a permanent foreign worker presence (roughly 6 percent of the population) will be a continuing feature of German politics.

Regionalism

Regionalism is another potential source of social and political division in contemporary Germany. The new Federal Republic is divided into 16 states (*Länder*), ten states in the West and six new states created out of East Germany, including the new city-state of Berlin. Many of the Länder are distinguished by their own historical traditions and social structure. The language and idioms of speech differentiate residents from the eastern and western halves of the nation. And no one would mistake a northern German for a Bavarian from the south—their manners and dialects are too distinct.

The decentralized nature of society and the economy reinforce these regional differences. Economic and cultural activities are dispersed throughout the country rather than concentrated in a single national center. The Federal Republic has more than a dozen regional economic centers, such as Frankfurt, Cologne, Dresden, Düsseldorf, Munich, Leipzig, and Hamburg. The mass media are organized around regional markets, and there are even several competing "national" theaters.

Unification has greatly increased the cultural, economic, and political variations between the various states. Indeed, the economic gap between regions was so large in the early 1990s that it required a revision of the constitutional guarantees of equal living standards across states, and the interstate financial transfers to produce this equalization. The economic and social tensions of German unification have reinforced the importance of regional differences within Germany. It is common to hear of "a wall in the mind" that separates Wessies (Westerners) and Ossies (Easterners). Easterners still draw on their separate traditions and experiences when making political decisions, just as Westerners do. At least in the short term, therefore, regional considerations remain an important factor in society and politics.

The Institutions and Structure of Government

The Basic Law adopted in 1949 supposedly created a temporary political system to serve the Federal Republic until both halves of Germany could be united. The preamble, for example, stated the intention "to give a new order to political life for a transitional period."

In actuality, the rapid disintegration of East Germany in 1990 led to the incorporation of the GDR into the existing political, legal, and economic systems of the Federal Republic. In September 1990 the Federal Republic and the German Democratic Republic signed a treaty agreeing to unify their two states, and the Basic Law was amended to accommodate the accession of new states from the East.

Thus the political system of the unified Germany functions within the structure of the Basic Law.

When the Parliamentary Council originally framed the Basic Law in 1949, it wanted to construct a stable and effective democratic political system.[10] One objective was to maintain some historical continuity in political institutions. Most Germans were familiar with the workings of a parliamentary system, and the framers wanted a federal structure of government.

Another objective was to design a political system that would avoid the institutional weaknesses that contributed to the collapse of Weimar democracy. The framers wanted to establish clearer lines of political authority and to create a new system with extensive checks and balances to prevent the usurpation of power that occurred during the Third Reich. Finally, Germany needed institutional limits on extremist and antisystem forces.

The Basic Law is an exceptional example of political engineering—the construction of a political system to achieve specific goals. It creates a parliamentary democracy that involves the public, encourages elite political responsibility, disperses political power, and limits the influence of extremists. A description of the FRG's institutions will illustrate how these goals were translated into a new constitutional structure.

A Federal System

One way to distribute political power and to build checks and balances into a political system is through a federal system of government. The Basic Law created one of the few federal political systems in Europe (see Figure 6.2). Germany is organized into 16 states (*Länder*). Political power is divided between the federal government (*Bund*) and the state governments. The federal government has primary policy responsibility in most policy areas. The states, however, have jurisdiction in education, culture, law enforcement, and regional planning. In several other policy areas the states and federal government share responsibility, although federal law takes priority in case of conflict. Furthermore, the states retain residual powers to legislate in areas that the Basic Law does not explicitly assign to the federal government.

FIGURE 6.2 The Structure of Germany's Federal Government

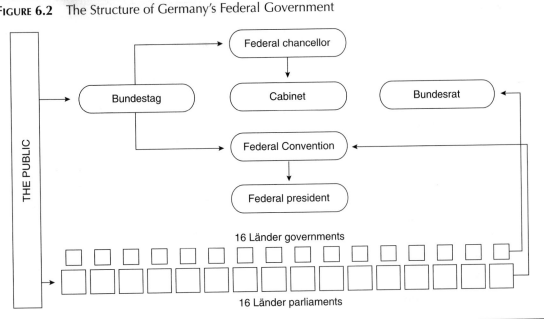

The state governments have a unicameral legislature, normally called a *Landtag*, which is directly elected by popular vote. The party or coalition that controls the legislature selects a minister president to head the state government. Next to the federal chancellor, the minister presidents are among the most powerful political officials in the Federal Republic.

The federal government is the major force in the legislation of policy, and the states are primarily responsible for policy administration. The states enforce their own regulations as well as most of the domestic legislation enacted by the federal government. The state governments also oversee the operation of local governments.

One house of the bicameral federal legislature, the Bundesrat, is comprised solely of representatives appointed by the state governments. State government officials also participate in selecting the federal president and the justices of the major federal courts. This federal system decentralizes political power by balancing the power of the state governments against the power of the federal government.

Parliamentary Government

The central institution of the federal government is the parliament. Parliament is bicameral: the popularly elected *Bundestag* is the primary legislative body; the *Bundesrat* represents the state governments at the federal level.

THE BUNDESTAG The 656 deputies of the Bundestag are the only government officials who can claim to represent the German public directly. Deputies are selected in national elections that are normally held every four years.

The Bundestag's major function is to enact legislation; all federal laws must receive its approval. The initiative for most legislation, however, lies in the executive branch. Like other modern parliaments, the Bundestag evaluates and amends the government's legislative program. Another important function of the Bundestag is to elect the federal chancellor, who heads the executive branch.

The Bundestag also provides a forum for public debate. Its plenary sessions consider the legislation before the chamber. Debating time is allowed to all party groupings according to their size; both party leaders and backbenchers normally participate. The Bundestag now televises its sessions, including live broadcasts on the Internet, to expand the public audience for its policy debates.[11]

The Bundestag also scrutinizes the actions of the government. The most common method of oversight is the "question hour" adopted from the British House of Commons. An individual deputy can submit a written question to a government minister: Questions range from broad policy issues to the specific needs of one constituent. Government representatives answer the queries during the question hour, and deputies can raise follow-up questions at that time. Bundestag deputies posed more than 17,000 oral and written questions during the 1994–1998 term of the Bundestag.

In addition to formal questions, deputies can petition for a special debate on a contemporary policy problem. These debates are often more informative than the plenary sessions, perhaps because debate is not focused on a specific legislative proposal. Finally, the Bundestag boasts a system of strong legislative committees. These committees provide the legislature with expertise to balance the policy experience of the federal agencies; the committees also conduct investigative hearings in their area of specialization.

The opposition parties normally make greatest use of these oversight opportunities; about two-thirds of the questions posed during the 1994–1998 term came from the opposition parties. Rank and file members of the governing parties also use these devices to make their own views known. On the whole, the Bundestag's oversight powers are considerable, especially for a legislature in a parliamentary system.

The Bundesrat   The second chamber of the parliament, the Bundesrat, reflects Germany's federal system. The state governments appoint its 69 members to represent their interests in Bonn. The states normally appoint members of the state cabinet to serve jointly in the Bundesrat; the chamber thus acts as a permanent conference of state ministers. Bundesrat seats are allocated to each state in numbers roughly proportionate to the state's population: from six seats for the most populous states to three for the

least. The votes for each state delegation are cast in a block, according to the instructions of the state government.

The Bundesrat is directly involved in the legislative process, although its legislative authority is secondary to that of the Bundestag. The federal government must submit all legislative proposals to the Bundesrat before forwarding them to the Bundestag. Bundesrat approval is required, however, only in areas where the states hold concurrent powers or where the states will administer federal laws. About two-thirds of legislative proposals now require Bundesrat approval. This is especially important for periods when one coalition controls the Bundesrat, while another coalition holds a majority in the Bundestag.

In summary, the parliament is mainly a body that reacts to government proposals rather than taking the initiative. In comparison to the British House of Commons or the French National Assembly, however, the Bundestag probably exercises more autonomy from the executive branch. Especially if one includes the Bundesrat, the German parliament has more independence and opportunity to revise government proposals. By strengthening the power of the parliament, the Basic Law intended to create a check on executive power. Experience shows that the political system has met this goal.

The Federal Chancellor and Cabinet

A weakness of the Weimar system was the division of executive authority between the president and the chancellor. The Basic Law resolved this ambiguity by strengthening the powers of the *federal chancellor (Bundeskanzler)*. Moreover, the incumbents of this office have dominated the political process and symbolized the federal government by their personalization of power. The chancellor plays such a central role in the political system that some observers describe the German system as a "chancellor democracy."

The chancellor is elected by the Bundestag and is responsible to it for the conduct of the federal government. This situation grants the chancellor substantial power. He represents a majority of the Bundestag and normally can count on their support for the government's legislative proposals. The chancellor usually heads his own party, directing party strategy and leading the party at elections.

Another source of the chancellor's authority is his control over the Cabinet. The federal government today consists of 14 departments, each headed by a minister. The Cabinet ministers are formally appointed, or dismissed, by the federal president on the recommendation of the chancellor (Bundestag approval is not necessary). The Basic Law also grants the chancellor the power to decide the number of Cabinet ministers and their duties.

The Basic Law's goal of avoiding the concentration of power that occurred at the end of Weimar can be seen in the relationship between the legislative and executive branches. For instance, the chancellor lacks the discretionary authority to dissolve the legislature and call for new elections, something that is normally found in parliamentary systems.

Equally important, the Basic Law limits the legislature's control over the chancellor. In a parliamentary system the legislature normally has the authority to remove a chief executive from office by a simple majority vote. During the Weimar Republic, however, extremist parties used this device to destabilize the democratic system by opposing incumbent chancellors. The Basic Law modified this procedure and created a *constructive no-confidence vote*.[12] In order for the Bundestag to remove a chancellor, it simultaneously must agree on a successor. This ensures a continuity in government and an initial majority in support of a new chancellor. It also makes removing an incumbent more difficult; opponents cannot simply disagree with the government—a majority must agree on an alternative. The constructive no-confidence vote has been attempted only twice—and succeeded only once. In 1982 a coalition of parties replaced Chancellor Schmidt with a new chancellor, Helmut Kohl.

The functioning of the federal government follows three principles laid out in the Basic Law. First, the chancellor principle says that chancellor defines government policy; the formal policy guidelines issued by the chancellor are legally binding directives on the Cabinet and the ministries. Thus, in contrast to the British system of shared Cabinet responsibility, the German Cabinet is formally subordinate to the chancellor in policymaking.

The second principle of ministerial autonomy gives each minister the authority to direct the ministry's internal workings without Cabinet intervention as long as the policies conform to the government's guidelines. Ministers are responsible for supervising the activities of their departments, guiding their policy planning, and overseeing the administration of policy within their jurisdiction.

The cabinet principle is the third organizational guideline. When conflicts arise between departments over jurisdictional or budgetary matters, the Basic Law calls for them to be resolved in the Cabinet.

The actual working of the federal government is more fluid than the formal procedures spelled out by the Basic Law. The number and choice of ministries for each party is a major issue in building a multiparty government coalition after each election. Cabinet members also display great independence on policy despite the formal restrictions of the Basic Law. Ministers are appointed because they possess expertise or interest in a policy area. In practice, they identify more with their roles as department heads than as agents of the chancellor; their political success is judged by their representation of department interests.

The Cabinet thus serves as a clearinghouse for the business of the federal government. Specific ministers present policy proposals originating in their departments in the hope of gaining government endorsement. The chancellor defines a government program that reflects a consensus of the Cabinet and relies on negotiations and compromise within the Cabinet to maintain this consensus.

The Federal President

Because of the problems associated with the Weimar Republic's divided executive, the Basic Law transformed the office of federal president (*Bundespräsident*) into a mostly ceremonial post. The president's official duties involve greeting visiting heads of state, attending official government functions, visiting foreign nations, and similar tasks.[13]

To insulate the office from electoral politics, the president is selected by a Federal Convention composed of all Bundestag deputies and an equal number of representatives chosen by the state legislatures. The president is supposed to remain above partisan politics once elected.

The reduction in the president's formal political role does not mean that an incumbent is uninvolved in the policymaking process. The Basic Law assigns several legal functions to the president, who appoints government and military officials, signs treaties and laws, and possesses the power of pardon. In these instances, however, the actions must be countersigned by the chancellor. The president also nominates a chancellor to the Bundestag and can dissolve Parliament if a government legislative proposal loses a no-confidence vote. In both instances, the president's ability to act independently is limited by the Basic Law.

Potentially more significant is the constitutional ambiguity over whether the president must honor certain requests from the government. The legal precedent is unclear on whether the president has the constitutional right to veto legislation, to refuse the chancellor's recommendation for Cabinet appointments, or even to reject a request to dissolve the Bundestag. Most analysts see these ambiguities as another safety valve built into the Basic Law's elaborate system of checks and balances.

The political importance of the federal president also involves factors that go beyond the articles of the Basic Law. An active, dynamic president can help to shape the political climate of the nation through his speeches and public activities. He is the one political figure who can rightly claim to be above politics and who can work to extend the vision of the nation beyond its everyday concerns. Johannes Rau was elected president in 1999 after serving as Minister President of North Rhine-Westphalia.

The Judicial System

The ordinary courts for criminal cases and regular legal disputes are integrated into a unitary system (see Figure 6.3). The states administer the three lower levels of the courts. The highest court, the Federal Court of Justice, is at the national level. These courts hear both civil and criminal cases, and all courts apply the same national legal codes.

The administrative courts hear cases in specialized areas. One court deals with administrative complaints against government agencies, one handles tax matters, and another resolves claims involving government social programs. Another court deals with labor-management disputes. Like the rest of the judicial system, these specialized courts are linked into one system including both state and federal courts.

The Basic Law created a third element of the judiciary: an independent *Constitutional Court*. This court reviews the constitutionality of legislation, mediates disputes between levels of government, and protects the constitutional and democratic order.[14] This is an innovation for the German legal system because it places one law, the Basic Law, above all others. This also implies limits on the decision-making power of the Parliament and the judicial interpretations of lower court judges. Because of the importance of the Constitutional Court, its 16 members are selected in equal numbers by the Bundestag and Bundesrat and can be removed only for abuse of the office.

The Federal Republic's judicial system follows the Roman law tradition that is fundamentally different from the common law Anglo-American system of justice. Rather than relying on precedents from prior cases as in the common law system, the legal process is based on an extensive system of government defined legal codes. The codes define legal principles in the abstract, and specific cases are judged against these standards. The system relies on a rationalist philosophy that justice is served by following the letter of the law.

Remaking Political Cultures

Consider for a minute what the average German must have thought about politics as World War II was ending. Germany's political history was hardly conducive to good democratic citizenship. Under the Kaiser, people were expected to be subjects, not active participants in the political process; this style nurtured feelings of political intolerance. The interlude of the Weimar Republic did little to change these values. The polarization, fragmentation, and outright violence of the Weimar Republic taught people to avoid politics, not to be active participants. Moreover, democracy eventually failed, and

FIGURE 6.3   Organization of the Courts

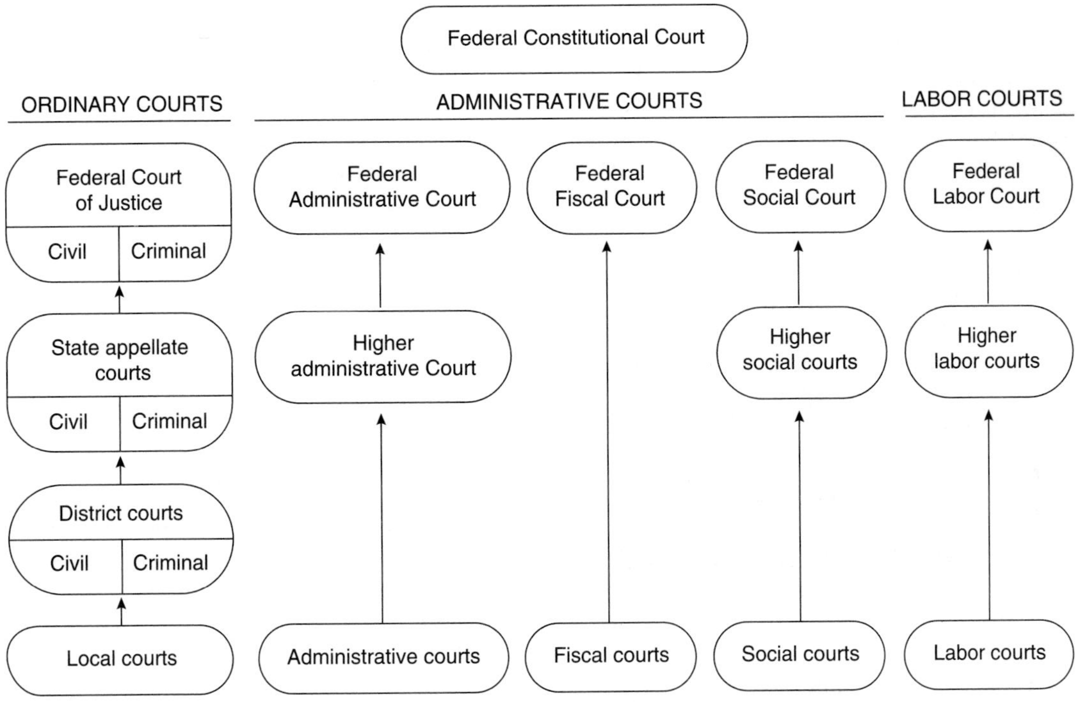

national socialism arose in its place. The Third Reich then raised another generation under an intolerant, authoritarian system.

Because of this historical legacy, the development of the Federal Republic is closely linked to the question of whether its political culture is congruent with its democratic system (see discussion in Chapter 2). During West Germany's initial years, there were widespread fears that the nation lacked a democratic political culture, thereby making it vulnerable to the same problems that undermined the Weimar Republic. Postwar public opinion polls in West Germany presented a negative image of public beliefs that was probably equally applicable to the East.[15] West Germans were politically detached, acceptant of authority, and intolerant in their political views. A significant minority were unrepentant Nazis, sympathy for many elements of the Nazi ideology was widespread, and anti-Semitic feelings remained commonplace.

Perhaps even more amazing than the Economic Miracle was the transformation of West Germany's political culture in little more than a generation. Confronted by an uncertain public commitment to democracy, the government undertook a massive program to reeducate the public. The schools, the media, and political organizations were mobilized behind the effort. The citizenry itself also was changing—older generations raised under authoritarian regimes were gradually replaced by younger generations socialized during the postwar democratic era. The successes of a growing economy and a relatively smoothly functioning political system also changed public perceptions. These efforts created a new political culture more congruent with the democratic institutions and process of the Federal Republic.

With unification Germany now confronts another serious cultural question. The communists tried to create a rival culture in the GDR that would support their state and its socialist economic system. Indeed, the efforts at political education in the East were more intense and extensive; they aimed at creating a broad "socialist personality" that included nonpolitical attitudes and behavior.[16] Young people were taught a collective identity with their peers, to nurture a love for the GDR and its socialist brethren, to accept the guidance of the Socialist Unity Party, and to understand history and society from a Marxist-Leninist perspective.

German unification means the blending of these two different political cultures, and the nature of this mixture is uncertain. Without scientific social science research in the GDR, we cannot tell if the government's propaganda was internalized by the Eastern public. Western influences also flowed eastward, and two decades of *Ostpolitik* increased the interchange between East and West. Furthermore, the revolutionary political events leading to German unification may have reshaped even long-held political beliefs. What does a communist think after attending communism's funeral?

The citizens in the West are deeply committed to liberal values and the democratic process, but can this culture assimilate 16 million new citizens with potentially different beliefs about how politics and society should function?

Nation and State

An essential element of the German culture has been a strong sense of German identity. A common history, culture, territory, and language created a sense of national community long before Germany was politically united. Germany was the land of Schiller, Goethe, Beethoven, and Wagner, even if the Germans disagreed on political boundaries. The imagery of a single *Volk* bound Germans together despite their social and political differences.

Previous regimes had failed, however, to develop a common political identity as part of the German political culture. Succeeding political systems were short-lived and were unable to develop a popular consensus on the nature and goals of German politics. Postwar West Germany faced a similar challenge: building a political community in a divided and defeated nation.

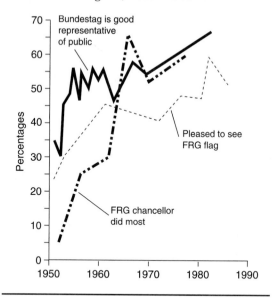

FIGURE 6.4   Increase in Support for the Democratic Regime, 1951–1986

Source: Russell J. Dalton, *Politics in Germany,* 2nd ed. (New York: HarperCollins, 1993), p. 121.

In the early 1950s large sectors of the West German public remained committed to the symbols and personalities of previous regimes.[17] Most people felt that the Second Empire or Hitler's prewar Reich represented the best times in German history. Substantial minorities favored a restoration of the monarchy or a one-party state. Almost half the population believed that if it had not been for World War II, Hitler would have been one of Germany's greatest statesmen.

Over the next two decades these ties to earlier regimes gradually weakened, and the bonds to the new institutions and leaders of the Federal Republic steadily grew stronger (see Figure 6.4). The number of citizens who believed that Bundestag deputies represent the public interest doubled between 1951 and 1964; public respect shifted from the personalities of prior regimes to the chancellors of the Federal Republic. By the 1970s an overwhelming majority of the public felt that the present was the best time in German history; West Germans became more politically tolerant, and feelings of anti-Semitism declined sharply. Other opinions displayed a growing esteem for the new political system.[18]

Even while Westerners developed a new acceptance of the institutions and symbols of the Federal Republic, something was still missing, something that touched the spirit of their political feelings. The FRG was a provisional entity, and "Germany" meant a unified nation. Were citizens of West Germany to think of themselves as Germans, West Germans, or some mix of both? In addition, the trauma of the Third Reich burned a deep scar in the Western psyche, making citizens hesitant to express pride in their nation or a sense of German national identity.

Because of this political stigma, the Federal Republic avoided many of the emotional national symbols that are common in other industrialized nations. There were few political holidays or memorials; the national anthem was seldom played; and even the anniversary of the founding of the FRG received little public attention. This legacy means that even today Germans are hesitant to openly expresss pride in the nation (see Figure 2.2)

The quest for a national identity also occurred in the East. The GDR claimed that it represented the "pure" elements of German history; it portrayed the Federal Republic as the successor to the Third Reich. Most analysts believe that the GDR succeeded in creating at least a sense of resigned loyalty to the regime because of its political and social accomplishments. Thus a 1990 study found that Eastern youth most admired Karl Marx (followed by the first president of the GDR), while Western youth were most likely to name Konrad Adenauer, the first Chancellor of the Federal Republic.

By the late 1980s, however, the GDR lacked a popular consensus in support of the state.[19] There were repeated purges against those who might oppose the GDR. The secret police (*Stasi*) kept files on more than 6 million people, government informers seemed omnipresent, and the Berlin Wall stood as a constant reminder of the nature of the East German state. The government found it necessary to use coercion and the threat of force to sustain itself. Once socialism failed, the basis for a separate East German political identity also evaporated.

Unification began a process by which the German search for a national political identity might finally be resolved. The opening of the Berlin Wall created positive political emotions that were previously lacking. The celebration of unification, and the designation of October 3 as a national holiday, finally gives Germans a positive political experience to celebrate. Germans in East and West remain somewhat hesitant to embrace an emotional attachment to the nation, and Easterners retain a lingering tie to their separate past. Yet the basic situation has changed. For the first time in over a century, nearly all Germans agree where their borders begin and end. Germany is now a single nation—democratic, free, and looking toward the future.[20]

Democratic Norms and Procedures

A second important element of the political culture involves citizen attitudes toward the system of government. In the early years of West Germany, the rules of democratic politics—majority rule, minority rights, individual liberties, and pluralistic debate—were new ideas that did not fit citizens' experiences. To break this model, the leaders of Federal Republic constructed a system that formalized democratic procedures. Citizen participation was encouraged and expected, policymaking became open, and the public gradually learned democratic norms by continued exposure to the new political system. Political leadership provided a generally positive example of competition in a democratic setting. As a result, a popular consensus slowly developed in support of the democratic political system. By the mid-1960s agreement was nearly unanimous that democracy was the best form of government. More important, the Western public has displayed a growing commitment to democratic procedures—a multiparty system, conflict management, minority rights, and representative government.

Political events occasionally have tested the long-term growth in democratic values in West Germany. For instance, during the 1970s a small group of extremists attempted to topple the system through a guerrilla warfare campaign. In the early 1980s the Kohl government faced a series of violent actions by anarchic and radical ecology groups. In both instances, however, the basic lesson was that the political system could face the onslaughts of political extremists and survive with its basic procedures intact, and without the public losing faith in their democratic process.

The propaganda of the East German government also stressed a democratic creed. In reality, however, the regime tried to create a political culture that was compatible with a communist state and socialist economy. The culture drew on traditional Prussian values of obedience, duty, and loyalty: People were again told that obedience was the responsibility of a good citizen, and support of the state (and the party) was an end in itself. Periodically, political events—the 1953 Berlin uprising, the construction of the Berlin Wall, and the expulsions of political dissidents—reminded East Germans of the gap between the democratic rhetoric of the regime and reality.

One reason the popular revolt may have grown so rapidly in 1989 was that the regime had lost the support of many citizens. For instance, studies of young Easterners found that identification with Marxism-Leninism and belief in the inevitable victory of socialism dropped off dramatically during the mid-1980s.[21] At the least, the revolutionary changes that swept through East Germany as the Berlin Wall fell nurtured a belief in democracy as the road to political reform. A 1990 public opinion survey found nearly universal support for the basic tenets of democracy among both West and East Germans, and these parallels persisted over the decade.[22]

One should be cautious about giving too much weight to expressions of support for democracy among Easterners, however. The true test of democracy occurs in the real world. Other studies suggest that Easterners' understanding of the democratic creed is limited, or at least different from the West.[23] Yet, the attachment to democratic values is markedly different from the situation in 1945. Rather than remaking this aspect of the East German culture, the greater need is to transform Eastern support for democracy into a deeper and richer understanding of the workings of the process and its pragmatic strengths and weaknesses.

Social Values and the New Politics

Another area of cultural change in West Germany involves a shift in public values produced by the social and economic accomplishments of the nation. Once West Germany addressed traditional social and economic needs, the public broadened their concerns to include a new set of societal goals. New issues such as the environment, women's rights, and increasing citizen participation attracted public attention. In the early 1980s a vibrant peace movement rekindled the debate on West Germany's international role.

Ronald Inglehart has introduced a theory of value change to explain the development of these new political orientations in the West.[24] He maintains that a person's value priorities reflect the family and societal conditions that prevail early in life. Older generations socialized before World War II lived at least partially under an authoritarian government, experienced long periods of economic hardship, and felt the destructive consequences of war. These older individuals are preoccupied with so-called materialist goals—economic security, law and order, religious values, and a strong national defense—despite the economic and political advances of postwar Germany. In contrast, because younger generations have grown up in a democratic political setting during a period of unprecedented economic prosperity, relative international stability, and now the collapse of the Soviet Empire, they are shifting their attention toward *postmaterial* or *New Politics* values. These new values emphasize self-expression, personal freedom, social equality, self-fulfillment, and maintaining the quality of life.

Although only a minority of Westerners hold these new values, they represent a "second culture" embedded within the dominant culture of FRG society. These values are even more limited among Easterners. Still, the evidence of political change is already clear. Public interest in New Politics issues has gradually spread beyond its youthful supporters and developed a broader base. Even in the East, many of the early demonstrations for democracy had supporters calling for *"Freiheit und Umwelt"* (freedom and the environment).

Two Peoples in One Nation?

Citizens in the East and West share a common German heritage, but 40 years of separation have created cultural differences that now must be integrated into a single national culture. Until recently, soldiers in the East German and West German armies viewed each other hostilely across the border; now they are comrades in arms. Bureaucrats raised in the communist system were suddenly expected to be FRG civil servants. And citizens in the East had to adjust to their new roles in a free and democratic state.

Because of these different experiences, the broad similarities in many of the political beliefs of Westerners and Easterners are surprising. Easterners and Westerners espouse support for the democratic system, its norms, and institutions. There is also broad acceptance of the principles of the market economy of the West. Thus the Federal Republic's second transition to democracy begins with an agreement on basic political and economic values that is markedly different from the situation after World War II.

Yet, other aspects of cultural norms present a potential source of division in a unified Germany. For instance, although residents in both the West and East endorse the tenets of democracy, it is harder to reach agreement on how these ideals translate into practical politics. The open, sometimes confrontational style of Western politics is a major adjustment for citizens raised under the closed system of the GDR. In addition, Easterners endorse a broader role for government in providing social services and guiding social development than is found among Westerners.[25]

There are signs of a growing gap in regional identities between East and West. The passage of time and harsh postunification adjustments have created a nostalgia for some aspects of the GDR among its former residents. Easterners do not want a return to communism or socialism, but many miss the slower and more predictable style of their former lives. Even while expressing support for Western capitalism, many Easterners have had difficulty adjusting to the idea of unemployment and to the competitive pressures of a market-based economy. There is a nostalgic yearning for symbols of these times, ranging from the Trabant automobile to consumer products bearing Eastern labels. In fact, public opinion surveys show that the percentage of Easterners who think of themselves as "East German" rather than "German" increased since unification. Easterners are developing a distinct re-gional identity that is similar to the feelings of Southerners in the United States.

Unification may have also heightened material/postmaterial conflicts within German society. The GDR had struggled to become a materialist success, while West Germany was enjoying its postmaterial abundance. Consequently, materialist goals such as higher living standards, security, hard work, and better living conditions are given greater weight today in the East. Most Easterners want first to share in the affluence and consumer society of the West, before they begin to fear the consequences of this affluence. The clash of values within West German society has now been joined by East-West differences.

Germans share a common language, culture, and history—and a common set of ultimate political goals—although the strains of unification may magnify and politicize the differences. Whether the nation can blend these two cultures successfully is a major factor in determining the fate and course of the new Germany.

Political Learning and Political Communication

If a congruent political culture helps a political system to endure, as many political experts maintain, then one of the basic functions of the political process is to create and perpetuate these citizen attitudes. The process of developing the beliefs and values of the public is known as political socialization. Researchers normally view political socialization as a source of continuity in a political system, with one generation transmitting the prevailing political norms to the next. The preceding discussion of political cultures described how socialization produced political change in postwar Germany. Now, German unification creates a new need for political relearning among the citizenry.

Family Influences

During their early years, children have few sources of learning comparable to their parents—normally the major influence in forming basic values. Family discussions can be a rich source of political information and one of the many ways that children internalize their parents' attitudes.

Basic values acquired during childhood often persist into adulthood.

In the early postwar years, family socialization did not function smoothly on either side of the German border. Many adults were hesitant to discuss politics openly because of the depoliticized environment of the period. Then, too, many parents were hesitant to discuss politics with their children for fear that the child would ask: "What did you do under Hitler, Daddy?" Furthermore, parents in West Germany were ill prepared to tell their children how to be good democrats, and Eastern parents were equally uncertain of the new communist system.

The potential for parental socialization has grown steadily since the years immediately after the war.[26] The frequency of political discussion increased in the West, and family conversations about politics became commonplace. Moreover, young new parents raised under the system of the Federal Republic could pass on democratic norms and party attachments held for a lifetime.

The family also played an important role in the socialization process of the GDR. Although the state bombarded young people with political indoctrination, parents were an important source of political and social cues. Researchers found that family ties were especially close in the East, and most young people claimed to share the same political opinions as their parents. The family also provided one of the few settings where people could openly discuss their beliefs, a private sphere where individuals could be free of the watchful eyes of others. Here they could express praise—or doubt—about the state.

Despite the growing openness within the family, both Germanies have experienced a widening generation gap in recent years. Youth in the West are more liberal than their parents, more oriented toward noneconomic goals, more positive about their role in the political process, and more likely to challenge prevailing social norms.[27] East German youth are also a product of their times; an autonomous peace movement and other counterculture groups flourished as part of the youth culture of the 1980s. The youthful faces of the first refugees exiting through Hungary or the democracy protests in Leipzig and East Berlin highlighted the importance of the youth culture within East Germany. Clearly, young people's values and goals are changing, often putting them in conflict with their elders.

Education

During the years when parental socialization was often lacking, the German governments used the educational system to fill part of this void.[28] In the West, the government enlisted the school system to reeducate the young into accepting democratic norms. Instruction aimed at developing a formal commitment to the institutions and procedures of the Federal Republic. Civics classes stressed the benefits of the democratic system, drawing sharp contrasts with the communist model. The educational system helped to remake the West German political culture.

Growing public support for the FRG's political system gradually made this program of formalized political education redundant. The content of civics instruction changed to emphasize an understanding of the dynamics of the democratic process—interest representation, conflict resolution, minority rights, and the methods of citizen influence. The present system has tried to better prepare students for their adult roles as political participants.

In the East, the school system also played a key role in the political education program, although the content was very different. The schools attempted to create a socialist personality that encompassed a devotion to communist principles, a love of the GDR, and participation in state-sponsored activities. Yet again, the rhetoric of education conflicted with reality. Government publications claimed that "education for peace is the overriding principle underlying classroom practice in all schools." However, paramilitary training became compulsory for ninth and tenth graders in 1978. The textbooks told students that the GDR endorsed personal freedom, but then they stared from their school buses at the barbed wire strung along the border. Many young people accepted the rhetoric of the regime, but the education efforts remained incomplete.

In addition to formal education, the GDR used other methods of political education. A cornerstone of the GDR's socialization efforts was a system of government-supervised youth groups. Nearly all primary school students were enrolled in the Pioneers, a youth organization that combined normal social activities—similar to those organized by the Boy Scouts or Girl Scouts in the United States—with a basic dose of political education. At age 14, about three-fourths of the young graduated into membership in the Free German Youth (FDJ) group. Politics was central to the activities of the FDJ, and the organization served as a training and recruiting ground for the future leadership of East Germany. Membership in the FDJ provided entree to the Communist Party and important professions for which party membership was a prerequisite. The politicization of social life even extended to sports. Like other communist states, the GDR was fond of staging mass sporting events that included an opportunity for political indoctrination, and used the Olympic medal count as a measure of the GDR's societal progress. In summary, most aspects of social, economic, and political relations came under the direction of party and state institutions. From a school's selection of texts for first grade readers to the speeches at a sports awards banquet, the values of the regime touched everyday life.

SOCIAL STRATIFICATION Another important effect of education involves its consequences for the social stratification of society, which differs in fundamental terms between West and East. The secondary school system in the West is stratified into three distinct tracks. One track provides a general education that normally leads to vocational training and working-class occupations. A second track mixes vocational and academic training. Most graduates from this program are employed in lower middle-class occupations. A third track focuses on purely academic training at a Gymnasium (an academic high school) in preparation for university education.

These educational tracks reinforce social status differences within society. Students are directed into one track after only four to six years of primary schooling, based on their school record, parental preferences, and teacher evaluations. At this early age family influences are still a major factor in the child's development, which means that most children assigned to the academic track come from

middle-class families, and most students in the vocational track are from working-class families.

Sharp distinctions separate the three tracks. Students attend different schools, minimizing social contact. The curricula of the three tracks are so different that once a student is assigned, he or she would find it difficult to transfer between tracks. The Gymnasia are more generously financed and recruit the best-qualified teachers. Every student who graduates from a Gymnasium is guaranteed admission to a university, where tuition is free.

There have been numerous attempts to reform West Germany's educational system to lessen its elitist bias.[29] Some states have a single comprehensive secondary school that all students may attend, but only about 5 percent of Western secondary school students are enrolled in these schools. Reformers have been more successful in expanding access to the universities. In the early 1950s only 6 percent of college-aged youths pursued higher education; today this figure is about 30 percent. The FRG's educational system retains an elitist accent, though it is now less obvious.

The socialist ideology of the GDR led to a different educational structure. Comprehensive schools were introduced in the 1950s, and by the 1960s ten-year comprehensive polytechnical schools formed the core of the educational system. Students from different social backgrounds, and with different academic abilities, attended the same school—much like the structure of public education in the United States. The schools emphasized practical career training, with a heavy dose of technical and applied courses in the later years. Those with special academic abilities could apply to the extended secondary school during their twelfth year, which led to university training.

The differences between the educational systems of the two states illustrate the practical problems posed by German unity.[30] Beyond the important differences in the content of education, the West lags in equalizing access to higher education. The Western educational system perpetuates social inequality and thus conflicts with the stated social goals of the Federal Republic. In contrast, the formal structure of the GDR's comprehensive schools was closer to the educational system of other European democracies, such as Britain or France, and was less elitist than the FRG's educational system. The unification treaty called for the gradual extension of the Western educational structure to the East, but the dissolution of comprehensive schools has generated dissatisfaction among Easterners. In 1994, the education ministers of the states agreed to put off plans for the further harmonization of East/West standards until after the year 2000. Ironically, unification is leading to new pressures for liberal reform within the Federal Republic's educational system.

Mass Media

The mass media have a long history in Germany: the world's first newspaper and first television service both appeared on German soil. Under previous regimes, however, the media frequently were censored or manipulated by political authorities. National socialism showed what a potent socialization force the media could be, especially when placed in the wrong hands.

The mass media of the Federal Republic were developed with the legacy of Nazi propaganda in mind.[31] After the war the Allied occupation forces licensed only newspapers and journalists who were free of Nazi ties. The Basic Law also guaranteed freedom of the press and the absence of censorship. There were two consequences of this pattern of press development. First, there was a conscious effort to create a new journalistic tradition, committed to democratic norms, objectivity, and political neutrality. This marked a clear departure from past journalistic practices, and it contributed to the remaking of the political culture.

A second consequence was the regionalization of the media. The Federal Republic lacks an established national press like that of Britain or France. Instead, each region or large city has one or more newspapers that circulate primarily within that locale. Of the several hundred daily newspapers, only a few—such as the *Frankfurter Allgemeine Zeitung, Welt, Süddeutsche Zeitung,* or *Frankfurter Rundschau*—have a national following. With unification, Western firms purchased most of the party or government-sponsored newspapers in the East, and some new independent papers were established. This created a new pluralism in the media

environment of the East, and interconnected the media network throughout Germany.

The electronic media in the Federal Republic have also followed a pattern of regional decentralization. Even in this age of new electronic media, public broadcasting networks still are the major television channels. Public corporations organized at the state or regional levels manage the public television and radio networks. To ensure independence from commercial pressures, the public media are financed mostly by taxes assessed on owners of radio and television sets.

The mass media are a primary source of information for the public and a communications link between elites and the public. The higher quality newspapers devote substantial attention to domestic and international reporting, although the largest circulation newspaper, *Bild Zeitung,* sells papers through sensationalist stories. The public television networks are strongly committed to political programming; about one-third of their programs deal with social or political issues. The most important new development is the expansion of privately owned cable and satellite television stations. Today, most German households receive these stations. This development is steadily eroding the government's control of the electronic media and pressuring public stations to devote more attention to consumer preferences. Many analysts see these new media offerings as expanding the citizen's choice and the diversity of information, but others worry that the quality of German broadcasting will suffer as a result.

Public opinion surveys show that Germans have a voracious appetite for the political information provided by the mass media. A 1998 survey found that 64 percent of the public claimed to read a newspaper on a daily basis and 70 percent said they watched television news programs daily. These high levels of usage indicate that Germans are attentive media users and well informed on the flow of political events.

Citizen Participation

Developing public understanding and acceptance of democratic rules was an important accomplishment for the Federal Republic. At first, however, the public did not participate in the new process; they acted like political spectators who were following a soccer match from the grandstand. The final step in remaking the political culture was to involve citizens in the process—to have them come onto the field and participate.

Certainly, German history was not conducive to developing widespread public involvement in politics. Not only had three regimes failed since the turn of the century, but supporters of the previous regime had suffered after the establishment of each new political order. These experiences probably convinced many Germans, in both the East and West, that political participation was a questionable, if not risky, pursuit.

Both German states tried to engage their citizens to participate in politics, although with different expectations about the citizen's appropriate role. The democratic procedures of West Germany induced many people to become at least minimally involved in politics. Turnout in national elections was uniformly high. Westerners became well informed about the democratic system and developed an interest in political matters. After continued experience with the democratic system, people began to internalize their role as participants. Most Westerners thought their participation could influence the political process—people believed that democracy worked.[32]

Changing perceptions of politics led to a dramatic increase in involvement. In 1953 almost two-thirds of the West German public never discussed politics; in the 1994 election about three-quarters claimed they talked about politics regularly. This expansion in citizen interest created a participatory revolution in the Federal Republic, as involvement in campaign activities and political organizations increased.

Perhaps the most dramatic evidence of rising participation levels has been the growth of *citizen action groups (Bürgerinitiativen)*.[33] Citizens interested in a specific issue form a group to articulate their political demands and influence decision makers. These groups often resort to petitions, protests, and other direct-action methods to dramatize their cause and mobilize public support. Parents organize for school reform, homeowners become involved in urban redevelopment projects,

taxpayers complain about the delivery of government services, or residents protest the environmental conditions in their locale. These groups expand the means of citizen influence significantly beyond the infrequent and indirect methods of campaigns and elections.

Under the GDR system, citizen involvement was widely encouraged, but individuals could be active only in ways that would reinforce their allegiance to the state. For example, elections were not measures of popular representation but offered the communist leadership an opportunity to educate the public politically. More than 90 percent of the electorate cast their ballots, and the government parties always won more than 95 percent of the votes. People were expected to participate in government-approved unions, social groups (such as the Free German Youth or the German Women's Union), and quasi-public bodies such as parent-teacher organizations. Hundreds of thousands of East Germans participated in government advisory bodies and representative committees. However, participation was a method not for citizens to influence the government but for the government to influence its citizens.

Although they draw on much different experiences, Germans from both the East and West have been socialized into a pattern of high political involvement (see Figure 6.5). Voting levels in national elections are among the highest of any European democracy. Nearly 83 percent of Westerners turned out at the polls in the 1998 Bundestag elections, as well as 80 percent of voters from the East. This turnout level is high by American standards, but it has declined from the nearly 90 percent voting in West German elections of the 1980s. High turnout partially reflects a popular belief that voting is part of a citizen's duty. In addition, the electoral system encourages turnout: Elections are held on Sunday when everyone is free to vote; voter registration lists are constantly updated by the government; and the ballot is always simple—there are at most two votes to cast.

Beyond the act of voting, many Germans participate in other aspects of politics. Data from a survey conducted in 1998 illustrate the participation patterns of Easterners and Westerners (see again

FIGURE 6.5   Participation Levels in West and East Germany

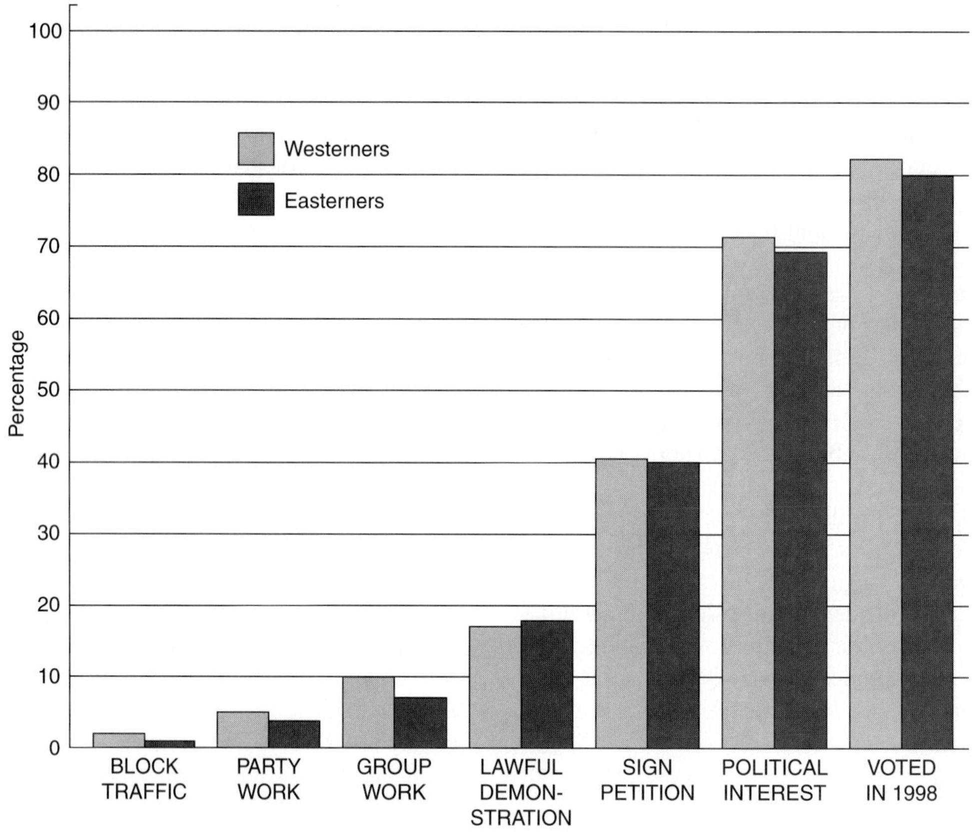

Source: 1998 ALLBUS Survey and government election turnout statistics; the survey is available through the Inter-university Consortium for Political and Social Research, University of Michigan.

Figure 6.5). Almost half of the public in West and East have signed a petition and about a fifth have participated in a lawful demonstration; these are high levels by cross-national standards (see Chapter 2). After the tumult of the GDR's collapse and the transition to democracy, political participation has decreased in the East. This underscores the point that the Western public is integrated into the democratic process, while Easterners are still learning to be democratic and participatory citizens.

There is also an interesting comparison between working with political parties and citizen action groups. A significant proportion of Westerners (5 percent) and Easterners (4 percent) say they have worked for a political party. In the Federal Republic, as in other Western European democracies, formal party membership is much more common than in the United States. Yet, work within a citizen action group—environmental groups, women's groups, or general citizen groups—is even more common among both Westerners (10 percent) and Easterners (7 percent). This indicates the expansion of political involvement to new modes of action.

Thus the traditional characterization of the German citizen as quiescent and uninvolved is no longer appropriate in either the West or the East. Participation has increased dramatically over the past 50 years, and the public is now involved in a

Box 6.2   Schröder's Political Career

Born in 1944, Gerhard Schröder is part of the new generation of German political leaders raised after World War II. When he was 19 years old, he joined the Social Democratic Party and became active in its youth organization. He attended night school to earn admission to the university, and worked as he studied for his law degree. In 1978 he became the national chairman of the Young Socialists, and two years later was elected to the Bundestag. He gained noteriety in his initial parliamentary speech when he became the first deputy to ever address the Bundestag without wearing a necktie. According to a well-known story, after a late night of drinking in Bonn he stopped outside the Chancellor's residence to shout, "I want in there!" He became Minister-President of Lower Saxony in 1990. In 1998 he fulfilled his earlier wish, gaining entry into the Chancellory by winning the Bundestag elections as the head of the SPD-Green coalition.

wide range of political activities. The spectators have become participants.

Politics at the Elite Level[34]

The Federal Republic is a representative democracy. Above the populace is a group of a few thousand political elite who manage the actual workings of the political system. Elite members, such as party leaders and parliamentary deputies, are directly responsible to the public through elections. Civil servants and judges are appointed to represent the public interest, and they are at least indirectly responsible to the citizenry. Leaders of interest groups and political associations participate in the policy process as representatives of their specific clientele groups.

Although the group of politically influential elites is readily identifiable, they do not constitute a homogeneous elite class. Rather, elites in the Federal Republic represent the diverse interests in German society. Often there is as much heterogeneity in policy preferences among the political elites as there is among the public.

Paths to the Top

Individuals may take numerous pathways to elite positions. Party elites may have exceptional political abilities; administrative elites are initially recruited because of their formal training and bureaucratic skills; and interest group leaders are selected for their ability to represent their group.

One feature of elite recruitment that differs from American politics is the long apprenticeship period that precedes entry into the top elite stratum. Candidates for national or even state political office normally have a long background of party work and officeholding at the local level. Similarly, senior civil servants spend nearly all their adult lives working for the government. The biography of the present chancellor, Gerhard Schröder, is a typical example of a long political career (see Box 6.2). Not all political careers are as illustrious as Schröder's, but they often are as long.

A long apprenticeship means that political elites have extensive experience before attaining a position of real power; elites also share a common basis of experience built up from interacting over many years. National politicians know each other from working together at the state or local level; the paths of civil servants frequently cross during their long careers. These experiences develop a sense of responsibility and regularity in elite interactions, as well as limiting the number of career shifts between different elite sectors. For instance, members of a chancellor's Cabinet are normally drawn from party elites with extensive experience in state or federal government. Seldom can top business leaders or popular personalities use their outside success to attain a position of political power quickly. This also contributes to the cohesion of elite politics.

Access to elite positions, of course, followed a much different pattern in the GDR. The prerequisites for elite positions in the former state—loyalty to the Socialist Unity Party and its communist ideology—conflict with the goals and values of the Federal Republic. Consequently, almost by definition, anyone in the East who was experienced in political decision making or public administration was compromised by ties to the communist state. Thus most political elites from the old regime have left office, and the new political leadership in the East is heavily drawn from the ranks of church leaders, dissident intellectuals, low-level Eastern officials, and Western politicians. Similarly, many individuals in the judiciary and civil service were laid off or given early retirement to allow new elites to enter positions of authority. Questions about the competency and legitimacy of Eastern elites will be a recurring aspect of politics in the new Germany.

Elites in East and West also differ in many of their policy priorities. For instance, Eastern elites are more likely to emphasize the need for greater social and economic equality, social security, and the integration of foreigners.[35] Creating a new political consensus is one of the challenges of unification.

Interest Groups

Interest groups are an integral part of the German political process, even more so than in the United States. Some specific interests may be favored more than others, but interest groups are generally welcomed as necessary participants in the political process.

A close relationship connects interest groups and the government. Doctors, lawyers, and other self-employed professionals belong to professional associations that are established by law and receive government authorization of their professional activities, making them quasi-public bodies. These associations, which date back to the medieval guilds, enforce professional rules of conduct.

The German system of formally involving interest groups in the policy process reaches further. Administrative law requires that government officials contact groups when formulating new policies that may affect their interests. These consultations ensure that the government can benefit from the expertise of interest group representatives. Other legislation gives interest groups a formal advisory role in the management of public broadcasting, or in other elements of policy administration.

In some instances the pattern of interest group activity approaches the act of governance. For example, when the government recognized the need for structural reform in the steel industry, it assembled interest group representatives from the affected sectors to discuss and negotiate a common plan. Group officials attempted to reach a consensus on the necessary changes, and then implemented the agreements, sometimes with the official sanction of the government.

This cooperation between government and interest groups is described as *neocorporatism*, a general pattern having the following characteristics:[36]

- Social interests are organized into virtually compulsory organizations.
- A single association represents each social sector.
- These associations are hierarchically structured.
- Associations are accepted as formal representatives by the government.
- Associations may participate directly in the policy process.

Policy decisions are reached in discussions and negotiations among the relevant association and the government—then the agreements are implemented by government action.

This neocorporatist pattern solidifies the role of interest groups in the policy process. Governments feel that they are responding to public demands when they consult with these groups, and the members of interest groups depend on the organization to have their views heard. Thus the leaders of the major interest groups are important actors in the policy process. Neocorporatist relations also lessen political conflict; for instance, strike levels and political strife tend to be lower in neocorporatist systems.

Another major advantage of neocorporatism is that it makes for efficient government; the involved interest groups can negotiate on policy without the pressures of public debate and partisan conflict. However, efficient government is not necessarily the best government, especially in a democracy. Decisions are reached in conference groups or advisory commissions, outside of the representative institutions of government decision making. The "relevant" interest groups are involved, but this assumes that all relevant interests are organized, and that only organized interests are relevant. Decisions affecting the entire public are often made through private negotiations, as democratically elected representative institutions—state governments and the Bundestag—are sidestepped and interest groups deal directly with government agencies. Consequently, interest groups play a less visible role in electoral politics as they concentrate their efforts on direct contact with government agencies.

Although interest groups come in many shapes and sizes, we focus our attention on the large associations that represent the major socioeconomic forces in society. These associations normally have a national organization, a so-called *peak association,* that speaks for its members.

Business

Two major organizations represent business and industrial interests within the political process. The *Federation of German Industry (BDI)* is the peak association for 35 separate industrial groupings. The BDI-affiliated associations represent nearly every major industrial firm, forming a united front that enables industry to speak with authority on matters affecting their interests.

The *Confederation of German Employers' Associations (BDA)* includes an even larger number of business organizations. Virtually every large or medium-sized employer in the nation is affiliated with one of the 66 employer and professional associations of the BDA.

Although the two organizations have overlapping membership, they have different roles within the political process. The BDI represents business on national political matters. Its officials participate in government advisory committees and planning groups, presenting the view of business to government officials and Cabinet ministers.

In contrast, the BDA represents business on labor and social issues. The individual employer associations negotiate with the labor unions over employment contracts. At the national level, the BDA represents business on legislation dealing with social security, labor legislation, and social services. It also nominates business representatives for a variety of government committees, ranging from the media supervisory boards to social security committees.

Business interests have a long history of close relations with the Christian Democrats and conservative politicians. Companies and their top management provide significant financial support for the Christian Democrats, and many Bundestag deputies have strong ties to business. Yet both Social Democrats and Christian Democrats readily accept the legitimate role of business interests within the policy process.

Labor

The German labor movement is also highly organized.[37] About half of the active labor force belong to a union. The *German Federation of Trade Unions (DGB)* is the peak association that incorporates 11 separate unions—spanning a range from the metalworking and building trades to the chemical industry and the postal system—into a single organizational structure. At the end of 1999, the DGB included about 8.3 million workers in all of Germany. This broad-based membership includes most organized industrial workers and many white-collar and government employees.

As a political organization, the DGB has close ties to the Social Democratic party, although there is no formal institutional bond between the two. Most SPD deputies in the Bundestag are members of a union, and about one-tenth are former labor union officials. The DGB represents the interests of labor in government conference groups and Bundestag committees. The large mass membership of the federation also makes union campaign support and the union vote an essential part of the SPD's electoral base.

In spite of their differing interests, business and unions have shown an unusual ability to work together. The Economic Miracle was possible because labor and management implicitly agreed that the first priority was economic growth, from which both sides would prosper. Work time lost through strikes and work stoppages has been consistently lower in the Federal Republic than in most other Western European nations.

This cooperation has been encouraged by joint participation of business and union representatives in government committees and planning groups. Cooperation also extends into industrial decision making through *codetermination (Mitbestimmung),* a policy mandated by federal law that requires half of the board of directors in large companies to be elected by the employees. The system was first applied to the coal, iron, and steel industries in 1951; in 1976 a modified form was extended to large corporations in other fields. When codetermination was introduced, there were dire forecasts that it would destroy German industry. The system generally has been successful, however, in fostering better labor-management relations and thereby strengthening the economy. The Social Democrats also favor codetermination because it introduces democratic principles into the economic system.

Religious Interests

Religious associations are the third major organized interest in German politics. Rather than being separated from politics, as in the United States, church and state are closely related. The churches are subject to the rules of the state, and in return they receive formal representation and support from the government.

The churches are financed mainly through a church tax collected by the government. The government adds a surcharge (about 10 percent) to an employee's income tax, and the government transfers this amount to the employee's church. A taxpayer can officially decline to pay that tax, but social norms discourage this step. Similarly, Catholic primary schools in several states receive government funding, and the churches accept government subsidies to support their social programs and aid to the needy.

In addition to this financial support, the churches are often directly involved in the policy process. Church appointees regularly sit on government planning committees that deal with education, social services, and family affairs. By law, the churches participate on the supervisory boards of the public radio and television networks. Members of the Protestant and Catholic clergy occasionally serve in political offices, as Bundestag deputies or as state government officials.

Although the Catholic and Protestant churches receive the same formal representation by the government, the two churches differ in their political styles. The Catholic Church has close ties to the Christian Democrats, and at least implicitly encourages its members to support these parties and their conservative policies. The Catholic hierarchy is not hesitant to lobby the government on legislation dealing with social or moral issues. With its abundant resources and tightly structured organization, the Catholic Church often wields an influential role in policymaking.

The Protestant Church is a loose association of mostly Lutheran churches spread across Germany. The pattern of the church's political involvement varies with the preferences of local pastors and bishops and their respective congregations. In the West, the Protestant churches have minimized their involvement in partisan politics, although they are seen as favoring the Social Democrats. Protestant groups also work through their formal representation on government committees or function as individual lobbying organizations.

The Protestant Church in the GDR played a more significant political role because it was one of the few organizations that retained its autonomy from the state. Churches were meeting places for people who wanted to discuss freely the social and moral aspects of contemporary issues. For instance, many churches organized "peace services" during the NATO missile controversy in the early 1980s and hosted meetings of the autonomous environmental movement. As the East German revolution gathered force in 1989, churches in Leipzig, East Berlin, and other cities granted sanctuary for citizens' groups; weekly services acted as a rallying point for opposition to the regime. Religion was not the opiate of the people, as Marx had feared, but one of the forces that swept the communists from power.

Despite their institutionalized role in the Federal Republic's formal system of interest group representation, the influence of both the Catholic and Protestant churches has gradually waned over the past several decades. Declining church attendance in both West and East marks a steady secularization of German society; about one-tenth of Westerners claim to be nonreligious, as are nearly half the residents in the East. The gradual secularization of German society suggests that the churches' popular base will continue its slow erosion.

New Politics Movement

In recent years, a new set of political groups has emerged under the label of the New Politics movement. Challenging business, labor, religion, agriculture, and other established socioeconomic interests, these new organizations have focused their efforts on the lifestyle and quality-of-life issues facing Germany.[38]

Environmental groups are the most visible part of the movement. Following the flowering of environmental interests in the 1970s, antinuclear groups popped up like mushrooms around nuclear power facilities, local environmental action groups proliferated, and new national organizations formed. Another part of the New Politics network has been the women's movement. That movement developed a dualistic strategy for improving the status of women: changing the consciousness of women and reforming the laws. A variety of associations and self-help groups at the local level nurture the personal development of women, while other organizations focus on national policymaking.

These political movements, and other New Politics groups, have distinct issue interests and their own organizations, but they are also elements of a common movement unified by their shared interest in the quality of life for individuals, whether it is the quality of the natural environment, the protection of human rights, or peace in an uncertain world. They draw their members from the same social base: young, better-educated, and middle-class citizens. These groups also are more likely to use unconventional political tactics, such as protests and demonstrations.

The New Politics movement does not wield the influence of the established interest groups, although their membership now exceeds the size of the formal membership in the political parties. These groups have become important and contentious actors in the political process. Moreover, the reconciliation of women's legislation in the united Germany and the resolution of the East's nearly catastrophic environmental problems are likely to keep these concerns near the top of the political agenda.

The Party System

The party system presents one of the clearest examples of the different political histories of the FRG and the GDR. Following World War II, the Western Allies created a democratic, competitive party system to guide the new political process in the West. The Allies licensed a diverse set of parties that were free of Nazi ties and committed to democratic procedures. The Basic Law further required that parties support the constitutional order and democratic methods of the Federal Republic.

Because of these provisions, the FRG developed a strong system of competitive party politics that was a mainstay of the new democratic order. Elections focused on the competition between the conservative Christian Democrats and the liberal Social Democrats, with the small Free Democratic Party often holding the balance of power. Elections were meaningful; control of the government shifted between the left and right as a function of election outcomes. When postmaterial issues entered the political agenda in the 1980s, a new political party, *the Greens,* emerged to represent these concerns.

Although the GDR ostensibly had a multiparty system and elections, this presented only the illusion of democracy—the Socialist Unity Party (SED) firmly held political power. In advance of an election, the SED would assemble a National Front list of candidates that would include representatives from the other parties and various social groups (such as the trade unions, women's groups, and youth groups). The SED decided the members of this list and each party's allocation of parliamentary seats before the poll. Thus the Christian Democratic, Liberal, and other parties in the East were mere extensions of the SED, and the elections themselves were largely symbolic acts.

When the GDR collapsed, its party system was drawn into this void. Support for the SED plummeted, and the party distanced itself from its own history by changing its name to the *Party of Democratic Socialism (PDS).* Many antigovernment opposition groups tried to develop into parties in order to compete in the March 1990 elections. Other new political parties represented interests ranging from the Beer Drinkers Union to a women's party. Very

FIGURE 6.6   Shares of the Party Vote (Second Vote), 1949–1998

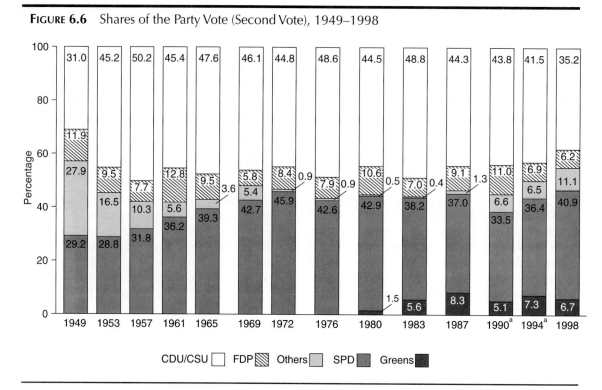

ᵃ 1990–1998 percentages combine results from Western and Eastern Germany.

soon, however, the West German parties usurped the electoral process, taking over the financing, tactics, organization, and substance of the campaign. Helmut Kohl made whistlestop tours for the conservative parties of the Alliance for Germany, while Willy Brandt and other SPD politicians campaigned for the Eastern SPD. The consolidation of the Western and Eastern party system was essentially completed with 1990 Bundestag election. Today the party system of the new Germany largely represents an extension of the Western system to the East.

Christian Democrats

The creation of the Christian Democratic Union (CDU) in postwar West Germany signified a sharp break with the tradition of German political parties. The CDU was founded by a mixed group of Catholics and Protestants, businesspeople and trade unionists, conservatives and liberals. Rather than representing narrow special interests, the party wanted to appeal

to a broad segment of society in order to gain government power. The party's unifying principle was that West Germany should be reconstructed along Christian and humanitarian lines. Konrad Adenauer, the party leader, developed the CDU into a conservative-oriented catchall party (*Volkspartei*)—a sharp contrast to the fragmented ideological parties of Weimar. This strategy succeeded; within a single decade the CDU emerged as the largest party, capturing 40 to 50 percent of the popular vote (see Figure 6.6).

The CDU operates in all states except Bavaria, where it allies itself with the *Christian Social Union (CSU)*, whose basic political philosophy is more conservative than the CDU. These two parties generally function as one in national politics (CDU/CSU), forming a single parliamentary group in the Bundestag and campaigning together in national elections.

The CDU/CSU's early voting strength allowed the party to control the government, first under the

TABLE 6.1   Composition of Coalition Governments

Date Formed	Source of Change	Coalition Partners[a]	Chancellor
September 1949	Election	CDU/CSU, FDP, DP	Adenauer (CDU)
October 1953	Election	CDU/CSU, FDP, DP, G	Adenauer (CDU)
October 1957	Election	CDU/CSU, DP	Adenauer (CDU)
November 1961	Election	CDU/CSU, FDP	Adenauer (CDU)
October 1963	Chancellor retirement	CDU/CSU, FDP	Erhard (CDU)
October 1965	Election	CDU/CSU, FDP	Erhard (CDU)
December 1966	Coalition change	CDU/CSU, SPD	Kiesinger (CDU)
October 1969	Election	SPD, FDP	Brandt (SPD)
December 1972	Election	SPD, FDP	Brandt (SPD)
May 1974	Chancellor retirement	SPD, FDP	Schmidt (SPD)
December 1976	Election	SPD, FDP	Schmidt (SPD)
November 1980	Election	SPD, FDP	Schmidt (SPD)
October 1982	Constructive no-confidence	CDU/CSU, FDP	Kohl (CDU)
March 1983	Election	CDU/CSU, FDP	Kohl (CDU)
January 1987	Election	CDU/CSU, FDP	Kohl (CDU)
December 1990	Election	CDU/CSU, FDP	Kohl (CDU)
October 1994	Election	CDU/CSU, FDP	Kohl (CDU)
September 1998	Election	SPD, Greens	Schröder (SPD)

[a] CDU: Christian Democratic Union. CSU: Christian Social Union. DP: German Party. FDP: Free Democratic Party. G: All-German Bloc Federation of Expellees and Displaced Persons: SPD: Social Democratic Party.

leadership of Adenauer (1949–1963) and then under Ludwig Erhard (1963–1966), as shown in Table 6.1. In 1966, however, the party lost the support of its coalition partner, the Free Democrats, and formed a Grand Coalition with the Social Democrats. Following the 1969 election, the Social Democrats and Free Democrats formed a new government coalition; for the first time in the history of the Federal Republic, the CDU/CSU became the opposition party.

In the early 1980s the strains of a weak economy increased public support for the party and its conservative economic program. In 1982 the Christian Democrats and the Free Democrats formed a new conservative government through the first successful constructive no-confidence vote that elected Helmut Kohl as chancellor. Public support for Kohl's policies returned the governing coalition to power following the 1983 and 1987 elections.

The collapse of the GDR in 1989 provided a historic opportunity for the CDU and Kohl. While others looked on the events with wonder or uncertainty, Kohl quickly embraced the idea of closer ties between the two Germanies. Thus, when the March 1990 GDR election became a referendum in support of German unification, the Christian Democrats were assured of victory because of the party's early commitment to German union. Kohl emerged victorious from the 1990 Bundestag elections, but his government struggled with the policy challenges produced by German unification. The governing coalition lost more than 50 seats in the 1994 elections, but Kohl retained a slim majority.

By the 1998 elections, the accumulation of 16 years of governing and the special challenges of unification had taken their toll on the party. Kohl was the longest-serving head of government in Europe, and his age showed. Many Germans looked for a change. The CDU/CSU fared poorly in the election, especially in the Eastern Länder that were frustrated by their persisting second-class status. The CDU's poor showing in the election was a rebuke to Kohl and he resigned the party leadership.

The CDU made some gains after the election and seemed posed to win several state elections in 1999 and 2000—and then lightning struck. Helmut Kohl was accused of accepting illegal campaign contributions and eventually admitted to this. Kohl's successor as CDU leader and his allies within the party were forced to resign, and the party's electoral fortunes suffered. To distance itself from these events, in 1999 the party selected Angela Merkel as party leader. Merkel is almost the opposite of Kohl: an Easterner, a relative newcomer to politics, a Ph.D. in physics, and a woman. She and the party now have the task of overcoming this scandal and restoring public confidence in the party, even while the legal resolution of the scandal remains uncertain.

Social Democrats

The postwar *Social Democratic Party (SPD)* in West Germany was constructed along the lines of the SPD in the Weimar Republic—an ideological party, primarily representing the interests of unions and the working class.[39] In the early postwar years the Social Democrats espoused strict Marxist doctrine and consistently opposed Adenauer's Western-oriented foreign policy program. The SPD's image of the nation's future was radically different from that of Adenauer and the Christian Democrats.

The SPD's poor performance in early elections (see again Figure 6.6) generated internal pressures for the party to broaden its electoral appeal. At the 1959 Godesberg party conference, the party renounced its Marxist economic policies and generally moved toward the center on domestic and foreign policies. The party continued to represent working-class interests, but by shedding its ideological banner the SPD hoped to attract new support from the middle class. The SPD transformed itself into a progressive catchall party that could compete with the Christian Democrats.

An SPD breakthrough finally came in 1966 with the formation of the Grand Coalition (see again Table 6.1). By sharing government control with the CDU/CSU, the Social Democrats alleviated lingering public uneasiness about the party's integrity and ability to govern. Political support for the party also grew as the SPD played an active part in resolving the nation's problems.

Following the 1969 election, a new Social Democrat–Free Democrat government formed with Willy Brandt (SPD) as chancellor. After a period of economic recession, Helmut Schmidt replaced Brandt as chancellor in 1974, and the SPD turned its attention toward the faltering economy. Although the SPD retained government control in the 1976 and 1980 elections, these were trying times for the party. The SPD and the Free Democrats frequently disagreed on economic policy, and political divisions also developed within the SPD. For example, many young middle-class SPD members opposed nuclear energy and large-scale economic development projects that were favored by the unions.

These policy tensions eventually led to the breakup of the SPD-led government in 1982. Once again in opposition, the SPD faced an identity crisis. In 1987 the SPD followed a centrist strategy but was unable to improve its vote share significantly. In 1990 it nominated Oskar Lafontaine as candidate for chancellor, someone who appealed to liberal, middle-class voters, but the SPD campaign was overtaken by events in the East.

Perhaps no one (except perhaps the Communists) was more surprised than the SPD by the course of events in the GDR in 1989–1990. The SPD had been normalizing relations with the SED as a basis of intra-German cooperation, only to see the SED ousted by the citizenry. The SPD and Lafontaine were ambivalent about German unification and stood by quietly as Kohl spoke of a single German *Vaterland* to crowds of applauding East Germans. The party's poor performance in the 1990 national elections reflected the SPD's inability either to lead or to follow the course of the unification process. In 1994 the SPD tried to project a reform image for the party. The public came to the brink of voting the SPD into office in 1994, and then pulled back.[40]

In the spring of 1998 the Social Democrats selected Gerhard Schröder to be their chancellor candidate against Kohl. Representing the moderate wing of the party, Schröder attracted former CDU/CSU and Free Democratic voters who were disenchanted with the government's performance. The party recorded broad gains in the September 1998 election and formed a new coalition government with the environmental Green Party. Since then, Schröder has tried to pursue a middle course for the government, but he has been pulled to the left by SPD activists and his coalition partners. The party's electoral fortunes have been bouyed by the CDU's party finance scandal, but the ultimate success of the government will depend on showing that they can be more successful than their predecessors in dealing with Germany's policy problems.

Free Democratic Party

Although the Free Democratic Party (FDP) is far smaller than the two major parties, it has often wielded considerable political influence. Government control in a multiparty, parliamentary system normally requires a coalition of parties, and the FDP often held enough seats to have a pivotal role in forming the government.

The FDP—created to continue the liberal tradition from the prewar party system—was initially a strong advocate of private enterprise and drew its support from the Protestant middle class and farmers. Its economic policies made the FDP a natural ally of the CDU/CSU (see again Table 6.1). In the mid-1960s the Free Democrats emphasized their liberal foreign and social programs, opening the way for the SPD-FDP coalition that began in 1969. Worsening economic conditions in the early 1980s led to a new coalition with the CDU/CSU that began in October 1982.

Because of the FDP's pivotal role in forming coalitions, the party had disproportionate influence on its larger coalition partners. The FDP generally acted as a moderating influence, limiting the leftist leanings of the SPD and the conservative tendencies of the CDU/CSU. This places the party in a precarious position, however, because if it allies itself too closely with either major party it may lose its political identity. The party struggled with this problem in the 1994 Bundestag election. The FDP won enough votes to return to parliament, but lost nearly half its supporters from 1990. In January 2001 Guido Westerwelle won the party leadership; his goal is to return the FDP to a role in the next government. The FDP moved to the opposition benches after the 1998 elections, and this has stimulated debates about the party's appropriate role in contemporary German politics.

The Greens

Environmental issues began to attract public attention in the 1970s, and the established parties generally were unresponsive to environmental concerns. The environmental movement therefore developed its own party representative: the Greens.[41] The party addresses a broad range of New Politics issues: opposition to nuclear energy and Germany's military policies, commitment to environmental protection, support for women's rights, and further democratization of society. The Greens differ so markedly from the established parties that one Green leader described them as the "antiparty party."

The party won its first representation in the Bundestag in 1983, becoming the first new party to enter Parliament since the 1950s. Using the legislature as a political forum, the Greens campaigned vigorously for an alternative view of politics, seeking much stronger measures to protect the environment and showing staunch opposition to the government's nuclear power program. The Greens also added a bit of color and spontaneity to the normally staid procedures of the political system. The typical dress for Green deputies is jeans and a sweater, rather than the traditional business attire of the established parties; their desks in Parliament sprout flowers and greenery, rather than folders of official-looking documents. The party's loose and open internal structure stands in sharp contrast to the hierarchic and bureaucratized structure of the established parties. Despite initial concerns about the impact of the Greens on the governmental system, most analysts now agree that the party brought necessary attention to political viewpoints that previously were overlooked.

German unification caught the Greens unprepared. The Western Greens opposed the simple eastward extension of the FRG's economic and political systems. Moreover, to stress their opposition to the fusion of both Germanies, the Western Greens refused to form an electoral alliance with any Eastern party until after the 1990 elections. The Eastern Greens/Alliance '90 won enough votes to enter the new Bundestag in 1990, but the Western Greens fell under the 5 percent threshold and failed to win any parliamentary seats on their own. The Greens' unconventional politics had caught up with them.

Box 6.3   A Party of a New Type

In preparing for the 1998 election the Greens platform included the following policies:

- To increase the price of gasoline to DM5 per liter (nearly $12 a gallon) in order to reduce the use of automobiles
- To encourage Germans to voluntarily limit their airline travel to one trip per year
- To close all nuclear power plants
- To legalize marijuana

- To decommission NATO's conventional and nuclear weapons and declare Europe a nuclear-free zone
- To tax Germans whose wealth exceeds DM 1 million to finance reconstruction in the East
- To provide grants to college students and to prohibit tuition
- To ban genetic engineering for use in agriculture and food production

---

After the 1990 election loss, the Greens charted a more moderate course for the party. Their commitment to the environment and an alternative agenda remained, but they tempered the unconventional style and structure of the party. The party regained entry to the Bundestag in 1994 with 49 seats.

By 1998 the moderates had won control of the Green Party and asked voters to support a new Red-Green coalition of SPD and the Greens (see Box 6.3). This Red-Green coalition received a majority in the election, and for the first time the Greens became part of the national government, holding four seats in Schröder's cabinet. The antiparty party is now struggling to balance its unconventional policies against the new responsibilities of governing. For instance, the party supported military intervention into Kosovo, despite its pacifist traditions. These issues have increased tensions between factions within the party and raised questions about the party's true goals among potential voters.

Communists to the Party of Democratic Socialism

The Communists were one of the first political parties to form in postwar Germany, and the party's history reflects the two paths Germany followed. In the West, the Communist Party (KPD) suffered because of its identification with the Soviet Union and the GDR. The party garnered a shrinking sliver of

the vote in the early elections, and then in 1956 the Constitutional Court banned the party because of its undemocratic principles. A reconstituted party began contesting elections again in 1969 but never attracted a significant following.

The situation was obviously different in the East. As World War II was ending, Walter Ulbricht returned to Berlin from exile in Moscow; he began to reorganize the Communist Party in the Soviet military zone. In 1946 the Soviets forced a merger of the eastern KPD and SPD into a new Socialist Unity Party of Germany (SED), which became the ruling institution in the East. The SED controlled the government apparatus and the electoral process; party agents were integrated into the military command structure; the party supervised the infamous state security police (*Stasi*); and party membership was a prerequisite to positions of authority and influence. The state controlled East German society, and the SED controlled the state.

In 1989 the SED's power collapsed along with the East German regime. Party membership plummeted, and local party units abolished themselves. The omnipotent party suddenly seemed impotent. To save the party from complete dissolution and to enable it to compete in the new democratic environment in the East, the party changed its name in February 1990 and became the Party of Democratic Socialism (PDS). The old party guard was ousted from positions of authority, and new moderates took over the leadership.

The PDS campaigned as the representative of those who feared the potential economic and social costs of German unity. In the 1990 Bundestag elections the PDS won 11 percent of the Eastern vote, although it captured only 2 percent of the national vote. The PDS won four district seats in the 1994 elections, and thus shared in the proportional distribution of Bundestag seats (see the following discussion of the electoral system).

The PDS fared even better in the 1998 election, winning four district seats and more than 5 percent of the nationwide vote. The party is now a distinctive representative of Eastern sentiment, especially among those who feel threatened by the new order or who still identify with the GDR.

The Electoral System

The framers of the Basic Law had two goals in mind when they designed the electoral system. One was to create a *proportional representation (PR)* system—a system that allocates legislative seats on the basis of a party's percentage of the popular vote. If a party receives 10 percent of the popular vote, it should receive 10 percent of the Bundestag seats. Other individuals saw advantages in the system of single-member districts used in Britain and the United States. They thought that this system would avoid the fragmentation of the Weimar party system and ensure some accountability between an electoral district and its representative.

To satisfy both objectives, a hybrid electoral system was developed. On one part of the ballot citizens vote for a candidate to represent their district. The candidate with a plurality of votes is elected as the district representative. Half the members of the Bundestag are directly elected in this manner.

On a second part of the ballot voters select a party. These second votes are added nationwide to determine each party's share of the popular vote. A party's proportion of the second vote determines its total representation in the Bundestag.[42] Each party is allocated additional seats so that its percentage of the combined candidate and party seats equals its share of the second vote. These additional seats are distributed according to lists prepared by the state parties before the election. Half of the Bundestag members are elected as party representatives.[43]

One major exception to this proportional representation system is the 5-percent clause, which stipulates that a party must win at least 5 percent of the national vote (or three district seats) to share in the distribution of party-list seats. The law is designed to withhold representation from the type of small extremist parties that plagued the Weimar Republic. In practice, however, the 5-percent clause handicaps all minor parties and contributes to the development of a few large parties.

This unique system has several consequences for electoral politics. The party-list system gives party leaders substantial influence on who will be elected to Parliament by the placement of candidates on the list. The PR system also ensures fair representation for the smaller parties. The FDP, for example, has won only one direct candidate mandate since 1957, and yet it receives Bundestag seats based on its national share of the vote. In contrast, Britain's district-only system discriminates against small parties; in 1997 the British Liberal Democrats won 16.7 percent of the national vote but only 6.9 percent of the parliamentary seats. The German two-vote system also affects campaign strategies. Although most voters cast both their ballots for the same party, the FDP traditionally encourages supporters of its larger coalition partner to "lend" their second votes to the Free Democrats. In recent federal elections these split ballots kept the FDP above the 5-percent hurdle.

Perhaps because of its mixed strengths, variations of the German electoral system have been used in the new democracies of Hungary and Russia; Italy, Japan, and New Zealand introduced versions of this system in the early 1990s.

The Electoral Connection

One of the essential functions of political parties in a democracy is interest representation. Elections provide individuals and social groups with an opportunity to select political elites who share their views. In turn, this choice leads to the representation of voter interests in the policy process because a party must be responsive to its electoral coalition if it wants to retain its support.

The alignment of the parties is shown in Figure 6.7. The figure displays where groups of East

FIGURE 6.7   Left-Right Placement of Party Supporters in 1998

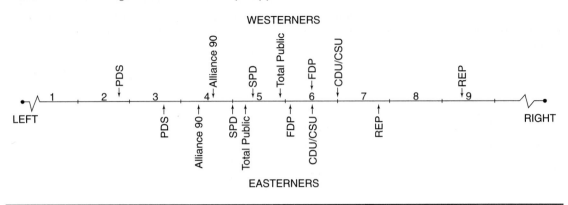

Source: *1998 German Election Study* conducted by the Wissenschaftszentrum Berlin.

and West party supporters position themselves on a left/right scale in 1998. The average Easterner is placed to the left of center (mean = 4.7), while the average Westerner is located at the center of the continuum (5.4). PDS supporters are the most leftist of all party groups, especially among Westerners; this reflects their continuing affinity for communist-socialist policies. Green voters and SPD supporters also position themselves to the left of the political spectrum, though the two parties represent different meanings of leftism in contemporary German politics. FDP and CDU/CSU partisans display their conservative orientations. The rightmost party group is the *Republikaner (REP)*, a neoconservative party that has advocated nationalist policies and antiforeigner propaganda.[44] The Republikaner have attempted to profit from the anxieties accompanying German union. However, the party has been unable to attract much of a national following.

The ideological differences among parties are also reflected in the patterns of support across social groups. Social differences in voting have gradually narrowed in the Federal Republic, and unification has added several million new voters and partially changed the composition of the electorate. Still, the political cues and policy preferences represented by social position influence voting choices. The voting patterns for the combined German electorate in 1998 reflect the traditional social divisions in German society and politics (see Table 6.2).[45]

The SPD's electoral coalition draws more voters from the liberal sectors of society, with disproportionate support from workers, union-member households, and Protestants. The party's strength is concentrated in central and north Germany, especially in the cities; the SPD is slightly underrepresented among voters from the East.

The CDU/CSU's base is almost the reciprocal of the SPD's voters: a large share of Union voters comes from the middle class, seniors, and residents of rural areas and small towns. Catholic voters also give disproportionate support to the party. In contrast to the two previous elections, the CDU fared poorly in the East in 1998.

The Greens have a very distinct electoral base heavily drawn from groups that support New Politics movements: the new middle class, the better educated, and urban voters. Even more striking are the age differences in party support; most (65.2 percent) Green voters are under 40. In 1998 the gender gap in Green support was also distinctive; 64.5 percent of Green voters were women.

The PDS also has a distinct voter clientele. In 1998 the party received more than 85 percent of its support from Easterners; all four of its directly elected Bundestag seats are in East Berlin. The PDS electorate draws heavily on the middle class, the better educated, and the nonreligious. The party of the proletarian revolution was actually a party

TABLE 6.2 Electoral Coalitions of the Parties in the 1998 Federal Elections

	SPD	Greens	CDU/CSU	FDP	PDS	Total Public
Region						
West	81.7	89.9	84.6	88.1	14.8	80.1
East	18.3	10.1	15.4	11.9	85.2	19.9
Occupation						
Worker	38.4	28.1	31.4	13.0	34.6	33.4
Self-employed	4.3	8.7	13.3	31.5	5.8	9.2
White collar/government	57.3	63.2	55.3	55.5	59.6	57.4
Union member in house						
Yes	32.5	24.6	16.4	3.2	37.0	24.5
No	67.5	75.4	83.6	96.8	63.0	75.5
Education						
Primary	42.1	16.2	38.1	36.5	18.5	37.5
Secondary	34.5	30.9	37.3	22.2	46.3	35.1
Advanced	23.4	52.9	24.6	41.3	35.2	27.4
Religion						
Catholic	29.3	28.1	45.6	26.4	3.7	33.8
Protestant	45.2	45.2	36.2	51.2	7.5	39.6
Other, none	25.5	26.7	18.2	22.4	88.8	26.6
Size of town						
less than 5,000	30.7	27.5	37.5	33.9	26.4	32.8
5,000–20,000	21.7	21.7	25.2	16.1	15.1	21.9
20,000–100,000	22.9	26.1	21.0	22.6	20.8	22.4
more than 100,000	24.7	24.6	16.3	27.4	37.7	22.8
Age						
Under 40	42.2	65.2	31.0	27.0	40.7	39.4
40–59	34.1	26.1	33.8	27.0	40.8	33.4
60 and over	23.7	8.7	35.2	46.0	18.5	27.2
Gender						
Male	49.2	35.5	54.0	57.1	47.0	50.4
Female	50.8	64.5	46.0	42.9	53.0	49.6

Source: September 1998 German Election Study; conducted by the Forschungsgruppe Wahlen for the Zweite Deutsche Fernsehen (weighted N = 1250). Some percentages do not total 100 because of rounding or missing cases. Dieter Roth provided access to these data.

benefiting the East German intelligentsia and party faithful, and this is reflected in its current patterns of voting support.

The FDP's voter base in 1998 illustrates the aging of the party and its narrow electoral appeal. The FDP drew an exceptionally large percentage of its voters from among the elderly and among the self-employed. In a nation with more than a third of the labor force employed in blue-collar occupations, the FDP won only 13 percent of the working-class vote. In addition, the FDP fails to appeal to many Eastern voters.

The incorporation of the new voters from the East is still producing strains within the German party system. The strength of the PDS in the East shows the continuing political divisions spawned by German unification. At the same time, the Greens and FDP have become distinctly Western parties in their voter appeal. The 1998 results suggest that East-West political divisions are continuing.

Party Government

Political parties deserve special emphasis in Germany because they are such important actors in the political process. Some observers describe the political system as government for the parties, by the parties, and of the parties.

The Basic Law is unusual because it specifically refers to political parties (the American Constitution does not). Because parties were suppressed during the German Empire and the Third Reich, the Basic Law guarantees their legitimacy and their right to exist—if they accept the principles of democratic government. Parties are also designated as the primary institutions of representative democracy, acting as intermediaries between the public and the government and functioning in place of provisions for direct citizen input such as initiatives and referendums. The Basic Law takes the additional step of assigning an educational function to the parties, directing them to "take part in forming the political will of the people." In other words, the parties are expected to take the lead and not just respond to public opinion.

The centrality of parties in the political process appears in several ways. There are no direct primaries that would allow the public to select party representatives in Bundestag elections. Instead, district candidates are nominated by a small group of official party members or by a committee appointed by the membership. Party-list candidates are selected at state party conventions. Thus the leadership has discretion in selecting list candidates and their ordering on the list. This power can be used to reward faithful party supporters and discipline party mavericks; placement near the top of a party list virtually ensures election, and low placement carries little chance of a Bundestag seat.

The dominance of party is also evident throughout the election process. Most voters view the candidates merely as party representatives rather than as independent political figures. Even the district candidates are elected primarily because of their party ties. Bundestag, state, and European election campaigns are financed by the government, with the parties receiving public funds for each vote they get. But again, government funding and access to public media are allocated to the parties, not the individual candidates. Government funding for the parties also continues between elections, to help them perform their informational and educational functions as prescribed in the Basic Law.

Within the Bundestag, the parties are even more influential. Organizationally, the Bundestag is structured around party groups (*Fraktionen*) rather than individual deputies. The key legislative posts and committee assignments are restricted to members of a party Fraktion. The size of a Fraktion determines its representation on legislative committees, its share of committee chairs, and its participation in the executive bodies of the legislature. Government funds for legislative and administrative support are distributed to the Fraktion, not to the deputies.

Because of these forces, the cohesion of parties within the Bundestag is exceptionally high. Parties caucus before major legislation to decide the party position, and most legislative votes follow strict party lines. This is partially a consequence of a parliamentary system and partially a sign of the pervasive influence parties have throughout the political process.

The Policy Process

The policymaking process may begin from any part of society—an interest group, a political leader, an individual citizen, or a government official. Because these elements interact in making public policy, it is difficult to trace the true genesis of any policy idea. Moreover, once a new policy is proposed, other interest groups come into play and become active in amending, supporting, or opposing the policy.

The pattern of interaction among policy actors varies with time and policy issues. One set of groups is most active on labor issues, and they use the methods of influence that will be most successful for their cause. A very different set of interests may assert themselves on defense policy and use far different methods of influence. This variety makes it difficult to describe policymaking as a single process, although the institutional framework for enacting policy is relatively uniform in all policy areas. A brief discussion of this framework will describe the various arenas in which policy actors compete, and clarify the balance of power between the institutions of government.

Policy Initiation

Most legislation reaches the formal policy agenda through the executive branch. One reason for this predominance is that the Cabinet and the ministries manage the affairs of government. They are responsible for preparing the budget, formulating revenue proposals, administering existing policies, and the other routine activities of government.

The nature of a parliamentary democracy further strengthens the policymaking influence of the chancellor and the Cabinet. The chancellor acts as the primary policy spokesperson for the government and for a majority of the Bundestag deputies. In speeches, interviews, and formal policy declarations, he sets the policy agenda for the government. It is the responsibility of the chancellor and Cabinet to propose new legislation that will carry out the government's policy promises. Interest groups realize the importance of the executive branch, and they generally work with the federal ministries—rather than Bundestag deputies—when they seek new legislation.

This focus on the executive branch means that the Cabinet proposes about two-thirds of the legislation considered by the Bundestag. Thirty members of the Bundestag may jointly introduce a bill, but only about 20 percent of legislative proposals begin in this manner. Most of the Bundestag's own proposals involve private-member bills or minor issues. A majority of state governments in the Bundesrat also can propose legislation, but they do so infrequently.

The Cabinet attempts to follow a consensual decision-making style in establishing the government's policy program. Ministers seldom propose legislation that is not expected to receive Cabinet support. The chancellor has a crucial part in ensuring this consensus. The chancellor's office coordinates the legislative proposals drafted by the various ministries. If the chancellor feels that a bill conflicts with the government's stated objectives, he may ask that the proposal be withdrawn or returned to the ministry for restudy and redrafting. If a conflict on policy arises between two ministries, the chancellor

may mediate the dispute. Alternatively, interministerial negotiations may resolve the differences. Only in extreme cases is the chancellor unable to resolve such problems; when such stalemates occur, policy conflicts are referred to the full Cabinet.

In Cabinet deliberations the chancellor also has a major part. The chancellor is a fulcrum, balancing conflicting interests to reach a compromise that the government as a whole can support. His position as government and party leader gives him substantial influence as he negotiates with Cabinet members. Very seldom does a majority of the Cabinet oppose the chancellor.

When the chancellor and Cabinet agree on a legislative proposal, they occupy a dominant position in the legislative process. Because the Cabinet also represents the majority in the Bundestag, most of its initiatives are eventually enacted into law. In the twelfth Bundestag (1994–1998), more than 90 percent of the government's proposals became law; in contrast, about 30 percent of the proposals introduced by Bundestag members became law.

The government's legislative position is further strengthened by provisions in the Basic Law that limit the Bundestag's authority in fiscal matters. The Parliament can revise or amend most legislative proposals. It cannot, however, alter the spending or taxation levels of legislation proposed by the Cabinet. Parliament cannot even reallocate expenditures in the budget without the approval of the finance minister and the Cabinet.

Legislating Policy

When the Cabinet approves a legislative proposal, the government sends it to the Bundesrat for review (see Figure 6.8). After receiving the Bundesrat's comments, the Cabinet formally transmits the government's proposal to the Bundestag. The bill receives a first reading, which places it on the agenda of the chamber, and it is assigned to the appropriate committee.

Much of the Bundestag's work takes place in these specialized committees. The committee structure generally follows the divisions of the federal ministries, such as transportation, defense, labor, or agriculture. Because bills are referred to the committee early in the legislative process, committees have

FIGURE 6.8 The Legislative Process

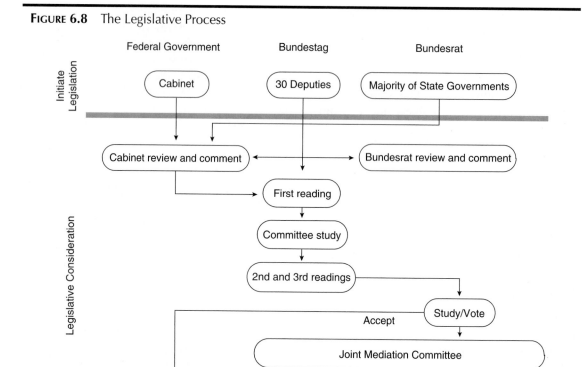

real potential for reviewing and amending their content. Committees evaluate proposals, consult with interest groups, and then submit a revised proposal to the full Bundestag. Research staffs are small, but committees also use investigative hearings. Government and interest group representatives testify on pending legislation, and committee members themselves often have expertise in their desig-

nated policy area. Most committees hold their meetings behind closed doors. The committee system thus provides an opportunity for frank discussions of proposals and negotiations among the parties before legislation reaches the floor of the Bundestag.

When a committee reports a bill, the full Bundestag examines it and discusses any proposed revisions. At this point in the legislative process, however, political positions already are well established. Leaders in the governing parties participated in the initial formulation of the legislation. The parties have caucused to decide their official position. Major revisions during the second and third readings are infrequent; the government generally is assured of the passage of its proposals as reported out of committee.

Bundestag debate on the merits of government proposals is thus mostly symbolic. It allows the parties to present their views to the public. The successful parties explain the merits of the new legislation and advertise their efforts to their supporters. The opposition parties place their objections in the public record. Although these debates seldom influence the outcome of a vote, they are nevertheless an important part of the Bundestag's information function.

A bill that passes the Bundestag is transmitted to the Bundesrat. The Bundesrat represents the state governments in the federal policy process. As previously discussed, the legislative authority of the Bundesrat equals the Bundestag in areas where the states share concurrent powers with the federal government or administer federal policies. In these areas the approval of the Bundesrat is necessary for a bill to become law. In the remaining policy areas that do not involve the states directly, such as defense or foreign affairs, the Bundesrat approval of legislation is not essential.

This sharing of legislative power between the state and federal governments has mixed political consequences. State leaders can adapt legislation to local and regional needs through their influence on policymaking. This division of power also provides another check in the system of checks and balances. With strong state governments, it is less likely that one leader or group could control the political process by usurping the national government.

The division of power between the two parliamentary bodies also presents problems. The Bundesrat's voting procedures give disproportionate weight to the smaller states; states representing only a third of the population control half the votes in the Bundesrat. Thus the Bundesrat cannot claim the same popular legitimacy as the proportionally represented and directly elected Bundestag. The Bundesrat voting system may encourage parochialism by the states. The states vote as a bloc; therefore, they view policy from the perspective of the state, rather than the national interest or party positions. The different electoral bases of the Bundestag and Bundesrat make such tensions over policy an inevitable part of the legislative process.

During most of the 1990s, the control of the two legislative bodies was split between different party coalitions controlling the Bundestag and the Bundesrat. In one sense, this division strengthened the power of the legislature, because the federal government had to negotiate with the opposition in the Bundesrat, especially on the sensitive issues of German union. But divided government also prevented necessary new legislation in a variety of areas.

As in the Bundestag, much of the Bundesrat's work is done in specialized committees where bills are scrutinized for both their policy content and their administrative implications for the states. After committee review, a bill is submitted to the full Bundesrat. If the Bundesrat approves of the measure, it transmits the bill to the chancellor for his signature. If the Bundesrat objects to the Bundestag's bill, the representatives of both bodies meet in a joint mediation committee and attempt to resolve their differences.

The mediation committee submits its recommendation to both legislative bodies for their approval. If the proposal involves the state governments, the Bundesrat may cast an absolute veto and prevent the bill from becoming a law. In the remaining policy areas, the Bundesrat can cast only a suspensive veto. If the Bundestag approves of a measure, it may override a suspensive veto and forward the proposal to the chancellor. The final step in the process is the promulgation of the law by the federal president.

Throughout the legislative process, the executive branch is omnipresent. After transmitting the government's proposal to the Bundestag, the federal ministers work in support of the bill. Ministry representatives testify before Bundestag and Bundesrat committees to present their position. Cabinet ministers lobby committee members and influential members of Parliament. Ministers may propose amendments or negotiate policy compromises to resolve issues that arise during parliamentary deliberations. Government representatives may also attend meetings of the joint mediation committee between the Bundestag and Bundesrat; no other nonparliamentary participants are allowed. The government frequently makes compromises and accepts amendments proposed in the legislature. The executive branch, however, retains a dominant influence on the policy process.

Policy Administration

In another attempt to diffuse political power, the Basic Law assigned the administrative responsibility for most domestic policies to the state governments. As one indicator of the states' central administrative role, the states employ more civil servants than the federal and local governments combined.

Because of the delegation of administrative responsibilities, federal legislation normally is fairly detailed to ensure that the government's intent is followed in the actual application of a law. Federal agencies may also supervise state agencies, and in cases of dispute they may apply sanctions or seek judicial review.

Despite this oversight by the federal government, the states retain discretion in applying most federal legislation. In part, they do so because the federal government lacks the resources to follow state actions closely. Federal control of the states also requires Bundesrat support, where claims for states' rights receive a sympathetic hearing. This decentralization of political authority provides additional flexibility for the political system.

Judicial Review

As in the United States, legislation in Germany is subject to judicial review. A Constitutional Court has the authority to evaluate the constitutionality of legislation and to void laws that violate the provisions of the Basic Law.

Constitutional issues are brought before the court by one of three methods. The most common involves constitutional complaints filed by individual citizens. Citizens may appeal directly to the court when they feel that their constitutional rights were violated by a government action. More than 90 percent of the cases presented to the court arise from citizens' complaints. Moreover, cases can be filed without paying court costs and without a lawyer. The court is thus like an ombudsman, assuring the average citizen that his or her fundamental rights are protected by the Basic Law and the court.

The Constitutional Court also hears cases based on "concrete" and "abstract" principles of judicial review. Concrete review involves actual court cases that raise constitutional issues and are referred by a lower court judge to the Constitutional Court. In an abstract review the court rules on legislation as a legal principle, without reference to an actual case. The federal government, a state government, or one-third of the Bundestag deputies can request review of a law. This procedure is sometimes used by groups that fail to block a bill during the legislative process. In recent years various groups have challenged the constitutionality of the national census (partially upheld), the unification treaty with the GDR (upheld), abortion reform law (overturned), the involvement of German troops in UN peacekeeping roles (upheld), and several other important pieces of legislation. Over the last two decades, the court received an average of two or three such referrals a year.[46] Judicial review in the abstract expands the constitutional protection of the Basic Law. This directly involves the court in the policy process and may politicize the court as another agent of policymaking.

Policy Performance

By most standards, the two Germanies could both boast of their positive records of government performance. The Federal Republic's economic advances in the 1950s and early 1960s were truly phenomenal, and the progress in the East was nearly as remarkable. By the 1980s West Germany had one of the strongest economies in the world, its living standard was among the highest of any nation, and nearly all indicators of material well-being had followed an upward trend. Other government policies improved the educational system, increased workers' participation in industrial management, extended social services, and improved environmental quality.

The GDR was the corresponding success story of Eastern Europe. Its economy ranked among the top 20 in the world, and postwar economic advances greatly improved the living standard of the average citizen. Despite this progress, the political and social systems in the East crumbled when the opportunity for change became apparent.

The 1990s has been a time of tremendous policy change and innovation as the Federal Republic adjusted to its new domestic and foreign policy circumstances. At this point, the outcomes are still uncertain. The integration of two different welfare systems, two different legal systems, two different military systems, and two different social systems cannot simply be resolved by the decision to unify.

Perhaps the best forecasts we can make for the future are based on the present policy programs and outputs of the Federal Republic, since these systems have been gradually extended to the East. Then after discussing the Federal Republic's policy record, we can consider the special policy challenges posed by German unification.

The Federal Republic's Policy Record

For Americans who hear politicians rail against "big government" in the United States, the size of the German government gives greater meaning to this term. Over the past half century the scope of German government has increased both in total public spending and in new policy responsibilities. Today, government spending accounts for almost half of the total economy, the federal government manages many economic enterprises, and government regulations touch many areas of the economy and society. Germans are much more likely than Americans to consider that the state is responsible for addressing social needs and to support government policy activity. In summary, total public expenditures—federal, state, local, and the social security system—have increased from less than DM 100 billion in 1960 to DM 741 billion in 1980, and over DM 1.8 trillion for a united Germany in 1998, which is nearly 50 percent of the gross domestic product.

It is difficult, however, to describe the activities of government in precise terms of revenue and budgets. A major complicating factor is Germany's extensive network of social services. Social security programs are the largest part of public expenditures; however, they are managed in insurance programs that are separate from the government's normal budget.

Another complicating factor is Germany's federal system. The Basic Law distributes policy responsibilities among the three levels of government. Local authorities provide utilities (electricity, gas, and water), operate the hospitals and public recreation facilities, and administer youth and social assistance programs. The states manage educational and cultural policies; they also hold primary responsibility for public security and the administration of justice. Policies that are best handled at the national level are assigned to the federal government, which includes foreign policy and defense, transportation, and communications. Consequently, public expenditures are distributed fairly evenly over the three levels of government. In 1998 the federal budget was DM 512 billion, the combined state budgets were DM 476 billion, and local authorities spent more than DM 277 billion.

Figure 6.9 describes the activities of government, combining public spending by local, state, and federal governments, as well as the expenditures of the social insurance systems in 1993. Public spending on social programs alone amounted to DM 840.6 billion, nearly as much as was spent on all other government programs combined. Because of these extensive social programs, the Federal Republic is often described as a welfare state, or more precisely a social services state. A compulsory social insurance system includes nationwide health care, accident insurance, unemployment compensation, and retirement benefits. Other programs provide financial assistance for the needy and individuals who cannot support themselves. Finally, additional programs spread the benefits of the Economic Miracle regardless of need. For instance, the government provides financial assistance to all families with children and has special tax-free savings plans and other savings incentives for the average wage earner. The unemployment program is a typical example of the range of benefits available (see Box 6.4). For much of the history of West Germany, politicians competed to extend the coverage and benefits of such programs. Despite efforts by the

FIGURE 6.9   The Distribution of Total Public Expenditures, 1993[a]

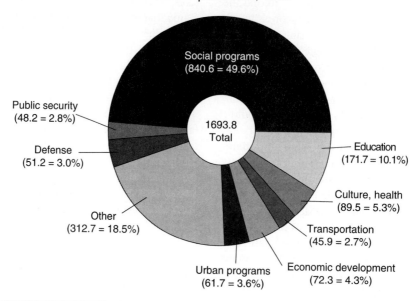

[a] In DM billions.
Source: *Statistisches Jahrbuch für die Bundesrepublik Deutschland 1996*, p. 487.

Box 6.4   German Unemployment Benefits

An unemployed worker receives insurance payments that provide up to 67 percent of normal pay (63 percent for unmarried workers) for up to a year. After a year, unemployment assistance continues at up to 57 percent of normal pay. The government pays the social insurance contributions of individuals who are unemployed, and government labor offices help the unemployed worker find new employment or obtain retraining for a new job. If the worker locates a job in another city, the program partially reimburses travel and moving expenses.

CDU government in the 1980s to scale back the scope of government activity, the basic structure of the welfare state has endured.

Unification has put this system (and the federal budget) to a new test. Unemployment, welfare, and health benefits for the East provided basic social needs during the difficult economic times following unification. But this has come at a cost of several hundred billion DM. This places new strains on the political consensus in support of these social programs, as well as the government's ability to provide these benefits.

The federal government is, of course, involved in a range of other policy activities. Education, for example, is an important concern of all three levels of government, accounting for about one-tenth of all public spending (see again Figure 6.9). The federal government is also deeply involved in communications and transportation. Much of the electronic media, television and radio, are owned or managed by the government. The federal government also owns and operates the railway system.

In recent years the government's policy agenda has expanded to include some new issues;

environmental protection is the most visible example. The Kohl government had been a surprising innovator for many environmental areas. Several indicators of air and water quality show real improvements in the past decade, and Germany has an ambitious recycling program. But many pressing environmental questions, such as nuclear power and the disposal of toxic wastes, remain unresolved. The SPD-Green government is now developing stronger policies for environmental protection.

Defense and foreign relations are another important activity of government. More than for most other European nations, the FRG's economy and security system are based on international interdependence. The Federal Republic's economy depends heavily on exports and foreign trade; in the mid-1990s over one-fourth of the Western labor force produced goods for export, a percentage much higher than that for most other industrial economies.

The FRG's international economic orientation has made the nation's membership in the *European Union (EU)* a cornerstone of its economic policy (also see Chapter 11). The FRG was an initial advocate of the EU and has benefitted considerably from its EU membership. Free access to a large European market was essential to the success of the Economic Miracle, and it is a continuing basis of the FRG's export-oriented economy. Participation in EU decision making gives the Federal Republic an opportunity to influence the course of European political development.

The Federal Republic is also militarily integrated into the Western alliance through its membership in the North Atlantic Treaty Organization. German troops are a mainstay of Western European defenses. Among the Europeans, the Federal Republic makes the largest personnel and financial contribution to NATO forces, and the German public strongly supports the NATO alliance. Over time, however, defense spending has decreased from about 13 percent of all public expenditures in the early 1960s to today's level of about 4 percent of public spending (or about 2 percent of the gross national product). The international treaties accompanying unification require a further reduction in military force for the new Germany.

TABLE 6.3 Satisfaction with Life Areas

Area	Westerners	Easterners
Housing	90%	82%
Work	88	86
Living standard	84	75
Leisure	83	73
Health	80	76
Household income	77	63
Social security	70	56
Environment	64	61
Physical security	58	41
Average	77	68

Source: *1998 Socioeconomic Panel;* this survey is available from the Zentralarchiv für empirische Sozialforschung, University of Cologne. Table entries are the percent satisfied with each area.

Public expenditures show the policy efforts of the government, but the actual results of this spending are more difficult to assess. Most indicators of policy performance suggest that the Federal Republic has been relatively successful in achieving its policy goals. Standards of living have improved dramatically, and health statistics show similar improvement. Although localized shortages of housing still appear in the West, overall housing conditions have steadily improved. Even in new policy areas such as energy and the environment, the government has made real progress. The opinions of the public reflect these policy advances (see Table 6.3). In 1998 most Westerners were satisfied with most aspects of life that might be linked to government performance: housing, living standards, work, income, social security, environmental quality, and public security.[47] Easterners are not as positive about their circumstances, but their evaluations have improved during the 1990s. By 1998, the gap between East and West has narrowed, but there are still considerable differences separating the two regions.

Paying the Costs

The generous benefits of government programs are not, of course, due to government largesse. The taxes and financial contributions of individuals and corporations provide the funds for these programs. Therefore large government outlays inevitably mean

FIGURE 6.10   The Sources of Public Revenues, 1993

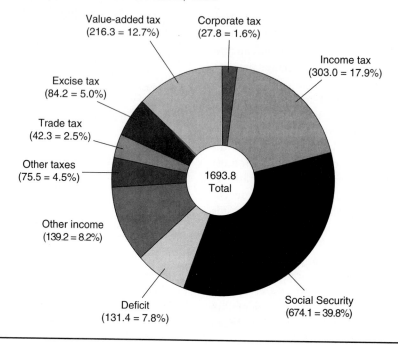

Value-added tax
(216.3 = 12.7%)

Corporate tax
(27.8 = 1.6%)

Income tax
(303.0 = 17.9%)

Excise tax
(84.2 = 5.0%)

Trade tax
(42.3 = 2.5%)

Other taxes
(75.5 = 4.5%)

1693.8
Total

Other income
(139.2 = 8.2%)

Deficit
(131.4 = 7.8%)

Social Security
(674.1 = 39.8%)

Source: *Statistisches Jahrbuch für die Bundesrepublik Deutschland 1994*, pp. 536, 519.

an equally large collection of revenues by the government. These revenues are the real source of government programs.

Three different types of revenue provide the bulk of the resources for public policy programs.[48] Contributions to the social security system represent the largest source of public revenues (see Figure 6.10). The health, unemployment, disability, retirement, and other social security funds are primarily self-financed by employer and employee contributions. For example, contributions to the pension plan amounted to about 19.2 percent of a worker's gross monthly wages, half paid by the employee and half by the employer. All the various insurance contributions combined account for about a third of the average worker's income, which is divided between contributions from the worker and from the employer.

The next most important source of public revenues is direct taxes—that is, taxes that are directly assessed by the government and paid to a govern-

ment office. One of the largest portions of public revenues comes from a personal income tax that the federal, state, and local governments share. The rate of personal taxation rises with income level, from a base of 25.9 percent to a maximum of 53 percent. After deductions and other allowances, the average worker pays about 18 percent of wages in direct income taxes. The government taxes corporate profits at a lower rate than personal income to encourage businesses to reinvest their profits in further growth.

The third major source of government revenues is indirect taxes. Like sales and excise taxes, indirect taxes are based on the use of income rather than wages and profits. The most common and lucrative indirect tax is the *value-added tax (VAT)*—a charge that is added at every stage in the manufacturing process and increases the value of a product. The standard VAT is 15 percent for most goods, with lower rates for basic commodities such as food. Other indirect taxes include customs duties, an energy tax, and liquor and tobacco taxes. Altogether, indirect taxes account for about two-fifths of all public revenues.

Indirect taxes—one of the secrets to the dramatic growth of government revenues—are normally "hidden" in the price of an item, rather than explicitly listed as a tax. In this way people are not reminded that they are paying taxes every time they purchase a product; it is also easier for policymakers to raise indirect taxes without evoking public awareness and opposition. Revenues from indirect taxes automatically rise with inflation, too. Indirect taxes are regressive, however; they weigh more heavily on low-income families because a larger share of their income goes for consumer goods.

The average German obviously has deep pockets to fund the extensive variety of public policy programs; U.S. taxation levels look quite modest by comparison. The marginal tax rate for the average German worker, including taxes and social security contributions, is over 50 percent, compared with a marginal rate in America of about 40 percent. When a German goes to the corner kiosk to buy a pack of cigarettes, 73 percent of the cost goes to taxes; taxes account for 66 percent of the cost of liquor and gasoline, 28 percent of the cost of a can of coffee, and 19 percent on a package of lightbulbs.

Even with these various revenue sources, public expenditures repeatedly have exceeded public revenues in recent years. To finance this deficit, the government draws on another source of "revenue"—loans and public borrowing—to maintain the level of government services. The CDU-led government limited the amount of deficit spending in the 1980s through budgetary restraint and new taxes. The costs of unification then increased the flow of red ink; a full accounting of public spending would show deficits averaging more than DM 100 billion a year since union.

The German taxpayer seems to contribute an excessive amount to the public coffers, and Germans are no more eager than other nationalities to pay taxes. Thus one of the major policy accomplishments of the Schröder government was new legislation in 2000 that broadly reduces income and corporate taxes. Still, the question is not how much citizens pay, but how much value is returned for their payments. In addition to normal government activities, Germans are protected against sickness, unemployment, and disability; government pension plans furnish livable retirement incomes. Moreover, the majority of the public expects the government to take an active role in providing for the needs of society and its citizens.

The Policy Challenges of Unification

Although economic and social development in the East lagged that of the West, the GDR had its own impressive record of policy accomplishments. East Germany developed a network of social programs, some of which were even more extensive than in the West. The GDR was the economic miracle of the Eastern bloc and the strongest economy in COMECON. East Germany was one of the few socialist nations that tried to develop new technologies, such as robotics and computers. Although the bright lights of West Berlin shone over the Berlin Wall, East Berlin itself was an economic showplace that impressed visitors from Poland, the Soviet Union, and other East European states.

Given this performance, most observers were surprised by the sudden and dramatic collapse of the East German economic and social systems in the wake of the November 1989 revolution. Most analysts expected that a new form of a socialist state with a human face would emerge from the communist system. Before that could happen, the entire socioeconomic structure fell apart. During the first half of 1990, the gross national product of the GDR decreased by nearly 5 percent, unemployment skyrocketed, and industrial production fell off by nearly 60 percent.[49]

The most immediate economic challenge after unification was the need to rebuild the economy of the East, integrating Eastern workers and companies into the social market economy of the West. The GDR economy looked strong in the sheltered environment of the socialist economic bloc, but it could not compete in a global marketplace. The GDR's impressive growth statistics and production figures often papered over a decaying economic infrastructure and outdated manufacturing facilities. A system that guaranteed everyone a job and had no real cost accounting method produced companies that were overstaffed, inefficient, and undercapitalized by Western standards. Similarly, the GDR was heavily dependent on trade with other COMECON nations. When COMECON ended with the collapse of communism in Eastern Europe, a major portion of the GDR's economy was destroyed.

The FRG took several steps to rebuild the economy of the East and then raise it to Western standards. The Currency Union in July 1990 was an experience in "cold turkey capitalism"—overnight the Eastern economy had to accept the economic standards of the Federal Republic. Even with salaries one-third lower in the East, productivity was still out of balance. Matching the Western economy against that of the East was like racing a Porsche against the GDR's antiquated two-cylinder Trabant—a race in which the outcome is foreordained.

To become more competitive, Eastern firms often reduced their labor force as a cost-cutting measure. This action increased the competitiveness of some firms and enabled them to survive, but the consequence was a dramatic rise in unemployment, which was especially shocking in a nation accustomed to guaranteed employment. Unemployment was further increased by cuts in the size of the Eastern civil service and other public sector employment.

Another step in the conversion process was the creation of the Trust Agency (*Treuhandanstalt*), which was charged with privatizing the 8,000 plus firms that the GDR government had owned. More than 80 percent of the GDR's economy was run by nationalized enterprises and the large state-owned cartels (*Kombinate*). The trust dissolved these cartels, converted individual enterprises into corporations, and sold them to private buyers, predominantly West German or other Western companies. However, privatization did not generate the capital for investment that was predicted by the government. Disputes about property ownership further slowed the pace of development. Massive subsidies from the FRG and the collapse of the Eastern property market meant that the sale of the GDR economic infrastructure generated a net loss for the nation. In retrospect, one wonders how politicians could have

been so optimistic about the prospects for an Eastern economic miracle.

The economic by-products of German unification affected other policy areas as well. The high levels of unemployment created great demands on the FRG's social welfare programs. Unemployed Eastern workers were drawing unemployment compensation, retraining benefits, and relocation allowances. Pensions and health insurance benefits in the East were assumed by the Federal Republic. West Germany had already been debating the limits to their welfare state before German unification; today the social services costs of unification continue to escalate, which has renewed this debate.

Nobody really knows what it will eventually cost to rebuild the East or to subsidize the economy through the reconstruction process. It is certain, however, that the costs will be staggering. It is equally clear that economic change cannot occur without large financial backing from the government. The government has spent massive amounts: from rebuilding the highway and railway systems of the East, to upgrading the Eastern telephone system to international standards, to moving the capital from Bonn to Berlin, which came with a price tag of billions of marks. The costs of renovating Eastern industry and agriculture are incalculable. Moreover, this renovation is likely to occur only with the protection of government financial subsidies and guaranteed loans.

Taken together, the aid from the West has been massive. In 1991, for example, the combined payments to the new Länder from official sources amounted to DM 113 billion (almost DM 7,000 per capita); this was more than twice Poland's per-capita disposable income for the same year.[50] Government statistics for 1999 showed that the net payments to the East had increased to DM 140 billion. All Germans still have to pay an extra 5.5 percent of income tax toward a "solidarity surcharge" that funds a party of the investment in the East. One attempt to estimate the total costs of unification calculated that DM 3 trillion in government and private funds will be required.

There have been substantial efforts to reconstruct the East's economy. The Treuhand privatized (or closed) nearly all the firms that it initially controlled and then dissolved itself by the end of

1994. A new transportation and communications infrastructure is developing in the East. Kohl proudly boasted during the 1994 campaign that 4 million new telephones had been installed in the East since 1990, which was more than twice what the GDR had installed during its entire history. New construction dots much of the Eastern landscape, and government incentives spur investment in the East.

Economic progress is being made. In the first half of 2000, economic growth rates in the East exceeded those in the Western states by a comfortable margin. But the East-West gap is still wide. Unemployment rates in the East are still more than double the rates in the West, and even after years of investment, productivity in the East still lags markedly behind the West. Although standards of living in the East have rapidly improved since the early 1990s, they also remain significantly below Western standards. Furthermore, the gap will continue. Even if the economy in the Eastern states grows at double the rate of the West, it will take decades for full equality to be reached.

German unification also creates new challenges for noneconomic policy areas. For example, the GDR had model environmental laws, but these laws were never enforced. Consequently, many areas of the East resemble an environmentalist's nightmare: untreated toxic wastes from industry were dumped into rivers, emissions from power plants poisoned the air, many cities lacked sewage treatment plants, and nuclear power plants used the technology of the Chernobyl reactor that had exploded in the Soviet Union in 1986. At the time of unification, some Eastern rivers had pollution levels more than 200 times above EU environmental standards. All of the deleterious health effects of these environmental conditions were covered up by the GDR.

The unification treaty called for raising the environmental quality of the East to Western standards—a difficult and expensive task. For example, several nuclear reactors in the East were closed for safety reasons, but this only placed a higher burden on the East's polluting, coal-fired power plants. In 1996 several of these coal-fired plants were also shut down for environmental reasons. The DM 200–400 billion price tag that is required to correct the GDR's environmental legacy competes against economic development projects for government funding. At least in the short term, unification is likely to intensify the political debate on the tradeoffs between economic development and environmental protection.

The social and economic costs of unification, and the changing international context, have also created new tensions between native Germans and the foreign population. Unification first meant a steady influx of Easterners into the Western sectors, which placed new demands on housing and employment in the West. Political instability in Europe led to rising numbers of foreigners seeking political asylum or legal immigration into the FRG. For instance, more refugees from the conflicts in the former Yugoslavia emigrated to Germany than to the entire rest of Europe.

Some Germans, in both East and West, treated foreigners as scapegoats for their personal problems or the nation's woes. Violent acts against foreigners increased in both halves of Germany, evoking horrendous memories of Weimar's collapse. Extreme right parties, such as the Republikaner, tried to flame the public's fears. The government's indecisiveness in dealing with this issue exacerbated the problem. Finally, the Federal Republic revised the asylum clause in the Basic Law in 1993 (making it closer to U.S. immigration policy), took more decisive action in combating violence, and mobilized the tolerant majority in German society. Today relations between Germans and foreigners have improved but this remains a sensitive area of politics.

Paralleling its domestic policy challenges, the new Germany is redefining its international identity and its foreign policy goals. The Federal Republic has linked its role in international politics to its participation in the NATO alliance and the European Union. Both relationships may change substantially as a result of German unity.

In mid-1990 Gorbachev agreed to continued German membership in NATO after unification. In return, Gorbachev won concessions on the reduction of combined German troop levels to a total of 370,000; the definition of the GDR territory as a nuclear-free zone; and Germany's continued abstention from the development or use of atomic, biological, and chemical weapons. In September 1990 the four World War II allies—the United States, Britain, France, and the Soviet Union—endorsed these agreements, granting Germany its sovereignty and essentially ratifying a peace treaty to finally end World War II. By the end of 1994 all four allies had removed their troops from Berlin, ending the last vestige of the occupation.

The new Germany will likely play a different military and strategic role as a result of these agreements and the changing international context. NATO existed as a bulwark of the Western defense against the Soviet threat; the decline of this threat will lessen the military role of the alliance. Moreover, Germany wants to be an active advocate for peace within Europe, developing its role as a bridge between East and West. The new Germany is also assuming a larger responsibility in international disputes outside the NATO region. In 1993 the Constitutional Court interpreted the Basic Law to allow German troops to serve outside of Europe as part of international peacekeeping activities—as they did in Somalia and the Balkans. With this expanding international role, the FRG has raised the issue of gaining a permanent seat on the UN's Security Council. Germany is now increasingly likely to exercise an independent foreign policy, within a framework of partnership with its allies.

Unification is also reshaping the Federal Republic's relationship to the European Union. The new Germany outweighs the other EU members in both its population and gross national product; thus, the parity that underlies the consensual nature of the Union will change. Moreover, Germany will have to walk a narrow line between being too active and too inactive in EU affairs. Some economic partners worry that Germany will attempt to dominate the European Union, pursuing its own national interests more aggressively. Other nations worry that Germany will turn its attentions eastward, diminishing its commitment and involvement in the EU's ambitious plans for the future.

Germany has attempted to assuage these fears: working to expand the powers of the EU, developing a common European currency and other integrationist policies, and expanding the Union's membership to other European states. Worries about German goals and commitments remain, however. At the least, it is clear that a united Germany will approach the process of European integration based on a different calculus than that which guided its actions for the previous 40 years.

After the Revolution

Revolutions are unsettling, both to the participants and the spectators. Such is the case with the German revolution of 1989. Easterners realized their hopes for freedom, but they also have seen their everyday lives change before their eyes, sometimes in distressing ways. Westerners saw their hopes for German union and a new peace in Europe answered, but at a substantial political and economic cost to the nation.

The Federal Republic is now forging a new social and political identity that will shape its domestic and international policies. Many Germans on both sides of the former border are hopeful, but still uncertain, of what the future holds for their nation. The Federal Republic's neighbors wonder what role the new Germany will play in European and international affairs. Addressing these questions will test the strength of the Federal Republic and its new residents in the East.

Unification has clearly presented new social, political, and economic challenges for the nation. One cannot merge two such different systems without experiencing problems. However, these strains were magnified by the inability or unwillingness of elites to state the problems honestly and to deal with them in a forthright manner. Even as voters were turning Kohl out of office in 1998, they differed on the new direction they wanted the government to follow. The new SPD-Green government must reforge the social and political consensus that was a foundation for the Federal Republic's past accomplishments.

Once this has been accomplished, Germans finally may be able to answer the question of their national identity. Unification has created a new German state linked to Western political values and social norms. Equally important, unity was achieved through a peaceful revolution (and the power of the DM), not blood and iron. The trials of the unification process are testing the public's commitment to these values. The government's ability to show citizens in the East that democracy and the social market economy can improve the quality of their lives may be necessary to solidify their democratic aspirations. If the revolution succeeds, this aspect of the German question may finally be answered.

✺ KEY TERMS ✺

Konrad Adenauer
Basic Law (*Grundgesetz*)
Bundesrat
Bundestag
Christian Democratic
  Union (CDU)
Christian Social
  Union (CSU)
citizen action groups
  (*Bürgerinitiativen*)
codetermination
  (*Mitbestimmung*)
Confederation of
  German Employers'
  Associations (BDA)
Constitutional Court

constructive no-
  confidence vote
Economic Miracle
  (*Wirtschaftswunder*)
European Union (EU)
federal chancellor
  (*Bundeskanzler*)
federal president
  (*Bundespräsident*)
Federal Republic of
  Germany (FRG)
Federation of German
  Industry (BDI)
Free Democratic Party
  (FDP)

German Democratic
  Republic (GDR)
German Federation of
  Trade Unions
  (DGB)
The Greens
guest workers
  (*Gastarbeiter*)
Adolf Hitler
Kaiser
National Socialist
  German Workers'
  Party (the Nazis)
Neocorporatism
Ostpolitik

Party of Democratic
  Socialism (PDS)
peak association
postmaterial values
proportional
  representation (PR)
Republikaner (REP)
Social Democratic Party
  (SPD)
Socialist Unity Party
  (SED)
Third Reich
value-added tax (VAT)
Weimar Republic

✺ SUGGESTED READINGS ✺

German Politics and Society Websites, compiled at the University of California, Irvine: www.democ.uci.edu/democ/germany.html

German Information Center Website: http://www.germany-info.org

Ash, Timothy Garton. *In Europe's Name: Germany in a Divided Continent.* New York: Random House, 1993.

Bark, Dennis, and David Gress. *A History of West Germany,* 2 vols., 2nd ed. London: Blackwell, 1993.

Childers, Thomas, and Jane Caplan, eds. *Reevaluating the Third Reich.* New York: Holmes & Meier, 1993.

Childs, David. *The GDR: Moscow's German Ally.* London: Hyman, 1988.

Craig, Gordon. *Germany 1866–1945.* New York: Oxford University Press, 1981.

Dalton, Russell. *Politics in Germany,* 2nd ed. New York: HarperCollins, 1993.

———, ed. *Germans Divided: The 1994 Bundestagswahl and the Evolution of the German Party System.* New York and Oxford, England: Berg, 1996.

Fulbrook, Mary. *Anatomy of a Dictatorship: Inside the GDR, 1949–1989.* New York: Oxford University Press, 1995.

Hampton, Mary, and Christian Soe, eds. *Between Bonn and Berlin: German Politics Adrift?* Lanham, MD: Rowman & Littlefield, 1999.

Hancock, M. Donald, and Helga Welch, eds. *German Unification: Process and Outcome.* Boulder, CO: Westview, 1994.

Hanreider, Wolfram. *Germany, America, Europe: Forty Years of German Foreign Policy.* New Haven, CT: Yale University Press, 1989.

Huelshoff, Michael, Andrei Markovits, and Simon Reich, eds. *From Bundesrepublik to Deutschland: German Politics After Unification.* Ann Arbor: University of Michigan Press, 1993.

Jarausch, Konrad. *The Rush to German Unity.* New York: Oxford University Press, 1994.

Katzenstein, Peter. *Policy and Politics in West Germany: The Growth of a Semisovereign State.* Philadelphia: Temple University Press, 1987.

Kolinsky, Eva. *Women in Contemporary Germany.* New York and Oxford, England: Berg, 1993.

Kopstein, Jeffrey. *The Politics of Economic Decline in East Germany. 1945–1989.* Chapel Hill: University of North Carolina Press, 1997.

Krisch, Henry. *The German Democratic Republic: The Search for Identity.* Boulder, CO: Westview, 1985.

Maier, Charles. *Dissolution: The Crisis of Communism and the End of East Germany.* Princeton, NJ: Princeton University Press, 1997.

Markovits, Andrei, and Philip Gorski. *The German Left: Red, Green and Beyond.* New York: Oxford University Press, 1993.

McAdams, James. *Germany Divided: From the Wall to Unification.* Princeton, NJ: Princeton University Press, 1993.

Merkl, Peter. *German Unification in the European Context.* University Park: Pennsylvania State University Press, 1993.

———, ed. *The Federal Republic at Fifty: The End of a Century of Turmoil.* New York: New York University Press, 1999.

Orlow, Dietrich. *A History of Modern Germany,* 3rd ed. Englewood Cliffs, NJ: Prentice Hall, 1995.

Padgett, Stephen. *Organizing Democracy in Eastern Germany.* Cambridge: Cambridge University Press, 2000.

Rohrschneider, Robert. *Learning Democracy: Democratic and Economic Values in Unified Germany.* New York: Oxford University Press, 1999.

Sheehan, James. *German History 1770–1866.* New York: Oxford University Press, 1989.

Sinn, Gerlinde, and Hans-Werner Sinn. *Jumpstart: The Economic Unification of Germany.* Cambridge, MA: MIT Press, 1992.

Smith, Gordon, et al. *Developments in German Politics 2,* 2nd ed. London: Macmillian, 1996.

Spielvogel, Jackson. *Hitler and Nazi Germany: A History.* Englewood Cliffs, NJ: Prentice Hall, 1988.

Turner, Henry. *Germany from Partition to Unification.* New Haven: Yale University Press, 1992.

✍ ENDNOTES ✍

1. The First German Empire was formed in the ninth century through the partitioning of Charlemagne's empire; see Kurt Reinhardt, *Germany: 2000 Years,* Vol. 1 (New York: Ungar, 1986).

2. Karl Dietrich Bracher, *The German Dictatorship* (New York: Praeger, 1970); Martin Broszat, *Hitler and the Collapse of Weimar Germany* (New York: St. Martin's, 1987).

3. Raul Hilberg, *The Destruction of the European Jews,* rev. ed. (New York: Holmes and Meier, 1985); Sarah Gordon, *Hitler, Germans and the "Jewish Question"* (Princeton, NJ: Princeton University Press, 1984).

4. Karl Hardach, *The Political Economy of Germany in the Twentieth Century* (Berkeley: University of California Press, 1980); Eric Owen Smith, *The German Economy* (London: Routledge, 1994).

5. Gregory Sandford, *From Hitler to Ulbricht: The Communist Reconstruction of East Germany, 1945–1946* (Princeton, NJ: Princeton University Press, 1983).

6. James McAdams, *East Germany and the West: Surviving Detente* (New York: Cambridge University Press, 1985); Stephen Larrabee, ed., *The Two German States and European Security* (New York: Macmillan, 1989).

7. Forschungsgruppe Wahlen, *Politbarometer* (monthly publications of the Forschungsgruppe Wahlen, Mannheim, 2000).

8. Commission of the European Communities, *Eurobarometer 19* (Brussels: Commission of the European Communities, 1983); see also Eva Kolinsky, *Women in Contemporary Germany* (Oxford, England, and New York: Berg, 1993).

9. Christian Joppke, *Immigration and the Nation-state: The United States, Germany, and Great Britain* (New York: Oxford University Press, 1999); James Hollifield, *Immigrants, Markets and States* (Cambridge, MA: Harvard University Press, 1993).

10. The Allied occupation authorities oversaw the drafting of the Basic Law and held veto power over the final document; see Peter Merkl, *The Origins of the West German Republic* (New York: Oxford University Press, 1965).

11. The English language URL for the Bundestag is: http://www.bundestag.de/btengver/e-index.htm

12. A second type of no-confidence vote allows the chancellor to attach a no-confidence provision to a government legislative proposal. If the Bundestag defeats the proposal, the chancellor may ask the federal president to call for new Bundestag elections; see Russell J. Dalton, *Politics in Germany,* 2nd ed. (New York: HarperCollins, 1993), p. 62.

13. Ludger Helms, "Keeping Weimar at Bay: The German Federal Presidency since 1949," *German Politics and Society* 16 (Summer 1998): 50–68.

14. Donald Kommers, *Constitutional Jurisprudence of the Federal Republic* (Durham, NC: Duke University Press, 1989); Donald Kommers, "The Federal Constitutional Court in the German Political System," *Comparative Political Studies* 26 (1994): 470–91.

15. Anna Merritt and Richard Merritt, *Public Opinion in Occupied Germany* (Urbana: University of Illinois Press, 1970); Ralf Dahrendorf, *Society and Democracy in Germany* (New York: Doubleday, 1967).

16. Christiane Lemke, "Political Socialization and the 'Micromilieu,'" in Marilyn Rueschemeyer and Christiane Lemke, eds., *The Quality of Life in the German Democratic Republic* (New York: M. E. Scharpe); Archie Brown and Jack Gray, eds., *Culture and Political Change in Communist States* (London: Macmillan, 1979).

17. Gabriel Almond and Sidney Verba, *The Civic Culture* (Princeton, NJ: Princeton University Press, 1963); David Conradt, "Changing German Political Culture," in Gabriel Almond and Sidney Verba, eds. *The Civic Culture Revisited* (Boston: Little Brown, 1980).

18. Conradt, "Changing German Political Culture," pp. 229–31; Kendall Baker, Russell J. Dalton, and Kai Hildebrandt, *Germany Transformed: Political Culture and the New Politics* (Cambridge, MA: Harvard University Press, 1981).

19. Henry Krisch, *The German Democratic Republic: The Search for Identity* (Boulder, CO: Westview, 1985); Gebhard Schweigler, "German Questions of the Shrinking of Germany," in Larabee, *The Two German States.*

20. Gerald Braunthal, *Political Loyalty and Public Service in West Germany* (Amherst: University of Massachusetts Press, 1990).

21. Walter Friedrich and Hartmut Griese, *Jugend und Jugendforschung in der DDR* (Opladen, Germany: Westdeutscher Verlag, 1990); Deutsches Jugendinstitut, *Deutsche Schüler im Sommer 1990* (Munich, Germany: Deutsches Jugendinstitut, 1990).

22. Russell J. Dalton, "Communists and Democrats: Democratic Attitudes in the Two Germanies," *British Journal of Political Science* 24 (1994): 469–93; Frederick Weil, "The Development of Democratic Attitudes in Eastern and Western Germany in a Comparative Perspective," in Frederick Weil, ed. *Democratization in Eastern and Western Europe* (Greenwich, CT: JAI Press, 1993).

23. Hans-Dieter Klingemann and Richard Hofferbert, "Germany: A New 'Wall in the Mind?' *Journal of Democracy* 5 (1994): 30–44; Robert Rohrschneider, *Learning Democracy: Democratic and Economic Values in Unified Germany* (New York: Oxford University Press, 1999).

24. Ronald Inglehart, *Modernization and Postmodernization* (Princeton, NJ: Princeton University Press, 1997); Ronald Inglehart, *Culture Shift in Advanced Industrial Society* (Princeton, NJ: Princeton University Press, 1990).

25. See Chapter 2; Russell Dalton, *Citizen Politics*, 2nd ed. (Chatham, NJ: Chatham House, 1996), Ch. 6.

26. Dalton, *Politics in Germany*, Ch. 5; Christiane Lemke, "Political Socialization and the 'Micromilieu,' " in Rueschemeyer and Lemke, eds., *The Quality of Life in the German Democratic Republic*.

27. Meredith Watts et al., *Contemporary German Youth and their Elders* (New York: Greenwood, 1989); Elizabeth Noelle-Neumann and Renate Köcher, *Die verletze Nation* (Stuttgart, Germany: Deutsche Verlag, 1987); Deutsches Jugendinstitut, *Deutsche Schüler im Sommer 1990*.

28. Sterling Fishman and Lothar Martin, *Estranged Twins: Education and Society in the Two Germanies* (New York: Praeger, 1987); Gert Glaessner, "The Education System and Society," in Klaus von Beyme and Hartmut Zimmerman, eds., *Policymaking in the German Democratic Republic* (New York: St. Martin's, 1984).

29. Max Planck Institute, *Between Elite and Mass Education* (Albany: State University of New York Press, 1982).

30. Rosalind Pritchard, *Reconstructing Education: East German Schools and Universities after Unification* (New York: Berghahn Books, 1999).

31. Peter Humphreys, *Media and Media Policy in Germany: The Press and Broadcasting Since 1945*, rev. ed. (New York and Oxford, England: Berg, 1994).

32. Dalton, *Politics in Germany*, Ch. 6; Max Kaase, "Partizipative Revolution: Ende der Parteien?" in Joachim Raschke, ed., *Bürger und Parteien* (Opladen, Germany: Westdeutscher Verlag, 1984).

33. Jutta Helm, "Citizen Lobbies in West Germany," in Peter Merkl, ed., *West European Party Systems* (New York: Free Press, 1980), pp. 576–96.

34. Wilhelm Bürklin, Hilke Rebenstorf, et al., *Eliten in Deutschland: Rekutierung und Integration* (Opladen, Germany: Leske and Budrich, 1997); Dietrich Herzog, Hilke Rebensstorf, and Bernhard Wessels, eds., *Parlament und Gessellschaft: Eine Funktionsanalyse der repräsentativen Demokratie* (Opladen, Germany: Westdeutscher Verlag, 1993).

35. Wilhelm Bürklin, "Einstellungen und Wertorientierungen ost-und westdeutscher Eliten 1995," in Oskar Gabriel, ed., *Einstellungen und politisches Verhalten in Transformationsprozess* (Opladen, Germany: Leske und Budrich, 1996); Rohrschneider, *Learning Democracy*.

36. Claus Offe, "The Attribution of Political Status to Interest Groups," in Suzanne Berger, ed., *Organizing Interests in Western Europe* (New York: Cambridge University Press, 1981), pp. 123–58; Volker Berghahn and Detlev Karsten, *Industrial Relations in West Germany* (New York and Oxford, England: Berg, 1989).

37. Kathleen Thelen, *Union in Parts: Labor Politics in Postwar Germany* (Ithaca, NY: Cornell University Press, 1991).

38. Ruud Koopmans, *Democracy from Below: New Social Movements and the Political System in West Germany* (Boulder, CO: Westview Press, 1995).

39. Gerard Braunthal, *The German Social Democrats Since 1969*, 2nd ed. (Boulder, CO: Westview Press, 1994).

40. Helmut Norpoth and Dieter Roth, "Timid or Prudent? The German Electorate in 1994," in Russell Dalton, ed., *Germans Divided: The 1994 Bundestagswahl and the Evolution of the German Party System* (Oxford, England: Berg, 1996).

41. Thomas Poguntke, *Alternative Politics: The German Green Party* (Edinburgh, Scotland: University of Edinburgh Press, 1993); E. Gene Frankland and Donald Schoonmaker, *Between Protest and Power: The Green Party in Germany* (Boulder, CO: Westview, 1992).

42. The electoral system also provides that a party that wins at least three district seats shares in the PR distribution of seats. In 1994 and 1998 the PDS won four district seats in East Berlin, which earned them additional seats through the PR distribution.

43. If a party wins more district seats in a state than it should have based on its proportion of the second vote, the party is allowed to keep the additional seats and the size of the Bundestag is increased. In 1998 the actual Bundestag membership was 669.

44. Hans-Joachim Veen, Norbert Lepszy, and Peter Mnich, *Die Republikaner Party in Germany: Right-Wing Menace or Protest Catchall?* (Westport, CT: Praeger, 1993); Hans-Georg Betz, *Rightwing Populism in Western Europe* (New York: St. Martin's 1994).

45. For evidence of voting patterns in prior elections, see Russell J. Dalton, "A Divided Electorate?" in Gordon Smith et al., *Developments in German Politics*, 3rd ed. (London: Macmillan, 1996).

46. Alec Stone, "Governing with Judges: The New Constitutionalism," in Jack Hayward and Edward Page, eds., *Governing the New Europe* (Oxford, England: Polity Press, 1995).

47. Statistiches Bundesamt, *Datenreport 1999: Zahlen und Fakten über die Bundesrepublik Deutschland* (Bonn, Germany: Bundeszentrale für politische Bildung, 2000), pp. 432–33.

48. Arnold Heidenheimer, Hugh Heclo, and Carolyn Adams, *Comparative Public Policy*, 3rd ed. (New York: St. Martin's, 1990), Ch. 6.

49. Gerlinde Sinn and Hans-Werner Sinn, *Jumpstart: The Economic Unification of Germany* (Cambridge, MA: MIT Press, 1992).

50. Sinn and Sinn, *Jumpstart*, pp. 24–25.

CHAPTER 7

POLITICS IN SPAIN

DONALD SHARE

Country Bio–Spain

POPULATION   40 Million
TERRITORY   194,896 square miles
YEAR OF INDEPENDENCE   1492
YEAR OF CURRENT CONSTITUTION   1978
CHIEF OF STATE   King Juan Carlos
HEAD OF GOVERNMENT   José María Aznar
LANGUAGE(S)   Castilian Spanish 74%, Catalan 17%, Galician 7%, Basque 2%
RELIGION   Roman Catholic 99%, other 1%

Policy Challenges

This chapter will argue that Spain has largely overcome the legacy of 40 years of authoritarian rule. By most measures, Spanish democracy is flourishing, and is arguably as healthy as any European political system. However, at the start of the twenty-first century Spanish democracy faces two serious policy challenges—Basque terrorism and chronic unemployment—that are directly related to that authoritarian legacy.

Twenty-five years after its transition to democracy, Spain continues to suffer from violence perpetrated by ETA, the pro-independence Basque terrorist organization. Spanish governments of the left and the right have so far been unable to either crush ETA or persuade it to lay down its arms. Attempts to destroy ETA have occasionally threatened the rule of law. During the Socialist governments of the 1980s top officials oversaw the creation of antiterrorist "death squads" whose attacks against suspected Basque terrorists resulted in the killing of innocent civilians. Discovery of the operation created an epic scandal and contributed to the electoral defeat of Felipe González and the Socialists in 1996 and the incarceration of a Socialist cabinet member. The conservative Popular Party of José María Aznar has fared no better in an attempt to stem terrorist violence. When Aznar announced the start of government-ETA negotiations in late 1988, there were high hopes that peace could be achieved. For about a year, Spain was free of terrorist violence. But negotiations broke down in late 1999 as ETA negotiators refused

253

to abandon their demand that the Basque Country be given the right to self-determination. A wave of terrorist killing ended the cease-fire and destroyed any hope for immediate peace. During the 2000 general election campaign Spanish courts appeared to threaten the right to free speech when they banned campaign material that was seen as supportive of ETA.

Basque terrorism has its roots in the particular brutality with which Francisco Franco treated the Basque Country during his dictatorship (1939–1975). It has been sustained by a deeply polarized political environment within the Basque Country, and the electoral success of Basque parties who support the goals (an independent Basque Country), if not the tactics, of ETA. With the failure of negotiations, Spanish governments face the prospects of escalating violence. Continued terrorist acts could undermine the legitimacy of Spanish democracy.

An equally vexing problem facing Spanish policymakers has been an unemployment level that has stubbornly remained about double the European average. In large part the high levels of unemployment were largely the result of Spain's transition from a highly protected economy under Franco to an increasingly global economy. Franco had achieved labor quiescence and near-full employment through a combination of repression, laws that prevented layoffs of workers, protectionism, and massive emigration. With Spain's democratization and integration into the European Union, governments of the right and left have worked cautiously (some argue too cautiously) to liberalize the economy, reducing the state role, making labor laws more "flexible," and ending subsidies to Spain's many inefficient industries. Despite these efforts, by 2000 Spanish labor laws were still among the most restrictive in Europe, and vestiges of Franco's statist economy were still evident. The results have been predictable: Unemployment rose from 4.5 percent on the eve of the transition, to 20.8 percent ten years later and has remained in double-digits since then. Moreover, unemployment has disproportionately affected young Spaniards: in 1995 almost half of those under 24 were unemployed.[1] Only in the late 1990s did Spain start to create new jobs at a pace sufficient to reduce unemployment. But current levels of unemployment (about 14 percent in 2000) are still the highest in Europe, and they pose a formidable challenge to Spanish policymakers.

The Historical Legacy

All U.S. schoolchildren learn the significance of 1492 in American history. That date is even more significant for Spain. In the events of that year we can observe the major themes that dominated Spanish history from the fifteenth century to the present.

First and foremost, the date represented the victory of the *Reconquista*, the Catholic reconquest of the Iberian Peninsula from the Moors, nomadic African Muslims who crossed the Straits of Gibraltar in A.D. 711 and occupied most of the peninsula for more than seven centuries. Their presence added immeasurably to Spanish culture and society, and the Moorish influence on architecture, music, cuisine, and language is still evident 500 years after their forced expulsion (along with Spain's Jews) in 1492. Spain's long isolation from the rest of Christian Europe led many Spaniards (including Francisco Franco, Spain's dictator from 1939–1975) to argue that Spain was (and should remain) fundamentally distinct from its European neighbors.

Second, the expulsion of the Moors was made possible by the political unification and centralization of a previously fragmented Iberian Peninsula. Ferdinand and Isabel, the monarchs of Spain's most important independent kingdoms, were married in 1492, uniting much of the peninsula in a single, centralized state. This unification is often credited with facilitating the building of Spain's vast global empire from the fifteenth to nineteenth centuries. However, a centralized Spain was never completely accepted by some Spaniards. Many formerly independent peoples, including the Basques and the Catalans, stubbornly resisted centralization and maintained separate languages, cultural identities, and even some political institutions, as noted in Chapter 1. The struggle between center and periphery in Spanish politics continues to this day.

Third, the fierce military struggle by Catholics to unify Spain and expel the Moors set a precedent for repressive authoritarian rule. The victorious Catholic monarchs immediately expelled all religious minorities from Spain and established the notorious *Spanish Inquisition,* a tribunal established in 1478 to enforce strict moral, religious, and political uniformity throughout Spain's empire. The dominant role given military leaders in the Reconquista and in the creation of Spain's vast American empire set the stage for numerous *pronunciamientos* (military uprisings) during the nineteenth and twentieth centuries.

Finally, 1492 marked the start of Spain's imperial experience, with the arrival of Columbus in the New World. The immensity and wealth of Spain's empire gave rise to a national pride (some would say arrogance) that rivaled British nationalism. When the rigidly centralized and overly bureaucratized empire began a slow and painful decline in the eighteenth century, many Spaniards were unable to accept that reality. The loss of Spain's last colonies, Cuba and the Philippines, in 1898, marked the end of the Spanish Empire. By then Spain had become an impoverished and peripheral European nation, but many Spaniards continued to wallow in Spain's past glory rather than accept the need for political and economic change. Some Spaniards blamed the forces of modernity for having accelerated the loss of empire and the subsequent economic decline. Others argued that the backwardness of Spain's economy and the rigidity of its political structures were responsible for Spain's demise. They called for economic reform and the democratization of Spanish political structures. This dispute between what have been dubbed the *two Spains* partly explains the political chaos of the nineteenth century, during which progressives (who tended to favor republican forms of government) and conservatives (who tended to favor authoritarian monarchies) repeatedly dislodged each other from power. The Constitution of 1812, for example, was one of Europe's earliest constitutions, and it embodied very progressive and democratic ideas for its time. It was short-lived, however, and was abolished by Ferdinand VII in 1814. Between 1812 and 1931 Spain had seven different constitutions, four of which were progressive and three conservative.

During the *Spanish Second Republic (1931–1936),* the forces of the two Spains met head on. Antimonarchical progressives founded the Republic, and its constitution contained protections for democracy, regional decentralization, and secularism. Conservative forces immediately felt threatened by the rapid political changes, especially measures that weakened the Catholic Church and the central state. Progressives controlled government from 1931 to 1933, while conservatives governed from 1934 to 1935. When a progressive coalition won the 1936 elections, forces of the right, led by a sector of the Spanish military, launched a rebellion against the Republic.

The *Spanish Civil War (1936–1939)* was the defining event of twentieth century Spanish history, and the brutality of that conflict traumatized an entire generation of Spaniards. When the rebels under the leadership of *Francisco Franco* declared victory, they set out to destroy the progressive movement in Spain once and for all. Franco was particularly vindictive when it came to identifying and punishing the losers of the war. He imposed laws that made it a crime to have supported the Republic, and his regime executed thousands of the Republic's supporters and exiled hundreds of thousands more. Political parties and independent trade unions were banned and strict censorship was imposed on the press. The regime centralized all political power in Madrid; fused executive, legislative, and judicial power; and made Franco dictator for life. The Catholic Church's official status and privileges were restored, and manifestations of regional culture, including the speaking of regional languages, were banned. The severe repression during the first three decades of Francoist rule quashed the democratic opposition. Franco eased the repression in the 1960s, and protest activity increased, but rapid economic growth during that period helped preserve the regime's strength.

Many feared that the death of Franco in 1975 would rekindle a conflict between the two Spains. Instead, Spain's transition to democracy between 1975 and 1978, after four decades of authoritarianism, evolved as what has been hailed as a model of

Box 7.1   Spain's Unusual Transition to Democracy

Spain's transition to democracy was unique. It took place fairly rapidly and occurred without major bloodshed. Moreover, leaders of the Francoist regime carried out a controlled and methodical transition, negotiating with the democratic opposition over the new rules of the game. As a result of this transition there were never any attempts to punish Francoist leaders for human rights abuses during authoritarian rule. Political scientists were quick to coin terms for this unique transition such as *transition through transaction, transition from above, negotiated transition*, and *pacted transition*. Spain's model of transition presents a nice contrast to neighboring Portugal, where in 1974 democracy was brought about by a coup of junior military officers. A social revolution and considerable violence followed. Spain also differs from Eastern Europe, where authoritarian regimes quickly disintegrated. The Spanish model of transition remains unique in Europe, but it was followed rather closely in countries on other continents such as Chile and South Africa.

peaceful regime change. The transition to democracy was not only peaceful, but it appears to have resolved two of the historical cleavages, regime type and church and state, that formed the basis of the struggle between the two Spains. The center-periphery cleavage persists but no longer directly threatens democratic rule (see Box 7.1).

Democracy and Spain's Historical Cleavages

Monarchy versus Republic, or Both?

The transition to democracy was accomplished peacefully because of several factors. First, members of the Franco regime, not the democratic opposition, initiated it. Opposition to Franco was strong and growing, but it alone could not force the regime to democratize. The transition to democracy was stewarded by *King Juan Carlos*, Franco's handpicked successor as head of state, and *Aldolfo Suárez*, a former Francoist bureaucrat and Juan Carlos's second prime minister. Second, the transition to democracy was carried out within the existing legal framework of the Franco regime. The laws that called for the first democratic elections and the dissolution of the Francoist legislature, for example, were passed according to the Francoist legal framework. Third, key leaders of the transition not only promoted democratic change, but they assumed a leading role in the early years of the new democracy. Adolfo Suárez, the last prime minister appointed by Franco, thus became the first elected prime minister. The last authoritarian head of state, Juan Carlos, became the first head of state under the democratic Constitution of 1978.

Finally, many aspects of the transition to democracy were negotiated between the Francoist reformers and the democratic opposition, giving rise to what has been elsewhere termed a "transition through transaction."[2] The negotiated nature of the transition helps explain why the Constitution of 1978 was purposely vague on a number of key issues, including regional devolution and certain social issues. Moreover, the negotiated nature of the transition meant that there were never any purges or prosecution of Francoist officials for human rights abuses or corruption, nor were there any official attempts to attack the Francoist past or to erase the symbols of Franco's regime. Herein lies what may be the chief asset of Spain's transition to democracy. The historical enmity between advocates of different types of political regimes has been virtually eliminated by Spain's transition. Francoist loyalists were assured that the Franco regime implemented (indeed legislated) the transition to democracy, and were assuaged by the continued presence of Franco's handpicked successor in the role of head of state. Today democrats can take comfort from the fact that Spain's democracy is now fully established and widely supported, even by the historically anti-democratic Spanish right. As will be noted later, Spain has a progressive constitution and legitimate political system. Both sides can be relieved that the change of regimes took place without much bloodshed, in marked contrast to the bitter precedent set during the Spanish Civil War.

Church and State: Bridging the Religious Divide

The feud over the proper role of the Catholic Church in society has been a crucial Spanish historical cleavage. Maintaining a key role in Spain's history, the Church was a central actor in the Counter-Reformation, and Spain was the birthplace of the Jesuit order. The Spanish Inquisition, an institution that epitomized religious intolerance, was run by the Spanish Church and was not abolished until the 1830s. Many liberals and progressives viewed Spain's decline as the result of its cultural and economic backwardness, and the dominant historical role of the Church was seen as a chief culprit. Church supporters rallied to defend their privileges and blamed the forces of secularism for Spain's problems. From the Napoleonic Wars of the early nineteenth century to the 1930s, Spain experienced a protracted and often violent struggle between the Church and political liberals. During this period, the Church begrudgingly accepted the end of the old regime and a loss of much of its power, but it was able to secure generous state financial support from weak liberal regimes, and dominance in important areas, like education. The religious cleavage reached its apogee during the Spanish Second Republic, when a radical republican regime attempted to secularize Spain and limit the Church's role in Spanish politics. The religious cleavage became highly dramatized and exaggerated during the Second Republic. Liberals and leftists, angered over historic Church support for authoritarian rule, and convinced of the need to modernize Spain, advanced a highly antagonistic anticlerical agenda that was deeply offensive to many Spaniards, and it turned many against democracy. Repression of the Church (including expulsion of religious orders and attacks on clergy) during the republic quickly turned the Church into one of the major supporters of Franco's Nationalist rebels.

Church support for Franco paid off handsomely. A thoroughly united church emerged "triumphant" from the Spanish Civil War, and it no longer needed to seek compromises with liberal regimes. The Franco regime was unabashedly confessional from the start, and all other religions were initially banned and repressed. The Church was given control over marriage, was allowed to run about half of all Spanish schools, and was handed the reigns of state censorship. The Francoist state lavished the Church with generous economic benefits.

The Church was a pillar of Franco's regime, but by the mid-1950s growing sectors of the Church began to distance themselves from authoritarian rule. Socially progressive currents of thought in Rome began to influence the Spanish Church, and in the 1960s parts of the Church came to represent one of the most serious sources of opposition to Franco. The Church thus entered Spain's transition to democracy as a disunited force. Some conservative Catholic organizations (like the secretive lay society, the Opus Dei) had advocated the continuation of authoritarian rule while other sectors of the Church wholeheartedly endorsed democratization. Given the historical intensity of the religious cleavage, many observers were surprised by the relatively neutral role assumed by the Church during the transition to democracy. However, as noted later in this chapter, there is lingering evidence of the presence of the religious factor in Spanish politics.

Resolving the Center-Periphery Cleavage

Another historical trademark of Spanish politics has been the center-periphery cleavage. In the twentieth century this issue was also associated with contending attempts to explain Spain's decline. Many readers may think of Spain as a single nation with a single language. However, most people in Barcelona, for example, would take issue with this characterization, noting that Spain currently contains many regional ethnic identities (*Basques, Catalans, Galicians, Castillians,* etc.), and that there are many Spanish languages (Basque, Catalan, Galician, etc.), including Castillian (what most people incorrectly call "Spanish"). An ardent advocate of centralism would likely flinch at this characterization of Spain. The role of regionalism in contemporary Spanish politics will be discussed in more depth later, but the composition of Spain and the degree of centralization and decentralization have long been subject to different interpretations.

There has been much speculation about the causes of Spain's intense regionalism, but many observers have noted that for centuries Spaniards have been more loyal to their families, towns, and regions than to the central state. Spain is one of Europe's largest countries, and its mountainous terrain and poor infrastructure historically isolated communities from one another. Car travel between Madrid and Barcelona (about 300 miles), Spain's two largest cities, took nine hours up until the late 1970s. There may also be historical reasons for the intensity of Spanish regionalism. The invasion of the Moors from North Africa in A.D. 711 shattered a budding national identity, and it forced the retreating Christians into isolated "statelets." During much of the long struggle to retake the Iberian Peninsula from Moslem forces, these isolated regions retained significant autonomy. Attempts to unify Spain under a centralized monarchy during the fifteenth century were far less complete than is often assumed, and the image of a unified Catholic Spain that was able to build a vast global empire ignores the reality of persistent regional identity.

Another foreign invasion, this time by Napoleon at the start of the nineteenth century, was also unable to extinguish regionalism despite the Napoleonic penchant for centralization. Attempts to abolish historic privileges of the Basque country, for example, gave rise to a fierce, politically conservative Basque nationalism, knows as Carlism. Two bitter and protracted wars waged by Carlist forces (1841 and 1876) were unable to restore regional privileges in the Basque Country, and they helped intensify the center-periphery cleavage. By the end of the nineteenth century, there was considerable popular support in the Basque Country and Catalonia, two of the wealthiest and most industrialized regions of Spain, for greater political autonomy from Madrid.

During the Spanish Second Republic, the center-periphery cleavage intensified. Republican leaders actively supported statutes guaranteeing autonomy to the Basque Country and Catalonia. These moves, and calls for outright independence by radical nationalists in both regions, frightened the Spanish right and helped precipitate the Spanish Civil War.

Basques and Catalans were cruelly punished for their support of the Republic, and both regions experienced some of the harshest repression during and after the Civil War. Perhaps the most famous symbol of this repression is Pablo Picasso's *Guernica*, a painting depicting the aerial bombardment of the Basque town of Guernica in 1937. Franco immediately revoked political and economic autonomy and harshly circumscribed the use of regional languages—street names were "Castillianized"—and cultural practices. This repression, particularly ruthless in the Basque Country, gave rise in the 1950s to new Basque separatist and terrorist movements.

The regional cleavage remained potentially explosive on the eve of Spain's transition to democracy. Strong regional movements were present in Catalonia and the Basque Country, and anti-Franco Basque violence had constituted the single greatest threat to the survival of the Franco regime. Spain's military and much of the Spanish right were vehemently opposed to any kind of federal system, and they steadfastly opposed threats to the "unity of Spain." As described later, the Constitution of 1978 would strike some unusual compromises in an attempt to resolve once and for all the regional question in Spanish politics.

Economics and the Weakening of Historical Cleavages

To a remarkable extent, Spain's transition to democracy has managed to overcome the cleavages of regime type, church and state, and center-periphery. However, by Franco's death in 1975 economic growth and the concomitant social and cultural changes had done much to erode the passions these schisms aroused. In comparative perspective Spain stands out because its transformation from an underdeveloped, largely agrarian country to a modern urban one occurred in a very short time period. At the turn of the century, most of the population lived in villages and small towns. By the 1960s, an economic boom that would be called the "miracle" turned Spain into a largely urban country; by 1994, 77 percent of Spaniards were living in urban settings.[3]

The economic boom also contributed to a more secular and less isolationist culture. During the 1960s, the inability of the Francoist economy to employ much of its population led to a massive emigration of labor, but during that same time, hordes of foreign tourists began to discover Spain's beaches. Tourist development combined with industrialization and economic growth thus created a new politically and socially tolerant middle class.

Structure and Process of the Political System

The Constitution of 1978: The Constitution of Consensus

As noted earlier, members of the Franco regime initiated Spain's democratization after the death of the dictator. The nature of the emerging regime, embodied in the Constitution of 1978, resulted from a set of complex negotiations between political forces. The writing of the Constitution was officially entrusted to the *Cortes*—the Spanish legislature—elected in June 1977. The constitutional committee of the Lower House of the Cortes then appointed a seven-member subcommittee of "experts" to write the document.[4] This contrasted markedly from previous Spanish constitutions, which were more partisan documents. The subcommittee operated secretly, and it produced a document that was full of compromises. A joint session of the legislature approved the Constitution of 1978 with more than 90 percent voting affirmatively, but there remained some opposition and considerable abstention by parliamentarians of the right and regional groups.

The Constitution gained considerable legitimacy in a referendum held in November 1978, when 87.8 percent of the voters approved it. Parties of the extreme right, and some regional leftist groups called for a "no" vote, while some more moderate regional groups called for abstention. The relatively high 32-percent abstention rate that resulted was considered by the Constitution's opponents to cast some doubt on its legitimacy, but the Constitution became law on December 27, 1978.

The Constitution that emerged borrows heavily from other European countries. It is the longest and most complex constitution in Spanish history, but observers have noted that some aspects of it are imprecise and vague, in part due to compromises required by Spain's unusual transition. Figure 7.1 provides an overview of the institutions of Spanish government as established by the Constitution.

The Monarchy

Perhaps the greatest compromise required of the Spanish left is exemplified in the constitutional provision establishing Spain as a parliamentary monarchy. In theory, the creation of a monarchy in the 1970s should have been anathema to the left not only because it is an unabashedly elitist institution, but because it installed Juan Carlos de Borbón, Franco's handpicked successor as king. Worse, Juan Carlos was not even the legitimate Bourbon heir to the throne. He was the grandson of Alfonso XIII, the last reigning Bourbon monarch and the son of the legitimate heir, Don Juan de Borbón. During the Francoist regime, Don Juan lived in exile and openly opposed the dictator. Curiously, he allowed his son Juan Carlos, at the age of 10, to be educated in Spain under Franco's tutelage. Under the close supervision of Franco, Juan Carlos was thoroughly socialized in the practices and protocol of authoritarian Spain. Despite the fact that Franco designated Juan Carlos to be his successor in 1969, Juan Carlos's father did not renounce his right to the throne until after Franco died, when the democratic reform was well underway. Juan Carlos's early willingness to be Franco's designated successor, and his accession to the throne after Franco's death in 1975, despite the opposition of his exiled father,

FIGURE 7.1   The Spanish Political Process

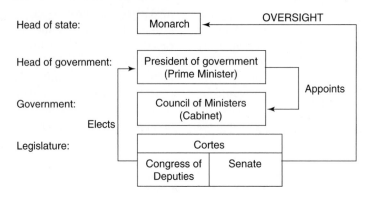

"tainted" the young prince in the eyes the democratic opposition.

In addition to being a hereditary post, Spain's monarchy is openly sexist: The constitution adopts the rule of primogeniture, giving the first born son of the monarch the right to accede to the throne and allowing for a queen only if there are no male heirs. However, during the transition to democracy, the left's assurance that it would preserve the monarchy was crucial to the success of Spain's negotiated transition, and it did much to create continuity between the authoritarian and democratic regimes.

Much of the left's initial resistance to a monarchy was mitigated by the strict limits placed on the institution, clearly spelled out in Articles 56–65 of the Constitution. Spain's monarchy is today a largely symbolic institution, and the powers of the monarch leave little room for discretion. The monarch is head of state but is more of an arbiter than a key actor. The monarch has no power to legislate but is entitled to a weekly meeting with the head of government in order to keep abreast of current affairs. The head of state does promulgate laws and issue decrees, but only those already approved by the parliament. One of the greatest powers enjoyed by the monarch, especially in the context of Spain's transition to democracy, is that the monarch is commander in chief of the armed forces.

As in the United Kingdom, Spain's monarch can, under certain circumstances exercise a degree of discretion. The Monarch is charged with appointing the prime minister from among the top candidates for the post, but except in rare circumstances the choice is strictly limited. The monarch must designate the leader of the largest party in the lower house as candidate for the prime minister's office. Ultimately, the legislature, not the monarch, determines who is to be head of government. The monarch's chief role is to act as Spain's ambassador to the world, a job in which Juan Carlos has excelled.

As noted before, for a variety of reasons the monarchy in general, and Juan Carlos in particular, initially had an authoritarian image. Juan Carlos's chief accomplishment has been to cautiously but deliberately democratize the monarchy in the eyes of a vast majority of Spaniards. His sacking of Franco's last prime minister, Carlos Arias Navarro, in July 1976 was widely applauded, but his replacement with Adolfo Suárez, former head of Franco's only legal political party and a career Francoist bureaucrat, brought howls of protest from the democratic opposition. In retrospect, however, it is clear that the King appointed a young politician with the will and skill to carry out a transition to democracy. While Juan Carlos took a low profile during much of the transition, there is little doubt that he backed Suárez unflinchingly.

Juan Carlos's performance as Spain's first democratic monarch has done much to win popular support for the monarchy. During the transition, Juan Carlos took great pains not to alienate supporters of the Franco regime. Up until the first

Box 7.2 The Role of Leadership in Spain's Democracy

The King's identification with democracy was further enhanced during the attempted coup of February 1981. Despite initial concerns (and obvious hopes from sectors of the military) that the King might support the coup, his actions to defend democracy were unambiguous. He forcefully ordered the military back to the barracks and was widely hailed by political leaders of every stripe. Had King Juan Carlos wavered the coup might have ended Spain's young experiment with democracy. His behavior underscores the importance of effective leaders in the consolidation of new democracies. Moreover it underscores the fact that undemocratic institutions like the monarchy can sometimes contribute to modern democracies. The King's role during the crisis strengthened the democratic system and gave the monarchy additional legitimacy

democratic elections of June 1977, Juan Carlos faithfully executed his duties as a Francoist head of state, never publicly rejecting the dictatorship (to which he owed his position), but gently supporting the democratic reforms implemented by Suárez. The King's credentials (he was trained in all three branches of the Francoist armed forces, and had sworn loyalty to Franco) made it easier for all but the most die-hard Francoists to support, or at least tolerate, the transition to democracy.

For the democratic opposition and much of the public, Juan Carlos has established a monarchy that is one of the world's most modern and least ostentatious and that is difficult to oppose. There is no royal court. The royal family pays taxes and lives relatively modestly, having refused to live in the Palacio de Oriente, a huge eighteenth-century palace in Madrid. By some estimations, Spain's monarchy is the least costly in Europe, costing less than half that of the UK monarchy. Juan Carlos is a very visible monarch, visiting towns throughout Spain on a regular basis, occasionally addressing audiences in local languages. He is admired as a great sportsman and is regularly seen on Spain's ski slopes.

The King has tended to avoid controversy, and his public statements are usually a masterpiece of diplomacy. He has, however, been an advocate of political compromise, calm, and common sense. He has denounced terrorism and has been an outspoken advocate of the democratic system. Opinion polls show that Juan Carlos is immensely popular and that a large majority of Spaniards support the monarchy and view it as an essential component of democracy.

Perhaps as a reflection of the King's popularity, the Spanish press treated the royal family with kid gloves up until about 1990, when some questions were raised about the "jet-setting" royal family; Spain's leading newspaper even suggested that the King might be having an affair. Still, the Spanish press has not savaged the monarchy to the extent witnessed in the United Kingdom (see Box 7.2).

The Legislature

Spain's Constitution specifies that the *Cortes Generales*, or parliament, is the repository of national sovereignty (Article 1.3). However, although Spain is formally a parliamentary system, its legislature has not turned out to be a very powerful political institution. The framers of the Constitution took great pains to create a strong executive and in the process weakened the legislature. Some researchers have claimed that this weakness stems in part from the political culture of Francoism, which was explicitly antiparliamentary.[5] Franco viewed parties as private interest groups that used the Cortes to subvert the national interest. Parliament was powerless under Franco, even though it did play a surprising support role in the transition to democracy. The frailty of political parties has no doubt contributed to the weakness of the Cortes.

The negotiated transition to democracy also weakened the Cortes. In order to avoid potentially dangerous political confrontation, most key policies during the first years of democracy were the result of an informal consensus among party elites. This consensus came to an end in 1979, and from 1979 to 1982 there was a precarious minority government. However, the failed military coup of 1981 delayed any resurgence of an independent parliament, and party leaders made agreements during this period without much regard for parliament. By 1982, when the Spanish Socialist Workers Party (PSOE) won the first ever absolute majority in the young democracy, the party easily controlled the Cortes because of its voting strength and the extraordinary party discipline within the governing Socialists. From 1982 to 1989 the Socialists had no effective political opposition, creating an incentive for them to ignore the opposition and further weakening parliamentary life. After 1989, as a result of the eroding Socialist majority, the weakening of party discipline, and a number of high-profile corruption scandals, the Cortes became more assertive.

Spain's legislature consists of two houses: the *Congress of Deputies* (lower house) and the *Senate* (upper house) (see again Figure 7.1). Each house elects a president, and the president of the Congress of Deputies is the equivalent of the Speaker of the House in the United Kingdom. The chamber presidents have the power to enforce the rules of each house. The King formally proposes prime ministerial candidates to the lower house president. Both houses are organized around "party groups," which are comprised of a minimum of 15 deputies (10 in the lower house), or 5 or more deputies who won at least 15 percent of the vote in a given region. Most parliamentary groups are made of deputies from the same party. All members who do not have a party group to join (members of small, mostly regional parties) are forced to join the "mixed group." Party groups, in turn, dominate the running of each chamber. They determine who is allowed to participate in debate, and who sits on committees. Party group leaders become the big hitters within the legislature, and in each house they sit on the Council of Party Spokesmen, chaired by the chamber president. This group sets the agenda for the legislature and assigns tasks to committees.

CONGRESS OF DEPUTIES The lower house of the legislature contains 350 members elected to four-year terms. Compared with their European counterparts Spain's parliamentarians are on the weaker end of the spectrum. Ninety percent of the laws passed by the Cortes originate with the government.[6] Only about 12 percent of initiatives from parliamentary groups are passed. The Cortes sets very strict limits on the activities of individual members, and officially designated parliamentary groups introduce almost all of legislation that originates within the Congress.

Spain's legislature has also failed to play much of a "watchdog" role and has generally been ineffective in controlling the executive. The Constitution's framers saw to it that the Cortes could not assert itself too boldly vis-à-vis the government. The *constructive vote of no confidence*, similar to that used in Germany, requires the Congress of Deputies to agree on a replacement for prime minister before voting out a head of government. To date no prime minister has been removed from office by such a vote. In its first 20 years the Congress of Deputies failed to produce many investigative commissions of real importance. However, in the last years of Socialist government, the Cortes began to assert itself more. As in the United Kingdom, Spanish members of parliament regularly question members of government during a weekly question time. Parliamentary groups may force a public debate on key policy issues in order to embarrass or challenge the government. Either house of parliament has the constitutional power to require testimony of government members at hearings. Parliamentary committees do play a crucial role in the legislative process. Every proposed law must be scrutinized and approved, and can be amended, by standing committees. Since the majority party in the Cortes has always dominated the committees, governments generally get their way with most legislation, but committees can and sometimes do substantially alter legislative outcomes.

The role of the Cortes as a recruiting mechanism for government positions is somewhat limited by the fact that government members do not need to be members of Parliament, though about 60 percent of ministers are in fact elected members. Indeed two leaders of political parties were not parliamentarians when chosen to head their parties (José Aznar, currently prime minister, and Julio Anguita of the Communist Party). There has been a high degree of turnover in the Spanish legislature. During the Socialists' tenure from 1982 to 1996, about a third of the deputies were first timers in the legislature, a proportion higher than in most Western European legislatures. This is in part due to the low prestige and few incentives attached to being a deputy. The Cortes is not well connected to the organized interests or decision-making centers, and a law issued in 1983 makes it illegal to be a member of Parliament and hold certain jobs. In addition, salaries are very low, and the power structure in the Cortes is very hierarchical, which means that newer members of Parliament have little power.

The weakness of the Cortes on a day-to-day basis should not obscure the important role it played in the consolidation of democracy in June 1977, when it functioned as the only elected body in the country and, at least initially, performed a crucial legitimation function. The relative balance among parliamentary forces encouraged cooperation among them. Initially, the Cortes played a key role in ratifying agreements, such as the Moncloa Pacts, a key set of macroeconomic accords agreed upon in 1978. Regional autonomy accords were pushed through by the parliamentary representatives from different regions. The constitution was in fact written by a small number of parliamentarians representing most political groups.

THE SENATE Spain's upper house is composed of 257 members, 208 elected under a plurality system that has made it far less representative than the lower house, and 49 indirectly elected through Spain's 17 *Autonomous Communities,* identified in the map at the beginning of this chapter. The Senate was originally intended to be representative of Spain's regions, but the parliaments of the Autonomous Communities, rather than the Senate, have performed this function. The Senate suffers from the fact that it is widely regarded as a superfluous body. Its main power is that it has two months to review bills passed by the Congress of Deputies. Senators themselves have called for an overhaul of the chamber to make it truly representative of the Autonomous Communities, but such reform will require a constitutional amendment.

It is Spain's lower house, the Congress of Deputies, that is charged with most important duties—formally electing the prime minister, approving or rejecting votes of confidence submitted by the prime minister, passing censure motions against the government, ratifying decree or laws, and authorizing states of emergency. The Senate can initiate legislation, but this has rarely happened, and it can amend lower house laws, but the amendments must always be hammered out in a joint Congress of Deputies-Senate committee. A simple majority in the Congress can override Senate amendments and vetoes of Congress legislation. The Senate can delay legislation for a maximum of 2 months for ordinary bills, and 20 days for urgent ones.

The Legislative Process

Most laws originate as Council of Ministers–sponsored *proyectos de ley* (government bills), although *proposiciones de ley* (private-member bills) occasionally pass. Figure 7.2 illustrates how such proposals become law. Once sent to the Congress of Deputies leadership and published in the official bulletin of Congress a proposed law is sent to legislative committees for amendments. A bill that survives this scrutiny must then be approved by a majority of the Congress. The Senate is then given 15 days to consider and amend the bill. Once obtaining a majority in the Senate, the bill is submitted to the monarch (who must ratify it within 15 days) and published in the official State Bulletin.

The Head of Government

Spain's head of government is officially called the *President of the Government,* although the officeholder is actually a prime minister. The "presidential" designation is significant since the framers of Spain's 1978 Constitution created one of the most powerful executives in Europe, clearly seeking to avoid the impotence of prime ministers during both previous republics. In both cases weak heads of government led to weak government and political instability.

The 1978 Constitution created a prime minister who is responsible only to the Cortes, which as we saw earlier has generally been a meek institution,

FIGURE 7.2 The Spanish Legislative Process

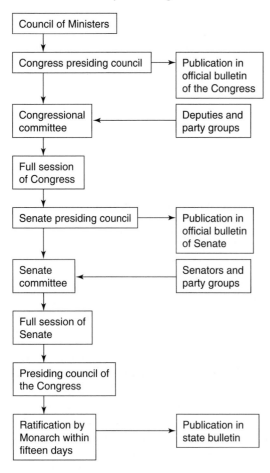

Source: Peter J. Donaghy and Michael T. Newton, *Spain: A Guide to Political and Economic Institutions* (Cambridge, England: Cambridge University Press, 1987), p. 59.

ter can also request that the monarch dissolve the legislature (only once per year, and not while a motion of censure against the government is being considered).

After parliamentary elections, the monarch selects a prime minister-designate who must then win a vote of investiture in the Congress of Deputies. Once elected, prime ministers may serve as head of government for a maximum of four years, but there are no limits to the number of times that a prime minister may be reelected. Prime ministers can request a vote of confidence at any time during their term of office. *Felipe González*, prime minister between 1982 and 1996, called and won such a vote in April 1990. As noted earlier, prime ministers may be ousted by the legislature only if legislators can agree on a replacement (Article 113). The legislature cannot simply remove an unpopular head of government via such a method: the entire government falls whenever a head of government is ousted, making the constructive vote of no confidence a measure that is likely to be employed rarely.

Table 7.1 lists the 11 governments and 5 prime ministers since the death of Franco. Two heads of government, Adolfo Suárez and Felipe González, have dominated the office and have gone a long way toward shaping its powers. Adolfo Suárez (1976–1981), despite having immense prestige associated with his stewardship of the transition to democracy, turned out to be a very weak head of government who was beholden to leaders of his coalition's factions. The minority status of both of his governments exacerbated his dependence on his squabbling coalition partners. Suárez's more conservative successor, Leopoldo Calvo Sotelo (1981–1982), was equally weak due to his lack of charisma, his coalition's rapid disintegration, and the continuing minority status of his government. Felipe González, a Socialist, was elected in 1982 in the first alternation of power in the young democracy. From 1982 to 1989 he presided over the first single-party majority government in Spanish history and was thus in a perfect position to enhance the powers of his office. Moreover, during much of that time he faced a disorganized and demoralized political opposition. Beginning with the elections of 1989, González's strength slowly began to erode, and from 1993 to 1996 González governed with a

especially when governments have enjoyed a majority in the legislature. Moreover, Spain's prime minister has unusually strong powers vis-à-vis the legislature. Article 98.2 gives the prime minister broad powers to form and lead a government and to appoint anybody to the Cabinet, whether or not a member of the Cortes, and whether or not a member of the governing party (both types of individuals formed part of governments of Felipe González between 1982 and 1996). The prime minister can add Cabinet members "without portfolio"—without parliamentary approval. The prime minis-

Table 7.1   Spanish Heads of Government, 1975–1996

Head of Government	Term	Party	Elected by Cortes After General Elections?	Minority, Coalition, or Majority Government
Carlos Arias Navarro	1974–1975	Appointed by Franco		n/a
Carlos Arias Navarro	1976–1976	Appointed by King		n/a
Adolfo Suárez	1976–1977	Appointed by King		n/a
Adolfo Suárez	1977–1979	UCD	yes	minority
Adolfo Suárez	1979–1981	UCD	yes	minority
Leopoldo Calvo Sotelo	1981–1982	UCD	no	minority
Felipe González	1982–1986	PSOE	yes	majority
Felipe González	1986–1989	PSOE	yes	majority
Felipe González	1989–1993	PSOE	yes	minority
Felipe González	1993–1996	PSOE	yes	minority
José María Aznar	1996–2000	PP	yes	minority
José María Aznar	2000–	PP	yes	majority

Source: Adapted from Paul Heywood, "Governing a New Democracy: The Power of the Prime Minister in Spain," *West European Politics,* 14, No. 2 (April 1991): p. 98.

minority in the legislature. Many observers argued that the immense powers granted to the government, the meekness of the legislature, and the Socialists' long tenure in power had created the conditions under which significant corruption thrived. Indeed, the corruption scandals that plagued Socialist administrations in the 1990s were largely responsible for their fall from power. The conservative José María Aznar was elected in 1996 but lacked a parliamentary majority. He was forced to work with regional parties in order to maintain a parliamentary majority until his party obtained an absolute majority in the March 2000 elections.

This brief overview clearly reveals that Spanish heads of government have been strongest when their parties are unified. Indeed, given the constitutional advantages enjoyed by prime ministers, it is fair to say that the most significant limits to their power come from within their own parties. Thus from 1982 to 1990 the Socialists maintained iron (some would say quasi-authoritarian) internal party discipline, and the power of Felipe González was greatly enhanced.[7] After 1990, when chief party whip Alfonso Guerra was implicated in a corruption scandal, internal party dissent increased, there were calls for an internal democratization of the PSOE, and González became somewhat less powerful.

Two Spanish prime ministers, Adolfo Suárez and Felipe González, used their immense personal charm and charisma to enhance their power in office. Unlike some parliamentary systems, Spain's prime ministers have generally remained aloof vis-à-vis the legislature and the prime minister's own party. González, for example, went long periods without appearing in the Cortes (there is no constitutional requirement for the prime minister to appear before the legislature), and near the end of his stint in power he was clearly much more interested in foreign than domestic affairs.

It would be a mistake, however, to argue that Spain's prime minister has limitless power, even though it seems valid to assert that the Cortes does not exercise much control over the head of government. During the first two decades of Spain's democracy, prime ministers often appeared to make decisions that represented compromises with entrenched political interests, both at the domestic and international level. As late as the 1980s, for example, prime minister González reversed his own (and his party's) position on taking Spain out of the North Atlantic Treaty Organization (NATO). He did so in part to mollify the Spanish military, which favored NATO membership, and in part to satisfy business interests, who viewed NATO membership and Spain's desired membership in the European Union (EU) as conjoined. On the domestic level, the unwillingness of the Socialists to liberalize Spain's restrictive abortion law, despite a legislative majority and widespread public support, suggests that the Church can exercise some limits on the government's power.

The Judicial System[8]

Reforming Spain's judicial system was one of the greatest challenges facing the democratic regime. Under Franco, the courts were identified with the harsh repression against opposition to the dictatorship. As late as September 1975, and despite an international outcry, Francoist courts sanctioned the execution without trial of Basque terrorists arrested under martial law.

The courts had little independence during the Franco regime, and most judges were appointed directly by Franco's government. In an attempt to depart from this authoritarian legal tradition, the 1978 constitution established a *Constitutional Court* as the supreme arbiter in political disputes and attempted to give it independence from the state. The Court consists of 12 members, all of them professional lawyers or judges. The Cortes selects eight of the judges (four per house, approved by three-fifths of both chambers), the government proposes two names, subject to the legislature's approval, and the General Council of the Judiciary (discussed later) names the final two. Its members must be independent of any party and cannot actively participate in them. Members are appointed to nine-year terms, with a third of the court renewed every three years. The government or legislature cannot dismiss Constitutional Court judges, and the Court has control over its own budget and organization.

The Constitutional Court can declare any law or government decree unconstitutional; it has the power to rule on a direct appeal by the prime minister, 50 members of either house, assemblies of Spain's Autonomous Communities, or lower court judges. In some cases, individual citizens may appeal to the Court if they feel that their constitutional rights have been violated. The legislature or the government may also ask the Court to rule on the constitutionality of pending legislation.

To date, the Constitutional Court has played a significant role in limiting Spain's powerful government. For example, in 1983 it ruled unconstitutional a major law intended to "harmonize" (and slow down) the devolution of power to Spain's Autonomous Communities. In 1993 it struck down key provisions of a government antiterrorism bill that would have facilitated police search of private homes. Despite this record of opposition to government measures, the Court has been criticized for lacking the political neutrality for which it was designed. During the long Socialist reign (1982–1996), the Socialist legislature was accused of packing the Court with its cronies. The massive backlog of cases and the lack of resources have hampered the effectiveness of the Court, an affliction suffered by all branches of the Spanish judiciary. The Constitution's ambiguity with regard to regional devolution has meant that the Court has been bogged down adjudicating countless disputes between the Autonomous Communities and the central government.

For matters that are not of a constitutional nature, the highest court is the *Supreme Court (Tribunal Supremo)*. This court has been in existence since 1834, but was completely overhauled in 1978 to rid it of its Francoist legacy. The powers of the Supreme Court have been eroded by the creation of the Constitutional Court (generally seen as the most powerful court in Spain), and by the devolution of many of its powers to the Autonomous Communities. Still, in the area of the enforcement of the penal code, the Supreme Court has the final word. In July 1988 the Supreme Court demonstrated its power and independence when it sentenced a former Socialist cabinet member to prison for his role in a government-sponsored antiterrorist death squad.

Each of the 17 Autonomous Communities has its own High Court of Justice *(Tribunales Superiores de Justicia)*, which oversee the administration of justice in each region. These are the highest courts at the regional level and are charged with, among other things, resolving electoral disputes. Each high court has three chambers dealing with civil/penal, administrative, and social matters.

One of the most interesting offices created by the 1978 Spanish Constitution is the *Defensor del*

BOX 7.3   Spain's Assertive New Judiciary

Some Spanish judges have become celebrities in the international arena as well as at home. Baltazar Garzón, a young, independent, and aggressive investigative judge of Spain's National Court, has become an international phenomenon due to his attempt to bring former Latin American military rulers to justice for human rights abuses committed against Spanish citizens during the 1970s and 1980s. Garzón formally requested the extradition of former Chilean dictator Pinochet (who was re-ceiving medical treatment in the United Kingdom) to Spain in 1998, provoking strong opposition from the Chilean government. Despite obvious opposition to Garzón's action (the Aznar government did not want to endanger Spain's close relations with Latin America) the government made no attempt to stop the extradition. The British ultimately refused to extradite Pinochet, but the incident was another sign of the growing independence and prestige of Spain's judiciary.

Pueblo, or Ombudsperson, appointed by the Cortes for a period of five years. Because the appointment requires the approval of a three-fifths majority in each house, the *Defensor* is intended to be a nonpartisan individual. The position was designed to be a watchdog over the administration and to investigate citizen complaints in their dealings with officialdom. The *Defensor* is required to report yearly to the Cortes with a summary of complaints against state agencies.

Despite the initial appointment of a prestigious lawyer, Joaquín Ruíz Giménez, the *Defensor*'s office has been a disappointment to date. Like the attorney general's office, it lacks a sufficient budget and staff. Its functions, only broadly outlined in the Constitution, have yet to be clearly defined. Early on the office was deluged with a huge number of cases, obviously reflecting the pent-up frustration of Spaniards with the bureaucracy. During the Socialist administration, there were complaints by the opposition that the position was an overly partisan one. Eyebrows were raised when the *Defensor* refused to challenge the government in the courts over the controversial Public Security Law, an antiterrorist measure that severely restricted civil liberties.

The Spanish judiciary is supervised by the General Council of the Judiciary, created in an attempt to insulate judges from political pressure. The Council has 20 members, 10 approved by each house of the legislature, for 5-year terms. The Spanish judiciary has clearly made a lot of progress since the Franco regime. Spanish judges cannot be easily removed by the government, are forbidden from holding any other public office, and cannot be members of any political party or trade union. In the 1980s and 1990s the judiciary has played an increasingly aggressive role in combating corruption and limiting the government. In a number of highly publicized corruption scandals beginning in 1990, Spanish judges were put in the spotlight, investigating and prosecuting cases against a variety of top Spanish officials. These investigations greatly enhanced the prestige of Spain's judiciary, converting some judges into national heroes with name recognition and popularity ratings rivaling the top political leaders (see Box 7.3).

While many Spaniards suspected that the Socialist government manipulated the judiciary, the government tended to view the judiciary and its increasingly assertive behavior as conservative and anti-Socialist. During the long Socialist tenure in office, the judiciary attempted to prevent government incursions against civil liberties. In the context of rapidly rising crime and the continued war against terrorism, and as an attempt to mollify the police and military, the Socialists passed the Public Security Law and gave permanent status to a controversial 1977 antiterrorism law. These measures, among other things, gave police broad powers to enter private homes without court order if they suspected criminal activity and to hold suspects incommunicado for long periods of time. In 1995

Prime Minister González admitted that police units had top political leaders under surveillance, increasing demands on the courts for protection of civil liberties against a powerful government. Spanish civil libertarians sought protection from the courts and were partly successful in weakening the law. In 1999 Spain's Constitutional Court dealt a blow to the Aznar government when it overturned the conviction of 23 Basque politicians who had been jailed for airing an election broadcast that supported Basque terrorists. In short, the tension between the government and the judiciary has been an important feature of Spain's political landscape in the 1990s.

The most serious obstacle to the Spanish judiciary has been financial deprivation, not government manipulation. Spain's judiciary is allocated a far smaller share of the budget than its European counterparts. As a result, there is a chronic backlog of cases. For example, in 1983 a fire at a Madrid discotheque killed 80 people, partly as a result of safety code violations, but the matter did not come to trial until 1993. An infamous scandal involving cooking oil poisoning that killed over 600 people in 1981 was still mired in the courts 13 years later.

The inefficiency of the Spanish legal system has damaged its prestige, and only serves to encourage the Spanish tendency to ignore laws and expect little from the administration of justice. Spain's democracy has so far been only partly successful in narrowing the gap between the citizen and the justice system. After two decades of delay, the first implementation of the constitutionally sanctioned jury system in June 1996 may be a first move toward involving Spanish citizens in the administration of justice.

Spain's Autonomous Communities

Despite the long history of regional nationalism, Spanish history offers no precedent for a successful decentralization of power from Madrid. Past attempts to give autonomy to Spain's regions (usually Catalonia and the Basque Country) alienated the Spanish right. The last attempt at decentralization during the Spanish Second Republic helped provoke the Spanish Civil War and precipitated the destruction of democracy. Under Franco all power was centralized in Madrid. Provincial governors, appointed by the dictator and under direct orders of the Ministry of the Interior, ran local government and appointed local officials.

Thus the founders of Spain's democracy after Franco's death sought to address this issue with caution. After protracted debate and much compromise, the 1978 Constitution attempted to establish a middle ground between federalism (favored by the left and regional nationalists) and a unitary state (favored by the right). The result, agree almost all observers, has been a confusing and often contradictory arrangement.

Spain's 1978 Constitution recognizes the right to regional autonomy through the Autonomous Communities (ACs), carefully avoiding the terms "state" or "nation," and without defining the meaning of that term or specifying the exact powers to be enjoyed by these communities. The Constitution left the nuts and bolts of the autonomy-granting process to future legislatures. Moreover, as a result of the interparty bargaining process (in which the Catalans were directly represented), the Constitution provided for a faster route to autonomy for "historic" regions like Catalonia, the Basque Country, and Galicia. These were regions with a history of separate languages and national identity. While all regions aspiring to AC status had to apply for it and complete a tedious set of procedures, the historic regions were presented with far fewer obstacles.

By 1979 autonomy statutes had been approved for Catalonia and the Basque Country, setting off a frenzy in which every region of Spain demanded autonomy. This resulted in the formation of 17 ACs through *devolution*, a chaotic process that frustrated regional nationalists and centralizing rightists alike, and may have encouraged the attempted coup of February 1981 (the *golpistas* had plans to rein in the devolution process). As a result of the attempted coup the governing center-right Union of the Democratic Center (UCD), together with the opposition Socialists, passed a controversial measure designed to slow down the devolution process. The measure gave Spanish law priority over AC law, even in the historic regions. The infuriated Basques and Catalans were able to get the Constitutional Court to throw out about a third of the law in 1983, effectively killing the measure. By then the governing Socialists were not as jittery about a military coup, and they began to expedite the devolution process. By February 1983 all 17 Autonomous Communities were in place, and by the end of that year all had held a regional election. (Catalonia, the Basque Country, Galicia, and Andalusia, the first four to obtain autonomy statutes, had held their first regional parliamentary elections earlier.) In most AC elections the Socialists were able to mirror their earlier success in general elections. With the Socialists a major player in most AC governments, the transfer of power from Socialist-dominated center to socialist-dominated periphery was facilitated.

Currently all ACs have their own statutes of autonomy and each has its own unicameral legislature, a president, an AC public administration, and an AC high court of justice. However, unlike purely federal systems each AC has slightly different powers depending on the negotiations between Madrid and the AC, and the timing and route to autonomy taken by the AC. Some scholars have referred to this arrangement as "asymmetric federalism." By the early 1990s the Socialist government made efforts to transfer identical powers to all ACs, raising fears from Catalans and Basques that they were being stripped of their special privileges as "historic" Autonomous Communities. Under current rules, regional and central governments share powers in many areas (education, health, law and order, civil service, among others), except for those specifically reserved for the central government (defense, foreign policy, and economic policy, among others). In practice the exact nature of the powers enjoyed by the central government and the ACs remains vague. This has further exacerbated the backlog at the Constitutional Court, the body charged with adjudicating disputes between the center and periphery.

Political Culture and Political Socialization

Spanish Political Culture

During Franco's traditional authoritarian regime, Spaniards were encouraged to stay out of politics and to focus their attentions on their families, their work, and other diversions such as sports and the state-censored television. Spain became a political desert, and fear of police repression kept it that way for the vast majority of Spaniards. Public opinion research conducted during Franco's rule documented the consequences of authoritarian rule for Spain's political culture. In 1966 when Spaniards were asked whether "it is better for one person to have all the authority and make all the decisions for us, or for a group of people elected by all citizens to make the political decisions," only 35 percent opted for the more democratic answer.[9] At the time of the democratic transition, about half of Spanish respondents gave authoritarian responses on this and other questions.

By the 1960s, however, Spain's isolation from the democratic world had ended due to emigration, increasing exposure to European ideas, and the concomitants of economic growth. Studies conducted in the 1960s and 1970s began to document the modernization of Spain's political culture. Still, on the eve of the transition, many scholars pondered whether a modern democracy could be constructed with Spain's authoritarian culture. The transition to democracy coincided with a severe economic recession that threatened to undermine the fragile legitimacy of the new democracy.

Such fears have proved to be unfounded. After two decades of democracy, the political culture of Spaniards is no longer that different from other European countries. By 1977, more than two-thirds of Spanish respondents disagreed with the notion that one person should rule, while a vast majority approved of allowing political parties to compete for power. A 1994 study found that while Spaniards were deeply polarized in their views about the Franco regime, they were far less polarized in their support for democratic rule.[10]

However, Spaniards do deviate from the European norm in the areas of political interest and activity. As would be expected, opinion research reveals that after an initial spurt in political interest Spaniards became less interested in politics as the transition has faded. In 1983, less than a decade after the transition, the interest of Spaniards in politics was below that of its European neighbors.[11] On a one-to-four scale (with four indicating the most interest in politics), Spaniards averaged 1.84, while the European Union average was 2.29. A 1984 study measured the frequency of political discussion and found that Spaniards discuss politics less than in other European countries. A 1991 poll found that 74 percent of Spaniards said they were bored or indifferent about politics, revealing a huge reservoir of cynicism among the Spanish public.[12] Perhaps a sign of the years under Franco and the elite-led transition, Spaniards still participate less in politics than their European counterparts.

Other studies confirm the weakness of all types of political associations in Spain compared with other advanced democracies. Some have argued that Spaniards naturally view the state and politics with suspicion, much as they feel an instinctive animosity toward the joining of associations.[13] However, this difference in political involvement is most pronounced among older Spaniards. Younger Spaniards, who were not subjected to Franco's depoliticization, score roughly the same as their European counterparts, suggesting that they have a different, more democratic political culture than their elders. Moreover, Spaniards' lack of political participation has not diminished voter turnout, as discussed elsewhere in this chapter.

The global sociopolitical orientations in Spain are broadly similar to European societies. Spaniards are moderately inclined toward social reformism, and very few take extreme positions on any issue. Indeed, in 1985 Spanish respondents were far less inclined toward conservative positions than in most other European Union countries. Spaniards generally rank the values of liberty and equality about equal.

A number of researchers have studied the major political cleavages in Spanish society. One study concluded that region, religion, and class, together with generational conflict, are the "master cleavages of Spanish politics."[14] However, in contrast with the Second Republic, Spain is now overwhelmingly urban, literate, and industrialized. Reduced church attendance, greater geographical mobility, emigration, and exposure to mass media have made Spain a less parochial society. The intensity of these "master cleavages," therefore, has diminished considerably, and they no longer threaten democratic rule.

Moreover, none of the cleavages are closely linked with partisan identification, a factor that has facilitated the consolidation of democracy.[15]

The regional cleavage, initially feared to be the intractable schism most likely to undermine Spanish democracy, has been shown to be less important than expected.[16] This has partly been the result of the massive internal demographic shift within Spain that brought many immigrants to the Basque Country and Catalonia. These immigrants tend to be less parochial and more attached to a Spanish national identity. Only in the Basque Country, and to a lesser extent, Catalonia, are there significant feelings of alienation toward the Spanish state. Because the regional cleavage is not strongly related to left and right (there is a weak relationship between regionalism and leftism), the danger posed by the regional cleavage has been lessened.

Until recently, most scholars argued that social class is not an important social cleavage in Spanish democracy, despite the fact that inequality in Spain ranks among the highest in Europe. They noted that the growth of a large middle class, the increased social mobility since the 1960s, and the long tenure in power of the Socialist Party (which enjoyed strong support from all social classes) have all helped to weaken this once divisive cleavage. However, a recent study concludes that social class has come to play a crucial role in determining support for Spain's two major parties.[17] Chhibber and Torcal attribute the growing political importance of social class to a strategy by party leaders. With democracy consolidated, party leaders of the left and right now feel comfortable appealing to social class in their party programs.

Several studies have pointed to the surprising continued strength of the religious cleavage in Spanish politics, and the percentage of Spaniards who claimed to have a religious affiliation actually increased slightly between 1978 and 1990. McDonough and his colleagues found that religion is a much stronger cleavage than class or region, even though the latter two are still important, and the religious cleavage appears to have been somewhat resistant to economic and social modernization. At the same time, Spanish society has rapidly become more secularized, and when it comes to politics, religious values no longer are of concern to the overwhelming majority of the public.[18] Religion no longer polarizes Spanish political culture as it once did. By the mid-1990s, McDonough and his colleagues concluded that "religious attachments have little do with popular attitudes toward democracy or toward government in Spain. . . . The day of mobilization against the political system on the basis of religion seems to be over."[19] Moreover, the importance of the religious cleavage is mitigated by the fact that those who are most religious tend to participate less in politics both in conventional political behavior (such as voting and party militancy) but also in protest behavior.[20] Finally, most studies of Spanish public opinion have shown that the intensity of social cleavages diminishes among younger Spaniards. A more secular and less divided Spain appears to be the way of the future.

A key aspect of Spanish political culture is that Spaniards do not feel capable of influencing the political process. However, Spain is rather similar to the rest of Europe in this respect. Public opinion research conducted in the 1990s shows a general lack of a sense of political efficacy among European publics.

In spite of this lack of efficaciousness, Spain's political culture is unique in the high level of support and confidence that people place in the democratic political system. By the time of a 1984 survey, 80 percent said that democracy was preferable to any other form of government. Antidemocratic attitudes were manifested by at most between 8 and 9 percent of respondents, a surprisingly low figure considering the recent experience with authoritarian rule and the persistent economic crisis in the first decades of democracy.[21] A 1999 survey showed that 68 percent of Spanish respondents were very or fairly satisfied with democracy, the fourth highest level within the European Union (the EU average was 56 percent).[22] Twenty-eight percent claimed to be unsatisfied with democracy in Spain, far less than the EU average of 40 percent. The fear that the economic crisis of the mid-1970s and the persistence of extraordinarily high levels of unemployment might erode the legitimacy of democratic rule proved unwarranted. Indeed, Spanish survey results demonstrate that "support for democracy rose despite poor state performance" and they confirm the conclusion of other scholars that the behavior of Spanish political elites and the centrist orientation of Spain's party system were able to prevent political polarization that might otherwise have overwhelmed Spain's young democracy.[23] A recent European Union study developed an aggregate indicator of support for and trust in national political systems. The results show that Spaniards' view of their political system is close to the European average.[24] Germans, Britons, and Danish citizens all had considerably more negative views of their political systems.

Education

Contemporary Spain is a highly educated and literate nation. Only 3.5 percent of Spaniards (mostly older citizens) are illiterate. Franco invested significant resources in education during the economic boom of the 1960s, and since democratization Spain's educational system has received a considerable boost. Unlike the United Kingdom, education in Spain has been remarkably accessible to people of all social classes, and to women (there are more women students than men in Spanish universities), and there is little of the elitism surrounding education that exists in the UK. The desire to obtain a college education, for example, does not vary considerably among classes. There is no Spanish equivalent of Britain's Oxford or Cambridge, and no well-established hierarchy among Spain's universities.

About one-third of Spanish schoolchildren are educated at private schools, half of which are owned by religious orders and the rest secular. Because of the shortage of schools in Spain, UCD governments like their predecessors from the Franco regime, allowed some Catholic private schools to provide state-subsidized places for students. This practice was expanded under the PSOE, and currently about 90 percent of secular private schools and 98 percent of religious schools are run with taxpayers' money. In return, the Socialists required private schools to set standardized admissions procedures and form representative governing bodies. In addition, teachers in these private schools had to be paid directly by the state, giving the state greater control. Students in these schools were given the option of not taking religion classes. These and other measures were deeply resented by many middle-class parents, and by the Catholic Church, as state encroachment on their educational freedom. Protests over Socialist educational policy produced some of the largest mass demonstrations of the democratic period, but the protests and an appeal to the Constitutional Court failed to stop the reforms.

The Socialists made educational reform one of their chief priorities, and in the early 1990s they overhauled the entire structure of Spanish education. The government attempted to alleviate a significant source of educational inequality by providing free preschool from ages 4 to 6. Since the recent reforms, Spanish children start primary education at age 6, and then progress to secondary education (ages 13 to 16). Students can then leave school or pursue a *Bachillerato* (high school diploma), from ages 16 to 18. After completing this degree, students can either enter university or attend state-funded vocational education.

The Socialists modernized the curriculum of Spanish schools as well. Foreign language training (English is now the predominant foreign language) is mandatory beginning at age 8. The Socialists added such topics as peace studies and environmental conservation, and eliminated gender discrimination from the traditional curriculum. New class size limits were imposed to reduce overcrowding.

About 30 percent of Spanish youth attend university, a higher percentage than in the UK and some other EU states, but given the high rate of course repetition (due to the high failure rate in Spanish university courses), the real figure is probably quite a bit lower.[25] The relatively open access to higher education has produced a serious condition of overcrowding at the relatively small number of Spanish universities. The Socialists tripled the number of university scholarships, but this has only exacerbated the overcrowding problem. The Socialists tried to clear the logjam by facilitating the establishment of more private universities.

The Role of the Media

Visitors to Spain often note the plethora of periodicals on news kiosks and are impressed with their variety and sophistication. However, a 1999 survey showed that only 26 percent of Spaniards read a newspaper daily, well below the EU average of 41 percent.[26] However, newspaper readership has grown quickly since the birth of democracy. Moreover, the relative absence of tabloids that are so popular in other European countries partly explains the low readership statistics. Even the most sensationalistic Spanish dailies contain serious news coverage. Despite small readership, the Spanish press has often played an important role in politics. During the PSOE tenure in office, when there was a strong majority and weak, meek legislature, the press brought a number of important scandals to the public's attention.

Television, however, is the most important medium in Spain, and it has been argued that "Spain is a nation of TV addicts."[27] After the British, Spaniards spend more time than any other Europeans watching TV. One study showed that about 70 percent of Spaniards formed their political views based on what they see on television.[28] Nearly all Spanish homes have TV sets, even in houses that lack other amenities: In Andalusia despite the torrid heat, more homes there had televisions than refrigerators as late as the 1980s.

Given the importance of television, control of that medium has been a political tempest since 1977. Prime Minister Suárez, a former director of the Francoist television monopoly, RTVE (Spanish Radio and Television), dragged his feet when it came to relinquishing state control of the electronic media. Parliamentary oversight has been mostly ignored. Once in office, the PSOE continued to manipulate the electronic media, as state television was unabashedly pro-government in the 1986 NATO referendum.

Slowly, however, the state monopoly of the electronic media has been reduced, in part because of the creation of regional television channels. Spain's state television monopoly ended in 1990 with the birth of private television channels. According to one expert on the media, privatization of television was granted begrudgingly by the Socialists but "is likely to be seen with hindsight as one of their most valuable contributions to the consolidation of democracy, comparable with their taming of the army."[29] Despite the proliferation of private television and radio since that time, two full decades after Franco's dictatorship the state is still the biggest owner of mass media. Private television has eroded the state monopoly, possibly contributing to the erosion of support for the PSOE, but by the end of the 1990s TVE-1 (the main state network) still topped the ratings.

The Importance of Family

The declining importance of the Church, the expansion and secularization of education, and the emergence of a modern media have all weakened traditional forms of socialization in Spain. However, the importance of family is one traditional value that remains surprisingly strong. Opinion research has demonstrated that Spaniards value their families far more than work, friends, leisure, religion, or politics.[30] The continued strength of the family is partially caused by the high rates of unemployment among youths, which has forced about 70 percent of 18- to 29-year-olds to live with their parents. The strength of family may have helped cushion the succession of changes that have swept over Spanish society in recent years, especially the dislocation caused by Spain's integration into the European Union.

Interest Groups

Under Franco, the state controlled virtually all interest groups and incorporated both employees and employers in a state-dominated organization. Even the Catholic Church, which enjoyed the greatest autonomy under Franco, was subject to state control. During the transition, organized interests played a secondary role and were not a crucial force pressuring for democratization.

Trade Unions

Franco's regime depended on labor repression and exclusion, despite some liberalization in the 1960s. Opposition trade unions differed in their approach to the Francoist trade union structure. The Communist *Workers' Commissions (CC.OO)* sought to infiltrate the official trade unions, while the PSOE-affiliated *General Confederation of Workers (UGT)* boycotted them. In the democratic period, these

two trade union organizations became the chief rivals for the allegiance of Spanish workers.[31]

Spain has the lowest union density (the percentage of the workforce affiliated with unions) in Europe, and unions have been divided ideologically, tactically, and regionally. Today only about one-tenth of salaried workers are unionized, down from a high of 57.8 percent in 1978; much higher figures are found in Italy, Greece, and Turkey.[32] The weakness of trade unions would lead one to expect a high level of labor conflict, and indeed Spain currently has one of the highest strike rates in Europe (see Figure 7.3).[33]

Although organizationally weak, Spanish trade unions have considerable influence. The 1980 Workers Statute codified worker representation in the workplace and gave trade unions a role in the process. In firms with 10 to 50 employees, workers are represented by up to 3 elected delegates. In larger firms workers councils are elected. Unions that elect at least 10 percent of council delegates are entitled to participate in collective bargaining negotiations. Thus, even though union membership is low, 80 percent of Spanish workers vote in workers' council elections. According to Schmitter, "Spanish unions have few members (and, therefore, precarious finances), but they exercise impressive power. They negotiate collective contracts that cover a very substantial proportion of the workforce; they regularly win most of the elections held for representatives at the enterprise level."[34] Collective bargaining in Spain by 1990 had covered 68 percent of workers, a very high percentage, but lower than in France (92 percent) or Portugal (79 percent).[35]

The best measure of the strength of individual unions comes from workers' council elections that are conducted in the workplace. In the 1999 union elections, the UGT and CC.OO each won just under 40 percent of the workplace delegates, with the remainder of the votes going to small (often regional) trade unions.

A major change in the role of trade unions has taken place during the first two decades of democracy. The UGT and the CC.OO entered the democratic period as "transmission belts" for the leftist

FIGURE 7.3 Labour disputes

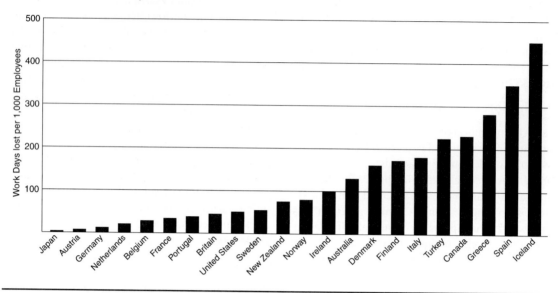

Source: *The Economist,* April 22, 2000.

parties with which they were affiliated. The desire to consolidate democracy took precedence over worker demands. The *Moncloa Pacts* of October 1977, a landmark economic accord between the UCD government and the leftist political parties, required trade unions to toe the party line and accept major sacrifices. Ties between the UGT and the PSOE were especially strong. PSOE members were required to join the UGT and to work with the union. A similar but somewhat looser relationship existed between the CC.OO and the PCE.

The UGT hoped to be compensated for its moderation and patience when the Socialists were elected to office in 1982. The PSOE program called for the creation of 800,000 new jobs. Instead, the Socialists embarked on a harsh austerity policy aimed at the internationalization of the economy and the creation of labor-market "flexibility." The UCD had been too weak to impose such harsh measures as a steep rise in energy prices and the radical streamlining of the steel and shipbuilding sectors. In the first four years of PSOE government, about three-quarters of a million people lost their jobs, and by 1987 Spain's unemployment rate reached 22 percent. The Socialists passed laws making it easier

for Spanish businesses to lay off workers and hire part-time labor.

By the mid-1980s, the UGT rejected the PSOE government's neoliberal economic policies. The CC.OO (Communist-affiliated Workers Commissions) and workers councils at the factory level had long been actively opposed to Socialist economic policy. Massive strikes throughout the 1980s failed to alter PSOE policy. The consistently high rates of unemployment under the Socialists had tested the patience of the UGT, but government attempts to cut welfare and unemployment benefits in 1988 pushed the UGT over the brink. By 1986 the UGT and PSOE were in open conflict. The UGT leader quit his PSOE seat in the Cortes and formally broke links with the Socialists. In the 1989 elections the UGT refused to endorse the Socialists. Since the late 1980s the UGT and CC.OO have often coordinated activities, and there has been talk of a possible merger.

Socialist economic policy not only infuriated the trade unions; it also ended the tripartite wage accords that from 1979 to 1987 had involved the government, unions, and employers. The general strike of December 1988, supported by all major trade unions, was the largest such protest since

1934: some 8 million workers refused to work for a day. The strike pitted organized labor against the Socialist government. Despite its impressive size, it failed to reverse Socialist policy although it undoubtedly weakened the PSOE in the 1989 general elections. Strikes called in the 1990s have to date been even less effective.

The future of the Spanish labor movement would appear to be mixed. On the one hand, prospects for coordinated action between historically rival unions are better than ever. On the other hand, unions remain weak, and despite massive strike activity they were unable to fundamentally alter government economic policy. Since the break between the UGT and the PSOE, unions no longer have the influence of strong political parties to rely on.

Business Organizations

Business associations have been stronger and more unified than organized labor. Near the end of the Francoist regime, a number of entrepreneurial organizations were tolerated, and the *Spanish Confederation of Entrepreneurial Organizations (CEOE)* emerged as the most important of these. The CEOE claims to incorporate 75 percent of firms and an even larger percentage of Spain's total production. It is probably the most successful peak business organization in all of southern Europe. Founded in 1977, the CEOE has 133 affiliated associations and 1.3 million affiliated firms. It includes a very wide spectrum of businesses. In 1983 it incorporated the main small and medium business organization, and most regional business groups have been brought within CEOE.

The CEOE took a hands-off approach to the democratic transition. Only after the attempted coup of 1981 did the CEOE make clear commitments to the democratic system.[36] However, the organization played an important role as spokesperson for business interests in the tripartite wage agreements during the late 1970s and early 1980s.

The CEOE has tended to maintain its distance from political parties. It has supported parties of the right and center, but its relationship with the PSOE has been far better than the PSOE–trade union relationship. The CEOE has been a pro-free market force, complaining about high energy costs and foreign competition. It has opposed tax policies that it believes hurt business and limit investment, and it has steadily assailed "unproductive" public spending. A constant goal of the CEOE is to revise what it views as overly restrictive laws regarding the hiring and firing of workers, many of which date from the Francoist era. Employers claim that they need more flexibility in hiring workers in order to compete with foreign enterprise.

Agricultural lobbies have been very weak in Spain, a reflection of the fact that the importance of agriculture in Spain has steadily declined. By 1994 agriculture employed only 10 percent of the population and accounted for less than 5 percent of the GDP. Agricultural lobbies are divided between high-tech interests that want further EU integration and smaller farmers who fear European competition.

The Armed Forces

Spain's military has a long history of involvement in politics. Since the early nineteenth century, military officers regularly tried to depose governments in support of both conservative monarchist and liberal agendas: From 1820 to 1936 there were 44 *pronunciamientos* (military uprisings), including the antidemocratic rebellion led by Franco. The humiliating defeats suffered by the military as Spain lost the last pieces of its empire, from Cuba to Morocco, made the armed forces defensive and sensitive to criticism by civilians. For most of the twentieth century, civilians accused of offending the military's honor were subject to military courts, and this measure was only repealed after democracy's restoration in 1978.

The Spanish Civil War was a turning point in the history of the armed forces. A significant minority of the military remained loyal to the democratic Republic, and this faction was purged under Franco's regime. The armed forces became a far more reactionary institution. Under Franco the military was given a prominent political role, though the Franco regime was never a pure military dictatorship: Thirty-two out of 114 Francoist cabinet posts were occupied by members of the armed forces. Military members sat on the boards of state-owned companies. Most importantly, the military gained control over all police forces, intelligence organizations, and customs.

Box 7.4   The Last *Pronunciamiento?*

On February 23, 1981, a detachment of Spain's *Civil Guard,* a militarized police force, burst into Congress and stopped a debate on the selection of a new prime minister. Millions of Spaniards following this debate on radio and television heard the gunshots and screams as members of the armed forces attempted to end Spain's democracy. Spain's outgoing prime minister and leader of the transition was pushed to the ground when he tried to resist the rebels. In Valencia, tanks occupied the streets and troops surrounded the Socialist Party headquarters. Most of the armed forces did not support the coup attempt, and King Juan Carlos ordered the rebellious soldiers back to their barracks. The coup attempt fizzled and democracy was saved, but the dramatic events of February 1981 reminded Spaniards that the military remained a serious obstacle to democratic consolidation. Since that time democratic leaders worked hard to discipline, reform, and reorient the Spanish armed forces. These measures have been highly successful, and the modernization and democratization of Spain's military is arguably the greatest achievement of Spain's democracy.

As a result of this beneficial treatment, the military was the group most consistently loyal to Franco.

During the transition, the military begrudgingly accepted the authority of Franco's designated successor, King Juan Carlos, and his prime minister, Adolfo Suárez. Military leaders, however, vigorously opposed aspects of the democratization process, especially the legalization of the Communist Party. Military hard-liners felt increasingly uneasy during the first UCD governments because of increased terrorism (usually directed against military members), rapid devolution of powers to Spain's regions, and squabbling and chaotic governments. Weak UCD governments failed to act decisively in the face of repeated acts of military insubordination.

Ironically, it was the Socialist Party that finally tamed the military. The strength and determination of the PSOE allowed it to act decisively vis-à-vis the military, and most observers would rank the Socialists' reform of the military as their single most important achievement in office. The Socialists streamlined and modernized the army. The PSOE decision to join NATO gave the Spanish military an international role and reduced its focus on domestic security. Most importantly, the PSOE consistently imposed severe punishment on members of the military for acts of insubordination. Spanish law now prohibits political or union activity by active military members, and military members must permanently leave the armed forces if they wish to run for office. The Spanish police forces have been thoroughly civilianized. The military presence in Spanish politics is now negligible.

During the first decades of democracy, a constant point of contention was the requirement that all Spanish males complete mandatory military service. In the 1980s several political parties (though not the PSOE) advocated abolition of the draft. The PSOE liberalized provisions allowing for conscientious objections and cut the length of military service. One of the first acts of the conservative Aznar government in 1996 was to announce a gradual elimination of conscription. Volunteers now make up almost one-half of Spain's armed forces, and by 2003 Spain's transition to an entirely professional military should be mostly complete.

Military spending in Spain rose steadily from 1975 to 1985 as a percentage of gross domestic product, a reflection of attempts to modernize the armed forces. Since 1985, the military budget has fallen steadily as a percentage of GDP. Spain currently spends only 1.3 percent of its GDP on the military, the second lowest in NATO[37] (see Box 7.4).

The Catholic Church

As noted earlier in this chapter, religion is still the strongest cleavage dividing Spaniards. The intensity of the religious question reflects the prominent role of the Catholic Church in Spanish history, and the resentment that this role has often created.

During the transition to democracy, the Catholic Church did not play an active political role. This neutrality reflected the fact that the Church had long ceased to be a unified supporter of authoritarian rule. By the mid-1950s, Catholic progressives began using the Church's autonomy to engage in social activism. By 1975, much of the Church, though not most of the top leadership, was actively opposed to the continuation of authoritarian rule. The bystander role taken by the Church during the transition was one reason that a successful Catholic political party never emerged.

In the democratic regime the Catholic Church has gradually become a more vocal participant in the political process. Church representatives weighed in during the writing of the Constitution, expressing their concerns on issues such as abortion and divorce. In the 1979 elections the Church fought hard to prevent a Socialist victory, publishing a number of documents warning of the dangers of a PSOE government. The Church's pugnacious stance on divorce helped spark the breakup of the UCD in the early 1980s. During the Socialist tenure, the Church reacted bitterly to proposed changes in education. On the eve of the March 2000 general election the Church angered many Spaniards when it openly endorsed the Popular Party.

Much of the defensive posture adopted by the Church has resulted from its weakening presence in Spanish society.[38] In a survey conducted in 1990, 87 percent of respondents said they were members of a religion (of which 99 percent were Catholic). However the data reveal a dramatic decline in religious practice. Slightly over 40 percent of Spaniards (and only about 22 percent of those under 35) claim to attend church at least monthly, a drop of more than 10 percent from a decade earlier. Moreover, church attendance is dropping quickly in the most urban and wealthy areas and among younger Spaniards. The number of Spaniards dedicating themselves to become priests and nuns is falling precipitously.

Democracy has meant a considerable loss of influence and wealth for the Church. Since 1976 Spanish heads of state no longer appoint Spanish bishops, and the revision of the Spanish-Vatican Concordat in 1979 prepared the groundwork for the separation of Church and state. State support for the Church will eventually be phased out, but no Spanish government has yet been willing to pull the plug entirely. Currently, Spanish taxpayers may opt to dedicate part of their taxes to the Church, but only about a third of taxpayers do so.

The ability of the Church to influence voter choice appears to be very weak in Spain. Few Spaniards believe that religious issues should be considered when voting.[39] This research also showed that large percentages of Spaniards opposed the official Church policy on a variety of issues.

As noted earlier, religion continues to be a very strong cleavage in Spanish politics, but the relationship between religiosity and voting is strongest at the political extremes: the PP does best among the most religious and the United Left does best among atheists. The relationship is weaker in the political center. Indeed, about a third of the most religious Catholics vote for the PSOE.

The Church, however, continues to be an important actor in Spanish politics. Pronouncements by the Bishops Conference, a top Church leadership body, carry considerable weight and are followed closely by the press. The Church continues to administer about one-third of Spanish schools, though it now has less control over curriculum in many of them. The Church publishes a daily newspaper and owns a radio network.

For decades Spaniards have also speculated about the power of *Opus Dei* (God's Work), a secretive Catholic lay organization founded in 1928. During the Francoist regime, this mysterious organization rose to prominence in Spanish business and education. *Opus Dei* members supposedly occupied about a quarter of university professorships during the Franco period. The *Opus Dei* runs an important private university, the University of Navarre, and a prestigious business school in Barcelona. Under Franco *Opus Dei* politicians became known for their technocratic authoritarian outlook. Several members of Aznar's cabinet have close ties to *Opus Dei*.

Other Groups

Since the return of democracy many interest groups have formed, and some have acquired significant political and economic power. One of the most fascinating and unusual examples is the Spanish Organization of the Blind (ONCE). Created by Franco's government in 1939 to employ the many who lost their vision while fighting in the civil war, ONCE was allowed to run tax-exempt lotteries throughout Spain. By 1950, ONCE used the profits to set up a welfare system for its own members. The organization was forced to reorganize and democratize after 1977 but has still managed to control Spanish lotteries. The wealth of ONCE has become immense, and the organization now invests in a plethora of Spanish business, including one of Spain's top private television stations. The wealth and power of the organization has led some to question the organization's tax-exempt status.

As in much of Europe, Spaniards have been attracted to a whole host of "single issue" interest groups. However, environmental, peace, and feminist groups, to mention a few, are less developed in Spain than in their European counterparts. The Franco regime's promotion of demobilization and apathy is partly responsible for the relative weakness of these organizations in Spain. Many political activists in the 1960s and 1970s focused their energy on the struggle against Franco, and this tended to weaken single-issue groups. In the 1980s a strong peace movement arose in opposition to Spain's participation in the North Atlantic Treaty Organization, but the decision of the governing Socialists to remain in NATO dealt the movement a major blow. Environmentalists have suffered from relatively low public awareness of and concern for environmental issues in Spain. Spain had no unified environmental organization until the 1993 creation of *Los Verdes* (Greens), and the Spanish environmental movement has yet to have the kind of impact that has occurred in other parts of Europe. As noted later in this chapter, Spanish women's groups have had significant success in the 1980s and 1990s, but the results have come more through the efforts of women in the established political parties (especially the Socialist Party) than through independent feminist groups.

Electoral Competition in Spain

The Political Party System

Political parties were banned during the four decades of authoritarian rule in Franco's Spain. The official Francoist National Movement never functioned as a mobilizing party; rather it operated bureaucratically, preempting the political space. Franco vilified modern political parties as parasitic organizations unable to act in the common interest. In the final months of the Franco regime, as late as the early 1970s, Francoist reformers agreed to tolerate highly restricted political "associations," but the dictator never legalized political parties. To a considerable extent, the nature of political parties in contemporary Spain—weak organizations with scant membership—can be explained by this long hiatus in party politics. Spanish parties thus tend to be ideologically vague and based as much on personality as ideology, and they are structured hierarchically with little room or incentive for popular participation.

Compared with their European counterparts, Spanish parties have very few members: no party has more than 200,000 members and most have under 100,000. They make relatively little effort to recruit new members. With the exception of the Spanish Communist Party (PCE), no party emerged from Francoism with a strong membership base. Given the clandestine conditions under which parties had to operate during the dictatorship, mass membership was not a goal pursued by Spanish parties. During the transition, hundreds of parties emerged on the left, right, and center of the political system. There were several parties claiming to be Socialist, several Christian Democratic organizations, and numerous parties of the extreme right. In the first elections in 1977, what distinguished these parties most was the popularity and name recognition of key leaders, not the size of their membership. It is also important to remember that the Spanish party system was created in the 1970s, well into the age of modern mass media. Unlike other European party systems, where traditions of mass membership parties predated the age of electronic media, Spain's party system emerged in an era where image mattered far more than organizational strength. Finally, given the negotiated nature of Spain's transition, the politics of mobilization was discouraged. Party leaders entered into a series of "bargains" with each other, and the building of mass party membership was not seen as facilitating such elite-level bargaining. Spain's political leaders remembered that in the Second Republic radicalized party masses had made such political compromise impossible.

The personalism of Spanish politics and the weak ideological content shares much in common with the trend in European politics as a whole. However, the same factors that have limited party membership in Spain have acted to exaggerate personalism. Memories of the Spanish Second Republic and the Civil War, still reasonably fresh in the memory of older Spaniards, emphasized the dangers of ideology. Four decades of Francoist authoritarianism stripped most Spaniards of ideological passion: The regime inculcated Spaniards with an apolitical orientation more than any particular ideological vision. During the transition, the emergence of hundreds of "new" political parties all competing for electoral survival meant that name recognition and simple slogans, rather than complex ideological messages, were at a premium. Personalism was better suited for political campaigns that depended largely on television advertising. Finally, Spanish political leaders purposely restrained themselves from presenting an ideologically charged image, fearing that ideological polarization would threaten the transition to democracy. As a result, political parties espoused vague commitments and once in office wandered far from official party platforms.

The hierarchical and rather authoritarian internal workings of Spanish political parties of today are partially related to the characteristics noted earlier. Low membership has facilitated strong internal control by party leaders. The importance of personalism, itself facilitated by ideological weakness, has tended to give party leaders (especially charismatic ones) excessive influence over their parties. Lack of ideology has often facilitated the formation of factions within each party seeking to impose a stronger ideological vision on the party. Such ideological struggles within parties have destroyed a number of political parties, including the Union of the Democratic Center (UCD), the governing party from 1977 to 1981, and have severely weakened others, such as the Spanish Communist Party (PCE). The electorate has consistently punished parties that displayed internal turmoil. Spain's most successful parties, consequently, have tended to limit internal dissent and impose strict party discipline. Hierarchical control

within parties has been facilitated by Spain's closed-list electoral system that gives party leaders (not the voters) control over the order in which party candidates for office appear on electoral lists. The electoral system also discriminates against small nationwide parties, making it more costly for dissatisfied party factions to bolt and form separate organizations. Finally, within the Cortes, there are procedural rules that severely penalize small parties, and that give almost no voice to party rank and file.

The Major Parties

Spain's political parties have undergone widespread and pervasive changes since the first elections in 1975. In order to simplify the discussion here, the parties are organized into several broad categories: the Communist left, the Socialists, parties of the center and right, and regional parties.

THE COMMUNIST LEFT During the Second Republic, the *Spanish Communist Party (PCE)* had been a marginal electoral force, but it came to play an important role in the unsuccessful defense of the Republic during the Civil War. Under Franco, the PCE, though illegal, was the only opposition force with any real presence inside Spain, conducting some guerrilla operations against the regime in the 1940s and 1950s. As a result, it was singled out for extremely harsh repression by the dictator. By the mid-1950s, the party had almost been eliminated within Spain.

In 1956 Santiago Carrillo, the PCE leader, changed the party's strategy to encourage alliances with other democratic forces in order to topple Franco. The PCE, more than any other clandestine force, began to organize workers and students. Official PCE ideology began to change as well. By the early 1970s, Carrillo had become one of Europe's foremost proponents of *Eurocommunism:* He distanced his party from the Soviet Union and from Marxist-Leninist tenets and accepted democratic electoral politics. Carrillo rejected the authoritarianism of both the Franco regime and the Soviet Union.

Adolfo Suárez's surprise legalization of the PCE on the eve of the first democratic elections infuriated the military and much of the right. However, during the transition the PCE exhibited exemplary behavior. It supported the monarchy, acted moderately and responsibly, and participated in the elite compromises that were required to write the Constitution. The moderate behavior of the PCE undoubtedly aided the consolidation of democracy, but it also alienated many party rank and file who saw the PCE as overly compromising.

The PCE had hoped to dominate the left after the 1977 elections. Instead it polled just under 10 percent, relegating the Communists to second place on the left, well behind the Socialists. Spanish voters were not entirely convinced of the moderation of the Communists. At the same time, the moderation of the PCE program made it appear similar to the Socialists, robbing the Communists of their distinctiveness. The PCE's failure to break out of the electoral ghetto led to internal dissent, but the party under Carrillo, despite its ideological democratization, remained very attached to democratic centralism. Ideological dissidents or critics of Carrillo's leadership style were purged from the party in 1981. Consequently, the PCE began to lose some of its most talented members, many of whom joined the Socialists.

The definitive blow to the PCE occurred in 1982 when the Communists were drubbed at the polls, winning only 4 percent of the vote in the 1982 general elections, down from almost 11 percent in the previous election. Carrillo stepped down as Communist leader, but the damage had been done. Bitter internal infighting began in 1983 and by 1985 Carrillo had left the party. The pro-Soviet faction of the party bolted as well. As a result of these schisms, PCE membership plummeted during the 1980s, declining from a high of 240,000 in 1978 to only 55,000 in 1991.[40]

In the aftermath of the PCE's decline the remains of the Eurocommunist wing of the party, together with other leftist parties, formed a coalition called *United Left (IU)*. The coalition was initially formed as an anti-NATO protest movement, uniting Communists, environmentalists, and feminists. After 1986, the IU became the only real leftist opposition to the Socialists, operating as a relentless and sometimes very effective critic of their economic policies. It argued that Socialist neoliberal economic policies disproportionately hurt the poor. The coalition's "green" and feminist emphasis also made it a strong critic of the Socialists in these areas.

After 1986 the IU gradually increased its number of seats, but there was still discontent within the PCE. In February 1988 Julio Anguita, the charismatic head of the PCE in Andalusia (a PCE stronghold), and a former mayor of Cordoba, became the PCE leader. Under Anguita the Communists mounted an energetic attack on the Socialist government over corruption charges. At the same time, Anguita purged most of the Marxist rhetoric from his public discourse. The new image for the PCE and IU paid off. In the 1996 election the IU polled over 10 percent of the vote, and with 21 seats had come close to the 23 seats that the PCE had won at its zenith in 1979. However, given the troubles experienced by the governing Socialists, the failure of the IU to gain more ground is puzzling. Moreover, the success proved short lived: the IU was the biggest loser of the 2000 general elections, dropping 13 of its 21 seats, and ceding its third-place status to the Catalan Minority.

As has been the case for all European Communist parties, the fall of Eastern European communism presented a crisis for PCE. Spain's Communists had long established independence from (and were often openly opposed to) those parties, but many within the PCE began to question whether the party should adopt a new name (as occurred in Italy) and alliance strategy. Despite its recent problems the PCE, now within the IU, has made a remarkable recovery since the crisis of the early 1980s, and it has survived the fall of the Berlin Wall.

THE SOCIALISTS   The *Spanish Socialist Workers Party (PSOE)* has been the dominant force during the first two decades of Spanish democracy.[41] Its long tenure in government—from 1982 to 1996—and its internal unity and discipline have made it highly successful.

The roots of the PSOE go back to 1879, when workers and intellectuals in Madrid founded what continues today as Spain's oldest existing political party. In its early years, the party's fierce anticlericalism and its rigid Marxist ideology limited its appeal. The party thus grew slowly, organizing among the working class and running candidates in national and local elections. Hampered by the small size of the Spanish working class, and the presence within the party of competing progressive as well as regional forces, the PSOE did not elect a single member of Parliament until 1910. The split of the Socialists and formation of the PCE in 1921, which mirrored the general European trend, weakened the PSOE and sapped much of its membership. The party gradually recovered its strength, and during the Second Republic the PSOE became the largest single party in Spain. However, it was badly divided between reformist social democrats (who were strongly anti-Communist and deeply committed to democratic procedures) and revolutionary socialists (whose main commitment was to the working class, and whose loyalty to the democratic Republic was "conditional"). The behavior of many Socialist leaders during the Republic was, in the words of Juan Linz, "accidentalist": They supported democracy only if it delivered the specific policy outcomes (workers' rights and the building of socialism) that they desired.[42] When the right won the elections of 1934, many of these leaders turned against the Republic and called for revolution, and the PSOE spearheaded a protracted armed uprising by workers in northern Spain. In the eyes of many contemporary Spanish socialist intellectuals, the divisions within the PSOE and the weak commitment to parliamentary rule contributed to the downfall of democracy and the rise of authoritarian rule. As a result, the PSOE suffered four decades of repression and exile during Franco's rule.

Throughout most of the Franco regime, the bulk of the Socialist leaders remained in exile, mainly in France or Mexico; the Socialists who remained in Spain attempted to reorganize but they were eclipsed by the better organized PCE and were repeatedly arrested by the Francoist police. Six entire executive committees were arrested between 1944 and 1953. Moreover, the Socialist movement continued to be badly divided around key leaders and ideological and strategic positions. United only by a fierce anticommunism and a desire to topple Franco, the Socialist Party in exile had ceased to have much importance.

It was up to a new generation of PSOE leaders based inside Spain to renovate the moribund PSOE. By the mid-1950s, young activists inside Spain took advantage of an easing of repression and in 1956 formed the underground Socialist University Group. University professors, intellectuals, and progressive Catholics began to organize into other groups that would produce many future Socialist leaders. In 1974 a group of young militants, led by Felipe González, wrested control of the PSOE. Under its new leaders, the party made spectacular gains in organizational strength from 1974 to the first elections in 1977. During that period its membership grew from 3,500 to 51,000, and then doubled again by 1979.[43]

The history of the PSOE between 1974 and 1977 has confused many students of Spanish politics. The new party leadership was young and espoused radical Marxist beliefs. Stylistically, they were trained in the combative rhetoric of the underground struggle against Franco. It appeared to many that the revitalized PSOE was far more leftist than the conservative PSOE in exile. As long as Franco's regime was intact, the radicalism of the PSOE platform was almost unavoidable. The rapid growth of PSOE membership had pushed the party rank and file to the left, and the December 1976 Party Congress adopted a radical socialist platform. Despite the radicalism of the rank and file, the young PSOE leadership moved toward the center for a number of reasons. The appointment of Adolfo Suárez in 1976, and his successful reform strategy, convinced Socialist leaders that a more confrontational strategy could be counterproductive. Suárez's legalization of political parties and call for elections in June 1977 forced the PSOE to worry about winning votes. The PSOE faced not only a strong center-right challenge from Suárez's party, but it feared significant competition on the left from the PCE and other socialist parties. After four decades of Francoist rule, the PSOE leadership knew that a highly ideological campaign would not win votes. Finally, the PSOE leaders, unlike their predecessors in the Second Republic, recognized that the consolidation of democracy was more important than ideological purity.

The PSOE's first electoral campaign in June 1977 contained no radical socialist content, and its slogan, "Socialism Is Liberty," emphasized the party's links to moderate, modern European socialism. Most of all, the party emphasized the face of its young leader, Felipe González. At meetings of party

TABLE 7.2   Seats in the Congress of Deputies, 1977–2000

	1977	1979	1982	1986	1989	1993	1996	2000
AP/CP/PP	16	9	106	105	106	141	157	183
UCD/CDS	166	168	12	19	14	0	—	—
PSOE	118	121	202	184	176	159	140	125
PCE/IU	20	23	4	7	17	18	21	8
CIU	2	8	12	18	18	17	16	15
PNV	2	7	8	6	5	5	5	7
Others	26	14	6	11	14	10	11	15
Total seats	350	350	350	350	350	350	350	350

Source: Anuario El País (various years) and *El País.*

faithful, PSOE leaders could still produce charged speeches, but for more general audiences, moderation prevailed. The PSOE's success in the first general elections exceeded all expectations: the Socialists took second place, with 28.5 percent of the vote and 33.7 percent of the seats in the Congress of Deputies (see Table 7.2). The PSOE all but eliminated contending Socialist parties, and by 1979 almost all had joined the PSOE. It trounced the PCE and clearly established itself as the hegemonic force of the left. The PSOE earned the right to play a large role in the writing of the new constitution, and much of that document resulted from elite-level bargaining between leaders of the governing UCD and the PSOE.

During the elite-level negotiations over the Constitution and the economy, the PSOE leadership abandoned much of its official platform, angering the party's left. In the 1979 general elections, Prime Minister Suárez shrewdly played on the contradictions between the leadership's moderation and the party platform's radical pledges. Partly as a result of this fear mongering, the PSOE increased its percentage of the vote very little, gaining only three seats. Party leaders, bolstered by electoral studies produced by the PSOE think tank, were convinced that a moderation of party ideology and tighter party discipline were needed to achieve an electoral breakthrough. Such changes were imposed at an Emergency Congress, held in 1979. Most important was the elimination of the Marxist, proletarian, and class-based definition of the party, and the affirmation of ideological pluralism within the PSOE. The

party's electoral platform was purged of some of its more radical proposals. Calls for mass mobilization were dropped, and the party pledged to become more of an interclass "catch-all" party. At the party's Twenty-Ninth Congress in October 1981, the PSOE presented itself as a unified, moderate political party. Delegates included far fewer members of the working class, and the party left was virtually excluded from the Congress. González and his entire executive committee were reelected with almost no opposition.

The more moderate party platform and the PSOE's virtual elimination of internal dissent (especially when contrasted with the internal chaos in Spain's other major parties) paid huge dividends in the 1982 elections. The PSOE victory was historical for several reasons. It signaled the first case of party alternation in the new democracy and the first government that contained no former Francoist leader. Second, the PSOE government was the first single-party majority government in Spain's history. Third, the Socialist victory brought to power a generation of young Spaniards who had not experienced the Spanish Civil War. Finally, the dimensions of the victory were unprecedented. The PSOE won 48.4 percent of the valid votes and 57.7 percent of the seats in the Congress of Deputies.

These factors gave the new Socialist government an unprecedented degree of control in a system that gives majoritarian governments extraordinary power. From the start of its term, the Socialists moved quickly to pursue a controversial neoliberal macroeconomic policy: The PSOE gave control over economics to the most conservative faction of the party. Miguel Boyer and Carlos Solchaga, the PSOE's first two economics ministers, were well connected with bankers. The PSOE economic policy in government clearly favored integration of Spain into the world economy, economic growth, and the building of infrastructure over cutting unemployment. The Socialists spent lavishly for the 1992 World's Fair in Seville and the Barcelona Olympics, including a controversial high-speed train from Seville to Madrid.

The hegemony enjoyed by the PSOE resulted in an aloofness and arrogance on the part of the government. Shortly after the Socialist victory, the right-wing death squads of the *Anti-Terrorist Liberation Groups (GAL)* began an intimidation campaign against the Basque terrorist group ETA. Eventually Spanish police were revealed to be organizers of the GAL and sentenced to long prison terms. They also implicated higher officials, beginning a snowballing scandal that has yet to be resolved and has badly tarnished the reputation of the PSOE.

Scandals involving the abuse of public offices continued to surface. Spaniards were shocked when in 1985 González vacationed with his family on Franco's former yacht. Throughout the 1980s the PSOE was dogged by accusations that it had raised funds illegally. In 1988 the government-appointed head of state radio and television was accused of spending tax dollars to buy clothes and jewelry for herself and for friends. In 1989, the brother of the deputy prime minister (and deputy leader of the PSOE) was accused of influence peddling, leading to the resignation of the deputy prime minister.

By the 1993 elections, the PSOE's majority was in jeopardy. The Socialists resorted to scare tactics (similar to those used against the PSOE in 1979) in an attempt to paint the Popular Party (PP) as a dangerous party of ex-Francoists. The Socialists won the elections but fell 17 seats short of a majority. The PSOE had to depend on centrist regional parties to prop up a minority government, partly explaining the Socialists' continued drift toward the right. In the post-election Cabinet, a third of the members did not even belong to the PSOE. In opinion polls taken during the first two years of conservative government, Felipe González remained very popular,

and was usually rated more highly than Prime Minister Aznar. It was therefore a shock when the veteran party leader announced his resignation as party leader to stunned delegates at the PSOE Thirty-Fourth Party Congress in June 1997. Joaquin Almunia, a veteran party leader, replaced him.

The PSOE is structured much like other Social Democratic parties in Europe, but it is an unusually centralized party. It is formally federal, with the local *agrupación* (party branch) being its primary structure, electing provincial and regional bodies. In 1979 the party leadership embraced a shift to a much more disciplined party structure. Rule changes were enacted to inhibit growth of factionalism and reinforce party stability. After the PSOE defeat in the 1996 elections many party members felt that the Socialist leadership had gotten out of touch with rank and file members. Consequently, at the PSOE's 1997 Party Congress a primary election system was adopted to select candidates for local and regional posts. The new PSOE Secretary General, Joaquín Almunia, chose to extend the primary system to the selection of the future Socialist candidate for head of government. To the dismay of Almunia and much of the PSOE leadership, the Secretary General was defeated in the primary election of April 1998 by a political rival, José Borrell. The use of party primaries to select candidates was a first for Spanish political parties, and it augured well for an internal democratization of the PSOE. Borrell soon resigned, and Almunia, his replacement, proved a lackluster candidate in the March 2000 elections. The PSOE's attempt to attack the PP under Aznar for cronyism proved hollow in light of the Socialists' recent history of corruption while in office. Socialist attempts to draw attention to growing concentration of wealth in Spain fell on deaf ears in the context of an economic boom. Moreover, Aznar's government had largely continued policies of privatization and liberalization begun under the Socialists. The PSOE drubbing in those elections (the PSOE lost 15 seats in the lower house, and over 1 million votes) led to Almunia's resignation and ignited a struggle for power within the Socialist Party. At the PSOE's thirty-fifth Congress held in July 2000, the Socialists elected 39-year-old *José Luis Rodríguez Zapatero* as their new leader. Zapatero, who in 1986 had become the youngest member of parliament ever, represents a new generation of Socialist "whiz kids" who seek to further democratize Party institutions and to resuscitate the PSOE's image. He quickly moved to bring in new blood to the PSOE leadership team and to repair damaged relations with the socialist trade unions.

PARTIES OF THE CENTER   On the eve of Spain's first elections in 1977, the political center was in disarray, with countless groups claiming to be "centrist." These included timid Francoist reformers who emerged in the twilight of the Franco regime, anti-Franco opposition figures, Christian Democrats, liberals, monarchists, and Social Democrats. In early 1977 a weak coalition of these groups was organized, its goal being to compete with both Francoist political right and the democratic left. The coalition lacked a well-known leader and was beset by political squabbling. On the eve of the historic June 1977 elections, Adolfo Suárez, the man responsible for stewarding the transition to democracy, agreed to lead this coalition, which took the name *Union of the Democratic Center (UCD)*. This marriage of convenience saved the political center from a sure electoral disaster, but many centrist leaders resented Suárez's last minute "occupation" of the center. Some refused to be associated with the last Francoist leader.

In the short term, however, the UCD experiment was immensely successful. Backed by the still powerful state media and bureaucracy, and fronted by Spain's most popular and charismatic leader, the UCD easily won the first two democratic elections. Running a campaign based solely on the image of its popular leader, the UCD advocated a cautious support for devolution of power to the regions, a separation of Church and state, military reform, and economic restructuring. It polled well among rural voters, women, and Catholics.

In retrospect, these victories were extremely important for the viability of Spanish democracy. The UCD brought to power a coalition of Francoist reformers and moderate democratic opposition members, thus bridging the gap between authoritarianism and democracy. It proved that those who had played a role in the Francoist regime could have a place in the new democracy. Indeed, in the first democratic legislature 44 UCD members of the Congress of Deputies were former members of the Francoist legislature, and 44 percent of the party's members were officeholders (mostly middle-level bureaucrats) under Franco.[44] Suárez and the UCD were thus in an ideal position to negotiate a democratic constitution that could appeal to a wide range of voters.

Once in power, however, the UCD proved to be an unwieldy beast. The ideological diversity of "centrists" was a fatal flaw, especially for a party that had to oversee constitutional compromise.[45] The tension between the Christian Democratic UCD right, and the Social Democratic left, eventually tore the party apart. Squabbling between Suárez and his "barons" was unabated. Suárez had alienated sectors of the military because of his role in the transition, and his government was unable to discipline the increasingly restive armed forces. Suárez resigned in January 1981, after he failed to acquire greater control over squabbling party leaders.

The attempted military coup of February 23, 1981, accelerated the intramural chaos in the UCD. Leopoldo Calvo Sotelo, long a top Suárez aide became the new prime minister. Soon the UCD Social Democrats bolted the party, some joining the PSOE, while some UCD Christian Democrats joined the rightist Popular Alliance. When Suárez quit the UCD to form a new centrist party, the Democratic and Social Center (CDS), the governing party's fate was sealed. The 1982 elections dealt the UCD a deathblow and was one of the largest electoral defeats of a governing party in Spain's electoral history. The UCD dropped from 168 seats to only 11!

Since the demise of the UCD, no centrist party has been able to achieve electoral success. The main reason for this failure has been that after the Socialist victory in 1982 the centrist political space grew smaller. The PSOE's move toward the center deprived other parties of that space, and the right's moderation and drift toward the political mainstream had a similar effect.

PARTIES OF THE RIGHT   Spanish parties of the right have a long history of disillusionment and disunity. Some have argued that the Spanish right has never had to organize given that its historical interests have usually been well protected. When its interests were threatened, the Spanish right supported authoritarian rule. During the Second Republic, the main party of the right eventually supported Francoist authoritarianism.

After 1977 the Spanish right was confronted with a difficult problem. It was initially unable and unwilling to distance itself from the Franco regime, and that identification hurt it at the polls. Attempts by rightist leaders to draw on the legacy of Spanish conservatism in the late nineteenth and early twentieth centuries had little resonance.

Spain's main party of the right, the Popular Alliance (AP), was founded in October 1976, drawing largely from recruits from the former top-level apparatus of the Francoist state. Manuel Fraga, a well-known minister under Franco, led the party. The well-organized and well-funded AP had high hopes for electoral success until Adolfo Suárez and UCD entered the 1977 electoral campaign. Compared with the UCD and the youthful Suárez, Fraga and his party appeared more authoritarian and less committed to democracy. The AP campaign stressed the need for order and continuity. It accepted regional autonomy but rejected federalism or regional independence. It opposed divorce and abortion, and advocated support for the police and armed forces. The AP performed poorly in the first democratic elections, winning only 16 seats of 350 in the Congress of Deputies, with only 8 percent of the vote. In the Basque Country and Catalonia, the AP won almost no support.

In retrospect it is clear that the post-Francoist right faced some serious obstacles. The right might have expected active support from the Catholic Church, but the Church (itself divided) refused to endorse any one political party. A more serious obstacle was the regional question. The Spanish right has a long history of opposing political decentralization, and this has meant that conservatives in Spain's most important regions have backed regional conservative parties. The absence of a single party capable of representing national and regional conservatives has weakened the right.

The dismal electoral results of 1977 encouraged the AP to ally with two small centrist parties (one Liberal and one Christian Democratic), under the name Popular Coalition (CP). Despite the reorganization, the CP won only nine seats in the Congress of Deputies and 6 percent of the vote in the 1979 elections, leading many observers to predict the disappearance of the right altogether. This might have been the outcome had the governing UCD not suddenly disintegrated in the 1982 election. The Popular Coalition in alliance with regional parties of the right reaped the benefits, winning 26 percent of the vote and 107 seats in the Congress of Deputies. About half of former UCD voters switched to the AP in 1982.[46] Despite the raised expectations, the CP failed to improve on its 1982 performance in the 1986 general elections, and the rightist coalition disbanded.

In 1988 the AP once again attempted to alter its image. It took a new name, the *Popular Party (PP)*, and sought to integrate former UCD leaders, but it failed to improve its percentage of the vote much in the 1989 elections. In 1990 the PP selected a new leader, *José María Aznar*, the young president of the Castilla-León Autonomous Community. Aznar promoted a modern Christian Democratic image and tried to purge the party of its extreme right. He also waged a relentless campaign against PSOE corruption. His steady, if not flamboyant, leadership of the PP paid dividends in the 1993 elections when the party made significant gains, and in the 1996 elections when the PP finally took power. In the 1980s the right had moved from being a vehicle for former Francoist elite to a more mainstream party. The PP's membership rose from 5,000 members in 1979 to 220,000 by October 1986, and younger Spaniards made up much of the new membership. The PP victory in the 1996 general elections finally enabled the Spanish right to demonstrate its credentials as a modern, democratic party. Aznar's first term in office allayed any fears that Spanish conservatives could not be trusted to uphold democratic rule. Under the PP Spain prospered, with annual growth rates averaging 3 percent, and unemployment falling by 8 percent. Aznar's willingness to enter into negotiation with Basque nationalists, coupled with his hard line during the bargaining process, won him much support. Voters in the March 2000 elections rewarded the PP. It became the first conservative party in Spanish history to win an absolute majority of legislative seats (see Table 7.2).

TABLE 7.3 Percentage of Votes (and Seats) in the Catalonian Legislature, 1980–2000

	1980	**1984**	**1988**	**1992**	**1995**	**1999**
CiU (Centrist Nationalists)	28 (43)	47 (72)	46 (69)	41 (70)	41 (60)	38 (56)
PP (National Conservatives)	13 (18)	8 (11)	9 (9)	7 (7)	15 (17)	10 (12)
ERC (Republican Left of Catalonia)	9 (14)	4 (5)	4 (6)	8 (11)	10 (13)	9 (12)
PSC-PSOE (Catalonian Socialists)	22 (33)	30 (41)	30 (42)	28 (40)	25 (34)	38 (52)
PSUC/IC (Catalonian Communists-United Left)	19 (25)	6 (6)	8 (9)	7 (7)	10 (11)	3 (3)

Source: Anuario El País, various years.

CATALONIAN PARTIES Spain's regional parties have played an important role in its democratic system, both within the Autonomous Communities, and to a lesser extent in the national party system. It is impossible here to cover all the regional groups, but it is important to touch on the major parties in the two most important regions, Catalonia and the Basque Country.

As is clear from Table 7.3, the Catalonian party system has been very stable from the start, dominated by the Democratic Convergence of Catalonia (CDC), which has run in elections together with a smaller group, the Democratic Union of Catalonia (UDC) in a coalition called *Convergence and Union,* or *CiU.* The CDC was founded in 1974 near the end of the Francoist regime, when political associations were being tolerated. CiU has been the leading electoral force in Catalonia since the advent of democracy, and it is currently the third largest electoral force in the national legislature.

The CiU has operated very much as a Catalonian "catch-all" party of the center. Its founder, Jordi Pujol, has dominated it from the start. Pujol spent two years in jail under Franco and he later became a leading force behind the Banca Catalana, a regional bank. Pujol won the first elections to the restored *Generalitat* (Catalonian Government) in 1980; he has won five consecutive elections since then, but won by the narrowest of margins in the 1999 regional elections.

Pujol's political longevity has given him immense prestige within Catalonia and considerable respect nationwide. However, his active promotion of Catalonian interests abroad has often angered Madrid. After the March 1996 elections, he lent his party's support to the PP government of Aznar despite the Spanish right's historical opposition to regional devolution. However, Pujol has always kept his distance from the national government, steadfastly refusing to accept cabinet positions. In addition, he was able to exact promises from the PP regarding regional devolution.

The CiU is best viewed as a centrist political party with a blend of Christian Democratic and nationalist ideology. It advocates a federal system but has come to accept the system of Autonomous Communities. It is a party that has also represented the small and medium-sized Catalonian bourgeoisie. Despite its early flirtation with Social Democratic ideas, it has generally promoted the market economy and free enterprise. A main emphasis of the CiU, and an area where it has had a significant impact, is its policy to restore the Catalan language to a position of dominance in Catalonia. By the mid-1980s, over 85 percent of the schools in the region offered some classes in Catalan, compared with about 3 percent at the start of the democratic period.

The CiU won every AC regional election between 1980 and the present, but in general elections the Catalonian Socialists (part of the PSOE) have generally been the leading party. The CiU has done best when national parties of the center are weakest, as was the case in 1982 and 1986, when it almost overtook the PSOE in Catalonia. Despite its electoral weakness on the national level, it has often played a crucial role in national government. After the 1979 elections, and again in 1981, the CiU helped sustain the UCD minority government with its votes in the Congress of Deputies, and it was rewarded with an acceleration of the devolution process. The CiU played a similar role after the PSOE lost its legislative majority: It agreed to back the government, but refused to join it. When the two largest parties have agreed on policy, however, the CiU has often been left out in the cold.

Table 7.4   Percentage of Votes (and Seats) in Basque Elections, 1980–2000

	1980	1984	1988	1992	1994	1998
PNV (Basque National Party)	38 (25)	42 (32)	24 (17)	29 (22)	29 (22)	30 (21)
EE (Basque Left)	10 (6)	8 (6)	11 (9)	8 (6)	—(—)	——
HB (Radical Basque Left)	17 (11)	15 (11)	18 (13)	18 (13)	16 (11)	18 (14)
EA (Moderate Breakaway from PNV)	—(—)	—(—)	16 (13)	11 (9)	10 (8)	9(6)
PSE-PSOE (Socialists)	14 (9)	23 (19)	22 (19)	20 (16)	17 (12)	18 (14)
PCE/IU (Communists)	4 (1)	1 (0)	1 (0)	1 (0)	9 (6)	6 (2)
NATIONAL RIGHT (PP)	13 (8)	9 (7)	8 (4)	9 (6)	14 (11)	20 (16)

Source: Anuario El País, various years.

Basque Parties   Unlike the Catalonian party system, the situation in the Basque Country has been very volatile and extremely polarized. As in Catalonia, the dominant party in the region has been a centrist force, the *Basque Nationalist Party (PNV)*. The PNV was an important regional force during the Second Republic, and it had a long history of opposition to and fierce repression by Franco during the authoritarian regime. Partially due to this painful history, and partially due to a strong and violent pro-independence movement, the PNV has been less accepting of the Autonomous Community status than the CiU in Catalonia, and unlike the CiU, the PNV formally opposed the Constitution of 1978.

The PNV has governed the Basque Country since the approval of the Basque Autonomy Statute in 1979, but since 1986 it has done so in coalition with the PSOE. The PNV was badly weakened by a party split in 1985. In national elections, the PNV has consistently made a strong showing, and like the CiU in Catalonia, it has done best when national centrist parties are weakest (see Table 7.4). Thus it has won as many as eight seats (in 1982), and in the last two general elections it has won five seats.

In contrast to Catalonia, there has been a consistently strong nationalist left presence in the Basque Country. The Euskadiko Euskerra (EE), or Basque Left, represented the regional left until it split during the transition to democracy. It lost much of its support to the Radical Basque Left party, Herri Batasuna (HB), the political arm of the terrorist organization ETA. Unlike the other Basque parties, the HB (renamed Euskal Herritarrok, or EH, in 1998) is an antisystem party, and like ETA it promotes the independence of the region from Spain.

It has done surprisingly well in regional and national elections, and won seats in every national election between 1979 and 1996, peaking with five deputies in 1986. Initially its elected members of the national parliament refused to occupy their seats as a sign of protest against the Spanish state. When HB deputies finally agreed to take their seats in 1989, they were expelled from the legislature for refusing to take the required oath to the Constitution. After 1986 the HB strength in national elections waned, and it won only two seats in the 1993 and 1996 elections. HB's successor, EH, boycotted the 2000 general elections and encouraged voters to abstain. However, Table 7.4 makes it clear that pro-ETA left continues to garner about one-fifth of the Basque vote in regional elections.

The Electoral System

Spain's electoral system was one of the many compromises that resulted from the negotiated transition to democracy. Adolfo Suárez negotiated the electoral laws with major opposition groups on the eve of the transition to democracy. The 1978 Constitution made some minor changes to the electoral law, but left it mostly intact. The left insisted on the use of proportional representation, while the right advocated a single-member district/plurality system. The compromise called for the use of proportional representation for the Congress of Deputies, but with strong "corrective" measures to favor the major parties and to prevent excessive fragmentation of the legislature. Conservatives won some additional victories. A plurality system was adopted for the Senate, and the voting age was set at 21, though it was reduced to 18 in 1979.

Spain's Congress of Deputies employs a modified system of proportional representation, using Spain's 50 unevenly sized provinces (generally smaller than the ACs) as constituencies. All provinces, regardless of size, receive a minimum of two deputies in the lower house, then additional seats for each 144,500 citizens. Conservatives initially saw this electoral system as prejudicial to the left, since urban areas that were thought to favor the left were underrepresented. However, the major consequence of Spain's electoral system is that it favors large parties over small ones, especially in smaller electoral districts. It also favors small parties whose vote is concentrated geographically, as is the case with Spain's many regional parties. Spanish parties must win over 3 percent of the vote to win seats in the legislature, a measure that also limits the success of small parties. In the first democratic elections the small size of electoral districts and the overrepresentation of conservative rural districts made it easier for the UCD to win elections. Spain's electoral system is, in the words of one scholar, "strikingly unproportional"[47]

Elections for the Congress of Deputies employ the closed list system of presenting candidates: the order and content of party lists are set by party leaders, not by voters. Moreover, candidates on party lists are not required to be members of that party. Both these provisions have tended to weaken party rank and file vis-à-vis party leaders.

The electoral system for the Cortes has had its intended outcome. It has often produced governments with a majority or plurality large enough to govern alone. Spain's party system is still highly fragmented, but it would undoubtedly be more so were it not for the electoral laws. Small parties have found it difficult to survive on the national level as a result of both the electoral system and Spain's system of party finance. On the national level at least, two large parties have dominated Spain's party system.

For elections to the Senate, voters select up to three names from a single list of all candidates who run in a given province, and the recipients with the most votes are elected. In addition, some Senate seats are appointed directly by the Autonomous Communities. The Senate electoral law will likely be changed in the near future, along with an overhaul of the functions of the upper chamber.

Strict laws govern the financing of political parties, but these laws have evidently not been followed very closely during the first two decades of Spanish democracy. Spain's political parties can raise their funds through public financing, membership dues, and strictly limited donations. The state reimburses parties for electoral expenses based on the number of seats they win in an election. The system clearly favors large incumbent parties, since campaign funds must be raised up front often by bank loans.

Since 1987, a parliamentary Audit Commission inspects party finances, but critics have argued that financing rules have been only sporadically enforced.[48] A series of party financing scandals made headlines in the 1980s and early 1990s as Spanish parties ran up gigantic debts. The incessant schedule of elections (national, regional, municipal, and European) began to take its toll on party coffers. With few dues-paying members, and almost no unpaid volunteers, both major parties were tempted to trade political favors for campaign contributions.

Campaigns and Elections

Unlike the United States, Spanish citizens of voting age are automatically registered to vote. The Central Electoral Junta is responsible for drawing up a list of eligible voters. An Electoral College, made up by citizens chosen randomly, counts the votes and oversees elections. Ultimately, the Constitutional Court is responsible for ensuring that elections are free and fair. As can be seen in Figure 7.4, Spaniards turn out to vote in large numbers, despite the daunting frequency with which elections are held.

Spanish electoral campaigns are short affairs. Until 1994, campaigns lasted three weeks, but since then they have been reduced to only two weeks, in order to save time and money. The day before elections is designated a "day of reflection," and all advertisements and campaign activities are banned.

FIGURE 7.4 Voting Turnout, 1977–1996

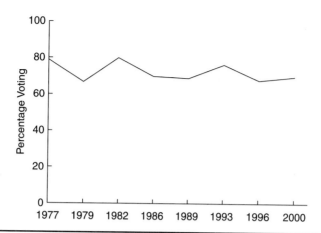

Source: *Anuario El Pais* (1994, 1995); the figure presents the actual voters as a percentage of potential voters.

In the early years of Spanish democracy, parties used mass rallies to build enthusiasm. In recent years, such mass electoral events have become rarities and parties rely heavily on the mass media to get out the word. Spanish parties are allocated free time on television according to their performance in the last election, thus favoring incumbents. Both the UCD and PSOE were criticized when in office for using the state media to enhance their political fortunes. The recent appearance of private television and radio would appear to have limited somewhat the ability of governments to manipulate the media in their favor.

A recent innovation that reflects the growing importance of television in electoral campaigns is the televised debate between party leaders. In the 1993 electoral campaign, Felipe González and José María Aznar engaged in a series of debates that drew a huge national audience, and that did much to enhance the image of the little known Aznar.

Spain's first electoral campaign in 1977 was a mild affair. Given the fragility of the transition to democracy, political elites from the major parties went out of their way not to polarize the political environment. Campaigns seemed drab and devoid of much content. There was relatively little in the way of personal attacks. In the 1979 electoral campaign Suárez shocked the opposition by launching a last-minute attack on the PSOE aimed at creating fears about a leftist victory. Since then, campaigns have tended to be more hard-nosed. During the Socialist tenure in office, opposition candidates harped on PSOE abuses of power, and there was more mudslinging. As its majority slipped away, the PSOE attempted to raise fears about a victory of the right, linking that group to the Francoist era.

The 2000 electoral campaign was relatively lackluster. The PP electoral slogan was *"vamos a mas"* ("Let's Take it to the Next Level"). The PP bitterly attacked the last-minute electoral pact between the PSOE and the IU, charging that a leftist government would damage Spain's relations with the EU and threaten Spain's economic growth. Moreover, during the campaign Aznar predicted that the coalition partners would be unable to work together. Resting on a comfortable lead in the polls, Aznar refused to engage in televised debates. The leftist coalition adopted the slogan *"lo próximo"* ("Coming Soon"), blamed Aznar for a growing concentration of income, called for a 35-hour work week, and proposed a tax on windfall profits accrued by privatized enterprises.

The Party System

During the first two decades of democracy, there was constant change in Spain's party system, with parties rising and falling almost overnight, as is best illustrated by the case of the UCD, and recasting and renaming themselves, as is illustrated by the rightist PP and the leftist IU. The presence of separate regional party systems in some of Spain's most important Autonomous Communities has made any simple characterization of the Spanish party system very elusive. As we have seen, regional parties also run in national elections, and in the last two elections these parties have had a crucial role in the viability of minority governments.

It is possible to point to some constant features of Spain's party system. First, since 1979 two major parties (though not always the same two) have dominated the electoral landscape (see again Table 7.2). Between 1977 and 1981, the UCD and PSOE were dominant; since then the PP and PSOE have dominated. This trend appears to be consolidated with the PP victory of 1996, which should put to rest fears that the Spanish right is incapable of contributing to democracy.

Second, there has been a growing fragmentation of the vote and a steady rise in regional parties throughout Spain. The success of such parties, which are largely based in the political center, goes hand in hand with the inability of a national centrist party to have achieved electoral success since the demise of UCD. This is something of a surprise in a country where the middle class has grown faster than any other class. It could be argued, however, that during its long term in office the PSOE acted very much like a party of the center. Since the PSOE's break with its trade union, the UGT, there is very little tying the Socialists to the working class.

Third, despite the fluctuation in the party system, the Spanish electorate has remained remarkably stable. Opinion research has consistently shown that Spanish voters are clustered just to the right or left of center. With the exception of the Basque Country (where antisystem parties have consistently drawn significant support), Spain's party system is less polarized than in many other European countries.

Consequently, a fourth feature of the party system is the failure of national parties that are perceived to be on the political extremes. The PCE (and later the IU) was unable to convince voters that it had moved toward the center, and as a result was condemned to receive no more than a tenth of the vote. The PP, in contrast, marginalized an older generation of leaders identified with Franco and has moderated its image.

Fifth, Spaniards are not very attached to political parties, and they have comparatively weak party identification, partly a result of the changing party landscape during the first decades of democracy.[49] Spanish political parties have very few members and are organizationally very weak. Finally, Spaniards place great weight on the popularity of party leaders, and in Spain's new democracy image means a great deal.

Another sign that the change in Spanish parties has not mirrored a change in voter orientation can be found in studies of electoral volatility. Morlino has calculated the degree of change in the way the Spanish electorate voted between elections.[50] Excluding the watershed election of 1982, the volatility of the Spanish voters has not been much higher than the average in other European elections. Another measure is "interbloc" volatility, which is the shift between right/center and left voting. Spain is a case where there has been high total volatility, but very low levels of interbloc volatility. Even in the party system realignment of 1982, relatively few voters crossed the divide between left and right.

The 1996 electoral results did little to change this description of the Spanish party system (Table 7.5). The PSOE actually received more votes than in 1993, but failed to win enough seats to form a government with the IU or the Catalan CiU. The PP gained 4 percent in its vote, but fell 19 seats short of a majority. Regional parties, like the CiU in Catalonia and the National Galician Bloc (BNG) in Galicia, made important gains, confirming the continued fragmentation of the party system. The IU lost three seats and fell below 10 percent of the vote,

TABLE 7.5   Vote Shares in Congress of Deputies Elections, 1993, 1996, and 2000

PARTY	1993		1996		2000	
	SEATS	VOTE (%)	SEATS	VOTE (%)	SEATS	VOTE%
PP	141	34.8	156	38.8	183	44.0
PSOE	159	38.8	141	37.5	125	34.0
CiU	17	4.9	16	4.6	15	4.2
IU	18	9.6	21	10.6	8	5.4
PNV	5	1.2	5	1.3	7	1.3
C. CANARIA	4	0.9	4	.9	3	1.0
BNG	—	0.5	2	.8	3	1.3
HB	2	0.9	2	.7	—	—
ERC	1	0.8	1	.7	1	.8
EA	1	0.6	1	.5	1	.4
U. VALENCIANA	1	0.5	1	.4	—	.2
OTHERS	1	6.5	0	3.3	3	7.4
Total	350	100	350	100	350	100

Source: *Anuario El País,* various years.

confirming that it occupies political space that most Spaniards view as too far left.

The 2000 elections consolidated the PP's control of government. The Conservatives won an absolute majority, and the PSOE and IU both suffered serious setbacks. The PP even won a number of electoral districts in Andalusia, the traditional Socialist stronghold. The Basque PNV gained two seats, and a number of small regional parties gained seats in the legislature.

Policy Performance and Outcomes

Do politics matter? Does public policy change when there is a change in political regime? The transition from Francoist authoritarianism to democracy in Spain provides an opportunity to examine this question. There has been a dramatic shift in public policy outputs between the two regimes. Under Franco, Spain lagged far behind other Western industrialized states in its levels of taxation and state public spending. As a result, the provision of many public services approached third world levels. By the mid-1980s, after only a decade of democracy,

Spain's public policy outputs were very close to the European norm. Figure 7.5 compares some measures of public policy outputs during two regimes.

The Size and Scope of Spanish Government

Spain is often identified with strong leaders like Ferdinand and Isabel, and Francisco Franco. Historically, however, the Spanish state has been weak compared to other European nations. It has often been unable to collect taxes or enforce laws. Even dictatorships were far from all encompassing in their power. Franco shelved the totalitarian project proposed by some of his supporters early in his regime. Part and parcel of this legacy is Spain's long history of bureaucratic inefficiency and stagnation, and the inability of governments to enact civil service reform has plagued authoritarian and democratic regimes alike.

Spain's recent Socialist government, armed with a parliamentary majority, tried hard to tame the bureaucracy. Under the Socialists the *reforma de los relojes* (reform of the clocks) required civil servants to work strict schedules, mandated that government offices remain open between 9 A.M. and

FIGURE 7.5   Patterns of Policy Development Across Regimes

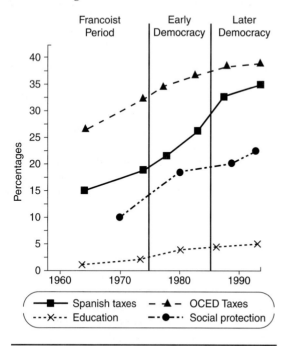

Source: Richard Gunther, "The Impact of Regime Change on Public Policy: The Case of Spain," *Journal of Public Policy* 16, No. 2 (1996): pp. 177, 179.

2 P.M., and attempted to streamline the bureaucratic maze facing Spaniards who seek government services. In 1984 the Socialists formally banned the practice of *pluriempleo* (multiple job holding). These reforms have been only partially successful. Moreover, with regional devolution state bureaucracies have often been replaced with Autonomous Community offices that may operate no more efficiently.

In 1990 there were about 2 million people dependent in some way on the public purse.[51] About a third were employed in the state's central administration (including the military, police, legal corps, and social security staff); about a quarter were employed by Autonomous Communities. By 1993 public sector employees represented just over 20 percent of the country's salaried workers, a figure that may seem large but is actually quite modest compared with other European nations.

Due in part to the Francoist legacy, the Spanish state owns and operates many business enterprises and continues to play an important role in many traditional (and declining) industries such as mining, iron, steel, and shipbuilding. In 1986 there were 180 companies in which the state held a direct majority share through three large state holding companies, along with 300 subsidiaries and more than 500 minority holdings. Together they accounted for about 5 percent of the total labor force and about 9 percent of the industrial sector labor force, which in comparative perspective is rather insignificant.

A major consequence of the long Socialist tenure in office was a gradual privatization of state holdings, beginning with the privatization of the automobile maker SEAT in 1986 (and later sold to Germany's Volkswagen). Privatization in Spain was not advocated for ideological reasons as was the case in Thatcher's Britain, and the scope of privatization has been far more limited. Rather, the PSOE sought to improve the state portfolio by improving the efficiency of state corporations. In a variety of profitable areas, like telecommunications, the Socialists were less willing to embrace privatization.

In the 1980s and 1990s there was a growing sense that the democratic state, especially under the powerful PSOE, was continuing the tradition of abuse and neglect that was evident under Franco. A series of scandals rocked the country, most of them broken by an aggressive press. Most troubling was the discovery that antiterrorist death squads in the 1980s were run by the police, possibly with the knowledge of higher-ups in the Spanish State.

Economic Performance

The economy in Spain stagnated for the first two decades of Franco's regime, and only in 1963 did real wages recover to the pre-Civil War level of 1936.[52] In the postwar era, Spain's regime was ostracized from the international community. The dictator pursued a policy of autarky (self-sufficiency through high levels of protectionism) that led to widespread suffering of the population. By the early 1950s this policy had failed and Spain was going bankrupt. Franco switched course and began to liberalize the economy in order to attract foreign capital. The result was the economic "miracle" in the

1960s. Spain's cheap labor (due to repression) and low taxes combined with state protection of key industries produced extraordinarily rapid industrial development.

By 1975 Spain was suffering from the side effects of this rapid growth. The OPEC oil crisis of the 1970s hit oil-dependent Spain particularly hard. Inflation, historically very low under Franco, was beginning to increase. Wages that had been kept artificially low during decades of authoritarian rule were now under pressure to rise. Spain's traditionally low budget deficit began to rise as governments during the transition to democracy sought to satiate pent-up demand for public services. Most ominous, however, was the widespread economic crisis symbolized by many of Spain's overprotected and increasingly obsolete industrial plants.

The first governments of the democratic period were unable to address the impending economic crisis. The UCD governments were too weak, and major economic policies were implemented through neocorporatist pacts negotiated between the UCD and parties of the left. The desire to consolidate democracy took precedence over economic reform. As a result, the economy stagnated from 1975 to 1982, and growth slowed to only 1.5 percent. Inflation soared, unemployment climbed, and industrial production and investment declined. The budget deficit skyrocketed. Spain's economic crisis at the time was the most severe in all of Western Europe.[53]

The rapid rise in unemployment since the transition to democracy has been the most alarming economic problem facing Spain. Unemployment rose from under 5 percent in 1975 to 16 percent in 1982. For most of the Socialist's tenure in office, unemployment consistently topped 20 percent (the 1996 rate was 22.7 percent). The Aznar government received much credit for reducing that rate to just over 15 percent by 1999, but Spain continues to have the highest unemployment rate in the EU.[54] There are many causes for this. Franco had been able to avoid high unemployment due to the massive migration of Spaniards to Europe, and the low number of women in the workforce. Europe's economic crisis in the 1970s and the return of democracy reversed this outflow of the labor force. With democratization there has been a rapid entry of

women into the workforce. Franco's use of state protectionism prolonged the life of many industries, but Spain's entry into the Common Market made continued state support for inefficient enterprises untenable. The Socialists' policy of closing down and streamlining such industries threw many Spaniards out of work. The rapid rise in wages after democracy was not accompanied by a rise in productivity, and many firms became less competitive as a result. The delayed effects of the 1960s baby boom that accompanied the economic "miracle" also swelled the labor market.

The Socialists' economic policy between 1982 and 1996 can be understood as an attempt to restructure Spain's economy and prepare it for a full integration into the international economy. In order to carry out this policy, tough austerity measures were implemented, many of which hurt poor Spaniards the most. A devaluation of Spain's currency and a dramatic rise in energy prices were announced on the PSOE's first day in power. The 1983 Law of Re-conversion and Reindustrialization started the process of closing down the most inefficient of Spain's industries. As noted earlier, the Socialists liberalized labor laws, giving employers more freedom to hire and fire workers and thus infuriating Spain's trade unions.[55] Spain's deficit was cut in half between 1982 and 1990, and the rate of growth in public expenditure fell dramatically. Tax reform increased the state's revenue, and inflation fell considerably. In the second half of the 1980s, the growth rate was about 5 percent annually, on average twice that of the European Community. In short, the Socialists were remarkably effective in reforming the Spanish economy. Ironically, these neoliberal measures were similar to the ones adopted by Thatcher's Conservative Party in Britain, although the Socialists insisted that they did so in a more humane fashion. The Socialists defended their record in office by noting the dramatic growth between 1982 and 1989 in expenditures on public pensions, public health, unemployment benefits, and education.[56] Indeed, the Socialists unquestionably made vast improvements in Spain's welfare state, even though their main concern was economic growth and European integration. The real wages of workers improved more than 6 percent during the Socialist period in office.[57] It is also true that once Spain joined the European Union in 1986 and endorsed the European Monetary System in 1989, it had little leeway in its macroeconomic policy.

However, critics have attacked the Socialist policies as hurting the poor and failing to reduce inequality. The percentage of people living in poverty in Spain stayed constant during their period in office, at about 20 percent of the population, far above the European Union average of 14 percent. GINI index data (measuring income inequality) show that levels of inequality declined sharply at the start of the democratic period but held constant (with a very slight decline) during the 16 years of Socialist government. However, as was shown in Table 1.2 in Chapter 1, it is clear that income in Spain is more equally distributed than in the United Kingdom, France, Germany, and Russia.

After 1996 the conservative government continued most of the Socialist economic policies, and it intensified others. In his investiture speech Prime Minister Aznar proposed an accelerated plan of privatization for state industries that would include some of the most profitable pieces of the public sector. Parts of the profitable state telephone and energy-generating monopolies were to be sold. The PP announced drastic budget cuts of $1.6 billion and called for the elimination of over 6,000 public sector jobs. The conservatives planned to reduce taxes on small and medium-sized enterprise and to reduce capital gains taxes to 20 percent.[58] Aznar pledged to reduce Spain's budget deficit, limit Spain's public debt, and tame inflation so as to comply with the EU standards required for participation in the proposed single European currency. By May 1997 Spain had met EU goals and by 1998 it qualified for participation in the new European currency. In recent years the trend of continued growth, declining inflation, and a dropping deficit, have been maintained (see Table 7.6). By June 2000 Spain had the fastest growing economy among the four largest nations in the Euro zone.[59]

The Spanish Welfare State

By the 1980s Spain was spending a greater proportion of national income on social security than did the United States, Britain, Canada, Switzerland, or

TABLE 7.6   Recent Spanish Economic Performance

	1993	1996	1999
Real GDP growth	−1.2	2.4	3.7
Inflation (consumer prices)	4.6	3.6	2.9
Unemployment (% of labor force)	23.7	22.2	15.4
Government deficit as % of GDP	7.0	4.6	1.4

Source: Anuario El País 1999, various years.

Australia, and it is currently in the middle of the pack among OECD nations.[60] This largesse is a relatively recent phenomenon and is mostly the result of the democratic regime. In 1960 Spain spent about 2 percent of its GDP on social security, but by 1990 that figure had risen to about 15 percent. During this period Spain's growth in social security spending was the highest in Europe. The data on social security spending make it clear that the biggest jump in spending accompanied the transition to democracy between 1977 and 1981. Likewise, education spending, which lagged during the Francoist regime, has risen dramatically, as was noted in Figure 7.5.

Democratic governments have overhauled and enhanced the welfare system. All citizens are now entitled to receive welfare benefits. A basic pension is guaranteed to all Spaniards regardless of the amount paid into the system by an individual. Spain's Social Security agency has seen its share of the national budget grow steadily, while the amount of its budget contributed by employers and employees has gradually declined (the state currently contributes about a third of the total cost of social security, similar to other European countries). Social security payments include health care, old age pensions, family support, and support to the disabled.

The National Health System created in 1986 replaced a variety of insurance schemes with an integrated public system that provides universal medical coverage. Universal coverage for all but the wealthiest 1 percent of the population was achieved by 1991 by the PSOE government. About a quarter of Spanish health care is private, and private providers are often contracted by the state to perform health services. A drawback to the extended coverage has been an increase in waiting lists, and investment in health care has not kept up with increased demand. Still, Spain is one of healthiest societies in the world and has the highest life expectancy in the EU. Infant mortality has plummeted and is lower than in the United States and most EU countries.[61]

In addition, the PSOE established a fairly extensive rural subsidy and jobs program, targeting Andalucia and Extremadura, the poor southern provinces. Though criticized for their inefficiency, these programs have significantly improved living standards in the south.

Spain's benefits for the elderly are among the most generous in the world. As a percentage of former earnings, only Sweden's are higher. With the economic crisis of the 1970s and 1980s, the pension system teetered on the verge of bankruptcy. The Socialists overhauled the system, restricting access to disability pensions and imposing stricter limits on the value of retirement benefits.

Spain's alarmingly high unemployment rate has focused attention on unemployment benefits. At the end of the Franco regime, only 62 percent of Spaniards were eligible for such benefits.[62] The Socialists steadily tightened up the criteria for receiving benefits, but in one of the few areas where they responded to trade union pressure, they raised that figure to about 70 percent by 1993. Under the Socialists, the number of Spaniards receiving unemployment benefits rose dramatically.[63] Unlike many European countries, there is no safety net for those who do not qualify for benefits. These individuals are forced to depend on their families for support. Spain's unemployment rate has been especially high among young people, and first-time job seekers do not qualify for unemployment benefits. Workers who qualify for benefits receive an amount that varies according to how much a worker has contributed to unemployment insurance over his or her career, but which is limited to six years. After six

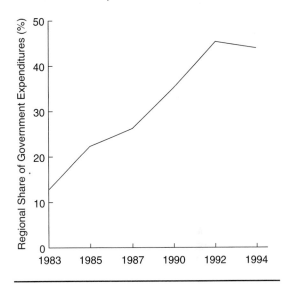

Figure 7.6   Growth in Regional Shares of Government Expenditures, 1983–1994

Source: *Anuario El Pois* (1991, 1993, 1994).

years, a very small unemployment "subsidy" (about $5,000 per year) is available.

Regional Devolution

Spain's democracy has gone a long way toward solving the historical conflict between center and periphery. But the solution has involved compromise, and a small minority of Spaniards remains dissatisfied with the constitutional solution. There can be no doubt that democratization has created a genuine devolution of power. A look at the shift in public expenditures from center to periphery clearly reveals that Spain's 17 Autonomous Communities get an increasingly large share of the pie (see Figure 7.6).

Between 1981 and 1991 the central government lodged Constitutional Court appeals against the ACs 120 times, while the regional government made appeals against the central government 127 times.[64] Most of these disputes involved the "historic" regions of Catalonia and the Basque country. The steady decline of such appeals in recent years (dropping from a high of 131 in 1985 to only 16 by

Box 7.5   The Persistence of Center-Periphery Issues in Spain

The center-periphery cleavage no longer threatens Spanish democracy, but it is still the source of serious tensions. For example, in 1992 the president of Catalonia, Jordi Pujol, infuriated the government in Madrid when he created a foreign policy delegate (similar to a foreign minister) within his government. Ads placed in foreign periodicals by the *Generalitat* (the Catalan government) affirmed "we are a nation." Pujol claimed that the 1992 Olympics were a victory for the Catalan nation. In his trips abroad Pujol has often been received more like a head of state than a state governor. More recently, the Aznar government angered regional officials when it claimed that school curriculums established by regional governments diminished the importance of Castile in Spain's history.

1993) suggests that a *modus vivendi* is slowly emerging in Spain.[65] However, the slow process of devolution and the ambiguous nature of the entire process have given rise to some serious tensions between center and periphery (see Box 7.5).

The most contentious issue between the central and AC governments concerns funding. The ability of ACs to receive revenue from Madrid and to raise it locally varies considerably from region to region. Under the Socialists, a gradual transfer of funds, especially in the areas of education and health care, began to take place, often raising cries of favoritism. The ability of ACs to levy their own taxes has yet to be fully resolved, and to date little AC revenue has been generated from internal taxes. Most of the AC budgets come from a portion of central government taxes collected in each region. Currently, the exact percentage of such taxes going to AC governments is determined by a complex and controversial formula that considers population, area, industrialization, migration patterns, and poverty levels. The bottom line, however, remains that ACs are still heavily dependent on the central state for their budgets, and far more so than states in Germany and the United States.[66]

One problem faced by the central government is income disparities among regions. Since the transition to democracy, many leaders in Madrid have sought to finance ACs in a way that would equalize the wealth among Spanish regions, similar to the European Union's policies toward its poorest members. Article 2 of the Spanish Constitution calls for a leveling of income between regions, and the Inter-Territorial Compensation Fund was established to achieve this. Since 1975, Spanish regions have become more equal, though this has in part resulted from equalization efforts of the European Union. However, Spain's two wealthiest regions and the regions with the greatest autonomy (the Basque Country and Catalonia) view such leveling as a drain on their economies. In addition, such solidaristic policies exacerbate the deep-seated view in both regions that Madrid has historically taken from these regions more than it has given back.

A more localized but still serious tension between center and periphery concerns the minority of individuals in the Basque Country (and to a much smaller extent, Catalonia) who continue to desire independence from Spain. In the Basque Country, *Herri Batasuna (HB)*, the political wing of the pro-independence Basque terrorist organization ETA (Basque Homeland and Liberty) has regularly received about 15 percent of the vote in that region. Those favoring independence are clearly in a small minority, but the persistence of pro-independence sentiment has alarmed many observers. Demands for independence in Catalonia have always been weaker, and in the 1999 regional elections the sole party advocating independence received only about 9 percent of the vote. The percentage of those desiring independence grew in the years following democratization, but plateaued in 1980 and has dropped steadily since then.[67] Even in the Basque Country and Catalonia, the two most pro-independence regions, the percentage of those polled favoring independence dropped from 32 and 15 percent respectively

Box 7.6   Devolution in Action

The success of Spain's devolution can be seen on many levels. In Catalonia, street signs appear in Catalan and a majority of children learn both Catalan and Castilian. The large majority of citizens in Catalonia now speak Catalan. In Catalonia and the Basque Country there are regional police forces and television and radio stations that broadcast in regional languages. All 17 ACs have their own elected governments and court systems, and each has control over territorial planning, social services, and cultural policy.

in 1979, to 15 percent and 8 percent respectively in 1987.

Opinion research has made it clear that only in two regions, Catalonia and the Basque Country, is there a large population with a truly dominant ethnic identity.[68] In other regions, citizens have clearly accepted both national and regional identifications. Even in the Basque Country and Catalonia, however, a sizable group, though not a majority, feel equally attached to Spain and the region. In Catalonia there is a significant percentage (13 percent) that feel only Spanish. As discussed earlier, only in the Basque Country is there significant electoral support for pro-independence parties.

The trend toward devolution now appears to be unstoppable. The central government in 1990 controlled only 65.6 percent of spending compared with 84.5 percent in 1979, one clear sign that the ACs are increasingly important. There is now a growing realization that Spain is moving toward a federal model of government, even if Spain's delicate transition to democracy was not able to acknowledge this at the outset. As a result, there have been renewed calls for revamping the Senate into a genuinely regional body. Concerns that the electoral victory of José María Aznar in 1996 would stem the devolution process were unfounded. Lacking a parliamentary majority, Aznar cut political deals with conservative regional groups that virtually guarantee a continuation of the devolution process.

The ability of the Spanish right to accommodate regional autonomy is one of the crowning achievements of Spanish democracy. After the 1996 elections, the PP's dependence on regional parties to sustain the Aznar government has facilitated this rapprochement. Aznar pledged to double the AC's

share of the national income tax, and will give ACs far greater control over education (see Box 7.6).

Terrorism

Terrorism—one of the most intractable problems of democracy in Spain—had its origins in the Francoist regime. The two main terrorist groups, *Basque Homeland and Liberty* (*ETA*—Euskadi ta Askatassuna) and the October First Revolutionary Antifascist Group (GRAPO), both emerged in opposition to Francoist repression. ETA carried out about 70 percent of the terrorist acts from 1976 to 1980, and about 90 percent after then. GRAPO, a tiny radical leftist group, was responsible for 14 percent of all acts before 1980, but has since disappeared.

Democracy has not solved the problem of terrorism, but the consolidation of democracy has coincided with a decline in the incidence of terrorism. As a result of democratization and devolution of powers to the regions, a major faction of ETA quit the armed struggle in 1977, backing a leftist Basque political party. Curiously, however, ETA continued to grow rapidly, and terrorist acts did not cease. Most targets of ETA terrorism have been members of the state security forces, but innocent bystanders are regularly murdered in ETA attacks. ETA's constant attacks on members of the military were a source of frustration for the armed forces and may have precipitated the attempted coup of 1981. ETA's strategy, in fact, has long been to provoke a military coup in an attempt to demonstrate the underlying authoritarian nature of Spanish democracy.

There has been much speculation about why democratization did not eliminate Basque terrorism.[69] Although it is thought to have no more than

Box 7.7   The Failure of Negotiations and the Tragic Consequences

In Northern Ireland negotiations led to a fragile political settlement that has ended decades of terrorist violence. To date, attempts at negotiations between the Spanish government and ETA have been unsuccessful. For the first time in its 30-year history ETA announced a unilateral cease-fire in September 1988 raising hopes that the end of Basque terrorism was imminent. During 1999 the Aznar government made some minor symbolic concessions to ETA (mainly concerning the relocation of ETA prisoners closer to the Basque Country), and direct contacts between ETA and the government took place in Switzerland. Two main factors led to the failure of these talks. First, ETA insisted that the government recognize the sovereignty of the Basque Country and its right to self-determination. ETA called for the removal of all Spanish police and military from the region. This demand was rejected by all major political forces in Spain, and was clearly unacceptable to Prime Minister Aznar, who has repeatedly claimed that Basques have more autonomy than any other ethnic minority in Europe. Second, arrests of ETA leaders after the announcement of the cease-fire, including one leader who had participated in talks with the government, angered ETA leaders and supporters and led to street violence in the Basque Country. Spanish police continued their attempt to smash ETA and arrest its members, and the success of those efforts hardened ETA's position. In December 1999 ETA ended its 14-month cease-fire and began a campaign of terror that rocked Spain. By the summer of 2000 ETA had murdered six Spaniards and set off explosions throughout Spain.

500 members, ETA's continued existence has been aided by its secretive structure (it is organized into small cells) and its constant campaign of robbery and extortion that have given the organization substantial resources. Popular support for ETA has also been important. The Constitution's failure to recognize the Basque Country's right to self-determination alienated many Basques. To some extent, Spain's democratic leaders until recently lacked the resolve to combat terrorism. Many leftists, and Basques of all political stripes, had sympathized with ETA during the dictatorship and found it hard to denounce the organization after 1977. The Basque Nationalist Party (PNV), for example, refused to refer to ETA as "terrorist." The Basque clergy condemned ETA, but often equated it with the police repression. In addition, ETA received support from foreign terrorist groups, and the French government tolerated the presence of Basque terrorists within its borders until the mid-1980s. ETA's political front, Herri Batasuna (HB), and more recently its successor Euskal Herritarrok (EH), have fared well in regional elections, winning 18 percent of the vote (and gaining four seats) in 1998.

Nevertheless, democratic leaders, while unable to stop terrorism, may be slowly winning the political battle. An accord between Spain and France in 1984 tightened the screws on ETA. Spain's entry into the European Union and NATO has afforded it important allies in the fight against terrorism. Most importantly, the tide of popular opinion within the Basque Country appears to have turned decidedly against ETA. The new Basque police force has also improved the image of government. In January 1988 all Basque political forces, except the pro-ETA HB, signed an antiterrorism pact. The leading Basque political party, the PNV, has been more openly critical of ETA, even though it often disagrees with the government in Madrid over how to best stop terrorism. Polls now regularly show that an overwhelming majority of Basques favor the disarming of ETA. In recent years, massive demonstrations against terrorism have become commonplace. Indeed, ETA's sudden announcement of a unilateral cease-fire in September 1988 (see Box 7.7) likely resulted from its growing isolation within the Basque Country. ETA's attempt to drive a wedge between political forces with the Basque Country has clearly failed.

Women in Spain

During the Franco regime, discrimination against women was blatant. Contraception, divorce, and abortion were all strictly illegal. Males had statutory power over women within Spanish families, and women needed permission from their husbands for a wide variety of activities. Women had no control over family assets. Penalties for adultery were far harsher for women than for men. Women's organizations, except for the absurd "Women's Section" of the official party (which sponsored courses on how to be a good wife and mother), were banned.

How successful has democracy been in promoting equality for Spain's women? The answer to this question is generally encouraging, but not without some important qualifications.[70] Much of the struggle for women's rights after 1975 was subordinated by the struggle to consolidate democracy. The first UCD governments abolished some of the most egregious legislation from the Francoist period, and the Constitution gave women and men legal equality, but many aspects of the document disappointed the women's movement. For example, the Constitution fudged on the issue of abortion by stating that "All have the right to life," implying possible inclusion of the fetus and rejecting the wording proposed by the left.[71] As noted earlier, the Constitution gives male heirs precedence over female heirs to the throne.

The consolidation of democracy did, however, facilitate the passing of laws that gave basic rights to women. By 1978 parliament had abolished some sexist laws, like criminalization of adultery for women, and had legalized contraceptives. Divorce was legalized only in 1981, and only after a bitter struggle that helped destroy the governing UCD. Other reforms had to await the election of the Socialists.

After 1982, the PSOE government actively sought to promote women's causes, and feminists were able to obtain important political positions. The most important innovation was the creation of the Spanish Women's Institute, the most powerful governmental institution to which Spanish women had access. With Cabinet backing, it pursued myriad actions to improve the lot of women. It attempted to eliminate all legislation that discriminated against women, improve women's health (a landmark 1985 health bill included provisions for state-funded family planning), promote women's participation in society, and encourage equal sharing of domestic responsibilities.

As a result, the lives of Spanish women in the first two decades of democracy have improved considerably.[72] As women have had increased opportunities to enter the labor market and as contraception has become widely available, there has been a rapid decline in birth rates: by 1990 Spain's birth rate was one of the lowest in Europe. Publicly funded preschool for 3- to 6-year-olds, a crucial issue for women, has been extensively implemented through Socialist policies. Spanish women have made enormous strides in higher education. By the end of the Francoist regime, only about a third of university students were women. Today over half of university students are women, making Spain one of Europe's leaders in this respect.

The Socialist record on abortion was far more mixed. Though pledging to legalize abortion, the PSOE introduced very timid legislation in 1983 that legalized abortions only if a woman's life or health is in danger, if the pregnancy results from rape, or if the fetus is gravely deformed. In practice abortions are hard to obtain in the National Health System. While doctors at private health clinics often interpret the law liberally (citing emotional distress to the mother as a health danger), many women are forced to seek illegal abortions or travel to other European countries where abortions are permitted. The Socialist plan to further liberalize abortion was shelved after the PSOE lost its majority in the 1993 elections and was forced to rely on support from more conservative regional forces.

Unemployment has been a matter of particular concern for women. Not only do women work disproportionately in lower paying and less secure jobs (in 1992 women on average earned only 72.5 percent of what men were paid), but the unemployment rate for women (about 30 percent) is almost double that of men and is the highest in Europe.[73]

Spain's Socialists can take credit for increasing the role of women in politics, a profession reserved for men until very recently. PSOE women were able to introduce a quota system requiring that a quarter of all party-controlled public posts be given to women. At the start of the Socialists' tenure in office, only 5 percent of political appointments went to women; by 1991 this figure had increased to 13 percent. One-fourth of the members of the Spanish legislature are women in the current legislature, well above the European average of 16 percent.[74]

Despite the continued strength of Spanish *machismo* and the persistence of discrimination against women, signs of change are everywhere. Women judges, Cabinet ministers, and (since 1993) bullfighters have changed the traditional image of Spanish women.

Foreign Policy

Spain was not an important international actor during the Franco regime. The international community ostracized authoritarian Spain during the first part of Franco's rule. The isolation was partly broken in the 1950s, when the United States began to value Spain's role as an anticommunist bulwark. A 1953 agreement between Spain and the United States gave the United States valuable military facilities on Spanish soil in exchange for American economic aid and political support. Membership in the United Nations came soon after, in 1955, and relations with Spain's European neighbors began to thaw (a trade agreement with the EEC was signed in 1970) but remained cool until after the death of the dictator in 1975.

Under the first UCD governments, Spain's relations with the world underwent a rapid normalization. Spain applied for membership in the European Community and NATO, improved relations with its neighbors, and formally renounced its last colonial claims in North Africa. After Spain's four decades of isolation the decision to join the European Union was supported by almost every Spanish political force and took on almost mythical significance. Spain, along with Portugal, joined the EU in 1986 after intense and protracted negotiations. Spain quickly became one of the strongest proponents for monetary integration. Despite the enormous sacrifices required over the last two decades in order to integrate into the EU, Spaniards continue

to be among the strongest supporters of European integration and a common foreign policy. Opinion research conducted in November 1999 showed that 64 percent of Spaniards supported the European Union, far above the average European level of support for the EU, and making the Spanish the fifth most pro-EU population (behind Ireland, Luxembourg, The Netherlands and Portugal).[75] Sixty-one percent of Spaniards believe that EU membership has benefited Spain, far above the EU average of 46 percent. Spaniards were also among the most enthusiastic backers of the new European currency, the Euro.

Integration into NATO proved far more controversial. Much of the left and a sector of the governing UCD were opposed to NATO membership when it was first proposed by the government in 1977, but they were unable to stop the process and Spain was formally admitted in May 1982. The PSOE opposed NATO membership and promised to hold a referendum on the issue if elected to power. The Socialists' resounding electoral victory in 1982 put Spain's membership in the Atlantic Alliance in question, as the new government froze military integration into NATO. However, Prime Minister Felipe González began to back away from his party's opposition to NATO. The reasons for this change of heart are complex, but fear of endangering Spain's EC application and a desire to democratize and modernize Spain's military were key factors. By mid-1984, González proposed a "compromise" whereby Spain would remain within NATO (but would not integrate into the military command structure), reduce the U.S. military presence in Spain, and ban nuclear weapons from Spanish territory. The PSOE kept its promise to hold a referendum on NATO—but now called on voters to ratify membership! Despite considerable popular opposition to NATO membership (many Spaniards favored neutrality, which had been the official policy of the PSOE in the 1982 electoral campaign), Spanish voters narrowly supported continued NATO membership in a March 1986 referendum. In 1988 the Socialists' carried through on the pledge to reduce the U.S. military presence by renegotiating Spain's military agreement with the United States. The 1995 appointment of Javier

Solana, a former Socialist cabinet minister, as the first Spanish NATO Secretary General, ended doubts about Spain's commitment to the organization. In 1996 the conservative government of Prime Minister Aznar guided a bill through the Cortes that fully integrated Spain into NATO's military command. Despite strong domestic opposition, Spain sent 1,000 troops to participate in NATO's Kosovo operation in 1999.

Spain is currently engaged in few international conflicts, but the most important unresolved foreign policy issue concerns the status of *Gibraltar*, a tiny (just over two square miles) British dependency on the southwest portion of the Iberian Peninsula that juts out into the Mediterranean Sea. Great Britain won the "rock" from Spain in 1704 but Spain claims sovereignty over Gibraltar. In protest over Britain's refusal to "return" Gibraltar, Franco closed the border between Gibraltar and Spain in an attempt to cut off and strangle the enclave. Instead, the policy only strengthened the resolve of Gibraltar's residents to remain British citizens. Only after the election of a Socialist government in 1982 was the border between Spain and Gibraltar normalized, but Spain has continued its claim over the rock. Fortunately, this issue no longer endangers Spain's relations with Britain, and the dispute is no longer imbued with the emotion that was present during the Franco years. An April 1999 accord between Spain and the United Kingdom has opened the way for future negotiations over the territory and promises to further ease tensions.

Spain continues to enjoy special ties to its former colonies in Latin America, having assumed the role of cultural leader of the 300 million Spanish speakers worldwide. It has attempted to represent the interests of Latin America within the European Union. In addition, democratic governments have been harsh critics of human rights violations in Latin America. Socialist support for Sandinista Nicaragua and Castro's Cuba (although Spain has been critical of both countries from time to time) created friction with the Reagan and Bush administrations during the 1980s. One of the first foreign policy acts of the conservative Aznar government was to cut off official Spanish aid to Cuba, an act that drew praise from the United States. However,

in 1997 the new conservative government locked horns with the democratic administration of Bill Clinton over U.S. Cuba policy. PP Foreign Minister, Abel Matutes, blasted U.S. attempts to penalize European investors in Cuba, threatening the United States with retaliation. Spain has played an active role in the negotiation and enforcement of peace proposals in Nicaragua and El Salvador, and has played a key role in United Nations missions in both countries.

In the mid-1990s Spanish foreign policy focused on two regional issues that were seen to directly threaten Spain's national security. Under Franco, millions of Spaniards emigrated to Europe seeking employment. The reverse trend occurred in the 1990s when a wave of job seekers from North Africa crossed the straits of Gibraltar, often illegally, raising concerns about Spain's ability to accommodate these immigrants. Racial tensions between African migrant workers and Spanish citizens exploded in southern Spain in February 2000, leading to considerable violence. Within the EU Spain has one of the smallest percentages of foreign residents (only .4 percent in 1998), and in opinion polls Spaniards view themselves as being among the least racist in Europe.[76] The recent violence has called into question Spain's racial tolerance, and immigration from Africa is likely to be an important issue in the near future.

The second issue involves the endangered health of the Mediterranean Sea. Spain has assumed an active role here, working closely with its neighbors to persuade the European Union to improve its Mediterranean environmental policy.

The Peaceful Disappearance of the Two Spains

For students of comparative politics, Spain's remarkable transition to democracy and its ability to overcome dangerous historical cleavages offers numerous lessons. Most importantly, the transition to democracy demonstrates that the art of politics—especially creative leadership and political compromise—can solve seemingly intractable political problems. The transition was successful in large part because of the ability of Juan Carlos and Adolfo Suárez to use Francoist political structures to promote democratic reform, and the willingness of democratic opposition leaders to tolerate such a strategy. Skilled political leadership was not the only explanation for Spain's successful democratization. As noted in Chapter 1, the relationship between economic development and democracy is a complex one, and this is certainly illustrated in the Spanish case. Rapid economic development under Franco after 1960 began to change Spanish society in ways that the dictator could not have foreseen. The urbanization, secularization, greater education, and increasing wealth of Spaniards all eroded historical cleavages. The opening of Spain to foreign investment ignited the economic boom, and the opening of Spanish society to foreign influence began to foster a democratic political culture.

Not all political cleavages have been mitigated by skilled leadership and economic modernization. As we have seen, the center-periphery issue continues to challenge Spanish democracy, but by the year 2000 only Basque terrorism remained as a reminder of this persistent problem. Small sectors of Spain's armed forces still admire Spain's authoritarian past, but the vast majority have accepted democratic rule. On the whole, however, the historic divide between the "two Spains" has been replaced by a united modern democracy that is undergoing a successful integration with its European neighbors.

✌ KEY TERMS ✌

Anti-Terrorist Liberation
    Groups (GAL)
Autonomous
    Communities
José María Aznar
Basque Homeland and
    Liberty (ETA)
Basque Nationalist
    Party (PNV)
Basques
King Juan Carlos
Castilians
Catalans
Civil Guard
Congress of Deputies
Constitutional Court

constructive vote of no
    confidence
Convergence and
    Union (CiU)
Cortes
Defensor del Pueblo
devolution
Francisco Franco
Galicians
General Confederation
    of Workers (UGT)
Gibraltar
Felipe González
Herri Batasuna (HB)
Moncloa Pacts
Opus Dei

Popular Party (PP)
President of the
    Government
Reconquista
José Luis Rodríguez
    Zapatero
Senate
Spanish Civil War
    (1936–1939)
Spanish Communist
    Party (PCE)
Spanish Confederation
    of Entrepreneurial
    Organizations
    (CEOE)
Spanish Inquisition

Spanish Second
    Republic
    (1931–1936)
Spanish Socialist Workers
    Party (PSOE)
Adolfo Suárez
Supreme Court
two Spains
Union of the Democratic
    Center (UCD)
United Left (IU)
Workers' Commissions
    (CC.OO)

✌ SUGGESTED READINGS ✌

Aguero, Felipe. *Soldiers, Civilians, and Democracy: Post Franco Spain in Comparative Perspective.* Baltimore: Johns Hopkins University Press, 1995.

Gunther, Richard, G. Sani, and G. Shabad. *Spain After Franco.* Berkeley: University of California Press, 1986.

Heywood, Paul. *The Government and Politics of Spain.* New York: St. Martin's Press, 1995.

Hooper, John. *The New Spaniards.* London: Penguin, 1995.

Lancaster, Thomas D., and Michael S. Lewis-Beck. "The Spanish Voter: Tradition, Economics, Ideology." *Journal of Politics* 48, No. 3 (August 1986): 648–74.

Lieberman, Sima. *Growth and Crisis in the Spanish Economy, 1940–1993.* London: Routledge, 1995.

McDonough, Peter, Samuel H. Barnes, and Antonio López Pina. *The Cultural Dynamics of Democratization in Spain.* Ithaca, NY: Cornell University Press, 1998.

Pérez-Díaz, Víctor M. *Spain at the Crossroads: Civil Society, Politics, and the Rule of Law.* Cambridge, MA: Harvard University Press, 1999.

Share, Donald. "Transitions to Democracy and Transition Through Transaction." *Comparative Political Studies* 14, No. 1 (January 1987): 525–48.

———. *Dilemmas of Social Democracy: The Spanish Socialist Workers Party in the 1980s.* Westport, CT: Greenwood Publishers, 1989.

———. *The Making of Spanish Democracy.* New York: Center for the Study of Democratic Institutions/Praeger Publishers, 1986.

Threlfall, Monica. "Feminist Politics and Social Change in Spain." In Monica Threlfall, ed., *Mapping the Women's Movement.* London: Verso, 1996, pp. 115–51.

ENDNOTES

1. Victor Pérez-Díaz, *Spain at the Crossroads* (Cambridge, MA: Harvard University Press, 1999), p. 106.

2. Donald Share, *The Making of Spanish Democracy* (New York: Praeger Publishers and the Center for the Study of Democratic Institutions, 1986), pp. 86–118.

3. United Nations, *World Urbanization Prospects* (New York: United Nations, 1995), p. 76.

4. The committee was more or less composed to reflect the strength of the various political forces in the legislature. As a result, the center-right Union of the Democratic Center had three seats, while the Socialist, Communist, and rightist Popular Alliance had one each. The Catalan minority (but, significantly, no Basque party) was given the final seat.

5. See J. Capo Giol, R. Cotarelo, D. López Garrido, and J. Subirats, "By Consociationalism to a Majoritarian Parliamentary System: The Rise and Decline of the Spanish Cortes," in Ulrike Liebert and Maurizio Cotta, eds., *Parliament and Democratic Consolidation in Southern Europe* (London: Pinter, 1990), pp. 92–129.

6. For a good overview, see Richard Gillespie, "The Break-up of the 'Socialist Family': Party-Union Relations in Spain, 1982–1989," *West European Politics* 13, No. 1 (January 1990): pp. 47–62.

7. Donald Share, *Dilemmas of Social Democracy: The Spanish Socialist Workers Party in the 1980s* (Westport, CT: Greenwood, 1989).

8. An outstanding overview is Thomas Lancaster and Michael Gates, "Spain," in Alan Katz, ed., *Legal Traditions and Systems* (New York: Greenwood Press, 1986), pp. 360–80.

9. Frederick Weil, "The Sources and Structure of Legitimation in Western Democracies," *American Sociological Review* 54 (October 1989): 691.

10. Peter McDonough, Samuel Barnes, and Antonio Lopez Pina, "The Nature of Political Support and Legitimacy in Spain," in *Comparative Political Studies* 27, No. 3 (October 1994): 356.

11. Thomas D. Lancaster and Michael S. Lewis-Beck, "The Spanish Voter: Tradition, Economics, Ideology," *Journal of Politics* 48, No. 3 (August 1986): 651.

12. Heywood, *Government and Politics of Spain*, (New York: Saint Martin's Press, 1995), p. 173.

13. Hooper, *The New Spaniards* (London: Penguin, 1995), p. 229 ff.

14. Peter McDonough, Samuel H. Barnes, and Antonio Lopez Pina, "Social Identity and Mass Politics in Spain," *Comparative Political Studies* 21, No. 2 (July 1988): 200–30.

15. McDonough, Barnes, and Lopez Pina, "Social Identity," p. 220.

16. McDonough, Barnes, and Lopez Pina, "Social Identity," p. 209.

17. Pradeep Chhibber and Mariano Torcal, "Elite Strategy, Social Cleavages, and Party Systems in a New Democracy: Spain," *Comparative Political Studies* 30, No. 1 (February 1997): 27–54.

18. Jorge Benedicto Millan, "Sistemas de valores y pautas de cultura predominantes en la sociedad espazola (1976–1985)," in Jose J Felix Tezanos, Ramon Cotarelo, and Andres de Blas, eds., *La transicion democratica espanola* (Madrid: Editorial Sistema, 1989), p. 649.

19. McDonough, Barnes, and Lopez Pina, "The Nature of Political Support," pp. 335–36.

20. McDonough, Barnes, and Lopez Pina, "Social Identity," p. 223.

21. Benedicto Millan, "Sistema de valores," p. 664.

22. *Eurobarometer*, 52, April 2000, p. 12.

23. Frederick Weil, "The Sources and Structure of Legitimation in Western Democracies," *American Sociological Review* 54 (October 1989): 696.

24. *Eurobarometer*, 47.1, December 1997.

25. Hooper, *The New Spaniards*, p. 269.

26. Hooper, *The New Spaniards*, p. 289.

27. *Eurobarometer*, 52, April 2000, p. 15.

28. Hooper, *The New Spaniards*, p. 307.

29. Hooper, *The New Spaniards*, p. 306.

30. Hooper, *The New Spaniards*, p. 177.

31. An excellent work on Spanish trade unions is Robert Fishman, *Working Class Opposition and the Return to Democracy in Spain* (Ithaca, NY: Cornell University Press, 1990).

32. Heywood, *Government and Politics of Spain*, p. 250; Philippe Schmitter, "Organized Interest and Democratic Consolidation in Southern Europe," in Richard Guther et al., *The Politics of Democratic Consolidation* (Baltimore: Johns Hopkins University Press, 1995), p. 294.

33. Lynne Wozniak, "The Dissolution of Party-Union Relations in Spain" *International Journal of Political Economy,* 22, No. 4 (Winter 1992–1993): 83.

34. Schmitter, "Organized Interest and Democratic Consolidation," p. 295.

35. Schmitter, "Organized Interest and Democratic Consolidation," p. 304.

36. Manuel Mella Marquez,"Los grupos de presión en la transición política" in José Félix Tezanos, Ramón Cotarelo, and Andrés de Blas (eds.), *La transición democrática española* (Madrid: Editorial Sistema, 1989), pp. 149–181.

37. *The Economist,* May 13, 2000, p. 51.

38. Hooper, *The New Spaniards,* p. 133.

39. José Ramón Montero, "Religiosidad, ideología y voto en españa," *Revista de Estudios Políticos* 83 (January–March 1994): 85.

40. Heywood, "The Spanish Left: Towards a Common Home?" in Martin Bull and Paul Heywood, eds., *West European Communist Parties after the Revolutions of 1989* (London: St. Martins, 1994).

41. On the PSOE, see Donald Share, *Dilemmas of Social Democracy.*

42. Juan J. Linz, "From Great Hopes to Civil War: The Breakdown of Democracy in Spain," in Juan J. Linz and Alfred Stepan, eds., *The Breakdown of Democratic Regimes: Europe* (Baltimore, MD: Johns Hopkins University Press, 1978), p. 166.

43. See Share, *Dilemmas of Social Democracy,* p. 28.

44. Kenneth Medhurst, "Spanish Conservative Politics," in Zig Layton-Henry, ed., *Conservative Parties in Western Europe* (London: MacMillan, 1982), p. 313.

45. Of the 165 UCD deputies elected to the Congress of Deputies in 1977, there were 49 Christian Democrats, 22 Liberals, 18 Social Democrats, 19 Regional Centrists, and 57 "Suáristas" (supporters of Suárez).

46. Heywood, *Government and Politics of Spain,* p. 204.

47. Richard Gunther, "Electoral Laws, Party Systems, and Elites: The Case of Spain," *American Political Science Review* 83, No. 3 (September 1989): 840.

48. Heywood, *Government and Politics of Spain,* p. 183.

49. Morlino, "Political Parties and Democratic Consolidation in Southern Europe," in *The Politics of Democratic Consolidation,* Richard Gunther, P. Nikiforous Diamandorous, and Hans-Jurgen Puhle, eds. (Baltimore: Johns Hopkins Press, 1995), pp. 331–32, discusses Spain's incredibly low party identification compared with its southern European neighbors (Portugal, Greece, and Italy). In 1985, the percentage of respondents with a party in Spain was only 47.5 percent, and by 1989 it had dropped to 30 percent, well below Spain's neighbors, all of which had identification levels near or above 50 percent. Indeed, Spain is the Western European country with the lowest level of party identification.

50. Morlino, "Political Parties," p. 319.

51. Heywood, *Government and Politics of Spain,* p. 122.

52. A good overview of the Spanish economy can be found in Sima Lieberman, *Growth and Crisis in the Spanish Economy, 1940–93* (London: Routledge, 1995).

53. José María Maravall, "Politics and Policy: Economic Reforms in Southern Europe," in Luiz Carlos Bresser Pereira et al., eds., *Economic Reforms in New Democracies* (Cambridge: Cambridge University Press, 1993), p. 89.

54. *Financial Times Survey,* June 24, 1996, pp. I–VI.

55. Spain's restrictive labor laws were a feature of Franco's regime. Workers had no real power within the Francoist syndical structure, but the regime attempted to gain the quiescence of workers through a system of near-guaranteed employment.

56. Maravall, "Politics and Policy," p. 111.

57. Maravall, "Politics and Policy," p. 108, argues that despite huge crisis and unemployment, earnings per worker actually rose from 1983 to 1991, up 6.2 percent in real earning power.

58. *El País Internacional,* May 13, 1996, p. 12.

59. *New York Times,* June 22, 2000, p. C4.

60. Francis G. Castles, "Welfare State Development in Southern Europe," *West European Politics* 2 (April 1995): 292. This is an excellent overview of the Spanish welfare state, from which this section draws heavily.

61. Hooper, *The New Spaniards,* p. 253.

62. Hooper, *The New Spaniards,* p. 245.

63. Maravall, "Politics and Policy," p. 106.

64. Heywood, *Government and Politics of Spain,* p. 147.

65. *Anuário El País* (1995), p. 96.

66. Heywood, *Government and Politics of Spain,* p. 152.

67. Heywood, "The Spanish Left," p. 161.

68. Eduardo López-Aranguren and Manuel Garcia Ferrando, "Nacionalismo y regionalism en la España de los autonomias," in José Beneyto Vidal, ed., *España a debate* (Madrid: Teenos, 1991), pp. 177–90.

69. Reinares, "Democratización y Terrorismo," p. 620.

70. The best overview of the women's movement in Spain, from which this section borrows heavily, is Monica Threlfall, "Feminist Politics and Social Change in Spain," in Monica Threlfall, ed., *Mapping the Women's Movement* (London: Verso, 1996), pp. 115–51.

71. Threlfall, "Feminist Politics," p. 120.

72. Threlfall, "Feminist Politics," p. 129.

73. Threlfall, "Feminist Politics," p. 141.

74. Based on information gathered from The Inter-parliamentary Union, http://www.ipu.org/

75. European Commission, *Eurobarometer Number 52* (April 2000), p. 26.

76. *El País,* February 14, 2000, p. 24, and European Commission, *Eurobarometer Number 47.1* (December 1997), p. 2.

RUSSIA

0	300	600 mi
0	482	964 km

DENMARK
NORWAY
SWEDEN
LATVIA
FINLAND
POLAND
BELARUS
ESTONIA
LITHUANIA
UKRAINE
Moscow
GEORGIA
ARMENIA
AZERBAIJAN
TURKMENISTAN
UZBEKISTAN
TAJIKISTAN
KYRGYZSTAN
IRAN
AFGHANISTAN

St. Petersburg
Barents Sea
Kara Sea
Ob
Volga
Caspian Sea
Aral Sea
Lake Balkash

K A Z A K H S T A N

C H I N A

ARCTIC OCEAN
East Siberian Sea
Laptev Sea
Bering Sea
Lena
Magadan
Yakutsk
Sea of Okhotsk

N

Omsk
Novosibirsk
Tomsk
Yenisey
Ob
Krasnoyarsk
Irkutsk
Lake Baikal
Khabarovsk

M O N G O L I A

JAPAN
Sea of Japan
NORTH KOREA

CHAPTER 8

POLITICS IN RUSSIA

THOMAS F. REMINGTON

Country Bio–Russia

POPULATION   146 Million

TERRITORY   17 million square kilometers

YEAR OF INDEPENDENCE   1991

YEAR OF CURRENT CONSTITUTION   1993

CHIEF OF STATE   President Vladimir Vladimirovich Putin

HEAD OF GOVERNMENT   Premier Mikhail Mikhaylovich Kasyanov

LANGUAGE(S)   Russian, other

RELIGION:

Orthodox: 71.8%, Muslim: 5.5%, Catholic: 1.8%, Protestant: .7%, Buddhist: .6%, Jewish: .3%, Other: .9%, No affiliation: 18.4%

Rebuilding Russia

On December 31, 1999, President Boris Yeltsin appeared on Russian national television to announce that he was resigning as president of Russia. Although Yeltsin's term was not due to expire until June 2000, he had decided to leave office early and turn the powers of the presidential office over to his prime minister, Vladimir Putin, who under the constitution was Yeltsin's successor. Parliamentary elections had just been held and had confirmed Putin's political strength. Yeltsin was leaving in such a way as to give Putin a strong advantage in the upcoming presidential election, which according to the constitution had to be held within three months of the president's leaving office. Putin's very first decree as acting president was to grant Yeltsin and his family lifetime immunity from all criminal prosecution. The manner in which the succession occurred was not illegal, but to many it smacked of an inside deal.

Yeltsin was first elected Russian president in 1991, a time of intense struggle between forces of change and the forces defending the old, communist order. By the end of 1991 those battles climaxed with the end of communist rule and the disintegration of the Soviet Union and Russia's independence as a national state. Yeltsin was reelected in 1996

307

under a new constitution adopted in 1993 and, despite growing infirmity, held on to power until his resignation in 1999; more than anyone else, Boris Yeltsin was the architect of Russia's transition from communism.

Russia's history as a post-communist state is brief: it dates only to the collapse of the Soviet Union in 1991. But Russia has existed as a state for over a thousand years, and for most of the twentieth century, Russia was the core of the larger communist state called the Union of Soviet Socialist Republics (USSR, or Soviet Union). Russia today shares many continuities of political culture and social structure with its Soviet and earlier past. At the same time, we should not underestimate how deeply Russia's political institutions have changed.

Russia's Political Agenda

Russia's leaders face an agenda of overwhelming proportions. The new political system has to cope with the onerous inheritance of communism. Under the old regime, the planners gave priority to military needs, leaving the rest of the economy to suffer from inefficient technologies and insufficient investment. Society was organized in such a way as to put it at the service of the state. System-level functions such as socialization, recruitment, and communication were shaped to meet the objectives set by the Communist Party. Although they claimed that they were building for a long-term communist future, in fact the rulers exploited the country's resources through wasteful and often destructive economic practices. At a deeper level, they reinforced values in the political culture which discouraged idealism, independence of thought, and civic-mindedness.

Russia's government today has not been able to solve the vast problems that it has inherited. In fact, its capacity to implement policy honestly and effectively is low. The wages and pensions of some of the most impoverished and vulnerable groups of the population, such as teachers, the indigent, and the elderly, often go unpaid for months at a time. Begging, homelessness, and delinquency have spread. Corruption and incompetence in the state bureaucracy are rife. Contract killings of state officials, journalists, and businessmen go unsolved. Many

banks have failed, taking depositors' savings with them. Meanwhile, large sums of earnings flee the country every year for off-shore banks, and a class of "new Russians" flaunts its wealth with fancy cars and trips abroad. Weakening of the social fabric has brought about rising alcohol abuse and crime, and a sharp increase in mortality rates since 1990.

For a majority of the population, living standards have fallen since the end of the communist regime, while uncertainty and anxiety have risen. As a result, confidence in the future is low. The most basic task facing Russia is to improve the quality of governance, so that political order is guaranteed through law, and not through fear or favor. If people's confidence in government can be raised, people will begin to build for a long-term future.

Changing Political Institutions

The Tsarist Regime

The Russian state traces its origins to the princely state that arose around Kiev (today the capital of independent Ukraine) in the ninth century of the present era. For nearly a thousand years, the Russian state was autocratic. That is, it was ruled by a hereditary monarch whose power was unlimited by any constitution. Only in the first decade of the twentieth century did the Russian tsar agree to grant a constitution calling for an elected legislature—and even then the tsar soon dissolved the legislature and revised the constitution unilaterally. State power in Russia was *absolutist*, meaning that the tsar wielded absolute power over the subjects of the realm. Tsarism was also influenced by *patrimonialism*, which refers to the idea that the ruler *owned* his realm as property.[1] Finally, tsarism allied itself with the Russian Orthodox Church. In Russia, as in other countries where it is the dominant religious tradition, the Orthodox Church supports the state authorities, identifying itself with the nation and exhorting its followers to show loyalty and obedience to the state.

Autocracy, patrimonialism, and Orthodoxy were not, however, the only major institutional features of Russia's political history. At times, Russia's rulers sought to improve Russia's military and economic potential by importing Western practices in technology, law, state organization, and education. Modernizing rulers such as Peter the Great (who ruled from 1682 to 1725) and Catherine the Great (1762–1796) had a powerful impact on Russian society, bringing it closer to West European models. This imperative was all the more pressing because of Russia's constant expansion through conquest and annexation of neighboring territories, and the ever-present need to defend its borders against outside powers. The state grew with the need to govern a vast territory: by the end of the seventeenth century, Russia was territorially the largest state in the world. But for most of its history, Russia's imperial reach generally exceeded its actual grasp, because its administrative capacity was riddled with inefficiency.

By comparison with the other major powers of Europe, Russia's economic institutions remained backward well into the twentieth century, but the trajectory of its development, especially in the nineteenth century, was toward that of a modern industrial society. By the time the tsarist order fell in 1917, Russia possessed a large industrial sector, although it was heavily concentrated in a few major cities; and the country had a sizable middle class consisting of merchants, industrialists, and professionals. They constituted but a small stratum, though, compared with the vast and impoverished peasantry and the radicalized industrial working class, and they were swept aside when the communists seized power in 1917.

The thousand-year tsarist era left a diverse and contradictory legacy. Rulers attempted to legitimate their absolute power by appealing to pride in tradition, empire, and divine right, and they treated constitutionalism and law as instruments of rule rather than sources of authority. The principle of the accountability of rulers to ruled and the doctrine that sovereignty resides in the will of the people were alien to Russian state tradition. Throughout Russian history, state and society have been more separate from each other than in Western societies. Rulers and populace regarded one another with mistrust and suspicion. This gap has been overcome at times of great national trials—above all in wars requiring great national mobilizations, such as the war against Napoleon and later the Great Patriotic War against Nazi Germany. Victory in those wars was celebrated as a triumphant demonstration of the unity of state and people. But Russia's political traditions also include alternative ideals, especially reflected in the writings of its great poets and writers. They reflect a yearning for equality, solidarity, and community, as well as for moral purity and sympathy for the downtrodden. And throughout the Russian heritage runs a deep strain of national feeling, based less on a sense of ethnic identity than on pride in the greatness of the country and the enduring strength of its people.

The Communist Revolution and the Soviet Order

The tsarist order fell because it could not cope with the severe strains of World War I. Tsar Nicholas II abdicated in February 1917 (March 1917, by the Western calendar), and the political vacuum was filled with a short-lived provisional government which in turn fell when the Russian Communists—Bolsheviks, as they called themselves—took power in October 1917 (November, by our calendar). Their aim was to create a socialist society in Russia and, eventually, to spread revolutionary socialism throughout the world. Socialism, the Russian Communist Party believed, meant a society without private ownership of the means of production, where the state owned and controlled all important economic assets, and where political power was exercised in the name of the working people. *Vladimir Ilyich Lenin* was the leader of the Russian Communist Party and the first head of the Soviet Russian government (see Figure 8.1).

Under Lenin's model of rule, the Communist Party controlled all levels of government. At each level of the territorial hierarchy of the country, full-time Communist Party officials supervised government. At the top, final power to decide policy rested in the CPSU (Communist Party of the Soviet Union) Politburo. Under *Joseph Stalin*, who took power after Lenin's death in 1924 and ruled until his death in 1953, power was even further centralized. Stalin instituted a totalitarian regime intent upon building up Russia's industrial and military might. Although the state survived the terrible test of World War II, ultimately pushing back the

FIGURE 8.1   Soviet Political Leaders, 1917–1991

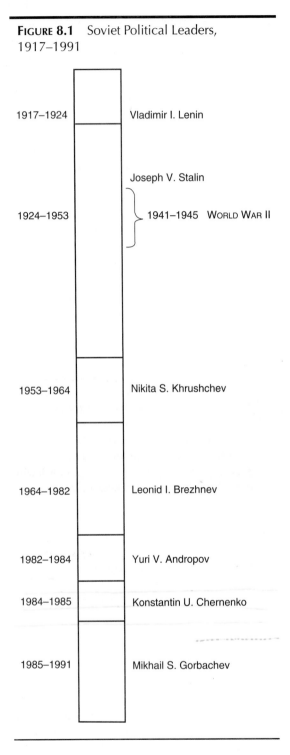

1917–1924	Vladimir I. Lenin
1924–1953	Joseph V. Stalin 1941–1945 WORLD WAR II
1953–1964	Nikita S. Khrushchev
1964–1982	Leonid I. Brezhnev
1982–1984	Yuri V. Andropov
1984–1985	Konstantin U. Chernenko
1985–1991	Mikhail S. Gorbachev

German army all the way to Berlin, the combined cost of war and terror under Stalin was staggering. The institutions of rule that Stalin left behind eventually crippled the Soviet state: they included personalistic rule, insecurity for rulers and ruled alike, heavy reliance on the secret police, and a militarized economy. None of Stalin's successors could reform the system without undermining communist rule itself.

The problem was that vast as the Soviet state's powers were, they were frustrated by bureaucratic immobilism. As in any organization, overcentralization undermined actual power, through distortions of information flow, tacit resistance to the center's orders by officials at lower levels who had their own interests, and the force of inertia. By the time *Mikhail Gorbachev* was elected General Secretary of the CPSU in 1985, the political system of the USSR had grown top-heavy, unresponsive, and muscle-bound.

The youngest member of the Politburo at the time he was named party leader—he was only 54 when he took over—Mikhail Gorbachev quickly grasped the levers of power that the system granted the General Secretary and moved both to strengthen his own political base and to carry out a program of reform.[2] Emphasizing the need for greater openness—*glasnost*—in relations between political leaders and the populace, Gorbachev stressed that the ultimate test of the party's effectiveness lay in improving the economic well-being of the country and its people. By highlighting such themes as the need for market relations, pragmatism in economic policy, and less secretiveness in government, he identified himself as a champion of reform. Gorbachev not only called for political democratization, but he pushed through a reform bringing about the first contested elections for local soviets in many decades. He legalized private enterprise for individual and cooperative businesses and encouraged them to fill the many gaps in the economy left by the inefficiency of the state sector. He called for a "law-governed state" (*pravovoe gosudarstvo*) in which state power—including the power of the Communist Party—would be subordinate to law. He welcomed the explosion of informal social and political associations that formed. He made major concessions to the United States in the sphere of arms control, resulting in a treaty which, for the first time in history, called for the destruction of entire classes of nuclear missiles.

Using to the full the General Secretary's authoritarian powers, Gorbachev quickly railroaded his proposals for democratization through the Supreme Soviet, and in 1989 and 1990 Gorbachev's plan for free elections and a working parliament was realized as elections were held, deputies elected, and new soviets formed at the center and in every region and locality. When nearly half a million coal miners went out on strike in the summer of 1989, Gorbachev declared himself sympathetic to their demands.

Gorbachev's radicalism received its most dramatic confirmation through the astonishing developments of 1989 in Eastern Europe. All the regimes making up the socialist bloc collapsed and gave way to multiparty parliamentary regimes in virtually bloodless popular revolutions, and the Soviet Union stood by and supported the revolutions! The overnight dismantling of communism in Eastern Europe meant that the elaborate structure of party ties, police cooperation, economic trade, and military alliance that had developed since Stalin imposed communism on Eastern Europe after World War II vanished. Divided Germany was allowed to reunite, and, after initial reluctance, the Soviet leaders even accepted the admission of the reunited Germany to NATO.

In the Soviet Union itself, meantime, the Communist Party was facing massive popular hostility and a critical loss of authority. The newly elected governments of the national republics making up the Soviet state one by one declared that they were sovereign, and the three Baltic Republics declared their intention to secede altogether from the union. Over 1989–1990, throughout the Soviet Union and Eastern Europe, Communist Party rule was breaking down.

Political Institutions of the Transition Period: Demise of the USSR

Gorbachev's reforms had consequences he clearly did not intend. The 1990 elections of deputies to the Supreme Soviets in all 15 republics, and for soviets in regions and towns all across the country, stimu-lated popular nationalist and democratic movements in most republics. In the core republic—Russia itself—Gorbachev's rival *Boris Yeltsin* won election as Chairman of the Russian Supreme Soviet in June 1990. As chief of state in the Russian Republic, Yeltsin was well positioned to challenge Gorbachev for preeminence.

Yeltsin's rise forced Gorbachev to alter his strategy. Beginning in March 1991, Gorbachev sought to find terms for a new federal or confederal union that would be acceptable to Yeltsin and the Russian leadership, as well as to the leaders of the other republics. In April 1991 he succeeded in concluding an agreement on the outlines of a new treaty of union with 9 of the 15 republics, including Russia. A weak central government would have remained to manage basic coordinating functions. But the republics would have gained the power to control the economies of their territories.

Gorbachev had underestimated the strength of his opposition. On August 19, 1991, his own vice-president, prime minister, defense minister, KGB chief, and other senior officials acted to prevent the signing ceremony of the treaty by placing Gorbachev under house arrest and seizing state power. This was a fateful moment for Russia. In Moscow and St. Petersburg, thousands of citizens rallied to the cause of democracy and Russian sovereignty. The coup collapsed on the third day and Gorbachev returned to office again as president. But his power was now fatally weakened. Neither union nor Russian power structures heeded his commands. Through the fall of 1991, the Russian government took over the union government, ministry by ministry. In November 1991, President Yeltsin issued a decree formally outlawing the Communist Party of the Soviet Union. By December, Gorbachev was a president without a country. On December 25, 1991, he resigned as president and turned the powers of his office over to Boris Yeltsin.

Political Institutions of the Transition Period: Russia 1990–1993

The Russian Republic followed the example of the USSR and adopted its own constitutional amendments creating a Congress of People's Deputies and Supreme Soviet, and soon after, a state presidency. Boris Yeltsin was elected President of the Russian Federation in June 1991. Unlike Gorbachev, Yeltsin was elected in a direct, popular, competitive election, which gave him a considerable advantage in mobilizing public support against Gorbachev and the central USSR government. (See Box 8.1: Boris Yeltsin—Russia's Great Campaigner.)

Like Gorbachev before him, Yeltsin demanded extraordinary powers from parliament to cope with the country's economic problems. Following the August 1991 coup attempt, he sought from the Russian Congress of People's Deputies, and was given, the power to carry out a program of radical market-oriented reform by decree. Yeltsin then named himself acting prime minister and proceeded to form a government led by a group of young, Western-oriented leaders determined to carry out a decisive economic transformation.

The new government's economic reforms took effect on January 2, 1992. Their first results were felt immediately as prices skyrocketed. Quickly a number of politicians began to distance themselves from the program: even Yeltsin's vice-president, Alexander Rutskoi, denounced the program as "economic genocide." Through 1992, opposition to the reform

policies of Yeltsin and Gaidar grew stronger and more intransigent. Increasingly, the political confrontation between Yeltsin and the reformers on the one side, and the opposition to radical economic reform on the other, became centered in the two branches of government. President Yeltsin exceeded the constitutional powers of his office in carrying out the reform program. Parliament refused to adopt a new constitution which would give him the powers he demanded. In March 1993 a motion to remove the president through impeachment nearly passed the Congress.

On September 21, 1993, Yeltsin declared the parliament dissolved, and called for December elections to a new parliament. Yeltsin's enemies then barricaded themselves inside the White House, as the building housing the parliament was popularly known. After a ten-day standoff, the dissidents joined with some loosely organized paramilitary units outside the building and assaulted the Moscow mayor's offices adjacent to the White House. They even called on their followers to "seize the Kremlin." Finally, the army decided to back Yeltsin and sup-

---

Box 8.1   Boris Yeltsin—Russia's Great Campaigner

Boris Yeltsin, born in 1931, graduated from the Urals Polytechnical Institute in 1955 with a diploma in civil engineering and worked for a long time in construction. From 1976 to 1985 he served as first secretary of the Sverdlovsk oblast (provincial) Communist Party organization.

Early in 1986 he became first secretary of the Moscow city party organization but was removed in November 1987 for speaking out against Gorbachev. Positioning himself as a victim of the party establishment, Yeltsin made a remarkable political comeback. In the 1989 elections to the Congress of People's Deputies, he won a Moscow at-large seat with almost 90 percent of the vote. The following year he was elected to the Russian republic's parliament with over 80 percent of the vote. He was then elected its chairman in June 1990. In 1991, he was elected president of Russia, receiving 57 percent of the vote. Thus, he had won three major

races in three successive years. He was reelected as president in 1996 in a dramatic, come-from-behind race against the leader of the Communist Party.

Yeltsin's last years in office were notable for his lengthy spells of illness and for the carousel of prime ministerial appointments he made. The entourage of family members and advisers around him, dubbed colloquially "the Family," seemed to exercise undue influence over him. Yet, infirm as he was, he judged that Russia's interests and his own would be safe in Vladimir Putin's hands. Instead of turning against Putin when Putin gained in power and popularity, Yeltsin chose to resign and turn the presidency over to Putin. His resignation speech was full of contrition for his failure to bring a better life to Russians. In retirement, Yeltsin entered a dignified private life, resurfacing with his old rival Mikhail Gorbachev for President Putin's inauguration on May 7, 2000.

press the uprising. The army launched an artillery attack against the White House, killing dozens of people inside.

The circumstances of the December 1993 parliamentary elections were hardly auspicious. Yeltsin's decree meant that national elections were to be held for a legislature that did not, constitutionally, even exist since the constitution establishing these institutions was also to be voted upon in December in a national referendum held in parallel with the parliamentary elections on December 12, 1993.

The Yeltsin Constitution of 1993

THE PRESIDENCY Yeltsin's constitutional draft was approved by the voters. The constitution established a system which Yeltsin called a "presidential republic." Figure 8.2 provides a schematic picture of the present constitutional arrangements.

In its combination of elements of presidentialism and parliamentarism, the Yeltsin constitution resembles that of the French Fifth Republic. As in France, the constitution provides for a dual executive in which the popularly elected president appoints a government which must have the confidence of parliament to remain in power. Russia's president has the power to issue decrees with the force of law although his decrees may not violate existing law and can be overridden by parliament. The president appoints the prime minister, subject to the approval of parliament. The Duma can refuse to confirm the president's choice, but if, after three attempts, the president still fails to win the Duma's approval of his choice, he dissolves the Duma and calls for new elections. Likewise the Duma may hold a vote of no confidence in the government. The first time a motion of no confidence carries, the president and government may ignore it, but if it passes a second time, the president must either dissolve parliament or dismiss the government. The president's power to dissolve parliament and call

FIGURE 8.2   The 1993 Russian Constitution

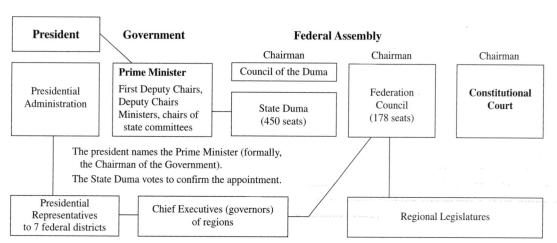

In 2000, President Putin created 7 federal super-districts, to each of which he appointed a presidential representative to monitor the observance of federal law in the regions.

Chief executives and heads of legislative assemblies in each of the 89 constituent territories of the federation were automatically made members of the Federation Council from 1995 until a new law passed in 2000. Under the new law, each regional chief executive and legislature chooses a permanent representative to the Federation Council.

for new elections is also limited by the constitution. He may not dissolve parliament within one year of its election, or once it has filed impeachment charges against the president, or once the president has declared a state of emergency throughout Russia, or within six months of the expiration of the president's term. Thus although the constitution gives the president the upper hand in relations with parliament, it is not an entirely free hand.

The constitution calls the president "head of state" and "guarantor of the constitution." He "ensures the coordinated functioning and collaboration of bodies of state power." He is not chief executive. Although the president's nominee for prime minister must be confirmed by parliament, the president can appoint and remove deputy prime ministers and other ministers without needing parliamentary consent. These decisions are, nonetheless, to be made "on the proposal" of the prime minister. Neither custom nor constitution bars the president, however, from removing the prime minister without parliamentary consent.

As in France, the Russian Constitution allows a variety of arrangements in the relations between president and prime minister, depending on the personalities and political tendencies of each. Also, the system is likely to evolve as precedents accumulate. As in France, it may be that the dual executive system works more harmoniously in practice if the two avoid competing for direct executive control over the same spheres of policy. In Russia, a division of labor has evolved between the president and the prime minister. The prime minister is directly responsible for economic management, while the president oversees foreign and security policy, provides overall direction to the course of economic policy, and enforces the loyalty of regional governments to the central government.

The two offices differ considerably in scope and power. The president's reach extends over a wide range of political institutions at the center and in the regions. He oversees a vast presidential administration which supervises the federal government and maintains liaison with regional governments. The "power ministries"—the Foreign Ministry, Federal Security Service (formerly the KGB), Defense Ministry, and Interior Ministry—answer directly to the president. There are also many official and quasi-official commissions and agencies funded and directed by the president which carry out a variety of supervisory and advisory functions. The president chairs the *Security Council*, which consists of a permanent secretary, the heads of the power ministries and other security-related agencies, the prime minister, and, more recently the finance minister and chairs of the two chambers of parliament. Its powers are broad but shadowy.

THE GOVERNMENT The government comprises around sixty ministries and other agencies which administer different branches of government such as the Ministry of Finance, the Ministry of Economics, the Foreign Trade Ministry, the State Committee on Privatization, and the Ministry of Defense.

The chairman of the government, equivalent to prime minister, has overall responsibility for the work of the government. He supervises the ministries and state committees through an intermediate layer of deputy chairs who supervise a particular bloc of ministries and state agencies, coordinating their work, and serving as liaison between the ministers in charge of particular ministries and the head of government.

In contrast to most parliamentary systems, in Russia the makeup of the government is not directly determined by the party composition of the parliament. The relationship between the distribution of party forces in the Duma and the political balance of the government can be loose. Most members of the government are career managers and administrators rather than party politicians. Overall, the government is not a party government, although to some degree, the makeup and policy direction of the government must reflect the balance of political forces in the parliament. This is because a newly appointed prime minister must be confirmed by parliament, and because the Duma has the power to deny the government its confidence, thus forcing either the appointment of a new government, or a new general election.

THE PARLIAMENT The parliament—Federal Assembly—has proven to be a modestly authoritative and effective body despite the turmoil surrounding its creation. Several features distinguish it from its predecessor institutions. One is the important role played by party factions in organizing its proceedings. Another is its bicameral structure; its two chambers differ markedly in their makeup and operations. The lower house, or *State Duma*, has the right to originate legislation except for certain categories of policy which are under the jurisdiction of the upper house, the *Federation Council*. As Figure 8.3 shows, upon passage in the State Duma, a bill goes to the Federation Council. If the upper house rejects it, the bill goes back to the Duma, where a commission comprising members of both houses may seek to iron out differences. If the Duma rejects the upper house's changes, it may override the Federation Council by a two-thirds vote and send the bill directly on to the president.

When the bill has cleared parliament, it goes to the president for signature. If the president refuses to sign the bill, it returns to the Duma. The Duma may pass it with the president's proposed amendments by a simple absolute majority, or override the president's veto, for which a two-thirds vote is required. The Federation Council must then also approve the bill, by a simple majority if the president's amendments are ac-

cepted, or a two-thirds vote if it chooses to override the president. On rare occasions, the Duma has overridden the president's veto and it has overridden the Federation Council's rejections more frequently. In other cases, the Duma has passed bills rejected by the president after accepting the president's amendments. Since 1994, the parliament and president have generally avoided provoking a conflict that could trigger a major constitutional crisis, although they have occasionally come close to the brink.

The Russian upper house, the Federation Council, is designed as an instrument of federalism in that (as in the U.S. Senate) every constituent unit of the federation is represented in it by two representatives. Thus the populations of small ethnic-national territories are greatly overrepresented compared with more populous regions. Until a major reform pushed through by President Putin in the spring of 2000, the Federation Council's members were the heads of the executive and legislative branches of each constituent territory of the federation; it would be as if the governors and assembly speakers of each state in the United States made up the members of

---

FIGURE 8.3   The Legislative Process: Overview

| State Duma | | Federation Council | | President |

The legislative process begins in the State Duma. Draft legislation can be submitted by the government, the president, or members of the Federal Assembly either individually or collectively. After a law is passed by the State Duma, it is considered by the Federation Council.

The Federation Council considers laws passed by the Duma. If it passes them, they go to the president for his signature. If it rejects a bill, the Duma may try to override the rejection. Or the two chambers form a conciliation commission to iron out the disagreements between the two chambers. The resulting compromise version is then voted on by both chambers. If both pass it, it is sent to the president for his signature.

The president decides whether to sign or reject laws sent to him by Parliament. If he signs a bill, it becomes law. If he rejects it, it is sent back to the Duma for further consideration. The Duma may vote to override a presidential veto. A two-thirds vote of each chamber is needed to override successfully. If the chambers cannot override the veto, normally they form a conciliation commission with representatives of the president and Parliament and agree on a compromise version.

the U.S. Senate. Now, however, each governor and each regional legislature is to name a representative to the Federation Council who will serve on a full-time basis.

The Federation Council has important powers. Besides acting on bills passed by the lower house, it is also called upon to approve presidential nominees for high courts such as the Supreme Court and the Constitutional Court. Its approval is required for presidential decrees declaring martial law or a state of emergency, and any actions altering the boundaries of territorial units in Russia. It must consider any legislation dealing with taxes, budget, financial policy, treaties, customs, and declarations of war. The Federation Council, not surprisingly, strongly defends the prerogatives of regional governments vis-à-vis the federal center.

The State Duma has emerged as an assertive and active body. Unlike the Federation Council, the Duma is organized by party faction. Representatives of its factions—one from each registered group regardless of size—comprise its steering body, the Council of the Duma. The Council of the Duma makes the principal decisions in the Duma with respect to legislative agenda and proceedings, and it acts on occasion to broker compromise agreements that overcome deadlocks among the deeply opposing political groups represented in the Duma. The Duma also has a set of 28 standing committees. Some, such as the budget committee, have become influential in shaping national economic policy. Both on distributive issues, such as the budget, and on regulatory policy, such as legal reform, the government and president often seek to compromise with the Duma in shaping legislation rather than reverting to the use of presidential decree power to break stalemates over policy.

EXECUTIVE-LEGISLATIVE RELATIONS The president's powers vis-à-vis parliament are great but should not be exaggerated. To be sure, the constitution makes it far harder for the parliament to remove the president than for the president to dissolve parliament. As in the United States, the legislature's sole device for forcing out the president is impeachment (see Box 8.2 on Impeachment Russian-Style).

Parliament's power to check the president has little to do with the threat of impeachment, however. Rather it stems from the need for the parliament's approval of all legislation, and the requirement of parliamentary confidence in the government. Since a presidential decree may not contradict federal law or the federal constitution, legislation is considered to have greater legitimacy in the eyes of the public and bureaucracy. A president would rather win parliamentary approval of his initiatives, therefore, than to enact them by decree.

The Russian president's ability to make policy against parliament's will faces certain constraints even in foreign and defense policy domains. This is because parliament can force the president to choose whether to dissolve the government or dissolve the parliament and call new elections in the event that a no-confidence motion carries twice within three months. The president must therefore calculate whether by dissolving parliament and holding new elections he will wind up with a friendlier or more hostile parliament. The balance of power, while asymmetrical, is by no means tilted in favor of the president as much as is often thought.

Relations between president and parliament have frequently been contentious throughout the 1990s; the first two Dumas, elected in 1993 and in 1995, tended to be dominated by party factions hostile to President Yeltsin and the policies of his government. This was particularly true in areas of economic and social policy. On other issues, however, such as reform of the judiciary and matters concerning federal relations, the Duma and president often reached amicable agreement—sometimes against the resistance of the Federation Council, whose members fought to protect regional prerogatives.

The election of 1999, however, produced a Duma with a pro-government majority. President Putin and his government found that they could generally count on majority support in the Duma for their legislative initiatives. This new relationship derived from the fact that the pro-government deputies depended heavily on the Kremlin for political support and career benefits. At the same time, the new balance of forces in the Duma had little ef-

---

Box 8.2   Impeachment Russian-Style

The 1993 Constitution provides for removal of a president through impeachment. The procedure consists of four basic steps. The State Duma must vote by a two-thirds majority (or 300 affirmative votes) in favor of impeachment; the Supreme Court must affirm that the president's actions constitute grave crimes or treason; the Constitutional Court must rule that no procedural violations were committed in the Duma's approval of the decision to impeach; and the Federation Council must vote by a two-thirds majority to remove the president. Initiating impeachment proceedings gives the Duma leverage over the president, in that once the Duma has approved (by the required two-thirds majority) the motion to impeach, the president may not dissolve the Duma and call new elections.

The communists in the Duma finally succeeded in placing impeachment on the agenda in 1998. The Duma voted to form a commission to examine five charges against Yeltsin: that he had committed treason by signing the agreement in December 1991 to dissolve the Soviet Union; that he had illegally initiated the war in Chechnia in 1994; that he had illegally dissolved the Russian Congress and Supreme Soviet in 1993; that he had destroyed Russia's defense capacity; and that he had committed genocide against the Russian people through the effects of the economic policies of his government since 1992. In March 1999 the commission approved all five charges and submitted them to the full chamber for its consideration. The Duma began debate on impeachment on May 13, 1999, and on May 15 voted on the five charges. Yeltsin used the full range of carrots and sticks at his disposal to avert impeachment, promising material rewards to some deputies in return for their support. None of the charges gained the required 300 votes, although the charge that Yeltsin had illegally initiated and conducted military operations in Chechnia came close, receiving 284 votes.

---

fect on the makeup of the government. Putin's own preferred party—Unity—contributed only one minister to the government. Nearly all the rest of the cabinet consisted of administrators with no partisan affiliation, and almost none were drawn from parliament. Thus, so far, there is little movement in the direction of a parliamentary-style system in which the government reflects the composition of the party majority in parliament.

THE CONSTITUTIONAL COURT   The 1993 constitution provides for judicial review by the *Constitutional Court*. Its 19 members are nominated by the president but are subject to confirmation by the Federation Council. The Court is empowered to consider the constitutionality of actions of the president, the parliament, and lower level governments. Through mid-2000, the court had not issued any decisions restricting presidential powers in any significant way, but it had decided several thorny constitutional issues, including the relations between the two chambers of parliament and the delineation of powers between the central and regional governments.

TOWARD CONSOLIDATION?   Russia's constitutional arrangements are still in flux. Presidents Yeltsin and Putin have generally acted within the constitution, but the system has considerable potential for instability in its design, stemming especially from the possibility of deadlock in relations between president and parliament. As political scientists have shown, a system in which the government is subordinate to the president, while it must simultaneously be able to command a majority in parliament, often produces severe confrontations between president and parliament.[3] It may be that in Russia, periods of stability in relations between president and parliament come about when there is no stable opposition majority that can provoke a crisis by forcing the government's fall through a vote of no confidence. In this instance, again, France may provide a model of stable development under a mixed parliamentary/presidential system.

The first few years of Russia's new constitutional order showed the potential both for democratic stabilization and a reversion to authoritarianism. The parties in the parliament were able to reach agreement on a number of difficult issues. Parliament and government succeeded in reaching agreement over some major legislation, such as the annual budgets, new civil and criminal codes of law, and a reform of the judicial system. President and government showed a willingness to bargain and compromise in their dealings with parliament. The traumatic events of September–October 1993 demonstrated that it was dangerous to take confrontation too far. The record of the operation of the new political institutions since 1993 encouraged some observers to express optimism about Russia's prospects for political stability. Parliamentary elections were held on schedule in 1995 and 1999, as were the presidential elections of 1996, and President Yeltsin surprised many observers when he voluntarily gave up power in 1999.

Nevertheless, as his health waned, President Yeltsin grew dependent on a coterie of powerful financial-media-industrial "oligarchs" for support. They have gained substantial influence over government. Still more dangerous than the high concentration of power in the presidency, it seems, is the loss of control and responsibility that can occur if the president does not command the powers of the office. When President Putin took over, he was faced with the dilemma of reasserting the power of the presidency without further weakening the tenuous system of checks and balances built into the constitution.

Central Government and the Regions

Despite the fears of many that Russia would break up along ethnic lines as had the USSR, the territorial integrity of the Russian Federation has weakened but not snapped. There are several reasons for this difference.

One is the demographic factor. The Soviet population was more ethnically heterogeneous than the Russian republic's population. Russia's population is 80 percent Russian. Its ethnic minorities represent only 20 percent of the total population, and none accounts for more than 4 percent of the total. The Soviet population was never an ethnic nationality, whereas Russia's national culture provided a historic identity which encouraged (and sometimes required) other national groups to assimilate to it.[4]

Like the USSR, the Russian Republic was also formally considered a federation under the old regime. But in contrast to the larger union, only some of its constituent members were ethnic-national territories. Most were pure administrative subdivisions, populated mainly by Russians. The non-Russian ethnic-national territories were classified by size and status into autonomous republics, autonomous provinces, and national districts; in many of them, the indigenous ethnic people comprised a minority of the population. Since 1991, the names and status of some of the constituent units in Russia have changed. As of 2000, Russia comprises 89 constituent territorial units; in Russian constitutional language, these are called the "subjects of the federation." Of these, 21 are republics, 6 are *krais* (territories), 10 are autonomous districts (all but one of them located within other units), 1 is an autonomous *oblast*, 2 are cities, and 49 are *oblasts*. Republics, autonomous districts, and the one autonomous *oblast* are units created specifically to give certain political rights to populations living in territories with significant ethnic minorities. *Oblasts* and *krais* are simply administrative subdivisions with no special constitutional status.

Republics jealously guard their special status. Over 1990–1992, all the republics adopted declarations of sovereignty and two made attempts to declare full or partial independence of Russia. In the mountainous region of the North Caucasus, between the Black and Caspian Seas, lies a belt of ethnic republics that includes the Chechen Republic (*Chechnia*). Its leadership declared independence of Russia in 1991, an act Russia refused to recognize but did not initially overturn by force. The other republic that sought to separate itself from Russia was the Tatar Republic, situated on the Volga, in an oil-rich and heavily industrialized region. Eventually Russia and Tatarstan worked out a treaty arrangement satisfactory to both sides, and the separatist movement in Tatarstan gradually subsided. In Chechnia, however, armed opposition failed to unseat the secession-minded leader. In December 1994 Russian forces then attacked the republic directly, subjecting its capital city, Groznyi, to devastating bombardment which forced tens of thousands of Chechen and Russian residents to flee the city and led to a protracted, destructive war. Fighting ceased in summer 1996 but resumed in 1999. Federal forces had established control over most parts of Chechnia by early 2000, but Chechen guerrillas continued to carry out ambushes against federal units.

The 21 ethnic republics have the constitutional right to determine their own form of state power so long as their decisions do not contradict federal law. All 21 have established presidencies. In many cases, the republic presidents have constructed personal power bases around appeals to ethnic solidarity and the cultural autonomy of the indigenous nationality. In several cases they have used this power to establish authoritarian regimes in their regions.

President Putin has made clear his intention to reassert the authority of the federal government over the regions. His reform of the makeup of the Council of the Federation was one step in this direction. Another law that Putin pushed through parliament in 2000 gave him the ability to remove a sitting governor if a court found that the governor had refused to bring his actions into line with the federal constitution and law. Needless to say, the governors strongly opposed these changes. But the Duma supported them and, with some modifications, they were passed into law.

Another action taken by Putin was his decree of May 13, 2000, creating seven new "federal districts." He appointed a special presidential representative to each district whose task was to monitor the actions of the governments of the regions within that district. The purpose of the reform was to strengthen central control over the activity of federal bodies in the regions; often, in the past, local branches of federal agencies had fallen under the influence of powerful governors. Critics of Putin's reform complained that it was a step in the direction of creating a hypercentralized, authoritarian system of rule. Defenders argued that many regions had effectively become dictatorial fiefdoms and that decisive steps were needed to bring them back under central control.

At the local level, Russia's constitutional order remains unsettled. The respective powers of regional and local governments still have not been fully worked out in law and practice. *Regional* governments resist allowing local governments to exercise any significant powers of their own, and regional governments have a great deal of clout. In many cases, the mayors of the capital cities of regions are political rivals of the governors of the regions. Moscow and St. Petersburg are exceptional cases because they have the status of regions. Therefore they are treated as "subjects of the federation" along with the other republics and regions. Other cities lack the power and autonomy of Moscow and St. Petersburg and must bargain with their superior regional governments for shares of power.

Regional chief executives (usually called *governors*) are elected in direct popular elections in their regions. Under a 1999 law, they cannot serve for more than two consecutive terms. Many governors' races are hotly contested, and the central government usually backs a candidate whom it thinks will support the Kremlin. In nearly every case, however, the winner seeks to develop strong, cooperative relations with the Kremlin. Party leanings or affiliations have little to do with how governors govern their regions.

Still, relations between the federal government and the governments of regions and republics are often contentious. Many regions have passed laws which violate the Russian constitution. For instance, several republics have declared that the republic has sovereign control—in effect, ownership—over the natural resources located in the republic. The Constitutional Court has struck down several laws adopted in republics and in ordinary territorial subjects that it found to conflict with the federal constitution, although it has also upheld several appeals from the regions against the unconstitutional intrusion of the federal government into the sphere of their legal power. In June 2000, the Court took advantage of President Putin's tough stance against regional separatism to strike down the claims to sovereignty that were asserted in the constitutions of several ethnic republics.

Thus the fears that Russia would split apart much as the Soviet Union did proved to be exaggerated despite the tragic case of Chechnia. Although Russia also underwent a wave of ethnic national mobilization within its national republics, separatism never reached the point where Russia itself as a national state was at the point of dissolution. However, the central government's power over regional governments is very weak, and in many areas, local authorities wield arbitrary power much as they did before communism fell. Reversing the central government's loss of control over the country in turn became President Putin's first great policy priority. Increasingly, Russian politics is becoming defined by the problems of federalism rather than by the struggle for democratic and market reform.

Russian Political Culture in the Post-Soviet Period

Over the last decade, survey researchers have found a sturdy core of commitment to democratic values in Russian society together with very high dissatisfaction with the current regime and very low levels of confidence in existing political institutions. Support for some features of a market economy is high but low for others, and dissatisfaction with the performance of the current economic system is even lower than that for the political regime. A number of studies have also found that a majority of the population supports the idea that the state should own heavy industry.[5]

But generally speaking, surveys show that there is a high level of support for principles associated with liberal democracy, including support for the values of political liberty and individual rights, rights of opposition and dissent, independence of the communications media, and competitive elections.[6] Political scientist James Gibson sums up the findings of a number of studies by drawing three conclusions: there is rather extensive support in Russia for democratic institutions and processes so long as people see these as rights for themselves; there is much less support for extending rights to unpopular minorities; and the segments of the population who are the most exposed to the influences of modern civilization (younger people, more educated people, and residents of big cities) are also those most likely to support democratic values. This would suggest that as Russia becomes more open to the outside world, support for democratic values will grow.[7]

Democratic aspirations set standards by which people judge the current regime harshly. Seventy-two percent of the respondents in a 1998 survey gave a positive rating to the pre-Gorbachev Soviet political system, and only 36 percent rated the current regime favorably.[8] But although many people remember the old regime in a positive light, few would want to bring it back: asked whether they would favor the restoration of the communist system, 41 percent agreed (completely or somewhat) and 59 percent disagreed.[9]

The support found for basic democratic principles challenges the widely held impression that Russian political culture is authoritarian, traditional, and influenced by decades of Soviet communist practice and indoctrination. Still, there is considerable continuity with the past in the level of support for the idea that the state should ensure society's prosperity and the citizens' material security.[10] More than in Western Europe or the United States, Russians continue to believe that the state is responsible for providing a just moral and social order, with justice being understood as social equality more than as equality before the law.[11] This pattern reflects the lasting influence of traditional conceptions of state and society on Russian political culture.

Russians have little confidence in present-day representative political institutions. Surveys over the past few years conducted have asked a battery of questions about how much Russians trusted various institutions to look after their interests. Table 8.1 reports the results of a 1998 survey on this question.[12]

The results suggest much higher levels of confidence in the army and Orthodox Church than in representative institutions. Parties and investment funds are the least-trusted institutions.

There is also a powerful backlash against Western influences and a strong tendency to blame the West, and especially the United States, for Russia's present woes. In a 1997 survey, 33 percent of the respondents agreed with a statement that Russia had become the victim of an international conspiracy against Russia; 47 percent rejected this idea. Most of the suspicious were elderly (and tended to be supporters of the Communist Party of the Russian Federation). Those opposed were mainly the young.[13]

The current disillusionment with the unsuccessful attempts to bring about market-oriented and democratic reform is not hard to understand. More interesting is the question of why the old regime was unable to transform Russian political culture along Marxist-Leninist lines. The answer to this question

TABLE 8.1   Trust in Institutions, 1998 (in %) (N = 2002)

	Trust	Neutral	Distrust
Army	34	22	44
Church	30	17	53
Courts	24	26	50
Television	23	24	53
Newspapers	22	25	52
Police	18	21	60
Local government	18	21	61
President of Russia	14	14	72
Trade unions	14	16	70
Duma	13	17	70
Private enterprises	11	17	72
Political parties	7	12	81
Privatization investment funds	5	9	85

may, in turn, shed some light on the longer-term dynamics of political culture. Three broad forces in particular should be noted: generational turnover, rising educational levels, and urbanization.

1. *Generational Change* Perhaps the single strongest factor in producing change in Soviet and post-Soviet political culture is the *succession of political generations.*[14] Whereas the Stalin-era population had shown relatively minor differences in opinion across generational and educa-tional cleavages, the gap between generations widened substantially by the time of the Brezhnev-era and Gorbachev-era studies. Not age (and hence life-cycle effects), but genera-tion, Donna Bahry finds, affects the shift in public opinion: "Those born after World War II, and especially after 1950, had fundamentally different values from their elders."[15]

2. *Rising Educational Levels* Over the 1960s, 1970s and 1980s, the proportion of the population who were 15 years of age and older and who had attained *at least* complete secondary education rose to over 60 percent. Moreover, a significant part of this growth has occurred among those with higher education. By 1989, over 10 percent of Soviet citizens aged 15 and over had higher educational degrees, approaching the U.S. level. It was precisely the most educated strata of the society who were the most

dissatisfied with the Brezhnev-era system. Similarly, all the studies of contemporary Russian values and attitudes find variance in educational levels to be one of the strongest predictors of democratic outlooks: the more highly educated, the more likely an individual is to support values and principles associated with liberal democracy.[16] Consequently, over time, as Russian society comprised more people with secondary and higher educational degrees, levels of support for democratic principles grew.

3. *The Urbanization of Society* Although old village mentalities and habits have retreated only slowly, Russian society has become predominantly urban in a very short span of time. By the late 1970s, more than two-thirds of the Russian population lived in cities; today, 73 percent of the population of Russia is classified as urban. But as recently as the late 1950s, the society was half urban, half rural. From 1950 to 1980 the urban population of the Soviet Union increased by nearly 100 million people—most of them immigrants from the countryside. The growth of the urban population has had some significant but subtle effects on political culture, among them the reinforcement of informal and cross-cutting social ties that nurture independent sources of public opinion and mediate the political messages sent out by the rulers.

Contemporary Russian political culture has thus been influenced by several factors, among them the thousand-year heritage of Russian statehood, the ambitious program of the Soviet communist regime to remake society along socialist lines, and the effects of social modernization which the communist regime generally encouraged but tried, with little success, to direct to its ends. We have noted the major lines of differentiation in society associated with differences in political attitudes: generation, education, and residence in city or countryside. The tumultuous events of Soviet history have affected different generations differently. Among the older generation, for instance, Stalin is viewed much more favorably than among the younger generations.[17] And to a large extent, these differences are mutually reinforcing: members of the older generation tend to have lower levels of education and less exposure to the more cosmopolitan way of life of cities.

Studies of Russian political culture have also called attention to the fact that support for democratic principles coexists with a profound discontent with the way reform has turned out in practice. Russian citizens value highly their right to vote, and they have exercised it actively in recent elections. Many, but not most, citizens would wish to return to the political order of the Soviet system. Attitudes about democratic and market institutions are strongly structured by age, education, and generation. Attitudes about political institutions are somewhat independent of citizens' evaluations of the performance of the current regime, but attitudes about the market economy have shifted markedly as the economy continues to slide downward. As time passes, support for democracy will therefore rest on two competing forces: the turnover of generations and the performance of the regime. The collapse of communist rule and the promise of democratic equality awakened expectations which have been cruelly disappointed. The long-term process of modernization and generational turnover has changed Russian political culture by creating new and higher standards for regime performance—standards which the current regime falls far short of meeting.

Political Participation and Social Capital

In a democracy, citizens take part in public life both through direct forms of political participation, such as voting, party work, organizing for a cause, demonstrating, lobbying and the like, and more indirect forms of participation, such as membership in civic groups and voluntary associations. Both kinds of participation influence the quality of government. By means of collective action citizens signal to policymakers what they want government to do, and it is through channels of participation that activists rise to positions of leadership. But, despite the legal equality of citizens in democracies, levels of participation across groups in the population vary with differences in resources, opportunities, and motivations. The better-off and better-educated tend to be disproportionately involved in political life everywhere, but in some societies the disproportion is much greater than in others.[18]

The Importance of Social Capital

A strong fabric of voluntary associations has been recognized since de Tocqueville's time as an important component of democracy. The stock of cooperation in a community or a society strongly affects the quality of government, as political scientist Robert D. Putnam has argued. Where a society is rich in social capital (that is, the network of ties among people in social associations) people are more willing to cooperate in endeavors that benefit the society. In societies where social capital is thick, the quality of government is better than in societies where the absence of trust and cooperation impedes people's ability to hold government accountable.

In Russia, however, social capital has been thin and state and society have been separated by mutual mistrust and suspicion. State authorities have usually stood outside and above society, extracting what resources they needed from society but not cultivating ties of obligation to it. To a large extent, the gap between state and society still exists today in Russians' attitudes and behavior. Although mass participation in voting is at a high level, participation in other forms of political activity is very low. Opinion polls show that most people believe that their involvement in political activity is futile and have little confidence that government serves their interests.

Since the late 1980s, political participation in Russia has seen a brief, intense surge followed by a protracted ebb. Compared with the surge of popular activism in the late 1980s, the long spell of low involvement in the 1990s appears to reflect a collapse of people's faith that life can be improved through the political process. In the longer perspective of Russian history, this is probably a reversion to a long-term pattern of political alienation of the populace from the state. Still, although few Russians are members of public associations and many are skeptical about their ability to influence government through political participation, the evidence suggests that Russians today *do* take elections seriously and value their freedom to participate in public life as they choose.

Participation in voluntary associations in contemporary Russia is extremely low: according to survey data, 90 percent of the population do not belong to any sports or recreational club, literary or other cultural group, political party, local housing association, or charitable organization. Only 1 percent report being a member of a political party. About 13 percent report attending church at least a few times a year, and about 17 percent report being members of labor unions. But even when these very passive forms of participation in public life are taken into account, almost 60 percent of the population still are outside any voluntary public associations.[19] Compare these figures with the United States: in the 1990s, even after several decades of steadily declining civic involvement, around 70 percent of Americans belonged to one or more voluntary associations and half consider themselves *active* members.[20] To be sure, the United States is still distinctive in the world for the high degree to which citizens actively take part in voluntary associations. But Russia stands out for the severe disengagement of its citizens.

This is not to say that Russian citizens are *psychologically* disengaged from public life. Half of the Russian adult population reports reading national newspapers "regularly" or "sometimes," and almost everyone watches national television "regularly" (81 percent) or "sometimes" (14 percent). Sixty-nine percent read local newspapers regularly or sometimes. Sixty-four percent discuss the problems of the country with friends regularly or sometimes, and 48 percent say that people ask them their opinions about what is happening in the country. A similar percentage of people discuss the problems of their city with friends.[21] Russians do vote in high proportions in national elections—higher, in fact, than their American counterparts.[22]

Moreover, Russians prize their right to participate in politics as they choose, including the right *not* to participate. Asked to compare the present regime to the old regime before Gorbachev, large majorities of Russians regard the present system as better in providing political freedoms: with respect to the right to say what one thinks, 73 percent think the present situation is "better" or "much better" than previously; concerning the right to join any organization one pleases, 75 percent consider the present regime "better" or "much better" than the old regime. On freedom of religion, 79 percent rate the present regime as better or much better, and 66 percent regard the present as better in allowing individuals to choose whether to participate in politics or not.[23]

The evidence suggests that Russians regard their regime with deep mistrust although valuing their political rights. Part of the reason for this may be the fact that the reforms of the Gorbachev period and the revolutionary breakdown of the old regime raised people's hopes to unrealistically high levels about how quickly conditions would improve. In the late 1980s there was a great surge of popular mobilization in Soviet society. It took multiple forms, including mass protest actions such as strikes and demonstrations, as well as the creation of tens of thousands of new informal organizations. But following the end of the Soviet regime, this wave subsided. The disengagement and skepticism reflected in public opinion today certainly reflects deep disillusionment with how conditions have turned out after the wave of public enthusiasm and mobilization in the late 1980s.

Elite Recruitment

Elite recruitment refers to the set of institutional mechanisms in a society by which people gain access to positions of influence and responsibility. It is closely tied to the forms of political participation in a society, because through participation people acquire interest and experience in politics and develop networks of friends and supporters. This was true as well in the Soviet regime, where the ruling party paid close attention to coordinating participation and recruitment. As a result, the breakdown of the old Soviet system of state-directed participation has strongly affected the way recruitment processes work in post-communist Russia.

Under the Soviet regime, the regime channeled the efforts of millions of citizens into officially approved forms of collective action, in organizations such as the Communist Party, youth leagues, trade unions, and women's associations. Through such organizations, the regime recruited potential leaders and gave them experience in organizing group activity. The party reserved the right to approve appointments to any position which carried important administrative responsibility or which was likely to affect the formation of public attitudes. The system for recruiting, training, and appointing individuals for positions of leadership and responsibility in the regime was called the *nomenklatura* system, and those individuals who were approved for the positions on *nomenklatura* lists were informally called, "the *nomenklatura.*" Many citizens thought of them as the true ruling class in Soviet society.

The democratizing reforms of the late 1980s and early 1990s made two important changes in the process of elite recruitment. First, the old *nomenklatura* system crumbled along with other Communist Party controls over society. Second, although most members of the old ruling elites adapted themselves to the new circumstances and stayed on in various official capacities, the wave of new informal organizations and popular elections brought about an infusion of new people into elite positions. Thus the contemporary Russian political elite consists of some people who were recruited under the old *nomenklatura* system together with a smaller share of individuals who have entered politics through new democratic channels. The political elite has not simply reproduced itself from the old regime to the new nor has it been completely replaced.[24] Rather, it has been expanded to accommodate the influx of new, often younger, politicians who have come in to fill positions in representative and executive branches. Many members of the old guard have successfully adapted themselves to the new conditions, and, drawing upon their experience and contacts, have found high-status jobs for themselves in business and government. At the same time, many young politicians have entered political life through the electoral process.

But there are two major differences between elite recruitment in the old system and the present. The *nomenklatura* system of the Soviet regime ensured that in every walk of life, those who held positions of power and responsibility were approved by the party. They thus formed different sections of a single political elite and owed their positions to their political loyalty and usefulness. But today, there are multiple, although overlapping, elites (political, business, scientific, cultural, etc.) with no one overarching mechanism for grooming and selecting their members. Moreover, today's political elite is made up of individuals from multiple streams of recruitment. Some are old-guard party and state officials who have found niches for themselves in state administration in the present regime. But others are new-wave politicians who have climbed the ladder of success in elections or who have entered the political elite after careers in business or science. Therefore, depending on which elite group we examine, we see a mixture of old and new channels of recruitment. Regions also differ in the degree to which the political elite is open to outsiders. Some regions have political regimes that have tended to preserve the old patterns of elite recruitment and the old political elite. In others, democratization and economic reforms have brought an intake of new people into the political elite.[25]

One of the most marked changes to have occurred since the fall of the Soviet regime has been the formation of a new business elite. To be sure, many of its members come out of the Soviet *nomenklatura,* as old guard bureaucrats discovered ways to cash in on their political contacts. Money from the Communist Party found its way into the establishment of as many as a thousand new business ventures, including several of the first commercial banks.[26] As early as 1987 and 1988, officials of the Communist Youth League (Komsomol) began to see the possibilities of cashing in the assets of the organization and started liquidating the assets of the organization in order to set up lucrative business ventures, such as video salons, banks, discos, tour agencies, and publishing houses.[27] They benefitted considerably from their insider contacts, obtaining business licenses, office space, and exclusive contracts with little difficulty.

Other members of the new business elite rose through channels outside the state. Many, in fact, entered business in the late 1980s, as new opportunities for legal and quasi-legal commercial activity opened up. A strikingly high proportion of the first generation of the new business elite comprised young scientists and mathematicians working in research institutes and universities. The new commercial sector sprang up very quickly: by the end of 1992 there were nearly one million private businesses registered, with some 16 million people working in them.[28]

Thus there has been a major shift in the pattern of recruitment of political elites. This is both because the formation of the political elite has become much more diverse than in the old regime, and because the old *nomenklatura* elite has accommodated itself successfully to the new system. Some of the old elites have gone on to high positions in the state bureaucracy in the new regime, but others have entered the business elite. Moreover, the new business elite is closely tied to the state. Powerful financial-industrial conglomerates have formed close and often collusive relations with ranking state administrators and legislators. Businesses need licenses, permits, contracts, exemptions, and other benefits from government; political officials in turn need financial contributions to their campaigns, political support, favorable media coverage, and other benefits that business can provide. The atmosphere of close and collusive relations between many businesses and government officials has nurtured widespread corruption and the meteoric rise of the business tycoons popularly known as "oligarchs." The rise of the new business elite has created numerous opportunities for government officials to enrich themselves.

Interest Articulation: From Statism to Pluralism

The political and economic opening of the last decade in Russia has had a powerful impact on the way social interests are organized. A far more diverse spectrum of interest associations has developed than existed under the old regime. At the same time, inequality in the political clout of weaker and stronger groups has also increased.

The old regime did not tolerate the open pursuit of any interests except those authorized by the state. Therefore the Soviet model of interest articulation was upset by *glasnost*. *Glasnost* stimulated an explosion of political expression which in turn prompted groups to form and to make political demands and participate in elections. It is hard today to appreciate how profound was the impact of *glasnost* on Soviet society: suddenly it opened the floodgates to a growing stream of startling facts, ideas, disclosures, reappraisals, scandals, and sensations. Gorbachev was clearly surprised by the range and intensity of the new demands that erupted. In loosening the party's controls over communication sufficiently to encourage people to speak and write freely and openly, Gorbachev also relinquished the controls that would have enabled him to limit political expression when it went too far.

As people voiced their deep-felt demands and grievances, others recognized that they shared the same beliefs and values, and made common cause with them, sometimes forming new, unofficial organizations. Therefore, one result of *glasnost* was a wave of participation in "informal"—that is, unlicensed and uncontrolled—public associations. Daring publications in the media allowed people with common interests to identify one another and encouraged them to come together to form independent associations. When the authorities tried to limit or prohibit such groups, they generated still more frustration and protest. Associations of all sorts formed: groups dedicated to remembering the victims of Stalin's terror; ultra-nationalists who wanted to restore tsarism; nationalist movements in many republics. The devastating explosion of the nuclear reactor at Chernobyl in 1986 had a tremendous impact in stimulating the formation of environmental protest, linked closely to nationalist sentiment in Belarus and Ukraine.[29]

The elimination of the state's monopoly on productive property resulted in the formation of new interests, among them those with a stake in the market economy. No longer does the state demand that organized groups serve a state-defined political agenda, as was the case under the old regime. Now groups can form freely to represent a diversity of interests, compete for access to influence and resources, and define their own agenda. By 1999, the Justice Ministry estimated that there were around 100,000 non-governmental organizations in existence in Russia.[30]

As new interest organizations have formed, they have entered into a variety of relationships with the state. Some organizations have survived into the new regime, clinging to their organizational assets and legacies and continuing to seek "insider" access to the state. Others that have sprung up from scratch also work closely with legislative and executive authorities, but others play "outsider" roles, trying to influence government by mobilizing public attention and support. The pattern of interest group activity is more pluralist than corporatist, because the very rapidity with which new associations have formed has defeated efforts by both government and interest groups to form monopolistic, stable, comprehensive umbrella organizations that the state could treat as the official voice of a particular interest. In most cases, interest associations are too numerous, too weak internally, and too competitive for corporatism to succeed.

Let us consider four examples of interest groups: industrial managers, women's groups, organized labor, and the new "oligarchs."

Industrial Managers

The directors of large industrial enterprises are powerful, but their *latent* influence is greater than is that of the organized associations which speak for them. One reason for the difficulty of uniting them in a single interest group is the widening division among them with respect to market competition: all large industrial firms were state-owned under the communist regime, but most have been privatized to a greater or lesser degree. Privatization and market reform have altered the playing field for industry. Firms that are competitive on the domestic and world markets seek greater freedom from state control, while others want the state to protect them from competition. They share a set of common interests with respect to privatization; generally the directors want to maximize their ownership of the enterprises they manage. But on other issues, such as state fiscal and monetary policy and the desirability of foreign investment in Russia, they are divided. These divisions have weakened the organizations that purport to represent them, such as the Russian Union of Industrialists and Entrepreneurs (RUIE). When the RUIE has thrown its support behind a political party in parliamentary elections, as it did in 1993 and 1995, it has failed abjectly. But behind the scenes it is an influential inside player in government decision making.

The government certainly reckons with the directors' interests. For example, the government designed privatization in such a way as to give directors of enterprises the opportunity to acquire substantial ownership rights over the firms they managed. Through this strategy, the government helped to ensure that the massive denationalization of state property met with virtually no resistance. This is a key to understanding why the transformation of Russia from communism was accomplished without a new revolution.

Thus as a *latent* interest group, the state industrial directors have benefited from state privatization policy, which was framed in anticipation of their preferences. But when called upon to act collectively in behalf of common *positive* goals, their efforts have been ineffective and incohesive. Their disunity reflects the widening division between winners and losers in economic reform.

Women's Groups

The Soviet regime sponsored several official women's organizations, but these mainly served propaganda purposes. During the *glasnost* period, a number of unofficial women's organizations sprang up. One was the *Committee of Soldiers' Mothers*. It formed in the spring of 1989 when some 300 women in Moscow marched to protest the end of student deferments from military conscription. Since then the movement has grown, focusing its energy on pressing the military to eliminate the use of soldiers' labor in its construction battalions, ending the brutal hazing of recruits which results in the deaths of hundreds of soldiers each year, and helping young men avoid being conscripted.[31] The onset of large scale hostilities in Chechnia in 1994–1996 and 1999–2000 stimulated a new burst of activity by the Committee. Through the 1990s, it became one of the most sizable and respected civic groups in Russia. One of the movement's greatest assets has been its moral authority as mothers defending the interests of their children; this stance has made it hard for their opponents to paint them as unpatriotic or power-hungry.

Notwithstanding its strong position against the draft and against the cruel hazing practices in the army, the Committee of Soldiers' Mothers has mainly concentrated its efforts on helping soldiers and their families deal with their problems. Other groups have sought to enter the political arena directly, publicizing their cause and running candidates for office. A case in point is the political bloc, Women of Russia, which formed to compete in the 1993 parliamentary elections.[32] Despite the fact that it had only two months in which to organize and campaign for the election, it was remarkably successful. Women of Russia won 8.13 percent of the party list vote and formed a parliamentary faction. However, it failed to sustain its political momentum. In the 1995 election, its vote share fell roughly in half, to 4.6 percent, and in 1999 its share fell by half yet again, to 2.04 percent. The dual strategy of playing an interest group's game and appealing to a particular constituency for support while at the same time seeking to win widespread vote support as a party had failed.

Because of the opening of the system to the outside world, women's groups have been able to form links to counterpart organizations abroad and to receive aid from international funding sources. This fact has had paradoxical effects. Outside help has enabled many groups to become active that might not otherwise have had a chance to organize. But at the same time, it has prompted some groups to concentrate more on cultivating their ties to the Western funders than to reaching out to potential constituencies at home. It has also fostered competition among groups, as each seeks its own exclusive share of resources. With time, however, women's groups have become more conscious of the need to cooperate, pool resources, and broaden their own indigenous bases of support.[33]

Organized Labor

The cases of industrial managers and women's groups illustrate the point that the old regime was rich in state-sponsored organizations but poor in autonomous social groups that could provide organizational resources to new interests seeking to organize and voice their demands. Official Soviet public organizations were mouthpieces of state policy and "transmission belts" for controlling society. Yet in some cases they served to foster skills and social ties that became important resources for interest organizations in the post-Soviet environment. RUIE was the successor of a Soviet association created under Gorbachev; Women of Russia was created by three women's groups, two of which were official state organizations under the old regime. Similarly, organized labor in Russia today also is strongly influenced by its predecessor organizations under the Soviet system. The old official federation of trade unions fractured, and some of its components became independent, while other trade unions sprang up as independent bodies representing the interests of particular groups of workers. As the 1990s ended, the successor organization to the old official umbrella group for labor remained the single largest trade union federation in Russia. Several other trade union organizations existed as well, but were much smaller in scale. Overall, organized labor was fragmented, weak, and unable to mobilize workers effectively for collective action.

To date, there has been much less labor protest than might be expected. Unrest did increase through the 1990s, mainly because of wage arrears. Surveys find that in the 1990s, in any given year, three-quarters of all workers received their wages late at least once.[34] Teachers have been particularly hard-hit by the problem of unpaid wages and have organized numerous local strikes. Waves of strikes by teachers shut down thousands of schools in 1997, 1998, and 1999. Over 1999–2000 teachers' protests subsided somewhat as wage arrears gradually were paid off due to the modest economic recovery.[35]

There was a considerable amount of organized labor protest in the 1990s. Yet we might wonder why there was not still more. Strikes were generally confined to particular occupations and particular localities. Why have trade unions been ineffective in mobilizing workers for collective action at the national level?

One reason is workers' dependence on the enterprises where they work for a variety of social benefits which are administered through the enterprise, such as pension contributions, cheap housing, and access to medical clinics and day care facilities.[36] Moreover, at some enterprises, workers can choose to affiliate with any of a number of competing labor unions and federations.

The *Federation of Independent Trade Unions of Russia (FITUR)* is the successor of the official trade union federation under the Soviet regime.[37] FITUR inherited its huge membership base and today represents around 95 percent of all organized workers. FITUR also inherited an empire of valuable assets from its Soviet-era predecessor organization, including thousands of office buildings, hotels, rest homes, hospitals, and children's camps. It also inherited the right to collect workers' contributions for the state social insurance fund. Control of this fund has enabled the official trade unions to acquire enormous income-producing property over the years. These assets and income streams give leaders of the official unions considerable advantages in competing for members. But FITUR no longer has centralized control over its regional and branch members. In the 1993 and 1995 parliamentary elections, for instance, member unions formed their own political alliances with parties. Thus internal disunity is another major reason for the relative weakness of FITUR as an organization.

Rise of the Oligarchs

The new capitalist opportunities presented by the opening of the Russian economy affected many people's interests. Even before the Soviet system collapsed, well-placed officials in the party, the KGB, and the Komsomol (Soviet Youth League) had been cashing in on their power, privileges, and connections in the Gorbachev period. Great fortunes were made almost overnight. Some called this wave of quasi-market activity "nomenklatura capitalism." By the time that the Soviet regime fell, some of the new *"biznesmeny"* had already entrenched themselves as powerful players.

Privatization of state enterprises then gave many who had gained wealth in the late 1980s an opportunity to convert it into shares of privatized enterprises and to assemble conglomerates of industrial, energy, financial, and media enterprises. The heads of these great empires became known as "oligarchs." They have a reputation for being power-hungry, unscrupulous, and immensely wealthy, and certainly during Yeltsin's presidency they gained considerable insider influence within the Kremlin itself. The most famous of them—Boris Berezovsky—was probably being more boastful than candid when he told the *Financial Times* a few weeks after Yeltsin appointed him deputy secretary of the Security Council (October 1996), that there was now a group of seven individuals, with substantial influence over government, who controlled banks and businesses which together controlled half of the economy. On several occasions, the oligarchs have shown that they were well able to cooperate when it served their common interest, as when they came together in 1996 to work for Yeltsin's re-election. Competitive as they are, even the oligarchs are able to join in collective action when it suits their needs.

New Sectors of Interest

We have seen that in a time when people's interests themselves are changing rapidly as a result of social change, both old and new organizations find it hard to stay united. In several fields new professional associations have formed. These act to set guidelines for professional practice, seeking to fend off onerous government restrictions and to regulate entry into their fields. Political consulting firms in Moscow, mayors of small cities, mayors of large cities, judges, attorneys, auditors, television broadcasters, and countless other professional and occupational groups have all formed associations to advance their goals.

The new competitive environment for interest articulation has made parliament an important site for interest group pressure. For example, the military's desires for more weapons spending, the agrarians' demands for subsidies and trade protection, the regions' demands for fiscal relief, and pensioners' demands for higher pensions all represent pressure on the budget. The budget process is under parliament's control, so that interest groups must lobby both government and parliament. Parliament is also pressured in the struggle over basic property rights, as well as over such matters as restrictions on foreign religious missionaries, whose activities the

Russian Orthodox Church has lobbied successfully to limit.[38]

Parties and the Aggregation of Interests

Interest aggregation refers to the combining of the demands of various groups of the population into programmatic options for government. Although other political institutions also aggregate interests, it is parties that are the quintessential agency performing this vital task. The question of how well parties in Russia aggregate interests, define choices for voters, and hold politicians accountable is therefore of critical importance to assessing the quality of democracy in Russia.

Many contemporary Russian parties grew out of the "informal" groups and movements that mobilized during the *glasnost* period.[39] Others emerged from the CPSU, as it fractured into hard-line and more liberal wings in 1989–1990. Many of these new organizations were politicized as they struggled to win legal registration, and began to articulate a broader, often radical, political program. Some allied themselves with the democratic movement, others with the hard-line wing of the Communist Party, and still others with extreme anti-Western nationalists. All three tendencies—democrats, communists, and nationalists—are represented in the spectrum of Russia's political parties today. Although specific party names and organizational identities continue to evolve rapidly, the ideological position of most parties can be located on a spectrum between the liberal, democratic parties at one end, and the anti-reform communist and nationalist groups at the other. In between are a number of parties that seek to stake out the elusive center ground.

The greatest impetus to the development of political parties as electoral organizations has been the parliamentary elections of 1989, 1990, 1993, 1995, and 1999. Each round of elections stimulated a burst of organizational activity.[40] Presidential elections, however, have not had a similar effect. Because Russia's presidential system encourages the president to avoid making commitments to parties, presidential elections have tended to concentrate attention on the candidates' personalities rather than their policy programs, and therefore have even undermined party development.

THE 1989 AND 1990 ELECTIONS   The elections of USSR deputies in early 1989 produced the first efforts by like-minded activists to elect democratically oriented candidates. When the USSR Congress of People's Deputies convened in May 1989, the democrats formed the first independent legislative caucus in Soviet history: the "Interregional Group of Deputies." In turn, it became the organizational nucleus for the formation of a still broader coalition of democratic candidates running for the Russian Congress of People's Deputies and for seats in lower soviets in the March 1990 elections; this coalition was called "Democratic Russia." Both the USSR and Russian parliaments in the transition period also had strong communist factions that fought against the dismantling of the state socialist system, but in neither 1989 nor 1990 did the communists form a cohesive electoral bloc that could rally voters to their cause. Likewise the transition parliaments had organized nationalist and agrarian factions that lacked nationwide electoral organizations. In 1993 these groups competed vigorously with the democrats for electoral support.

THE 1993 ELECTIONS   Yeltsin's decrees of September and October 1993 dissolving parliament and calling for new elections in December gave political parties an impetus because the electoral law that he enacted by decree introduced a strong proportional representation element into the election of new deputies. Elections in the past had used a *single-member district* system exclusively. The new 1993 system divided the seats in the lower house of parliament, the State Duma, into two categories. Each voter would have two votes, one for a candidate running for that electoral district's seat, the other for one of the registered parties putting up candidates on party lists. Half, or 225, of the seats in the Duma would be filled by the winners of single-member district seats. The other 225 seats would go to candidates nominated on party lists, according to the share each party received in the proportional representation ballot, so long as the party won at least 5 percent of the valid party list vote. Table 8.2 indicates how the results of the 1993

TABLE 8.2 December 1993 Duma Elections and 1994 Duma Faction Affiliations

Party	Party List Vote %	Party List Seats Held	District Deputies Affiliated	Total Seats (April)	As % of Duma
Russia's Choice (RC)	15.51	40	33	73	16.22
Party of Russian Unity and Accord (PRES)	6.73	18	12	30	6.67
Yabloko	7.86	20	8	28	6.22
Liberal Democratic Union of December 12	0	0	26	26	5.78
Democratic Party of Russia (DPR)	5.52	14	1	15	3.33
Women of Russia (WOR)	8.13	21	2	23	5.11
New Regional Policy (NRP)	0	0	66	66	14.67
Agrarian Party of Russia (APR)	7.99	21	34	55	12.22
Liberal Democratic Party of Russia (LDPR)	22.92	59	5	64	14.22
Russia's Way	0	0	14	14	3.11
Communist Party of the Russian Federation (CPRF)	12.4	32	13	45	10.00
Parties failing to meet 5% threshold*	12.94	–	–	–	–
Unaffiliated deputies	–	–	10	10	2.2
Total	100	225	224	449	100

Note: The Liberal Democratic Union of December 12, New Regional Policy, and Russia's Way were formed after the new Duma convened in order to represent deputies elected from single-member districts, many of whom had been nominated by parties that failed to receive seats in the PR ballot.
*Includes votes cast against all parties.

elections were translated into representation for parties in the Duma.

Note that deputies were free to affiliate with factions and in practice have treated faction membership very loosely. Even deputies elected on one party's list sometimes leave that party's Duma faction, and join another. During the first few weeks of a new Duma's life, members are constantly drifting in and out of factions. Therefore a party that is entitled to a certain number of seats in the Duma because of the share of the vote its list obtained in the election, and whose candidates have won a certain number of single-member district races, might wind up with many more or many fewer members in its Duma faction than it would have had if its election results had been translated directly into seat shares in the Duma. For this reason, Tables 8.2, 8.3, and 8.5 show the distribution of Duma seats by faction and electoral mandate type several weeks into the new Duma's term in order to show the balance of political forces after the initial dust has settled.

The distribution of seats by faction is a product of the outcome of the voting in the two ballots. As the table indicates, eight parties which ran candidates on party lists won seats. Five failed to clear the threshold and did not receive seats. Nearly all of the deputies who won single-member district seats joined one or another faction. Some joined one of the eight party factions (often because they had run in their districts with that party's support). Others, rather than joining existing parties, formed groups serving single-member district deputies.

THE 1995 ELECTIONS Over the 1994–1995 period, some Duma factions lost members, and other factions formed. The major party factions retained their influence and identity throughout the life of the 1994–1995 Duma, however. Each faction in turn then developed a campaign organization and list of candidates to compete for seats in the new Duma that was to convene in January 1996. Altogether 400 (90 percent) of the deputies ran for re-election to the Duma and 158 (40 percent) were successful.

The December 1993 elections, Yeltsin decreed, were to elect a transitional Duma. Elections were to be held again two years later, in December 1995, for a new Duma that would have the right to serve out its full, constitutionally mandated four-year term unless it was dissolved prematurely. The elections were held on schedule on December 17, 1995.

This time an immense array of political groups competed to elect deputies—far more than could possibly be accommodated given that the same 5 percent threshold rule was kept. Some forty-three organizations succeeded in registering and winning a spot on the ballot. But in the end, only four parties crossed the 5 percent threshold: the communists, Zhirinovsky's LDPR, the "Our Home Is Russia" bloc formed around Prime Minister Chernomyrdin, and the Yabloko bloc led by Grigorii Yavlinsky. Of these, the communists were the most successful, with 22.3 percent of the party list votes. Zhirinovsky's party won 11.4 percent; Our Home Is Russia (NDR, in its Russian initials) took 10.1 percent, and Yabloko 6.9 percent (see Table 8.3). The proliferation of reform-oriented parties associated with prominent personalities split much of the pro-reform vote among them, with the result that 8.2 percent of the votes went to four small democratic parties that failed to cross the 5 percent barrier. Another 11.5 percent went to centrist groups which also failed to clear the threshold.

Altogether, half of the votes were cast for parties which failed to win any seats on the party list ballot. These votes were redistributed to the parties that did clear the threshold, as is usual in proportional representation systems. As a result, each of the four winners gained about twice as many seats as they would have been entitled to had there been no wasted votes. Moreover, the communists were quite successful in winning district seats, taking more than fifty. Combined with the seats they won through the party list vote, they wound up with one-third of the seats in parliament, the highest share that they or any party had held in the previous Duma.

THE 1996 PRESIDENTIAL ELECTION The 1995 parliamentary election was considered to be a test of strength for Russia's parties and leaders. The big unknown was how Yeltsin would perform. At the beginning of 1996 his popularity ratings were extremely low: in early March, Yeltsin was preferred by only 8 percent of the electorate, while 24 percent said they supported Ziuganov.[41] Over the course of the campaign, however, Yeltsin successfully shaped

TABLE 8.3   December 1995 Duma Elections and 1996 Duma Faction Affiliations

Party	Party List Vote %	Party List Seats Held	District Deputies Affiliated	Total Seats (Feb.)	As % of Duma
Yabloko	6.89	31	15	46	10.5
Our Home Is Russia (NDR)	10.13	45	20	65	14.8
Regions of Russia	–	0	41	41	9.3
LDPR	11.4	50	1	51	11.6
Agrarian	–	2	33	35	8.0
People's Power	–	2	35	37	8.4
CPRF	22.3	95	54	149	33.9
Parties failing to meet 5% threshold°	49.28	–	–	–	–
Unaffiliated deputies	–	–	16	16	3.6
Total	100	225	215	440	100

Note: The Regions of Russia, Agrarian, and People's Power groups were formed after the new Duma convened in order to represent deputies elected from single-member districts, many of whom had been nominated by parties that failed to receive seats in the PR ballot.
*Includes votes cast "against all" parties.

the agenda, emphasizing that voters were choosing between him and communism. The message was that none of the other candidates had a chance of beating Ziuganov, so that if voters wanted to prevent the return of communism, they had no choice but to vote for Yeltsin.

This strategy worked. Yeltsin's displays of vigor during the campaign, his lavish promises to voters while out on the campaign trail, and his domination of media publicity all contributed to a remarkable surge in popularity. In the first round, Yeltsin received 35 percent to 32 percent for Gennadii Ziuganov, his communist rival.[42] In the second round, Yeltsin received almost 54 percent of the vote to Ziuganov's 40.3 percent.[43] (See Table 8.4.) Russia's great campaigner had won his last election.[44]

THE 1999 ELECTIONS   The fact that 43 parties ran for election on the party list portion of the ballot in 1995 was discouraging from the standpoint of

hopes for the consolidation of a party system. But politicians drew lessons from 1995 and began to form larger coalitions aimed at clearing the 5 percent threshold. For instance, democratically oriented candidates formed a bloc called the "Union of Right Forces" which united several prominent liberal political leaders. In the end, 26 parties appeared on the party list ballot.

A measure of the weakness of Russian political parties was the fact that they had very little impact on single-member district races. Only the communists had much presence in local races, running candidates in two-thirds of the districts. Party competition tended to be far more focused on the party list vote than on winning single-member district seats.

Six parties cleared the 5 percent threshold in the party list vote. Three had been in the previous two Duma; three were new players (although including some politicians with previous Duma experience). Among them, they won just over 81 percent

TABLE 8.4   Presidential Election Results (in percent)

	First Round (June 16, 1996)	Second Round (July 3, 1996)
Boris Yeltsin	35.28	53.82
Gennadii Ziuganov	32.03	40.31
Aleksandr Lebed'	14.52	
Grigorii Yavlinskii	7.34	
Vladimir Zhirinovsky	5.70	
Svyatoslav Fedorov	0.92	
Mikhail Gorbachev	0.51	
Martin Shakkum	0.37	
Yurii Vlasov	0.20	
Vladimir Bryntsalov	0.16	
Aman Tuleev	0.00	
Against all candidates	1.54	4.83

of the list vote, so that there were far fewer "wasted" votes than there had been in 1995. This suggested that voters, too, were beginning to learn to discriminate between the more viable and less viable parties. Table 8.5 indicates the breakdown of votes and Duma seats for the parties in the 1999 election.[45]

PUTIN AND THE 2000 PRESIDENTIAL RACE   The presidential election of 2000 was held earlier than scheduled due to President Yeltsin's early resignation. Under the constitution, the prime minister automatically succeeds the president upon the premature departure of the president, but new elections for the presidency must be held within three months. Accordingly, the presidential election was scheduled for March 26, 2000. The early election gave the front-runner and incumbent, *Vladimir Putin*, an advantage because he was able to capitalize on his popularity and the country's desire for continuity. Putin ran the Russian equivalent of a "rose garden" campaign, preferring to be seen going about the normal daily business of a president rather than going out on the hustings and asking for people's votes. He counted on the support of officeholders at all levels, a media campaign which presented a "presidential" image to the voters, and the voters' fear that change would only make life worse. His rivals, moreover, were weak. Several prominent politicians prudently chose not to enter the race against him. Putin's campaign managers' real con-

cern was to convince voters to turn out for the election, wanting to ensure a broad mandate for their candidate.

In the event, Putin won an outright majority on the first round, with a reasonably high turnout of 69 percent. Table 8.6 shows the results.

Party Ideologies

Despite the high turnover in the array of parties and candidates competing for vote support in Russian parliamentary and presidential elections, there is continuity in the ideological tendencies they represent. Moreover, voters appear to be able to make coherent choices among parties and candidates reflecting their own assessments of where the parties stand on the basic issues. The main political families of parties can be classified in four basic types: democratic, centrist, communist, and nationalist.

DEMOCRATIC PARTIES   This category comprises parties that promote liberal democratic political values and market-oriented economic values; they want to dismantle the political and economic framework of state socialism and replace it with a political system guaranteeing individual freedom and the rule of law and an open, free market economy based on property rights.

Russia's democrats first mobilized in the *glasnost* era and formed a movement called *Democratic*

TABLE 8.5   December 1999 Duma Elections and 2000 Duma Faction Affiliations

Party	Party List Vote %	Party List Seats Held	District Deputies Affiliated	Total Seats (Mar.)	As % of Duma
Union of Right Forces (SPS)	8.52	24	8	32	7.2
Yabloko	5.93	16	5	21	4.7
Unity	23.32	65	17	82	18.3
People's Deputy	–	1	57	58	13.0
Fatherland-All Russia (OVR)	13.33	30	17	47	10.5
Russia's Regions	–	6	34	40	8.9
LDPR	5.98	15	1	16	3.6
Agro-Industrial Group	–	16	26	42	9.4
CPRF	24.29	50	39	89	19.9
Parties failing to meet 5% threshold°	18.63	–	–	–	–
Unaffiliated deputies	–	2	18	20	4.5
Totals	100	225	222	447	100.0

Note: The Agro-Industrial Group, People's Deputy, and Russia's Regions were deputy groups formed after the new Duma convened in order to represent deputies elected from single-member districts, many of whom had been nominated by parties that failed to receive seats in the PR ballot.
*Includes votes cast "against all" parties.

TABLE 8.6   Presidential Election Results, March 26, 2000 (in percent)

Vladimir Putin	52.94
Gennadii Ziuganov	29.21
Grigorii Yavlinskii	5.8
Aman Tuleev	2.95
Vladimir Zhirinovsky	2.70
Konstantin Titov	1.47
Ella Pamfilova	1.01
Stanislav Gororukhin	0.44
Yuri Skuratov	0.43
Alexei Podberezkin	0.13
Umar Dzhabrailov	0.10
Against all	1.88

Russia to compete for seats in the Russian parliament in 1990. Soon they split up into different groups, but in 1993 a number of democratic figures allied under the name *"Russia's Choice"* headed by the architect of economic reform, Egor Gaidar. Russia's Choice counted on a major electoral success in 1993 and was bitterly disappointed when it took only 15.5 percent of the list vote. As time passed, its electoral fortunes sagged further. In 1995, (renamed Russia's Democratic Choice) it took only 3.9 percent—not enough to qualify for seats in the Duma.

As the 1999 elections drew near, a number of politicians from Russia's Choice and other groups pooled their resources and formed a new electoral alliance called the *Union of Right Forces* (SPS, for its Russian initials). They put a trio of younger, appealing leaders at the top of their party list, and their campaign emphasized that Prime Minister Putin had vaguely endorsed their economic program. Their strategy paid off, and they entered parliament with 8.5 percent of the list vote. Their success showed that Russia's democrats, hammered and discredited by the results of the economic reforms with which they were associated, still commanded a significant following among Russia's voters.

Yabloko, headed by the prominent political leader Grigorii Yavlinsky, promotes itself as the "democratic opposition" to the government. It espouses a socially oriented economy and a pro-Western external policy. Yavlinsky himself ran for the presidency in 1996 and again in 2000, receiving around 7 percent of the vote in 1996 and 5.8 percent in 2000. Yabloko has been an active force in parliament, sponsoring much legislation and forging tactical alliances with other parties to get bills passed, but until recently it resisted forming any permanent alliance with other groups. Then in June 2000, it announced that it was entering into a formal alliance with the Union of Right Forces to coordinate their legislative agenda in parliament.

CENTRIST PARTIES One of the paradoxes of Russian politics over the past decade is the fact that no viable centrist party has arisen despite the fact that survey research regularly shows that voters favor policies and values that could form the basis for such a party. In particular, despite the apparently strong base of support that a social-democratic party would enjoy, no one has succeeded in creating a major, lasting social-democratic party—one advocating a strong role for the state in protecting social welfare while also preserving political freedoms and private property rights. This is not for want of trying. Numerous political leaders, among them former USSR President Mikhail Gorbachev, have launched parties with an explicitly social democratic platform. None has managed to win more than a negligible share of the vote.

However, the state authorities have formed a series of "official" parties with broadly centrist platforms as a way of keeping themselves in power. An example of this type of party was *Our Home Is Russia*. It originated in 1995, when President Yeltsin's

political advisers proposed using the Kremlin's political resources to create a pro-government, centrist but moderately reformist, political movement. Yeltsin asked then-Prime Minister Chernomyrdin to head it. Benefitting from government support and promoting a reassuring image of stability and pragmatism, Our Home did succeed in crossing the 5 percent threshold in December 1995, with 10.3 percent of the list vote. However, Our Home never succeeded in defining a clear program, and was mostly a coalition of officeholders. It soon became known as the *"party of power."* Once Chernomyrdin was dismissed from the government in 1998, Our Home began to collapse. In 1999 it only won 1.2 percent of the list vote.

At least three "parties of power" ran in the 1999 parliamentary election. Besides Our Home Is Russia, two other blocs also competed that had strong links to the state authorities. The *Fatherland-All Russia* alliance united several powerful regional leaders and its list was headed by former Prime Minister Evgenii Primakov. But the real phenomenon of 1999 was *Unity*. Unity formed only three months before the election, with the active assistance of President Yeltsin's entourage in the Kremlin. Its trump card was Vladimir Putin. Appointed prime minister on August 9, 1999, Putin helped create the new movement and commented publicly that he intended to vote for it. Thus state officials who wondered which was the "true" party of power could safely back Unity, particularly as Putin's public popularity soared. As the once-dominant Fatherland-All Russia bloc's ratings fell, Unity's support soared, and it received 23.3 percent of the vote on election day.

The history of these "parties of power" illustrates the point that when parties depend on official support, they avoid formulating their own appeals to voters or building independent bases of organizational support. Their policy positions are vague, and when their major sponsors in the state lose power, they vanish. There is little doubt that if President Putin were to lose popularity or power, Unity would disintegrate.

COMMUNIST PARTIES The communists have consistently opposed Russia's president and government since 1991, so they have had to rely on their own resources for support. The *Communist Party of the Russian Federation (CPRF)* is the major successor party to the old CPSU. It has evidently decided to make use of the rules of the parliamentary game to influence national policy, operating with a long-term strategy. It opposes the market reforms and privatization programs of the last decade, and demands restoration of state ownership and planning in heavy industry. The CPRF also attacks Western influence in Russia. Its leader, Gennadii Ziuganov, has also worked to align the party with the religious and spiritual traditions of Russian culture, ignoring Marx's and Lenin's hatred of religion. Ziuganov frequently invokes the traditional mutual support between the Russian state and the Russian Orthodox Church. So far, however, the Patriarch has refrained from endorsing the Communist Party.

The CPRF is the most party-like of Russia's parties. Unlike any other party, it has a substantial organizational base, a well-defined electoral following, a large membership (estimated at around a half million), a large network of local party newspapers, and, probably most important, the heritage of Communist Party discipline. Divisions within the party are muted by the party's ability to speak and act with one voice. But it has clear weaknesses as well. Its voters tend to be older than average, and it appeals to them by its association with the old regime. Moreover, it is ideologically straitjacketed: if it moves too much to the center of the political spectrum, it will lose its distinctiveness as a clear alternative to the government, but if it moves further to the left, it will marginalize itself. The result is that the CPRF has a rather stable share of the electorate, but one which (so far, at least) prevents it from winning a majority in parliament or capturing the presidency.[46]

NATIONALIST PARTIES The most visible nationalist party, the *Liberal Democratic Party of Russia (LDPR)*, which is often referred to as Zhirinovsky's party, differs from the communists in certain important respects. Zhirinovsky's party stresses the national theme, even more than the communists, appealing to feelings of injured ethnic and state pride. Zhirinovsky calls for aggressive foreign policies and harsh treatment of non-Russian ethnic minorities. However, his economic policy is much fuzzier. Zhirinovsky distances himself from the socialist economic system of the past and poses as a "third force," which is neither tied to the old communist

regime nor to the new order. Finally, he also sends a clear message that he is seeking the presidency, the powers of which he will use dictatorially to right wrongs and settle accounts with Russia's enemies.

Zhirinovsky cultivates a vivid, theatrical public persona, which works effectively on television. He appeals to many voters who are angry over the current situation but unenthusiastic about returning the communists to power. However, as he has come to be identified with the Moscow political establishment, his party's vote support has fallen. From its strong showing in 1993, when his party won almost 23% of the list vote, its vote share has dropped roughly by half in each of the next two elections: to 11.4% in 1995, and less than 6% in 1999. Zhirinovsky's decline is also reflected in the votes he has received in presidential elections: 5.8% in 1991, 5.7% in 1996, and 2.7% in 2000.

The LDPR has been the most successful of the parties competing for the nationalist vote. Many other parties have also attempted to build successful followings around themes such as the need to restore the Soviet Union, or to make Russia a great world power again, or to cleanse Russia of the ethnic "outsiders" who contaminate it. But these parties have either failed in their bid for parliamentary votes and then splintered and faded, or have concentrated their efforts on forming a small but dedicated corps of militant (sometimes armed and militarily organized) followers.

Party Strategies and the Social Bases of Party Support

Survey researchers have also found distinct differences in party support among various categories of the population. Both age and education levels are correlated with party preferences; younger voters are likely to support the democratic camp or Zhirinovsky's party than are older voters, while older voters are disproportionately drawn to the communists. In 1999, well educated voters were likelier than others to prefer Yabloko and the Union of Right Forces, while less educated voters were likelier than the average voter to support the communists or Zhirinovsky. A strong influence on party preference is household income. Most of the communists' support has come from voters whose household income is below the median, while most of the support for the Union of Right Forces and Yabloko comes from voters in the upper half of the distribution.[47] Table 8.7 indicates how the parties differed in the social bases of their support. Note that the table should be read downward. For example, it tells us that 48 percent of communist supporters were men and 52 percent were women; in contrast 62 percent of Zhirinovsky's supporters were men, and only 38 percent were women.

Table 8.7 indicates revealing differences in the appeal of the different parties. The communists took over half of their support from citizens 55 years old and older; none of the other parties depended so heavily on pensioners. Similarly, the parties have markedly different profiles by income category, with the market-oriented Union of Right Forces (SPS) drawing a substantial amount of its support from better-off citizens, and the communists from among those who are barely scraping by. Finally, education

also strongly affects party support. Note that the liberal Yabloko and SPS parties draw 80 percent of their support from people with secondary and higher educational levels, whereas the communists get half of their support from among people with less than a full secondary education.

Russia's parties also differ in the ways they compete for vote support. The communists rely on their inherited organizational networks, their habits of party discipline, a clear-cut ideological profile, and their association with the socialist legacy of the old regime. The various "parties of power," such as Our Home Is Russia, Fatherland-All Russia, and Unity, depend almost completely on the patronage of executive officeholders and almost not at all on an ideological platform or indigenous party organization. LDPR and Yabloko have relatively weak electoral organizations but have well-known, visible political leaders and defined programmatic appeals.

TABLE 8.7   Social Bases of Party Support, 1999

	CPRF	Unity	Fatherland	Yabloko	Right Forces	Zhirinovsky
Age						
18–24	5	10	10	12	25	18
25–39	17	38	29	40	37	42
40–54	26	24	25	29	23	23
55 +	53	28	36	19	15	18
Gender						
Men	48	50	44	47	42	62
Women	52	51	56	54	58	38
Education						
Elementary or less	15	8	8	5	3	10
Incomplete secondary	36	24	26	16	17	26
Secondary	20	27	22	24	26	30
Vocational	18	25	21	28	29	29
Higher plus	11	16	23	27	25	5
Economic Situation						
Barely make ends meet	45	33	28	24	17	32
Have enough for food	40	41	46	41	44	37
Enough for food & clothes	13	23	21	30	31	28
Can buy durables easily	2	3	5	6	8	3

Source: VTsIOM pre-election polls, December 1999. Total N = 6400
(From www.russiavotes.org/ October 1, 2000.)
Note: Table columns read vertically and indicate the share of each party's supporters who belonged to one of the row categories in each set of social groups. Thus, for example, 48 percent of communist supporters were men, 52 percent women; in contrast 62 percent of Zhirinovsky's supporters were men, and only 38 percent were women.

Toward Consolidation of the Party System?

Party development in Russia has been hampered by the constitutional arrangements. Since the president does not need a majority in parliament to exercise his substantial policymaking powers, he is tempted to win a personal mandate rather than a mandate for a party. Both Yeltsin and Putin have stayed outside party politics, sometimes conferring their blessing on one or another party, but never joining a party or seeking its endorsement. As a result, parties are weak at performing the functions of aggregating the interests of citizens and formulating practical policy options. Parties often find it more rewarding to concentrate on extravagant criticism of government, distancing themselves from responsibility for its policies, or to make vague emotional appeals that cannot be translated into meaningful policy actions. Under these circumstances, where parties never take responsibility for government, voters have no way to measure their performance as policymakers.

Politicians face a parallel situation. Why should they form durable commitments to building up parties, if parties will never reward them with political office? Politicians treat parties as disposable objects, good for one-time use, but not intended for repeated or long-term use. Often they have formed a party for a single election; once it has served its purpose, it is discarded. As a result, there has been substantial turnover in the array of parties running in each of the parliamentary elections since 1993. Only four parties have contested all three, the CPRF, LDPR, Yabloko, and Women of Russia. And only the first three managed to clear the threshold each time.

Yet notwithstanding the high turnover and low accountability in Russia's party system, a slow consolidation of the party system is taking place. The electoral law has a powerful effect on the party system, encouraging parties to enter the arena through the party list ballot and to build broad bases of support to overcome the 5 percent hurdle to winning seats. Moreover, deputies in parliament have an incentive to unite in parliamentary factions, because by doing so they acquire important privileges, such as office space and funding for staff support, as well as a voice on the powerful Council of the Duma which directs the work of the Duma. Parties use the parliament to showcase favored bills or an investigation or resolution, to hold press conferences and parliamentary hearings, and to force a vote or to prevent a vote. Parties thus use parliament for their policy and electoral purposes. Individual members of parliament who want to further their political careers or to shape policy need to affiliate with one or another parliamentary party. The complementary interests of voters in supporting a particular organized political entity and of officeholders in affiliating themselves with a particular party organization to win power are thus influencing the development of Russia's nascent democracy to move, although slowly, toward a competitive party system.

The Politics of Economic Reform

The Dual Transition

A major reason Russia's transition has been so wrenching is that the country is remaking both its *political* and *economic* institutions. The relationship between the political and economic dimensions of this transformation is complex. Considering the dismal economic performance of communist regimes, few doubt that a market economy leads both to higher growth and greater dynamism in an economy over time. But in view of the tensions a transition from a state-controlled economy to a market system generates, many observers wonder whether it is preferable to keep a firm hand on the tiller while opening the economy up to private property and market competition, and only at a later stage open the political system up to democracy.

STABILIZATION Russia pursued two major sets of reforms in the early 1990s, macro-economic stabilization and privatization. *Shock therapy* refers to the stabilization program. Stabilization, also called structural adjustment, is an austerity regime for the economy in which the government seeks to restore a macro-economic balance between what society spends and what it earns. Stabilization gives the national currency real value, which requires eliminating chronic sources of inflation. Doing so requires drastic cuts in state spending, increases in taxation, the end of price controls, and an open foreign trade regime so that foreign products can compete with domestic ones. Structural reform of this kind always lowers the standard of living for some or most groups of the population, at least in the short run. Therefore in Russia, the reform program was nicknamed "shock therapy."

Those who are made worse off are not the only enemies of reform. In many post-communist countries, it has been the "early winners" from reform who step in to block subsequent measures to open the economy to free competition. These include officials who have acquired ownership rights to monopoly enterprises and then work to shut out potential competitors from their markets, or state officials who benefit from collecting "fees" to issue licenses to importers and exporters or permits for doing business.[48]

The question for the architects of reform therefore is what mixture of policies and institutions is most likely to launch the economy on a path of growth and development and keep it on that path despite political opposition. Reformers may have only a very short window of opportunity in which to act, and they must be politically realistic. If they alienate too many powerful interests, a strong coalition of opponents is likely to block reform. But if they give away too much to the "early winners," reform may stall partway.

FROM COMMUNISM TO CAPITALISM Communist systems differed from other authoritarian regimes in ways that made their economic transitions more difficult. This has been particularly true for the Soviet Union and its successor states. For one, the economic growth model followed by Stalin and his successors tended to seek economies of scale by concentrating large shares of the production of particular goods in particular enterprises. This means that many local governments are entirely dependent on the economic health of a single employer: almost half of Russian cities have only one industrial enterprise, and three-fourths have no more than four.[49] The enormous commitment of economic re-

sources to military production in the Soviet Union has further complicated the task of reform in Russia, as has the vast size of Russia. Rebuilding the decaying infrastructure of a country as large as Russia is staggeringly expensive.

Russia's economic reform program began on January 2, 1992, when the government undertook a major initiative to push Russia toward a market system by abolishing most controls on wholesale and retail prices and cutting government spending sharply. Almost immediately, opposition began to form to the new program. Economists and politicians took sides. Dispassionate analysis of the effects of the stabilization program became virtually impossible to get. The "shock therapy" program was an easy target for criticism, even though there was no consensus among critics about what should be done. It became commonplace to say that the program was all "shock" and no "therapy."

For the advocates of macro-economic stabilization, the great enemy is hyper-inflation.[50] They argue that once inflation is under control, then the economy can be restored to health, whereas high inflation will wreck both democracy and productivity because it undermines all faith in the currency and in the future. They regard inflation as a far worse ill than the recession that stabilization causes. By cutting government spending, letting prices rise, and raising taxes to squeeze inflationary pressure out of the economy, stabilization aims at creating incentives for producers to increase output and encouraging them to look for new niches in the marketplace where they can make and sell products for a profit. Increases in production should in turn bring prices back down. But if producers do not respond by raising productivity, society suffers from a sharp, sudden loss in purchasing power. People go hungry; bank savings vanish. This is what happened in Russia; the producers did not respond to the new economic incentives as the theory dictated they should, and the economy fell into a protracted slump.

As factories cut back on production, reduced workforces, and stopped paying their bills and taxes, the economy went into a severe recession. Those directors of state and private enterprises who did want to retool or expand operations, however, faced a severe credit crunch. The state cut back on the supply of easy money in an effort to get inflation under control. Organized crime rackets preyed on any firm enjoying even a little success in the market. Firms that were politically connected were able to survive by winning cheap credits and production orders from government, which dampened any incentive for improving productivity. Some critics even said that the West was deliberately trying to sabotage Russia by forcing it to follow the "shock therapy" prescription. Communists and nationalists got a rise out of audiences by depicting the 1992 government as the traitorous hirelings of a malevolent, imperialist West.

Privatization   Stabilization was followed shortly afterward by the mass privatization of state assets. In contrast to the "shock therapy" program, privatization enjoyed considerable public support, at least at first. *Privatization* is the transfer to private owners of legal title to state firms. Economic theory holds that under the right conditions, private ownership of productive assets is more efficient for society as a whole than is state ownership, because in a competitive environment owners are motivated by an incentive to maximize their property's ability to produce a return.

In Russia's first phase of privatization, buyers bought shares of companies with cash. But cash privatization had the effect of making the rich richer and giving ownership of enterprises to the officials who had run them before. Ordinary citizens often were excluded from the most profitable opportunities as insiders acquired the stock of the most promising firms. And the poor, of course, had no chance at all to buy shares.

In April 1992, Yeltsin decreed that a program of voucher privatization would begin later that year. Under the program, every citizen of Russia would be issued a voucher with a face value of ten thousand rubles (a little over $30 at the time). People would be free to buy and sell vouchers, but they could only be used to acquire shares of stock in privatized enterprises or shares of mutual funds investing in privatized enterprises. The program was intended to ensure that everyone became a property owner instantly. Politically, the aim was to build support for the economic reforms by giving citizens a stake in the outcome of the market tran-

sition. Economically, the government hoped that privatization would eventually spur increases in productivity by creating meaningful property rights.[51]

Beginning in October 1992, 148 million privatization vouchers were distributed to citizens. By June 30, 1994, when the program ended, 140 million vouchers had been exchanged for stock out of 148 million originally distributed.[52] Some 40 million citizens had become property owners. The next phase was to privatize most remaining state enterprises by means of auctions of shares for cash. By 1996, around 90 percent of industrial output was being produced by privatized firms, and around two-thirds of all large and medium-sized enterprises had been privatized.[53]

Consequences of Privatization   How much did privatization transform Russia's economy? It is fair to say that the actual transfer of ownership rights was far less impressive than it appeared. This is for several reasons. The dominant pattern was acquisition of title through "insider privatization," rather than through open competitive bidding. Management of many firms did not change; they continued to be closely tied to state life-support systems such as cheap loans and subsidies.[54]

The program allowed a great many unscrupulous wheeler-dealers to prey on the public through a variety of financial schemes. Some investment funds promised truly incredible rates of return; most investors in Western companies would have regarded these claims as outrageous and fraudulent. Many people lost a great deal of money by investing in funds that went bankrupt or turned out to be simple pyramid schemes, where the dividends for the early investors were supplied by the contributions of later investors. The Russian government lacked the capacity to protect the investors. Many people were disenchanted with the entire program as a result.

Privatization has yet to bring a viable capital market into being: the mechanism for mobilizing private savings into investment in Russian companies works very poorly. Enterprises that are starved for working capital fail to pay their wages and taxes on time and trade with one another using barter. By 1998, at least half of enterprise output was being "sold" through barter trade.

Moreover, the government's own long-term and short-term goals competed with one another. At the same time the government was trying to auction off shares in enterprises, it was also trying to raise revenues by issuing bonds at extremely high rates of return.[55] The market for the lucrative bonds crowded out the capital market for investment in industry. The government fell into an unsustainable debt trap. To pay off the interest on the loans it had taken, it needed to raise still more cash, which it did through foreign borrowing, issuing high interest-bearing domestic bonds, and selling off state enterprises. As lenders became increasingly certain that the government could not make good on its obligations, they demanded ever higher interest rates, deepening the trap. Ultimately the bubble burst: in August 1998, the state could not honor its obligations. It declared a moratorium on its debts and let the ruble's value collapse against the dollar. Overnight, the ruble lost two-thirds of its value and credit dried up.[56] The government bonds held by investors were almost worthless. Importers went out of business. The effects of the crash rippled through the economy. The sharp devaluation of the ruble made exports more competitive and gave impetus to domestic producers but also significantly lowered people's living standards.

Privatization has not extended to land, because of the opposition to allowing property rights in land by the communist-agrarian-nationalist forces in parliament. Over 90 percent of agricultural land continues to be owned by the old collective and state farms.[57] Almost all of these have been legally transformed into joint stock companies but continue to be run as in the past. Many of the institutional forms necessary for capitalist development are lacking, particularly the legal right to use land as a security to guarantee a loan, despite repeated attempts by reformers to pass a law establishing mortgages as a legal form of secured debt, the communists and their allies have managed to impose severe restrictions on mortgage loans. As a result, it is difficult to secure a loan to buy personal or commercial real estate property with a deed to the property itself. The weakness of a market for mortgages inhibits the development of market relations in land and other real property.

In addition, despite the goal of encouraging widespread property ownership through the mass privatization program, capital became highly concentrated as financial capital merged with industrial capital. A small number of powerful "financial-industrial groups" (FIG's) gained concentrated ownership of Russian industry. Financial-industrial groups are holding companies in which a leading bank owns controlling shares in a number of enterprises in a particular branch.[58] Some are controlled by the "oligarchs" we mentioned earlier.

Overall, then, privatization through vouchers and cash has created property rights and a class of property owners. This class is still narrow, however, as ownership of many assets is concentrated in the hands of the few rather than the many. Capital markets have been extremely slow to get off the ground, and the August 1998 crash set back the development of both stock and debt markets. Yet 1999 and 2000 brought signs of recovery; if President Putin carries through on his commitment of creating an equal playing field for all market players, privatization may well come to be regarded as a painful but necessary passage to the birth of a market economy in Russia.

Economy and Society

As we have seen, economic production fell sharply over the decade of the 1990s. Table 8.8 shows that there was a slight recovery in 1997, but it was wiped out by the financial collapse of 1998. The crash resulted in an inflationary shock, as the price of the dollar and of goods purchased for hard currency rose three to four times in relation to the ruble. Thus, as Table 8.8 indicates, inflation rose sharply in 1998 while output fell. In 1999 the economy began to recover.

The very structure of the economy has shifted. Much more of Russia's economic activity is occurring in the sphere of services and less in industry and agriculture. Since services are much easier to conceal from the authorities, the service sector might even have grown overall, if unrecorded transactions are included. There is certainly a great deal of off-book economic activity taking place, some of it legal but outside the scrutiny of the tax police, and some of it illegal. A conservative estimate of the scale of output of unregistered goods and services is 20 percent of GDP, but some place the figure as high as 40 percent.[59]

TABLE 8.8   Russian Annual GDP Growth and Price Inflation Rates, 1991–1999

	1991	1992	1993	1994	1995	1996	1997	1998	1999
GDP*	−5.0	−14.5	−8.7	−12.6	−4.3	−6.0	0.4	−11.6	3.2
Inflation**	138.0	2323.0	844.0	202.0	131.0	21.8	11.3	84.4	36.5

*GDP is measured in constant market prices.
**Inflation is measured as the percentage change in the consumer price index from December of one year to December of the next.
Source: Press reports of Russian State Statistical Service.

Still, the fact remains that Russia's economy sank into deep depression by the mid-1990s, was hit further by the financial crash of 1998, and then began to recover in 1999–2000. Russia's economic decline was far more severe and more protracted than was the Great Depression experienced by the United States or Western Europe following 1929. It is about half as severe as the catastrophic drop caused by the effects of World War I, the Bolshevik Revolution, and the Civil War.[60] Although economic reform caused an initial drop in economic performance throughout Eastern Europe, Russia was one of the only former socialist economies in which output continued to fall as of the end of the 1990s.[61]

Yet Russia has bounced back from the August 1998 financial crash with surprising speed. Much of the reason for the recovery is that world oil prices have risen. Another reason is that domestic industries such as food processing have benefitted from the steep increase in the prices of imported goods. Also, recovery has been helped by the fact that even a small infusion of cash into the economy has a multiplier effect, as enterprises are able to pay off arrears in back wages and taxes, in turn allowing government to pay off its backlog of wages and pensions, in turn allowing consumer demand for industry's products to rise, and so on. For the first time in many years, unemployment in 2000 fell as enterprises added workers. Bank savings increased. Still, there has been no systematic restructuring of the financial system, so the economy is vulnerable to a downturn if, for instance, world oil prices fall again.

SOCIAL CONDITIONS   These economic changes have had an enormous impact on living standards. A small minority have become wealthy, and some households have improved their lot modestly. A majority of the population, however, has suffered a net decline in living standards as a result of unemployment, lagging income, and nonpayment of wages and pensions.

A much larger share of the populace lives in poverty than was the case in the Soviet era. Several factors have brought this about, including unemployment and the lag of incomes behind prices. Unemployment stood at about 13 percent of the workforce in June 2000, a drop of about half a million unemployed by comparison with the previous year.[62] This rate—which is high even by West European standards[63]—was especially high for a country accustomed to nearly full employment and lacking an extensive state-funded social safety net.

As elsewhere in the former communist countries, unemployment has affected women more severely than men: in Russia two-thirds of the unemployed are women and young people (and these are, of course, overlapping categories).[64] Women are less likely than men to find offsetting employment.[65] Since the vast majority of single-parent households are headed by women, rising unemployment has pushed more women and children into poverty.[66] One estimate is that 55 percent of households headed by a single mother with small children live in poverty.[67] Also vulnerable to the economic trends of the past few years have been groups whose incomes are paid directly out of the state budget, such as those living on pensions and disability payments, as well as teachers, scientists, and health care workers. Although they have received periodic increases in pay, these often have been insufficient to keep up with increases in prices.

Both poverty and inequality have grown sharply since the end of the Soviet era. Over 40 percent of the Russian population live in poverty.[68] But while most people were suffering falling living standards, others were becoming wealthy. One commonly used measure of inequality is the Gini Index, which is an aggregate measure of the total deviation from perfect equality in the distribution of wealth or income in a country. In a highly egalitarian country such as Finland, Sweden, or Norway, the Gini Index for income distribution stands at about 20. Countries with moderately high levels of income inequality, such as Great Britain, France, and Italy, are at about 30. High-inequality countries such as the United States have a Gini Index of around 34. In Russia, in 1993, the equivalent index reached 48, double the level of 1988, and higher than any other postcommunist country except for Kyrgyzstan.[69] We can only imagine the degree of anger and frustration that this rapid change has brought about in a society used to high social equality.

Tied to the deteriorating economic performance has been the erosion of public health. Mortality rates have risen, especially among males. Life expectancy for males in Russia is at a level comparable with poor and developing countries. The State Statistics Committee estimated in 1999 that life expectancy at birth for males was 58 and for females 71, a remarkable discrepancy, generally attributed to the higher rates of abuse of alcohol and tobacco among men. Demographers warned that although life expectancy was beginning to rise again, at the present rate of mortality, 40 percent of Russia's 16-year-old boys would not reach their sixtieth birthday.[70] Other demographic indicators are equally grim. Every year Russia's population declines by as many as half a million people or more due to the excess of deaths over births. By early 2000, there were twice as many deaths per year as births.[71]

PUTIN'S AGENDA Vladimir Putin has repeatedly stated that he intends to set the economy firmly on the path of growth again and that he means to do so by leveling the playing field for all economic actors. He has called for honoring principles such as the rule of law and respect for property rights. Clearly, an efficient, competitive market economy would benefit nearly all groups in Russia's society. But, as is the case with fair, effi-

cient, and honest government as well, the groups who profit from the status quo are strong and well organized, giving them an advantage in the political arena over the large but unorganized interests that would be made better off from a successful economic reform. The task of carrying the promise of economic reform through now falls to President Putin.

Rule Adjudication: Toward A Constitutional Order

The Law-Governed State

One of the most important goals of Gorbachev's reforms was to make the USSR a *law-governed state* (*pravovoe gosudarstvo*) rather than one in which state bodies and the Communist Party exercised power arbitrarily. Since 1991, the Russian leaders have continued to assert that the state must respect the primacy of law over politics—even when they took actions grossly violating the constitution. The difficulty in placing law above politics testifies to the deep divisions which persist in society and the lingering impact of the old regime's abuse of the legal system.

The struggle for the rule of law did not begin with Gorbachev.[72] Even under the post-Stalin regime, the party and police could and did use legal procedures to give the mantle of legal legitimacy to acts of political repression. Alternatively the authorities sometimes resorted to the practice of declaring a particular individual mentally incompetent and forcing him into a mental hospital. The continuation of these practices until the late 1980s shows that the law failed to protect the rights of individuals whom the party and KGB chose to suppress.

The Judicial System

Full establishment of a law-governed state would mean that no arm of the state would be able to bend or violate the law for political ends. In turn, this requires that the judiciary be independent of political influence. Changes since 1991 have gone far toward establishing an independent judicial branch.

THE PROCURACY Russia's legal system traditionally vested a great deal of power in the *procuracy;* the procuracy was considered to be the most prestigious branch of the law. The procurator is the official corresponding to a prosecutor in U.S. practice. Procurators are given sweeping responsibilities for fighting crime, corruption, and abuses of power in the bureaucracy, and for both instigating investigations of criminal wrong-doing by private citizens and responding to complaints about official malfeasance. One of the procuracy's assigned tasks is to ensure that all state officials and public organizations observe the law. Moreover, the procuracy is charged with overseeing the entire system of justice, including the penal system. The procuracy has traditionally been seen as the principal check on abuses of power by state officials. But it has usually been inadequately equipped to meet the sweeping responsibilities that the law assigns to it, because of the difficulty of effectively supervising the vast state bureaucracy and overcoming the entrenched political machines of party and state officials.

THE JUDICIARY In contrast to the influence that the procuracy has traditionally wielded in Russia, the bench has been relatively weak. Trial judges are usually the least experienced and lowest paid of the members of the legal profession, and the most vulnerable to external political and administrative pressure. Successful judicial reform requires greater independence and discretion on the part of courts. If judges are to supervise the legality of arrests, ensure fair trials, and render just decisions in the face of intense external pressure, they will need greater legal training, experience, and social esteem. Judges are being called upon to raise their standards of professionalism, moreover, at a time of rapid change in law, legal procedure, and social conditions: in a few instances, judges have been murdered when they attempted to take on organized crime. Many judges have left their positions to take higher paying jobs in other branches of the legal profession, but caseloads have risen substantially as a result of the widening of judicial power.

Policymakers recognize the importance of an independent judiciary: this is one of the points on which reformers and conservatives tend to agree. They disagree, however, on the conditions needed

to achieve it. In the past, judges were formally elected by the local soviet of the jurisdiction in which they served, although in fact they were selected by the party through the nomenklatura system. Reforms beginning in the late 1980s attempted to increase judges' independence of local political forces by lengthening their term of office and placing their election in the hands of the soviet at the next-higher level to that of the jurisdiction in which they served. But this still allowed powerful regional executives to sway judicial decision making. Therefore reformers worked to pass a major reform of the judicial system which puts the power of appointment of judges into the president's hands (although the president is to select judges from among candidates who have been approved by boards of judges). An important aspect of the reform is that all courts of general jurisdiction are federal courts, and must uphold federal law throughout the country.

THE HIERARCHY OF COURTS The Russian judiciary forms a unitary system of federal legal authority. All courts of general jurisdiction are federal courts, except for local justices of the peace. Most trials are held in district and city courts, which have original jurisdiction in most criminal proceedings. Higher-level courts, including regional and republic-level courts, hear appeals from lower courts and have original jurisdiction in certain cases. In turn, the Russian Supreme Court hears cases referred from lower courts and also issues instructions to lower courts on judicial matters. The Supreme Court does not have the power to challenge the constitutionality of laws and other official actions of legislative and executive bodies. That power is assigned by the constitution to the Constitutional Court. Under the constitution, the judges of the Supreme Court are nominated by the president and confirmed by the Federation Council of the Federal Assembly.

There is a similar hierarchy of courts hearing cases arising from civil disputes between firms or between firms and the government; these are called "commercial courts" (*arbitrazhnye sudy*). Like the Supreme Court, the Supreme Commercial Court is both the highest appellate court for its system of courts as well as the source of instruction and direction to lower commercial courts. As with the

Supreme Court, the judges of the Supreme Commercial Court are nominated by the president and confirmed by the Federation Council. In recent years, the Supreme Commercial Court has handed down a number of major decisions that clarify the new rules of the economic game.

Overseeing the court system and providing for its material and administrative needs is the Ministry of Justice. Its own influence over the judiciary is limited, however, because it lacks any direct authority over the procuracy.

CONSTITUTIONAL ADJUDICATION   One of the most important reforms in post-communist Russia's legal system is the establishment of a court for constitutional review of official acts of federal and lower governments. The Constitutional Court has established its authority to interpret the constitution in a variety of areas. It has ruled on several ambiguous questions relating to parliamentary procedure. It has overturned some laws passed by ethnic republics within Russia and struck down a provision of the Russian Criminal Code that limited individual rights. Generally, in disputes between individuals and state authorities, the court finds in favor of individuals, thus reaffirming the sphere of individual legal rights. It has consistently upheld the sovereignty of the federal constitution over regional governments.

However, the most important challenge for the court has been the huge domain of presidential authority. The court has been reluctant to challenge the president. One of its first and most important decisions concerned a challenge brought by a group of communist parliamentarians to the president's edicts launching the war in Chechnia. The court ruled that the president had the authority to wage the war through the use of his constitutional power to issue edicts with the force of law. However, in other, less highly charged issues (which did not touch directly on national security), the court has established legal limits to the president's authority. For instance, the court ruled that the president may not refuse to sign a law after parliament has overridden his veto (see Box 8.3: Yeltsin and the "Trophy Art" Law). The court seems to be gradually establishing its status as a legitimate source of

judicial review power which might one day check potential abuses of power by the executive and legislative branches, regional governments, and the bureaucracy.

THE BAR   Change of another sort has been occurring among those members of the legal profession who represent individual citizens and organizations in both criminal and civil matters: "advocates" (*advokaty*). They are comparable to defense attorneys in the United States. Their role has expanded considerably with the spread of the market economy. They long enjoyed some autonomy through their self-governing associations, through which they elect officers and govern admission of new practitioners. In the past, their ability to make effective use of their rights was limited, but in recent years, their opportunities have risen markedly. Lawyers have begun forming law firms. New colleges of advocates have formed and have begun to compete with one another. The profession has become attractive for the opportunities it provides to earn high incomes.

Statutory Reforms

In addition to these changes in judicial institutions, an entirely new legislative foundation for the legal system has begun to be established. The new law codes prescribe the principles needed for the protection of civil rights, private property, and meaningful federalism. To a surprising degree, this statutory foundation of a democratic society has been achieved by the laborious process of bargaining and consensus building among interested opposing groups rather than by decree or dictate. The area of consensus is larger than might be imagined, given the deep division between those who want to advance Russia toward a democratic, market-based society, and those that want to preserve socialism. The goal of a "law-governed state" is one that both reformers and conservatives can support. They can also agree that Russia requires a mixed economy with both market institutions and state administrative controls. On other basic legal issues, however, reformers and the opposition cannot agree. The most important is the question of private ownership of land.

Box 8.3   Yeltsin and the "Trophy Art" Law

The Constitutional Court issued an important ruling in April 1998 limiting the president's right to withhold his signature when both chambers of parliament voted by the required two-thirds majority to override a presidential veto.

The case concerned a law which would prohibit the return of any art works or cultural artifacts seized by Soviet armed forces in World War II to their country of origin. This law was strongly opposed by President Yeltsin on the grounds that it undercut his ability to reach agreements with Germany and other countries on the exchange of art works taken out of the two countries during the war, and thus would prevent Russia from reacquiring some of the treasures it had lost when German forces occupied Russia. However, the law enjoyed strong support on nationalist grounds in both chambers of parliament. Yeltsin vetoed the bill in March 1997 but both houses voted to override his veto and sent it back to him for his signature in May. In June he vetoed the bill again, claiming that the procedures used by the parliament in passing the law had been unconstitutional. He cited the fact that the Federation Council had sent the ballot out to its members by mail for their vote, which was not permitted under the constitution, and that the State Duma had allowed members to vote for their absent colleagues by using their electronic voting cards, again in violation of the Duma's own procedural rules. Parliament appealed to the Constitutional Court to adjudicate, claiming that the president had no right to judge the constitutionality of the parliament's voting procedures, and that in any case he had no right to withhold his signature when the parliament had duly overridden his veto.

The Constitutional Court in April 1998 ruled that the president must indeed sign the law. He could simultaneously seek a judgment from the court as to the constitutionality of the voting procedures used by parliament and as to the constitutionality of the substance of the law. But he had no right not to sign it. President Yeltsin duly complied with the court's decision and signed the law nine days later. But he immediately appealed to the court to rule that the law itself was unconstitutional, both in its substance and due to the method of its passage.

In July 1999 the court ruled on the president's appeal. The court struck down some provisions of the law but allowed others to stand. The result was to give the president some discretion to negotiate with foreign governments over the return of particular cultural artifacts while not challenging parliament's right to pass legislation in this area. As to the Duma's informal practice of allowing deputies to vote for absent colleagues—a practice which is not allowed under the rules but has been tolerated as an indispensable means of getting business done—the court rendered a Solomonic judgment. It held that for deputies to vote for other deputies was indeed unconstitutional. But the court refrained from striking down the trophy art law on the basis of the irregularity of the Duma's voting methods since this would have required the court retroactively to overturn most of the legislation passed over the past several years on the same grounds. Instead, the court warned the Duma that if proxy voting was needed in the future, the Duma should formalize it in the rules of procedure.

Nevertheless, a number of other major legal questions have been decided through the parliamentary process. Parts I and II of an entirely rewritten Civil Law Code have been passed by parliament and signed into law; the third and final part—dealing with property in land—remains mired in controversy. It was notable that communists and reformers alike could agree on a set of legal principles defining a new body of civil law. Another important achievement was the new Criminal Code, finally signed into law by President Yeltsin in June 1996 following a year and a half of negotiations and deliberations among specialists, concerned state bodies, the presidential administration, and members of parliament. The new code brought the criminal law into closer conformity with the demands of the post-Soviet, post-communist environment.

Obstacles to the Rule of Law

How close has the Soviet system come to realizing the ideal of a "law-governed state"? While substantial change has occurred, structural barriers to the full triumph of law remain. Three problems in particular should be noted.

The first is the continuing power of the security police. Until October 1991 the agency with principal responsibility for maintaining domestic security was called the KGB (State Security Committee). Under Soviet rule, the KGB had excercised very wide powers, including responsibility for both domestic and foreign intelligence. Since 1991 its functions have been split up among several agencies. The main domestic security agency is called the Federal Security Service. A series of reorganizations have altered the structure and mission of the security organs, but never were they subjected to a thorough-going purge of personnel. Although many of the archives containing documents on the activities of the secret police in the past have been opened to inspection, exposing many aspects of the regime's use of terror, no member or collaborator of the security service has ever been prosecuted legally for these actions. None of the KGB's informers has been exposed to public judgment. The position taken by the security police is that they were themselves victims of arbitrary rule and terror under Stalin, and for that reason today uphold the rule of law. Whether this position is credible is another matter.[73]

The second impediment to the primacy of law is the immense inertia of a heavily bureaucratized state. The lawmaking authority of parliament is frequently undermined by the power of administrative regulations issued by executive agencies. The profusion of rules and regulations, complementing, interpreting, and often contradicting one another, creates ample opportunities for evasions, as well as generating pressures for intervention through the authority of powerful individuals to cut through the jungle of red tape. Patronage and protection often serve to compensate for the paralyzing effects of anonymous bureaucratic power.

The final threat to the primacy of law is the willingness of the president to enact decisions in pursuit of his policy goals that violate constitutional or statutory principles. An example is President Yeltsin's set of decrees in September and October 1993 that dissolved parliament. They were unconstitutional, even though they called for a national referendum to determine the constitutional principles that Russia was to adopt for the future. Another example is the massive military engagement in Chechnia. Here President Yeltsin's use of his decree-making authority was upheld by the Constitutional Court but was widely criticized as an excessive response to the situation.

Apart from these cases, there is another, less spectacular threat to the primacy of law in the president's power. The constitution grants the president the right to issue decrees (*ukazy*) which have the force of law unless the parliament passes legislation that supersedes them. Presidential decrees may not contradict existing law, however. President Yeltsin used his decree power extensively in matters such as privatization, social spending, and reorganization of the executive branch, although he often invited the Federal Assembly to adopt substitute legislation in these areas. Opponents have accused both Yeltsin and Putin of exceeding their constitutional authority to issue decrees. The president's decree power means that he can set policy by decree and use his veto power to block parliament's initiatives. When there is a strong opposition majority in parliament, however, parliament can override his veto.

The institutional legacy of authoritarian rule—a powerful and autonomous security police, wide discretion by government agencies to issue rules and regulations that interpret and implement laws, and a broad, unconstrained grant of power to the chief executive—has proven very difficult to dismantle. In the end, it may defeat the cause of a law-governed state. Rampant corruption, poverty, inequality, and other social problems may sway public opinion to sacrifice legal rights for security under an authoritarian order. The spread of political and economic competition in society, however, make it more likely that most groups will prefer to achieve social stability through the rule of law.

Is Russia a Democracy?

Russia's thousand-year history of expansion, defense, and state domination of society has left behind a legacy of autocratic rule. Its transition from communist rule, moreover, is bound up with the reconstruction of Russia as a national state. Russia historically tied its national existence with the political mission of building and maintaining a multi-national, imperial state. This was true in the

Soviet period as well, when the regime imposed a strongly Russian national identity on Soviet society, disguised as "Soviet nationality." The reconstruction of national identity thus complicates Russia's progress toward democracy since the transition is not occurring within historically settled national borders.

Throughout Russian and Soviet history, the state has played the dominant part in initiating phases of intense social change, and personal leadership has been crucial in moving the state. Gorbachev and Yeltsin illustrate this pattern in their attempts to use power in an arbitrary way to achieve democratic goals such as democratization and a market economy. Using autocratic power to impose democracy, of course, undermines the very institutions it endeavors to create. For that reason, the changes that have occurred in Russia over the last decade have been more effective in breaking down the fabric of the old system than in constructing a new institutional framework to replace it.

Russia's post-communist transition has been difficult and incomplete. Within Russia, many are disenchanted with the promise of democracy. Organized crime continues to flout the law with apparent impunity. At the same time, the end of communism has stimulated groups to organize for the protection of their interests. New institutions for articulating and aggregating these interests remain fragile. But the spread of political and property rights has resulted in the emergence of a more pluralistic environment.

Russia's vast size, weak government capacity, and cultural legacy of state domination make it likely that democratic consolidation in the post-communist era will be slow and uneven. At the same time, international factors such as the end of the ideological confrontation between democracy and socialism and the dense network of international communications linking societies, together with the effects of domestic social changes such as rising educational levels, make a return to dictatorship unlikely. Although sometimes it appears that Russian politics boils down to the incestuous interplay of a few powerful Kremlin cliques, groups and leaders are increasingly acting as though they believe that they are all better off accepting a common framework of democratic institutions in which to articulate their demands and resolve their differences.

Chronology of Major Political Events: Russia, 1989–2000

1989:

March. Elections to USSR Congress of People's Deputies. Yeltsin wins Moscow seat by a landslide.

1990:

March. USSR Congress of People's Deputies elects Gorbachev president of the USSR.

March. Elections to Russian Republic Congress of People's Deputies, and to local soviets throughout Russia; elections to republic and local soviets in other republics. Democratic and nationalist forces score dramatic victories.

May–June. First Russian Congress of People's Deputies convenes, elects Yeltsin chairman of the Supreme Soviet, adopts Declaration on Sovereignty.

1991:

June. Election of Russian president. Yeltsin wins with outright majority.

June. New Treaty of Union is initialed by Gorbachev and heads of seven republics.

August. Gorbachev goes to Crimea for scheduled vacation.

August. New Union Treaty is published in press; official signing set for August 20.

August 19–21. "State Committee on the State of Emergency" puts Gorbachev under house arrest, seizes power, declares state of emergency, suspends constitution. Coup fails as military withholds full support; Yeltsin rallies opposition. Coup leaders surrender. Gorbachev returns to Moscow, resumes nominal powers as USSR president but is fatally weakened. Yeltsin's stature strengthened.

November. Russian Congress of People's Deputies grants Yeltsin extraordinary decree powers to enact economic measures. Yeltsin appoints himself head of government. Names team of young radical reformers as deputy prime ministers. Readies program of radical economic reform.

December 1. Ukraine holds referendum on independence; issue passes with 90 percent of the vote.

December 8. Yeltsin meets with heads of Ukraine and Belorussia; they declare USSR dissolved and form a new "Commonwealth of Independent States" in its place. Later Kazakhstan and other Central Asian states join.

December 25. Gorbachev addresses country on TV, announces resignation as USSR president, gives powers of office to Yeltsin. USSR flag replaced by Russian tri-color on top of Kremlin.

December 26. Russian Supreme Soviet renames RSFSR the "Russian Federation."

December. USSR seat on the UN Security Council assumed by Russia.

1992:

January. "Shock therapy" program of radical economic stabilization takes effect.

October. Distribution of vouchers for mass privatization begins.

December. Russian Congress of People's Deputies refuses to confirm Gaidar as prime minister. Yeltsin nominates Viktor Chernomyrdin as prime minister; Congress confirms the nomination. Agrees to hold national referendum on new constitution.

1993:

March. Congress of Russian People's Deputies votes to cancel referendum, reject constitutional amendments giving Yeltsin full power to name and remove government ministers.

March. Yeltsin threatens to dissolve Congress, declare presidential rule.

March. Congress by narrow margin fails to pass motion to remove Yeltsin through impeachment. Then approves motion to hold referendum on approval of Yeltsin and his policies.

April. Referendum on Yeltsin and his policies held; 59 percent express approval of Yeltsin; 53 percent approve policies of his government.

June. Yeltsin convenes special constitutional assembly to draft new constitution.

July. Constitutional assembly completes work on draft of new constitution providing for strong presidency.

September. Yeltsin decrees dissolution of Congress of People's Deputies and Supreme Soviet; annuls deputies' mandates; calls for new parliamentary elections in December along with national referendum on new constitution based on draft developed by constitutional assembly. Opposition parliamentary leaders barricade themselves inside "White House" (parliament building), hold rump Congress.

October. Opposition leaders break through barricades, join with anti-Yeltsin paramilitary forces outside, smash through neighboring building, break into offices of state television tower; army suppresses uprising. Army shells White House.

December. Elections to new Federal Assembly held; referendum on new constitution. Constitution approved by majority of voters.

1994:

January. New Federal Assembly convenes. State Duma elects Ivan Rybkin (moderate communist, member of Agrarian party faction) chairman.

December. Yeltsin sends federal ground and air forces into Chechnia to suppress independence movement of President Dzhokar Dudaev.

1995:

December. Elections to State Duma held. Communists win one-third of seats.

1996:

January. State Duma convenes, elects communist Gennadii Seleznev chairman.

March–June. Yeltsin runs vigorous campaign for reelection.

June. First round of presidential election. Yeltsin and Ziuganov win most votes. Yeltsin names Alexander Lebed new Secretary of Security Council.

July. Second round of presidential election, won by Yeltsin. Yeltsin suffers new heart attack on eve of second round.

October. Cease-fire agreement with Chechen leaders signed. Yeltsin fires Lebed for attempting to exceed allotted powers.

November. Yeltsin undergoes heart surgery.

September–December. Elections of chief executives held in 50 regions.

1997:

March. President Yeltsin delivers extended address to joint session of Federal Assembly, promises sweeping reform of executive branch, financial system. Names Anatolii Chubais and Boris Nemtsov first deputy prime ministers with mandate to carry out radical restructuring of collapsed financial system.

1998:

March–April. President Yeltsin dismisses entire government. Appoints Sergei Kirienko prime minister. State Duma confirms the appointment on the third and final vote.

April–July. Financial crisis. Government demands deep spending cuts and tax increases. IMF approves rescue credit.

August 17. Default and devaluation: Government declares moratorium on interest payments on internal debts and allows the ruble to fall against the dollar. Financial markets collapse.

August 23. President Yeltsin dismisses Prime Minister Kirienko and the entire government. Appoints Viktor Chernomyrdin acting prime minister.

August–September. Stock share prices, ruble exchange rate tumble; prices rise sharply. Trading on stock and currency markets repeatedly suspended.

September 11. After President Yeltsin withdraws nomination of Chernomyrdin and names Foreign Minister Primakov as candidate for prime minister, Duma confirms Primakov as head of government with 317 affirmative votes. Primakov names communist Yuri Masliukov as first deputy prime minister in charge of economic policy.

1999:

May. Yeltsin dismisses Primakov government; nominates Sergei Stepashin as next prime minister; Duma votes on 5 articles of impeachment of president, none receives required minimum 300 votes; Duma then confirms Stepashin as prime minister.

August. Yeltsin dismisses Stepashin government, nominates Vladimir Putin as prime minister. Duma confirms Putin.

December 19. Duma elections

December 31. Yeltsin resigns as president. Putin becomes acting president.

2000:

March 26. Presidential elections. Vladimir Putin is elected in first round.

✌ KEY TERMS ✌

Chechnia
Committee of Soldiers' Mothers
Communist Party of the Russian Federation (CPRF)
Constitutional Court
Federation Council
Federation of Independent Trade Unions of Russia (FITUR)

glasnost
Mikhail Gorbachev
governors
law-governed state
Vladimir Ilyich Lenin
Liberal Democratic Party of Russia (LDPR)
nomenklatura

party of power
presidential decrees (*ukazy*)
privatization
procuracy
Vladimir Putin
Security Council
shock therapy

single-member districts
Joseph Stalin
State Duma
Unity
Yabloko
Boris Yeltsin

✑ SUGGESTED READINGS ✑

Bahry, Donna. "Comrades into Citizens? Russian Political Culture and Public Support for the Transition." *Slavic Review* 58, No. 4 (1999): 841–53.

Bahry, Donna. "Society Transformed? Rethinking the Social Roots of Perestroika." *Slavic Review* 52, No. 3 (Fall 1993): 512–54.

Blasi, Joseph R., Maya Kroumova, and Douglas Kruse. *Kremlin Capitalism: Privatizing the Russian Economy.* Ithaca, NY: Cornell University Press, 1997.

Bremmer, Ian, and Ray Taras, eds. *New States, New Politics: Building the Post-Soviet Nations.* Cambridge: Cambridge University Press, 1997.

Bunce, Valerie. *Subversive Institutions: The Design and the Destruction of Socialism and the State.* Cambridge: Cambridge University Press, 1999.

Colton, Timothy J. *Transitional Citizens: Voters and What Influences Them in the New Russia.* Cambridge, MA: Harvard University Press, 2000.

Cook, Linda J. *The Soviet `Social Contract' and Why It Failed: Welfare Policy and Workers' Politics from Brezhnev to Yeltsin.* Cambridge: Harvard University Press, 1993.

Fish, Stephen M. *Democracy from Scratch: Opposition and Regime in the New Russian Revolution.* Princeton: Princeton University Press, 1995.

Frye, Timothy. *Brokers and Bureaucrats: Building Market Institutions in Russia.* Ann Arbor, MI: University of Michigan Press, 2000.

Gaddy, Clifford G., and Barry W. Ickes. "Russia's Virtual Economy." *Foreign Afffairs* 77 (September–October 1998): 53–67.

Gustafson, Thane. *Capitalism Russian-Style.* Cambridge: Cambridge University Press, 1999.

Hellman, Joel S. "Winners Take All: The Politics of Partial Reform in Postcommunist Transitions." *World Politics* 50, No. 1 (January 1998): 203–34.

Hough, Jerry F. *Democratization and Revolution in the USSR.* Washington, DC: Brookings Institution, 1997.

Huskey, Eugene. *Presidential Power in Russia.* Armonk, NY: M. E. Sharpe, 1999.

Kolsto, Pal. *Political Construction Sites: Nation Bulding in Russia and the Post-Soviet States.* Boulder, CO: Westview, 2000.

Laitin, David D. *Identity in Formation: The Russian-Speaking Populations in the Near Abroad.* Ithaca, NY: Cornell University Press, 1998.

McFaul, Michael. *Russia's 1996 Presidential Election: The End of Polarized Politics.* Stanford, CA: Hoover Institution Press, 1997.

Remington, Thomas F. "The Evolution of Executive-Legislative Relations in Russia since 1993." *Slavic Review* 59, No. 3 (Fall 2000): 499–520.

Remington, Thomas F. *The Russian Parliament: Institutional Evolution in a Transitional Regime, 1989–1999.* New Haven, CT: Yale University Press, 2001.

Rose, Richard. *Getting Things Done with Social Capital: New Russia Barometer VII.* Glasgow: Centre for the Study of Public Policy, University of Strathclyde, 1998.

Shleifer, Andrei, and Daniel Treisman. *Without a Map: Political Tactics and Economic Reform in Russia.* Cambridge, MA: MIT Press, 2000.

Sperling, Valerie. *Organizing Women in Contemporary Russia: Engendering Transition.* Cambridge: Cambridge University Press, 1999.

Stoner-Weiss, Kathryn. *Local Heroes: The Political Economy of Russian Regional Governance.* Princeton, NJ: Princeton University Press, 1997.

Treisman, Daniel S. *After the Deluge: Regional Crises and Political Consolidation in Russia.* Ann Arbor: University of Michigan Press, 1999.

Weigle, Marcia A. *Russia's Liberal Project: State-Society Relations in the Transition from Communism.* University Park, PA: Pennsylvania State University Press, 2000.

White, Stephen, Richard Rose, and Ian McAllister. *How Russia Votes.* Chatham, NJ: Chatham House Publishers, Inc., 1997.

Woodruff, David. *Money Unmade: Barter and the Fate of Russian Capitalism.* Ithaca and London: Cornell University Press, 1999.

www.columbia.edu/~sls27/Content/Russia/Russia Intro.html

www.msu.edu/M~herrone2/links.htm

www.rferl.org/newsline/search/

www.russiatoday.com/

www.solar.rtd.utk.edu/friends/home.html

www.ucis.pitt.edu/reesweb/

∽ ENDNOTES ∽

1. Richard Pipes, *Russia Under the Old Regime*, 2nd ed. (New York: Penguin Books, 1995).

2. Archie Brown, *The Gorbachev Factor* (New York: Oxford University Press, 1996).

3. Matthew Soberg Shugart and John M. Carey, *Presidents and Assemblies: Constitutional Design and Electoral Dynamics* (Cambridge: Cambridge University Press, 1992).

4. Ian Bremmer and Ray Taras, eds., *New States, New Politics: Building the Post-Soviet Nations* (Cambridge: Cambridge University Press, 1997).

5. Stephen Whitefield and Geofrey Evans, "The Russian Election of 1993: Public Opinion and the Transition Experience," *Post-Soviet Affairs* 1994 10: 46–49; William Zimmerman, "Markets, Democracy and Russian Foreign Policy," *Post-Soviet Affairs* 10 (1994): 103–26; Donna Bahry, "Society Transformed? Rethinking the Social Roots of Perestroika," *Slavic Review* 52, No. 3 (Fall 1993): 511–54.

6. James L. Gibson and Raymond M. Duch, "Emerging Democratic Values in Soviet Political Culture," in Arthur H. Miller, William M. Reisinger, and Vicki L. Hesli, eds., *Public Opinion and Regime Change* (Boulder, CO: Westview, 1993), pp. 69–94; William M. Reisinger, Arthur H. Miller, and Vicki L. Hesli, "Political Values in Russia, Ukraine and Lithuania: Sources and Implications for Democracy," *British Journal of Political Science* 24 (1994): 183–223; and Jeffrey W. Hahn, "Continuity and Change in Russian Political Culture," *British Journal of Political Science* 21, No. 4 (1991): 393–421.

7. James L. Gibson, "The Resilience of Support for Democratic Institutions and Processes in the Nascent Russian and Ukrainian Democracies," in Vladimir Tismaneanu, ed., *Political Culture and Civil Society in Russia and the New States of Eurasia* (Armonk, NY: M. E. Sharpe, 1995), p. 57.

8. Richard Rose, *Getting Things Done with Social Capital: New Russia Barometer VII*, paper no. 303, Studies in Public Policy (Glasgow, UK: Centre for the Study of Public Policy, University of Strathclyde, 1998), pp. 40–43. Richard Rose's New Russia Barometer is a series of opinion surveys of a nationally representative sample of adult Russians conducted by Russia's premier survey research organization, the All-Russian Center for Public Opinion Research. The number of survey respondents is 2,000.

9. Rose, *Getting Things Done*, p. 44.

10. James R. Millar and Sharon L. Wolchik, "Introduction: The Social Legacies and the Aftermath of Communism," in James R. Millar and Sharon L. Wolchik, eds., *The Social Legacy of Communism* (Washington, DC and Cambridge: Woodrow Wilson Press and Cambridge University Press, 1994), p. 16.

11. Marcia A. Weigle, *Russia's Liberal Project: State-Society Relations in the Transition from Communism* (University Park, PA: Pennsylvania State University Press, 2000), pp. 432–41.

12. Reported by Richard Rose, *Getting Things Done*, pp. 58–59. VTsIOM conducted the study in March–April 1998. The interviewers provided respondents with a 7-point scale with 1 indicating great mistrust and 7 indicating great trust. Anyone whose score was from 1 to 3 was coded as not trusting, and anyone with a score from 5 to 7 was coded as trusting. A score of 4 was coded as neutral.

13. From a survey by the Public Opinion Foundation reported in *Segodnia*, February 10, 1997.

14. Bahry, "Society Transformed?" pp. 512–54.

15. Ibid., p. 544.

16. Gibson and Duch, "Emerging Democratic Values," p. 86; William M. Reisinger, Arthur H. Miller, Vicki L. Hesli, and Kristen Hill Maher, "Political Values in Russia, Ukraine and Lithuania: Sources and Implications for Democracy," *British Journal of Political Science* 24 (1994): 216–18; Jeffrey W. Hahn, "Continuity and Change in Russian Political Culture," in Frederic J. Fleron, Jr. and Erik P. Hoffmann, eds., *Post-Communist Studies and Political Science: Methodology and Empirical Theory in Sovietology* (Boulder: Westview Press, 1993), pp. 319–22.

17. Reisinger, Miller, Hesli, and Maher, "Political Values in Russia, Ukraine and Lithuania," p. 200.

18. Sidney Verba, Norman H. Nie and Jae-on Kim, *Participation and Political Equality: A Seven-Nation Comparison* (Cambridge: Cambridge University Press, 1978).

19. Rose, Richard, Getting Things Done, pp. 60–62.

20. Robert D. Putnam, *Bowling Alone: The Collapse and Revival of American Community* (New York: Simon & Schuster, 2000), p. 59.

21. Rose, *Getting Things Done with Social Capital*, pp. 32–33.

22. Turnout levels in American presidential elections in the 1970s, 80s, and 90s averaged 52–54 percent. Turnout for congressional elections was much lower.

23. Rose, *Getting Things Done with Social Capital*, pp. 35–36.

24. David Lane and Cameron Ross, *The Transition from Communism to Capitalism: Ruling Elites from Gorbachev to Yeltsin* (New York: St. Martin's Press, 1999).

25. Sharon Werning Rivera, "Elites in Post-communist Russia: A Changing of the Guard?" *Europe-Asia Studies* 52, No. 3 (2000): 413–32.

26. Igor M. Bunin, ed., *Biznesmeny Rossii: 40 istorii uspekha* (Moscow: OKO, 1994), p. 373.

27. Steven L. Solnick, *Stealing the State: Control and Collapse in Soviet Institutions* (Cambridge, MA: Harvard University Press, 1998), pp. 112–24.

28. Bunin, *Biznesmeny Rossii*, p. 366.

29. Jane I. Dawson, *Eco-Nationalism: Anti-Nuclear Activism and National Identity in Russia, Lithuania, and Ukraine* (Durham, NC: Duke University Press, 1996).

30. RFE/RL Newsline, May 24, 1999.

31. Article 59 of the 1993 Constitution provides that young men of conscription age who are conscientious objectors to war may do alternative service rather than being called up to army service, but legislation that would specify how this right is to be exercised still has not been passed,

due to the strong opposition from the military itself. Thus would-be conscientious objectors and courts are in a legal limbo.

32. See Valerie Sperling, *Organizing Women in Contemporary Russia: Engendering Transition* (Cambridge: Cambridge University Press, 1999), pp. 118–29.

33. Sperling, *Organizing Women*, pp. 255–56.

34. Richard Rose, *New Russia Barometer VI: After the Presidential Election* (Glasgow: Centre for the Study of Public Policy, University of Strathclyde, Studies in Public Policy no. 272), p. 6; Richard Rose, *Getting Things Done*, p. 15. In 1996, the question was: at any point during the past 12 months, have you received your wages or pension late? In 1996, 78 percent responded yes, 21 percent no. In 1998, the question was: at any point during the past 12 months, have you received your wages late? 75 percent responded yes, 25 percent no.

35. RFE/RL Newsline, January 13, 1997; January 17, 1997; February 18, 1997; November 25, 1998; January 14, 1999; January 27, 1999; September 15, 1999; June 26, 2000.

36. Linda J. Cook, *Labor and Liberalization: Trade Unions in the New Russia* (New York: The Twentieth Century Fund Press, 1997), pp. 76–77.

37. This was called the All-Union Central Council of Trade Unions, or VTsSPS for its Russian initials.

38. Harold J. Berman, "Religious Freedom and the Rights of Foreign Missionaries under Russian Law," *The Parker School Journal of East European Law* 2, Nos. 4, 5 (1995): 421–46.

39. M. Stephen Fish, *Democracy from Scratch: Opposition and Regime in the New Russian Revolution* (Princeton: Princeton University Press, 1995); Michael Urban, with Vyacheslav Igrunov and Sergei Mitrokhin, *The Rebirth of Politics in Russia* (Cambridge: Cambridge University Press, 1997).

40. Good accounts of the political campaigns surrounding the 1989 and 1990 elections include Brendan Kiernan, *The End of Soviet Politics: Elections, Legislatures, and the Demise of the Communist Party* (Boulder: Westview Press, 1993); and Michael McFaul and Sergei Markov, *The Troubled Birth of Russian Democracy: Parties, Personalities, and Programs* (Stanford: Hoover Institution Press, 1993).

41. Stephen White, Richard Rose, and Ian McAllister, *How Russia Votes* (Chatham, NJ: Chatham House, 1997), p. 254.

42. Based on results published in *Rossiiskaya gazeta* on 22 June 1996, and taken from the OMRI Daily Digest of 25 June 1996. The percentages are calculated based on the number of voters participating in the voting (75, 587, 139), the method used in the 1995 Duma elections.

43. *Segodnia*, 10 July 1996.

44. White, Rose, and McAllister, *How Russia Votes*, pp. 241–70.

45. In nine electoral districts, including Chechnia, the elections were declared invalid either because turnout fell below the minimum 25 percent threshold, or because voters cast more votes "against all" than for any of the candidates on the ballot. New elections were held in these districts in 2000.

46. On the CPRF, see Richard Sakwa, "Left or Right? The CPRF and the Problem of Democratic Consolidation in Russia," *Journal of Communist Studies and Transition Politics*, 14,

Nos. 1, 2 (March–June 1998): 128–58; Joan Urban and Valerii D. Solovei, *Russia's Communists at the Crossroads* (Boulder: WestviewPress, 1997).

47. Rose, Munro, and White, The 1999 *Duma* Vote, pp. 20–25.

48. Joel S. Hellman, "Winners Take All: The Politics of Partial Reform in Postcommunist Transitions," *World Politics* 50, No. 1(January 1998): 203–34.

49. Aslund, *How Russia Became a Market Economy*, p. 154.

50. Economists generally say that once prices start rising by 50 percent a month and more, the economy is in a state of hyper-inflation.

51. The goals of the privatization program are laid out in a volume of essays by its chief Russian designers and their Western advisers. See, in particular, Anatoly B. Chubais and Maria Vishnevskaya, "Main Issues of Privatisation in Russia," and Maxim Boycko and Andrei Shleifer, "The Voucher Programme for Russia," in Anders Aslund and Richard Layard, eds., *Changing the Economic System in Russia* (New York: St. Martin's Press, 1993), pp. 89–99 and 100–111.

52. Radio Free Europe/ Radio Liberty Daily Report, July 1, 1994.

53. Joseph R. Blasi, Maya Kroumova, and Douglas Kruse, *Kremlin Capitalism: Privatizing the Russian Economy* (Ithaca, NY: Cornell University Press, 1997), p. 50.

54. Blasi, Kroumova, and Kruse, *Kremlin Capitalism*; Michael McFaul, "State Power, Institutional Change, and the Politics of Privatization in Russia," *World Politics* 47 (January 1995): 210–43.

55. In spring 1996, when the presidential election campaign was at its height, Russian state treasury obligations were selling at ruinously high interest rates—over 200 percent effective annual yields on six-month bonds. Little wonder that investors were uninterested in the stock market. Because of the instability of the political climate and the fear of default, the great bulk of this paper was short term.

56. Thane Gustafson, *Capitalism Russian-Style* (Cambridge: Cambridge University Press, 1999), pp. 2–3, 94–95.

57. European Bank for Reconstruction and Development, *Transition Report 1995: Investment and Enterprise Development* (London: 1995), p. 55.

58. Ol'ga Kryshtanovskaia, "Finansovaia oligarkhiia v Rossii," *Izvestiia*, January 10, 1996, p. 5. The author is a respected sociologist who heads the sector for the study of the elite of the Institute of Sociology of the Russian Academy of Sciences. Also see Blasi et al., *Kremlin Capitalism*, pp. 155–57.

59. OMRI Daily Digests for April 20 and May 30, 1995; Gustafson, *Capitalism*, p. 25.

60. The Russian Civil War (1918–1921) was fought between the Bolshevik ("Red") forces and the anti-communists ("Whites") following the communist revolution. The Whites comprised a diverse set of enemies of the new regime—among them both monarchists and socialists—whose inability to unite against the Bolsheviks ensured their ultimate defeat at the hands of the Red Army.

61. Branko Milanovic, *Income, Inequality and Poverty during the Transition from Planned to Market Economy* (Washington, DC: World Bank, 1998), pp. 25–27.

62. RFE/RL Newsline, June 21, 2000.

63. As of summer 2000, unemployment stood at 11.2 percent in Belgium, 9.6 percent in France and Germany, 10.7 percent in Italy, and 14.1 percent in Spain. *Economist*, August 5, 2000, p. 98.

64. OMRI Daily Digest, January 12, 1995.

65. Khibovskaia, "Rossiiane stali," *Segodnia*, July 26, 1995.

66. Gail Kligman, "The Social Legacy of Communism: Women, Children, and the Feminization of Poverty," in James R. Millar and Sharon L. Wolchik, eds., *The Social Legacy of Communism* (Washington, DC: Woodrow Wilson Center Press and Cambridge University Press, 1994), p. 261; Mary Buckley, "The Politics of Social Issues," in Stephen White, Alex Pravda, and Zvi Gitelman, eds., *Developments in Russian and Post-Soviet Politics*, 3rd ed. (London: Macmillan, 1994), pp. 192–94.

67. G. Pirogov and S. Pronin, "The Russian Case: Social Policy Concerns," in Yogesh Atal, ed., *Poverty in Transition and Transition in Poverty: Recent Developments in Hungary, Bulgaria, Romania, Georgia, Russia, Mongolia* (New York: Berghahn Books/ Paris: UNESCO Publishing, 1999), p. 189.

68. *Segodnia*, July 4, 2000.

69. Milanovic, *Income, Inequality and Poverty*, p. 41.

70. REF/RL Newsline, March 8, 1999.

71. RFE/RL Newsline March 23, 2000.

72. A seminal study of the influences on the development of law in the Soviet Union is Harold J. Berman, *Justice in the U.S.S.R.*, rev. ed. (Cambridge, MA: Harvard University Press, 1963).

73. Two books, one by a Western scholar, the other by a Russian journalist who has followed the activities of the KGB for many years, emphasize the continuing clandestine power of the KGB and its successor organizations. The first is J. Michael Waller, *Secret Empire: The KGB in Russia Today* (Boulder: Westview, 1994); the second is Yevgenia Albats, *The State Within a State: The KGB and Its Hold on Russia, Past, Present and Future*, trans. Catherine A. Fitzpatrick (New York: Farrar, Straus, Giroux, 1994).

POLAND

0   50   100 mi
0   80   160 km

SWEDEN

LATVIA

*BALTIC
SEA*

N

LITHUANIA

RUSSIA

BELARUS

- Gdynia
- Slupsk
- Gdańsk
- Koszalin
- Elblag
- Olsztyn
- Augustów
- Szczecin
- Grudziadz
- Toruń
- *Norew*
- Lomża
- Bialystok
- *Notéc*
- Bydgoszcz
- *Vistula*
- Plock
- *Bug*
- Poznań
- *Warta*
- Warsaw
- Siedlce
- Zielona Góra
- Kalisz
- Lódz
- Radom
- Lublin
- Wroclaw
- Piotrków Trybunalski
- Chelm
- *Odra*
- Częstochowa
- Kielce
- Zamość
- Opole
- Katowice
- *San*
- Rzeszów
- Cracow
- Tarnów

GERMANY

CZECH REPUBLIC

UKRAINE

SLOVAKIA

CHAPTER 9

POLITICS IN POLAND

RAY TARAS

Country Bio–Poland

POPULATION   38.7 Million

TERRITORY   120,700 sq. mi.

YEAR OF INDEPENDENCE   1918

YEAR OF CURRENT CONSTITUTION   1997

CHIEF OF STATE   President Aleksander Kwasniewski

HEAD OF GOVERNMENT   Prime Minister Jerzy Buzek

LANGUAGE(S)   Polish

RELIGION   Roman Catholic 95%, Eastern Orthodox, Protestant, and other 5%

Over a decade has passed yet 1989 remains a remarkable year, an *annus mirabilis* in Central and Eastern Europe. When that year began, communist parties ruled in eight countries: Poland, Czechoslovakia, East Germany, Hungary, Bulgaria, Romania, Yugoslavia, and Albania. By Christmas day, when Romanian dictator Nicolae Ceausescu and his wife Elena were executed, communist leaders remained firmly in control of only Albania. With the opening of the Berlin Wall in November, communist East Germany was about to disappear. The defeat of the communist candidate in presidential elections in Slovenia in 1989 signaled the imminent breakup of socialist Yugoslavia. The year 1989 marked not only a historic regime change in the region, therefore, but a reconfiguration of countries and borders as well.

An often-repeated aphorism describing the sequence of change in Central Europe was the following: whereas it took Poland ten years to overthrow communism, it took Hungary ten months and Czechoslovakia just ten days (the so-called "velvet revolution"). Yet few specialists on the region would disagree that if Poland had to struggle longer to end communist rule, it was precisely by virtue of this fact that the other overthrows were swifter. Dominos would not have fallen the way they did had Polish society not taken the lead in repeatedly demonstrating the illegitimacy of communist rule. Moreover, had the Solidarity movement not been organized in Poland in 1980 to express public discontent with communist policies, it may not have become clear to the leadership in the Soviet Union, which controlled the communist parties of Eastern Europe, how unpopular these parties had become. Without Solidarity, therefore, there may never have been Mikhail Gorbachev, a man selected to lead the USSR and breathe life into a moribund political system, but who inadvertently brought about its demise.

We can agree that Poland was pivotal to the chain of events that produced the 1989 breakthrough. It is more difficult to make the case that developments in Poland since 1989 have had a similar impact on the region's political and economic evolution. Is Poland the model democracy in today's Central Europe? Even if it is its spectacular economic recovery that has been the envy of the region, it is important to acknowledge that Central Europe consists today of fully independent states that relish the hard-fought freedom of pursuing courses of action that are distinct to each. Therefore we need to study Poland in terms of whether it furnishes an ideal-type case of transition to democracy, not whether it is representative of or a model for the other states that formed part of the *annus mirabilis*.

Current Policy Challenges

Democratic Poland faces pressing problems as well as grand opportunities. Like the citizens of most new democracies, Poles must search for the right institutional tools to forge ahead. First among the Third Republic's challenges is the need for fine-tuning free market reform. While Poland's progress toward a free-market, capitalist system is among the most impressive in Central Europe (as we describe in a section on policy outcomes later), this very progress has brought with it a new set of problems centered around growing social inequality. Economic transformation has engendered an ever-widening division between those who turn out to be the winners (largely well-educated urbanites) in this new game and those who find themselves the losers. The losers—the poorly educated, inhabitants of less prosperous regions, rural dwellers—require social programs and spending that may clash with the goals of building a liberal free-market economy as quickly as possible. The problems of Polish agriculture—heavily labor-intensive and inefficient—

are particularly glaring and have resulted in regular, sometimes violent protests. The threat of overwhelming foreign ownership of Polish companies is also taken seriously by many citizens.

Finding new security solutions in a changing geopolitical environment has been an important concern of Polish policymakers. Joining NATO in 1998 may have been the single most important step in assuring Polish security, but the responsibilities of alliance membership have created a host of new challenges. NATO's increasing interventionism in conflicts in the Balkans, the peacekeeping commitments that ensue, the backlash these create in Russia, and the ambiguous security architecture in place for Poland's neighbors like Ukraine and Lithuania add up to new security dilemmas for the country. While Poland is undoubtedly more secure today than at any time in the twentieth century, the Polish tendency to doubt in others' commitment to the defense of the country's territorial integrity has not vanished.

Europeanization, which can refer specifically to the prospect of becoming a full member of the European Union (EU) or at a more general level to less tangible issues of assimilation into European identity, is the third and unquestionably the most complicated policy challenge. Poland's leaders are overwhelmingly in the pro-Europe camp but so were Denmark's, and it did not prevent the Danes in September 2000 from voting against European monetary union. Poland confronts an enormous set of tasks in aligning its institutions and practices in accordance with EU requirements. How patient the public will be with this already protracted process is difficult to gage. Should Poland's bid for EU membership get sidetracked, serious political problems will follow. The country most likely will meet the challenge of accession, but it is less prepared to deal with an EU rebuff should that occur.

The Making of Modern Poland

Every nation takes a selective approach to its own history: it focuses on a handful of recorded events, great leaders, and rival peoples, and transforms them into a core history. Often this core history is thought of as establishing the political traditions of a nation. In its selectivity and simplification, such history can assume a mythmaking function, having influence on contemporary political attitudes and behavior while distorting historical development.[1] Especially if a country has undergone regime change, as Poland did after 1989, there will be efforts to legitimate the new system by reference to past traditions. What are the most salient aspects of Polish history that have popular currency today and help give legitimacy to (or bring into question) the country's present political development?

Defining Features

Today's Poland occupies a location centered in the lowlands of the Northern European Plain that is almost the same as that of the first Polish state a millennium ago. Geographically it is the "heart of Europe"[2] and, therefore, it is accurate to regard Poland as part of Central Europe. Because the eastern part of the country was ruled by Russia throughout the nineteenth century, and the Polish state between 1945 and 1989 was integrated into the Soviet bloc, Poland has also been described as Eastern European for geopolitical reasons. In terms of surface area Poland is large by European standards, just slightly smaller than unified Germany.

Poland's population is close to 40 million, the vast majority of whom are Catholic. In the 1970s the communist authorities claimed that Poland was among the top ten industrial countries in the world, with its specialization in metallurgy, chemicals, and shipbuilding. Since the end of the communist system in 1989, the service sector has grown exponentially and has now overtaken the industrial sector. Agriculture is Poland's chief natural resource now that coal use has declined worldwide. About one-third of the population is rural. The capital, Warsaw, has become a financial hub as well as the home of state administration since a free market was created in the early 1990s. Other major cities are Lodz, Krakow, Wroclaw, Poznan, and Gdansk. Rapidly increasing trade with the West has transformed much of Poland, especially the cities, and it is visibly more cosmopolitan than in the 1980s, with visitors from the advanced industrial states but also from the former Soviet Union present in greater numbers.

Poles form part of the Slavic world. Their language belongs to the western Slavic group that includes Czech and Slovak. An eastern linguistic group is made up of Russians, Belarusians, and Ukrainians, and a southern one of Serbs, Croatians, Slovenes, and Bulgarians. Some historical evidence indicates that the original home of all Slavs was territory that came to be ruled by Polish kings by the fourteenth century. Accordingly, Poles frequently give the impression that they represent the heart of the Slavic world, more than the far larger Russian nation does. Poland (along with the Czech Republic) forms the western boundary of Slavdom so Poles also claim that, in contrast to Russians, they are an integral part of the European tradition.

The importance of Poland's first king, *Mieszko I,* comes as much from what he did—his conversion to Christianity in 966—as from the challenges he faced. External relations during his 26-year reign foreshadowed subsequent Polish history. His conversion was aimed at bolstering Poland's alliances in the face of the Germanic threat. But it was a Rus invasion in 981 that stripped the country of much of its lands. Mieszko then turned to the Apostolic See for protection and obtained its recognition of Poland as a separate kingdom. Mieszko's key dilemmas of international politics and his room for maneuver are strikingly similar to those of a thousand years later. This fact is not lost on Poles, who exhibit a fatalism born of what they perceive as a disastrous geopolitical position and the external security threat it engenders.

An important historical debate touches on whether Poland has constituted an ethnically homogeneous country or has been a multinational state. History provides ambiguous evidence on this matter. For the first four centuries, under the Piast dynasty, Poland consisted largely of related tribes. But in 1370, a Polish-Lithuanian union was created that transformed the ethnically homogeneous state of the Piasts into a multinational one under the new Jagiellonian dynasty. The union's expansive borders stretched from the Baltic Sea in the north to the Black Sea in the south. Within this Polish-dominated state, most Lithuanians were Catholic, though they were not Slav. By contrast, large Ukrainian and Belorussian groups (who were Slavs) were incorporated into this mini-empire; they belonged predominantly to the Eastern Orthodox faith.

The adage that to be Polish means to be Catholic is, therefore, historically inaccurate given the ethno-religious makeup of Poland in medieval times. During the Reformation of the sixteenth century, Protestantism was given legal recognition (in 1555) and religious toleration and equality was proclaimed (in 1573). While the numbers of Lutherans and Calvinists considering themselves Polish were limited, then and now, about 80 percent of the world's Jews lived in Poland in the Middle Ages. One writer observed how "in no other country than ancient Israel, have Jews lived continuously for as many centuries, in as large numbers, and with as much autonomy as in Poland."[3] During the June 1997 pilgrimage of Polish-born Pope John Paul II to his native country, he celebrated the culture that Catholic and Jewish Poles had helped forge over the centuries. He drew attention to the idea that Polishness was not the sole possession of Catholic Poles. The widespread interwar attitude that Jews were "among us" but not "of us" had to end, he exhorted, even if the country's current Jewish population was small, numbering under 20,000.

The ecumenical approach of Pope John Paul II departs from a more proprietary attitude traditionally taken by the Catholic Church toward Poland. The role of Catholicism in the making of the Polish nation was evident from the time of Mieszko's conversion, but in the mid-fifteenth century the ruling gentry began to define Poland's role in Europe in terms of an *antemurale christianitatis*—that is, the easternmost bulwark of Roman Catholicism. Poland was regarded as a nation lying on the faultline of Western and Eastern civilizations, under the constant threat of becoming absorbed by the East. Poland's task was to contain the non-Catholic East. Over the next centuries, a Polish version of manifest destiny was interpreted to encompass secular, political aspects. In this view the country stood as the outpost of European civilization generally. To its east, the culture of Rus, Byzantinium, Asia began. A philosophy evolved to systematize this mission. Called *Sarmatianism* (from an ancient Slavic tribe that came to dominate other peoples), it assigned a special mission to Poland as a shield protecting Christianity from paganism.

Both religious and secular versions of the *antemurale* myth have been stressed in Polish historiography. In 1648 the Ukrainian Cossacks revolted against Polish rule, auguring "The Deluge": In quick succession Tatars, Turks, Russians, and Swedes went to war against Poland. The Swedish army swiftly overran most of the country but a successful last-ditch defense of the monastery at Czestochowa in 1655 was attributed to the intercession of the Blessed Virgin whose icon, the Black Madonna, was (and is) kept there. The best example of Poland's historic mission as defender of Western Christian civilization came in 1683 when King Jan Sobieski defeated the Turkish armies outside of Vienna, thereby saving Europe from Islam.

The beginning of Jagiellonian rule in 1370 marked a change in the structure of power within the kingdom, the consequences of which still have relevance today. Jagiello had become king with the support of the nobility and, from then on, the Polish throne was to be subject to elective confirmation by this class. Two centuries later, Poland's political system had embraced a type of democracy that was to be exercised mostly by and for the nobility. Regional assemblies made up of nobles (*szlachta*) asserted increasing influence in the affairs of central government. This class had long recognized the legal equality of everyone within its ranks without regard to wealth or power. Its ranks were remarkably diverse: "In it were the great lords, holders of the highest positions in the state, owners of substantial landed estates, possessors of considerable wealth. . . . At the other end of the spectrum were the poor gentry, descendants of medieval knights, warriors or courtiers, entitled to noble rank and privileges but frequently possessing little or no land."[4]

When the last of the Jagiellonians died in 1572 without leaving an heir, the monarchy became even more beholden to the nobility. To select a successor as king, the *szlachta* adopted a radical new formula: "one nobleman, one vote." Power was now formally vested in this class and a crude kind of democracy—what was to be known as *szlachta democracy*—emerged. Although it was restricted to men of status, it nevertheless empowered a wider group than in most other European states of the period, making Poland a spectacular exception to the rule of absolute monarchies of the late Middle Ages. The system of elective kings became the political cornerstone of the Republican Commonwealth, this quasi-democratic kingdom, that lasted until the partitions of Poland in the late eighteenth century.

Such a political system carried the seeds of self-destruction and, indeed, it hastened the demise of the Commonwealth by the end of the eighteenth century. On the one hand, constitutional laws that incorporated the ideas of liberty, equality, and government based on the consent of a significant part of the nation enshrined the important principle of the rule of law (*non Rex sed lex regnat*). In 1505 the principle of *nihil novi* was introduced into Polish jurisprudence, requiring that no new legislation could be enacted by the king unless it received the consent of parliament. England was still some time away from recognizing the supremacy of parliament. However, such political arrangements, though ahead of their time, contributed to a general breakdown of authority and to a popular belief that Poland was governed by unrule. Foreign adversaries in Russia and Prussia were to employ the argument that Poland was ungovernable to justify its dismemberment.

The fear of absolutist government more than a precocious commitment to democratic ideas contributed most to a growing state of "unrule" in the country. It was behind the adoption of the best known principle of the Commonwealth, the *liberum veto*. This procedure allowed a single member of the *Sejm* (or parliament) to veto any act presented to this body. One historian explained the *szlachta*'s rationale for exercising this right: "The *liberum veto* would defend the sovereignty of the individual. God and Europe would defend that of the Republic."[5] The flaw in the logic was, of course, that God and Europe did not rescue Poland from political oblivion following the partitions—at least for 125 years. Although the Polish state had devised an ingenious system of checks-and-balances intended to preserve the democracy of the gentry, if abused this system would destroy itself. If skillfully exploited by Poland's foes, it would lead to destruction from without.

Partitions and Resistance

Between 1772 and 1795 Polish lands were *partitioned* among its powerful neighbors until an inde-

pendent Polish state ceased to exist. Stanislaw Kosciuszko's national insurrection of 1794 was a romantic highpoint of resistance but it foundered and led to bloody reprisals by Russian troops. By the third partition signed by Russia, Prussia, and Austria in October 1795, all remaining Polish lands were divided up, the king was forced to abdicate, and the name Poland was supposed to disappear from world maps forever.

How did Poles respond to the loss of statehood? Adam Mickiewicz, a nineteenth-century romantic writer acclaimed as national poet, compared Poland to Christ, destined to suffer on the cross to redeem the sins of other nations so that they, too, might become worthy of liberty. Mickiewicz broached an important theme running through modern Polish history, that of *romantic insurrectionism*. Its origins lay in a series of events extending from the partition period to our time. In late 1830 another national uprising was launched against Russian rule. Crushed by Russian forces within a year, severe repression and forced russification of Poles followed. But other uprisings followed: in 1846 in Austrian-occupied Galicia, and in 1848, during Europe's "springtime of nations," in various parts of Poland from Poznan in the west to Lwow in the east. In January 1863 Polish insurgents launched one more desperate attack on Russian garrisons. By fall, they had been routed and the principal leaders hanged.

A more pragmatic approach to rebuilding the Polish nation followed.[6] The beginnings of industrialization in the second half of the nineteenth century led to a shift toward positivism—the belief that use of reason and intelligence promotes progress. An offshoot of positivism in Poland was "organic work"—a spirit of industriousness that would raise the social, economic, and cultural level of the nation and, in this way, make Poland strong again. Late nineteenth-century positivism was a manifestation of Poles seeking to forge a civil society—fusing the individual's private and public spheres while remaining outside the reach of alien state structures. One writer put it this way: "Poland never had an autonomous State in modern times. The idea of civil society thus provided the only ideological alternative to foreign domination."[7] The task of constructing an independent civil society was resumed almost a century later, when Poles found no other way to confront communist rule.

Interwar Poland

When Poland regained independence in November 1918, it had less to do with romantic insurrectionism, positivism, or the building of a civil society; it owed more to the collapse of empires and to the role played by the Western Allies. The tsarist empire in Russia disintegrated in November 1917 when the Bolsheviks seized power, and Austria and Germany were defeated a year later to end World War I. For a time at least, Poland's nemeses were gone. To be sure, in 1920 Polish leader *Jozef Pilsudski*, considered the father of the reborn Polish state, faced off against Russian armies intent on bringing Bolshevism to the country. In the "miracle on the Vistula," the Polish commander turned the imminent capture of Warsaw into a rout of the Bolsheviks, advanced eastward rapidly, and contemplated striking at Moscow itself. In the end he was satisfied with incorporating large parts of Ukraine and Belorussia into Poland.

This expanded state turned out to be ethnically more heterogeneous than Woodrow Wilson had anticipated in his *Fourteen Points*, outlined in January 1918, that provided a framework for peace. In the thirteenth point, he foresaw a "united, independent and autonomous Poland with free unrestricted access to the sea" and situated on "territories inhabited by an indubitably Polish population." Nevertheless, in 1921 about 70 percent of the population was ethnically Polish and the rest minorities. The latter included up to 6 million Ukrainians, 3 million Jews, 1.5 million Belorussians, and more than 1 million Germans. A corridor linking Poland to the Baltic Sea and the international city of Danzig (or Gdansk), where many Germans lived, was approved by the West. This would sow the seeds of disaster when Hitler embarked on German expansion in the 1930s. In addition, deprived of statehood for over a century, the new leaders of independent Poland gave priority to nation building rather than ensuring the rights of minorities. Anti-Semitism never became official government policy, but it was never combated with much energy by the interwar governments.

The constitutional system of the reconstituted Polish state was modeled on the French Third Republic and fell prey to the same failings as that country in the interwar years. The president was given little authority, the legislature was made powerful but suffered from a proliferation of political parties (in 1925, 32 out of 92 registered parties had representatives in the Sejm), and cabinets turned over in rapid succession. The prime minister of the first national government was Ignacy Paderewski, more celebrated as a concert pianist than as a father of the *Second Republic*, the term used to describe interwar Poland. The first president, Gabriel Narutowicz, was assassinated in 1922, two days after being sworn in; this had never happened to a Polish king. Free elections were held in 1919 and 1922 but Pilsudki's *May 1926 coup* put an end to eight years of fledgling democracy.

Pilsudski's regime was a personal dictatorship concealed in parliamentary guise. Rigged elections, harassment, and even internment of opposition officials, and widespread censorship brought his misnamed *sanacja* ("purification") regime into disrepute. After his death in 1935, the "colonels' regime" abandoned all pretense of being a democracy and fascist tendencies surfaced. Fear of communism increased, strikes were violently suppressed, and living conditions of the peasantry worsened. Foreign policymakers were at a loss to develop an alliance structure that would address the dual threats emanating from Nazi Germany and Stalinist Russia.

Poles' historical anxiety about partition was awakened by two insidious international agreements signed just prior to and toward the end of World War II. In August 1939 a secret protocol of the *Ribbentrop-Molotov pact*, officially announced as a nonaggression treaty between Hitler's Germany and Stalin's Soviet Union, set a provisional line of partition of Poland by the two totalitarian states. When the Germans invaded Poland on September 1, 1939, and the Russians marched in from the east on September 17, each claimed its prearranged spoils.

The very existence of the Polish nation was in doubt during German and Russian occupation between 1939 and 1945. One-fifth of Poland's prewar population, more than 6 million people, was killed between 1939 and 1945, the highest casualty rate of any nation in the war. Some 3 million Polish Jews (90 percent) were exterminated, together with 3 million other Poles. Total battle deaths were 660,000, about the total number suffered by British and U.S. forces combined. Resistance to German occupation was relentless during the war but two insurrections stand out. It took one month of savage repression for German forces to liquidate the Jewish ghetto of Warsaw in April and May of 1943. In all, 60,000 Jews were killed. In the 63-day long Warsaw uprising of 1944, nearly 200,000 Poles lost their lives. Russian forces remained on the other side of the river as the capital was destroyed, offering no help. Russian occupation of eastern Poland during the war added terribly to the nation's suffering. From the experience of World War II, Poles learned that insurrections did not lead to national independence; agreements concluded among the great powers, as happened at Yalta, did.

The *Yalta agreement* was the second deleterious international event for Poland in the twentieth century. The February 1945 meeting of Churchill, Roosevelt, and Stalin at the Crimean resort of Yalta informally incorporated Poland into the Soviet political bloc and deprived it of political independence, if countenancing satellite state status. Britain, the United States, and the Soviet Union set up an interim government for Poland, to be composed of Soviet-backed Polish communists and a handful of representatives from the Polish government-in-exile in London. Churchill was persuaded that "free and unfettered elections" called for by the Yalta accord would indeed take place. When, by the summer of 1945, the composition of the provisional government was stacked in favor of the communists, the United States and Britain extended diplomatic recognition to it anyway.

Communism and Its Collapse

The sovietization of Poland was jumpstarted when the Red Army entered the country in 1944 to liberate it from German occupation, but the process accelerated during Stalin's last years. By the time of the dictator's death in March 1953, all political freedoms and political opposition had been erased, and Poland's system—its institutions, processes, ideology, economy—resembled that of the USSR. A communist party—called the *Polish United Workers' Party*

(PUWP)—headed by an all-powerful Politburo and its leader, the first secretary, had a monopoly over decision making, captured in the slogan "the party's directive role in society." Within the PUWP, the more pro-Soviet leaders began to purge those suspected of harboring a Polish nationalist "deviation."

The post-Stalin thaw in the Soviet Union provided an opportunity for Polish leaders who wished to ease the Kremlin's hold on the country and effect some political liberalization. In 1956, seeing the PUWP leadership in disunity, workers in Poznan staged protests demanding bread and freedom. While swiftly quashed, the unrest allowed a victim of the Stalinist purges, Wladyslaw Gomulka, to take power in October of that year. The celebrated *Polish October*, with widespread expectations of political change, turned out to be a deception as Gomulka made few significant changes to the system.

In an uncanny repeat of the Polish October, strikes in shipyards located on the Baltic coast in December 1970—again brutally repressed by the communist authorities—propelled Edward Gierek to power. The new party boss spoke of a technocratic approach to the country's problems and closer relations with Western countries allowed Poland to obtain massive credits with which a mini-economic boom was financed in the mid-1970s. Gierek established a working relationship with the much-loved Primate of the Catholic Church, *Cardinal Stefan Wyszynski* who, until his death in 1981, had personified opposition to Marxist ideology. In turn, Gierek's *noblesse oblige* style provided a cue to political dissidents to organize without having to fear for their lives. To be sure, strikes in June 1976 claimed more victims, but they also led to the establishment of the *Committee for Workers' Self-Defense (KOR)*, bringing together a score of dissidents who were to figure prominently in the Solidarity organization in 1980 and later, in 1989, in the roundtable talks that ushered in democracy.

When the Polish economy began to decline in the late 1970s, opposition to the communist system coalesced. In the summer of 1980 strikes spread throughout the country. Initially putting forward only economic demands (higher wages, lower prices for food products), by the time workers laid down their tools in the shipyards the protests had become politicized. In August 1980 shipyard electrician *Lech Walesa* became spokesman for an independent trade union made up of workers from factories across the country. The union called itself *Solidarnosc (Solidarity)* and presented 21 demands, economic and political, to the communist authorities. After a tense standoff, Walesa's resolve forced the communist rulers to recognize for the first time the independence of an organization not subordinated to the party. Violence was avoided but Gierek was made a scapegoat for the crisis and removed.

From September 1980 to December 1981 Poland experienced a political revolution. Solidarity mushroomed into a social movement having close to 10 million members. Nowhere else in Eastern Europe had a communist party been forced to share power with noncommunists since World War II. Under pressure from the Kremlin, the PUWP drew up contingency plans to crush Solidarity, beginning with the promotion of *General Wojciech Jaruzelski*, then defense minister, to the post of prime minister in February 1981. By October he had also become party first secretary, and by mid-December he was ready to act. *Martial law* was declared on December 13, Solidarity leaders were rounded up and interned, and the trade union was made illegal. For the next seven years Jaruzelski did not allow Solidarity and its leaders back into political life. Although some liberalization occurred after martial law was suspended, the communist regime was unable to solve the country's worsening economic crisis.

It is true that Eastern European economies had lagged well behind their Western counterparts even before communism was introduced into the region. Andrew Janos provided data indicating that around 1800 the ratio of the aggregate national product per capita between Eastern and Western Europe was in the order of 80:100. By 1910, the per capita income gap between six Eastern European and six Western European nations had worsened to about 48:100. The period between 1926 and 1934 produced further deterioration in the ratio of 37:100 (for Poland, 35:100). Janos estimated the 1980 per capita income ratio for Poland to be 34:100—that is, almost unchanged from the 1926–1934 period, but the economic crisis of the 1980s was devastating. Janos concluded that "Communist economies were drifting downward from the relative position their coun-

tries had held in the world economy prior to the Second World War."[8] The economic transformation of Poland after communist collapse reduced gross domestic product (GDP) further, by 18 percent up to 1992. Janos's final estimate was of a historically low (25:100) ratio between Eastern and Western Europe at the end of 1992.

The communist system could boast of some successes between 1945 and 1989. The proportion of the labor force employed in the agricultural sector was halved, from 54 percent in 1950 to 27 percent in 1990.[9] Employment in agriculture now ranked behind both the industrial and service sectors, each of which employed about 36 percent of the active work force. Still, communist Poland's service sector remained about half the size of its counterparts in the West, such as the United States and the Netherlands, where about 70 percent of the labor force was employed in this sector. Longitudinal aggregate data presented in Table 9.1 on such subjects as GNP per capita, urbanization, educational attainment (number of students enrolled in primary, secondary, and higher education), and media diffusion (circulation of newspapers and number of radio and television sets) also were claimed by communist authorities as achievements. The data indicated an increasingly better-educated, more-informed population (the falloff in the number of high school and college graduates in the 1980s was primarily the result of demographic factors and not a sign of educational regression).

Other successes claimed by the communist regime were that real income had nearly tripled between 1955 and 1981—the peak year. Living standards improved between 1946 and 1990: meat consumption—historically a reliable indicator of living standards—quadrupled while consumption of potatoes was halved (there was some regression in the conditions of austerity in the early 1990s; see Figure 9.1). But again, if we focus on the late communist period (see Table 9.2), growing poverty affected all social groups. Real income fell by one-third between 1981 and 1990—a bottom line that, more than any other single factor, explains why the communist leadership wished to extricate itself from crisis and share responsibility for performance with Solidarity.[10]

TABLE 9.1   Indices of Economic and Social Change, 1946–1999

	1946	**1950**	**1960**	**1970**	**1980**	**1990**	**1999**
Economy							
Per capita gross domestic product	—	$271	$564	$955	$4,276	$4,099	$8,671
Urban population (%)	33.9	36.8	48.3	52.3	58.8	61.8	61.8
Workforce outside of agriculture (%)	—	46.4	56.7	65.7	70.3	73.2	72.9
Education							
Students in primary schools (000s)	3322	3360	4963	5389	4260	5276	3958
High school graduates (000s)	26	111	105	365	552	440	554
College graduates (000s)	4	15	21	47	84	52	215
Communications[a]							
Newspaper and magazine sales	—	73	62	90	98	74	113
Registered radios	20	59	176	173	243	286	245
Registered televisions	—	—	14	129	223	260	238
Telephones	5	8	18	33	54	86	261

[a]Communication statistics are number of each medium per 1000 people.
Source: Glowny Urzad Statystyczny, *Rocznik Statystyczny* (Warsaw: GUS, yearbooks from 1950 to 1999), as calculated by the author. Net material product rather than GDP before 1980; GDP based on purchasing power parity after 1990.

FIGURE 9.1   Changing Patterns of Food Consumption over Time

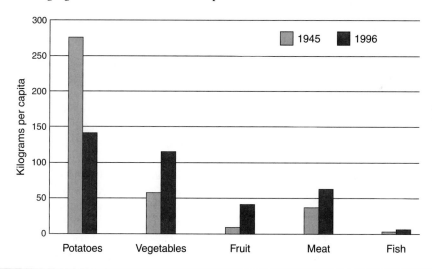

Source: Bozena Bulbicka, Instytut Ekonomiki Rolnictwa. Reported in *Donosy,* No. 1957 (November 28, 1996).

Resistance to communism, of course, was driven by noneconomic factors, too, not least of which was the moral bankruptcy of Marxism.[11] Organized resistance reflected the contrasting political traditions of the country: revolutionary romanticism and political pragmatism; a preference for nonauthoritarian methods; recognition of the need to coexist with externally determined autocratic rulers; a multinational, civic understanding of the state and an ethnic, religious one; an orientation toward Western Europe and self-consciousness about lying on the eastern edge of western civilization. At the turn of the 1990s, the pragmatic, democratic, civic, Western-oriented traditions embedded in Polish

TABLE 9.2   Poverty and Wealth Measured by Per Capita Income According to Socio-Occupational Group, 1982 and 1988

| | INCOME | | | |
| | 1982 | | 1988 | |
Socio-occupational Group	Low	High	Low	High
Professionals	0.6	21.6	10.7	27.7
Intermediate nonmanual	4.3	8.5	15.1	18.7
Skilled workers	9.0	8.1	23.5	10.1
Unskilled workers	9.6	6.3	31.7	2.9
Private farmers	12.8	15.3	40.2	11.7
Others in private sector	1.6	31.1	10.1	30.4

Note: Low income = less than 50 percent of average per capita household income; high income = more than 150 percent of average per capita household income.
Source: Edmund Wnuk-Lipinski, "Nierownosc, deprywacje i przywileje jako podloze konfliktu spolecznego," *Polacy '88: dynamika konfliktu a szanse reform* (Warsaw: IFIS PAN, 1989).

history became dominant. They provided the metaphysical context for regime change. The practicalities were to be worked out between rival elites, as described in the next section. Poland's 1996 Nobel Prize–winning poet, Wislawa Szymborska, captured the eternal moral strain underpinning Polish history in her poem, "Possibilities."

I prefer when I like humans,
Than when I love humanity.
I prefer not to believe,
That reason is responsible for everything.
I prefer moralists, who promise me nothing.
I prefer conquered to conquering countries.
I prefer the hell of chaos than the hell of order.[12]

The Democratic Transition

A paradoxical aspect of the 1989 democratic breakthrough in Poland is that it was not the result of popular revolution. There had been failed societal uprisings against the communist system in 1956, 1970, and 1980; in 1989 little or no mass political mobilization occurred. Strikes had recurred in the summer of 1988 but they never approached the scale of the summer of 1980, when Solidarity was born. While the year 1989 is associated in Eastern Europe with images of large-scale popular protests in Prague, Bucharest, Vilnius and, of course, Berlin, it is important to remember that the democratic

breakthrough in the region was recorded in Poland first, and in circumstances where the public played an inconspicuous role. Regime change in Poland was jumpstarted by way of a pacted transition between rival communist and opposition elites.

The first indication of serious change in the communist party leadership's approach to resolving crisis came with the television address in August 1988 of the Interior Minister (responsible for state security). He called for *roundtable talks* with representatives of various social groups: "I stipulate no preconditions regarding the subject of the talks nor regarding the composition of participants."[13] "Talks about talks" began in August 1988 and soon included an informal meeting between the Minister and Walesa. The first tangible public product of Czeslaw Kiszczak's offer was a debate on state television between Walesa and the head of the communist trade union on November 30, 1988. A nonperson for seven years, Walesa scored a debating victory and showed that Solidarity was poised to return to center stage.

In January 1989, the PUWP Central Committee voted in favor of political and trade union pluralism, thereby giving a green light to full-scale roundtable talks. The decision resulted only after Jaruzelski threatened to resign from his posts—as party leader, President of the Council of State, and Commander-in-Chief—and leave the party leaderless. Hard-line members felt double-crossed by what they considered dealmakers in the party.

Jaruzelski's role in pursuing roundtable talks and the democratic breakthrough that they produced was, therefore, pivotal. One leading Solidarity activist cited a remark made by Jaruzelski: " 'Please remember that only General de Gaulle was capable of getting France out of Algeria.' " The writer drew the obvious conclusion: "This was a portentious statement because it meant that only General Jaruzelski could get the PUWP out of Poland."[14]

The roundtable of February–April 1989 consisted of two sides and three subgroups. Representatives of the communist leadership were called the "coalition-government" side, those of the democratic movement the "opposition-Solidarity" side. The Catholic Episcopate was officially not involved in the roundtable talks and declared its neutrality, though its representatives invariably backed positions advocated by Solidarity. The three subgroups of the talks included one on socioeconomic policy, another on trade union pluralism, and the third on political reform. Six hundred individuals had participated in the roundtable negotiations by the time the talks adjourned two months later. Probably the most important discussions, related to conditions for a *pacted transition*, involved private meetings between top party and Solidarity leaders held at a villa in *Magdalenka*. Walesa took part only in these while Jaruzelski never directly participated. The secretive nature of discussions at Magdalenka caused some observers to claim that a surreptitious deal was worked out between two elite groups. For example, an allegation regularly made in the 1990s was that in exchange for extricating itself from politics, the ruling communist class (the *nomenklatura*) would have free reign in appropriating economic assets previously owned by the state for itself.

At the center of roundtable negotiations was legalization of Solidarity and its future role in politics. Having failed to coopt Solidarity into government, the party tried other ways to get Solidarity into the legislature. The one finally agreed to was that in elections to the Sejm 35 percent of the seats would be contested and the remaining 65 percent set aside for the communists and their allies. The elections for the 35 percent of seats were to be "nonconfrontational" which, in practical terms, signified that the communists should not be the target

of negative campaigning. Finally, this *contract Sejm* was to be a one-time arrangement, with the understanding that the next legislative elections would be fully free. The agreement stated: "The sides will do everything to ensure that the composition of the next parliament will be determined completely by the will of the voters."[15]

Apart from seeking to recruit Solidarity into a communist-dominated coalition, regime negotiators proposed the restoration of the presidency that had been abolished in 1952. The assumption was that the president could serve as a stabilizing force and as a symbol of continuity in the transition period. The party's obvious candidate was Jaruzelski, and even much of Solidarity recognized the advantages of having the long-serving Polish leader preside over a protracted transition period. When Solidarity won all the contested seats for the Sejm in June 1989, it proposed the arrangement: "your President, our Prime Minister." More contentious than who would occupy the post were the powers to be conferred upon the president. The ruling coalition proposed extensive powers that would have created a presidential system. Presidentialism would compensate for whatever influence communists lost in a multiparty, partially freely elected Sejm. The opposition acknowledged that the president should be given responsibility for defense and foreign policy, but otherwise his powers had to be limited. To break the deadlock, the communist side proposed reestablishing an upper house, the Senate, abolished in 1948. The Senate could become the freely elected body where Solidarity could show off its widespread popular support.

The finely struck balance contained in the roundtable agreement, which was signed on April 5, 1989, was welcomed even in Moscow. As Jacques Levesque noted, "Soviet reactions to the results of the Roundtable were positive, even enthusiastic. Izvestiia, for example, stated that the accords had 'dealt a death knell to the myth that socialism cannot be reformed.' "[16] This optimistic interpretation was based on the calculation that a pact containing so many mutual checks and balances could not possibly produce a lopsided defeat for the communists. The agreement was designed to ensure that transition would proceed gradually and would pose no risks to either the old or new elite. Moreover the semifree elections scheduled for June left the two sides with little time to prepare full-fledged electoral campaigns. The PUWP had never competed in competitive elections, while the Solidarity opposition was neither legal nor even a political party just a few months earlier.

At the time of roundtable negotiations, some advisers to the communist leadership predicted that the party might obtain about one-quarter of votes cast. It might even win a majority of the openly contested seats to the Senate since rural areas were overrepresented in the upper chamber and Solidarity's strength had always lay in the cities. In terms of distribution of the popular vote, the June election results proved the party forecast half-right. The government coalition obtained just over one-quarter of all valid votes cast (26.8 percent) and Solidarity 69.9 percent (the remainder went to independents). Solidarity swept all Sejm seats and 99 out of 100 Senate seats. Worse for the party, even of the 65 percent of seats set aside for the government coalition, the majority of party-backed candidates did not win the 50 percent of votes required to avoid going into a second round.

Turnout for the first round of this historic election was a disappointing 63 percent of eligible voters. One explanation was that the public perceived the election as an arrangement of two establishment parties—the communists and Solidarity. The same suspicions aroused by the talks in Magdalenka—"elites talking to elites"[17]—may have spread to sections of the population as they contemplated whether voting really was meaningful.

The election results produced a domino effect on other provisions of the roundtable agreement. Jaruzelski announced he would not be a candidate for the revamped presidency but, after Walesa announced that he did not intend to stand at this time (partly so as to allay Kremlin fears that too much change was happening too quickly), he reversed his decision and, on July 19, was elected by a bare majority of the two houses—270–233 with 34 abstentions. This left one other issue to be resolved in the summer of 1989—the formation of a government. Since the communist bloc held a working majority in the contract Sejm, Jaruzelski nominated his Interior Minister to the post. This, however, would have

left both major offices in the hands of the electorally repudiated communist party. Following the surprise defection of two small pro-communist parties from the government camp, Walesa announced on August 17 that Solidarity was prepared to form a coalition government with them. Exactly a week later *Tadeusz Mazowiecki*—Catholic intellectual, editor of an important opposition newspaper, and long-time Walesa adviser—was appointed prime minister, the first non-Communist one in East Europe since Stalin's time. With all but hardline communists accepting the new political reality, his nomination was endorsed in the Sejm by 378 to 4, with 41 abstentions.

Eleven of 23 ministerial posts in Mazowiecki's government were taken by Solidarity, only four were given to the PUWP, and the rest went to the small parties and one independent. To be sure, communist ministers were to hold on to the pivotal defense and security portfolios. The Sejm vote approving this government now had no opposition: 420–0, with 13 abstentions. Few participants at the roundtable talks of a few months earlier could have foreseen this course of events and this final outcome.

Structure of the Political System

What distinguishes a democracy from an authoritarian system of government? Political freedom is a crucial factor, as shown in Chapter 1 (Figure 1.8), Poland ranked high on this index in 1995–1996. Another distinguishing characteristic of democracy is that political outcomes are determined by rules of the game, designed and accepted by all major political actors. These rules are written into a country's constitution, they can be found in laws passed by an elected assembly or approved in a general referendum, and they can be based on conventions and traditions established over time. Rules identify the jurisdiction and powers of various governmental institutions—president, prime minister, cabinet, parliament. Rules also determine how officeholders in such institutions are to be picked.

The interwar experience was influential in the crafting of a new democratic system. In the flush of triumph after the 1989 democratic breakthrough, it was natural for the architects of the post-communist system to look to Poland's experiment with democracy after 1918 for guidance. Poland's name was changed from "People's Republic" to simply "Republic," as it had been in 1918; if the interwar system had constituted the Polish Second Republic, the post-communist period was called the *Third Republic*. The 45-year People's Republic was thus treated as an anomaly—as not really having been a Polish state—and was facetiously referred to as the "Second-and-a-Half Republic."

The structure of the new government, illustrated in Figure 9.2, did, however, have to incorporate compromises with its communist predecessor. Democratizing the political system meant designing new institutions and formulating legal provisions in place of communist ones. Among the institutional changes were: (1) replacing the constitution of July 22, 1952; (2) introducing an electoral law for a multiparty system; (3) changing the official symbols and terms of the communist system (the country's official name, coat of arms, flag, and anthem); (4) introducing such new political institutions as the presidency, the Senate, and a reformed local government system; (5) providing the legal framework for private ownership; and (6) safeguarding the independence of the judiciary and enshrining principles incorporating civil rights.

The need for a new constitution was most pressing since most other changes would follow from it. There was widespread disagreement about what the new constitution should include. The preamble itself would prove contentious: opinions differed whether it was the Polish nation, or all citizens of Poland, that were the subjects of the document; and whether the special role of Catholicism in the country should be explicitly mentioned (as was the case in the Irish constitution) or not. The constitution finally adopted in May 1997 incorporated references to both the Polish nation and its citizens, and to both Catholicism and other faiths.

Between 1989 and 1992 only piecemeal constitutional change was possible, producing a much-amended version of Stalin's 1952 constitution. The so-called *Little Constitution* of October 1992 represented a more sweeping attempt at change, but even its title, referring to Poland's earlier provisional constitutions, underscored the transitional nature of the document.[18] Suffering from constitutional burnout, when a new constitution was submitted for public approval in a referendum in 1997, only 43 percent of the electorate turned out at the polls, of which just 53 percent voted in favor of its adoption.

The distribution of power between branches of government called for by the 1992 Little Constitution resembled that of the interwar republic to 1926. The power of the executive branch—defined as including both president and prime minister—was circumscribed. A form of "Sejmocracy" emerged in the first years of the new system. Little could get done without legislative approval, and even the famous *Balcerowicz plan* of January 1990 which created a free market would have never passed had not its author, finance minister Leszek

FIGURE 9.2   Structure of Poland's Government

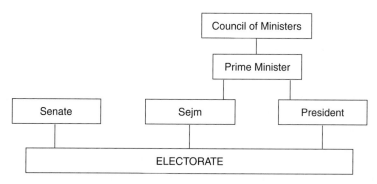

Balcerowicz, surprised the Sejm with a bill he demanded immediate approval of.

Walesa, who became president in December 1990 after direct elections, liked to refer to the interwar experience. The chaos and paralysis that a powerful legislature had produced then had convinced Pilsudski that a strong executive was essential to political efficacy and stability; that was why he undertook the coup. There is no evidence that Walesa was plotting a coup to wrest power from the legislature, but he clearly was in favor of a strong presidency. Accordingly, during his five-year term as president, he undermined the authority of a succession of prime ministers, in the process heightening the political instability he condemned. He did his best to prevent a parliamentary system from being institutionalized, but the Sejm rebuffed his attempts to expand presidential powers and also defeated him on the key issue of the electoral law, which legislators insisted should be more proportional than Walesa wanted.[19]

The 1992 Little Constitution, granting the president modest authority, was not the legal framework that Walesa had in mind. When, in 1995, the Sejm began to consider various drafts of a new constitution, Walesa's was the only version of seven that proposed a presidential system. His failure to get reelected in December 1995 was, in large measure, a popular vote against establishing a strong executive branch. The new president, *Aleksander Kwasniewski*, stressed how he was a "parliamentarian" and was content to preside over rather than dominate Polish politics. Walesa's defeat signified not only a shift in power from Solidarity to ex-communist forces, but also a change from an active to a passive presidency.[20]

The President

The constitutional role of the presidency in the new system is circumscribed. The 1992 Little Constitution termed Poland "a Presidential-parliamentary system of government," but the *constitution of 1997* dropped this phrasing. Article 10.1 of Chapter I declares that "the system of the Polish Republic is based on the separation and balance of legislative authority, executive authority, and judicial authority."[21] The presidency is recognized as part of the ex-ecutive branch, together with the government, or *Council of Ministers* (Article 10.2), but certain powers of ministerial appointment were stripped from the office by the 1997 act.

The president is elected directly by majority vote. If no candidate obtains a majority, a second round of elections is held two weeks later between the top two vote-getters from the first round. The term of office is five years, with a two-term limitation. There is no vice-president, and in the event of the president's incapacity or death the Marshal of the Sejm (similar to Speaker of the House) temporarily holds the office until new elections are held.

The constitution designates the president as head of state and commander-in-chief of the armed forces. A political convention has emerged that the president should not formally belong to a political party. Chapter 5 of the 1997 constitution enumerates the specific powers of the president. Article 126.1 declares that the president is "the supreme representative of the Polish Republic and guarantees the continuity of state authority." Enumerated powers include the right to designate the prime minister (though not cabinet ministers), initiate legislation, veto bills (which the Sejm can override by a three-fifths majority), refer bills to the Constitutional Court for a ruling as to their constitutionality, under certain conditions dissolve parliament and call early elections, call a referendum, oversee defense (indirectly through the defense ministry and through appointing the Chief of the General Staff of the armed forces) and national security matters (together with the National Security Council), declare martial law if the Sejm is unable to meet quickly, and represent the state in foreign relations. The president can issue decrees and administrative acts, the latter requiring the prime minister's countersignature. The officeholder has a constitutionally recognized Presidential Chancellory (Article 142.2b) to help carry out duties. Despite these various functions, the Polish president cannot be said to be at the top of a semipresidential system as exists in contemporary France.

The Legislature

The legislative branch is made up of two chambers: the lower house (Sejm) consists of 460 deputies and the upper house (*Senate*) is made up of 100 members (Chapter IV of the constitution). On some occasions the two meet together as the National Assembly. Direct elections to both houses must be held no more than four years apart. Early elections can be held if (1) a government cannot be formed; (2) a vote of no confidence in an existing government is passed (however, the notion of a "constructive" no-confidence vote, which is not mentioned in the constitution but has been used in Poland and resembles that found in Germany, would only mean that the present government should resign or reconstitute itself—not that elections should follow); or (3) the president decides, under certain conditions, to dissolve the legislature. As in most parliamentary systems, the prime minister, or head of the government, seeks to influence the timing of elections so as to coincide with an upswing in his or her party's fortunes.

The Sejm enacts legislation through three readings of a bill, after which it is sent to the Senate for approval. The Senate can make changes to the bill or even vote it down, but the Sejm can have its way by enacting the bill again with a simple majority vote. The bill becomes law when the president signs it. The power of the Senate is limited, and some have called for its abolition. We should recall how it was little more than a bargaining chip at the roundtable to address political contingencies of the time.

The Sejm, then, is the locus of Polish politics. It is where the competitive party system functions for most of the year (the Sejm recesses briefly in summer). The extended, often-heated debates on legislative bills give the lower house the constant visibility that the presidency does not possess. The most controversial issues of Polish politics after 1989 have been debated *in extenso* in the Sejm: enacting a new constitution, defining the official place of the Catholic church in society, determining women's access to abortion, drafting legislation on the privatization of state-owned industry, clarifying the public role that former communist officials could play in a democratic Poland (through the so-called lustration law that required a "background check" of candidates for high office to determine whether they had worked secretly with the former security apparatus), reorganizing local government (from 47 to 16 regions), ratifying membership in NATO and, of course, the passing of government budgets.

If the Sejm makes or breaks prime ministers and their cabinets, it can also serve as the stage where the performance of a backbench parliamentarian is noticed, leading to her or his promotion to a ministerial post. Deftness as chair of a Sejm committee is also a basis for political advancement. Each of the major parties has a parliamentary caucus that in great measure determines who will hold positions of leadership, and it looks to a deputy's Sejm record (attendance, speeches, bills proposed, voting) for guidance. One of the most overlooked factors smoothing the process of democratic transition was the shift in power in 1989 within the communist party from its own bureaucratic apparatus (Politburo and Central Committee) to its representatives in the Sejm. The PUWP caucus was the forum that allowed future President Kwasniewski and future Prime Minister Jozef Oleksy to rise to prominence. It is no exaggeration to claim, then, that in addition to its all-important legislative function, the Sejm is also kingmaker.

Prime Minister and Cabinet

According to Article 146.1 of the constitution, "The Council of Ministers carries out the domestic and foreign policies of the Polish Republic"; Article 146.2 also gives it residual powers not assigned to other bodies. Another key function of the Council of Ministers (synonymous with government or cabinet) is deciding on the annual budget. Article 157 introduces the doctrine of the collective responsibility of this body to the Sejm, and of the individual responsibility of each minister for the work of his or her department, also to the Sejm. By the 1997 constitution, both the government and the prime minister can issue decrees within their own areas of jurisdiction.

The prime minister is officially nominated by the president but, in practice, is usually the leader of the largest party in parliament. It has happened, however, that the candidate was not drawn from the ranks of the strongest party. Thus, ironically, both the Solidarity camp in 1992 and the ex-communists, calling themselves the Alliance of the Democratic Left (SLD), in 1993 opted for the leader of the pivotal Polish Peasants' Party (PSL), Waldemar

Pawlak, to be prime minister. Although the new political system is only a decade old, it appears that the office with the highest stakes is that of prime minister. President Walesa's power was neutralized when parliament and prime minister were controlled by the opposing camp (the SLD) between 1993 and 1995. Similarly, President Kwasniewski was at a disadvantage when parliament and prime minister were under the control of the opposing Solidarity Electoral Action (AWS) following the 1997 elections.

No one party was able to obtain an absolute majority of parliamentary seats in the 1990s, so prime ministerial turnover and cabinet reshuffles were commonplace until 1997 (see Table 9.3). Between 1989 and the end of 1997, ten persons were nominated to be prime minister and form a government: Kiszczak as the last communist party nominee; Mazowiecki as first noncommunist prime minister; the first economic neoliberal, Jan Krzysztof Bielecki; the first prime minister to be ousted by the president, Olszewski; Pawlak, who could not form a government the first time he was asked; the country's first woman prime minister,

Hanna Suchocka; Pawlak again, this time as nominee of the resurgent ex-communist coalition; Oleksy, the first prime minister who came from the ex-communist party (SLD) but also the first to fall victim to charges (unproved subsequently) that he worked with Soviet and Russian intelligence agents; Wlodzimierz Cimoszewicz, the first to fail in a presidential bid (in 1990) but return as prime minister; and Jerzy Buzek, chosen to form a new government following the victory of Solidarity Electoral Action in the September 1997 Sejm elections. Only Buzek who, ironically, was not even head of the AWS (Marian Krzkalewski was its leader), managed to keep the job of prime minister for more than a year and a half.

It is unclear whether this turnover of governments produced real political instability. The complex six- and seven-party coalition governments of the early 1990s with their "carousels" of incoming and outgoing ministers have given way more recently to two-party coalitions where ministerial shuffles are rarer. The electoral law adopted in 1993 rewarded parties winning the most votes with a disproportionate number of parliamentary seats (as in

TABLE 9.3 Presidents and Prime Ministers of Poland Since 1989

Presidents	Took Office	Supported By	Left Office
Wojciech Jaruzelski	August 1989[a]	postcommunists	Dec. 1990
Lech Walesa	December 1990	Solidarity	Dec. 1995
Aleksander Kwasniewski	December 1995	postcommunists	Dec. 2005[d]
Prime Ministers	**Appointed**	**Supported by**	**Left Office**
Tadeusz Mazowiecki	August 1989	Solidarity	Dec. 1990
Jan Krzysztof Bielecki	December 1990	KLD, PC	Dec. 1991
Jan Olszewski	December 1991	PC, ZChN, PL	June 1992
Waldemar Pawlak	June 1992[b]	PSL	July 1992
Hanna Suchocka	July 1992	UD,KLD,ZChN,PSL	May 1993[c]
Waldemar Pawlak	September 1993	PSL, SLD	March 1995
Jozef Oleksy	March 1995	SLD, PSL	Jan. 1996
Wlodzimierz Cimoszewicz	February 1996	SLD, PSL	Oct. 1997
Jerzy Buzek	November 1997	AWS, UW	Oct. 2001[d]

[a]Jaruzelski was elected indirectly, by the National Assembly.
[b]Pawlak was nominated as prime minister but could not form a government.
[c]Suchocka lost a vote of confidence in May but remained in office until September.
[d]Scheduled date for leaving office.
Note: See list of political parties and their abbreviations following Key Terms at the end of this chapter.

simple-majority electoral systems), and the Sejm could now insist on the accountability of governments to it. It could force changes in prime ministers and their cabinets to ensure responsive government in a way that even the much-praised British system of responsible government does not.

Ultimately it is the grounds on which a government falls and another one is constituted that tells us about the health of a democratic system. Poland clearly has moved away from government crises triggered by dangerous and destabilizing struggles for power between president and prime minister (as in the case of Walesa versus Prime Minister Olszewski during spring 1992) to crises grounded in policy differences between coalition partners (as on taxation between the AWS and UW in 2000). The political rules of the game have taken root and differences are compressed within those parameters.

The Judicial Branch

Chapter 8 of the 1997 constitution delineates the system of courts and tribunals as a separate branch of authority independent of all others. The judicial system is made up of the Supreme Court, general courts, administrative courts (including the Supreme Administrative Court), and military courts. Supreme Court judges are appointed by the president on the advice of the National Judicial Council. They have life terms, cannot be removed, are dependent on no one, and cannot belong to a political party or trade union. An additional body is the *Constitutional Tribunal* which, as in France or Germany, rules on the constitutionality and offers binding interpretations of laws, delimits the jurisdiction of different branches of government, and undertakes other kinds of judicial review. The Constitutional Tribunal consists of 15 judges elected by the Sejm for one term lasting nine years. In its first decade in existence it saw its mission as laying the foundation for a democratic law-based state and, for the most part, succeeded in gaining widespread credibility.

Another important judicial body is the Tribunal of State, to which leaders of national institutions—the president and the prime minister, individual ministers, heads of the National Bank, members of the National Radio and Television Council, the head of the Chief Inspectorate (or NIK, which controls the work of the state administration and other state institutions), and the head of the armed forces—must answer for the constitutionality of their acts. During the 1990s both the Supreme Court and the Constitutional Tribunal issued rulings that upset both the executive branch of government and lawmakers. For example, in 1997 the Constitutional Tribunal concluded that the previous year's law easing restrictions on abortion did not fully comply with Poland's constitutional framework. The ruling could only be overridden by a two-thirds majority in the Sejm, but the conservative AWS government decided not to pursue the matter.

The Polish Third Republic also has a Civil Rights Ombudsperson. The official is chosen by the Sejm for a five-year term and is responsible for determining whether citizens' rights and freedoms are promoted or infringed upon by state bodies. The first three Ombudspersons (one was a woman) were legal scholars who won much praise for their work. About 50,000 letters from citizens per year were received by the office. The majority dealt with such issues as housing, pensions, taxes, and workers' rights. The 1997 constitution also established an Ombudsperson for Children's Rights. In these ways the new system has dramatized the break with the previous one by providing a panoply of institutional mechanisms for protecting civil rights.

The Advantages of Institutional Experimentation

There is something to be said for Poland's trial-and-error approach to institution-building since 1989. Organizational theorist Douglass North tried to understand why some societies develop efficient, adaptive, growth-promoting institutions and others do not. He thought the answer lay in a society's openness to institutional innovation as well as its commitment to institutional elimination: "It is essential to have rules that eliminate not only failed economic organization but failed political organization as well. The effective structure of rules, therefore, not only rewards successes, but also vetoes the survival of maladapted parts of the organizational structure."[22] Given Poland's recent economic success and political stability, it appears that the country has skillfully carried out creative and flexible institutional adaptation since 1989.

Many other political structures have been overhauled since the democratic breakthrough. Some were completely discarded and replaced by new structures. Functional ministries such as defense, foreign affairs, and internal affairs have been remodeled and restaffed. The Supreme Court and the Constitutional Tribunal have been given added responsibilities. A new State Security Agency, *Urzad Ochrony Panstwa (UOP)* has replaced the communist security apparatus. The UOP was at the center of a controversy in 1995 and 1996 when several of its officials backed the internal affairs minister's claim that then Prime Minister Oleksy had worked for Soviet intelligence. The charges were not proved and the security apparatus again came under attack, as in the communist period, for playing dirty politics.

Other institutions inherited from the antecedent regime have, sometimes surprisingly, survived, if in an overhauled form. These include the Central Office of Planning, the Main Statistical Office, the National Bank, the Chief Inspectorate (NIK), the Ombudsperson, and the Office of the Council of Ministers. New institution-building has been aimed at speeding up economic transformation. It has included the Economic Committee of the Council of Ministers, the Social Committee of the Council of Ministers, the Ministry of Property Transformation (or Privatization), the Ministry of Foreign Economic Cooperation, and the Anti-Monopolies Office. Conversely, institutional elimination has occurred when the changing context required it. Thus the privatization ministry was eliminated in 1996 to reflect the fact that the state should not be in the business of promoting market relations. For the most part, then, the institutional design with which Poland entered the twenty-first century provided grounds for optimism about Polish democracy.

Political Culture

In her 1999 book on Poland, Frances Millard concluded that "if the state institutions and political elites were quite successful in adapting themselves to the procedural requirements of liberal democracy, they were less successful in forging links with

society."[23] Are elites only "procedurally" committed to democracy, reticent for whatever reason to be swayed by the electorate's opinions? Or can it be that the same Polish society that toppled communism finds itself estranged at present from its elected representatives, embracing a value system distinct from that of leaders? Studying political culture can provide answers to these questions.

Contained in the meaning of political culture is the notion that political values, attitudes, and behavior are deeply embedded in—not transient to—a particular nation. Political culture is rooted in the more enduring political orientations of a country. Electoral results that we consider next suggest that Poles' political preferences have been rather fickle since the democratic breakthrough. Findings of attitudinal surveys conducted since 1989 reflect a different value system in existence today compared with the recent past. On the basis of short-term trends, can we speak of a culture shift toward democratic values in Poland, or has an irreversible cultural break with the past yet to occur?

Values and Identity

Norms about the community a citizen lives in are crucial in a postmodern world dominated by fragmentation and transience. Have Poles been able to maintain a strong sense of national identity and continue to take pride in their nation and state? Or, with so much global culture shift generally, and the rapid shift from a political identity imposed by Russia to one shaped by the values of the West in Central Europe specifically, are Poles unclear and anxious about the community they live in?

In the World Values Survey conducted between 1991 and 1993 that encompassed 43 societies throughout the world, Poland ranked third in terms of identifying "the country as a whole" as "the geographical group you would say you belong to first of all."[24] In answer to the question "How proud are you to be Polish?" 69 percent answered "very proud"—ranking fourth out of 43 countries (see again Figure 2.2).[25] Paradoxically, though, Poles ranked next-to-last when questioned whether they trusted their own nationality.[26] Both a sense of national identity and of patriotism seemed unproblematic for Poles in the 1990s.[27]

Also noteworthy is the inclusive rather than exclusionary understanding of citizenship that Polish respondents have provided. Whereas sharply drawn ethnic boundaries and their enforcement would reflect a less open attitude to minorities, inclusiveness would suggest tolerance and liberalism. In a fall 1994 survey, respondents were asked who, in their view, was Polish. The leading answers were someone who speaks Polish (cited by 96 percent of respondents), whose citizenship is Polish (92 percent), whose parents were Polish (82 percent), or who lives in Poland (80 percent). Surprisingly, not much more than one-half of the sample (57 percent) said that a Pole was someone who was Catholic.[28] These answers on national identity indicate a considerably more liberal orientation than those warning us of Polish nationalism and xenophobia would lead us to believe. If political culture reflects the types of relationships that prevail between members of different groups, then we can say that tolerance, a core concept of Western liberalism, has grown since the 1990s.

Democratic Norms

A central component of political culture is citizen attitudes toward the system of government. Polish political scientist Andrzej Rychard suggested that a democratic transition posits no specific normative model.[29] A consolidated democracy does, however, as reported in Chapter 2 (Figure 2.3), and Poland now receives high scores in terms of democratic values (support for a multiparty system and a free press). For a democratic culture to take root in Poland then, liberal values need to appear and authoritarian ones to fade.

A more participant culture where citizens are informed about politics and make political demands is a further sign of a modern democratic system. Some scholars have highlighted the deferential, subject culture of many Slavic societies where citizens passively obey government officials and the law that was reinforced by Soviet-style authoritarianism.[30] Thus both the communist and precommunist pasts in Eastern Europe were characterized by lack of elite responsiveness to the public will.[31] Others have stressed the distinctiveness of national cultures—in the case of Poland, the experience of insurrectionism and antiauthoritarianism—

and their general incompatibility with the communist normative system.[32] Others still point to the more recent experience of building a civil society—a private sphere of life for citizens free of governmental interference—that was undertaken in Poland in the mid-1970s, earlier than in other states in the region. Learning how to organize outside of the structures of power facilitated the transition to democratic procedures and laid the groundwork for the spread of liberal values. When Polish society was freed from an imposed model of communist political culture, therefore, it was difficult to predict which types of political values would take hold.

Early on in the transition, Poles expressed comparatively little confidence in the emergent system (Table 9.4). In 1992, at a time of political uncertainty and economic recession, it was surprising to discover that less than half of Poles expressed an interest in politics—considerably lower than among citizens in the United States or most other Western countries. A democracy assumes a variety of institutions aggregating citizen interests; yet, in a 1992 poll only 26 percent said "there are now organizations, associations, or unions in Poland that serve the interest of people like you," and 53 percent of respondents answered negatively. A Polish political scientist gave an ominous interpretation of these results: "Frustration leads to attitudes more compatible with authoritarianism than with democracy, at least in the version practiced in Poland."[33] In December 1999 the public opinion research center CBOS reported that "The majority of Poles do not feel that politicians currently in charge of the country sufficiently represent their interests. The institutions accused of lack of sufficient care for public needs are the central authorities, the government, and also, to a lesser degree, the provincial authorities."[34] If in 1992, 7 percent of respondents believed they "had influence on the country in general," the proportion rose to 19 percent in 1997 but dropped to 16 percent in 1999 (with 82 percent saying they had no such influence). The sense of political efficacy remains rather low in Poland, then.

A decade after the democratic breakthrough, Poles still expressed ambiguous feelings about the new and old systems. On the one hand, they were more critical than others in the region about the

TABLE 9.4 Confidence in the Country's Political System in 1990

Country	GENDER			AGE			EDUCATION			POLITICAL AFFILIATION		
	Total	M	F	16–29	30–49	50+	Primary	Secondary	College	Left	Center	Right
Eastern Europe												
Poland	9	10	9	14	9	7	10	9	7	14	11	7
Bulgaria	29	31	26	25	25	36	41	26	23	34	28	23
Czechoslovakia	44	45	43	40	44	47	42	44	47	30	41	59
Former Soviet Union												
Belarus	23	24	22	17	22	29	35	18	23	21	21	31
Russia	46	42	48	35	42	58	58	44	40	37	49	48
Baltic												
Lithuania	13	12	13	8	10	20	16	12	15	na	na	na
Latvia	18	15	21	17	18	21	25	19	15	na	na	na
Estonia	17	15	19	17	14	22	20	16	16	na	na	na
North America												
Canada	38	37	38	35	37	40	37	34	44	38	39	43
United States	55	58	53	53	49	63	57	51	59	53	57	61

Note: Numbers represent the percentage asserting "a great deal" or "quite a lot" of confidence.
Source: Ronald Inglehart, Miguel Basanez, and Alejandro Moreno, *Human Values and Beliefs: A Cross Cultural Source Book* (Ann Arbor, MI: University of Michigan Press, 1997), Table V285, Political System.

functioning of their democracy (see Figure 9.3). On the other hand, they were more glad than others that communism had been laid to rest: when asked in 1999 to reflect on whether the collapse of communism was a good thing, 80 percent of Poles (a figure similar to that of West Europeans) said yes and only 6 percent said no. Other Central Europeans gave an approval rate nearer to 70 percent.[35]

The early 1990s' World Values Survey highlighted another aspect of Polish exceptionalism: "almost all of the socialist or ex-socialist societies . . . are characterized by (1) survival values, and (2) a strong emphasis on state authority, rather than traditional authority. Poland is a striking exception, distinguished from the other socialist societies by her strong traditional-religious values."[36] It is a "hyper-Catholic society . . . manifesting relatively traditional cultural values across a wide range of areas. Not only in religion, but also in politics, gender roles, sexual norms, and family values, their values are far more traditional than those generally found in industrial societies."[37] Religion was the single most important factor determining the outcome of the 1995 presidential elections and the 1997 leg-

islative ones, with Catholic Poland strongly supporting Catholic-oriented candidates. But this was less true for the 2000 presidential and 2001 parliamentary elections, perhaps indicating that society was breaking with the traditional-religious value system.

Social and Economic Values

To what extent did the prescriptive communist value system take hold in Poland? If we assume that the core values of this system were social justice and egalitarianism, then large sections of Polish society internalized such ideals during the communist period.[38] But communist values also prescribed deference to authority, the centrality of the common good, and, officially at least, a nonmaterialist (more accurately, nonconsumerist) way of life. In these areas, Polish political culture proved resilient to the regime's indoctrination efforts.

At the outset of the 1990s, Poland ranked twenty-eighth out of 43 societies in terms of espousing post materialist values. Let us recall the meaning of this term and of its opposite, materialism. "Materialist priorities are tapped by emphasis on such

FIGURE 9.3 Rating the Functioning of the Political System, June 2000

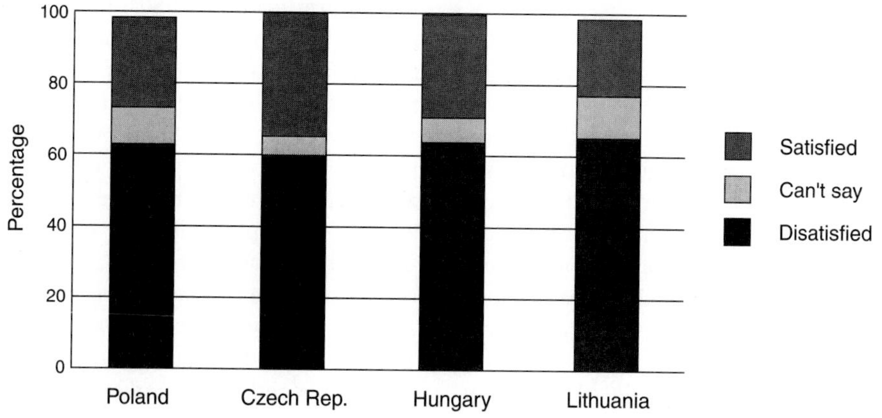

Source: Centrum Badania Opinii Spolecznej (CBOS), "Evaluation of the functioning of democracy in Poland, the Czech Republic, Hungary, and Lithuania" and "The state and the citizens' interests in Poland, the Czech Republic, Hungary and Lithuania," June 2000. (URL is www.cbos.pl).

goals as economic growth, fighting rising prices, maintaining order and fighting crime; while *post materialist values* are reflected when top priority is given to such goals as giving people more say on the job or in government decisions, or protecting freedom of speech or moving toward a less impersonal, more humane society."[39] The economic shock therapy that Polish society experienced in the early 1990s forced citizens to shift to materialist priorities. This contrasted with the more idealistic project of building a civil society initiated by dissidents in the 1970s and 1980s.

Early in the 1990s the uncertain consequences of the transition to a market economy and democracy were reflected in a body of public opinion that revealed considerable anxiety. Egalitarianism, the core value of the socialist normative order, carried over to the democratic system though with weaker societal commitment to it. One study in the first years of the transition discovered that the issues considered important by the public were egalitarian in character: unemployment, inflation, agriculture, poverty, crime, and housing.[40] Another study found that decommunization was ranked last of 11 priorities identified by respondents (only 9 percent mentioned it). When asked what type of society was

preferable—one in which individual interests dominated or where the state provided citizens with guarantees—Polish respondents displayed a slight preference for the latter (36 percent to 30 percent, with 29 percent attracted to a middle road).[41] Statist attitudes holding that it is the duty of the state to safeguard minimum living standards for everybody survived regime change. But in the second half of the decade the egalitarian mindset weakened as large numbers of Poles found employment in the more remunerative, opportunities-filled private sector. A February 2000 CBOS report concluded that Poles would put freedom before equality in social life if they were faced with such a choice (57 percent and 35 percent respectively).[42]

Today's political culture reflects the effects of over a decade of democratic experience. Some statist values remain but among young people in particular they have given way to individualist ones. Political behavior, a central aspect of political culture, is now channeled through the ballot box, though public demonstrations (against abortion and EU agricultural products, for health care reform and farm subsidies) also reflect the more open participatory culture. Some skeptics have detected a lag between the precocious growth of democratic institutions and a slower transformation of societal values in Poland. But by the turn of the new century this seemed an exaggerated concern.

Political Socialization

The transition to democracy entailed both a different form of and a different content to political socialization. The communist regime had assigned high priority to political indoctrination (called "agitprop," short for agitation and propaganda) work. An elaborate network of interlocking organizations was set up to carry out communist political teaching. As in other societies, the education system was invested with a curriculum and an incentive system rewarding those that internalized—or at least paid lip service to—socialist values. Socialization into the Marxist system of values was artfully pursued, extending from inexpensive state-run creches and child care facilities allowing both parents to work and making them aware of the magnanimity of the communist welfare system, to universities and vocational colleges where students were trained to move smoothly into the labor market.

Parallel to the school system were youth organizations that prepared members for leadership roles in society and, for a select number, entrance into the ruling communist party. On taking up employment, individuals were recruited into officially independent trade unions, workers' councils, and employees' committees. In fact, these organizations served as the schools of socialism, as Lenin had referred to unions. When not at school or work, citizens were encouraged to take part in the self-management of publicly owned housing blocks where they lived. A hierarchical structure of residents' committees, from the floor one lived on to the neighborhood that one resided in, existed both to invite citizen participation and to control citizens' behavior. All these agents of socialization were supposed to ensure that social justice, order, and equality of condition were maintained.

The media, too, were in the hands of the party-state. For many decades Poles' sole source of political information was radio, television, and newspapers, all subject to the scrutiny of censors. The propaganda of success permeated news content, reaching its apogee in the 1970s during a mini-economic boom but continuing in a more subtle form into the 1980s. Political socialization now countenanced a consumer culture, proclaiming that communist economic planning was laying the foundation for a society of plenty. The virtue of austerity inculcated in the 1950s and 1960s was replaced by the call for people to enrich themselves and join the ranks of the "red bourgeoisie." Films and books supplemented the other media in portraying the value of *arrivisme*, going from humble origins to affluence by whatever means were necessary. A short-lived attempt was made in the early 1980s, under the martial law regime, to attack speculators and black marketeers. But this quickly gave way to a system of "material incentives" designed to keep society content with communist economic performance.

Communist propagandists were never averse to stressing the desirability of patriotic sentiments among citizens. To be sure, the meaning of patriotism was blurred by the seemingly contradictory ideas of proletarian internationalism and a special relationship with the Soviet Union. From the origins of the Polish People's Republic in the mid-1940s to the martial law regime of the early 1980s, tension between the value of patriotism and that of Russophilism was discernible in propaganda. It even caused divisions within the communist elite and the chiefs of staff. This strain was never fully resolved and contributed to the collapse of communism, a system perceived by much of society as an alien, Russian-imposed ideological aberration.

It was not just the content of political socialization, then, but the preferred methods of carrying it out that changed with the transition to democracy. Agents of socialization located in the public sphere—schools, mass organizations, the workplace, neighborhood groups, and the media—became secondary, and more traditional sources of values—peer group, family, church—returned to the forefront. The privatization of public life occurred in step with the privatization of the economy. Children of working-class families were likely to be taught the value of solidarity, while those of the middle class were taught individualism. More than ever, peasant children were brought up to be good

Catholics. Many children of the economic and social elite were now sent to schools in the West so as to internalize Western values (to be sure, part of the communist elite had done likewise).

As in the West, young people rebelled against the values of their elders, and peer pressure had a multiplier effect on this rebellion. In the early 1990s some of the worst outbreaks of political violence were of young anarchists—many of them indistinguishable from street punks—attacking public buildings, even though these now housed Solidarity leaders. Initial enthusiasm about politics, triggered by regime change, was soon displaced by disinterest among the young in the wrangling over political issues of their parents' generation. The number of drug users grew, and young victims of AIDS were often forced onto the streets to beg since there were no treatment centers for them. The pervasiveness of Western youth culture was seen in styles of dress (from preppy khakis to cargo pants), ways of speaking (creeping anglicisms), and tastes in music. Indigenous popular musical forms emerged (for example discopolo, popular among rural youth), but in the cities it was American-style rap that enjoyed widest appeal.

An ethnic revival occurred in the country as people discovered long-suppressed identities—Jewish, German, Silesian, Ukrainian, Lemko, Kashub. The religious and cultural institutions of minority peoples were revived and began to function as agents of socialization. For minority groups, the family, especially when it transmitted a maternal language and distinct cultural heritage, reemerged as a chief instrument of value dissemination.

Did the Catholic Church continue to successfully inculcate Christian values after the democratic breakthrough? Studies have shown that many Poles regarded the church as too influential in political life in the 1990s (see following discussion). Outward signs of religiosity–attendance at Mass, receiving first communion, making pilgrimages to the monastery at Czestochowa, turning out in enormous numbers for visits by the Pope—have been clearly visible. But Pope John Paul II and *Cardinal Jozef Glemp*, Primate of the Catholic Church since 1981, cautioned against submitting to the materialism and loss of spirituality occurring in society. If Poles remained largely a devout, believing people, they began to differentiate faith in God from faith in the church's role in politics.

The rise of anticlericalism has not, however, indicated a rejection of Catholic dogma or of the social teachings of the church. It was sparked by the church's attempt to replace the state as the dominant form of political socialization. Jan Winiecki provides an analysis of the role of the church: "Catholicism has once again shown itself as a historical factor making pro-capitalist changes harder. Its communalism, pressure to subordinate the interests of the individual to those of the community, its dislike of the creation and use of wealth by the individual . . . were an important binding agent of dislike of the 'new.' "[43]

The church sided with losing conservative parties in a series of elections (the exception was in 1997). Its intervention in the abortion issue triggered a backlash against it. Moreover, large sections of society were disappointed in the leadership of the church offered by Cardinal Glemp, who was viewed as too conservative and nationalistic. Many Poles were upset at the ineptness Glemp showed in dealing with successive controversies involving the Nazi death camp at Auschwitz: first, the plan to build a Carmelite convent close by, then the improvised erection of crosses by ultranationalist Poles on a nearby hillside to highlight the deaths of Catholics there, and finally a developer's proposal to construct a shopping plaza in the vicinity. Many believed that the Catholic Primate should have showed greater resolve and a spirit of ecumenism by siding with Jewish groups' protests.

Catholicism continues to exert great influence on the value system internalized by individual Poles and the Polish family. Under tremendous stress due to the economic hardships caused by the transition, the Catholic family has, more than ever, performed the role of support group for its members. It may now be the most important agent of socialization professing collective, as opposed to individualistic, values. The notion of a common good is an important value in a time of upheaval and, in this respect, the Polish family may play a key role in safeguarding it.

The church in Poland is sometimes accused of playing an insidious role in the socialization of women. Whereas the communist system and Marxist ideology treated the economic liberation of women as a high priority, Catholicism has stressed the unique role that women have to play as mothers and as the nucleus of the family. If the communist system effectively imposed a double burden on women—as indispensable participants in the labor market and as homemakers—the church has taken a more one-sided view, seeing women as givers of life, raising children to be practicing Catholics, and forming the hearth of the family. If the communist regime, officially at least, sought to radicalize women and invited their participation in politics, the church encouraged the traditional women's roles of childrearing, cooking, and going to church.[44] Clearly the church failed in the first task: the fertility rate fell from 2.2 children per woman in 1987 to 1.4 in 1998. Higher living costs and child expenses, together with some women's deliberate choice to work rather than rear children, accounted for falling demographics (seen elsewhere in Central Europe as well).

In the 1990s women were the main victims of the transition to a market economy, accounting for nearly two-thirds of the nonmanual unemployed. Finding new employment was much more difficult for them. In addition, the dismantling of the state-run child care system presented many women with little choice but to return to the home. None of this has been the direct result of the church resocializing females to take up their traditional roles. But ecclesiastical leaders have not concealed their glee that economic imperatives have succeeded in changing women's roles in line with Catholic teachings. Compulsory religious education and an ultraconservative abortion law were the church's doings, moreover; in addition, because women account for a greater proportion of believers, they faced more moral agonizing than men when deciding whether to conform with Catholic teachings. By internalizing Catholic values, Polish women may thus be tempted to reject some of the emancipatory ideas commonplace in Western countries today. Even when Catholic values lead to conservative attitudes among Polish women,

it does not follow that they are any less emancipated than their Western cohorts.

Apart from the church, the mass media are a major form of socialization. The political knowledge of Polish citizens has expanded as previously government-controlled media have been democratized or privatized. However by 1996 few daily newspapers were owned by Polish concerns, and if a bias existed, it resulted either from foreign ownership (French, German, Italian) or the efforts of the church to promote a Catholic worldview. Perhaps because of such biases, the most widely read newspaper, *Gazeta Wyborcza* ("Electoral Gazette"), is Polish-owned and secular-oriented. It was established in 1989 by dissident Adam Michnik to break the state monopoly on the media. An attempt to gain greater control over publishing in democratic Poland was a law passed by the Sejm banning pornography. The bill would have provided for two-year jail sentences to newsagents who sold such "soft porn" as *Playboy*, and five-year sentences for stocking hard porn. Inspired by the church, the bill was vetoed in 2000 by President Kwasniewski.

Control over television has sparked a number of political battles. Between 1993 and 1997 the SLD government stacked the committee overseeing the media (the National Broadcasting Council) and filled the post of director of state television with their own supporters. Yet the AWS-led Buzek government tried to do much the same between 1997 and 2001. The tug-of-war over top positions in the Polish media had little effect on the flow of information to citizens because they had other channels (including many from Western Europe) to tune in to. The state owned or controlled two television channels, a number of national radio stations, and a nationwide newspaper (*Rzeczpospolita*), but these were numerically overwhelmed by privately owned mass media. Even the church, led by Franciscan monks, planned to launch its own family television network in 2001 in response to complaints of too much violence and sex on the main networks.

The expansion of the Internet and of on-line sources of information has further increased the flow of information to Polish citizens. Inevitably, the pressure to make profits has forced all mass media to cater to the tastes of the reading, viewing, listening, and wired public. This has in turn produced a tendency to package fluff, a tried-and-true formula of Western media.

Political Participation

The transition from communism to democracy involved a fundamental change in the nature of political participation. The communist system exhorted citizens to take part in politics through voting in elections, attendance at mass rallies and meetings, and membership in many different types of organizations that supposedly made inputs into the political system. Statistics were compiled showing how many citizens took part in the political process, but voting was purely a ceremonial function, attending rallies was of no more than symbolic importance, and joining various organizations was primarily a form of manipulated participation.

The piecemeal adoption of electoral democracy meant that voting now had real significance. In the space of 12 years Poland had five parliamentary elections (1989, 1991, 1993, 1997, and 2001) and three direct presidential elections (1990, 1995, and 2000). Two referenda, in 1996 and 1997, were also held. As meaningful participatory opportunities expanded under democracy, the rate of participation dropped off (Figure 9.4). However, turnout for presidential contests (which involved a first round and a runoff between the largest vote-getters two weeks later) ranged from a low of 53 percent in the 1990 second round to a high of 68 percent in the 1995 Walesa-Kwasniewski runoff. With the exception of the June 1989 semifree parliamentary election (few people realized at the time that their votes would prove so historic) when 63 percent of voters cast ballots, successive parliamentary elections have generally drawn about one-half of the electorate to the polling stations. The 1996 referendum was invalidated because only 32 percent of those eligible voted, while the referendum in 1997 to approve a new constitution brought out only 43 percent, a turnout described as "tragic" by former President Walesa. As elsewhere in electoral democracies, voting in local elections in Poland seldom exceeds the 10- to 25-percent range.

There are many explanations for nonvoting by citizens. The new political parties have not offered clear and consistent programs, making partisan identification difficult. There is near consensus among parties that market reform, less government, and NATO and EU membership are indispensable, blunting voters' interest. By and large, the new political leaders have lacked charisma. Exhaustion with politics after the struggles with the communist regime in the 1980s led to greater citizen apathy. The opportunity to live one's life exclusively in the private sphere and ignore political involvement altogether is welcome after the constant mobilization and countermobilization of that decade. Many citizens are now enjoying the right to turn down opportunities for political participation, a right that did not exist under communism when not voting often led to harassment by the authorities.

In what ways does the public take part in politics today? The demise of the communist party in 1990 has left no mass-membership political parties in existence in Poland. Political participation is now rarely channeled through a party—a reaction against the demands made by communist leaders at all levels of their rank-and-file members. Parties today are in the first place electoral ones, seeking to win over voters, and once they secure representation in the Sejm, they become parliamentary ones, seeking to influence policymaking. Combined with a falloff in membership in mass organizations (trade unions, farmers' groups, student organizations) and a widespread unwillingness to participate in civil society under post-communist conditions, citizens have become less effective in aggregating their interests. Intermediary organizations between state and society are lacking (some that do exist are discussed later in this chapter). To be sure, direct political action as through demonstrations is more frequent and does not involve the danger it did under communism. But it often meets with a disdainful response on the part of the present political elite, which contrasts with the overreaction to such action by communist authorities. In short, with few and generally ineffective intermediary organizations, Poles experiencing democracy for the first time see the elite's reliance on the ballot box to settle disputes as devious. If citizen activity is limited to the

FIGURE 9.4   Turnout in Elections and Referenda, 1989–1997

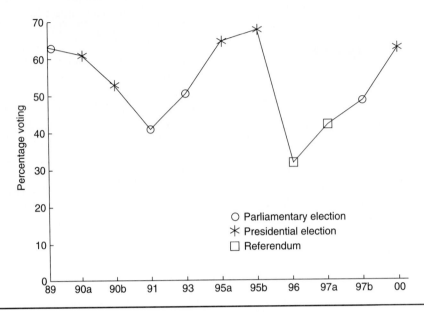

ballot box, it can be taken as a positive sign that the political system is not overloaded with demands. At the same time, the general disaffection with politics discernible in many established democracies seems to be catching up with Poland. Whether this is a longer term trend or one that can undermine the legitimacy of its political leaders is difficult to foresee.

Leadership Recruitment

Who are Poland's new political elites and where are they recruited from? If we focus on those individuals who have held executive power (as either president or prime minister), we arrive at a very heterogeneous group in socio-occupational terms. One president was an electrician by profession (Walesa), the other an *apparatchik* in the former communist bureaucracy specializing in youth and physical education (Kwasniewski). Prime ministers have included a Catholic intellectual and journalist (Mazowiecki), a businessman (Bielecki), a Solidarity lawyer (Olszewski), a farmer (Pawlak), a law professor (Suchocka), a Marxist-trained economist (Oleksy), a farmer with a doctorate in law who had been a Fulbright scholar (Cimoszewicz), and a

chemistry professor (Buzek). The marshal, or speaker, of the Sejm has included a professor of civil law and a specialist in labor law. Most of these very well-educated individuals (Bielecki the businessman had a degree in economics, Pawlak the farmer held an engineering degree, though Kwasniewski the president never completed his M.A.) completed their university studies when Poland was a communist system. Their different training symbolizes the pluralist nature—and the varied political leanings—of today's political elite.

Interesting patterns emerge if one looks at the social background of a wider political elite—those elected to parliament in 1993.[45] In terms of age, nearly half of all deputies were between 40 and 49 years of age—that is, they were members of the baby boom generation whose political memories did not reach back to the Stalinist period. The distribution of deputies older and those younger than this core group was equal. In 1993, 87 percent of the 460–member Sejm were men, down insignificantly from 90 percent in 1991. About 20 percent of elected deputies from left-of-center parties were women. In the communist regime, women usually made up 25 percent or more of parliamentarians.

TABLE **9.5**   Public Opinion on Selected Institutions in Poland, March 2000 (in Percent)

Institution	Positive Evaluation	Negative Evaluation	Hard to Say
Firefighters	85	5	9
State radio	82	6	12
State television	76	13	12
Postal service	73	16	12
President	67	18	15
National sports lottery	57	9	34
Roman Catholic Church	57	26	18
Local government	41	37	22
Ombudsperson	41	19	41
Tax agency	35	33	33
State security agency	34	17	49
Police	29	57	13
Courts	20	57	23
Senate	18	55	28
Solidarity trade union	16	57	27
National Trade Union Accord	15	42	43
Public health service	14	78	8
Parliament	13	65	22
Government	13	68	19
National football team	10	60	30

Source: Pracownia Badan Spolecznych, "Instytucje i urzedy w Polsce, czerwiec 2000."
http://www.pbssopot.com.pl/wyniki_instytucje062000.html. The survey was carried out in March 2000.

Seventy-eight percent of deputies had completed higher education, and nearly 20 percent had a doctorate. The best-represented occupations were farmer (13 percent), manager (12 percent), and university professor (9 percent). Lawyers and private businesspeople were further down the list, each accounting for 3.7 percent of deputies. Only three deputies of 460 reported they did not know any foreign language. Nearly 50 percent said they knew two languages and another 20 percent claimed to know three or more. Of languages identified, Russian was purportedly known by 82 percent of deputies, English by 44 percent, German by 40 percent, and French by 14 percent. Knowledge of Russian was not surprising, but knowledge of English reflected both the practicality and attraction of this language (some Poles are anglophiles, but the vast majority is americanophile). Polish deputies seemed to be exceptionally well educated compared with their Western counterparts, and they seemed to be an extraordinarily cosmopolitan group if we ac-

cept their self-described linguistic abilities at face value. On the other hand, we need to be cautious and not draw too close a linkage between language skills and a cosmopolitan world outlook: the fact that a vast majority of deputies spoke Russian did not produce Russophile policies and, if anything, may have inclined the Sejm to proceed cautiously when dealing with Russia.

Eighty-six percent of deputies had first been elected to the Sejm in 1991 or later, representing a new political elite. Even if we make allowances for the fact that only the leading dissidents who had organized against the communist regime had a chance to be elected to parliament in 1989 (and, of course, not even them before that date), the fact is that people completely new to politics now constituted the majority of the parliamentary elite. Dissidents who had been active in Solidarity and KOR (the Committee for Workers' Self-Defense—a misnomer since nearly all its members were intellectuals) had as much difficulty getting elected as did older communist party members. During the democratic transition, many leading members of the movements that opposed the communist elite found that they had outlived their usefulness in politics. The new skills required of politicians comprised consensus building rather than oppositional tactics.

The disappearance of the old elite, along with the political inexperience of the many new party leaders and parliamentary deputies who appeared on the political scene in the first half of the 1990s, allowed Walesa for a time to bully friends and foes alike. After 1995, however, the pluralistic elite emerging in parliament had honed their skills, were prepared to challenge the few remaining established leaders, and became a force to be reckoned with. A consensus-building president, like Kwasniewski, reflected the style of the new elite.

It is unlikely that the ruling elite will consist of such a well-educated, professional group of people in the future. As formal educational qualifications slip into second place in a market economy behind entrepreneurial and managerial skills, so elite recruitment is likely to tap the pool of businesspeople more than that of academics and professionals. In any case, higher education is not the elitist preserve it used to be and the number of colleges, and of college graduates, has increased greatly in recent years. Over the next decade, the new professional schools will turn out graduates who are attracted to political careers. Poland will face the same questions that have been debated for years in the United States and other Western democracies. Do economic and political elites overlap, or has a pluralism of elites emerged?

Interest Groups

There were no true interest groups under the communist system, even though Western scholars occasionally stretched the meaning of the term to include organizations under the control of the state, such as trade unions, youth associations, women's leagues, and even government ministries.[46] These organizations had identifiable institutional interests of their own but they could at any time be ignored or even eliminated by the communist leadership. Their participation in the policy process was primarily symbolic and represented a form of manipulated participation. That was why reluctant state recognition of the independent trade union Solidarity in fall 1980 was such a breakthrough. An interest group had come to exist in a communist state.

The democratic breakthrough in 1989 was accompanied by a surge of associational activity in Eastern Europe, conceptualized by Sharon Wolchik as a "repluralization of politics."[47] One study found over 2,000 voluntary associations in existence in Poland in the early 1990s,[48] another estimated that there were up to 500 environmentalist groups alone,[49] and a third concluded that in 1995 "there were about 40 groups which could be sensibly called women's groups."[50] In the heady years following the democratic breakthrough, more powerful institutions like the Catholic Church and labor and business organizations believed that they could play a direct role in politics so they put forward candidates for parliament and concluded alliances with political parties.

Most of the new, spontaneously created groups were short of the resources (membership numbers, finances) and skills (quality of leadership, negotiation skills) needed to engage in effective policy concertation. As with the initial proliferation of political parties (370 were registered in 1997 when the law on political parties was changed), aggregate numbers were unreliable indicators of the place held in the political system by voluntary associations. Before we examine some of the most important socioeconomic organizations in Poland today, let us consider the part played by two long-powerful institutions in the country, the Catholic Church and the military.

The Catholic Church

The role assumed by the Catholic Church in Polish politics has nearly always been historic. No one trivializes its importance in engaging the communist regime in a battle for the minds of citizens from the 1940s to the 1980s—a battle that the church won handily. More than any other institution, the church adopted a triumphalist attitude when the communist regime collapsed. Indeed, the church violated the terms of the roundtable agreement of April 1989 which specified that the partially free parliamentary elections were to be noncompetitive: the church used every means at its disposal—the pulpit, its printing facilities, its meeting rooms, its many voluntary workers, above all its good name—to persuade citizens to vote against all communist candidates. Communist rulers, who had so often tricked others to make deals that the rulers had no intention of keeping (such as promising to register Solidarity as a legal trade union in the fall of 1980 and then backing away from the idea), were themselves taken in by the church's pledge to act as an impartial mediator of the 1989 election.

However, the role of the church in the politics of the Third Republic has become increasingly questioned. The highly unpopular, restrictive abortion bill that had to be vetoed by the president, the requirement that public schools provide religious education (though pupils do not have to take it), the principle that Christian values should permeate public broadcasting, and the tough law on pornography that again required a presidential veto alienated many of the faithful, not to mention non-Catholics. Occasional anti-Semitic sentiments discernable in members of the Episcopate, lay Catholic groups, and individual priests have further discredited the church as a whole. The general arrogance of the Episcopate and of some parish priests has rankled many citizens. Radio Maryja, a nationalist Catholic radio network, has also polarized much of society.

A survey carried out in 1994 found that 71 percent of respondents agreed that the church had too much influence in public life. From being the most trusted of all institutions in Poland throughout most of the 1970s and 1980s, the church had by the end of 1994 fallen in rank, to a position behind the army and the police in terms of trustworthiness: from a 90 percent confidence level in the church before communism's fall, to only about 50 percent by 1994. Kwasniewski explained his hostility to the church: "We are not going to have a theocratic state in the middle of Europe at the end of the twentieth century."[51] Whenever in the mid-1990s parliament debated drafts of a new constitution, the church made the case for a preamble identifying Christian values as the basic principles underlying Polish society, official recognition of its special role in the

country, an outright rejection of the notion of a secular state, and a constitutional ban on abortion. The church's reduced political influence has been evident in its inability to have most of these proposals enshrined.

Another test of the church's future political role—equal in importance to the writing of the constitution—is the *Concordat* signed in July 1993 between President Walesa and Pope John Paul II but not approved by the Sejm until early 1998. The 1993 draft consisted of 29 articles beginning with the assertion that "The Catholic religion is practiced by the majority of the Polish population." A similar clause in the constitution of the Second Republic was a source of controversy since, at the time, Poland had several large ethnic and religious minorities. Catholic education in schools was formalized by this document, and church marriages were to have the same legal status as civil ones (though the church was prudent enough not to press for changes to existing divorce laws).

Probably the most contentious item in the agreement was Article 22, a cryptic clause dealing with restitution of church property. A special church-state commission was to be set up to make changes in legislation. Moreover, "The new regulation will take into account the needs of the Church given its mission and the practice hitherto of church life in Poland." Added to this was Article 27: "Matters requiring new or additional treatment will be regulated by new agreements or understandings." In this way Sejm approval of the Concordat could provide the church with a *carte blanche* to make additional changes. Opponents of the Concordat, largely on the left of the political spectrum, alleged that many of its provisions were in violation of the European Union treaty. One Polish writer put it this way: "Anyone who naively believes today that church-state conflict was invented by the communists and, with their demise, this chapter is closed for all time is making a major and possibly costly mistake."[52]

Even after a leftist coalition made up of the SLD and PSL took power in 1993, it was careful not to antagonize Pope John Paul and Cardinal Glemp on the question of Concordat ratification. The backbone of the PSL constituency was the peasantry, largely Catholic and conservative on social issues. SLD prime ministers and an SLD president tread carefully, therefore, in seeking revisions to the Concordat. The Pope's visit to Poland in June 1997 created new momentum to approve the Concordat. Critics of the SLD leaders who were so solicitous toward John Paul II were quick to point out that the party's precursor—the communist PUWP—had also often struck deals with the church. One of the right-of-center Buzek government's first decisions on taking power in late 1997 was to submit the Concordat to the Sejm for ratification. Left-of-center President Kwasniewski quickly signed it into law in 1998.

The church has been aware that as part of its plan to integrate with Western Europe, Poland will have to become a more secular country. The general wealth of the church in Poland—indeed its sheer opulence as symbolized by the spate of grand church buildings constructed in poor parishes in the 1990s—is at odds with the hardships suffered by many of the faithful during economic shock therapy and after. The Polish Pope, who had helped mastermind the end of communism in his country,[53] was personally as revered as ever but had lost some influence in a Poland modeling itself on Western Europe, where the separation of church and state was a centuries-old way of life.

The Military

A central issue in the politics of most states but especially those new to democracy is civil-military relations. A democracy requires civilian oversight over the military since civilian leaders are elected, military ones are not. In the case of Poland, fulfilling eligibility requirements for NATO entailed meeting its standards for democratic civilian control over the military establishment.

Complicating the problem in Poland of civil-military relations is the influence and visibility that the army had in politics in the last years of communist rule. With the imposition of martial law in December 1981 to crush the Solidarity movement, Polish generals violated a long-standing rule of communist systems—that the military would always remain subordinated to civilian, communist party leaders. The military-party distinction became blurred when in a short period of time General

Jaruzelski went from being defense minister to prime minister (in February 1981) to communist party leader (in October 1981) to head of the Military Council for National Salvation (in December 1981)—the body that ruled Poland for a year when martial law was imposed. Jaruzelski was also elected by the Sejm as the first president of democratic Poland (July 1989) and held the office until direct elections were held in December 1990. It was easy to marginalize Jaruzelski in the new democratic system; only in October 1996 did a Sejm committee finally determine that the general would not face charges stemming from his imposition of martial law 15 years earlier. We should remember, however, that it was another military figure, Pilsudski, who served as a role model for President Walesa. It has therefore been difficult to eradicate the idea, popular in certain left-wing and conservative circles alike, that the military has a legitimate right to intervene in politics.

The temptation that presents itself to leaders of a new regime is to mimic the behavior of their predecessors while simply favoring a different political elite. This indeed seemed to be what occurred in the so-called "Parys affair" of April 1992 that highlighted the controversial nature of *civilian control* of the military. An upstart politician, Jan Parys, was named as defense minister by the right-of-center, virulently anti-communist government of Olszewski. Not surprisingly, Parys announced shortly after being appointed that he would purge the military of what remained of former Soviet and communist party agents. Since the interim constitution gave the president powers in defense and security matters, however, the president's chancellery also laid claim to carrying out civilian oversight. President Walesa selected General Tadeusz Wilecki—someone congenial to the military—as his candidate to become the new Chief of the General Staff. Prime Minister Olszewski and Defense Minister Parys objected on the grounds that the government had not been given a say. There were even accusations from the Olszewski camp that Walesa was planning a coup d'etat with the help of military leaders. The military felt that it was caught up in a power struggle between the executive and legislative branches of government and that its professional autonomy was suffering. The Olszewski-Walesa rivalry was resolved in dramatic fashion shortly afterward: the president galvanized enough deputies in the Sejm to demand the Olszewski government's resignation, which was submitted in June 1992.

Parys was not the only defense minister to fall victim to political intrigues. With the election of the ex-communists to power in September 1993, Navy Admiral Piotr Kolodziejczyk, who had been pensioned off by Parys in 1992, became defense minister. His personnel policy seemed to favor ex-communists. He also removed controls on the military when these were exercised by conservative forces and in this way, at least, contributed to greater military autonomy. Since the General Staff had already obtained considerable autonomy from the defense ministry, Kolodziejczyk's maneuvers became suspect and were viewed as setting up a new "commissarocracy"—rule by communist party commissars. Even though a Sejm committee exonerated Kolodziejczyk of such allegations, Walesa nevertheless fired the defense minister.

Walesa's move increased the autonomy of the General Staff from the defense ministry but shortly thereafter, by removing Wilecki as Chief of the General Staff in 1997, President Kwasniewski reinforced civilian control, a prerequisite for NATO membership. As defense minister Janusz Onyszkiewicz, a mathematician and former Solidarity press spokesman, kept a tight grip on the ministry from 1997 to 2000 while becoming widely unpopular among his subordinates. The bottom line was, however, that NATO membership, as well as civilian control, was secured in this period.

A note of caution is in order. Having presided over a 50-percent cut in the size of the armed forces, continuous budgetary cutbacks (until 1995), and clumsy civilian meddling in personnel matters, the General Staff has reason to question the wisdom of civilian control of defense. According to one author, "the history of political involvement by the Polish military, the communist-era concept of professionalism, the trauma of the post-1989 restructuring, and the sense of alienation from the civilian authority have fostered a siege mentality among the Polish senior officer corps."[54] It is difficult to criticize the General Staff for its belief that in recent years civilian control has produced greater political wrangling than respect for the military's professional interests.

Trade Unions

We have considered the part played by two "quintessentially Polish" institutions, the church and the military, in politics. Since it was a trade union organization, Solidarity, that was directly responsible for bringing down the communist regime, it seems appropriate to ask whether labor unions still exert great influence in the new democracy.

From its peak of nearly 10 million in 1981, membership in Solidarity declined throughout the 1980s when it was banned by the communist authorities. Surprisingly, however, membership continued to fall off after the democratic breakthrough and by 1998 it numbered only about 1.3 million. An economic recession, a widening private sector, growing unemployment, major cuts in the size of state industry, and a global decline in unionized labor reduced the proportion of union membership in Poland to one-third of the labor force by 1998. Successive Polish governments including SLD ones have pursued a subtle policy of reducing union influence in politics, a populist strategy that, like Britain under Thatcher and the United States under Reagan, elicits support for incumbents.

In democratic Poland, ironically, the much-disparaged former pro-communist trade union movement—the *National Trade Union Accord (OPZZ)*—exchanged places with Solidarity to become the largest labor organization with up to 4.7 million members (25 percent of the economically active workforce) in 1994. The political role of the OPZZ has even exceeded its membership numbers. It enjoyed a privileged representational status as a core group making up the parliamentary caucus of the SLD—the largest bloc in the Sejm following the 1993 and the 2001 elections. Accounting for 61 of the SLD's 171 seats in 1993, the OPZZ was at once, then, a coalition partner of the government and its potential adversary, in the Tripartite Commission negotiating labor policy (see discussion in this chapter) and elsewhere. A system of corporatism, discussed in greater detail later in this chapter, consists of the state determining representation for interest groups. In Poland corporatism was stood on its head: it was the interest structure (the OPZZ) that helped determine state representation (the ruling SLD coalition).

Further explaining OPZZ resurgence was leadership recruitment and a non–blue-collar constituency. Gone were the *apparatchiks* who ran the union during communist times. A fiesty new chairwoman and parliamentary deputy, Ewa Spychalska, attracted many supporters in the 1990s. Furthermore, contrary to popular perception, the largest unions in the OPZZ were not those representing blue-collar workers but white-collar schoolteachers (565,000 members) and farm workers (411,000)—neither group usually associated with labor militancy.[55]

A Polish sociologist concluded that "Systemic transformation disintegrates older interest structures and forms new ones."[56] With capitalist transformation, workers' interests have been "decomposed" into specific occupations—textile worker, coalminer, lathe operator—and, further, into particular firms.[57] Interest structures of the future are likely to reflect such differentiated socio-occupational categories of workers, so the future of centralized trade unions is not promising. Organized labor in Poland, once of legendary stature, has become fragmented even if still institutionalized in the country's political parties. Trade union membership is down, but organized labor is the heart of Poland's two-party system, with Solidarity forming the core of the AWS and the OPZZ a major player in the SLD.

Business Groups

Many organizations have been established to represent the interests of Poland's new entrepreneurial class. Proprietors and executives of private businesses can choose membership in such organizations as the Business Center Club, the Business Roundtable, the Club of Polish Capital, the Confederation of Polish Employers, the Polish Business Council, and the Polish Convention of Entrepreneurs. Small business has locally organized Enterprise Clubs. In October 1994, the first local business lobby, the Polish Federation of Independent Entrepreneurs, was founded.[58]

The question arises whether Polish employers are better off in a unified and centralized organization that transmits its interests to the government, as in France or Germany, or an individualistic, highly decentralized business lobby as in Britain or the United States. Efforts have been made to revitalize a national Chamber of Commerce that all firms would be mandated to join. Still, whether business interests become more confederated or are decentralized may not ultimately determine how much influence they have on public policy. As in any democracy, a more important issue is whether a pro-business or pro-labor party is in power.

Ethnic Groups

Limited ethnic politics exist in Poland. About one-half of the forty or so minority associations registered in the country are German-language groups. They are mostly based in provinces bordering on the reunited Federal Republic, where the vast majority of people of German ancestry lives. As a measure intended to institutionalize minority representation in national politics, beginning with the 1993 parliamentary elections a new electoral law excepted parties of national minorities from having to reach the newly imposed 5 percent threshold for obtaining Sejm representation. As a result, the German coalition won four seats in the Sejm (it won nine in 1991), to go with one in the Senate. While western Poland has generally voted for leftist candidates in elections held in the 1990s, districts with a large German population have supported more conservative candidates like Walesa.

The most influential German organization is the Social-Cultural Association of the German Minority in Silesia. German Chancellor Helmut Kohl's visit to Poland in July 1995 confirmed the Polish government's acceptance of Germany's role as an unofficial patron of Silesians.[59] Largely as a result of extending more autonomy to the German minority, the Polish population from the eastern provinces transplanted to the recovered territories after the war, though it remains a majority in this region, has felt threatened by these developments.

Ukrainian, Lithuanian, and Belarusan minority associations are centered in their respective areas of ethnic settlement like the Bieszczady, Suwalszczyzna, and Bialostockie regions. In the 1993 elections, Belarusans lost their only legislative seat, while Ukrainians and Lithuanians have not elected deputies to parliament.

Jewish cultural associations were formed in the 1990s, among them a veterans' organization. While a number of Jews have been elected to the Sejm, they have been members of national parties, like the UW, rather than a specifically Jewish party. Earlier we referred to the debate about whether Polish national identity is so defined as to include its Jewish population, or whether, as in Russia and elsewhere in the region, assimilationist forces have been so strong as to blur Jewish identity. Since the democratic breakthrough, mutual efforts have been undertaken by leaders of both groups to overcome negative stereotypes of each other. Still, stereotypes die hard: after the Catholic Church, it was Jews that Poles rated as having too much influence in contemporary politics.

Political Parties

Democracy is often equated with political pluralism, a multiparty system, and free elections. In Poland the development of a *competitive party system*, where two or more parties look for electoral support to gain political influence, took many twists and turns in the 1990s. Parties splintered frequently; just as often, they entered into electoral pacts with other parties in order to capture votes. They adopted different names when contesting elections. Their elected members formed clubs once they entered parliament with even different names. Let us take the example of the Christian National Union (ZChN), a conservative, clerical party. It ran in the 1991 parliamentary elections under the label Catholic Electoral Action (the Polish acronym was WAK). For the 1993 parliamentary elections, a similar Catholic alliance was called "Fatherland." For the 1995 presidential elections, the ZChN formed part of the Alliance for Poland. For the 1997 legislative elections the party joined with Solidarity to call itself *Solidarity Electoral Action "S" (AWS)*. In similar fashion, numerous peasant parties have formed parliamentary blocs and electoral pacts. Even the SLD is a coalition of various political groups tracing their origins to former communist organizations. Until recently, the fluidity of individual parties and party alliances made keeping track of them very difficult.

The changed electoral law for the 1993 legislative elections reduced political fragmentation and helped consolidate a more stable party system. It deprived smaller parties (those obtaining under 5 percent of the popular vote) of any representation in the Sejm. It also rewarded the major vote-getting parties by allocating to them a disproportionate number of seats in parliament. Ironically, it was the ex-communists who were quickest to adapt to the new law. Presenting a unified leftist coalition, they capitalized on being the strongest electoral party to become the dominant parliamentary party. Table 9.6 lists Poland's major parties in 2001.

The Changing Party System

All major parties in Poland share some common characteristics. One is that "perceptions are dominated by a super-sensitivity to Western reactions."[60] In political and economic terms this means that the major parties have the same starting point: the desire for Poland to join the EU and become part of Europe. No major party criticizes the country's membership in NATO. Furthermore, and of crucial importance to democracy, nearly all political groups have accepted the rules of the game and abide by outcomes generated by these rules. There is no threat, even by the former communists, to employ extraparliamentary means in order to obtain power.

The most important lesson learned by political parties in Poland after 1989 is the need to form a broad-based coalition in order to obtain a bloc of seats and gain influence, and even power, in parliament. The AWS, for example, is really a *catch-all party*, that is, an umbrella organization for numerous political groups and advancing a broad political program. It was formed in June 1996 after an agreement was concluded by about twenty small conservative groups (which had no representation in parliament) and the Solidarity trade union. This was an odd combination to be sure by Western standards, where conservative parties and the labor movement are generally at odds with each other. Political expediency—to drive the ex-communists from power in the 1997 parliamentary elections—united these forces. The AWS leader came from its dominant component, the Solidarity union. *Marian Krzaklewski* chaired the famous Solidarity Congress of 1981 that had confirmed Walesa as leader and established a free trade union within a communist

TABLE 9.6   Main Political Parties, Programs, and Leaders in Poland, 2001

Party (Acronym)	**Alliance of the Democratic Left** (*Sojusz Lewicy Demokratycznej* or SLD); political party created in 1999; formerly an electoral alliance led by the Social Democracy of the Republic of Poland (*Socjaldemokracja Rzeczypospolitej Polskiej* or SdRP), the successor to the communist party		**Solidarity Electoral Action** (*Akcja Wyborcza Solidarnosc* or AWS); coalition of several center-right parties, unions, and other organizations including the Solidarity trade union (*NSZZ Solidarnosc*), Social Movement AWS (RS AWS), Conservative-Peasant Party (SK-L), Christian National Union (ZChN), and the Agreement of Polish ChristianDemocrats (PPChD)
Policy Orientation	Social market economy, secular		Syndicalist, socially conservative, Christian, democratic
Leader	Leszek Miller		Marian Krzaklewski
Party (Acronym)	**Freedom Union** (*Unia Wolnosci* or UW); 1994 merger of Democratic Union (*Unia Demokratyczna* or UD) and (*Kongres Liberalno-Demokratyczny* or KLD)	**Union of Labor** (*Unia Pracy* or UP) Leftist wing of former Solidarity trade union	**Polish Peasant Party** (*Polskie Stronnictwo Ludowe* or PSL) Former satellite of the communist party
Policy Orientation	Reformist, ethical, secular, divided on economic policy	Social-democratic, pro-labor	Agrarian, protectionism, state interventionism
Leader	Bronislaw Geremek	Marek Pol	Jaroslaw Kalinowski

system. Krzaklewski led the AWS to victory in the 1997 elections but he himself declined to be prime minister, appointing Buzek instead. The alliance was so broad that over the next four years it was plagued by internal disputes which, in turn, engendered disaffection among voters.

Before the formation of the AWS, the most important catch-all party was the *Freedom Union (UW)*. Founded in December 1990 as the Democratic Union (UD), it posted the strongest electoral showing of any party in 1991, owing in large measure to the ironic claim of its leaders that it had no ideology or program. The UD consisted of a left-of-center, welfare-state orientation represented by former KOR dissident Jacek Kuron; a centrist group comprised of Mazowiecki supporters; and for a time a right-wing faction. The first post-communist government of Mazowiecki was a UD protege, as was the Suchocka government, in power from July 1992 to September 1993.

Electoral defeat in September 1993 convinced the UD to add the Liberal Democratic Congress (KLD), an economically neoliberal group made up largely of businesspeople, to its ranks in 1994. The renamed Freedom Union chose Kuron as its presidential candidate in 1995. His poor result led the UW to select Balcerowicz as its party chair. The UW is hard pressed still to repair the schism between those in its ranks who support a German-type social market approach and those clinging to Thatcherism. Defection of several leading figures from the left-wing Union of Labor (UP) to the UW in 1998 further broadened its ideological spectrum. Still, the party has enough of a history and a core following, especially among the better-educated, secular, urban public, to assure it a central place in Polish politics. This was seen after the 1997 election when it joined with the AWS to form a government.

After 1993, the largest party in terms of both membership and vote-getting was the *Alliance of the*

Democratic Left (SLD), the social-democratic successor of the former communist party. Because its origins lay in the communist regime, it was frozen out of all government coalitions formed up to 1993. The SLD had to gain power through electoral appeal, not by playing the coalition game in parliament, and its electoral successes began with a victory in the 1993 elections. While in appearance the Alliance resembled a catch-all organization, with various unions and parties in it, in practice it was dominated by the Social Democratic Party; other groups wishing to bandwagon with it were welcome. In 1999 the post-communist leadership dissolved the SdRP and turned the SLD into a political party. Today a plurality of Poles (43 percent) see the SLD as resembling a Western European social democratic type with only one-third clinging to the view that it is a successor party of the communists.[61]

A coalition partner of the SLD between 1993 and 1997 was the Polish Peasant Party (PSL), which established itself as the strongest political organization in rural Poland. Also a descendant of a communist-era party, the PSL defends private farmers (the communists had been unable to collectivize land) whose economic interests are threatened by the transition to a market economy (in particular, the disappearance of the state as the largest purchaser of agricultural production). Given that the rural population in Poland accounts for over one-third of the electorate, the PSL has the potential to play a strategic role in politics, although its showing in 1997 was a disaster.

If we have observed a consolidation of the party system, it is less certain that the interests of voters have been consolidated within this party system. Table 9.7 depicts the bases of left/right division within Polish politics. There is a perceptible political geography of voting[62] as well as that based on class. To be sure, workers have been able to choose between an ex-Solidarity (UP) and an ex-communist party (SLD), as can farmers (PSL) and the urban intelligentsia (UW). By contrast, the expanding business class has little choice: either to support the UW (with its unappealing left-of-center faction) or the AWS (heavily influenced by the church and statist in orientation). In 2001, therefore, a pro-business political organization, Citizens' Platform (*Platforma Obywatelska*) was set up to fill this void.

TABLE 9.7 Principal Political Orientations of the Polish Electorate

Left of Center	Right of Center
Western	Nationalist
Secular	Clerical
Urban	Rural
Business	Agrarian
Civil rights	Social order
Social liberalism	Christian values
Political liberalism	Authoritarian
Meta-communist	Anti-communist
Interdependence	National interest

It is interesting to consider, then, which parties are absent in Poland today. Despite numerous efforts to create one, a Christian democratic party has never enjoyed electoral success. So many Poles are Catholic that such a party would not incorporate salient political differences. A social democratic party not originating in communism, of the kind found in Britain or Germany, has also never got untracked. The Labor Union (UP) faltered after a promising start, failing to mark out a left-wing constituency distinct from the SLD. Likewise a conservative party embracing social and economic conservatism was stillborn. Poles supporting family values or low taxes are forced to choose one of the catch-all parties, and then they must expect it to run against such a voter's preference on other issues. In sum, no one a decade ago could have predicted today's party system in Poland, and it would be risky to claim that in a decade from now the SLD and AWS will remain the core parties in parliament.

Election Results

Some political scientists consider a democratic system to be consolidated when a minimum of two free elections are held. In Poland, four completely free parliamentary elections have taken place. There have also been three free and direct presidential elections. By this criterion, Poland's democratic system seems firmly rooted.

Other political scientists believe that a successful turnover of government, from incumbents to opposition, has to occur before we can speak of a consolidated democracy. This has also happened in Poland with both parliament and president. In the September 1993 legislative elections the Solidarity coalition government was defeated at the polls and replaced by a coalition government led by former communists. In 1995 the elections to the presidency produced an identical outcome: Walesa, a founder of the Solidarity trade union, suffered a narrow defeat at the hands of former communist party member Kwasniewski. Although Kwasniewski won a second term in October 2000, the government switched hands again in 1997 going to Solidarity. In 2001 the SLD was poised to recapture power.

Poland's electoral outcomes have required that several parties negotiate in order to form a government majority. In a few of the larger countries of Western Europe, electoral verdicts in themselves prove decisive: In 1997 the Labour Party swept to power in Britain and the Socialist Party in France. As was discussed in Chapter 3 (and shown in Figure 3.5), many elections in Western Europe have not produced legislative majorities for any single party, making post-election bargaining crucial. So Poland is not exceptional, and a political party generally

must do well both in elections and in coalition building to gain a share of power. Let us briefly review the Third Republic's electoral history.

PRESIDENTIAL ELECTIONS   To win the first direct presidential election, held in 1990, a strong organizational basis was crucial. Solidarity's organization (known as Citizens' Committees) served as the pillar of Walesa's election bid, but Catholic parties also endorsed Walesa from the outset. His most serious rival was Prime Minister Mazowiecki, who lacked a prior organization for his presidential campaign and depended on his Citizens' Movement for Democratic Action to establish campaign committees. The SLD, suffering from its communist pedigree, still had a relatively large membership (about 60,000) and selected Cimoszewicz as its presidential candidate. The largest party in terms of membership (about 400,000) was the PSL. It too sought to shake off its communist past and nominated its leader, Roman Bartoszcze.

Walesa topped the other candidates in the first round but was well short of the 50 percent needed to avoid a runoff (Table 9.8). The greatest shock was

TABLE 9.8   Presidential Election Results, 1990–2000 (Top Five Vote-Getters)

	First Round (%)	Second Round (%)
1990 Candidate (Party)		
Lech Walesa (Solidarity KO)	40.0	74.3
Stanislaw Tyminski ("X")	23.1	25.7
Tadeusz Mazowiecki (ROAD)	18.1	
Wlodzimierz Cimoszewicz (SdRP)	9.2	
Roman Bartoszcze (PSL)	7.2	
1995 Candidate (Party)		
Aleksander Kwasniewski (SLD)	35.1	51.7
Lech Walesa (non-party)	33.1	48.3
Jacek Kuron (UW)	9.2	
Jan Olszewski (RdR)	6.7	
Waldemar Pawlak (PSL)	4.3	
2000 Candidate (Party)		
Aleksander Kwasniewski (SLD)	53.9	
Andrzej Olechowski (non-party)	17.3	
Marian Krzaklewski (AWS)	15.6	
Jaroslaw Kalinowski (PSL)	6.0	
Andrzej Lepper (non-party)	3.1	

the second-place showing of outsider Stan Tyminski, a Polish emigrant to Canada who claimed to have established successful businesses there and in Peru, and the elimination of Mazowiecki. The second round runoff produced the expected result: Walesa received 74 percent of votes cast to Tyminski's 26 percent. This has been the one and only time that a wildcard has had a major impact in Polish politics.

In 1995, 13 candidates contested the first round of the presidential elections. The three-month campaign was notable for a dramatic surge in popularity for Walesa who closed in on longtime front-runner Kwasniewski. The incumbent was able to establish himself as the only "electable" candidate of the center-right. His campaign posters accurately depicted the choice in the election: "There are many other candidates. There is only one Walesa." In the first round, just over two-thirds of all votes cast were split between Kwasniewski (35 percent) and Walesa (33 percent). Two centrist candidates were next. The momentum seemed to favor Walesa: unifying the Solidarity bloc in the second round would have mathematically put him over the top. Two television debates reversed this trend. Kwasniewski's youthfulness (he was 41), eloquence, and good manners stood in sharp contrast to a particularly ill-tempered and agitated Walesa. It was especially ironic that the former communist charged Walesa with being a man of the past. Even though Walesa was more composed for the second debate, Poles had been reminded of how irascible and unrefined the shipyard electrician could be.

With a high turnout in the second round, Kwasniewski won by a very slim margin: 51.7 percent to 48.3 percent. Walesa had so antagonized his former associates in Solidarity that many of their supporters refused to vote for him in the runoff. For example, over 40 percent of Kuron voters turned away from Walesa to the ex-communist. The decline in Walesa's fortunes was brought home in Popowie, the town in which he was born, where he lost by a margin of 13 percent. While he won the majority of votes cast by those over 50, by private entrepreneurs, pensioners, and housewives, and by those with primary and those with higher education, Kwasniewski registered a sizable margin of victory among the twenty-somethings and the baby-boomers. Farmers, office workers, manual laborers, and the unemployed backed the ex-communist. While rural women supported Walesa for being a devout Catholic, Kwasniewski was preferred by secular-oriented, urban, and better-educated women. Most importantly, however, the election verdict was neither a repudiation of capitalism nor nostalgia for communism. It was primarily a retrospective verdict—a rejection of "five more years of this."

The 2000 election held none of the suspense of the previous one. Early on the saying was that the only person who could defeat Kwasniewski was his wife. Even the probability of a runoff if no candidate captured half the votes in the first round was far fetched. Nevertheless the turnout (61 percent) was only slightly lower than in the previous election, and voters were aware that giving Kwasniewski a mandate to be head of state for a second five-year period would be a consequential decision. Twelve candidates contested the election but only three received support in the double digits: Kwasniewski (54 percent of votes cast), independent Andrzej Olechowski (17 percent), and the AWS's Krzaklewski (16 percent). Former President Walesa managed just 1 percent support (Table 9.8).

As predictable as the result was, the reelection of a president was a milestone in recent Polish history. It demonstrated that a party system based on the distinction drawn at the 1989 roundtable between a left-wing bloc and a Solidarity camp was anachronistic. The top two vote getters were communist-era officials but, as Kwasniewski emphasized in a post-election television interview. "Poles voted for the future in these elections; the historical baggage of the past had no significance." Capturing the irony of the changed political conditions, he added that those who were hostages to ideology—the anti-communist variant, of course, not Marxism—were the biggest losers, as were those who opposed Poland's membership in the European Union. In fact the combined vote of anti-EU candidates was around 5 percent. (Table 9.9)

The election revealed the weakness of the Polish right. The AWS lost over one-third of the support it had received three years earlier in parliamentary elections. Krzaklewski as leader had come across as both arrogant and ineffectual. The patched-together AWS coalition itself seemed to be lacking a *raison*

TABLE 9.9 Share of Support for 2000 Presidential Candidates Coming from Different Demographic Categories (in Percent)

	Kwasniewski	Olechowski	Krzaklewski	Kalinowski	Lepper
Age					
18–24	16	19	10	11	14
25–39	27	31	23	31	28
40–59	41	39	39	43	41
60+	17	11	28	15	17
Sex					
Women	53	52	54	45	34
Men	47	48	46	56	66
Residence					
Cities (above 200,000)	23	35	27	5	9
Towns (50–200,000)	20	19	17	5	10
Towns (under 50,000)	26	24	24	13	17
Rural	30	22	32	78	65
Education					
Primary	13	7	16	23	25
Vocational	27	17	24	34	40
Secondary	45	47	40	34	30
University	15	30	20	9	4
Occupation					
Manager	11	20	12	6	3
Enterpreneur	8	13	8	4	5
Farmer	5	2	6	37	31
Blue-collar worker	17	11	13	13	19
Clerical	13	15	10	8	4
Housewife	4	3	4	4	3
Retired	26	16	35	18	22
Students	9	15	8	6	5
Unemployed	7	5	5	5	8

Source: Polish Television (TP SA). "Election Studio" program (October 8, 2000). http: 157.25.180.53 wybory2000.

d'etre and it was unclear how long it would survive as a political force. While the runner-up, Olechowski, was described as a center-right candidate, his admission that he had cooperated with the secret police, as well as his service as a bureaucrat during the communist era, put him outside the pale for the political elite on the right. The center-right UW had failed to put up a candidate of its own; most observers concluded that the UW's informal support for the independent Olechowski (64 percent of UW voters in 1997 cast their ballots for him) was less important than his appeal to well-educated, upwardly mobile, urban voters and his well-run campaign. The results also confirmed the weakness of leftists who were not former communists. It became evident that the Labor Union (which supported Kwasniewski) was a spent force while the Polish Socialist Party (PPS) was not a force at all (its candidate won 0.2 percent of votes). Dissatisfied peasants were divided between two protectionist options: the more mainstream PSL candidate and the wildcard candidature of Andrzej Lepper, frequent organizer of illegal and often violent agrarian protest actions. Even if it lacked drama in itself, the 2000 election revealed more dramatically than ever the need for radical reconfiguration of the Polish party system.

PARLIAMENTARY ELECTIONS The first parliament to be elected freely, untainted by deals reached with the communists (as in June 1989), was subjected nevertheless to a complicated electoral law. In 1991 voting for the Senate was simple: electors would choose two senators by plurality in each of the country's 47 provinces, and three each from the densely populated metropolitan areas of Warsaw and Katowice, for a total of 100 seats. For the Sejm elections, 37 constituencies were to provide anywhere from 7 to 17 members each depending on their size, for a total of 391 seats.[63] Sixty-nine other deputies would be elected indirectly. Parties would provide "national lists" of candidates and would be apportioned seats based on the number of votes they received in the constituencies.[64]

The electoral law was sensitive to votes given to small parties since no minimum threshold was required to obtain Sejm representation; there was no such thing as a wasted vote. Designers of the new system wanted to make sure that no political force went unrepresented and that each could expect greater gains from participating in the electoral process than from carrying on political activity outside of it. At this time groups had more to lose from opting out of the electoral process than from staying in; if they faired poorly in one election they could always hope to do better the next time.

The 1991 elections were contested by parties having markedly different programs. Some (like the UD) attracted liberals, while others (the PSL) appealed to opponents of economic neoliberalism. The SLD attracted voters because of its anticlericalist policies while right-wing parties campaigned largely on an anti-communist platform. Christian democratic and nationalist orientations were also represented within a broad electoral alliance. The 1991 election results demonstrated how the electorate took advantage of this menu for choice (Table 9.10). There was no overwhelming support for any one political orientation. Prime Minister Olszewski campaigned on a single issue, decommunization, but failed to win widespread support. It was up to parties and leaders with coalition-building skills to forge a new government out of the parliamentary fragmentation. When this Sejm was dissolved by Walesa in 1993, 29 parties were represented.

The electoral law adopted for the 1993 elections was intended to limit fragmentation and it changed the balance of power in the Sejm. Individual candidates rather than party lists became more important: 391 seats were to be contested in multimember constituencies and 69 other seats were to be distributed to parties receiving more than 7 percent of the national vote.[65] Only one electoral coalition (the SLD) cleared the 8 percent threshold set for alliances to send deputies to parliament. Just five parties not running as part of an electoral alliance were able to cross the 5 percent threshold required for a party to be represented in parliament. A party representing the German minority in Silesia also sent four deputies to the Sejm, its position secure by Poland's electoral law, which exempts parties representing Poland's minorities from the 5 percent requirement.

Were it not for personal rivalries and internal disputes within the Solidarity camp, the election result would not have been a stunning victory for the ex-communists. To be fair, the ex-communists had completed a remarkable comeback. In the mining center of Sosnowiec, for example, support for the SLD multiplied from 3 percent in the 1990 presidential elections to 19 percent in the 1991 parliamentary ones to 34 percent in 1993. In Warsaw, SLD leader Kwasniewski placed far ahead of other party leaders in votes received, more than doubling that for Bronislaw Geremek, a historian and former Solidarity leader who went on to become a highly respected foreign minister and as of 2001, leader of the UW.[66] Shock therapy had created a political backlash: the SLD got much mileage from its slogan: "It doesn't have to be like this". The coalition government formed by the SLD and PSL was headed by PSL leader Pawlak. Kwasniewski moved aside to concentrate on the upcoming presidential election.

In 1997 it was the turn of the head of Solidarity to replace a former communist in power. The breakdown in voting between left and right was not much different than it had been in 1993, but running this time as an electoral coalition allowed the conservative forces to win. In a dull campaign devoid of controversy, Krzaklewski's AWS won by a comfortable margin of nearly 7 percent over the SLD. Fifty-two of the AWS seats went to representatives of the Solidarity trade union, 45 to Catholic activists in it, and the remainder to various conservative and nationalist

TABLE 9.10   Parliamentary Election Results, 1991 to 1997

Party	1991 Election			1993 Election			1997 Election		
	Vote Percent	Sejm (N=460)	Senate (N=100)	Vote Percent	Sejm (N=460)	Senate (N=100)	Vote Percent	Sejm (N=460)	Senate (N=100)
Alliance of the Democratic Left (SLD)	12.0	60	4	20.6	171	37	27.1	164	28
Polish Peasant Party (PSL)	8.7	48	8	15.3	132	36	7.3	27	3
Democratic Union (UD)	12.3	62	21	10.7	74	4	—	—	—
Freedom Union (UW)	—	—	—	—	—	—	13.4	60	8
Union of Labor (UP)	—	—	—	7.2	41	2	4.7	0	0
Confederation for an Independent Poland (KPN)	7.5	46	4	5.6	22	0	—	—	—
Nonparty Bloc for Reform (BBWR)	—	—	—	5.4	16	2	—	—	—
German minority	—	—	—	0.6	4	1	0.6	2	0
Fatherland Alliance	—	—	—	6.4	0	1	—	—	—
Movement for Reconstruction (ROP)	—	—	—	—	—	—	5.6	6	5
Solidarity	5.1	27	12	4.6	0	9	—	—	—
Solidarity Electoral Action (AWS)	—	—	—	—	—	—	33.8	201	51
Center Accord (PC)	8.7	44	9	4.5	0	1	—	—	—
Liberal Democratic Congress (KLD)	7.5	37	6	3.8	0	1	—	—	—
Catholic Election Action (WAK)	8.7	49	9	—	—	—	—	—	—
Peasant Accord (PL)	5.5	28	7	—	—	—	—	—	—
Friends of Beer Party (PPP)	3.3	16	0	—	—	—	—	—	—
Other parties and independents	11.9	43	20	14.8	2	7	7.6	0	5

Sources: *Monitor Polski,* No. 41 (December 5, 1991); No. 50 (October 4, 1993). *Rzeczpospolita* (September 25–26, 1997).

groups like the ZChN, sometimes likened to Henri Le Pen's National Front in France.

The government of Prime Minister Cimoszewicz was replaced by one led by Jerzy Buzek. A native of Silesia, Poland's most industrialized region, an academic and union activist like Krzaklewski, Buzek was also an Evangelical Lutheran, highlighting reli-gious diversity in the AWS movement that had too often been portrayed as Catholic and clerical. The real reason why Krzaklewski did not welcome the chance to be prime minister was his preference to concentrate on the 2000 presidential contest. He was subsequently criticized for weakening representative government in Poland.

To obtain a governing majority in the Sejm, the AWS needed a coalition partner. After some hesitation it reached agreement with the underachieving but ambitious Freedom Union. The UW garnered just 13 percent of the vote and 60 seats in 1997, but its leadership included Balcerowicz of shock therapy fame and former Prime Ministers Mazowiecki and Suchocka. Aware that it held the balance of power in parliament, that it had a prestigious past, and that its leaders were well known and popular with Western politicians, the UW was able to obtain influential ministerial posts for joining the AWS in a coalition. Balcerowicz reassumed his former posts of deputy prime minister and finance minister; his party colleague Geremek became foreign minister, Suchocka, a lawyer, was appointed Justice Minister and Procurator General; and Onyszkiewicz got back the defense portfolio he had held in an earlier coalition government. The AWS-UW coalition was a conspicuous example of the tail wagging the dog.

The Buzek government survived longer than any other in the Third Republic, and as a result it was able to carry out a series of far-reaching reforms. In local government the number of provinces (or *wojewodztwo*) was reduced from 49 to 16. Provincial prefects were given wider powers than under the communist system but, in common with it, they became political appointees of the party in power in the Sejm. Other reforms enacted in 1999 reduced state involvement in health service and education. Also in 1999, faced with a resignation threat from finance minister Balcerowicz, the AWS adopted a tax reform law reducing income and corporate tax rates and abolishing loopholes. The pension program was also changed: set up in 1999, 21 new private pension funds were able to amass close to $1 billion in assets within a year, mostly through investments in government bonds and bills. That exceeded the total amount that mutual funds had accumulated over nine years. Buzek also sought to modify the privatization process by adopting the mass enfranchisement program that allowed up to 7 percent of stocks in privatized companies to be distributed to average Poles.

The coalition government split in mid-2000 when longstanding differences between the AWS and UW came to a head. The direct catalyst for the split was Buzek's claim that the Warsaw city council's government had ceased to function. Against the objections of the UW he replaced it with an administrator. The political context, however, was the UW's switch of coalition partners in Warsaw in March of that year from the AWS to the SLD. For some time observers had been saying that a UW-SLD coalition, even at the national level, seemed more natural, given the parties' common liberal economic policies and anticlericalism, than one between the AWS and UW. Buzek decided to punish the UW for its desertion of the AWS in Warsaw and it brought on the UW's desertion at the national level, too. The coalition had further been split when AWS deputies torpedoed a 3 percent value-added tax on agricultural products proposed by Balcerowicz.

The minority Buzek government limped toward the next parliamentary elections scheduled for 2001 with less and less public support (even if the UW had promised not to bring it down). President Kwasniewski did not need to dissolve parliament since the SLD that he once belonged to gained continuously in opinion polls. After so much alternation in government since 1989, it looked that as the new century began former communists would be more entrenched in power in Poland than ever.

The Policymaking Process

In a democratic system we should be able to identify four distinct phases to the policymaking process: policy initiation, the legislation process, policy implementation, and judicial review. Citizen and interest groups play an important role in the initiation of policy phase. To be sure, in Poland's new democratic system, it has taken time for groups to acquire the competence and the confidence to engage in agenda setting and advance policy initiatives. More often, it is the central actor in the second phase, the legislators, that initiate or at the least formulate policy. Each of these bodies has standing and ad hoc committees to help draft legislative bills. The president can also, with the help of his Chancellory, introduce a bill and have it enacted.

The legislative process, the second phase of policymaking, is very similar to that in Western parliamentary democracies. Bills with the highest probability of being enacted into law are those initiated by the government, proposed on the floor of the Sejm by a minister and voted for by all members of the party, or coalition of parties, that make up the government. The most partisan debate on the bill takes place during the second reading; it is at this stage that party discipline is most crucial in affecting the fate of the legislation. The degree of party discipline differs from party to party, with the SLD (the communist successor) usually most unified as a bloc (though it was rare that it could count on its coalition partner, the PSL, for unanimous support). In general, Polish parties are not as disciplined as in Britain (with its system of three-line whips requiring MPs to vote as party leaders require) or as lax as in the United States (with crossover voting a regularity).

After a bill has received second reading in the Sejm, both the third reading and the Senate debate that follows involve more technical, rather than partisan, consideration. But enactment still requires the president's signature, and he may send the bill back to the Sejm for substantive changes he desires. This legislative process offers interest groups three key occasions to influence policy: (1) when the government is drafting a bill for introduction in the Sejm; (2) between the first and second readings, when the bill is being studied by a Sejm committee; and (3) before the president signs it into law. In the first case lobbying is directed at the party of government as well as at the various advisory bodies connected to the cabinet (especially the Economic Committee of the Council of Ministers). In the second case, interest groups engage in lobbying Sejm committee chairs, parliamentary caucus leaders, and backbench deputies. In the third case, the president's Chancellory is likely to be the target of intense lobbying. This is not to suggest that Polish interest groups have professionalized their lobbying techniques on the scale of their U.S. counterparts. Even policy cases we consider later, such as the Enterprise Pact, have involved ramshackle groups taking their first steps in the policymaking process.

A third phase is the carrying out of policy. This is the role of the state and local bureaucracy, with the Council of Ministers and individual ministers overseeing the process. Most of the top posts in the state administration have gone to officials unconnected with the old communist system, although the SLD government was repeatedly accused of appointing ex-communists to high positions. Still, even under the communist system and, more so under a democratic one, civil servants have generally had to be accountable to political leaders for administering policy.

The fourth phase occurs when policy comes under judicial review—for example, for infringing upon an individual's constitutional rights. This is the function of Poland's overhauled judicial system.

Policymaking involves many political actors. This seeming pluralism may disguise the real distribution of power in the process, however. Corporatist structures—interest groups largely controlled by the state—have not disappeared altogether with the end of communism. This raises the question whether the state ultimately gets its way on issues it assigns priority to. Or are political institutions designed to encourage inputs into the policy process by various groups? What is the relationship between the state and interest groups during democratization? To answer these questions, it is helpful to introduce the concept of *corporatism* into our analysis.

The classic definition of corporatism was provided by Philippe Schmitter: "a system of interest representation in which the constituent units are organized into a limited number of singular, compulsory, noncompetitive, hierarchically ordered and functionally differentiated categories, recognized or licensed, if not created, by the state and granted a deliberate representational monopoly within their respective categories in exchange for observing certain controls on their selection of leaders and articulation of demands and supports."[67]

Schmitter distinguished between corporatism, understood as the process of interest intermediation, and concertation, the process whereby "affected interests . . . become incorporated within the policy process as recognized, indispensable negotiators and are made co-responsible (and occasionally completely responsible) for the implementation of policy decisions."[68] Concertation is, therefore, the institutional process in which peak labor and business organizations, together with the state, negotiate social pacts and formulate public policy. It is a type of policy formation rather than an example of pressure group politics.[69] The benefits of corporatist systems of negotiation and interest representation may include fewer strikes and less unemployment. Corporatist policy formulation is likely to be more in evidence in the early stages of post-communist political and economic development when "mini roundtables" bring together many interested parties to discuss a variety of still-unresolved issues.

The best example in Poland of the use of a corporatist system of negotiation is the Pact on State Enterprises concluded in 1992. This so-called Enterprise Pact, promoted by minister of labor Kuron and signed by a number of trade unions and by representatives of business and state structures, was aimed at bringing labor peace to the country. It gave rise in turn to the Polish Tripartite Commission on Socioeconomic Issues whose task was to draft legislation following consultations and negotiations among representatives from business and labor organizations and the state. This commission sought to institutionalize a form of concertation in the making of employment policy.

As desirable as the process of *tripartism* might be, problems arose in how influence was to be distributed among parties involved in negotiations. By 1994 the Polish trade union movement was so decentralized that labor's representatives to tripartite negotiations came from different organizations. Four were to be selected by Solidarity, four by the OPZZ, and at least seven smaller unions were to name one representative each. Even then, representation of workers in the policy process remained incomplete. Unorganized labor, employed by the private sector, would not have participants at such talks.

The business side was also not fully represented on the Tripartite Commission. The Confederation of Polish Employers (CPE) was the major group representing business and sent four delegates to such talks. But the level of centralization of business interests in the CPE was low, primarily because it did not represent the rapidly expanding private sector that employed nonunionized workers. Given incomplete representation and the low level of centralization of interests, it seemed unlikely that policy concertation would become a central institutional feature of the policymaking process.

Not surprisingly, the most influential organizations sought to ensure for themselves a more direct role in policymaking. The Solidarity union was the core group in AWS and reasoned that there was no better way of shaping policy than having a large bloc of deputies elected to parliament. Tripartism as a vehicle of policy concertation was, therefore, of secondary interest to the union. Failing to obtain a large bloc of seats, another strategy for an interest group like a trade union was to establish close interorganizational links between itself and a major political party. The OPZZ's institutional linkage within the SLD coalition is an example of this strategy. Thus, when an interest group has representatives in parliament promoting its objectives, the strategy becomes one that offers higher, more immediate payoffs than tripartism. It says something about the health of Polish democracy that organizational actors wish to be catapulted directly onto the political stage.

The process of forging interorganizational links between business groups and a pro-business political party is incomplete because, as described earlier, there is no real conservative party in Poland. This is not to say that business does not have its representatives in parliament. In the neoliberal global climate of the post–Cold War years, business interests are effectively promoted through the influence projected by external actors (the IMF and EU), by the functional imperatives of economic transformation (privatization), and even by left-of-center governments and presidents. For business, corporatist structures are largely redundant and vacuous.

Some observers have been concerned about the lack of intermediary structures in the policymaking process. But from this we cannot conclude that existing political institutions in Poland are failing to perform their functions. If anything, it is the continuing centrality of state institutions, like the Sejm, that have made policymaking an open, transparent, and democratic process.

Policy Outcomes

The discussion here has focused on the many different choices—concerned with the constitution, institutions, parties, and leaders—that the new political system in Poland has faced. In this final section, the focus shifts to three major policy issues that have concerned the country's rulers. One is the promotion of a free market economy, the second is the framing of a new security policy, and the third is integration into Europe. Steps have been taken in all three areas but work remains if Poland is to consolidate into a liberal, democratic state.

Free Market Reform

Economic reforms had begun in Poland while the communist party was still in power. In February 1987 the United States lifted the last of the economic sanctions leveled at Poland as punishment for the imposition of martial law in 1981. Shortly afterward a leading communist party official traveled to Washington to discuss debt rescheduling and request a new line of credit for Poland. Later in 1987 Poland was admitted to the World Bank. Under the last two communist prime ministers, the first steps were taken toward economic decentralization and price liberalization.

One of the two questions contained in the referendum—a milestone for a communist country—held in November 1987 was whether the public supported rapid economic changes over a two- or three-year period (the other question concerned "deep democratization"). Two-thirds of voters (though only 44 percent of eligible ones) supported rapid economic change. In February 1988 further moves toward price liberalization were taken with increases in food prices (by 40 percent) and energy (by 100 percent). This was followed by widening the autonomy of large state firms, especially in conduct of foreign trade. In November 1988 parliament adopted a law promoting private enterprise; in the first half of 1989, 1,302 joint ventures were registered. Many of these were set up by members of the communist nomenklatura.

The Solidarity-based governments from the second half of 1989 to the fall of 1993 accelerated the economic transformation begun by the communists. Policies included restricting the money supply, controlling hyperinflation while freeing prices of nearly all products from state controls, limiting the budget deficit (5 percent of GDP was the target), promoting currency convertibility (helped by the creation by Western institutions of a *zloty* stabilization fund), and developing incentives for private enterprise.

Poland's economic policy was shaped by the IMF and overseen by Balcerowicz, appointed minister of finance and economic reform head in September 1989. In January 1990 he introduced a crash stabilization package, popularly termed shock therapy. Its core features were a balanced government budget, strict fiscal, monetary, and income policies, and convertibility of the *zloty*, the Polish currency. Anti-inflationary measures were predicated on inducing short-term recession and lowering real income. IMF aid was made contingent on keeping close to the 5-percent target.

Balcerowicz's stabilization package also envisaged structural adjustment of the economy. Sweeping privatization would be a prerequisite for structural adjustment and, indeed, a privatization law was enacted in July 1990 (after 17 different drafts had been considered), followed in September by a law transforming 40 percent of state firms into public corporations. Economist Winiecki persuasively argued that privatization of state-owned industrial juggernauts was poorly conceived but, fortunately, it was not critical to successful economic transformation. Instead, Poland's remarkable economic recovery in subsequent years owed most to "creating conditions for virtually unrestricted entry of private firms into all sectors of the economy and fields of activity."[70]

Harvard economist Jeffrey Sachs, an adviser to the Polish government at the time, recommended shock therapy, or the "big bang" approach to economic reform. He recognized the quandary of such reform: "Why should something 'so good' feel 'so bad?' "[71] Sachs was one of the first to draw the comparison between Poland's and Spain's economic development after 1950. Both countries had similar economic conditions then: comparable population size, large agricultural sectors, peripheral regions of Europe lagging behind in modernization, Catholic. "Spain shot ahead of Poland in the next thirty-five years. Spain started to catch up with the rest of Western Europe, while Poland fell farther behind."[72] Economic integration with Europe was the key factor behind Spain's success.

One critic, Adam Przeworski, however, attacked both the assumptions and the process of shock therapy. "The architects of reform were persuaded that their blueprint was sound—no, more: the only one possible."[73] Reform was unresponsive to public preferences: "Radical reform was a project initiated from above and launched by surprise, independently of public opinion and without the participation of organized political forces" and, accordingly, "had the effect of weakening democratic institutions."[74] The best example was passage of the Balcerowicz plan in December 1989. The Sejm was "given sixteen pieces of legislation and told that it must approve the nine most important before the end of the month to meet the IMF conditions."[75]

The process of reform might have been contentious but the success of the reforms was undeniable. GDP growth was 4 percent in 1994, and from 1995 onwards 6 percent annually. Already in the early 1990s Poland had become a market economy. It was the first in Central Europe to resume economic growth after 1989 and the first to have GDP surpass the 1989 level. It also had the most privatized economy in the region, a buoyant stock market, and robust consumer demand. Only privatization of the colossal, state-owned industrial enterprises proved laboriously slow.

Capitalism produces losers as well as winners and in the year 2001 unemployment remained at high levels (about 15 percent of the labor force) and inflation was still not under control (at around a 10 percent annual rate). One of the reasons that the electorate supported the SLD was the belief it would be more sensitive to newly disadvantaged social groups. But the SLD government was in the advantageous position of reaping the rewards of painful economic reforms enacted by its predecessors. It was not about to discard a policy producing results that were the envy of the region.

By the end of the 1990s Poland had become the biggest attractor of foreign direct investment in the region. In 1998 alone it drew in over $5 billion. That represented about 18 percent of all capital invested in the country, the rest accounted for by domestic investment. In one survey in early 2000, chief executives at the world's largest companies ranked Poland as the fifth most attractive place for foreign direct investment (after the United States, Britain, China, and Brazil). Privatization of the energy sector was cited as one of the main reasons. But the Polish government also

cashed in on privatization: in 1999 its revenues from sell-offs totaled $8.3 billion. The one alarming statistic in the country's economy performance was the current account deficit. From a 4 percent surplus in the current account balance in 1995 it had reached a deficit of 8 percent of GDP by 2000. Part of the explanation lay in falling exports (the crash of the Russian market), but a larger issue was how competitive Polish-made goods really were.

Security Policy

The idea of *antemurale christianitatis*, discussed earlier in this chapter, has strong contemporary resonance in security matters. Since the democratic breakthrough, Polish politicians have debated what role the country should play in Europe. The foreign policy debate, highlighting Poland's security needs, has had a major impact on domestic politics. The consensus has been that Poland should press for swift integration into European economic and security structures. Fearing Russian revanchism that could quickly spread into Belarus, Moldova, Ukraine, and the Baltic states, many political leaders in the country believe that Poland's role should, once again, be that of a rampart defending Western civilization against the less civilized East.

Significant changes having a major impact on Poland's security occurred on the country's borders in the early 1990s. The number of neighboring states increased from three (the USSR, Czechoslovakia, and East Germany) to seven (Russia, Lithuania, Belarus, Ukraine, Slovakia, the Czech Republic, and Germany). Just as important as the increase in the number of neighbors was the nature of the nations with whom Poland now shared borders. In the west it was with a critical member of the NATO alliance—the reunified Federal Republic of Germany. By contrast, in the east and south Poland's borders are shared primarily with states suffering from varying degrees of political and economic instability. Given the re-sovietization processes occurring in Belarus, Poland's border with that state is sometimes considered a de facto border with Russia. In the north, Poland has a border with Russia itself—the Kaliningrad oblast (or region).

TABLE 9.11   Who Central Europeans Feared the Most

Nation	Minorities	Immigrants	Neighbors	Russians	Germans	Americans
Poles	35	41	62	63	68	11
Hungarians	26	51	64	13	6	3
Czechs	44	38	35	38	38	6
Slovaks	53	23	46	26	21	5
Slovenes	13	61	60	3	3	14
Croats	57	28	62	34	3	6
Bulgarians	46	0	61	5	3	4
Belarusans	30	22	20	13	14	13
Ukrainians	24	6	10	19	3	4
Romanians	60	16	67	62	13	10

Source: Polityka, No. 32 (August 7, 1993): p. 20.

Not surprisingly, Poles are suspicious about their eastern neighbors (Table 9.11), while leaders have been unenthusiastic about regional cooperation schemes, such as (1) the *Visegrad group* which consists of Poland, the Czech and Slovak Republics, Hungary, Slovenia, and Romania; and (2) the Central European Free Trade Association (CEFTA) comprising the 90 million people living in the six Visegrad states. The dominant orientation of foreign policy has been westward.

Poland's strategic position is self-evident. Since it is situated in the central lowlands of Europe with no natural borders in the east or west, the country was squeezed in between NATO and Russia. During his visit to Warsaw in June 1995, U.S. Defense Secretary William Perry called Poland "the key to European security." For Poland the key to European security was always membership in NATO. After the Cold War, the military alliance's role changed. Apart from providing a security umbrella, NATO promoted democratic values eastward. Supporters of Poland's membership in the alliance stressed this point, and also that NATO enlargement would signify the obliteration of the division of Europe agreed upon at Yalta. Successive Polish governments argued against a new division of Europe based along either the Oder (Poland's western border) or Bug (its eastern border) rivers. They disclaimed any interest in becoming a front-line state, an *antemurale occidentalis,* though in practical terms that is what NATO ending at Poland's eastern border may

turn the country into. Hence Poland has given a high priority to promoting the security interests of its eastern neighbors Lithuania and Ukraine. Already in the early 1990s Poland signed bilateral treaties of friendship and cooperation with all neighboring states. Designed to guarantee a framework for cooperation, these treaties at a minimum affirmed the principle of the inviolability of state borders as they currently existed, and at a maximum they provided for freer trade (as within CEFTA) and for cooperation in defense industries (as with Ukraine).

The process of drawing Poland into NATO began with a NATO commitment in 1994 to integrate select Central European states into its defensive structures. In 1997 Poland was officially invited to become a member, and in spring 1998 the U.S. Senate approved the inclusion of Poland (together with the Czech Republic and Hungary) in the NATO treaty. The one catch to NATO membership for Poland has been that it has antagonized Russia. Since 1998 Polish-Russian relations have been correct, but problems have surfaced regularly. For example, in January 2000 the Polish government expelled nine Russian diplomats for spying. In March of that year pro-Chechen demonstrators vandalized the Russian consulate in Poznan, which led to the temporary recall of Russia's ambassador. In April 2000 in a report that was supposed to be secret, Poland's security service warned that Russian intelligence was stepping up activity in the country. Not surprisingly, a CBOS report published that month found that only 2 percent of Poles considered relations with Russia to be good; 40 percent claimed they were bad.[76] From these trends it is risky to conclude that Poland's security and national interests are problem-free following NATO accession.

European Integration

In March 1998 the EU opened accession negotiations with Poland and four other Central European candidates. Polish leaders had talked of entry into this exclusive club of nations from the time of the 1989 breakthrough, and hopes were raised by the start of formal negotiations. But in October 1999 European Commission President Romano Prodi presented progress reports on the candidates and indicated that they had achieved little in the two years since it had issued its initial opinions which had been very encouraging for Poland. He announced that the Commission would monitor applicants' claims about progress more closely, implying less trust in their reports. Prodi emphasized that the accession timetable would be based on merit rather than politics. Although Poland claimed it had done much to adapt its laws and structures to EU criteria, the 1999 Commission report contended that it "has not progressed significantly." Moreover, it observed "a notable lack of progress" in reforming such areas of contention as state aid for ailing industries, steel restructuring, agriculture, and fisheries. Poland missed the December 1999 EU deadline for enacting a law on state aid that would define when the state could help companies and when it could not. The coalition government in Poland was split between state interventionists in the larger party and neoliberals led by Balcerowicz in the smaller one.

In addition Poland's infrastructure was singled out as below EU standards. Let us consider the example of highways. Poland had one of the lowest levels of interstate highways per land area in all Europe. In 1994 the government approved a program to construct 1,500 miles of privately financed turnpikes but by 2000 only 65 miles had been finished. The state's involvement became urgent and a new law established a National Motorway Fund that would use public money to build highways.

In mid-2000 Poland submitted a detailed timetable to the 15-member EU on enacting 150 laws needed to prepare for membership. The Polish government's target for admission into the EU was 2003 but the EU Enlargement Commissioner stated that 2005 was more likely. Negotiations on the thorniest issues had not even begun and criteria for assessing candidates' records were not finalized. Wealth levels, environmental standards, legal harmonization, unrestricted movement of workers, regional development, and agricultural policy were the crucial problems affecting accession. Disagreements on how much funds Poland and other applicants could tap from the EU's agricultural and structural funds had also to be resolved. Haunting Europe was the fear of large-scale westward migration from Central and Eastern Europe, a salient issue in many EU states and most vividly illustrated by the success of Jorg Haider's far-right Freedom Party in Austria. Would Polish workers look for jobs in Western Europe should the country enter the EU? In 1992 Portugese workers, who had roughly one-half of the income of their German counterparts, migrated to the richer EU states when their country became a member. In 2000 Poles' incomes were only one-sixth of those in Germany. If there is indeed a direct relationship between income gaps and migration, then one German think tank's forecast of 500,000 Central Europeans moving to Western Europe per year if borders were fully opened cannot be ruled out.

What has proved most frustrating for Poland's Europhiles is how far the country has already traveled to meet European standards. The European Commission gave Poland a top grade for meeting its political criteria but faulted it for persisting corruption. In its report for 2000 *Transparency International* ranked Poland only forty-third of 80 states in its corruption perceptions index.[77] A 2000 World Bank report identified corruption "at the highest levels" as Poland's most serious problem. Based on interviews with government officials and the national audit office, the 1999 World Economic Forum survey ranked Poland fifty-second out of 59 countries in terms of governmental favoritism and forty-third in terms of insider trading (not much different from other Central and Eastern European states). And a European Bank for Reconstruction and Development (EBRD) report on the legal systems of Central European states published in 2000 found that the perception of the effectiveness of laws was largely negative. In the case of the law on bankruptcy, for example, only 40 percent of Polish lawyers surveyed thought it was sound, placing Poland thirteenth of the 16 Central and East European states studied.

A history of democracy, plus wealth, inhibit corrupt practices in a country. Poland has had neither. Credible political institutions also help; Poland's are only a decade old. When Poland has to resolve such diverse shortcomings as corruption, highways, agriculture, and harmonization of laws with the EU, it is easy to see why much of Polish society is skeptical about the accession process. In May 2000 only 30 percent of Poles expressed "definite support" for the EU while 29 percent were skeptical and 41 percent ambiguous.[78] The good news for EU advocates was that these proportions reflected an increase in support after a steady decline from 1997 on. Still, compare these figures with support for NATO: 68 percent for, 13 percent opposed, in February 2000. Polish leaders were faced with the conundrum, then, of keeping morale on the EU high, negotiating a good deal for Poland, and maintaining the EU's interest in enlargement.

Conclusion

Studying democratic consolidation is important in a country that was a precocious exponent of the idea but also regularly fell victim to authoritarian rule. Zbigniew Brzezinski has cautioned us that "Though the notions of 'democracy' are fashionable, in much of the world the practice of democracy is still quite superficial and democratic institutions remain vulnerable."[79] In similar fashion, Seymour Martin Lipset warned against equating democratic breakthrough with democratic consolidation. To a great degree, new democratic regimes are judged by their current performance, thereby making them more vulnerable to collapse in the face of economic or social crisis. Citizens in new democracies frequently fail to distinguish between the source of political authority (such as the constitution) and the agent of authority (the current government). Lipset noted that the failures of a particular government become equated with the flaws of the political system, and new democracies have been helpless to rebut this presumption since, by definition, they cannot invoke a record of past successes.[80]

This chapter has clearly illustrated that Poland has made great strides in consolidating its democracy. The country has recorded greater progress in institutional and economic development than in cultural transformation. The policy process is squarely based on political institutions universally regarded as providing for fair, impartial outcomes. In economic terms, history has vindicated Adam Smith in his stress on the intimate relationship between commerce and liberty.[81] Or as Barrington Moore put it, there can be no democracy without a bourgeoisie.[82] But does the Polish population favor the growth of a bourgeoisie?

Sociologist Piotr Sztompka dramatized the implication of this uneven development between institutional and cultural growth: "To be already in Europe, in a political and even an economic sense, is not yet the same as becoming a fully fledged European citizen. Joining the realm of European states and markets is not the same as *entering European civil societies*. Only the latter will signify a true and ultimate return to Europe."[83] For all its efforts at forging and consolidating democracy, Poland still seems confronted with the catch-22 dilemma of having to culturally resemble Western Europe in order to be integrated with it wholly. Becoming a NATO garrison state by itself does not resolve this dilemma. Although it has been reduced, it is the cultural divide between Western and Central Europe that is in need of greater mutual accommodation.

KEY TERMS

Alliance of the Democratic Left (SLD)
antemurale christianitatis
apparatchik
Balcerowicz plan
catch-all party
civilian control
Committee for Workers' Self-Defense (KOR)
competitive party system
constitution of 1997
Constitutional Tribunal
Concordat
contract Sejm
corporatism

Council of Ministers
electoral law of 1993
Fourteen Points
Freedom Union (UW)
Cardinal Jozef Glemp
General Wojciech Jaruzelski
Marian Krzaklewski
Alesander Kwasniewski
liberum veto
Little Constitution of 1992
Magdalenka
martial law
May coup 1926
Tadeusz Mazowiecki

Mieszko I
National Trade Union Accord (OPZZ)
nomenklatura
pacted transition
Partitions
Jozef Pilsudski
Polish October
Polish United Workers Party (PUWP)
post materialist values
Ribbentrop-Molotov pact
romantic insurrectionism
roundtable talks
Sarmatianism

Second Republic
Sejm
Senate
Solidarity (*Solidarnosc*)
Solidarity Electoral Action (AWS)
szlachta democracy
Third Republic
tripartism
Visegrad group
Lech Walesa
Cardinal Stefan Wyszynski
Yalta agreement

LIST OF PARTY ABBREVIATIONS

AWS Solidarity Electoral Action (*Akcja Wyborcza Solidarnosc*)
BBWR Nonparty Bloc for Reform (*Bezpartyiny Blok Wspierania Reform*)
BdP Bloc for Poland (*Blok dla Polski*)
KLD Liberal Democratic Congress (*Kongres Liberalno-Demokratyczny*)
KO Citizens' Committees (*Komitety Obywatelskie*)
KPN Confederation for an Independent Poland (*Konfederacja Polski Niepodleglej*)
OPZZ National Trade Union Accord (*Ogolnopolskie Porozumienie Zwiazkow Zawodowych*)
PC Center Alliance (*Porozumienie Centrum*)
PK Conservative Party (*Partia Konserwatywna*)
PL Peasant Accord (*Porozumienie Ludowe*)
PO Citizens' Platform (*Platforma Dbywatelska*)
PPP Friends of Beer Party (*Partia Przyjaciol Piwa*)
PSL Polish Peasant Party (*Polskie Stronnictwo Ludowe*)

RdR Movement for the Republic (*Ruch dla Rzeczypospolitej*)
ROAD Citizens Movement for Democratic Action (*Ruch Obywatelski Akcja Demokratyczna*)
ROP Movement for Poland's Reconstruction (*Ruch Odrodzenia Polski*)
SdRP Social Democracy of the Polish Republic (*Socjaldemokracja Rzeczypospolitej Polskiej*)
SK-L Conservative-Peasant Party (*Stronnictwo Konserwaytwno-Ludowe*)
SLD Alliance of the Democratic Left (*Sojusz Lewicy Demokratycznej*)
UD Democratic Union (*Unia Demokratyczna*)
UP Union of Labor (*Unia Pracy*)
UPR Union of Political Realism (*Unia Polityki Realnej*)
UW Freedom Union (*Unia Wolnosci*)
WAK Catholic Electoral Action (*Wyborcza Akcja Katolicka*)
ZChN Christian National Union (*Zjednoczenie Chrzescijansko Narodowe*)

SUGGESTED READINGS

Ascherson, Neil. *The Polish August.* Harmondsworth, England: Penguin, 1983.

Connor, Walter D., and Piotr Ploszajski, eds. *The Polish Road From Socialism.* Armonk, NY: M. E. Sharpe, 1992.

Davies, Norman. *God's Playground: A History of Poland*, Vols. 1–2. New York: Columbia University Press, 1984.

Ekiert, Grzegorz, and Jan Kubik. *Rebellious Civil Society: Popular Protest and Democratic Control in Poland, 1989–1993.* Ann Arbor, MI: University of Michigan Press, 1999.

Elster, Jon, ed. *The Roundtable Talks and the Breakdown of Communism (Constitutionalism in Eastern Europe).* Chicago: University of Chicago Press, 1996.

Hicks, Barbara. *Environmental Politics: A Social Movement between Regime and Politics.* New York: Columbia University Press, 1996.

Kaminski, Bartlomiej. *The Collapse of State Socialism: The Case of Poland.* Princeton, NJ: Princeton University Press, 1991.

Kurski, Jaroslaw. *Lech Walesa: Democrat or Dictator?* Boulder, CO: Westview, 1993.

Michnik, Adam. *Letters From Freedom: Post-Cold War Realities and Perspectives.* Berkeley, CA: University of California Press, 1998.

Millard, Frances. *Polish Politics and Society.* London: Routledge, 1999.

Milosz, Czeslaw. *The Captive Mind.* New York: Vintage Books, 1990.

Podgorecki, Adam. *Polish Society.* New York: Praeger, 1994.

Sachs, Jeffrey. *Poland's Jump to the Market Economy.* Cambridge, MA: MIT Press, 1994.

Slay, Ben. *The Polish Economy: Crisis, Reform, and Transformation.* Princeton, NJ: Princeton University Press, 1994.

Staar, Richard F., ed. *Transition to Democracy in Poland*, 2nd ed. New York: St. Martin's, 1998.

Taras, Ray. *Consolidating Democracy in Poland.* Boulder, CO: Westview, 1995.

Wnuk-Lipinski, Edmund, ed. *After Communism: A Multidisciplinary Approach to Radical Social Change.* Warsaw: ISP PAN, 1995.

1. On the role of history in creating unique social characteristics in Poland, see Adam Podgorecki, *Polish Society* (New York: Praeger, 1994), Ch. 4.

2. This is the title of a history of Poland: Norman Davies, *Heart of Europe: A Short History of Poland* (New York: Oxford University Press, 1984).

3. Earl Vinecour, *Polish Jews: The Final Chapter* (New York: New York University Press, 1977), p. 1.

4. Andrzej Wyczanski, "The Problem of Authority in Sixteenth Century Poland: An Essay in Reinterpretation," in J. K. Fedorowicz, ed., *A Republic of Nobles* (Cambridge: Cambridge University Press, 1982), p. 91.

5. Jerzy Lukowski, *Liberty's Folly: The Polish-Lithuanian Commonwealth in the Eighteenth Century, 1697–1795* (London: Routledge, 1991), p. 25.

6. The romanticism versus pragmatism dichotomy is described by Adam Bromke, *Poland's Politics: Idealism vs. Realism* (Cambridge, MA: Harvard University Press, 1967).

7. Adam B. Seligman, *The Idea of Civil Society* (New York: Free Press, 1992), p. 8.

8. Andrew Janos, "Continuity and Change in Eastern Europe: Strategies of Post-Communist Politics," *East European Politics and Societies* 8, No. 1 (Winter 1994): 3–4.

9. Data reported in Irving Kaplan, "The Society and Its Environment," in Harold D. Nelson, ed., *Poland: A Country Study* (Washington, DC: U.S. Government Printing Office, 1984), p. 107.

10. Glowny Urzad Statystyczny, *Rocznik Statystyczny 1991* (Warsaw: GUS, 1991), pp. 24–26, 26–38.

11. See John Clark and Aaron Wildavsky, *The Moral Collapse of Communism: Poland as a Cautionary Tale* (San Francisco: Institute for Contemporary Studies Press, 1990).

12. This is my translation.

13. *Zycie Warszawy* (August 27–28, 1988). Kiszczak added that those who rejected the constitutional order of the Polish People's Republic could not participate.

14. Jacek Zakowski, *Rok 1989: Geremek odpowiada, Zakowski pyta* (Warsaw: Plejada, 1990), p. 214.

15. *Porozumienie okraglego stolu* (Warsaw: NSZZ Solidarnosc, Region Mazurski, 1989), p. 7.

16. *Izvestiia* (6 April 1989). In Jacques Levesque, *The Enigma of 1989: The USSR and the Liberation of Eastern Europe* (Berkeley, CA: University of California Press, 1997), p. 115.

17. Jadwiga Staniszkis, *The Dynamics of the Breakthrough in Eastern Europe: The Polish Experience* (Berkeley: University of California Press, 1991), p. 199.

18. See Richard F. Staar, ed., *Transition to Democracy in Poland*, 2nd ed. (New York: St. Martin's, 1997), Chs. 3, 5.

19. See Frances Millard, "The Polish Parliamentary Elections of October 1991," *Soviet Studies* 44, No. 5 (1992): 838–40.

20. For an analysis of the role of the presidency, see Krzysztof Jasiewicz, "Poland: Walesa's Legacy to the Presidency," in Ray Taras, ed., *Postcommunist Presidents* (Cambridge, England: Cambridge University Press, 1997), pp. 130–67.

21. For the text of the 1997 constitution, see "Konstytucja Rzeczypospolitej Polskiej," *Rzeczypospolita* (April 3, 1997).

22. Douglass C. North, *Institutions, Institutional Change, and Economic Performance* (Cambridge, England: Cambridge University Press, 1992), p. 81.

23. Frances Millard, *Polish Politics and Society* (London: Routledge, 1999), p. 177.

24. Ronald Inglehart, Miguel Basanez, and Alejandro Moreno, *Human Values and Beliefs: A Cross Cultural Sourcebook* (Ann Arbor, MI: University of Michigan Press, 1997), Table V320. See also Inglehart, *Modernization and Postmodernization: Cultural, Economic, and Political Change in 43 Societies* (Princeton, NJ: Princeton University Press, 1997). The alternatives were to identify with one's town or with the world as a whole. Argentina and South Korea preceded Poland on this value.

25. Inglehart, Basanez, and Moreno, *Human Values and Beliefs*, Table V322. Ahead of Poland were Ireland, the United States, and India.

26. Inglehart, Basanez, and Moreno, *Human Values and Beliefs*, Table V340. With an 82-percent rate of trust in one's own nationality, Poles were approximately 15 percent below the mean, but still 27 percent ahead of the most trustless nation, the Russians, at 55 percent.

27. See Ray Taras, "Redefining National Identity After Communism: A Preliminary Comparison of Ukraine and Poland," in Ray Taras, ed., *National Identities and Ethnic Minorities in Eastern Europe* (London: Macmillan, 1998).

28. Centrum Badania Opinii Spolecznej (CBOS) Public Opinion Research Center (Fall 1994).

29. Andrzej Rychard, "Spoleczenstwo w transformacji: koncepcja i proba syntezy analiz," in Rychard and Michal Federowicz, eds., *Spoleczenstwo w transformacji: ekspertyzy i studia* (Warsaw: IFiS PAN, 1993), p. 7.

30. For a discussion of the congruence between a country's history of authoritarianism and communist totalitarianism, see Stephen White, John Gardner, and George Schopflin, *Communist Political Systems: An Introduction* (New York: St. Martin's, 1987), Ch. 2.

31. See Hugh Seton-Watson, *The East European Revolution* (Boulder, CO: Westview Press, 1983).

32. See Janina Frentzel-Zagorska, "Civil Society in Poland and Hungary," *Soviet Studies* 42, No. 4 (October 1990): 759–77.

33. CBOS survey. Cited by Jerzy J. Wiatr, "Social Conflicts and Democratic Stability: Poland in Comparative Perspective," in Jerzy J. Wiatr, ed., *The Politics of Democratic Transformation: Poland After 1989* (Warsaw: Scholar Agency, 1993), pp. 14–15.

34. Centrum Badania Opinii Spolecznej, "Sense of Representation of Interests and Control of Public Affairs" (January 2000). www.cbos.pl

35. Reported in *Business Central Europe* (December 1999/January 2000), p. 59.

36. Inglehart, Basanez, and Moreno, *Human Values and Beliefs*, p. 27.

37. Inglehart, Basanez, and Moreno, *Human Values and Beliefs*, pp. 30–31.

38. George Kolankiewicz and Ray Taras, "Poland: Socialism for Everyman?" in Archie Brown and Jack Gray, eds., *Political Culture and Political Change in Communist States* (New York: Holmes and Meier, 1979), pp. 101–30. See also James R. Kluegel, David S. Mason, and Bernd Wegener, eds., *Social Justice and Political Change: Public Opinion in Capitalist and Post Communist States* (The Netherlands: Aldine DeGruyter, 1995).

39. Inglehart, Basanez, and Moreno, *Human Values and Beliefs*, p. 19. See Table V405 for country rankings.

40. Ireneusz Bialecki and Bogdan W. Mach, "Orientacje spoleczno-ekonomiczne poslow na tle pogladow spoleczenstwa," in Jacek Wasilewski and Wlodzimierz Wesolowski, eds., *Poczatek parlamentarnej elity: poslowie kontraktowego Sejmu* (Warsaw: IFIS PAN, 1992), pp. 129–31.

41. Mary E. McIntosh and Martha Abele MacIver, "Coping with Freedom and Uncertainty: Public Opinion in Hungary, Poland, and Czechoslovakia 1989–1992," *International Journal of Public Opinion Research*, 4, No. 4 (Winter 1992): 381–85.

42. Centrum Badania Opinii Spolecznej, "Freedom and Equality in Social Life" (February 2000). www.cbos.pl

43. Jan Winiecki, "The Reasons for Electoral Defeat Lie in Non-Economic Factors," in Jan Winiecki, ed., *Five Years After June: The Polish Transformation, 1989–1994* (London: Centre for Research into Communist Economies, 1996), p. 87.

44. For a detailed study, see Marilyn Rueschmeyer, ed., *Women in the Politics of Post-Communist Eastern Europe* (Armonk, NY: M. E. Sharpe, 1994).

45. Data are taken from *Sejm Rzeczypospolitej Polskiej: II Kadencja-Przewodnik* (Warsaw: Wydawnictwo Sejmowe, 1994), pp. 240–46.

46. For a pioneering work, see H. Gordon Skilling, *Interest Groups and Communist Politics* (Boston: Little, Brown, 1971).

47. Sharon Wolchik, "The Repluralization of Politics in Czechoslovakia," *Communist and Post-Communist Studies* 26, No. 4 (December 1993): 412–31.

48. Grzegorz Ekiert and Jan Kubik, *Rebellious Civil Society: Popular Protests and Democratic Consolidation in Poland, 1989–1993* (Ann Arbor, MI: University of Michigan Press, 1999).

49. Piotr Glinski, "Environmentalism Among Polish Youth: A Maturing Social Movement," in *Communist and Post-Communist Studies*, Vol. 27, No. 2 (June 1994): 156–58. See also Barbara Hicks, *Environmental Politics: A Social Movement between Regime and Politics* (New York: Columbia University Press, 1996).

50. Millard, *Polish Politics and Society*, p. 121.

51. Survey data and Kwasniewski's statement are from Tom Hundley, "Catholic Church Losing Clout in Poland," *Chicago Tribune*, November 13, 1994.

52. Stanislaw Podemski, "Zadowoleni i niespokojni," *Polityka* 32 (August 7, 1993): 1.

53. On this topic, see Carl Bernstein and Marco Politi, *His Holiness: John Paul II and the Hidden History of Our Time* (New York: Doubleday, 1996).

54. Andrew A. Michta, "Civil-Military Relations in Poland After 1989: The Outer Limits of Change," *Problems of Post-Communism* 44, No. 2 (March–April 1997): 64.

55. Data are from Mariusz Janicki, "OPZZ przetrzymalo: w jednym Sejmie," *Polityka*, December 4, 1993, p. 14.

56. Wlodzimierz Wesolowski, "Transformacja charakteru i struktury interesow: aktualne procesy, szanse i zagrozenia," in Andrzej Rychard and Michal Federowicz, eds., *Spoleczenstwo w transformacji: ekspertyzy i studia* (Warsaw: IFIS PAN, 1993), p. 138.

57. Wesolowski, "Transformacja charakteru i struktury interesow," p. 133.

58. This list is taken from "Business Group Buffet," *Business Central Europe* (November 1994): 33.

59. Silesians are a clearly distinguishable group having a German background. But one Polish politician remarked in 1995 that given Germany's present citizenship law extending citizenship to anyone with a grandparent of German origin, millions of other Poles could also be regarded as German. The migratory movement that this conception of Deutschvolk could set off would clearly not be in either Germany's or Poland's interest.

60. Judith Gentleman and Voytek Zubek, "International Integration and Democratic Development: The Cases of Poland and Mexico," *Journal of Interamerican Studies and World Affairs* 34, No. 1 (Spring 1992): 72.

61. Centrum Badania Opinii Spolecznej, "The Image of the SLD: About the Identity of the New Party" (February 2000). www.cbos.pl

62. As the 1995 presidential election highlighted, the highly industrialized western and northern parts of the country tend to vote left-of-center, while the more rural, Catholic southern and eastern parts vote conservative.

63. Each party would receive a certain number of seats for a constituency based on (1) number of seats available multiplied by

64. votes received; (2) the product divided by total votes cast. Remainders were used to distribute the balance of seats.

65. To be eligible for national seats, a party had to win seats in at least five separate constituencies or have polled 5 percent of the national vote. Alliances between party lists were permitted.

66. *Ordynacja wyborcza do Sejmu i Senatu Rzeczypospolitej Polskiej* (Gdansk: Temida, 1993).

67. Data are taken from Janina Paradowska, Mariusz Janicki, and Radoslaw Markowski, "Krajobraz po wyborach: mapa mandatow," *Polityka* (October 2, 1993): 14–15.

68. Philippe C. Schmitter, "Still the Century of Corporatism?" in Schmitter and Gerhard Lembruch, eds., *Trends Toward Corporatist Intermediation* (London: Sage, 1979), p. 13.

69. Philippe C. Schmitter, "Reflections on Where the Theory of Neo-Corporatism Has Gone and Where the Praxis of Neo-Corporatism May Be Going," in Gerhard Lehmbruch and Phillipe C. Schmitter, eds., *Patterns of Corporatist Policy-Making* (London: Sage, 1982), p. 263.

70. This point is made by Jonathan A. Terra, "Policy Concertation, Interest Representation, and Democratic Consolidation in Postcommunist East Central Europe" (unpublished paper, Department of Political Science, Stanford University, 1996).

71. Jan Winiecki, "The Sources of Economic Success: Eliminating Barriers to Human Entrepreneurship—A Hayekian Lesson in Spontaneous Development," in Winiecki, *Five Years After June*, p. 41.

72. Jeffrey Sachs, "Western Financial Assistance and Russia's Reforms," in Shafiqul Islam and Michael Mandelbaum, eds., *Making Markets: Economic Transformation in Eastern Europe and the Post-Soviet States* (New York: Council on Foreign Relations Press, 1993), p. 146.

73. Jeffrey Sachs, *Poland's Jump to the Market Economy* (Cambridge, MA: MIT Press, 1994), p. 25.

74. Adam Przeworski, "Economic Reforms, Public Opinion, and Political Institutions: Poland in the Eastern European Perspective," in Luis Carlos Bresser Pereira, Jose Maria Maravall, and Adam Przeworski, eds., *Economic Reforms in New Democracies: A Social-Democratic Approach* (Cambridge: Cambridge University Press, 1993), p. 183.

75. Przeworski, "Economic Reforms, Public Opinion, and Political Institutions," p. 180.

76. Przeworski, "Economic Reforms, Public Opinion, and Political Institutions," p. 176.

77. Centrum Badania Opinii Publicznej, "Poles on the Relations between Poland and Russia and the Political Situation in Russia" (April 2000). www.cbos.pl

78. See www.transparency.de. Poland was tied with Belarus, El Salvador, Lithuania, and Malawi for forty-third place.

79. Centrum Badania Opinii Spolecznej, "Opinions on the Results of Poland's Integration with the European Union and the Process of Accession Negotiations" (July 2000). See www.cbos.

80. Zbigniew Brzezinski, *Out of Control: Global Turmoil on the Eve of the 21st Century* (New York: Collier Books, 1993), p. 216.

81. Seymour Martin Lipset, *Political Man: The Social Bases of Politics* (Baltimore, MD: Johns Hopkins University Press, 1981).

82. For an introduction to Smith's general theory, see Donald Winch, *Adam Smith's Politics: An Essay in Historiographic Revision* (Cambridge, England: Cambridge University Press, 1978).

83. Barrington Moore, *Social Origins of Dictatorship and Democracy* (Boston: Beacon Press, 1966), Ch. 7.

84. Piotr Sztompka, "The Intangibles and Imponderables of the Transition to Democracy," *Studies in Comparative Communism* 24, No. 3 (September 1991): 311.

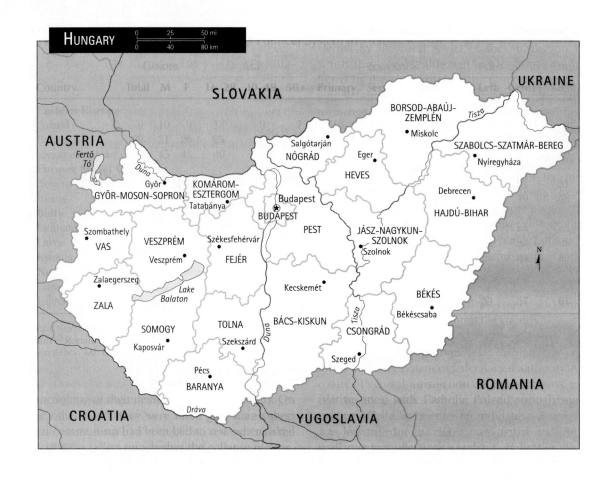

HUNGARY

0   25   50 mi
0   40   80 km

SLOVAKIA

UKRAINE

AUSTRIA

Fertö
Tó

Duna

Győr

GYŐR-MOSON-SOPRON

KOMÁROM-
ESZTERGOM

Tatabánya

BORSOD-ABAÚJ-
ZEMPLÉN

Tisza

Miskolc

Salgótarján

NÓGRÁD

Eger

SZABOLCS-SZATMÁR-BEREG

Nyíregyháza

HEVES

Debrecen

Budapest

BUDAPEST

HAJDÚ-BIHAR

Szombathely

VESZPRÉM

Székesfehérvár

PEST

JÁSZ-NAGYKUN-
SZOLNOK

VAS

Veszprém

FEJÉR

Szolnok

N

Zalaegerszeg

Lake
Balaton

Kecskemét

BÉKÉS

ZALA

Békéscsaba

Tisza

SOMOGY

TOLNA

Duna

BÁCS-KISKUN

CSONGRÁD

Kaposvár

Szekszárd

Szeged

Pécs

ROMANIA

BARANYA

CROATIA

Dráva

YUGOSLAVIA

CHAPTER 10

POLITICS IN HUNGARY

KATHLEEN MONTGOMERY

Country Bio-Hungary

POPULATION   10.1 Million

TERRITORY   Total Area: 93,030 kilometers (35,919 sq. miles)

YEAR OF INDEPENDENCE   1001

YEAR OF CURRENT CONSTITUTION   1949

CHIEF OF STATE   President Arpád Göncz

HEAD OF GOVERNMENT   Prime Minister Viktor Orbán

LANGUAGES(S)   Hungarian 98.2%, other 1.8%

RELIGION   Roman Catholic 67.5%, Calvinist 20%, Lutheran 5%, atheist and other 7.4%

ETHNIC COMPOSITION   90 percent Hungarian (Magyar); 4% Roma (Gypsy); 2.6% German; 2% Serb; 0.8% Slovak; 0.6% Romanian.

It has been said that the Hungarian democratic revolution of 1989–1990 took place without "breaking a single window pane."[1] It has also been said that Hungary lacked some of the drama and charismatic leadership found in the revolutions in neighboring states. There was no bloodshed; no dissident playwright emerged to lead the democratic forces, as in Czechoslovakia's velvet revolution; and no single group united society against communist rule, as did Poland's Solidarity. Rather, reformist elements within the communist leadership entered into negotiations with a relatively weak and fragmented opposition. Their compromises led to free, multiparty elections in which the communists lost power for the first time in over forty years.

This is not to say that the Hungarian transition was uneventful. There were moments of high drama—among them, when Foreign Minister Gyula Horn decided to allow East German citizens passage to the West via Hungarian borders. In little more than a month, 50,000 East Germans had voted with their feet, crossing Hungary to enter Austria. This triggered the fall of the Berlin Wall and provided a symbolic end to the Cold War. Hungary then had its place in Eastern Europe's *annus mirabilis.* But in a perhaps uniquely Hungarian fashion, change took place through negotiation and the continuation of a process of gradual, top-down reform that began in the 1960s.

This particular mode of transition raises interesting questions for social scientists. On the one hand, a high degree of elite bargaining might improve the chances of democratic consolidation by reducing conflict and managing social tensions. On the other hand, it might result in an incomplete transformation of the elite, making it possible for the old guard to simply return in new clothing. A history of reformism might also make it possible to avoid radical economic restructuring and thereby hinder the transition to a full-fledged market.[2] What can we say about Hungary a decade after the negotiated revolution?

Scholars generally divide the post-communist countries of Eastern Europe into two camps: a set of more or less consolidated and prosperous democracies, including Poland, Czech Republic, and Slovenia, and a group of semi-free and economically peripheral nations, such as Serbia, Albania, and Bulgaria. Hungary clearly belongs in the former category. It is the only East European country that has not seen a single post-communist government fall prior to scheduled elections, and that stability has paid off in the realm of economic policy. A 1999 IMF Report described Hungary as the miracle economy of the region.

The style of democracy that is developing in Hungary, however, differs from other countries in the consolidated democracies group. Where Poland, for example, is consolidating toward a pluralist and confrontational model of democracy, with frequent strikes and high levels of popular mobilization, post-communist politics in Hungary has been marked by "low levels of political mobilization, relatively high levels of elite consensus and bargaining, and a generally. . .pragmatic political discourse."[3] Whether key features of this model persist over time may depend on several current developments.

Current Policy Challenges

While most Western observers of Hungarian politics are preoccupied with monitoring the dual economic and political transition, Hungarian leaders insist that their country should no longer be viewed as an emerging democracy but rather as a political and economic system that is *converging* with the rest of Europe. The issues that preoccupy Hungarians are therefore much the same as the issues that concern citizens in other post-industrial democracies. Hungarians worry about how to balance economic growth while preserving social welfare and how to have political freedom without sacrificing public order. Television and print media carry frequent stories about single mothers, and the high divorce, suicide, and alcohol rates in the country. These same social problems are the focus of discussion and policy in other countries as well. The difference for Hungary, as a post-communist democracy, is that behind virtually every discrete policy debate looms the question of European integration.

Prior to the fall of communism, Hungary was heavily dependent on the Soviet Union and the other CMEA countries for trade. The Soviets bought Hungarian food products, computer technology, and buses. Hungary, in turn, was heavily dependent on the Soviet Union for the provision of important industrial and agricultural inputs (including about 95 percent of its natural gas, 90 percent of its oil and iron ore, and 75 percent of its fertilizers). With the dissolution of the Soviet bloc, Hungary turned westward, and integration into the European Union became an explicit goal. Hungary eagerly embraced NATO membership, hoping this would serve as an antechamber to EU admission. The country resolved several long-standing disputes with neighboring states and took important steps toward democratization. In order to enter the EU (and qualify for IMF loans), however, Hungary has also needed to demonstrate that it can reduce its expenditures for social welfare, which exceed those of the affluent Western welfare states.

From the 1960s on, Hungarian citizens had come to expect universal education, health care, pensions, and family benefits. The constitution guaranteed these as "citizens' rights." With privatization and a shift to market economics, these expensive programs have required a very high tax rate. Within Europe, only Swedish citizens pay higher taxes than Hungarians do. High taxes are unpopular, but so are reductions in social programs. Populist political parties have gained growing support by promising to lower taxes while preserving extensive social safety nets. Liberals and some Socialists have called for lower taxes along with an at least partial retrenchment of the welfare state. They have justified this as both an economic necessity and a precondition for integration with Europe.

In 1995, the Socialist-led government introduced an austerity economic reform package called the "Bokros package," named after the finance minister who launched it. The reform plan called for students in higher education to start paying tuition. It raised the retirement age to 62 (from 60 for men and 55 for women), eliminated the child welfare allowance that had been paid to all families with children under the age of 3, and introduced means testing. These measures sparked student protest, the formation of pensioner's groups, and even sit-ins at some local welfare offices. Angry women demanded that welfare be returned to the status of a "motherhood right." Rightist parties decried the negative effect that reductions in family allowances would have on the already low birthrate. And several features of the Bokros package could not be immediately implemented due to challenges in the Constitutional Court.

A more thoroughgoing pension reform still looms on the horizon (there will be nearly 80 pensioners for every 100 workers by the year 2016) and Hungary has yet to tackle the job of reforming its ailing health care system. Hungary spends more on healthcare than most OECD countries but has life expectancy rates well below the OECD average. Campaigns have been launched to improve public health, by among other things, restricting tobacco use in public places (alcohol and tobacco consumption in Hungary are above the OECD average). But no government has yet been willing to take the unpopular step of reducing expenditure, a move that would certainly lead to a loss of jobs in a sector where unemployment has been much lower than the nationwide average.

In order to join the European Union, Hungary must also show that it is able to comply with the *acquis communitaire* (the large body of EU legislation). (See Chapter 11.) The government must demonstrate, among other things, that it can maintain friendly relations with its neighbors, that it is reforming the agricultural sector and fighting corruption, that there will be a free and independent media, and that there will be an effort to rectify the problems of the gypsy minority.[4] Progress in several of these areas has been challenged recently by struggles over the distribution of power and the proper role of government in a democratic system.

In 1998, a rightist coalition of parties came to power, led by the *Alliance of Young Democrats—Hungarian Civic Party* (commonly referred to as *Fidesz*) and its controversial president, Viktor Orbán. The personal style of Orbán has been more authoritative and combative than the style of previous prime ministers. Though all three post-communist governments have been accused of overcentralizing power, the Fidesz government is unique in that it has managed to enact institutional changes that codify a concentration of power in the office of the prime minister. Egged on by smaller, more staunchly rightist parties, Fidesz has sought to further consolidate its power through attacks against media and cultural organizations associated with its leftist and liberal opponents. These moves directly contradict the laws and norms of the EU and provide new challenges for the consolidation of democracy.

Historical Development and Political Experience in Hungary

No country is free from its history. According to political economist Douglass North, history *matters* because it shapes the context in which modern political actors make choices and behave.[5] In order to understand democratic and market developments in Hungary today, we must first ask what Hungarian elites and citizens have learned from the past. What institutional choices were (and were not) available to Hungarian constitutional crafters? And, which historical issues are continuing to shape Hungarian political prejudices and expectations?

At face value, Hungarian history follows the pattern found in much of Western Europe. Hungary took part in all of the European developmental experiences—feudalism, the Renaissance, the Reformation and Counter-Reformation, and the Enlightenment—but it did so differently and less fully than most of the Western European states.[6] The twin revolutions of urbanization and industrialization that helped modernize the rest of Europe came late to Hungary, which remained a semifeudal and comparatively backward society into the twentieth century. A late and unsatisfying nation-building experience led to a potent brand of frustrated nationalism, while protracted foreign rule interrupted the gradual development of democratic institutions. Hungary was able to survive as a nation only through a process of adaptation and compromise.[7] Novelist Tibor Dery once noted that "the spirit of Hungary has been marked, more than anything, by its historical destiny. Hungary was always the weakest, always came off second best in conflicts with other peoples, in historic struggles, and its revolutions. . .That experience has imbued the Hungarian character with. . .sober realism."[8]

The Struggle for Independence: Defeat, Adaptation, and Compromise

Sometime around the end of the ninth century, approximately 250,000 Hungarians (*Magyar*) ended a long migration from the Ural Mountains region and came to rest in the Carpathian Basin, a large plain located at the crossroads of the European continent. Other nomadic groups, such as the Huns and Avars, had also swept into the unprotected region, but only the Magyars managed to establish a permanent presence. They did this through a process of adaptation and modernization that was imposed from above. After a crushing defeat in 955 at the hands of German forces, King István (Stephen) unified the Magyar tribes and began a process of sedentarization. He adopted Christianity and showed that he was willing to spread it by means of force. In 1001, his efforts were rewarded with a crown from the Pope. Hungary officially became a Christian nation, and Latin replaced Hungary's unique native language (*magyarul*) as the language of administration (see Box 10.1).

For the first 500 years after the coronation of St. Stephen, the leadership of Hungary passed through a variety of different families—some native, some foreign—as the boundaries of the nation shifted. Then, in 1526, Ottoman Turks defeated Hungarian troops in the battle at Mohács. This led to a three-way partition of Hungarian lands. Muslim Turks ruled the central portion of Hungary for the next 150 years; Western lands came under the control of Catholic and Counter-Reformationist Habsburgs; and the region known as Transylvania became a relatively autonomous Turkish vassal state.

Hungarian lands were finally reunited in 1699 when Hungary became part of the Austrian Habsburg Empire. The Habsburgs encouraged the spread of German speakers into Hungarian territory as a means of unifying the vast multinational Empire. That policy inadvertently helped to mobilize Hungarian national leaders around the issue of cultural preservation. The nationalist sentiment that swept Europe in the Napoleonic wars touched Hungary as well, and in 1848, Hungarian leaders demanded the

---

BOX 10.1   The Hungarian Magna Carta

Unlike France and China, attempts in Hungary to centralize absolutist power invariably failed. In 1222 (just seven years after the British Magna Carta), King András (Andrew) II issued a Golden Bull which stated the limits of the monarch's powers. It contained 31 articles that reaffirmed rights previously granted to nobility and clergymen and set forth new privileges. The charter compelled the king to convoke the diet (predecessor to the modern parliament) regularly, forbade him to imprison a noble without a trial, and denied him the right to tax the estates of nobility or the Church. Foreigners were prohibited from owning landed estates, and (after 1231) Jews and Muslims were prohibited from holding public office. Nobles no longer had to serve in the king's army abroad without pay. The king's county officials could be dismissed for misconduct, and their positions could no longer become hereditary. Finally, if the king or his successors violated the provisions of the Golden Bull, the nobles and bishops had the right to resist without being punished for treason. After 1222, all Hungarian kings were to swear to uphold the Golden Bull. With more auspicious geography, this might have led to the type of gradual democratic development that Britain experienced.

right of self-determination. Less than a year later, Lajos Kossuth proclaimed Hungary an independent republic. The Austrian Emperor responded by enlisting the support of some 200,000 Russian troops to crush the incipient revolution.

Eventually, a combination of internal and external pressures forced the Habsburgs to negotiate with Hungarian leaders. The product of these negotiations was the Great Compromise (*Kiegyezés*) of 1867. Hungary would become part of a dual monarchy ruled by the "Emperor of Austria and Apostolic King of Hungary." To some Hungarians, acceptance of this compromise seemed like treason; they wanted nothing short of full independence. Dualism, however, turned out the be a time of extraordinary creativity and advancement for Hungary. Budapest became one of the great capitals of Europe, and Hungary modernized in the areas of industry, commerce, communication, and education. Hungarian national leaders, who had gained administrative control over lands that included large national minority populations, launched intense programs of *Magyarization* in which the key to social and economic mobility was a willingness to adopt Hungarian culture, including the language. Large numbers of Germans and Jews assimilated (often voluntarily). In less than 120 years, the Hungarian population tripled to roughly 10 million. Hungary, however, still lacked the independent statehood it craved. Large Romanian, Slovak, Croatian, Ruthenian, and gypsy populations resisted assimilation, and at the outbreak of World War I, Magyars comprised less than half the population in their territory.

The problem of independence was finally resolved with the collapse of the Habsburg Empire at the end of World War I. Hungary became a Republic with Count Mihály Károlyi as its minister-president. Weakened by inflation, territorial losses, and refugee pressures, this fledgling democracy fell in 1919 to a Hungarian Soviet Republic headed by Béla Kun. The Kun regime, which lasted only 133 days, launched a radical nationalization program and violently repressed its perceived enemies. The Red Terror was followed by a White Terror, during which reactionary forces executed and imprisoned anyone suspected of involvement with Bolshevism, particularly Jews.

On November 14, 1919, Admiral Miklos Horthy—a representative of the old semifeudal ruling class—stepped in to fill the political void. He was elected as Regent of a nominal Hungarian Monarchy and remained so throughout the interwar period, even as prime ministers and governments changed. Horthy promised an era of stability, but external decisions made by more powerful countries would render that impossible. At the Trianon palace at Versailles, Hungarian representatives were forced to sign the *Trianon Treaty*, a peace agreement in which Hungary would retain only a third of its original territory. Seven out of every twenty Hungarians—a total of 3.3 million people—were placed under foreign rule, and Hungary was left to nurse irredentist claims against its neighbors.

Trianon amounted to a second partition in the minds of many Hungarians and came to be associated in the popular consciousness with national humiliation and continued domination by foreign powers. This, coupled with the negative experience of Bolshevism during the Kun regime, elevated the appeal of rightist solutions. From 1921 to 1931, a Christian national movement ruled the country with the support of rural landowners and the Catholic Church, whose members constituted two-thirds of the post-Trianon population. This government passed anti-Semitic legislation to appease populists and the rural peasantry but rarely enforced these laws.

The global depression at the end of the decade undermined the agrarian base of the moderate-conservative regime, and that paved the way for the radical right-wing government of Gyula Gömbös, an anti-Semite and populist, whom critics referred to as "Gömbölini," after the Italian dictator Mussolini.[9] Gömbös moved Hungary closer to the German Third Reich and allowed a fascist group, the Arrow Cross, to gain strength. In 1939, the Arrow Cross became the second largest party in parliament.

Territorial revisionism naturally led Hungary to enter World War II on the side of the Axis Powers. At first, the strategy paid dividends. Hungary assisted in the dismemberment of Czechoslovakia and Yugoslavia and received as compensation prized territory in Northern Transylvania (located in modern Romania) and the Vojvodina region of

Serbia. By the summer of 1941, Hungary had regained half the territory it had lost at Trianon and was allied with the Axis forces in the war against the Soviet Union. It would later declare war on the United States. Hungary, however, proved an unreliable ally. In the final year of the war, Horthy attempted to withdraw Hungary from the Axis, but Hitler would not allow it. In March of 1944, German forces occupied Hungary.[10]

The Soviets liberated Hungary later that year and, in 1945, allowed the first free election in Hungarian history. The sizable peasant and small landholder interests gave the Independent Smallholders' Party an outright majority of seats in the National Assembly. This new rightist government took power in the shadow of Soviet tanks and was shortly forced to sign a peace accord that reasserted Trianon borders. Meanwhile the Communist Party, which held only 76 out of 415 seats in the Assembly, was able to secure changes in the electoral rules that helped it to win a plurality (22 percent) in 1947. The Communists, with Soviet support, used this position to purge political enemies and take control of the state.

By 1949, Hungary had become a political and economic satellite of the Soviet Union (see Figure 10.1). Its political system reflected the Soviet requirement of Communist Party monopoly on power, a ban on "factions," and democratic centralism. Its economy was transformed along the Stalinist model of central planning and agriculture was largely collectivized. Hungary joined the Council for Mutual Economic Assistance (CMEA) where trade relations heavily favored the Soviet Union, and foreign policy was tied to Soviet interests through the Warsaw Pact. Mátyás Rákosi, the Moscow-trained Party First Secretary, imposed the Soviet system through coercion, widespread terror, and massive political "reeducation" programs.

Through it all, Hungarian national aspirations persisted. The death of Stalin and the process of de-Stalinization in the region led Hungary to test the boundaries of Soviet tolerance for "independent roads." The challenge emanated from the top of the Hungarian political system and was led by the reformist prime minister, Imre Nagy. It began as a fairly conservative effort to "nationalize" communism, but soon thousands of students became involved, and their demands became increasingly radical. In 1956 they called for multiparty elections and the immediate withdrawal of Soviet troops from Hungarian soil. The Soviet Union's unwillingness to discuss national roads to socialism forced Nagy toward increasingly radical steps, including withdrawal from the Warsaw Pact.

The Soviet response was swift and brutal. On November 3, 1956—for the second time in little more than a century—Russian forces invaded Hungary to crush a revolution. The Soviets installed János Kádár as General Secretary of the Hungarian Socialist Workers' Party. Under their orders, he lured Imre Nagy from safety in the Yugoslav Embassy with promises of immunity, then had him summarily tried, executed, and buried in an unmarked grave. A hastily recruited internal police force rounded up insurgents and suspected sympathizers. An estimated 25,000 were imprisoned, nearly 230 were executed, and some 200,000 fled the country.

The failed revolutions of 1848 and 1956 became fused in the Hungarian national consciousness and set the stage for another major instance of Hungarian adaptation and compromise that came to be known as *Kádárism* or *goulash communism*. At first it seemed that Kádár would use traditional methods of coercion to reassert Soviet hegemony. Over time, however, he proved far more pragmatic. He realized that the way to maintain control in Hungary was to provide stability and prosperity. He did this by essentially negotiating a dual pact between the Hungarian Communist Party—officially known as the *Hungarian Socialist Workers Party* (*HSWP*)—and the Soviets, on the one hand, and the Party and Hungarian society, on the other. Kádár offered Moscow a Hungary that would not openly challenge Soviet domination. In return he sought limited freedom to introduce nationally tailored economic and social reforms.

The cornerstone of this unique Hungarian form of communism was an economic reform package launched in 1968 called the *New Economic Mechanism* (*NEM*) which introduced various market elements to an otherwise centrally planned economy. Like the earlier *kiegyezés*, this compromise did not fulfill Hungary's dreams of full independence,

FIGURE 10.1   Major Hungarian Political Events Since World War II

Year	Event
1948	Hungary becomes a satellite of the Soviet Union. Rákosi holds positions as Communist Party Secretary and Prime Minister.
1953	Imre Nagy becomes Prime Minister.
1956	Érnö Gerö becomes Party Secretary. Hungarian Uprising János Kádár installed as Party Secretary.
1968	New Economic Mechanism (NEM) introduced.
1985	Forty independent candidates elected in parliamentary elections.
1987	Károly Grósz becomes Prime Minister; HDF formed.
1988	Kádár is ousted; Károly Grósz becomes Party Secretary.
1989	Miklós Németh becomes Prime Minister; AFD and Fidesz form. Roundtable talks announced.
1990	József Antall selected as Prime Minister after free elections.
1993	Péter Boross becomes Prime Minister.
1994	Gyula Horn selected as Prime Minister after election.
1998	Fidesz wins largest number of seats in Assembly and forms right-wing coalition. Viktor Orbán selected as Prime Minister. HSP enters opposition with 134 seats.

but it did allow Hungarians to develop a better standard of living than most of their communist neighbors. With goulash communism Hungary became jokingly known as the "happiest barracks" in Eastern Europe.

The NEM, however, was never fully implemented. It lurched forward and back in measures primarily designed to meet the party's political needs, and, in the end, the promise of better material conditions was purchased through foreign borrowing rather than economic growth.[11] By the early 1980s, the country had accrued some $20 billion in external debt, growth had stagnated, and social spending as a percent of GDP had well exceeded the OECD average. As goulash communism began to fall noticeably short of its promises, the legitimacy of Kádár's rule increasingly relied on the perception that he was the best guarantor of protection against arbitrary Soviet intervention.

The rise to power of Mikhail Gorbachev in the Soviet Union—and his calls for *perestroika* and *glasnost* at home—revealed the bankruptcy of the Kádárist pact. When it became clear that the Soviet Union would no longer enforce the Brezhnev Doctrine of military intervention, Kádár went from being Hungary's liberator to the primary obstacle to freer politics.[12] This loss of legitimacy provided space in which fledgling opposition groups and reformist elements within the Party could begin a process of negotiation.[13]

Hungary's Negotiated Revolution

There were several turning points or critical moments in this process. In 1985, various strands of the anti-communist opposition met together for the first time. During that same year, some forty independent candidates were elected to the parliament. These deputies fought for reforms that would transform the legislature into more than a mere rubber-stamp for Communist Party decisions. In 1987, unofficial publications (*samizdat*) became increasingly bold in calling for political pluralism, freedom of the press, and radical economic reforms. That same year, the populist wing of the opposition defied the official ban on factions and met in the village of Lakitelek to form the *Hungarian Democratic Forum* (HDF). This group did not initially see itself as a po-

litical party or a direct challenge to the HSWP. In fact, reformist members of the Communist Party, such as Imre Pozsgay, attended the gathering.

The HSWP was initially divided over the appropriate response to this burgeoning pluralism. In April of 1988, four prominent reformist intellectuals were expelled from the Party. Hardliners called for a Special Party Conference in May to regain control over events in the nation. At the end of that conference, however, it was Kádár who got ousted from power. He was replaced by the apparently more reform-minded Károly Grósz. With this, the Party hoped to manage the crisis by making reform concessions. This process of top-down reform continued throughout the transition, pressed forward by growing social pluralism.

In the autumn of 1988, the HDF held a second meeting. At around the same time, the "Network of Free Initiatives," a coordinating center for a number of dissident opposition movements, established a party called the *Alliance of Free Democrats* (AFD). Discussion clubs in the Budapest law and economics faculties formed a party of Young Democrats (commonly known by its Hungarian acronym Fidesz). Several parties with roots in the pre-communist period—notably the *Independent Smallholders' Party* (ISP) and the *Christian Democratic People's Party* (CDPP)—also reestablished themselves.

Reform elements of the party responded by trying to remain out in front of the growing popular demands. In January of 1989, Imre Pozsgay called for the exhumation and identification of the remains of Imre Nagy and launched an official reevaluation of the previous 40 years of history. The events of 1956 would no longer be referred to as a "counter-revolution" but an "uprising" against oligarchic rule, and members of the Committee for Historical Justice would be allowed to organize a ceremonial reburial of Imre Nagy (see Box 10.2).

Less than one month later, the HSWP backed its symbolism with a formal acknowledgment that Hungary would become a multiparty democracy. It also agreed to enter power-sharing negotiations with representatives from the main social organizations (for example, official Trade Unions) and the eight most important opposition groups. These negotia-

---

Box 10.2   The Struggle for Independence: 1848, 1956, and 1989

Timothy Garton Ash, a Western journalist on hand at the ceremony to rebury Imre Nagy, described the following scene:

"Heroes' Square, 16 June, 1989. The great neo-classical columns are wrapped in black cloth. From the colonnades hang huge red, white, and green national flags, but each with a hole in the middle, a reminder of how the insurgents of 1956 cut out the hammer and sickle from their flags. Ceremonial flames burn beside the six coffins arrayed on the steps of the temple-like Gallery of Art: five named coffins for Imre Nagy and his closest associates, the sixth, a symbolic coffin of the Unknown Insurgent. . .the crowd, perhaps some 200,000 strong, is still quiet, subdued, when the raven-haired

Viktor Orbán of the Young Democrats [takes the stand shouting]: "Citizens! Forty years ago, although starting from Russian occupation and communist dictatorship, the Hungarian nation just once had a chance, and the strength and courage, to realize the aims of 1848. . .we can put an end to the communist dictatorship; if we are determined enough we can force the Party to submit itself to free elections; and if we do not lose sight of the ideals of 1956, then we will be able to elect a government that will start immediate negotiations for the swift withdrawal of Russian Troops."

Source: Timothy Garton Ash, *The Magic Lantern* (New York: Random House, 1990).

---

tions were called *Roundtable Talks*, following the Polish example. They began on June 13, 1989, and ended in mid-September with an agreement to hold free multiparty elections, revise the Constitution, and establish a new electoral law.

As talks moved toward the announcement of free elections, the reform wing of the party dissolved the HSWP and founded a new party without the word "Workers" in its title. Imre Pozsgay became the leader of this new *Hungarian Socialist Party (HSP)*. During the campaign, he tried to distance the reconstituted party from the mistakes of the past, while retaining the positive reformist legacy. That strategy failed, and the 1990 elections made the Hungarian Democratic Forum the largest party in the new democratic parliament. The HDF, in turn, formed a center-right coalition with two smaller parties and set about the enormous task of transforming Hungary into a working democracy and market economy.

The new coalition proved unable to address the economic crisis it had inherited, however; and by 1993, the government was near collapse. The populist wing of the HDF had been expelled from the party's parliamentary benches; a minor coalition partner, the Smallholders, had split in two; and the

popular Prime Minister, József Antall, had died of cancer. The government nevertheless managed to survive until regularly scheduled elections in 1994 when voters, nostalgic for the material security of goulash communism, gave the reformed Hungarian Socialist Party (HSP) a landslide victory.

Despite holding a majority of seats in the Assembly, the HSP chose to enter a coalition with its former enemy, the Alliance of Free Democrats. Together, the Socialists and the Free Democrats introduced a shock therapy style economic reform package that had nearly immediate results. Hungary went from a growth rate in 1991 of −11 percent to positive growth in the first year of the reforms.

The HSP entered the 1998 elections confident voters would reward it with another electoral victory. The Alliance of Young Democrats—Civic Party (Fidesz—HCP), however, had meanwhile moved to the right of the ideological spectrum. It promised to continue economic reform but with less social pain. It also promised to more vigorously protect Hungary's cultural inheritance from (among other things) declining birthrates, excessive foreign influence in the economy, and an over-zealous retrenchment of the welfare state.

In May of 1998, voters rewarded Fidesz with the largest number of seats in the Assembly. Lacking a majority, the party formed a coalition with the more populist Independent Smallholders' Party and a small group of HDF members, many of whom had been jointly sponsored by Fidesz. Viktor Orbán assumed the role of prime minister.

Contradictory Lessons of Hungarian History

The free multiparty elections of 1990 marked the end of one period of political development in Hungary and inaugurated a new era of independence and democracy, but the slate of history was not wiped clean with a single stroke. Critical events— the failed revolutions, Dualism, Trianon, communist takeover, and negotiated revolution—continue to shape the path of Hungarian development. The precise contours of that path, however, depend on how Hungarians today interpret the lessons of their history and adapt those lessons to the uncertainties of a transitional society.

Years of partition and foreign domination have taught Hungarians that their nation is weak when it stands alone. One policy implication is that Hungary should seek protection within the economic and security organizations of the West. According to 1998 data, 68 percent of Hungarians favor NATO membership and 86 percent want their country to join the European Union (EU). Most notably, 61 percent say they believe that EU membership will contribute to the nation's *political* stability.[14]

Failed revolutions have taught leaders to be pragmatic and citizens not to challenge authority directly. The result is that problems are often addressed through negotiation at the elite level. Continuing this pattern, the post-communist political parties have engaged in a number of informal pacts and have built imperatives for negotiation into their formal institutions, often forging agreements across government and opposition lines.

Other lessons, of course, may be drawn from the same historical facts. Many rightist voters and politicians take a romantic view of Hungary's historical struggles. They conclude that forces within and outside the country threaten the survival of the Hungarian nation. This "elegaic romanticism"[15]

vies against Dery's "sober realism" and the drive for European integration, and recently it seems to have gained strength. The right-wing populist *Hungarian Justice and Life Party (HJLP)* managed to cross the threshold for parliamentary representation for the first time in 1998, espousing, among other things, that Hungary should maintain independence from the European Union and international financial institutions. This is an extreme position, but all of the rightist parties emphasize the importance of cultural preservation to one degree or another. Whether romantic nationalism or pragmatism will come to dominate Hungarian politics depends on the social impact of transition and the degree to which parties find it expedient to mobilize popular dissatisfaction.

Social Forces in Transition

The democratic and market revolution of 1989 constitutes one of the major events in Hungarian history, but it was not (nor was it intended to be) a social revolution, like the communist takeover of 1949 that forced Hungary through a rapid process of industrialization and modernization. Postcommunist Hungary therefore continues to reflect many of the basic demographic features established by the communist regime by the 1960s. Hungary has an aging population, caused by declining birthrates and improved life expectancy. Since the 1960s, the number of professional and skilled workers has been increasing and the number of agricultural workers declining. Today, only about 7 percent of Hungarians are employed in agriculture, and only about 3 percent can be categorized as self-employed peasants. Hungary also has a highly educated population with a high level of female workforce participation and extensive social welfare commitments. These features have not changed in any substantial way since the fall of communism. In spite of efforts to reduce public expenditures for social welfare, Hungarians can still expect to receive subsidized health care, state pensions, and family benefits. Hungarians are also continuing the patterns of work and leisure established under goulash communism. Hungarian men typically work several jobs to better the material welfare of their families;

women continue to experience an exhausting dual burden, engaging in paid employment as well as hours of unpaid labor in the home.

More dramatic social change has come in the area of the economy. The collapse of the centrally planned economy has led to a rapid expansion in private employment, with all that entails. There have been winners and losers in this transition. Traditionally marginalized groups, such as gypsies, are falling further behind, and integration in Western markets helps some regions of the country while pushing others to the periphery.

Social Structure and Income Inequality

The state-socialist regime was dedicated to the creation of an egalitarian society. Under the surface, however, social class divisions continued to be a potent source of resentment. The top members of the party-state apparatus—the *nomenklatura*—had access to greater privileges than ordinary citizens had.[16] Goulash communism offset this to some extent by making social welfare benefits universal and offering a wide array of citizens the opportunity to improve their living conditions through participa-

tion in the unofficial or "second" economy. That promoted the development of a middle class.

Since transition, there is evidence that this middle stratum has expanded and moved into the private sector. There has been dramatic growth in the number of individuals who claim to be entrepreneurs, and the largest growth in employment has come from small to middle-sized private enterprises. The percent of the population categorized as self-employed merchants and artisans, a category almost eliminated (at least officially) during the communist era, has returned to 1949 levels. All of this is encouraging, given the importance of a relatively autonomous middle class for the development of stable parliamentary democracy.

On the downside, class differences hidden during the communist regime have come into the open and grown wide.[17] The GINI coefficients presented in Figure 10.2 show that, while income disparities decreased from the early seventies through the last years of Kádárism, they have expanded steadily since the transition. According to one study, net household income has declined among the poorest groups all the way up through the middle class; only the top 20 percent have experienced gains.[18]

FIGURE 10.2   Distribution of Household Income

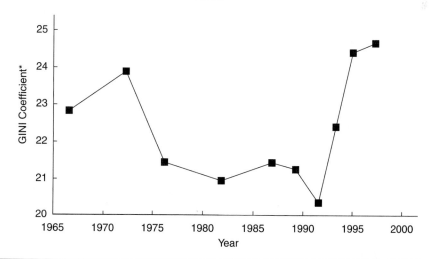

*GINI coefficient measures social inequality on a scale of 0–100, where 0 = perfect equality and 100 = perfect inequality.
Source: UN/WIDER-UNDP World Income Inequality Database.

Regional Disparities

The capital city, Budapest, shows more evidence of the benefits of marketization than the provincial cities and towns. With nearly 20 percent of the nation's inhabitants, Budapest forms an administrative, economic, and cultural center. Approximately half of all foreign trade comes to Budapest, and the city is Hungary's largest employer. According to data compiled by the Hungarian Central Statistical Office in 1998, Budapest has the highest per capita GDP of any county in the nation. The simple visual difference between Budapest and the provinces is striking. When you leave the capital, Western billboards disappear and the trendy pubs and American-style restaurants are replaced by traditional *sörözők* (beer bars).

The country as a whole is increasingly divided between a Western region, that has prospered in transition due to its proximity to natural resources and Western markets, and a stagnant industrial rust belt in the North and East. The agricultural region in the central plains has suffered from a loss of government subsidies and a decline in agricultural production, but without question the most economically depressed areas are the industrial cities in the northeastern part of the country. The counties of Nógrád, Szabolcs, and Borsod (see the map at the beginning of the chapter) have the lowest per capita GDP in the country. Steel cities, such as Ózd near the Slovakian border, were built by the communist regime to produce a single major industrial product. The loss of state subsidies with the fall of communism has forced the inefficient and bloated industries in these cities to shut down. Unemployment in some cases has risen to 40 and 50 percent. The northeastern cities also face the worst pollution and crime problems in the country and have the largest concentration of gypsies, many of whom are illiterate and poor.

Ethnic Minorities

The communist regime officially prohibited expressions of nationalism and anti-Semitism. This should have been easy to enforce, since Magyars form the overwhelming majority of the population. Less than 1 percent of the current population is Jewish, while Germans, Slovaks, Ruthenians, Serbs, Croats, and others (including gypsies or *Roma*) account for approximately 3.5 percent. Hungary lost its minority nations in the Treaty of Trianon, and the postwar Jewish and Roma populations are very small due to the genocide committed against them during World War II.[19] Approximately 200,000 Hungarian Jews and 30 percent of the prewar gypsy population were murdered in the Holocaust (what the Roma refer to as the *Devouring*).[20]

The roots of anti-Semitic and anti-gypsy sentiments run very deep, however. Roma have always existed outside the dominant culture. Historically, they were nomadic and worked in nonagrarian trades (blacksmiths, musicians, palm readers, and contract miners). The communist regime forced them to settle in housing projects built by the State. Populists saw this as special treatment and claimed that gypsies were becoming affluent through crime, misuse of state resources, and "Jew work" (work that makes money without manual labor).

Jews, for their part, were largely assimilated by the outbreak of World War II. Originally recruited to Hungarian cities to carry out the work of modernization, they eventually formed the core of an affluent, urban middle class. This made them ready targets for frustration.

Populist parties have resurrected those resentments in the post-communist period to paint their liberal and Socialist opponents as somehow less Hungarian. They have accused the liberal parties, which are primarily based in Budapest, of being "too Jewish." Anti-Semitism is sometimes couched in attacks on intellectuals and Bolsheviks.

At the same time, there has been a rise in violence against Roma and dark skinned foreigners. Racist violence takes place on the fringes of society, but its ideological partner, radical populism, has found some mainstream expressions. The so-called "mother" of the skinhead movement, Izabella Király, was a member of parliament from 1990 to 1994. The Hungarian Justice and Life Party contains members with open ties to skinhead organizations (what they euphemistically refer to as "short-haired young men with strong national feelings").

Growing income inequalities may exacerbate resentments toward the small Jewish and Roma minorities. Less-educated groups who are marginalized by the market transition look for someone to blame. Jews have historically filled that role. Growing poverty and unemployment among Roma are leading to higher crime rates within that population. That, in turn, heightens the perception among the majority population that Roma are dangerous and alien. The success of the populist right in the 1998 elections may be a testament to the enduring appeal of scapegoat politics, especially in times of growing economic inequality and uncertainty.

Women in Transition

Women were supposed to be emancipated under communism through their mass participation in the paid labor force, a feat made possible by state subsidized day care, liberal abortion laws, free education, paid leaves to care for sick children, and the guarantee of a job after maternity leave. The reality of women's lives stood in stark contrast to the promise, however. Men remained the primary breadwinners in most two-parent households; women were concentrated in lower-pay, lower-prestige jobs and continued to do much of the cooking, shopping, cleaning, and childcare often without the benefit of household conveniences.[21] This dual burden became triple with the additional responsibility of all socialist citizens to engage in political activity.

Since transition, there has been a widely noted retraditionalization of social values, including attitudes regarding the proper role of women in society.[22] This pattern, found throughout post-communist Eastern Europe, reflects both a resurgent nationalism and a backlash against communist policies of directive emancipation, which reduced women's equality to mandatory participation in the paid labor force. Implementation of the Bokros program has only heightened the appeal of a retreat to domesticity for many women. The rapid and dramatic retrenchment of social welfare programs has left families vulnerable and reinforced the dual burden for women. Few families can afford to lose female wages, so women continue to participate in paid labor at very high rates, but they now have even less support for this.

The New Democratic Structures

New democratic institutions have been put in place to ensure democratic representation. It is the task of these new institutions to accommodate the interests of groups that have been disadvantaged by the transition. New institutions must be structured in such a way that democratic procedures will be viewed as fair and legitimate. They must be representative but at the same time they must be able to efficiently resolve conflicts through public policy. After nearly a decade, what can we say about the design and performance of Hungary's democratic institutions?

As earlier sections of this chapter have already suggested, the institutions of Hungary's post-communist democracy developed through a process of negotiation epitomized by (but not limited to) Roundtable Talks. At one level, this process reflected the efforts of transitional actors to secure the most advantageous place possible in the new democratic landscape. It must also be seen as manifestation of Hungary's broader historical orientation toward elite level compromise. The entire institutional negotiation phase—though hardly conflict free—was marked by a widespread commitment by the major actors to reach agreement. Often this resulted in compromises that maintained the balance of power among actors and created imperatives for future cooperation.

Among the most important of these bargains was an agreement to set aside a certain number of "laws of constitutional force," laws that would require a special majority (two thirds of the full chamber) for passage. These laws included everything from the media and state budget to new parliamentary rules (Standing Orders) and adoption of a revised constitution. The Socialists, fearing that they would fail to gain two thirds of the legislature in democratic elections, and the opposition groups, who believed they would lose the election, in turn agreed to establish a strong and independent Constitutional Court. This court would be able to counterbalance a powerful cabinet in a unicameral parliamentary system, a system that had been established through another series of interparty agreements.

These institutions—the strong court, two-thirds laws, and cabinet government (as opposed to a presidential or semi-presidential system)—created further incentives for negotiation after the 1990 election. That election failed to produce a majority cabinet. The Hungarian Democratic Forum (HDF) chose to form a coalition with two minor parties, leaving the second largest party, the Alliance of Free Democrats (AFD), in opposition. In order to govern under these circumstances, the HDF and the AFD-led opposition negotiated a *Little Pact*. The AFD agreed to accept a *constructive vote of non-confidence*, after the German model. This meant that a government would only fall if a majority of the Assembly could agree on a replacement. In return, the HDF agreed that the new president would be AFD member, Árpád Göncz.[23] The parties also agreed to allocate chamber representation in such a way that opposition members would hold key committee chairmanships and chamber leadership positions. The parties also tacitly agreed to avoid recurrent legislative stalemate on two-thirds laws.

Since the HDF-led coalition barely held 50 percent of the seats in the Assembly, it was never able to achieve the necessary two-thirds support for new Standing Orders; and it did not attempt to ratify a fully revised constitution. The two-thirds problem should have become moot in 1994 when the victorious Socialist Party invited the Alliance of Free Democrats to form an oversized coalition. Together, the two governing parties had enough votes to clear the two-thirds hurdle for achieving constitutional and rules revisions. Following the norm of consensus, however, the government did not press its advantage. It granted the opposition *overrepresentation* on key constitutional and parliamentary rules drafting committees. The government even went so far as to make a written offer to the opposition, which essentially stated: "Although we are entitled to amend the constitution with our 2/3 majority, we believe that the opposition should be fully involved in the drafting of the new constitution. Therefore we will only amend the constitution if we can achieve either a 4/5 majority or the support of all parties minus one."[24]

In the end, this high threshold could never be achieved. The Socialists wanted language that would strengthen the institutional representation of peak associations like Trade Unions; the Democratic Forum wanted to include references to Hungarian minorities in neighboring states. Both parties withdrew their support from the draft constitution when it became clear that a final document would not include their preferred wording, and so Hungary continues to operate with the 1949 Soviet-inspired constitution that was modified by the last communist parliament in preparation for the transition to multiparty democracy.[25] In a sense, this is another instance of compromise politics, since the end result was to continue with a constitution that reflects no party's ideal but provides a stable solution for all. The government elected in 1998 lacks a two-thirds majority, so it has tabled the matter, achieving constitutional changes instead through court challenges and legislative initiative.

The Hungarian constitution today identifies parliament as the leading decision-making body in the country and endows it with the power to elect both the prime minister *and* the president of the republic. It also outlines a powerful and independent court, a system of regional governance, and an Ombudsman's Office. While negotiation and pact-making continue to shape Hungarian politics, those features have become firmly entrenched in the post-communist system.

The Legislature

A National Assembly existed under communist rule but, in keeping with the basic Soviet party-state model, it was not a genuine working legislature. Its deputies were elected directly and did not give up their original occupations. At an ideological level, this was a way of ensuring the representation of workers and those with direct knowledge about local matters. At a practical level, it was made possible by short and infrequent legislative sessions (assembling every three to four years for no more than a few days). Plenary sessions did little more than ratify policy decisions made in the executive bodies of the party and state, the Politburo and Presidential Council.

Since the transition, the Hungarian National Assembly (Országgyülés) has become a full-time legislature and the central institution of government (see Figure 10.3). It passes legislation, debates policy issues, and elects the prime minister and the president. The ornate parliament building sits on the left bank of the Danube River in Budapest. It seats 386 members. Members of parliament (MPs) serve a four-year term unless the parliament is dissolved early.

The need for sweeping legislative changes during the transition elevated the significance of the assembly's legislative function. Legislators spend more time working on legislation than any other area of parliamentary work, including government oversight and constituency service. In the first parliament alone, over three hundred laws were enacted.[26] Many of these were hastily prepared and required significant modification, leading observers to criticize the parliament as a "law factory." Still, the ability of this fledgling democratic legislature to so quickly establish a legal framework for the political and economic transition stands as an impressive accomplishment.

In addition to passing legislation, the National Assembly also serves as a forum for public debate.

The Standing Orders stipulate that parties may comment on a given piece of legislation (within a strict time frame) and MPs may offer speeches before the session's work begins. These speeches rarely pertain to any item on the agenda, but because they are televised, they have become one of the most lively—if least productive—activities in parliament.

The Hungarian public, unused to open debate and conflict, has tended to assess the "talking function" of the legislature negatively. They see half-empty plenary sessions (a normal feature of many parliaments) and politicians making personal attacks on their rivals. This makes democracy appear inefficient and unwieldy. It will take some time before citizens become comfortable with the procedures (and even sometimes the follies) of democratic governance.

During Roundtable Negotiations, the Assembly's role in overseeing and scrutinizing the activities of the government was seen as one of the most important institutional features for a new democratic legislature. As a result, there are several formal oversight instruments in the National Assembly, including three types of parliamentary questions, political debate, and investigative committees. Though MPs (particularly those in opposition benches) make wide use of these tools, the oversight function

FIGURE 10.3 The Structure of Hungary's Unitary Government

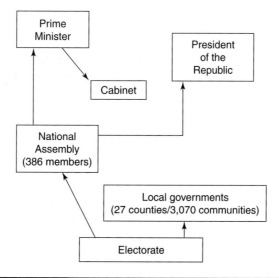

of the Hungarian legislature has been relatively weak. Votes of confidence cannot be readily used as tools of oversight, due to the "constructive" requirement. The extraordinary volume of legislation and decrees reduces the ability of members to engage in careful scrutiny. Finally, pacts between government and opposition in 1990-1994 and 1994-1998 emphasized cooperation across government and opposition benches. This weakened the ability of the parliament to control government.

The norm of cooperation "across the benches" seems to be breaking down somewhat in the post-1998 parliament. Party discipline in the chamber has increased over the post-communist period. This is leading to a more adversarial mode of interaction. Furthermore the leading party in government, Fidesz, believes that parliamentary politics will be improved by the clarification of party programs into sharp left-right alternatives and a clear demarcation between government and opposition. Fidesz refused, for example, to cede the chairmanship of Committee on EU Affairs to the opposition, even though it had held that position while in opposition in 1994-1998. The party's president, the current Prime Minister Viktor Orbán, had even chaired that committee. The Fidesz government also recently changed the parliamentary meeting schedule from "weekly" to "every third week." This curtails the opportunities for opposition parties to criticize the government and advertise their positions. The tendency of Fidesz to press its procedural advantages breaks from the pattern of bargaining that has characterized post-communist politics within the Assembly.

Prime Minister

Nowhere is this more apparent than in the office of the prime minister. Orbán changed the government's structure by creating the Office of the Prime Minister. The head of this office holds ministerial rank and enjoys substantial powers. Opposition parties immediately criticized the enlargement of prime ministerial powers the new office would entail; however, the change is consistent with the language and the spirit of the constitution, which places the lion's share of policymaking control in the hands of the prime minister. The prime minister

is elected by the National Assembly and thus represents a majority of parliament while directing the executive branch of government.

The constructive vote of non-confidence also strengthens the preeminence of the prime minister. As in Germany, the prime minister does not depend on maintaining a majority on all of his legislative proposals to remain in power. This certainly augmented Hungary's governmental stability during transition. When József Antall died in December of 1993, his replacement, Péter Boross, inherited a mere two-vote majority in the Assembly. On one occasion Boross was actually booed from the podium from which he was addressing the chamber, but due to the constructive vote of non-confidence, the fragile government did not fall. Hungary became the only Eastern European country to finish its first full parliamentary cycle without having to call early elections.

On the downside, the constructive vote reduces the government's ability to push through its policy agenda. Members of the governing majority may withdraw their support for government policies without the threat that the government will fall. Hence, party leaders complain about the difficulty of getting members to show up for important votes, and the government cannot always ensure a majority for its proposals.

The Cabinet

According to the constitution, the prime minister selects his cabinet, which is formally called the Council of Ministers, and decides the number of ministers to include. (There is also an informal cabinet that refers to a smaller working body of ministers.) The prime minister has formal discretion to choose individuals to serve in the Council of Ministers. Motions of no confidence may only be raised against the government as a whole and not against individual ministers.

Practically speaking, cabinet formation is another element of interparty negotiation and pact making in Hungary's multi-party democracy. In order to get the AFD to agree to enter the coalition in 1994, the Socialist Party was forced to accept AFD members in key ministries (for example, Gábor Kuncze as Minister of the Interior) and to join the

AFD in implementing an economic stabilization program. More recently, Fidesz was forced to make the controversial leader of its minor coalition partner, Smallholders president József Torgyán, Minister of Agriculture. It was also forced to vastly expand the jurisdiction of that ministry and grant the Smallholders' Party the right to nominate the next Hungarian president.

Partly as a consequence of this, prime ministers often propose legislation and issue decrees without the consultation or approval of the cabinet. Socialist Prime Minister Gyula Horn was accused of excluding his coalition partners from policymaking when he issued a response to the Constitutional Court on a major economic ruling without even showing it to AFD ministers. The practice of excluding ministers has become considerably easier during Orbán's watch, since the Office of the Prime Minister has desks that mirror each ministry's jursidiction. This strengthens the power of the prime minister vis-à-vis the cabinet to such an extent that observers now compare the Hungarian system to German "chancellor democracy." Orbán also expanded his power by filling about half of his cabinet with ministers who have no real loyalty to or background in the governing parties. Most of his cabinet is personally loyal to him.

The power of the prime minister in a multiparty cabinet, however, has important limitations. The two-thirds laws, in particular, can exaggerate the influence of minor coalition parties in government policies. In a recent example, the Smallholders' Party threatened to withdraw support for the 2000 budget unless the share for agriculture was increased. Over the protest of the Finance Ministry, agriculture's share of the budget was ultimately doubled over the figure originally proposed.

President

According to the constitution, "The head of state of Hungary shall be the President of the Republic, who shall represent the unity of the nation and safeguard the democratic functioning of the state organization."[27] The president, who is elected by parliament to serve a five-year term, must relinquish any other state, social, or political office. Many presidential powers are strictly ceremonial: the president confers titles and medals, appoints the rectors of universities, promotes generals, receives ambassadors, and enters into international agreements on behalf of Hungary. These appointments and signatures are made on the advice of ministers and with the consent of the Assembly.

The president also possesses several potentially substantive powers, including the right to sit in on parliamentary sessions, initiate legislative proposals and plebiscites, and refer laws to the Constitutional Court. President Árpád Göncz, elected in 1990 and reelected in 1995, has made wide use of his right to introduce legislation and to refer legislation to the Constitutional Court. Most of the legislation adopted in the Assembly emanates from the government, so the president has little real policy influence in that regard, and the precise role of the president is somewhat ambiguous in the Constitution. Much depends on the personality of the individual who holds the office and whether that person will adopt a maximalist interpretation of the role. Constitutional revisions, if they had passed, would have clarified the role of president by, among other things, rescinding the right to introduce legislation. Without a new constitution, the presidency retains the possibility of being something more than a symbolic head of state; however, recent trends suggest that it is unlikely that the presidency will develop as an effective check on the already powerful court and prime minister.

Local Governments

Hungary has never been a federal system, but it does have a history of regional representation that dates back to medieval times. The traditional structure of local governments continued to operate during the communist era but largely as an instrument of applying central government guidelines to the localities. Under strong popular pressure, the new democratic parliament passed a law in 1990 that granted greater autonomy to towns and villages. Under the new system, local governments are popularly elected in 19 counties and 8 cities with county status, including the capital city, Budapest, which is further subdivided into 22 districts. The county units are broken down into some 3,070 communities, each of which has a directly elected local council. All of these governments form a single layer. County governments do not have any greater autonomy or authority than the smallest community council.

On paper, these local governments are granted a degree of autonomy unusual even in Western Europe. In practice, they have fallen short of citizen expectations for local representation. Many of the local governments represent very small communities—over 50 percent cover populations of no more than a thousand. These small entities rely heavily on the central government for funding. The larger towns also receive a large percentage of their operating budgets from the central government. This allows local leaders to eschew the politically painful option of raising taxes and, at the same time, reduces the practical autonomy of the governments.

Citizens who find that they cannot get the help they need at the local level are forced to press their grievances at the national level, through MPs and letters to ministers and the Ombudsman. This increases the demand load of the central government. At the same time, the activities of the national and the local governments have not been well coordinated. Local governments are often controlled by different parties than the national legislature and, despite the creation of regional oversight boards, there still is no clear-cut legal framework to guide intergovernmental relations. As a consequence, dis-parities in health and social welfare are widening across the regions.[28] (See Box 10.3).

The Judicial System

A law-governed state has been one of the chief aims of the democratic transition. During Roundtable Negotiations, the HSWP argued for a relatively weak Constitutional Court, half of which would be drawn from the existing socialist parliament and half to be determined by the majority in a newly elected democratic parliament (a majority which the socialists still believed they could control).[29] Representatives of the fledgling opposition groups, however, pressed for a strong court, based on the German model, which would limit the legislative authority of the National Assembly and ensure that the decisions of lower-court judges conform to the law of the land. In the end, all sides agreed that a powerful court would act as a check against whatever party might control the cabinet.

The 15-member Court that they designed contains justices who may serve a 9-year term, with one opportunity for reelection. These members are selected through a two-thirds vote in the National Assembly; they, in turn, select a president and vice president from within their own ranks to serve a three-year term. A candidate may not have served as a leading member of government, been a paid

---

Box 10.3   Hungary's Ombuds(wo)man

Chapter Five of the Hungarian Constitution provides for an Ombudsman's Office including a Commissioner of Civil Rights and a Commissioner for National and Minority Rights. There is also now a Commissioner for Data Protection. In 1995, the parliament finally filled the civil rights post with Katalin Gonczol, a legal scholar and professor. Gonczol, who has virtually unlimited powers to investigate, criticize, and recommend corrective action—including the power to submit cases to the Constitutional Court—also understands that her role is to connect citizens with democratic governance and teach the values of human rights and rule of law. She has said that ordinary citizens are ". . .ill-prepared for the risks they must face every day in a modern market economy. . .I must teach them to defend their rights and homes and livelihoods in the absence of paternalistic protection by the state. Just as I must teach authority how to exercise power in the interest of the citizen." Already, her department receives some 800 complaints a month. More than two-thirds of these cannot be resolved through her office. In those cases, her office prepares a reply explaining why the Ombudsman's Office cannot help, who can, and how they should be approached.

Source: Thomas Land, "Hungary's Guardian of Human Rights," *Contemporary Review*, 275: p. 23 (July 1999).

employee of a political party, or held a top position in the state administration during the four years prior to the first democratic election. This final exclusion rule eliminated the possibility that the communists would control the new court and use it as a means of stifling opposition.

The Constitutional Court has been operational since January 1990 and has acted as a significant brake on executive power. In the 1990–1994 parliamentary cycle, the court received 260 decisions to investigate (including 21 parliamentary acts and 12 governmental decrees); it declared 31 percent of these unconstitutional. Seven laws were sent to the court by the president of the republic and six of these were overturned.[30] Given this record, the Hungarian court is considered by some analysts to be one of the boldest and most authoritative in the world.

The rest of the judicial system (consisting of county, municipal, and district courts) is monitored by the Justice Ministry and the Supreme Court. The president of the Supreme Court and the chief public prosecutor are elected by the National Assembly; judges are appointed by the president of the republic.

Hungary has a strong tradition of legal scholarship and vests a great deal of authority in the hands of judges.[31] There is no jury system and no exclusionary rule for evidence admission. Judges must therefore be trusted to have the wisdom and training to make prudent decisions based on legal statutes.

A Democratic Political Culture in the Making?

Political culture studies are particularly interesting in the context of new democracies because they can help us to predict both the viability and the style of democracy that will develop (see Chapter 2). Hungary, like most of its neighbors, has had only limited experience with democratic governance—in the immediate aftermath of World War I and just prior to the communist takeover. Those governments were doomed, at least in part, because they were caught in the grip of ideological and power politics. Nonetheless, it is clear that one of the causes for the breakdown of interwar democracy

was the absence of a democratic political culture. Fascist authoritarianism was palatable for a majority of Hungarians because it promised to further Hungary's national goals and restore prosperity. Populists and conservative nationalists favored discriminatory solutions that made Jews and foreigners scapegoats for Hungary's problems; in addition, many citizens craved a strong father figure who would lead Hungary out of chaos.

The German electorate displayed many of the same cultural characteristics prior to the establishment of democracy (see Chapter 6). However, the postwar West German culture was remade and now displays strong and stable support for democratic values and institutions. Can Hungary achieve the same transformation? Is there evidence of a culture shift since 1990? In order to address these questions, it is first necessary to examine the contours of the political culture Hungarians brought with them into the new democratic era.

The Cultural Legacy of Soft Dictatorship

The success of center-right parties in 1990—and particularly the historical Smallholders' Party—created a popular impression that Hungary had returned to pre-communist social alignments and cultural patterns. The underlying assumption was that communist rule had acted as a sort of lid that repressed and covered up earlier cultural patterns without fundamentally altering them. Modern Hungarian political culture naturally has antecedents in the pre-communist past, but this observation underplays the impact of Kádárism on Hungarian expectations and patterns of political involvement.

The period of goulash communism, in fact, reinforced the longer-term trend of social depoliticization. During the Rákosi era, citizens were forced to participate. There were massive reeducation efforts designed to purge adult citizens of their prior political affiliations, and children were indoctrinated through communist pioneer organizations and the schools. Seminar attendance was mandatory and citizens could expect to be visited by agitation and propaganda teams. Martial music and Soviet songs were played over loudspeakers in the public squares.

Kádár shifted the focus away from coercion. He summed up the difference in his approach to political socialization in the now famous statement, "whereas the Rákosiites used to say, those who are not with us, are against us, we say that those who are not against us are with us."[32] Hungarian citizens, exhausted from forced political participation and demoralized by the failure of the 1956 revolution, willingly withdrew from public life and into the private sphere of family and friends. They traded participation and political voice for the promise of a more comfortable material life for themselves and their families.

The Kádár regime still used various propaganda techniques to inculcate the basic communist values of building socialism, anti-Westernism, antinationalism, and antiindividualism.[33] But, the official ideological message was contradicted by the promise of goulash communism to repay political apathy with material rewards. The end result was that, rather than creating a new socialist morality of collective discipline, altruism, and revolutionary consciousness, the post-1956 communist regime developed an introverted and materially oriented brand of individualism.

The *European Value Systems Study* conducted in 1982 asked respondents in more than twenty countries about their attitudes regarding individualism versus altruism and sociability. Figure 10.4 displays the percent of respondents answering "no" to the question "Is there anything that you would sacrifice yourself for, outside your family?" Hungarians were noticeably less sociable and altruistic than citizens in Western European democracies. This legacy of goulash communism affects the way that citizens view the post-communist system and how they relate to other citizens and the institutions of democracy.

Citizen Attitudes Toward the New System

At the broadest level, analyses of political culture are concerned with citizen values regarding the political system as a whole. Due to the dual nature of transition, the question of support for democracy is intimately tied with support for market reforms. Hence we must ask about both the degree to which Hungarians trust and support their governments and the degree to which they support the transition to a market economy. Do they wish for a return to communist rule or the emergence of a strong leader who can "get things done"? Do they see democracy as able to perform well and fulfill the promise of prosperity offered by market economics? The answers to these questions are not entirely straightforward in the Hungarian case.

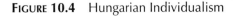

FIGURE 10.4   Hungarian Individualism

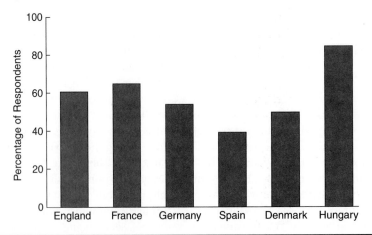

Note: Percentage shown responded "No" to the question "Is there anything you would sacrifice yourself for, outside your family?"
Source: 1982 *European Value Systems Survey* reported in Elemer Hankiss, *East European Alternatives* (Oxford, England: Clarendon Press, 1990), p. 208.

TABLE 10.1   Approval of the Current Market System in Eastern European Countries

	1991	1992	1994	1995	1998
Hungary	37	29	27	27	40
Poland	31	39	50	68	61
Czech Republic	57	55	66	71	38
Slovakia	41	34	31	43	31

Note: Numbers represent the percentage of the public that approve of the current economic system in each nation.
Source: New Democracies Barometer 1995 and 1998.

Hungarians have an international reputation for being pessimistic. According to a 1995 international Gallup survey, only Mexico can challenge Hungary for the title of "most dissatisfied nation."[34] This pessimism (or sober realism, as Hungarians might argue) is reflected in citizen evaluations of the new market and democratic systems.[35] Recent surveys indicate that the concrete economic situation of Hungarians has improved since 1991.[36] More and more Hungarians are beginning to claim that they make enough money from their regular job to make a living; that is, fewer are having to rely on income from the black economy or moonlighting. There has also been a continued increase in consumption of consumer durables (televisions, cars, and household appliances) that began with goulash communism.

In spite of all this, popular evaluations of the present economic system are notably low (see Table 10.1). The 40 percent approval rating posted in 1998 is a dramatic improvement over prior years and certainly reflects the recent economic upturn. It should be noted, however, that approval of the current market system still pales by comparison with approval for the old system, which runs around 70 percent. Seventy-two percent believe that their living standard has gone down since the introduction of a market economy.

Evaluations of the democratic system appear similarly bleak. In a 1994 survey, only 22 percent of respondents in Hungary said they were satisfied with the way that democracy is working in the country and only 23 percent said that they believe the country is moving in the right direction.[37] A 1998 survey shows that Hungarians are less likely to approve of the "current system of government with free elections and many parties" than citizens in Poland, the Czech Republic, and Romania. Positive evaluations of the *soft dictatorship*, on the other hand, are consistently high.

This would appear to bode ill for democratic consolidation in Hungary, since a reserve of antiauthoritarian legitimacy can provide a new democratic government with much needed time to resolve key issues and develop a performance record. The emerging Hungarian political culture, however, suggests an interesting paradox. Citizens are dissatisfied with the present economic and governmental situation, and they are pessimistic about future improvements. But they do not embrace change, either in the form of a return to the previous communist system or some other suspension of parliamentary rule. Data presented in Figure 10.5 show that the gap between nostalgia for the former communist regime and approval for a return to authoritarian government is higher in Hungary than in any of the other post-communist regimes in Eastern Europe. Nostalgia for the past and pessimism about the current situation do not add up to a lack of support for democracy.

The high degree of nostalgia that Hungarians feel for the previous regime clearly stems from their experience of soft dictatorship. Goulash communism provided a virtual guarantee of employment and universal social welfare benefits, and Hungarians, unlike their neighbors, did not have to wait in long lines for food and shoddy consumer goods. The limited marketization launched under the NEM did not provide the best of both worlds, but it did provide some of the benefits of both types of economic system—the stability and commitment to egalitarianism of the socialist economy with some

FIGURE 10.5 Nostalgia and Reaction in East-Central Europe, 1994

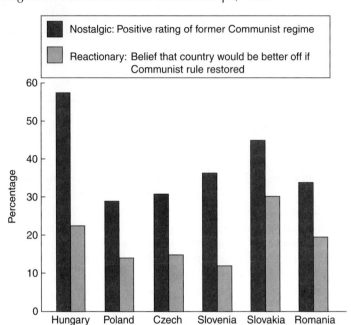

of the consumer goods available in market systems. It is hardly surprising then, that Hungarians have been overwhelmingly positive about their experience of the command economy, while Czechs, Slovenes, and particularly Poles have been far less nostalgic.

As mentioned previously, this apparent longing for the old system should not be confused with a rejection of democracy. Since the transition, Hungarians have consistently rejected the notion of suspending parliament and the multiparty system (with less than 30 percent ever claiming to support such a proposition).[38] The stability of this trend is important because it suggests that support for democracy is a basic cultural value. The widely held belief that the democratic legislature ought to be upheld may help to transcend the impact of unpopular policies or leaders.

Citizen Participation

Participation forms a key element of democracy. Through it, citizens express their preferences, choose their representatives, and shape public policies. In Hungary, however, citizens have been reluctant to engage in either the activities associated with representative democracy (namely voting) or participatory democracy (signing petitions, protesting, and other forms of direct citizen action). Under Kádár, Hungarian citizens were encouraged to value material well-being over political freedom and participation. This has carried over to the post-communist era. Immediately after the transition, when citizen interest in politics seemed to be high throughout the region,[39] Hungarians generally ranked participation and having a say in political matters far below the values of "having a life without worries" and being "well-off" (see Table 10.2). More recent survey data suggest that this trend is continuing. Hungarians consistently value social order and price stability over participation and freedom of speech.[40] They also continue to emphasize the importance of family and friendship networks as sources of satisfaction.

TABLE 10.2 Rank Ordering of Political Values During the 1989–1990 Regime Transition

Value	Importance Rating
How important is it in life that people. . .?	
Can live without worries	93
Can work	90
Be well-off	86
Can learn and have access to culture	85
Can freely tell their opinions	79
Be equal	72
Can have leisure and entertainment	71
Are not exposed to the will of the authorities	69
Have no great income differences	65
Have a say in dealing with public matters	62
Can live their lives without state interference	50
Can freely establish organizations to defend their interests	49

Source: János Simon, "Post-Paternalist Political Culture in Hungary," (1993): 237. *Communist and Post-Communist Studies* 26: No. 2.

Communist era depoliticization therefore continues to mark Hungarian political culture. This is most clearly reflected in the fact that Hungary posted the lowest voter turnout in Eastern Europe in 1990 (63 percent in the first round and 46 percent in the second). In 1991–1992, several by-elections had to be declared invalid due to less than 10-percent popular participation. In the 1994 parliamentary elections, the situation was slightly better, with 68 percent turnout in the first round and 55 percent in the second. In 1998, the situation deteriorated again. Only around 56 percent turned out for the first and second rounds, despite the fact that there was a very tight race to control the next parliament.

Voter apathy is matched by a reluctance to participate in nonconventional activities such as demonstrations or signing petitions. Historically, nonconventional participation in Hungary has been limited primarily to elite groups. Both the 1848 and 1956 uprisings were directed by individuals within the political and intellectual elite. There was little grassroots support for (or even awareness of) the samizdat produced by small groups of dissidents during the seventies, and Hungary produced nothing like the Solidarity-led strikes in Poland.

Since the establishment of parliamentary democracy, a few small protests have been staged around the new issues such as gay rights, minority rights, and environmental protection. Agricultural workers picketed outside the Assembly during the debate on land privatization. Nationalist groups have staged demonstrations during traditional Hungarian celebrations. And a major spontaneous outburst nearly brought the first government to a standstill. In October 1990, taxi and truck drivers communicating via short-wave radio called for a blockade of bridges, border crossings, and towns. The strike received widespread popular support, but it was quickly absorbed into and resolved by elite level bargaining.

Strike activity is relatively infrequent in Hungary. Studies comparing Hungary and Poland find that Hungarians engaged in overt protest (demonstrations, strikes, and protest campaigns) less than half as many times in the period 1989–1994; that strikes constituted only a small fraction of Hungarian protest activity; and that Polish strikes were more forceful and violent.[41] Comparatively weak trade unions and the establishment of an Interest Reconciliation Council help to account for the low levels of confrontational citizen action in Hungary, but there is also an attitudinal component. Surveys show that citizens do not believe activities such as protests and letter writing will be very effective. A 1991 cross-national survey asked respondents whether they felt they could do something about measures that violate their interests.[42] Hungarians expressed feelings of helplessness similar to those found in the developing world. Results of a 1994 survey confirm continuing anomie and political alienation, particularly among women, the elderly, and the less educated.

Most of the time, conflicts are managed preemptively through elite negotiation. When strikes occur, they tend to emanate from major state-controlled sectors, such as transportation, energy, and education. They are quickly resolved through compromise with the government, and often give the impression of "scripted theater."[43] Members of parliament, in fact, expect that interests will be articulated in this manner, indicating on surveys that they view direct lobbying as an illegitimate source of pressure.[44]

In some ways, popular quiescence and the ability to manage conflicts through negotiation has given the post-communist governments room to implement unpopular reforms, such as shock therapy. On the down side, however, some important issues are left outside the scope of elite bargaining. One could list here the problems of the Roma minority, pensioners, the poor, the unemployed and homeless, large families, and women. Their issues are not readily picked up by any of the major parties, and some have likened this to a communication breakdown between government and society.[45]

Citizen Expectations of Government

Governments exist to serve specific needs but what those tasks should be is a matter for debate. What is the proper scope of government activity? How much should the state become involved in the regulation of the economy and in the provision of social welfare? Citizen expectations in these areas vary from country to country. Interestingly, though, the dilemmas faced by Western and Eastern European governments have converged since the fall of communism. Extensive tax and welfare states developed on both sides of the Iron Curtain. So, new and established democracies alike must find ways to balance citizen expectations for social welfare (and lower taxes) with the need to balance budgets and compete in global markets.

In Hungary, universal welfare benefits were first extended under Kádár as a part of the social pact. By 1972, approximately 99 percent of the population had social insurance; by 1975, every Hungarian citizen was entitled to free health care. The percentage of preschool-aged children getting placed in the daycare system rose to nearly 90 percent and the number of doctors and hospital beds surpassed the levels found in most Western industrial states. It is clear, in retrospect, that much of this was made possible by foreign loans and substandard provision of services. The guarantee of so-

cial welfare has nevertheless become a deeply ingrained expectation for Hungarian citizens who otherwise favor free markets.

In 1991 László Bruszt and János Simon found that fully 71 percent of Hungarians agreed with the statement "The capitalist economy based on free private initiative is the best for our country."[46] However, a majority of citizens still expected a strong government role in providing universal employment, regulating prices, and reducing inequalities between the rich and poor. The 1998 New Democracies Barometer Survey shows that Hungarians still believe in a strong role for the state in equalizing social conditions. Fully 65 percent of survey respondents said that they believe that "the State should be responsible for everyone's economic security." The percent agreeing with that statement in Poland and Czech Republic was only 52 and 45 respectively.

Table 10.3 demonstrates two important trends in public attitudes toward the welfare state: (1) the overwhelming majority favor programs such as family allowances, three-year paid maternity leaves, sickness pay, and free medical care; and (2) Hungarians prefer universal, comprehensive benefits to means-testing.[47] With the exception of pensions, citizens expect the government to pay for benefits regardless of work status or income. In other words, they favor a Scandinavian-style social democratic welfare system to an American or British model.

Pensions provide an exception for several reasons. Under Kádár, poverty rates among pensioners were reduced. Today, when child poverty is on the rise, some may perceive that elderly pensioners (who are emerging as a powerful interest since the transition) are getting more than their fair share. In addition, a contributory pension scheme was introduced over twenty years ago. That has generated a cultural acceptance of contribution leading to entitlement in this area. Finally, the demographic bulge of pensioners expected to hit by the year 2016 will strain the present pension system beyond capacity. Hungarians thus accept the need for pension reform (specific policy responses will be discussed later in this chapter). The important point, in terms of political culture, is that Hungarians have the same expectations for their government as citizens

TABLE 10.3   Citizen Expectations of the Government's Role in Social Welfare

Statement	Percentage Agreeing
Family Allowance Should Go To . . .	
Every family with children, regardless of whether the parents are working	68.3
Only families where one of the parents works	31.0
No one	0.7
Pensions Should Go To . . .	
All retired citizens	23.7
Only those with a 20 year work record at age of retirement	33.6
Only those who paid the pension contribution for twenty years prior to retirement	42.7
Free Medical Care Should Go To . . .	
Every citizen	73.5
Only those who have worked	22.1
Only those who can pay a fee	4.4
Other Opinions	
Sick pay should not be a part of social insurance but the responsibility of the worker	5.3
Only those mothers who are below the poverty line should receive the maternity benefit	19.8
The maternity leave policy should be terminated	4.1
They should tighten up on access to pensions	42.7

Source: *Társadalomkutatási Informatikai Egyesülés (TÁRKI),* 1995 survey (N = 980). Reported in Péter Róbert, *A szociálpolitikával kapcsolatos attitüdök alakulása* [Changing Attitudes on Social Welfare]. 1996, in Magyarorszdág politikai évkönyve [Political Yearbook of Hungary] (Budapest: Hungarian Center for Democracy Studies, 1996).

in many of the more affluent Western European (particularly Scandinavian) countries. Such demands could prove overwhelming to a new democratic parliament that is also trying to cope with a wide range of economic reforms.

Elite Level Politics

The term "revolution" suggests that one political elite has been replaced by another. The Hungarian revolution, however, is better described by Timothy Garton Ash's neologism—"refolution." This combination of reform and revolution raises questions about whether Hungary has recruited a fundamentally different political and economic elite or whether the old elite has simply recycled itself through the negotiated revolution.

Evidence suggests that the post–1990 Hungarian elite does represent a break with the communist era power structure. The process of change has been gradual, however. It started in the 1980s, when turnover in key economic positions doubled the rate it had been in previous decades. From that point on the "old elite" ceased to exist. The most

profound changes since that time include the declining significance of party affiliation and working-class background. It is no longer necessary to be a member of any particular party to be part of the economic elite. Nomenklatura lists ended with the fall of communist rule, and older forms of status seem to have returned. In 1990, half the economic elite had working-class fathers; by 1993 that figure had dropped to 35 percent. The post-communist economic elite is also younger, since young people have had the kinds of training, travel experience, and language skills which make them valuable in the global economy. The transformation, of course, has not been complete. Consistently about half of the members of the economic ministries, banking, and State Enterprise boards held similar positions prior to 1989.

Though there are notable exceptions, the political elite has turned over as well. One indication of this is the decline in representation of women, workers, and peasants. Under communist rule, the National Assembly was a symbolic mirror of society, and quotas were used to achieve the appropriate balance of various social groups. Quotas became less pronounced after the introduction of a new electoral law in 1983, but the last communist legislature still consisted of nearly 35 percent blue collar workers and over 20 percent women. When citizens were finally given the opportunity to freely express their preferences, they returned Hungary to Western norms of recruitment. That is, they chose a less representative institution in terms of social groups, favoring highly educated male candidates of the dominant ethnicity.

Hungarian voters initially preferred young, inexperienced candidates as well—political outsiders who were not tainted by participation in the old regime. Over 95 percent of the political class recruited in the 1990 elections had never served in a national legislature. The median age was only 45 and several members from the Young Democrats Party (Fidesz) were in their early twenties. Few had any sort of direct political experience and most held degrees in the humanities, theology, and the social sciences. Candidates with strong local ties and name recognition also fared well in the first elections. Nearly 50 percent of MPs represented constituencies located in the county of their birth and many were drawn from locally based occupations, such as veterinary medicine, dentistry, and elementary education.

The 1994 and 1998 elections have continued the pattern of rewarding highly educated, male candidates. However, there has been a voter backlash against inexperience. Over one-third (139) of the MPs elected in 1994 were incumbents, and it has been estimated that as many as eighty members of the Socialist Party's parliamentary group had been members of the apparatus of the Communist Youth League or of the HSWP before 1989.[48] Many others gained their political experience as representatives of local government or mayors. This trend of starting a political career at the local level appears likely to continue since the Assembly recently adopted a law permitting panachage (holding local and national office simultaneously).

The disappearance of political amateurs is also reflected in the occupational and educational backgrounds of the MPs. The number of members trained in the humanities and social sciences has gone down, while the number of lawyers and economists has increased. Party affiliation has also become far more important than it was in the 1990

election, when the party labels still meant very little.[49] In 1990, ten MPs were elected either without a party affiliation or with multiple party sponsors. In 1994 and again in 1998, only one member was elected in this manner.

Hence, in less than a decade, Hungary has not only ousted the former communist elite, it has established a new political class based on criteria very similar to those that guide the voting choices of most democratic electorates. When given an opportunity to genuinely choose their representatives, Hungarian voters prefer politicians who they believe will have the time and training to be full-time representatives (often male lawyers and economists). While this trend is disturbing from the point of view of minority and female representation, it does stand as a testament to the change from an authoritarian system, in which the legislature was largely ceremonial, to genuine parliamentarism.

Interest Groups in Transition

Democracy requires mechanisms for articulating the interests of citizens and groups. But this area of political life—often described by political scientists as "civil society"—had only a limited chance to develop in Hungary prior to the transition. Under the state-socialist regime, official interest groups, from trade unions to women's and youth organizations, were thoroughly coopted and controlled by the Communist Party. When communism fell, they lost their official position in society. Today, some are struggling to establish themselves as legitimate representatives of their constituents in an open political environment. Others, like the Communist Youth League (KISZ), have disappeared entirely and been replaced by a myriad of new organizations formed on the basis of shared interests (for example, sports, music, hobbies).

Hungary's present interest group system defies simple classification. During the Roundtable period, the liberal opposition argued fiercely on behalf of rules that would encourage pluralism; they believed this was the surest means of undermining single-party control. The socialists, the HDF, and the historical parties, on the other hand, favored a corporatist model along Dutch-Belgian lines. Ultimately, it was agreed that corporate interests would be represented through a series of chambers (*kamarák*) or peak associations that would meet with government representatives in an Interest Reconciliation Council (IRC). This, however, has not led to the consolidation of groups into a few peak associations. The old official groups have splintered and new groups have proliferated. Today, there exist some twenty thousand independent interest associations, more than double the number that existed in 1989, just after the communist government fell.

Until recently, Hungary was the only post-communist country with an effective interest reconciliation body. All of the Central European countries had adopted some form of corporatist bargaining institution, but only the Hungarian IRC amounted to much. If the Socialist government had been successful in achieving its preferred draft constitution, the role of the IRC would have been guaranteed. Since that effort failed, the competence of the IRC depends on the government in power; and the Orbán government has all but dismantled it.

The following discussion will focus on the chief successors of the traditional interest groups—labor and employers' associations, the churches, women, and youth. It will also discuss a few of the more important groups that existed outside the communist system of interests, such as minority interests and new politics groups. The military, which was a powerful entrenched interest in many communist countries, never played much of a role in Hungary and thus will not be discussed here.

Labor and Employers

Trade unions held a place of pride in the former communist system. They existed as an arm of the party-state bureaucracy and could provide benefits for their members. Since the regime change, the trade union structure has splintered and some six national trade union associations have come into being. The largest of these is the National Federation of Hungarian Trade Unions (MSZOSZ), the lineal descendant of the counterfeit labor movement in the old regime. MSZOSZ has strong ties to the Hungarian Socialist Party (HSP). The two largest new labor associations are the League of Independent Trade Unions (LIGA) and the National Federation of Workers' Councils (MOSZ).

The older unions have come under sharp political attack for their cooperation with the former regime. However, they still enjoy strong support from employees. This point was made clear in the May 1993 elections for the supervising boards of the social security system. Almost half of the votes cast were for MSZOSZ representatives, while 10 to 12 percent went to both LIGA and MOSZ.

Though the descendants of the old unions and the new unions are beginning to cooperate, the post-communist trade-union movement in Hungary is usually described as weak and divided. Barely a quarter of Hungarian workers belong to a trade union. The railway strike in 1999 was the country's longest strike since World War II; it lasted only five days and involved only one of the nation's main rail unions. In the end, the strike was declared illegal, the strikers went back to work, and the government did not give in to demands for higher wages.

As weak as the trade unions seem to be, employers' associations probably enjoy even fewer historical precedents and social roots. A Chamber of Commerce existed during the communist regime, but in practice there was no genuine institutional representation for entrepreneurs, particularly those working in the unofficial second economy. With the fall of communism and the move to marketize, a revamped Chamber of Commerce emerged to represent state-owned companies. Privatization created a constituency for other employers associations, as well. The larger private firms have organized under the National Association of Manufacturers (GYOSZ). The National Association of Entrepreneurs (VOSZ) has emerged to represent small and medium-sized private enterprises. These organizations are beginning to gain strength, but they remain smaller and less effective than the larger trade union associations.

The Churches

Though religion remains a salient social cleavage in Hungary, churches play a less significant role in politics than elsewhere in the region. One reason is that Hungary has a majority church (over 60 percent Roman Catholic), but not a dominant one. Protestants (mostly Calvinists and Lutherans) account for nearly 30 percent of the religious population. Another reason is that much of the population is secularized. Only about 11 to 15 percent of adults go to church regularly. Finally, Hungarian churches under Kádár never really played an oppositional role. Unlike the Catholic Church in Poland, Hungarian churches did not challenge the regime for the loyalties of the population or actively create space for civil society formation.

Despite all this, churches were nonetheless eager to flex their muscles in the new political space created by democracy. Local churches seized school buildings to compensate for property confiscated by the communists. Churches were also vocal in seeking a more restrictive abortion law, and they won the restoration of some former church assets while a rightist government held power between 1990 and 1994.

In an era of pluralism, the historical churches cannot claim the exclusive franchise to represent people of faith. New churches—Mormons, evangelical Protestant groups, Hare Krishna, and Christian Scientists—are all gaining a foothold in Hungary. The Protestant churches (particularly the Calvinists) are losing members most quickly, both to the new religious groups and to atheism. The Catholic population has been holding its own.[50]

If the Hungarian population is becoming more secular overall, but at a higher rate among Protestants, and if Protestants (especially the Calvinists) are associated with a liberal worldview, then the denominational shift has implications for political affiliation among people of faith. The religious cleavage in Hungary is increasingly a divide between traditional-minded Catholics and irreligious voters. The former group finds representation in the nationalist-Christian and populist parties. This point is discussed further in the section on political parties.

Women

Women were officially represented in communist Hungary through a Party organization and a womens' political caucus in the legislature. The purpose of these institutions was to subsume women's interests to the interests of the party as articulated by the topmost, almost exclusively male, leaders.

Since the fall of the communist regime, the official women's organization has been replaced by a variety of groups expressing heterogeneous policy preferences. A few small feminist organizations formed to fight planned legislative restrictions on abortion, and female members of the Alliance of Free Democrats formed an organization called MONA.

Conservative women are better organized. The Christian Democrats and the Independent Smallholders' Party maintain women's auxiliary organizations. These groups emphasize the traditional role of women as the bearers of Magyar language and culture and, in a very literal sense, the reproducers of the Hungarian nation. In 1993, a tiny National Party of Hungarian Mothers formed to advocate the father-headed household and encourage women to stay in the home.

The main way that women can exert a voice in the Hungarian system is through the ballot box. All of the major parties make rhetorical commitments to women, but so far they have been far less willing to promote female politicians.[51] At the high point of Kádárism, women held around 30 percent of the seats in the legislature. That figure dropped to 7 percent in the 1990 election. The success of the Socialist Party and its liberal ally in 1994 increased female representation to 11 percent, but the figure declined again in 1998 to 8 percent. This places Hungary below the average for European Union countries and below several of its post-communist neighbors.

Women are also underrepresented in local government, forming only about 11 percent of municipal council members. Currently there is only one woman in the national government, Ibolya David, the Minister of Justice, who is also the only female party president. Women are virtually absent from the leadership of Trade Unions and other important "peak associations."

All of this has important ramifications for the post-communist policy agenda. With a divorce rate higher than the European Union average, Hungary has many single-parent (usually female-headed) households. Studies have shown that these households are at highest risk for poverty. Since large families are also likely to slip below the poverty line, the impact on children is obvious. It is estimated that nearly 50 percent of children and teenagers now fall into the lowest two deciles of household income.[52] Women might be expected to emphasize this issue. Another issue of particular concern to women is pension reform. Already the age of retirement for women has been raised. Debates over health care reform will also be of interest to women, since women are disproportionately employed in the state health care sector and make widest use of leaves to care for sick children and relatives.

The main political parties have tended to reduce "women's issues" to a set of consumer demands, promising that a successful transition to the market will bring prosperity and thereby make household conveniences more widely available. This, they say, will reduce the dual burden and improve women's lives. In the meantime, women, who are most heavily dependent on the welfare state (as both clients and employees), are bearing a disproportionate amount of the cost associated with marketization.

These circumstances would seem ripe for the formation of a pro-equality women's movement, but to date nothing of substance has emerged. Post-communist citizens are suspicious of Western-style feminism, because the communist regime used the same rhetoric to reduce equality to mandatory employment. Many women say that they have had enough of that kind of equality. At the same time, the parties on the right of the ideological spectrum—parties that are not apt to promote gender equity—are promising the continuation of social safety nets for vulnerable groups. This has strong appeal for women. The apparent passivity of women's interests furthermore mirrors the general situation in post-communist Hungary. Aside from anomic outbursts, as when a handful of women staged a sit-in at a local welfare office to protest the introduction of means-testing,[53] women (like workers) have been largely silent when key areas of interest have been challenged. With so few women in the legislature or in leadership positions in the parties, women (as an interest group) have little impact on government policy.

Minorities

Ethnic minorities have never had political representation in Hungary. At best, they were restricted to the right of privately preserving their cultural heritage. This has changed under the democratic system. In 1993, the Assembly passed an Act on National and Ethnic Minority Rights that is considered one of the most liberal in Europe. The drafters of the law hoped that it would set an example for neighboring states with Magyar minorities. They also hoped that the law would help to curb violence against minorities, which reached a peak in 1993 when 48 skinheads went on a rampage in which they beat a man they mistook for a Roma, seriously injured three blacks, and attacked a Roma pub.

As the largest minority group in Hungary, the Roma stand to gain the most from the law. Coordinated political activity, however, has proved elusive. Literally dozens of rival interest groups and proto-parties have emerged to represent the Roma minority. These groups fight bitterly among themselves (often along clan lines) and the majority of the Roma community resists political organization entirely. Several minority groups entered the 1998 elections together under the umbrella "Minority Forum," but they failed to gain any representation.

The major political parties usually deal with the "Gypsy problem" when they are discussing the "crime problem." Little has been done to address the fact that hundreds of thousands of Roma are living on the periphery of Hungarian society in concentrated pockets of poverty, illiteracy, and unemployment. These disenfranchised people have yet to find their place in the new democratic system. But with much higher birthrates than the population at large, their plight is one of the issues that the democratic system will have to face in coming years.

New Politics Groups

As in Western Europe, groups representing the so-called new values issues have emerged in Hungary.[54] The most substantial of these is the Green movement, which has its roots in the late-communist era. In the 1980s, groups such as the Danube-Circle managed to block the planned construction of the Gabčikovo-Nagymaros hydraulic power dam on the Danube River between Bratislava and Budapest. This marked a major milestone in the emergence of pluralism in Hungary.

In many ways, the Green movement was part of a broader backlash against the communist regime. Many citizens associated environmental degradation with insensitive regime policies that failed to take into consideration the health and lifestyle concerns of the population. Central planners were willing to manipulate the natural environment as they saw fit in order to meet plan targets set forth arbitrarily by central authorities. The Green movement unified against these actions. Since the transition, the policy issues are more diverse and the movement has become less unified. Numerous environmental parties and groups now exist but the "Green Force" in Hungarian politics has largely failed to materialize.[55]

Democratic Elections and the Emerging Party System

Genuinely independent interest groups serve democracy by articulating citizen demands and interests. Parties, in turn, aggregate those interests and represent them in the political process by recruiting and nominating candidates and structuring voter choices. In Hungary, parties have already come to play an important and legitimate role in parliamentary government.[56] After three elections, Hungary has settled into a moderately fragmented party system, and voters look to parties to structure their voting choices.

The parties also structure voting behavior in the parliament through party caucuses or fractions (*frakciók*). Until recently, any party winning 15 seats could form a parliamentary fraction. The Orbán government challenged that rule, as it would have prevented the Hungarian Justice and Life Party (with 14 seats) from forming a fraction. That, in turn, would have prevented the HJLP from partaking in all of the benefits of fraction membership: participation in the allocation of committee seats and chamber leadership positions, access to resources from the state budget to fund party activities and staff, and an increase in members' salaries. The Constitutional Court held the 15-member rule unconstitutional and declared that any party clearing the 5 percent parliamentary threshold may constitute a fraction.

The party system and the rules for party operation continue to undergo revision, but the changes at this point are relatively minor. The success of Hungary's party system development has been largely attributed to the early choice of an electoral system that reduced the number of political parties competing for power and narrowed the field to a handful of relatively moderate alternatives. This helped make it possible to govern in the first few years without calling for new elections.

The Electoral System and Its Consequences

Like the other institutional arrangements discussed in this chapter, Hungary's electoral system emerged from elite bargaining and compromises. At the Roundtable Negotiations, the Hungarian Socialist Party (HSP) called for plurality elections in single-member districts, arguing that a pure proportional representation (PR) system would be "impersonal, inimical to voters in the provinces. . .it would be enough for 'listed' candidates to send their photos to the voting district."[57] Parties resurrected from the pre-communist period wanted PR with county-based party lists—the same system that was used in 1945 and 1947. No group was strong enough to impose its will, so they compromised and came up with one of the most complicated systems in the world.

There are three means through which a candidate may gain a seat in the National Assembly: (1) 176 seats are filled through two-round elections in single-member electoral districts. In the first round, a majority (50 percent plus 1) is required to take the seat. Seats that cannot be filled through this method (and most cannot) go to a second round in which the top three candidates compete for a plurality of the vote; (2) 152 seats are allocated through PR ballots in the 19 historical counties (*megyek*) and Budapest; and (3) the remaining seats are allocated on a national list according to a proportional distribution of *scrap votes* (*töredék szavazatok*) or votes that were insufficient to elect a member in the territorial contests.[58] The national lists tend to be allocated to the second and third most successful parties in the territorial contests.

The combination of PR and local constituency representation provided a familiar model for Hungarians. Many elites admired the German hybrid system, so often praised for its role in the success of democracy in that country. Hybrid electoral rules were also familiar to voters, because they had been used seven times in Hungary's electoral history, including the last communist election in 1985 when a number of members were elected from a national list.

As in the German system, only those parties that gain 5 percent of the total vote cast in the territorial contests can participate in the PR element. The threshold was intended to discourage potentially dangerous party fragmentation and to reduce the likelihood that an extremist party would enter the Assembly. To take this a step further, the Hungarian hybrid system (unlike the German) is noncompensatory. If a party were to win all of the district seats, it would still be allowed to participate in the proportional allocation of seats on either the county or national lists. The outcome is less proportional overall than what occurs in Germany (see Chapter 6).

From the voters' perspective, the system is relatively straightforward. Each voter receives two ballots, one with the names of individual candidates running in the district and one with party lists for the county. Voters cannot change the rank ordering of the candidates on the list; they simply check the name of the party that they prefer. Parties may run candidates in districts and place the same names on a county list and the national list. Multiple candidacies are commonplace, but positions on the national list are usually reserved for top party elites as a safeguard against defeat in the territorial contests. This virtually guarantees that party leaders will be represented in the National Assembly.

The 5-percent threshold and plurality elements of the law have helped to reduce fragmentation in the party system and to exclude extremist parties from parliament (including the hard-line communist Workers' Party). Nearly fifty parties registered to contest the founding democratic elections, including a Winnie-the-Pooh Party and a Beer Lover's Union. Only six of these ultimately achieved parliamentary representation (see Figure 10.6). The

FIGURE 10.6   Party Strength in Parliament, 1990, 1994, 1998.

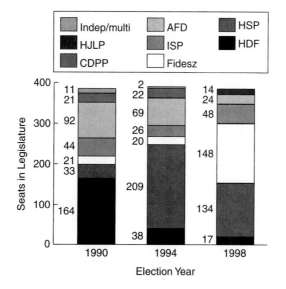

Hungarian Democratic Forum (HDF) received 164 seats, the largest number in the National Assembly; the second largest party was the Alliance of Free Democrats (AFD), with 92 seats. It wound up in the opposition alongside the Young Democrats (Fidesz), another party that was disappointed with the results of the campaign.

Without question, however, the biggest losers in 1990 were the successor parties to the communist regime. The newly christened Hungarian Socialist Party (HSP) had difficulty convincing voters that it was a genuinely reformist party. It received a disappointing 33 seats in the parliament. The remains of the party's hard-line ran under the old Hungarian Socialist Workers' Party (HSWP) label and failed to gain a single seat in the legislature.

The same six parties returned to parliament in 1994. (See again Figure 10.6.) The HSP won a landslide victory, taking 209 seats, a sufficient number to form a governing majority on its own. It chose instead to form a coalition with the liberal AFD, which had retained 69 seats. The HDF lost nearly 80 percent of the seats it had held in the first parliament and became the largest party in a four-party opposition that together controlled no more than 28 percent of the seats.

In the 1998 elections, government and opposition benches switched places again, but this time the Assembly would be far more balanced between left-wing and right-wing forces (see again Figure 10.6). The HSP retained 134 of its 209 seats, but it was nonetheless overcome by a new constellation of political forces on the right. Viktor Orbán's Fidesz, now calling itself the Young Democrats-Civic Party (Fidesz-MPP), moved to the ideological right and went from 20 seats to 148. The right-wing Independenendent Smallholders' Party (ISP) nearly doubled its seat share, but other members of the rightist coalition from 1990 did not fare as well. The Christian Democratic People's Party (CDPP) disappeared from parliament, while the HDF gained only 17 seats, just slightly more than the extreme-rightist Hungarian Justice and Life Party (HJLP), which cleared the 5-percent threshold for the first time. Orbán assumed the position of prime minister and formed a government with the ISP and

the handful of HDF deputies. The extremist Hungarian Justice and Life Party (HJLP) was left out of the coalition. It refused to join the opposition, however, and supports the governing coalition on many issues.

Nostalgia and Backlash

The complete reversal of government and opposition benches in each post-communist election provides scholars with an excellent opportunity to observe the dynamics of party system formation in general and in the particular post-communist context. Classic analyses of party system formation describe parties as representing intense cleavages in society. Parties arise to resolve social conflicts and are therefore rooted in particular social groups and interests. In the post-communist systems, however, 40 years of state socialism atomized society. Old social categories were eroded, and the parties that emerged during the transition to contest newly declared elections did not effectively perform their interest aggregation function. The Hungarian Democratic Forum provided a loose umbrella for populist writers, nationalists, moderate conservatives, and reform communists. The communist successor party, the HSP, found it difficult to claim its traditional base among workers and was therefore unsure about whom it would represent. Even the historical parties with social groups in their names—the Independent Smallholders and Christian Democrats—could hardly point to clear social bases of support. In the last pre-communist election, when the Smallholders won the largest number of seats in the Assembly, nearly half of the working population could be described as "self-employed peasants"; by 1990, that figure had dropped to 1 percent. The ability of the Smallholders to join the first post-communist government had little to do with a return to older cleavage patterns.

The Social Bases of the Hungarian Parties

Though the Hungarian party system has been criticized for its shallow root system,[59] the parties do represent divergent worldviews. All of the major parties agree that Hungary should move toward a marketized economy, and all wish to increase the prominence of Hungary's cultural heritage after years of Soviet domination. Importantly though, they differ over the appropriate degree of state intervention in the economy and the relative emphasis they place on individual liberties versus collective obligations to family, church, and nation. The Alliance of Free Democrats (AFD) has been the staunchest advocate of a shock therapy style of economic transition, though the economic crisis of the mid-nineties pushed the Hungarian Socialist Party (HSP) toward radical reform, and the success of those reforms has encouraged the Young Democrats—Hungarian Civic Party (Fidesz) to continue on the same path. The Independent Smallholders' Party (ISP) and the Hungarian Justice and Life Party (HJLP) prefer protectionist trade policies and greater government subsidy of farms, industries, and social welfare. Parties and politicians on the individualist side of the spectrum (the AFD and HSP) are oriented toward issues of civil rights and liberties and tend to welcome Western ideas and investment. The parties that emphasize collective obligations (ISP, HJLP, Christian Democrats, Fidesz, and HDF) tend to be suspicious of foreign influences, to promote the traditional family as the source of national culture, and to highlight traditional values.

Though party loyalties are still in flux, there do exist a couple of identifiable patterns of support for these broad worldviews. Generally speaking, older voters and frequent churchgoers support the parties on the rightist-traditional end of the spectrum (the Independent Smallholders, Democratic Forum, Christian Democrats, and now Fidesz). Rural voters also support these parties, but this does not reflect an occupational cleavage. The Smallholders draw only about 20 percent of their support from agricultural workers. The Socialists, by contrast, receive slightly less support from rural voters, but their urban support comes primarily from nonmanual (rather than urban industrial) workers.

Social groups that tend to support traditionalist parties are unlikely to shift their vote to the liberal AFD, but across elections, a large proportion of voters has been either uncommitted or weakly committed to any particular party. Between 1990 and 1994, it is estimated that less than one-fifth of the voting age population was attached to any single party.[60] These floating voters seem to look for promises of economic and social security and to shift their support accordingly. Such voters arguably found appeal in the HDF's 1990 promise to be a "calm force" between the old Socialist and the new, more radical liberal alternatives. In 1994, the HSP was able to lure some 43 percent of the weakly attached voters with an appeal to nostalgia for the security of "goulash communism." In 1998, the floating voters shifted right again—literally between electoral rounds—to support a revamped Fidesz that promised softer economic reforms. This shift did not dramatically affect the Socialists who maintained much of their 1994 support (percent of the vote in 1994 was 32.99 and dropped to 32.92 in 1998). The HSP lost seats primarily due to superior cooperation among rightist parties and the complications of the electoral system. The AFD, on the other hand, suffered a large-scale voter defection.

Data on class and religious bases of party support displayed in Figure 10.7 suggest that the most successful parties rely on heterogeneous bases of support. (Note that the religion columns do not add up to 100 because "other parties" were included in that sample.) In 1994, the victorious HSP was able to pick up support from upper and lower classes and religious and non-religious voters. The AFD and the CDPP, on the other hand, had clear social bases. The AFD's support emanated almost exclusively from affluent and irreligious voters (Budapest intellectual circles). The CDPP had no appeal whatsoever among nonreligious voters, yet religious voters also supported the HDF, ISP, and even the HSP.

The HDF, HSP, and Fidesz have more heterogeneous bases of support and have been alternately successful in drawing uncommitted voters away from other alternatives. The problem with this sort of success is that the coalition of support must be rebuilt in each election. This renders prediction about future elections difficult. Provincial, religious, older, and less-educated voters will probably continue to lean toward parties that embody a collectivist/soft reform worldview. There are more parties of this type in Hungary than liberal or socialist

FIGURE 10.7   Social Bases of Support: Class and Religious Cleavages

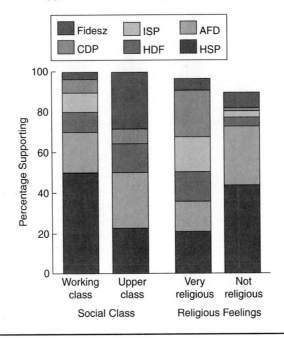

Source: Ferenc Gaszó and István Stumpf, *Parties and Voters After Two Elections* (Report of the Institute of Political Science, Hungarian Academy of Sciences, 1994).

alternatives. It is unclear, however, just how solid Fidesz support is today. It has typically had the smallest proportion of committed voters. In the near term, we can probably expect more volatility. Electoral outcomes will depend on which party or group of parties is able to most effectively mobilize feelings of nostalgia and insecurity among voters (see Box 10.4).

The Parties

ALLIANCE OF FREE DEMOCRATS   The AFD began its life as a small organization comprised mostly of intellectuals (economists, sociologists, and lawyers) who had produced *samizdat* materials throughout the 1970s and early 1980s. The party developed a nationwide following virtually overnight, drawing a number of supporters when it exposed the "Danube-gate" scandal (the continued tapping of opposition party leaders' telephones by the security services). The resulting cleavage between the core of

intellectual founders and the mass membership erupted into open conflict in 1991 when the party president János Kis resigned, and the membership chose Péter Tölgyessy to replace him instead of one of the dissident old guard. Several of the AFD's founders responded by leaving the party's executive.

The election of Iván Pető to replace Tölgyessy in 1992 put an end to most of the internal fights. The intellectuals receded from decision making, and several chose not to seek reelection in 1994. Gábor Kuncze, a relatively unknown politician with a teddy-bear charm and a large mustache, was chosen as the AFD candidate for prime minister in the 1994 elections. This provided further evidence that the party's urbanist and intellectual roots had become less pronounced.

In the early stages of party formation, the AFD's dissident core favored a classical liberal ideology, including a rapid transition to market economics. Yet, there were always differences of opinion be-

---

Box 10.4   Campaign Graffiti

Campaign posters provide a key means for Hungarian parties to form an image in the minds of voters; they also provide an opportunity for citizens to respond. The Alliance of Free Democrats Party, with its largely urban electoral base, has long been labeled a "Jewish party" among populists. Its posters are frequently spray-painted with the Star of David and the word "zsid(" (Jew). When Fidesz began shifting to the right of the ideological spectrum, its posters were scrawled with the words "MDF Szolgák" (HDF servants). The Socialists' 1994 campaign provided a particularly good target for graffiti. Their candidate for Prime Minister, Gyula Horn, was supposed to appeal to voter nostalgia. As Foreign Minister in the last years of the communist regime, Horn had established his credentials as a reformer by opening Hungary's borders and signing the document that would withdraw Soviet troops from Hungarian soil. Horn, however, had also been accused of being a member of the pufajkás (the volunteer police force charged with rounding up insurgents and sympathizers in the 1956 uprising). Hence, posters featuring a picture of Horn under the words "Vote Socialist to Add My Expertise to Government" were modified to read: "Vote Socialist to add a pufajkás to government!" The allegation that Horn (as a pufajkás) had kicked a young boy in the mouth also made it to the billboards. A vandal blackened the front teeth of a smiling little girl on one poster and inserted the caption "Horn fog" (a play on words meaning both "Cape Horn" and "Horn tooth") above the official slogan describing the Socialists as the "Reliable Solution."

Source: Kurtán Sándor, et al., eds. *Magyarország politikai évkönyve*, 1995 [Political Yearbook of Hungary, 1995]. Budapest: Center for Democracy Studies, 1996, pp. 127-135.

---

tween those who preferred a Thatcherite approach to the economy and those who took a more social-liberal (even social democratic) view.[61] The latter position was elevated in the 1994 platform with references to increased state intervention in the economy to create jobs and calls for transforming maternity and pension benefits into "citizens' rights," and creating an "adequate social minimum" through universal health care and special subsidies for families of school-aged children.

The AFD is sharply differentiated from the nationalist-conservative parties in terms of worldview. It is generally pro-Western. It favors open trade, foreign investment, religious freedom, and low taxes. Some of its MPs have been leaders in the effort to protect the rights of groups who have suffered from discrimination, such as Roma, homosexuals, and Jews.

In 1994, the AFD won nearly 20 percent of the popular vote and joined the HSP in a governing coalition. The long-developing economic decline reached a crisis point in late 1994, forcing the HSP and left-leaning elements within the AFD to adopt radical neoliberal reforms. These reforms helped to inaugurate the most impressive economic recovery in the region but also created a great deal of social pain.

It appears that voters in 1998 primarily blamed the AFD for the painful aspects of transition, giving the party only 7½ percent of the vote and 24 seats. In response, the AFD leadership has brought in a successful female lawyer to help rewrite the party's platform. The AFD is particularly concerned about shedding its image as insensitive and overly intellectual. The party has also adopted a regional quota for its party lists in an attempt to gain greater representation of the provincial interests.

The AFD has very little competition for the "liberal vote"—there are a couple of other minor liberal parties, including János Palotás's Republic Party and Tamás Nagy's Agrarian Union. The problem for the AFD is that liberalism has never enjoyed widespread support in Hungary (or anywhere in Eastern Europe for that matter). Unless it can broaden its appeal, the party could slip from the parliamentary scene.

ALLIANCE OF YOUNG DEMOCRATS—HUNGARIAN CIVIC PARTY (FIDESZ)   Fidesz, more than any of the other major parties, has searched for an ideological and social cleavage to represent. It was initially formed as an alternative to the Communist Party youth organization, with its membership restricted to those 35 years of age or younger. This stipulation has been dropped but the party's electoral support is still strong among voters in the 19 to 35 age bracket.

From its inception, Fidesz had an advantage over the other parties; it had perhaps the only truly charismatic leader in the Hungarian transition, Viktor Orbán. During the first parliament, Fidesz became a tight-knit parliamentary group, holding its lead in public opinion polls from 1991 through the end of 1993. The party's electoral base and organization, however, never seemed to fully take root. Fidesz failed to win any of the five by-elections held in the 1990–1994 parliament and there were serious divisions within the leadership. One branch of the party, led by Orbán, wanted to retool the anti-Communist youth organization into a party that could be elected to government. In order to do this, he thought that the party should move toward the ideological right. The other wing of Fidesz sought to maintain the cafe-intellectual roots of the party and to pursue a social-liberal program.

The Orbán wing ultimately prevailed. In 1993, Fidesz rejected its previous ties with liberal parties like the AFD and began to talk to the HDF's populist leader, Sándor Lezsak; it also added "Civic Party" to its title, and there has been some speculation that it may drop the word "young" from its name altogether. Voters are rejecting political amateurs, so the perception of inexperience is now a liability. Moreover, the youth generation has turned out to be an unstable cleavage basis for a political party. The party would prefer to establish a firm place on the ideological spectrum as "moderate-conservative," an alternative to the Socialists and the shock therapy advocating AFD, on the one hand, and the more extreme nationalist parties, on the other.

Whether Fidesz will be able to keep the coalition of support it was able to rally in 1998 is still in question. After taking power, the party's popularity dropped. That is not at all unusual for a governing party, but Fidesz has also faced an increase in incidents of organized crime (an issue of concern to many voters). There have been charges of corrup-

tion and cronyism leveled against the government. The Smallholders continue to cause trouble for the coalition, and Orbán is a controversial figure, often depicted as arrogant and unsympathetic. He has attempted to gain control over a media that he says is dominated by his opponents (leftists and liberals). He secured constitutional changes that strengthen the role of the Prime Minister and then made his friend and former professor Head of the Office of the Prime Minister. The perception among many that Orbán fancies himself king may prove problematic for the party in future elections (see Box 10.5).

THE CHRISTIAN DEMOCRATIC PEOPLE'S PARTY (CDPP)
The CDPP is one of several historical parties that emerged in the run-up to the 1990 election. It was the last of the six parliamentary parties to declare itself a party, but it made up for the lost time and ran 105 candidates, winning 21 seats. It joined the HDF in 1990 in a right-of-center Christian and nationalist government.

Throughout most of the four years in government, the CDPP remained a more or less silent partner. It did launch a "Buy Hungarian" campaign on its own in 1993 in order to combat unemployment, but its platform was otherwise kept intentionally vague. László Surján (Minister of Social Welfare in the HDF coalition and CDPP president) wanted to position the CDPP as a potential coalition partner for whichever party might win the 1994 elections.

The party's organizational capacity had improved by 1994, so it ran candidates in 163 individual constituencies and all the county races. Nevertheless, it won only 22 seats in the Assembly and wound up in the parliamentary opposition. The CDPP was competing for many of the same voters as the HDF and the ISP. It was more successful than those parties only in attracting elderly voters (those over the age of 70) and women (who made up 62 percent of CDPP voters). In 1998, the party split over the degree to which it should cooperate with larger rightist parties. The lack of internal cohesion and narrow voter base kept the CDPP from crossing the 5-percent threshold.

THE HUNGARIAN DEMOCRATIC FORUM (HDF) Perhaps more than any other party in Hungary, the HDF fit the definition of an "umbrella party." This

Box 10.5 Crowngate

On January 1, 2000—one day after the official start of a new millenium—Hungary celebrated its own millenium. One thousand years earlier, Pope Sylvester II had presented a golden Sacred Crown to Saint Stephen (Szent István), Hungary's first Christian king. The millennial celebrations, planned by the Fidesz-led government and costing some 140 million dollars, included moving the crown of St. Stephen from the national museum to a display case in the parliament. That move touched off a Budapest within-the-beltway controversy that came to be known in the press as "Crowngate." Members of the Alliance of Free Democrats (AFD) and the reformed Hungarian Socialist Party (HSP) accused the government of politicizing a national symbol and sending a dangerous message to Hungary's neighbors and nationalist elements within the country. Government representatives responded by saying that they only wanted to give the historic crown a place of honor and sniped that the AFD always opposes anything having to do with traditional values.

The importance of the crown itself has always resided more in what it represents than what it is. It is unlikely that the crown was ever actually worn by St. Stephen, since it contains gold bands of a more recent vintage, and two of its famous painted icons depict rulers who held the throne after Stephen's death. It none the less has become the most enduring symbol of the Hungarian nation and its legitimate, if beleaguered, claim to statehood. Over the centuries, the crown has been bent, lost on a roadside, stolen and then ransomed back, moved between Habsburg capitals, buried (in 1848), and kept in Fort Knox, Kentucky to prevent it from falling into Soviet hands. President Carter finally had it returned to Hungary's national museum in 1978. Today, according to one Budapest joke, Prime Minister Orbán has moved it again: this time closer to his office, so he can try it on at night!

Source: Donald G. McNeil Jr., "Hungary's Millennium Fireworks," *The New York Times*, January 3, 2000.

term—coined to describe broad movements of communist opposition, such as Poland's Solidarity or the Czech Civic Forum—captured a phenomenon of the transition period. Political tendencies and social groups that under normal political conditions would have been rivals were joined together in a common cause. The HDF brought together populist writers, reformist elements in the Communist Party, moderate Christian Democrats, and extreme nationalists. Initially, the Forum was reluctant to describe itself as a political party, seeing itself instead as a broad grassroots movement. When free elections were scheduled, the HDF finally registered as a party. It sought to differentiate itself from others in the field by claiming to be the "calm force" in Hungarian politics, a break from the communist past but an advocate of more gradual change than the radical opposition.

József Antall took leadership of the party in 1990, and many believed that he was the one person who could cement the party's disparate elements. At times, he seemed to rely on the populist rhetoric of nationalism and anti-Semitism, but after

the 1990 elections it became clear that he would pursue a moderate conservative path. As prime minister, he marginalized the populist wing led by extreme nationalist István Csurka.

With the expulsion of the Csurka faction, the HDF seemed to have resolved its internal problems. Extremist elements in the party had been purged and took relatively little of the party's base with them. However, the devastating defeat of 1994 split the party again. A new populist branch argued that the Torgyán-led Smallholders had capitalized on the HDF's movement away from its Lakitelek roots—the populist themes of national identity and cultural heritage. Moderates responded that "if you want to win an election, you need to offer a moderate, professional party, an alternative to the more ideological Smallholders,"[62] splitting off to form the Hungarian Democratic People's Party (HDPP).

The HDPP clearly sought to evoke the "Antall legacy," which is popular among voters who associate the Antall years with gradual change and stability. But the new party was unable to compete with Fidesz for the center ground in 1998. The HDF, for its part, chose to cooperate with Fidesz rather than challenge it as the moderate-conservative alternative to the Socialists, Liberals, and Ultra-nationalists. As a result, the party is back in government but this time as a very junior member of the coalition. It failed to cross the threshold for parliamentary representation but did gain some 17 seats through single-member district contests. The party, currently led by the only female party president, Ibolya David (the Minister of Justice), has not asserted as strong a voice as the ISP, preferring at times to play the role of peacekeeper within the coalition.

THE HUNGARIAN JUSTICE AND LIFE PARTY (HJLP)

The HJLP formed from the populist wing of the HDF. In August of 1992, István Csurka (a member of parliament in the HDF) published an article in which he argued that social tensions were being exploited by an international conspiracy of liberals, former Communists, and Jews. Less than a year later, he refused to sign a new Hungarian-Ukrainian Basic Treaty that would assent to the immutability of Hungary's modern borders. The leader of the HDF, József Antall, responded by expelling Csurka and three other right-wing deputies from the party. In July 1993, a group of MPs formed the Hungarian Justice and Life Party (HJLP), which was to be supported by Csurka's new grassroots organization, the *Magyar Ut* (Hungarian Way). During the 1994 electoral campaign Csurka held joint rallies with the Torgyán-led Smallholders that drew large crowds, but the HJLP failed to clear the threshold for representation in parliament.

The party entered the Assembly for the first time in 1998, winning 14 seats. It was not asked to join the rightist coalition, due to its openly xenophobic orientation and its ties to skinhead organizations and radical right wing parties in places like France and Austria. Neither did it join the HSP-led opposition. Fidesz has often counted on HJLP votes. That, coupled with HJLP affinities to the ISP, has given the party disproportionate influence in the government, particularly on issues having to do with culture, Hungarian minorities abroad, and the media. The HJLP is the only major party that opposes Hungarian membership in the European Union. The party also opposes foreign ownership of Hungarian farmland, and calls for the nation's independence from international financial institutions.

HUNGARIAN SOCIALIST PARTY (HSP)

The HSP is the direct descendant of the Hungarian Communist Party (HSWP after 1956). Its history is virtually synonymous with post-1949 Hungarian history until the Fourteenth Party Congress in October 1989, when it accepted that it would no longer serve a "leading role" in society. Gyula Horn took over the post of party president in May 1990 and became the prime minister when the HSP won the parliamentary majority in 1994.

The party's platform changed when it dropped the word "Workers'" from its name in October 1989. It now espouses a European-style social democratic approach that includes mixed forms of property within a market economy. It differs very little from the other mainstream parties in its support for market reforms and its willingness to join Western economic and security organizations. With acceptance into the Socialist International, the HSP effectively eclipsed the Social Democratic Party of Hungary as the main leftist alternative. Old party functionaries still play a role in the party, particularly in the middle ranks, but most of the orthodox communists abandoned the HSP in 1989-1990 to join the reconstituted HSWP (now called the Workers' Party).

Today the HSP claims about thirty-five thousand members. It has maintained a fairly unified fraction in parliament, but there are occasional differences between the national and local party leaderships and among platforms represented within the party. The left-wing platform is a neo-Marxist group with little support outside a small circle of Budapest intellectuals. The author of the party program leads another grouping called the "Social Democratic Community." This platform has a great deal of influence within the party but few members are actually involved in it. The pragmatic "Socialist Group" has larger support among the party cadres. It is led by the former head of Hungary's largest Trade Union (MSZOSZ), Sándor Nagy.

The HSP's electoral fortunes seemed bleak after the 1990 elections, but (other than the defection of Imre Pozsgay in 1993) the parliamentary fraction remained intact and performed well in its opposition role. The party's image began to improve in 1993 and it ultimately overtook Fidesz as the leading party in the polls. Early in 1994, the HSP began to forge ties with key social groups, promising leaders of these groups (including MSZOSZ) a place on the party lists in exchange for their electoral support.

By the May 1994 election, the HSP clearly emerged as the strongest political force, the only party with sufficient nominations to contest every seat in the country. It won almost 33 percent of the votes cast. Its support spread across the social spectrum (though it was less popular among the very old and the very young) and it won a plurality in every county throughout Hungary. In declining industrial areas, like the steel town of Dunaújváros, it was even more successful, securing nearly 50 percent of the vote.

Four years later, the strong economic recovery seemed to suggest another Socialist victory. The HSP therefore aimed at winning an outright majority in the Assembly. The Socialist campaign openly criticized the party's minor coalition partner, the AFD, laying the blame for the painful aspects of transition at that party's feet. The rightist parties, led by Fidesz, had meanwhile established themselves as a credible alternative and entered agreements of mutual support for one another. The election turned into a major defeat for the governing parties. The HSP lost only slightly in terms of the popular vote, but it ended up with only 134 seats—compared to 148 for Fidesz and 48 for the Smallholders.

The defeat, though it hardly represented a popular backlash, placed the HSP in the opposition benches and caused concern within the party leadership. At a September 1998 Party Congress, former Prime Minister Gyula Horn stepped down as party leader. The popular ex-Foreign Minister László Kovács defeated Sándor Nagy for leadership of the party.[63]

THE INDEPENDENT SMALLHOLDERS' PARTY (ISP) Today's ISP is the descendent of the Smallholders' Party that won the last pre-communist election. It is one of many parties claiming to represent Hungary's important agricultural interests, yet its disastrous policies and internal factional fights ironically may have contributed to the present agricultural troubles.

In February 1989, the ISP expelled four members, and in March it let them back in. Just before the 1990 elections, the National Smallholders' Party split away. The ISP was ultimately able to use its historical reputation and a populist platform of land restitution to achieve a minor electoral success; it gained 44 seats in the Assembly and entered into a coalition with the HDF.

The fragility of this coalition gave the ISP the leverage to force the introduction of its main electoral promise—that property, especially land, would be returned to the 1947 owners or their heirs. The policy was extremely unpopular in the Assembly because it would have placed large portions of Hungary's most valuable natural resource into the hands of nonfarmers and would ratify ownership based on the pre–1947 liquidation of Jewish property. Appeals to the Constitutional Court eventually derailed the ISP plan.

This angered József Torgyán, who in the meantime had taken control of the ISP leadership through rather suspicious means. He threatened to boycott the vote and leave the coalition. Thirty-three ISP members in parliament openly opposed Torgyán and voted to pass the government's compromise restitution plan. In February 1992, Torgyán responded by expelling those members from the fraction. This group which, with the addition of a few more members, came to call itself the "Smallholders' Thirty-Six," remained in the government. Torgyán took the party's name and resources and used them to win a minor victory in the 1994 elections.

Five other Smallholders' parties ran in 1994; Torgyán distinguished his party in two ways. First, every campaign poster featured his picture. He became perhaps the best-known politician in the country. Second, he forged links with other populist groups such as Csurka's Hungarian Justice and Life Party (HJLP). The strategy paid off and the Torgyánist party was the only Smallholders' group to clear the 5-percent electoral threshold. It gained 26 seats in the new parliament and joined three other parties in forming a parliamentary opposition.

Torgyán's campaigns have focussed on national pride and the fight against profiteering. This has struck a chord against the backdrop of rapidly proliferating American fast-food chains (McDonald's, Burger King, Pizza Hut, Dunkin' Donuts, to name a few) and grocery store shelves filled with German detergents and Pepsi. However, his message also contains xenophobic and intolerant elements, blaming foreigners and those communists who remained in power for a range of social ills, from unemployment and crime to the breakdown of the Hungarian family. He has called for a policy of "complete accounting" for those who have benefited from privatization, and his persistent recusancy has given him the reputation of a hot-head.

Fidesz had hoped to form a moderate conservative alternative to the ISP, but the outcome of the 1998 election forced it to look for a coalition partner. Fidesz rejected the possibility of a grand coalition with the HSP and therefore turned to the ISP, the third largest party in the Assembly. The ISP has proven to be an unusually assertive junior partner: ISP-led ministries overspent the agriculture budget in 1999, tried to ban all dairy imports based on an unsubstantiated claim of contamination, and opposed the Fidesz plan to remove agricultural colleges from the authority of the agriculture ministry. The economics minister had the dairy ban lifted before it could take effect and undermine Hungary's EU commitments, but the EU's ambassador in Budapest none the less decried the incident and criticized the handling of EU grants administered by Smallholder-led ministries.[64]

In some respects, the Smallholders' version of "compassionate conservatism" appeals to Fidesz leaders, who feel they won the 1998 election on the claim that the former government's economic success had been purchased through too much social pain and foreign advice. The ISP's actions, however, undermine the moderate conservative agenda of European integration, and Torgyán openly opposes Fidesz on a variety of issues. He resisted, for example, Fidesz attempts to transfer State-run football clubs to a new youth-and-sports ministry, arguing that he ought to retain the right to subsidize Ferencvaros, a popular club historically linked to the farm ministry. Torgyán's unabashed nepotism has also embarrassed the government. He placed family members in the State Lottery Board and put his daughter-in-law on the board of the Hungarian airline, MALEV. He justified the latter move by saying that she had experience in the airline industry, because she used to sell tickets in a travel agency. Antics like that have undermined the ISP's popular support, which stands at about 6 percent. Torgyán nevertheless claims that his party will defeat Fidesz and the HSP in the 2002 general election.

Policy Process and Performance

One of the keys to the success of multiparty parliamentary democracy in Hungary is the government's ability to create public policies that resolve social conflicts and achieve economic prosperity. Despite some initial difficulties, institutions and processes have developed rather quickly for doing just that.

The idea for a new policy may emerge from a variety of sources—a university study, an MP who sees a problem in his constituency, or an individual citizen. In practice, however, the Hungarian policy process (as in most countries) is dominated by government proposals and those of the prime minister in particular. Legislation can be initiated by MPs, committees, the president of the Republic, and the government. But private initiatives are placed on the agenda only if they have the approval of a committee appointed by the speaker.

Once a bill has been initiated, it must go through three readings (see Figure 10.8 for details of the process). In the first reading, the bill is placed on the legislative calendar and assigned to the relevant committee(s). Any committee or MP can submit amendments to the bill at this time. The committee of jurisdiction takes an especially active role at this stage of the process. It can call on interest groups and ministerial representatives to testify on the proposal and initiate investigative hearings.

There are Twelve Standing Committees in the National Assembly and approximately six special committees. There is also a "supercommittee" which must review all legislation to ensure that it adheres to legal and constitutional norms. The standing committees more or less follow the ministerial divisions and adhere to the Western norm of specialization. Members of the Budget Committee tend to be economists and so forth.

FIGURE 10.8 The Legislative Process

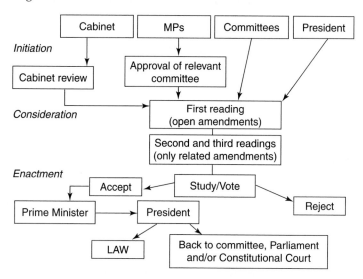

Committee seats are divided in proportion to party strength in the parliament. We might therefore expect voting within the committees to reflect the will of the government. However, since committee chairs and vice chairs are divided between the government and opposition parties, policy-making in committees tends to follow a model of interparty consensus. Fractions maintain a high degree of authority in this process. They bring their own experts and specialists to committee hearings and caucus before the vote in order to establish the party's position.

Once a bill has reached the second and third readings, only amendments related to those made in the first reading can be submitted. This recently enacted rule has reduced the overburden of legislative amendments that created logjams in the first parliament. MPs have made wide use of amendments in the past to raise issues of local concern, but new rules now require that MP-sponsored amendments receive the support of at least one-third of the relevant committees in order to be voted upon.

When a bill has been through the committee hearings, it is studied and voted upon in a plenary session of the Assembly. If it is approved, it then goes to the prime minister for approval into law.

The president must also review the law and has the right to challenge it by sending it back to the committee or to parliament for further discussion, or in some cases referring it to the Constitutional Court. On certain occasions the president has used this power to stall and obstruct legislation that he did not favor. In most cases, however, proposals emanating from the executive pass the Assembly (often in highly modified form) and are enacted into law.

Policy Outputs

Prior to the fall of the communist empire in the early 1990s, no political system had ever attempted a wholesale shift from central planning to market economics. Privatization of state-owned enterprises was a feature of Thatcherism in Britain, but that project took place on a small scale *within* a stable democracy and a market economy. The task in Hungary has been to build stable democracy while moving from a primarily state-owned economy (with some market elements) to a fully developed capitalist system.

Until recently, Hungary was cited as the chief example of a gradualist approach to economic transition in the post-communist world.[65] Usually posed in contrast to the Polish "shock therapy" program, Hungarian economic policy in the first democratic parliament was based on the notion that it was not necessary to articulate a comprehensive reform plan. Reforms already enacted before the formation of Antall's government had moved Hungary well past its neighbors. These reforms, starting with the New Economic Mechanism, had significantly liberalized the price structure, deregulated private, state, and cooperative enterprises, introduced private forms of property[66] and a personal income tax, commercialized the banking system, and introduced a securities market and unemployment compensation.

Hungary's early head start helped it to privatize a large percentage of the economy (today well over half of the economy is in private hands) and to capture the majority of foreign investment in Eastern Europe, but gradualism began to draw criticism as the economy slumped. Between 1990 and 1993, real incomes continuously declined and the GDP plummeted some 19 percent. Industrial and agricultural outputs fell by 40 and 50 percent respectively. Inflation rose to around 20 percent per year, and serious budget and current accounts deficits developed. Black market activity in the early nineties accounted for 30 percent of Hungary's GDP, and, in March 1993, unemployment reached a peak of nearly 14 percent nationwide. Tax and welfare reforms carried out before the transition allowed Hungary to defer painful cuts in public expenditures and to privatize extensively without undercutting the old political-economic class.[67]

In 1995, the Socialist Party reluctantly adopted the position of its coalition partner, that the economy required a shock-therapy–type austerity policy to reverse the negative economic trends, secure international loans, and reverse the denigration of Hungary's position in relation to its neighbors. Prime Minister Horn appointed László Békesi as finance minister but quickly clashed with him over the levels of state support that should be retained in the economy. Békesi wanted to balance Hungary's books by cutting government spending. In 1995 Horn replaced Békesi with Lajos Bokros, a 41-year-old former banker. Bokros followed closely in the footsteps of his predecessor and set forth a package of austerity measures referred to in the popular press as the *Bokros*

csomag (*Bokros package*). The package included large spending cuts, devaluation of Hungarian currency by 28 percent, a reduction in real wages, the privatization of most of the country's electricity and gas utilities, and a plan to revamp the nation's public sector, particularly the welfare system. The basic framework of the *Bokros csomag* was passed by parliament in March 1995 but subsequently delayed in a series of Constitutional challenges. Clashes with the socialist leadership and trade unions over welfare cuts caused Bokros to resign his post in February of 1996.

During his brief tenure, the Bokros package posted important successes, and the HSP-AFD government ultimately adhered to its core provisions. The most prominent area of government activity still remains the provision of social welfare (see Figure 10.9). In 1998 the Hungarian government spent more of its total budget on social programs than defense, public safety, transportation, and culture combined. Unemployment remains high, particularly in certain regions. But Hungary has been able to reduce its budget deficit, curb inflation, and most importantly, it has posted positive growth rates over the past several years. Positive economic performance—not the least, Hungary's improved position vis-à-vis the economies of its neighbors—has been associated with increasingly positive citizen evaluations of democracy.

A Decade After the Revolution

Hungary has emerged from transition with remarkably stable political institutions. After three elections, there is little to indicate that the parliamentary system will be upended. Hungary, for all of its pessimism, seems to have escaped the darker legacies of its authoritarian past. The question therefore is not "whither democracy?" but rather "what kind of democracy?" will take shape in Hungary.

This will be determined in large measure by the level of voter tolerance (for social inequalities and the loss of social protections) and the political alternatives that develop. Under the leadership of Viktor Orbán, new elements of conflict and confrontation

FIGURE 10.9   Distribution of Total Public Expenditures, 1997; In Forint/Billions (total 3,644.2 billion excluding 831 Ft/billion for "other" expenditures)

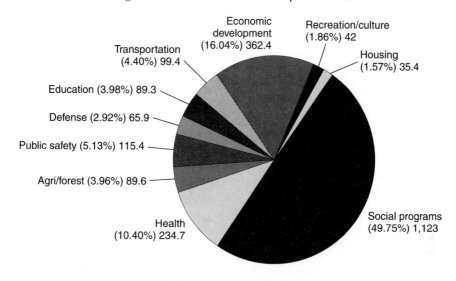

Economic development (16.04%) 362.4
Recreation/culture (1.86%) 42
Transportation (4.40%) 99.4
Housing (1.57%) 35.4
Education (3.98%) 89.3
Defense (2.92%) 65.9
Public safety (5.13%) 115.4
Agri/forest (3.96%) 89.6
Health (10.40%) 234.7
Social programs (49.75%) 1,123

Source: *Government Financial Statistics Yearbook* (International Monetary Fund, 1998).

have been introduced to the traditionally consensual Hungarian political practice. It is not yet clear whether these will become lasting features of Hungarian democracy. Fidesz is proving remarkably tranformist in its aspirations and has often bowed to the demand of more extreme right wing parties in parliament. The 1998 elections showed that the populist message is resonating among the nearly two-thirds of the population that has experienced a decline in living standards. If Hungary is able to maintain its economic miracle, however, and if enough Hungarians experience the fruits of that success, then the intolerant and populist strands of Hungarian political tradition may be eclipsed. Hungary has developed many of the characteristics of established Western European democracies. It has a relatively stable multi-party system, and even the great policy challenge of post-communism—economic transition—is now beginning to converge with the Europe-wide concern about how to balance economic growth with citizen demands for extensive social welfare systems.

✎ KEY TERMS ✎

Alliance of Free Democrats (AFD)
Alliance of Young Democrats-Civic Party (Fidesz)
Bokros *csomag* (Bokros package)

Christian Democratic People's Party (CDPP)
constructive vote of non-confidence
goulash communism

Hungarian Democratic Forum (HDF)
Hungarian Justice and Life Party (HJLP)
Hungarian Socialist Party (HSP); the main successor to the HSWP

Hungarian Socialist Workers Party (HSWP); the former Communist Party
Independent Smallholders' Party (ISP)

Kádárism

Kiegyezés

Little Pact

Magyar

magyarization

New Economic

   Mechanism (NEM)

nomenklatura

Roma

Roundtable Talks

samizdat

scrap votes

soft dictatorship

Trianon Treaty

∽ SUGGESTED READINGS ∽

Andorka, Rudolf, Tamás Kolosi, Richard Rose, and György Vukovich, eds. *A Society Transformed: Hungary in Time-Space Perspective*. Budapest: Central European University Press, 1999.

Bozóki, András, András Körösényi, and George Schöpflin, eds. *Post-Communist Transition: Emerging Pluralism in Hungary*. London: Pinter, 1992.

Deacon, Bob. "Developments in East European Social Policy." In C. Jones, ed. *New Perspectives on the Welfare State in Europe*. London: Routledge, 1993.

Hankiss, Elemér. *East European Alternatives*. Oxford: Clarendon Press, 1990.

Heinrich, Hans-George. *Hungary: Politics, Economics, and Society*. London: Frances Pinter, 1986.

Janos, Andrew C. *The Politics of Backwardness in Hungary, 1825-1945*. Princeton: Princeton University Press, 1982.

Király, Béla, and András Bozóki, eds. *Lawful Revolution in Hungary, 1989–1994*. New York: Columbia University, 1995.

Kornai, János. *The Socialist System: The Political Economy of Communism*. Princeton: Princeton University Press, 1992.

Lendvai, Paul. *Hungary: The Art of Survival*. London: I. B. Tauris, 1988.

Olson, David M., and Phillip Norton, eds. *The New Parliaments of Central and Eastern Europe*. London: Frank Cass, 1996.

O'Neil, Patrick. *Revolution from Within: the Hungarian Socialist Worker's Party and the collapse of Communism*. Northampton, MA: E. Elgar, 1998.

Rothschild, Joseph. *Return to Diversity: A Political History of East Central Europe Since World War II*. New York: Oxford University Press, 1993.

Tökés, Rudolf L. *Hungary's Negotiated Revolution: Economic Reforms, Social Change, and Political Succession: 1957-1990*. Cambridge: Cambridge University Press, 1996.

White, Stephen, Judy Batt, and Paul G. Lewis. *Developments in East European Politics*. Durham, NC: Duke University Press, 1993.

∽ ENDNOTES ∽

1. János Simon, "Post-Paternalist Political Culture in Hungary: Relationship Between Citizens and Politics During and After the 'Melancholic Revolution' (1989–1991)," *Communist and Post-Communist Studies* 26, No. 2 (1993): 226–38.

2. Anders Aaslund, "Why Goulash-Communism Is a Liability Now," *Transition: The Newsletter About Reforming Economies* 5, No. 5 (May-June 1994): 6.

3. Anna Seleny, "Old Political Rationalities and New Democracies: Compromise and Confrontation in Hungary and Poland" in *World Politics* Vol. 51, No. 4, 1999, p 488. Seleny sets forth the notion that Hungary represents a corporatist bargaining model of consolidation and outlines the ways in which both the formal and informal manifestations of this model emanate from pre-transition political rationalities and discourses.

4. "Hungary: On the Road to European Union," A World Bank Country Study (Washington D.C.: The World Bank, 1999).

5. A number of political scientists now draw upon the notion of "path dependency" to explain institutional choices, arguing that political actors may choose their institutions but they do not do so under conditions of their own design. This idea has its origins in the work of Douglass North; see, for example, his *Institutions, Institutional Change, and Economic Performance* (Cambridge, England: Cambridge University Press, 1992).

6. George Schöpflin, "The Political Traditions of Eastern Europe," *Daedalus* 119, No. 1 (Winter 1990).

7. For background on Hungarian history, see Peter F. Sugar, Péter Hanák, and Tibor Frank, (eds.), *A History of Hungary* (Bloomington: Indiana University Press, 1990); Nigel Swain, *The Rise and Fall of Feasible Socialism* (London: Verso, 1992); Ivan Volgyes, *Hungary: A Nation of Contradictions* (Boulder: Westview Press, 1982); William Shawcross, *Crime and Compromise: Janos Kadar and the Politics of Hungary Since the Revolution* (New York: E. P. Dutton & Company, 1974); William F. Robinson, *The Pattern of Reform in Hungary: A Political, Economic, and Cultural Analysis* (New York: Praeger, 1973); Hans-Georg Heinrich, *Hungary: Politics, Economics, Society* (Boulder: Lynne Reinner, 1986); and Elemer Hankiss, *East European Alternatives* (Oxford: Clarendon Press, 1990).

8. Quoted in Paul Lendvai, *Hungary: The Art of Survival* (London: I. B. Tauris, 1988), p. 12.

9. For this reference and a useful summary of Hungarian political history, see Tamás Kolosi and Richard Rose, "Introduction: Scaling Change in Hungary" in Rudolf Andorka, et al.,

(eds). *A Society Transformed: Hungary in Time-Space Perspective* (Budapest: Central European University Press, 1999).

10. For a detailed discussion of this point, see Joseph Rothschild, *Return to Diversity* (Oxford: Oxford University Press, 1993) pp. 3–24.

11. János Kornai, *The Road to a Free Economy: Shifting from a Socialist System: The Example of Hungary* (New York: Norton, 1990).

12. András Bozóki, András Körösényi, and George Schöpflin, eds., *Post-Communist Transition: Emerging Pluralism in Hungary* (London: Pinter, 1992);

13. Béla Király and András Bozóki, eds., *Lawful Revolution in Hungary* (New York: Columbia University Press, 1995); Patrick O'Neil, "Revolution from Within: Institutional Analysis, Transitions from Authoritarianism and the Case of Hungary," *World Politics* 48, No. 4 (1996).

14. Richard Rose and Christian Haerpfer, *New Democracies Barometer V: A 12-nation Survey*. Glasgow: University of Strathclyde Centre for the Study of Public Policy, Study No. 306, 1998).

15. Laszlo Foldenyi and Michael Blumenthal, "Dependency by Way of Rejection (The Revolutions of 1989: Lessons of the First Post-Communist Decade," in *East European Politics and Societies*, Spring 1999 v 13 i2 p 364(1).

16. Ákos Róna-Tas, "The First Shall Be Last? Entrepreneurship and Communist Cadres in the Transition from Socialism," *American Journal of Sociology* 100, No. 1 (July 1994): 40–69.

17. T. Kolosi, "Gazdagabbak lettünk?" [Are we richer?], in Népszabadság (September 25, 1993), p. 14.

18. See Éva Ehrlich and Gábor Révész, *Hungary and Its Prospects: 1985–2005* (Budapest: Akadémia Kiadó, 1995).

19. Paul Lendvai, *Anti-Semitism Without Jews: Communist Eastern Europe* (Garden City, NY: Doubleday, 1971).

20. Martin Gilbert, *Atlas of the Holocaust* (New York: MacMillan, 1982), p. 44; Martin Gilbert, *The Holocaust: A Record of the Destruction of Jewish Life in Europe During the Dark Years of Nazi Rule* (New York: Noonday Press, 1975), p. 22.

21. Barbara Einhorn, *Cinderella Goes to Market: Citizenship, Gender and Women's Movements in East Central Europe* (London: Verso, 1993); Chris Corrin, ed., *Superwomen and the Double Burden: Women's Experience of Change in Central and Eastern Europe and the Former Soviet Union* (London: Scarlet Press, 1992); Marilyn Rueschemeyer, *Women in the Politics of Post-Communist Eastern Europe* (Armonk NY: M. E. Sharpe, 1994).

22. Beth Stark, Sue Thomas, and Clyde Wilcox, "Popular Support for Electing Women in Eastern Europe," in Richard Matland and Kathleen Montgomery, eds., *Women's Access to Political Power in Post-Communist Europe* (Oxford University Press: London forthcoming, 2002).

23. On this point, see Patrick O'Neil, "Presidential Power in Post-Communist Europe: The Hungarian Case in Comparative Perspective," *The Journal of Communist Studies* 9, No. 3 (1993).

24. MP interview quoted in Seleny, 1999, p. 496.

25. Attila Ágh, "The Permanent 'Constitutional Crisis' in the Democratic Transition: The Case of Hungary," in Joachim Jens Hesse and Vincent Wright, *Constitutional Policy and Change in Europe* (Oxford: Oxford University Press, 1995), pp. 296–326.

26. Records of parliamentary activities are available to the public in Hungarian through the *Országgyülési Napló* (Parliamentary Diary) and the *Országgyülési Almanach* (Parliamentary Almanac).

27. *The Constitution of the Republic of Hungary*, Chapter III, Section 29.

28. Statistical Yearbook on CECs 1998-A Statistical View of Central Europe (Luxembourg: Eurostat Press Office).

29. Schiemann, John, *Myopic Bargains, Transitions to Democracy, and Democratic Consolidation: The Negotiated Origins of Hungary's Constitutional Court* (Paper prepared for the Midwest Political Science Association Meeting, Chicago, April 23–25, 1998).

30. Ágh, "Democratic Parliamentarism," p. 19.

31. Csaba Varga, *Transition to the Rule of Law: On the Democratic Transformation in Hungary* (Budapest: Project on Comparative Legal Cultures of the Faculty of Law of Loránd Eötvös University and the Institute for Legal Studies of the Hungarian Academy of Sciences, 1995).

32. Cited in Bennett Kovrig, *Communism in Hungary*, from Kun to Kádás. Stanford Calif: Hoover Institution Press, 1979. p. 350.

33. On communist-era political socialization, see Iván Völgyes, *Political Socialization in Eastern Europe: A Comparative Framework* (New York: Praeger, 1975).

34. Results of the survey are reported in Jim Kharoul, "Home of World Class Bad Moods," *Budapest Business Journal* (July 7, 1995): 6.

35. John Hibbing and Samuel Patterson, "Public Trust in New Parliaments of Central and Eastern Europe," *Political Studies*, XLII (1994), pp. 570–92; Judith Pataki, "Hungarians Dissatisfied with Political Changes," *RFE/RL Research Report*, (November 1992), pp. 66–70.

36. Richard Rose and Christian Haerpfer, "Change and Stability in the New Democracies Barometer: A Trend Analysis," *Studies in Public Policy 270* (Glasgow: Centre for the Study of Public Policy, 1996).

37. *Central and Eastern European Eurobarometer* No. 5 (Autumn 1994): Questions 1, 6.

38. Rose and Haerpfer, "Change and Stability," p. 35.

39. According to the 1991 Times-Mirror "Pulse of Europe" Survey, Hungarians displayed the lowest interest in politics of any of the Eastern or Western European countries in the survey.

40. Andorka, "Dissatisfaction and Alienation" in Andorka et al., p. 149.

41. Seleny (1999) summarizes several studies on this point.

42. Simon, "Post-Paternalist Political Culture in Hungary," p. 235.

43. Seleny (1999) notes that the railroad workers strike every year just before the budget negotiations in order to influence the upcoming budget. This, according to members she has interviewed, has become "regular showbiz."

44. See David Judge and Gabriella Ilonszki, "Member-Constituency Linkages in the Hungarian Parliament," *Legislative Studies Quarterly* 20, No. 2 (1995); Kathleen Montgomery, "Interest Group Representation in the Hungarian Parliament," in Attila Ágh and Gabriella Ilonszki, eds., *Parliaments and Organized Interests: The Second Steps* (Budapest: Hungarian Centre for Democracy Studies, 1996).

45. Zsofia Szilagyi, "Communication Breakdown Between the Government and the Public," in *Transition: Events and Issues in the Former Soviet Union and East-Central and Southeastern Europe* 2: 6 (March 1996), pp. 41–43.

46. László Bruszt and János Simon, "The Change in Citizens' Political Orientations During the Transition to Democracy in Hungary" (Budapest: Institute of Political Science of Hungarian Academy of Sciences, 1990–1991); Hankiss, *East European Alternatives*, p. 204.

47. Péter Róbert, "A szociálpolitikával kapcsolatos attitüdök alakulása" [Changing Attitudes on Social Welfare] in *Magyarország politikai évkönyve* [Political Yearbook of Hungary] (Budapest: Hungarian Center for Democracy Studies, 1996).

48. Edith Oltay, "The Former Communists' Election Victory in Hungary," *RFE/RL* 3: 25 (June 24, 1994).

49. Barnabas Racz and István Kukorelli, "The 'Second Generation' Post-Communist Elections in Hungary in 1994," *Europe-Asia Studies*, 47, No. 2 (1995): 251–79.

50. Miklós Tomka and István Harcsa, "Religious Denomination and Practice," in Andorka, et al., eds., *A Society Transformed: Hungary in Time-Space Perspective.* (Budapest: CEU, 1999), pp. 61-72.

51. Kathleen Montgomery and Gabriella Ilonszki, "Weak Mobilization, Hidden Majoritarianism, and Resurgence of the Right: A Recipe for Female Under-Representation in Hungary" in Richard E. Matland and Kathleen A. Montgomery (eds). *Women's Access to Political Power in Post-Communist Europe* (Oxford University Press, London: Forthcoming, 2002).

52. Ehrlich and Révész, *Hungary and Its Prospects*, p. 88.

53. Lynne Haney, "'But We Are Still Mothers: Gender and the Construction of Need in Post-Socialist Hungary." *Social Politics* (1997): 209-244.

54. Ronald Inglehart, *Modernization and Postmodernization* (Princeton: Princeton University Press, 1997).

55. Éva Hajba, "The Rise and Fall of the Hungarian Greens," in Terry Cox and Andy Furlong, eds., *Hungary: The Politics of Transition* (London: Frank Cass, 1995).

56. Mihály Bihari, "*Stabil demokrácia, alacsony fokú legitimáció, élezödö konfliktusok*" [Stable Democracy, Low Levels of Legitimacy, Sharpening Conflicts], in Kurtán, Sándor, and Vass, eds., *Magyarország politikai évkönyve* [Political Yearbook of Hungary] (Budapest: Center for Democracy Studies, 1995).

57. István Kukorelli, "The Birth, Testing, and Results of the 1989 Hungarian Electoral Law," *Soviet Studies* 43, No. 1 (1991): 143.

58. By now the details of the Hungarian electoral system and its consequences have been summarized in numerous articles. For example, see John R. Hibbing and Samuel C. Patterson, "A Democratic Legislature in the Making: The Historic Hungarian Elections of 1990," *Comparative Political Studies* 24, No. 4 (January 1992); Kukorelli, "The Birth, Testing, and Results of the 1989 Hungarian Electoral Law"; András Körösényi, "Hungary," *Electoral Studies* 9, No. 4 (December 1990); John T. Ishiyama, "Electoral System Experimentation in the New Eastern Europe: The Single Transferable Vote and the Additional Members System in Estonia and Hungary," *East European Quarterly* 29, No. 4 (Winter 1995).

59. Angelusz and Tardos, "Politikai és Kulturális Választóvonalak a Parlamenti Pártok Szavazótáborában" [Political and Cultural Cleavages in the Electoral Bases of Parliamentary Parties], *Tásadalomkutatás 1*; Gábor Tóka, "Kakukk Fészke: Pártrendszerek és Törésvonalak Magyarországon" [Cuckoo's Nest: Party Systems and Cleavages in Hungary], *Politikatudományi Szemle* [Journal of Political Science], (1992); András Körösényi, "Stable or Fragile Democracy? Political Cleavages and Party System in Hungary," *Government and Opposition* 28, No. 1 (Winter 1993).

60. Ferenc Gaszó and István Stumpf, "Parties and Voters after Two Elections," in *Hungarian Parliamentary Election 1994*, a report of the Institute for Political Science of the Hungarian Academy of Sciences, 1994.

61. The AFD was finally granted membership in the Liberal International in September 1993 after three years of confusion over whether the party should be considered liberal or social democratic.

62. Iván Szabó quoted in Duncan Shiels, "MDF Split Opens Up Hungary's Center Ground," *Reuters World Service* (March 11, 1996).

63. See information provided by European Forum http://www.europeanforum.bot-consult.se/cup/hungary.

64. "Hungary: The Price of Power" in *The Economist* (US), Nov 6, 1999 v 353 i8144 p 54.

65. Ben Slay, "Rapid Versus Gradual Economic Transition," *RFE/RL* 3: 31 (12 August, 1994); Josef Brada, "The Transformation from Communism to Capitalism: How Far? How Fast?" *Post-Soviet Affairs*, 9: 2 (1993), p. 93; Olivier Jean Blanchard, Kenneth A. Froot, and Jeffrey D. Sachs, eds., *The Transition in Eastern Europe, Volume 2: Restructuring* (Chicago: University of Chicago Press, 1994).

66. For example, before the Antall government came to power, taxis, restaurants, hotels, and small shops were allowed to operate under private ownership or rental bases. Small scale industrial enterprises with 20 (and later as many as 40) were also allowed, but the large, heavy industries (the nation's major employers) remained in state hands. In the 1980s, however, even these were broken down into smaller units. For example, the shoe and meat industrial conglomerates or trusts were broken into member companies that were granted independence. This organizational decentralization was expected to aid in the process of privatization and was seen as a leg-up over countries like Russia and Czechoslovakia.

67. David Stark, "Path Dependence and Privatization Strategies in East Central Europe," *East European Politics and Society* 6 (1992): 17–54; and Aaslund from footnote 2.

CHAPTER 11

POLITICS IN THE EUROPEAN UNION

The *European Union* (*EU*) represents a remarkable attempt by the nation-states of Europe to construct a framework of governance in which together they make collective decisions about a broad range of issues. As an organization, the EU is far more legally authoritative and institutionally sophisticated than any other international body. The 15 member nations have not, however, renounced the vigorous pursuit of their "national interest" in any policy area. Yet by agreeing to pursue that interest within an organization as constraining as the European Union, the member-states have recognized the ultimate superiority of multilateral, as opposed to unilateral, decision making and action in a variety of policy arenas.

The European Union is often used interchangeably with the term European Community. The original European Economic Community (EEC) established with the Treaty of Rome in 1958 gradually came to be known as the European Community (EC). The Treaty of Maastricht changed the name of the EC to the European Union. In certain legal contexts, however, the term European Community is still used. In this chapter, usage is determined by what seems most appropriate given the historical period being discussed.

Although the European Union resembles an international organization in certain ways, it is in fact very different. To begin with, it includes institutions that are not directly controlled by the member-states and that exercise real power in the policymaking process. In a similar vein, although the EU has clear similarities to a traditional national political system, it is clearly distinct from the other political systems discussed in this book. For example, it does not have its own military or its own police force nor does it have a prime minister or an elected government.

National governments believe that by becoming members of the Union, they can achieve both peace and prosperity for themselves and for Europe. The Union is an experiment in "pooling sovereignty." National governments have over time agreed to restrict their own ability to make decisions independently at home by participating in a collectivity in which each national voice is heard but must of necessity compromise both with other national voices and with the institutions of the Community that do not represent national governments. A national government, when outvoted by other governments, can be legally required to comply with the decision it opposed. This process does not cover all policy areas, but it does cover many. Unilateral decision making by national governments has become less frequent as the EU's policy agenda has gradually expanded.

The consequences of belonging to the European Union are serious for governments and member-states. In 1991, for example, more laws affecting France were adopted at the Community level than at the national level. In fact, some analysts have calculated that "today only 20 to 25 percent of the legal texts applicable in France are produced by the [French] parliament or the government in complete autonomy, that is, without any previous consultation in Brussels."[1] Membership in the Union is not to be taken lightly, for it changes the policy processes and the policy outcomes of national political systems. Membership carries with it serious binding commitments so that individual nations belonging to the Union can be increasingly thought of as member-states.

Why "Europe"?

Why have the individual nation-states of Europe—among the oldest in the world—decided to "pool their sovereignty"? Why have they accepted the sharing of power with institutions not directly controlled by the member-states? After all, political scientists tend to argue that the protection and maintenance of sovereignty is the top priority of governments throughout the world. Why did the process of European integration begin in the first place?

National leaders initiated the drive for European integration out of fear—the fear that history would repeat itself unless they succeeded in finding a new way in which to live together. At its core, the Union is rooted in the desire to transcend European history, a history filled with "rivers of blood" to use Winston Churchill's famous phrase. European integration is an attempt to change the geopolitics of Europe. By entangling the domestic institutions of individual nation-states within the institutions of the European Union, integration has changed (hopefully forever) the relations between European

states. Such a change in international relations, however, has "fed back" into national political systems, so that domestic policies, institutions, and modes of governance have been changed by virtue of belonging to the Union.[2]

The effort at integration is anchored in the belief that integration represents the best answer to what is known as "the German Question." That is, integration (rather than confrontation) is the best way to keep Germany firmly in the company of peaceful democratic nations and to keep it from playing a destructive role in European geopolitics. The attempt to ensure that Germany will be a cooperative rather than a threatening neighbor has led to a historic restructuring of relations among European states, which has also had a significant impact on domestic politics and policy.

Although the fear of potential German aggression was the main motive for European integration, other important spurs to integration have more recently come into play. The fear that European business firms were losing competitiveness with regard to American and Japanese firms has been one such spur. A growing acceptance that international problems such as environmental pollution, illegal immigration, and organized crime require transnational solutions has been another. The less than stellar European role in dealing with the various Balkan crises, including Kosovo, has pushed governments to increase their coordination in the defense area. Government leaders have acknowledged, sometimes reluctantly, that together they can have a much greater impact on problems than through individual action. Essentially, they have had to decide whether they wanted to exercise "a share of more effective power or [have] exclusive control over a less effective or wholly ineffective power."[3] Old-fashioned sovereignty—that is exclusive control over policymaking—has become associated with "naive sovereignty."[4] The result is that Brussels, the city that symbolizes the European Union, has gradually come to supplement, constrain, lead, and at times supplant national capitals.

The international (European) relations and the domestic politics of the members of the European Union have become increasingly intertwined. While the Union cannot be viewed as the "United States of Europe," it is such an important form of government that the global role of its member-states, their policymaking, and the political and economic choices available to their elected leaders are so entangled with the European Union that a complete analysis of politics in any member-state must consider the impact of the Union.

National governments have sometimes led this effort at integration. At other times, they have acquiesced in accepting it, but they have also resisted it. Whatever their stance toward European integration, however, national governments have played a key role in shaping and directing it. The institutions of the Community not controlled by the member-states, including the European Court of Justice, have also played a role in keeping the process of integration moving, especially when the member-states did not exercise leadership.

The European Union is now so important that much of what happens in national capitals cannot be understood without taking Brussels into account. However, neither can one understand what happens in Brussels without taking national capitals into account.[5] Brussels is not nearly as divorced from national politics as is Washington from the politics of state capitals in the United States.[6]

The European Union's political system is entangled with the politics of its constituent member-states while simultaneously having its own separate institutional identity and political dynamics. It is that balance between entanglement and autonomy that makes it both complex and fascinating. The "separateness" of the Union's political dynamics is rooted in the role of the various institutions involved in the policymaking process at the Union level, institutions that form a highly sophisticated and complex policymaking machinery. Most of those institutions do not strictly represent the interests of national governments, which means that national governments operating within the framework of the Union need to accommodate, respond to,

and compromise with institutions representing the "supranational" interest. Figure 11.1 diagrams the interaction of factors.

Historical Origins

Precisely because of the linkage between national systems and the European Union discussed earlier, the Union is considered to be *sui generis.* Although it is recognizable to students of federal systems such as the United States and the Federal Republic of Germany, it is also recognizable to students of international organizations such as the United Nations. In fact, the Union as a political system stands somewhere between a federal system and an international organization. To understand why—and why it is still moving along that continuum—it is important to understand its historical origins. Those origins have shaped subsequent developments much as the historical underpinnings of the American constitution have shaped American politics. Its historical origins help explain why the Union does not look more like a traditional state, why the electorate plays an indirect role, and why the national governments play such an important role in a framework that does have strong supranational elements to it.

The European Union is the most important institutional manifestation of the process of European integration. It has succeeded in moving toward an integrated Europe, whereas other institutions (such as the completely separate Council of Europe) for whom some had such hopes have not. The desire for integration is rooted in European history, much of it the result of the numerous and bloody centuries-old conflicts between what is now Germany and France. A quick look at recent history makes it clear why so many in postwar Europe were afraid that the past would continue to haunt Europe's future. Between 1870 (the Franco-Prussian War) and 1945, France and Germany had fought three times, twice in conflicts so vast that they were known as "world" wars. Only 21 years separated the end of World War I (1918) from the beginning of World War II (1939), and both France and Germany had been involved in the traumatic

Figure 11.1   The Structure of the European Union

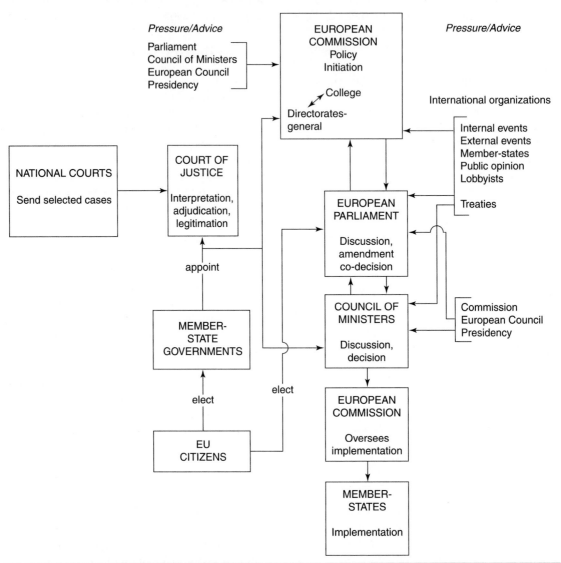

Source: Taken from John McCormick, *European Union: Politics and Policies* (Boulder, CO: Westview Press, 1996), p. 207.

Spanish Civil War (1933–1936), which foreshadowed the world war to come.

European integration as currently understood in Europe is linked to the creation of institutions that have some autonomy apart from the member governments. While member governments continue to be pivotal, they are not the only important ac-

tors. Institutions that have some independence from the member governments are also important. The existence of such independent institutions—cohabiting with institutions that are more tightly controlled by member governments—is known as "supranationality." Intergovernmentalism, by contrast, refers to institutional arrangements in which only national governments matter in the making of policy. European integration therefore is symbolized by the fact that a supranational component exists alongside an intergovernmental one. It is the symbiotic relationship between the two—within an institutional framework designed to enhance cooperation—that makes the politics of European integration so intriguing.

Supranational Integration: Schuman, Monnet, and the European Coal and Steel Community

The effort toward European integration—understood as having a supranational component—dates from May 9, 1950 and the *Schuman Plan*. On that day, French Foreign Minister Robert Schuman proposed the creation of an international organization to coordinate activity in the coal and steel industries. Designed to ensure Franco-German reconciliation and representing "a first step in the federation of Europe," Schuman's proposal represented a reversal of French foreign policy toward Germany—from one of unremitting hostility to one of reconciliation. Rather than viewing Russia/USSR as the key to constraining German power (the view historically taken by France), Shuman's proposal envisioned a Germany embedded in an integrated framework as the way to constrain German might. That view was a radical break with the past and helps explain why today's European Union represents such an extraordinary development. At its core, the Union has attempted to break the underlying dynamics of European geopolitical history.

Above all, the Schuman Plan was, in Schuman's own words, "a leap into the unknown."[7] France declared its willingness to restrict its own sovereignty in the fields of coal and steel in order to ensure that German sovereignty would be equally limited. Reconciliation would be tried as an alternative to the "balance of power" international game that had brought so much death and destruction to Europe in the past. Schuman hoped that war would become "politically unthinkable and economically impossible."[8]

That "leap into the unknown" had been designed by Jean Monnet, then general commissary for the French Plan of Modernization and Equipment, in an atmosphere of tremendous secrecy. Monnet was to play a critical role in the process of European integration throughout the following decade and beyond, so much so that he is sometimes referred to as "Mr. Europe." It was Monnet who underscored the strategic importance of having a "supranational" component in any initiative designed to achieve integration. In his view, supranationality was necessary to prevent the old interstate balance of power dynamics from becoming preeminent. His role in articulating the importance of supranationality in European integration was so important that many consider Monnet to be "the most important single architect of the European Community."[9]

The Franco-German relationship lay at the core of the Schuman plan, and that relationship still remains the central one within the process of European integration. France is Germany's key interlocutor in Europe, and Germany is France's key referent. When they agree on the need for further integration, France and Germany provide the political energy, the driving force, the momentum for achieving further integration.

In addition to reversing French foreign policy toward Germany, the Schuman Plan invited democratic nations in Europe to join in forming an organization that would implement the vision outlined in Schuman's declaration. Germany, Italy, Belgium, Luxembourg, and the Netherlands (the latter three known as the Benelux countries) responded. Negotiations began a month later, and the Treaty of Paris, which established the European Coal and Steel Community (ECSC), was signed on April 18, 1951. Although the ECSC was overshadowed by future developments in integration, it represented the first key step in overcoming the ancient divisions of continental Europe.

Negotiating Europe

The European Coal and Steel Community focused on economics as the most appropriate arena for integration. In particular, interstate trade and the prosperity that was thought to flow from such trade was to be fostered by integration. In turn, integration would be fostered by the results of such

Box 11.1   Robert Schuman: A True "European" (1886–1963)

Born in Luxembourg and raised in German-speaking part of Lorraine

Attended German universities

Drafted into German Army in World War I

Became French citizen in 1919 when Alsace-Lorraine was restored to France under Treaty of Versailles.

Elected to French Parliament

Refused to serve under Vichy Regime

Imprisoned by Gestapo for condemning expulsions of French population of Lorraine

Escaped in 1942 and became active in French Resistance

Helped to found Christian Democratic Party (MRP) in 1944

November 1947–December 1952–served as either premier or foreign minister of France

November 1950–Proposed the Schuman Plan, the catalyst for European integration

1958–1963–served as a member of the European Assembly, the forerunner of the European Parliament

trade. This view has shaped the evolution of European integration and its substantive policy core: economics, economic policy, and trade in the pursuit of economic prosperity. Underlying this concern with prosperity was the notion that prosperity facilitates peace. Because the interwar years (1918–1939) had seen economic tumult throughout much of Europe and the simultaneous rise of fascism and Nazism, it is not surprising that economic prosperity should be thought of as necessary for both democracy and peace.

The negotiations over the Schuman Plan did not involve only economic issues, however. Both domestic and foreign policy were major considerations. Foreign affairs—closely intertwined with domestic politics—emerged as a critical concern for all heads of state after World War II. It is useful to briefly consider why the countries that accepted Monnet's invitation did so. Here we find an often entangled combination of political/economic and geopolitical reasons—the Siamese twins of Europe. Economics played an important role in the first attempt at integration and has remained as a critical factor. It might be argued that integration proceeds fastest when the political/economic and geopolitical reasons reinforce one another.

Why Join Europe?

European integration was not inevitable. It represented a political choice. If different leaders had been in power, it might well not have occurred. While integration addressed the needs of the political leaders who accepted Schuman's invitation, these leaders were also predisposed to the idea. It is important to note that all of the leaders who decided to accept Schuman's invitation were from the Christian Democratic Party. (Schuman was a Christian Democrat as well.) Their party affiliation gave them a common bond and a set of ideological referents and beliefs that provided a basis for similar views of the world, a cognitive lens through which leaders and followers could define problems and choose solutions. The leaders who agreed had a great deal in common.

Schuman's own life experience encouraged him to shape "French foreign policy to his vision of a Europe in which France and Germany were reconciled and the suffering of the border provinces ended."[10] (See Box 10.1.) For Konrad Adenauer, who became German Chancellor in 1949, the proposed community represented a way for Germany to become an accepted and respectable member of both Europe and the international system. Personally, he was anxious to have closer ties with France. He was also confident that the German coal and steel producers were in a strong enough position that their interests would be safeguarded. In both strategic and personal terms, therefore, Schuman's proposal was attractive. By contrast, Kurt Schumacher, the postwar leader of the German Social Democratic Party, opposed integration with France. Although other key members of the Social Democrats supported European integration and the European Coal and Steel Community, he strongly opposed both. He saw the ECSC as both too capitalist and too dominated by the Christian Democratic Party.[11] The fact that Adenauer rather than Schumacher was chancellor when Schuman made his proposal was undoubtedly significant in shaping the history of European integration.

For the Benelux countries, dependent on trade with their neighbors, Schuman's proposal represented an attractive way of solving the German Question. The Dutch Foreign Ministry saw the Schuman Plan as creating "the capability for Europe to profit by Germany's strength without being threatened by it."[12] Once Belgium was able to obtain special treatment of its coal mines, the Benelux countries were on board.

The Italian Christian Democratic premier Alcide de Gasperi made a different calculus.[13] He viewed integration with the West as a way both to escape Italy's fascist past and to keep the strong Soviet-linked Italian Communist Party from coming to power. (The Communist Party opposed the Schuman Plan, viewing it as increasing American domination in Europe.) Eventually, European integration also represented a way to modernize the country, partially by ensuring export markets and partially by ensuring that millions of Italians would be allowed to emigrate and work in the rest of Europe.

Although in 2001 nearly all of Western Europe was in the European Union and Eastern European countries were clamoring for admission, in 1950 the governments of only six countries saw European integration as being in their interest.

Why Stay Out of Europe?

The countries that did not join in 1951 made their decisions on a variety of grounds. Spain and Portugal were under dictatorships and thus did not qualify for membership, while Greece was experiencing a civil war. The Scandinavians were uninterested in "supranational" schemes: the Nordic Union was based on cooperation rather than integration. The Eastern European countries were in the Soviet sphere of influence and were simply unable even to consider answering Schuman's invitation. All of these countries were to join the drive toward European integration much later. The United Kingdom, the most important country to absent itself from the ECSC, did not join for a variety of reasons. Perhaps the most important was that Britain saw itself as a world power, the leader of an empire, rather than as a state that needed to be concerned with its "European" role. The British rejection of the French government's invitation to participate in the ECSC negotiations was to be a defining moment for the future relationship of Britain with an integrated Europe.[14]

The Cold War, the United States, and European Integration

American influence on European integration in the 1950s was expressed in a number of ways. The United States, the "maker" of the international system, decisively shaped global institutions so as to break down trade barriers, protectionism, and imperial preferences and thereby create a liberal international economic regime.[15]

The United States also influenced Europe more directly. The postwar period, especially between 1947 and 1950, was a crucial one for institutionally linking the United States to Europe. On June 5, 1947, the outlines for what came to be the *Marshall Plan* (1948–1951) were announced. By insisting that Europe coordinate requests for Marshall Plan aid rather than allow each recipient country to deal bilaterally with the United States, the plan helped set the stage for European integration, "not least in the fostering of new modes of thinking."[16] Later, the United States would provide strong support for both the Schuman Plan and the European Economic Community.[17]

While the Marshall Plan linked the United States and Europe economically, the Americans also became involved in the military field. In April 1949, the Atlantic Pact was signed and the *North Atlantic Treaty Organization* (*NATO*) was born. Through NATO, the United States and Canada were committed militarily to European defense.

Six weeks after Schuman made his historic announcement on May 9, 1950, war broke out when North Korea invaded South Korea. The Korean War proved to be a pivotal event in the American relationship to Europe and thereby for the future of European integration. The American government feared that the Soviet Union would invade Western Europe via Germany. The United States therefore backed German rearmament, announced (in September 1950) that American troops would be incorporated into the NATO defense force, and that German divisions would be put under NATO command.

The European Defence Community (EDC) emerged as a counterproposal, in which a European army would be formed into which all German forces would be incorporated. However, the French parliament definitively rejected the proposal on August 30, 1954. Although the EDC was dead, German rearmament was still on the agenda. In May 1955 Germany was recognized as a sovereign state and accepted as a member of NATO. The dream of a European army was stillborn. In a similar vein, the possibility of an independent European role in international politics was remote, for "the European state system was, for the first time since the seventeenth century, firmly embedded in an international order dominated by others."[18]

The incorporation of both American troops and Germany in NATO within the context of the Cold War set the framework within which security and defense issues would be considered even after the end of the Cold War. Those issues were in a sense taken off the agenda of European integration.[19] The Bretton Woods system had for its part taken international monetary policy off the agenda. The path of integration was profoundly shaped by the fact that European integration took place within the "NATO-Bretton Woods system" in which the United States exercised hegemony in the West.[20]

It was not until the 1980s (in response to the breakdown of the Bretton Woods system) that the Community seriously addressed the issue of international finance (in the form of exchange rates) from an integrationist perspective. And the issue of security and defense policy was to remain within a transatlantic arena of discussion. It was not until 1999 that Europe began seriously discussing the creation of a separate European military force to be used for crisis management and even that would be linked to NATO. The process of European integration, therefore, has, until very recently, incorporated

only selected issues rather than concerning itself with all those issues traditionally considered "high politics." The exclusion of such issues ensured that European integration would not lead to the establishment of a European state in the traditional sense.

The European Economic Community

In May 1955, the Assembly of the ECSC asked the foreign ministers of the Six to draft new treaties to further European integration. The *Treaty of Rome* established the *European Economic Community* (*EEC*) and came into force on January 1, 1958. One of the French negotiators, Robert Marjolin, articulated the hopes and symbolism attached to the signing of the Treaty of Rome:

> I do not believe it is an exaggeration to say that this date [March 25, 1957] represents one of the greatest moments of Europe's history. Who would have thought during the 1930s, and even during the ten years that followed the war, that European states which had been tearing one another apart for so many centuries and some of which, like France and Italy, still had very closed economies, would form a common market intended eventually to become an economic area that could be linked to one great dynamic market?[22]

The Treaty of Rome included a much wider range of economic arenas and modified the institutional structure of the ECSC in important ways. Unlike the superseded ECSC, the European Economic Community has remained at the core of the integration process. The close working relationship that gradually developed among the six countries operating within the ECSC transferred over into the EEC. The Treaty of Rome called for the creation of a common market—the free movement of people, goods, services, and labor—among the six signatories as well as for a common agricultural policy (the latter provision had been included in order to convince the French parliament to ratify the treaty). It also called for measures to move the EEC beyond a mere common market. It embodied both economic and political objectives: "Whilst the Treaty of Rome is virtually exclusively concerned with economic cooperation, there was (and remains) an underlying political agenda. There is no doubt that its architects saw it . . . as another step on the road to political union."[23]

The Expansion of Europe

Two models of "Europe" developed during the 1960s. The first was that symbolized by the EEC, with its supranational dimension. The second was symbolized by the *European Free Trade Association (EFTA)*. EFTA was established in 1960 with Britain playing a leading role in its birth and Norway, Sweden, Denmark, Switzerland, Austria, and Portugal joining the British-led initiative. It was entirely intergovernmental, lacked any supranational element, and was concerned only with free trade. Whereas EFTA did not compromise sovereignty, the ECC created an entanglement and a fusion between national and community powers.[24] Over time, the supranational model eclipsed the intergovernmental, with only Iceland, Norway, and Switzerland remaining in EFTA. The decline of EFTA was presaged by the UK's decision to apply for membership in the EEC, and after two vetoes by President De Gaulle of France, the British, along with Ireland and Denmark (for whom the UK was a key trading partner), finally joined in 1973. Norway had also applied and been accepted, but its electorate rejected membership in a referendum in 1972.

In 1981 Greece joined and in 1986 Spain and Portugal did the same. The accession of all three was viewed as consolidating their transition to democracy and as widening European integration to the Mediterranean. In 1995, Austria, Sweden, and Finland joined; Norway's electorate again refused accession in a referendum. Of the four poorest countries included in enlargement, Ireland, Spain, and Portugal are typically viewed as "success" stories while Greece, by contrast, has been far more problematic for the Union. Its internal politics have been such that the fit between Brussels and Athens has been far from an easy one.[25]

Beyond the Treaty of Rome

The dismantling of tariffs within the Community did indeed increase trade among the six signatories of the Treaty of Rome. However, the increased volatility of financial markets, rooted in the breakdown of the Bretton Woods system established immediately after World War II, threatened the expansion of trade. In 1979 a Franco-German initiative designed to minimize the fluctuations in exchange rates gained the support of the Six. The European Monetary System (EMS), which was to serve as the foundation for a common currency and Economic and Monetary Union (EMU) was established. Britain, however, declined to join the EMS's key mechanism, the exchange rate mechanism. Again, the Six had taken the process of European integration one step further, but without British participation. Britain was to remain outside until October 1990, just before Margaret Thatcher was forced out of office by her own political party.

While the British government did not want to tie the British pound to the currencies of the Six, it did share the concern of the Six with the declining competitiveness of European industry with its American and Japanese counterparts. Beginning with the election of Margaret Thatcher as prime minister in 1979, political elites in Europe gradually became more sympathetic to the idea that the opening of markets was necessary both to spur economic growth and to improve the competitiveness of European firms in the emerging global economy. The election of Christian Democratic Chancellor Kohl in Germany in 1982 and the ill-fated fortunes of the French Socialist government's policies from 1981 to 1983 led to an emerging consensus that Europe needed to establish a true common market, one in which so-called nontariff barriers were dismantled. Markets were increasingly seen as promoters of economic growth rather than simply as a mechanism from which workers needed extensive protection.

This emerging consensus was crystallized by the new president of the European Commission, Jacques Delors. Delors, whose own father was left for dead by German troops in World War I, played a key role in the next decade's movement toward European integration. Appointed in 1985, Delors seized on the idea for an internal market (the new name given to the "common market" with the connotation of removing nontariff barriers). The internal market project revitalized the Community, ensured Delors's place in the history of European integration, and gave the Community a much

FIGURE 11.2 Population of the European Union by Member-States

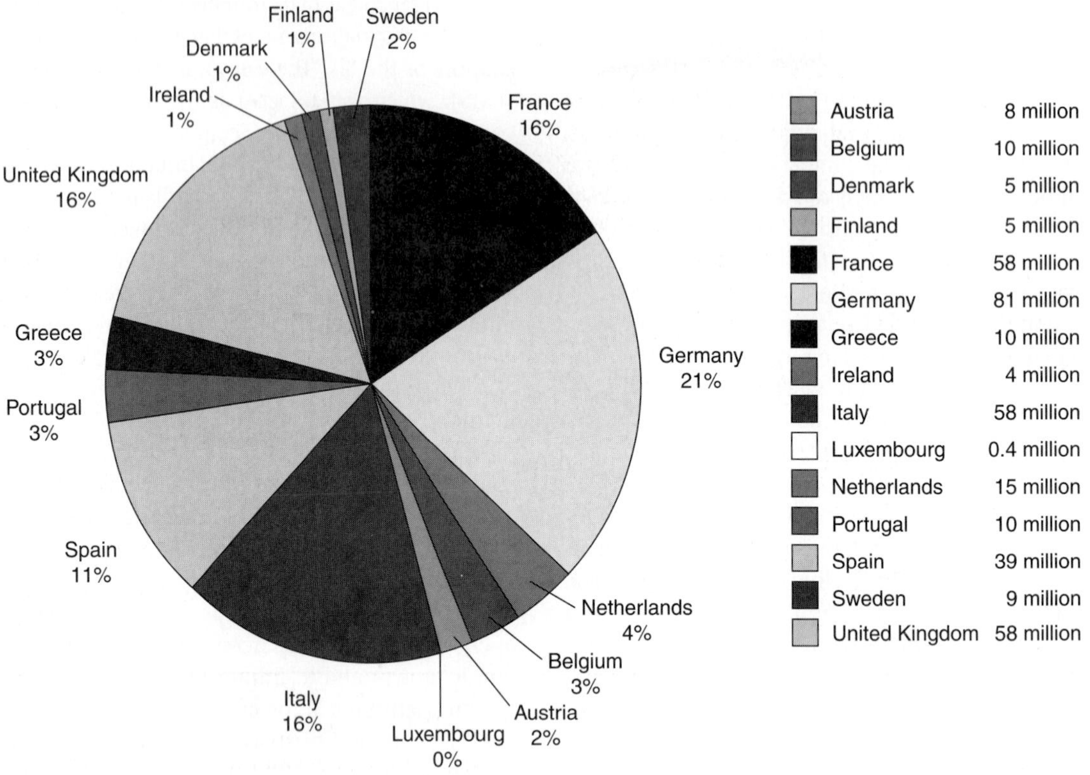
Finland 1%
Sweden 2%
Denmark 1%
Ireland 1%
France 16%
United Kingdom 16%
Greece 3%
Portugal 3%
Germany 21%
Spain 11%
Netherlands 4%
Belgium 3%
Italy 16%
Austria 2%
Luxembourg 0%
Austria 8 million
Belgium 10 million
Denmark 5 million
Finland 5 million
France 58 million
Germany 81 million
Greece 10 million
Ireland 4 million
Italy 58 million
Luxembourg 0.4 million
Netherlands 15 million
Portugal 10 million
Spain 39 million
Sweden 9 million
United Kingdom 58 million

[a]Sixty-two votes are needed for a qualified majority.
Source: Survey European Union," *The Economist,* May 31–June 6, 1997, p. 12.

higher profile than it had previously had. The process led to the Single European Act, a major amendment to the Treaty of Rome. For Delors, the single-market project was using economics strategically so as to pursue a political agenda. As he explained in a radio interview in 1993, "If this job was about making a single market I wouldn't have come here in 1985. We're not here just to make a single market—that doesn't interest me—but to make a political union."[26]

The Single European Act

The decision to amend the Treaty of Rome was made in 1985, and the *Single European Act* (*SEA*) came into force in 1987. The SEA changed the decision rules for legislation designed to create the internal market in that qualified majority voting rather than unanimity was to apply to such legislation. (A qualified majority requires more votes for approval than does a simple majority.) A national government would be unable to veto legislation introduced for the explicit purpose of creating the market (the veto had been legitimated in January 1966 in the Luxembourg Compromise). Furthermore, the powers of the European Parliament were increased as were the Community's powers in the area of environmental protection.

The drive for the single market came to be known as the "1992" Project—1992 being the deadline for the adoption of Community legisla-

FIGURE 11.3   Territory of the European Union by Member-States

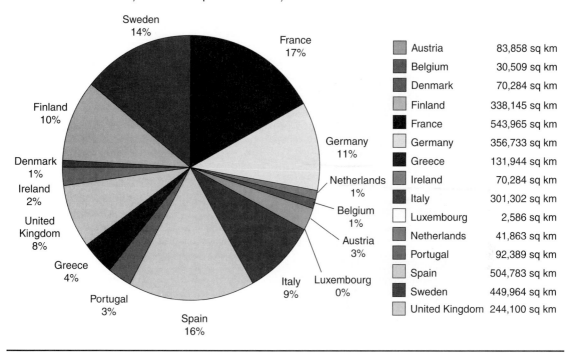

Austria	83,858 sq km
Belgium	30,509 sq km
Denmark	70,284 sq km
Finland	338,145 sq km
France	543,965 sq km
Germany	356,733 sq km
Greece	131,944 sq km
Ireland	70,284 sq km
Italy	301,302 sq km
Luxembourg	2,586 sq km
Netherlands	41,863 sq km
Portugal	92,389 sq km
Spain	504,783 sq km
Sweden	449,964 sq km
United Kingdom	244,100 sq km

tion needed to remove nontariff barriers. The adoption of a single market represented a milestone in the history of European integration. It can be thought of as analogous in importance to the "interstate commerce clause" in the American constitution. Just as that clause undergirded the growth of federal power in nineteenth-century America, the single market represented a major step in the integration of Europe and the power of the Community institutions.

A single market is designed to minimize nontariff barriers. Such barriers accumulate over time and are often closely tied to cultural traditions, which means that overriding them can be politically sensitive. It is for that very reason that the single market has been so important. By examining barriers from the perspective of whether they inhibit the possibilities open to an exporter to a certain country, the single market opens to scrutiny many institutional arrangements in both the public and private sectors which have been accepted over time without much

thought. Germany could not exclude beer made in an "unGerman" way, Italy could not exclude pasta made with "foreign" wheat, and so forth.

The 1992 Project was above all a project of regulatory reform—national deregulation combined with re-regulation at the Community level. Market forces were to be strengthened in order to improve the ability of European firms to compete globally. Regulation would often be implemented in Brussels rather than the national level. The European Community began setting up regulatory agencies—such as the European Agency for the Evaluation of Medicinal Products to regulate pharmaceuticals—that have complemented national regulatory frameworks. Although national economic systems were deregulated, re-regulation occurred in Brussels. Furthermore, environmental regulation has been increasingly concentrated at the Community level. Finally, the Commission began to exercise its powers in the area of competition policy (which covers antitrust and state aids) much more aggressively.[27]

FIGURE 11.4 Gross National Product of the European Union by Member-States

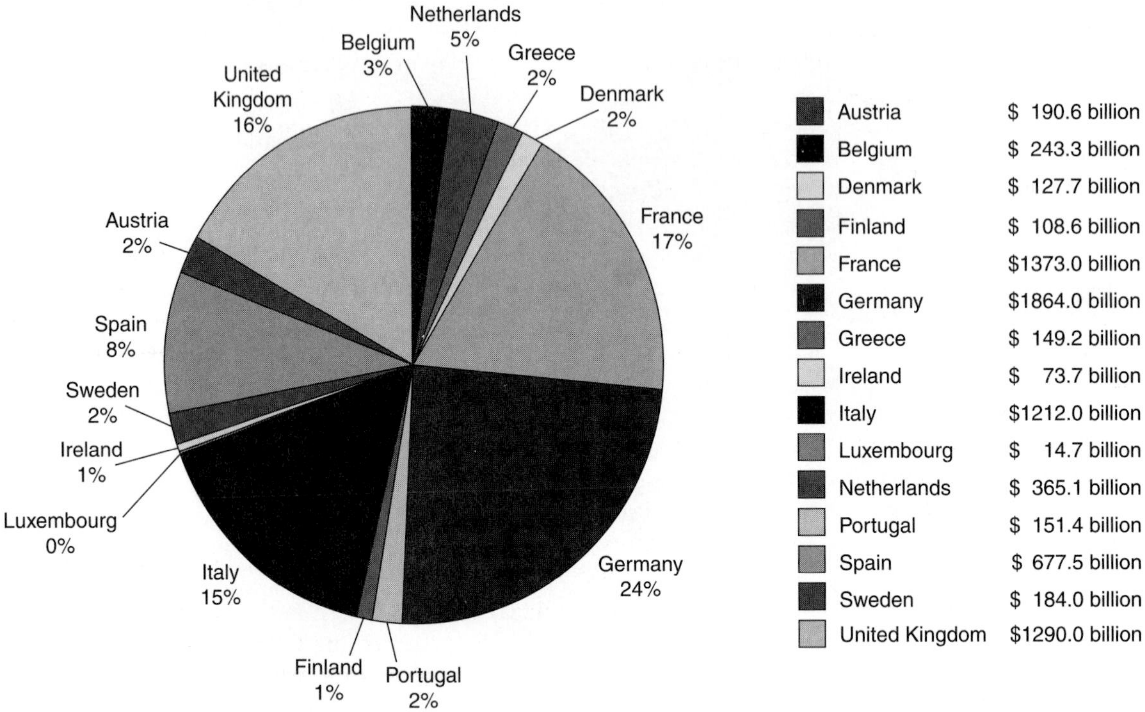
Netherlands 5%
Belgium 3%
Greece 2%
United Kingdom 16%
Denmark 2%
France 17%
Austria 2%
Spain 8%
Sweden 2%
Ireland 1%
Luxembourg 0%
Italy 15%
Germany 24%
Finland 1%
Portugal 2%
Austria $ 190.6 billion
Belgium $ 243.3 billion
Denmark $ 127.7 billion
Finland $ 108.6 billion
France $1373.0 billion
Germany $1864.0 billion
Greece $ 149.2 billion
Ireland $ 73.7 billion
Italy $1212.0 billion
Luxembourg $ 14.7 billion
Netherlands $ 365.1 billion
Portugal $ 151.4 billion
Spain $ 677.5 billion
Sweden $ 184.0 billion
United Kingdom $1290.0 billion

Protected markets, such as those in the telecommunications sector, were gradually liberalized. By the late 1990s, the Community's regulatory reach was so important that some analysts considered it a "regulatory state."[28]

The Maastricht Treaty

The single market of the late 1980s was largely viewed as a success. Business investment climbed, and Europe seemed to enjoy a new sense of economic optimism. Under these circumstances, an initiative to move to a European central bank and a common currency as an extension of the single market began to attract support. Central bank governors, under the chairmanship of Jacques Delors, began to lay out a framework by which a common currency could be achieved.

While that effort was underway, the Berlin Wall fell in November 1989. German unification, once barely considered, now became a reality. A new Germany was on the scene. Would it continue to face westward—to Brussels—or would it face toward the East? What role would the new Germany play in a Europe fundamentally changed by the end of the Cold War? How could Europe "contain" this economic powerhouse that had just added more than 16 million inhabitants? These questions were especially pressing, as the problems—and especially the huge costs—associated with German unification were still unacknowledged by most observers.

One response to a new iteration of the old "German Question" was to move toward a new treaty that would tie Germany even more firmly to the West by further entangling German institutions with those of the Community. The purpose was to ensure that a "European Germany" would not be supplanted by a "German Europe." Helmut Kohl, the Christian Democratic chancellor of Germany, for whom memories of World War II were still keen, strongly supported embedding Germany in a more deeply integrated European Community. The result was the *Treaty of European Union* (*TEU*), usually referred to as the *Maastricht Treaty* after the small Dutch town in which the final negotiations took place in December 1991.

The Maastricht Treaty, which came into effect in November 1993, represented another milestone in the history of European integration, moving the process of European integration into two critical new arenas as well as entrenching the Community's jurisdiction over the pivotal area of monetary policy. The treaty is complex. It changed the name of the European Community to that of the European Union (EU). Most importantly, it changed the structure of the Community by establishing three "pillars" in which the Community institutions played different roles; that same structure was retained in the Treaty of Amsterdam which was negotiated subsequent to the Treaty of Maastricht and came into effect in 1999. In both Maastricht and Amsterdam, the European Council and the Council of Ministers were important in all three pillars, whereas the other Community institutions were central only in pillar one. The more federally inclined members of the Union saw the pillar structure as a transition phase, one that would ultimately lead to all three areas of policy being brought under the Community's institutions. The more intergovernmentalist members viewed the pillar structure as a safeguard against precisely that kind of evolutionary development.

Pillar One: The Extension of the Treaty of Rome

Pillar one as defined by Maastricht encompassed the creation of the *Economic and Monetary Union* (*EMU*)—including a new European Central Bank and a common currency (the Euro) as well as incorporation of all the policy areas previously falling under the Community's jurisdiction. The *acquis communautaire*—all the accumulated laws and judicial decisions adopted since the signing of Treaty of Rome—belonged to the first pillar. For example, the single market, agriculture, environmental policy, regional policy, research and technological development, consumer protection, trade policy, fisheries policy, competition policy, and transportation policy all fell under pillar one.

Decision-making procedures within pillar one were firmly rooted within the traditional European Community institutions while expanding the Parliament's decision-making power. Policy areas that were designated as falling under the jurisdiction of pillar one were dealt with within the institutional machinery of the Commission, the Parliament, the Council of Ministers, the Presidency, the European Court of Justice, the European Council, and the new European Central Bank. Under Maastricht, however, the UK and Denmark were allowed to "opt out" of the common currency as well as several other provisions if they so wished. In September 2000, the Danish public voted against joining the Euro so that Denmark will not be a member of the eurozone for at least some time. In general pillar one under Maastricht included everything which the "old" European Community included plus the new European Central Bank.

Pillars Two and Three: An Intergovernmental Compromise

Pillars two and three expanded the scope of what became renamed the European Union by encompassing policy areas which previously had been outside the scope of European integration. The institutional structures which governed pillars two and three differed from those found in pillar one. Pillar two referred to the area of the *Common Foreign and Security Policy* (*CFSP*) and pillar three referred to what in Europe is known as *Justice and Home Affairs* (internal security). In both pillars, the Council of Ministers rather than the Commission was primarily responsible for action, unanimous voting was required, the Parliament was largely excluded, and the European Court of Justice did not exercise jurisdiction.

The fact that the Council of Ministers rather than the European Commission was established as the key institution represented a compromise between those countries that favored a more "federal" model of integration and therefore supported giving the Commission its traditional powers in these areas and those governments (Britain and France) that are worried about sovereignty. Pillars two and three therefore were brought within the process of integration but were to be governed by the European Council and the Council of Ministers, the

---

Box 11.2 Justice and Home Affairs (JHA) Pillars 1 and 3

The Treaty of Amsterdam and the 1999 European Council Summit in Tampere, Finland, resulted in much deeper integration in the sensitive area of internal security. The level of intergovernmental cooperation was increased and the powers of the Commission and the European Court of Justice were broadened to such an extent that Justice and Home Affairs is now viewed as a key component of an integrating Europe. Included among the important new initiatives in this area were:

EUROPOL given significant new powers to initiate criminal investigations

Police and immigration officials given cross-national legal powers in all EU member-states

Network of Union public prosecutors (Eurojust)

European Police College to train law enforcement officials

Joint investigative teams to combat terrorism and drug trafficking

Task force of senior police officers

Development of

- common EU asylum and immigration policy
- harmonized approach to dealing with refugees (including a European refugee fund)
- standardized methods of combating illegal immigration
- tougher laws against money-laundering
- policies to ensure that court judgments issued in one country are enforceable throughout the Union

---

most intergovernmental institutions within the Community's institutional framework.

Treaty of Amsterdam

The *Treaty of Amsterdam* came into effect in 1999 and significantly changed the policy and institutional landscape established by the Maastricht Treaty. First of all, most areas of what had been pillar three under Maastricht were now placed within pillar one, significantly strengthening the policy reach of the Commission and the influence of the European Court of Justice. Along with that expansion, the power of the Commission President *vis à vis* the other Commissioners was enhanced. Secondly, the power of the European Parliament was also increased by both simplifying and expanding the use of co-decision in a wide range of issue areas. Thirdly, the powers of the EU in several policy areas, including public health (critical to the European welfare state) and CFSP, both of which are very sensitive for national sovereignty, were enhanced. Public health is firmly under the Union's institutions in pillar one while CFSP is firmly in the intergovernmental pillar two.

The transfer of most policy areas within the "old" pillar three to pillar one represented a very significant step in the process of European integration. Internal security is traditionally viewed as absolutely central to

national sovereignty. In the post-Amsterdam period, issues such as asylum, immigration, and judicial cooperation in civil matters came within the policy remit of the Commission and, with some restrictions, the jurisdiction of the European Court of Justice. Whereas in Maastricht the member-states had given up their sovereignty in the area of monetary policy by accepting the Euro but had been very reluctant to "Europeanize" internal security, the Treaty of Amsterdam represented their new willingness to "pool" their sovereignty in the area of Justice and Home Affairs. (In the United States, the Department of Justice is concerned with most of the same issue areas.) The intergovernmental pillar three of the Maastricht Treaty was widely viewed as having been a failure so that the Treaty of Amsterdam signaled the new willingness of the member-states to try to make it more effective by bringing it under the Commission's umbrella.

In a similar vein, in October 1999 the member-states met at a special summit in Tampere, Finland, and agreed to numerous initiatives which mark a major turning point in the degree of integration which the member-states are willing to accept in this extremely sensitive area. (see Box 11.2). Only two policy areas remain within the "new" pillar three after Amsterdam—police cooperation (including the European Police Office known as EUROPOL which

TIMETABLE

May 1950–Schuman Plan
1952–Treaty of Paris (European Coal and Steel Community) (ECSC)
1958–Treaty of Rome – European Economic Community (EEC)
1966–Luxembourg Compromise
    (Legitimated use of national veto, thereby requiring unanimity to adopt legislation)
1979–Direct election of European Parliament
1987–Single European Act (SEA)
- Introduced qualified majority voting, single market – "1992" project
- EEC becomes European Community (EC)

1993–Maastricht Treaty
- Acceptance of single currency (Euro) and of European Central Bank
- Three pillars expand the reach of integration
- EC becomes European Union (EU)

1999–Introduction of Euro as a "virtual" currency
    Treaty of Amsterdam
- Significant integration in Justice and Home Affairs
- European Security and Defense Policy
- European Parliament able to participate in co-decision in a wide range of areas
- High Representative for the EU Common Foreign and Security Policy ("Mr. CFSP")

2002–The Euro is introduced into daily use, replacing the currencies of those member-states which have joined the Euro-zone

under Amsterdam was given stronger powers and a more operational role) and judicial cooperation in criminal matters, and even here the member-states were willing to be less intergovernmental. Whereas the European Court of Justice had been completely excluded in the old pillar three, it was given a limited role in the post-Amsterdam pillar three. Furthermore, the Commission as well as the member-states has the right of initiative in all matters falling under pillar three, an expansion of the role of the Commission. Some convergence of criminal legislation is now possible, so that Amsterdam is viewed by some as contributing "towards creating a common European criminal law."[29]

With regard to pillar two of the Maastricht Treaty, Amsterdam enhanced the powers of the Union in the area of a common foreign and security policy. Institutionally, the Secretary-General of the Council of Ministers was also appointed as the High Representative for the EU Common Foreign and Security Policy ("Mr. CFSP"). Javier Solana, widely respected in his previous post as NATO Sec-

retary-General was appointed to that position when the Treaty of Amsterdam came into effect in 1999.

The Institutions

The institutional structure of the European Union is based on the complex divisions represented by the three pillars (see Figure 11.5). The sophisticated policymaking process normally associated with the Community resides in pillar one—including key policymaking institutions such as the European Commission, the Council of Ministers, the European Parliament, the European Council, European Court of Justice, and the European Central Bank.

Whereas the other institutions all interact with one another, the European Central Bank (located in Frankfurt, Germany) is very independent from all the other institutions. However, Justice and Home Affairs within pillar one still excludes the Parliament so that the Commission and the Council are the central policymaking actors in areas such as immigration, visa policy, and asylum policy. In pillars

FIGURE 11.5   The Three Pillars of the European Council

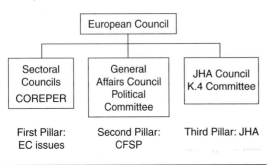

First Pillar:
EC issues

Second Pillar:
CFSP

Third Pillar: JHA

Source: Fiona Hayes-Renshaw and Helen Wallace, *The Council of Ministers,* the European Union Series (London: Macmillan, 1997), p. 163.

two and three, the European Council and the Council of Ministers are the key institutional actors.

The European Commission

The *European Commission,* located in Brussels, is the Community's most visible institution in day-to-day policymaking. Its institutional mission within the Community is to promote integration. Toward that end, the Commission is made up of the College of Commissioners, the decision-making body within the Commission, and civil servants that do the work typical of all bureaucracies. The College of Commissioners is the political (although not in a partisan sense) component of the Commission while the civil servants are the administrative sector. The term "Commission" is used in the press to refer either to the civil servants, the College, or both.

The Commission is composed of 20 commissioners who collectively make up the College of Commissioners. Each commissioner is appointed by the prime minister or president of the member-states. The United Kingdom, France, Germany, Spain, and Italy each have two commissioners; all other member-states have one. Each commissioner has one vote, serves for a five-year term, and can be reappointed if the national government so wishes. Each is in charge of certain policy areas (environment, agriculture, research and technology, transport, or telecommunications, for example) and

when they meet collectively every Wednesday, they are known as the College of Commissioners.

The president of the Commission is the most important commissioner and his influence within the Commission was enhanced by the Treaty of Amsterdam. He is proposed by a member-state but is chosen by a unanimous vote of all the prime ministers and heads of state meeting in the European Council. Typically a president from a large country is succeeded by a president from a small country. Strong Commission presidents leave an imprint: Walter Hallstein, the first president, and Jacques Delors (1985–1995) both led the Commission in ways that increased its profile and prestige. Commission presidents, however, are constrained by the fact that they do not appoint their fellow commissioners and have little formal control over them. Even Jacques Delors at the height of his power and prestige was unable to convince some governments to reappoint commissioners he would have liked to have returned to the Commission.

The role of the president of the Commission is not similar to that of a prime minister. The president is not accountable to Parliament in the way that a national prime minister is and does not become president of the Commission through an election. He is appointed by the national governments rather than being elected, as are prime ministers. In a similar vein, the Commission is not a "government" in that it is not selected by the voters or legislature as a result of an election.

The Commission has a number of important powers, but its most pivotal is contained in pillar one: It is the only institution that can propose legislation in pillar one. Neither the Council of Ministers nor the European Parliament can initiate legislation; the monopoly exercised by the Commission over policy initiation is one of its most important formal powers. Although that power is circumscribed by the power of the Parliament to ask for a legislative proposal, the fact that it must be the Commission which drafts the proposal gives it important leverage in the legislative process. This power thus enables the Commission to help set the policy agenda. The Commission also manages the Community's budget, is involved in external relations, monitors the application of Community law in the member-states, and generally is expected to make the arguments and proposals necessary to promote further integration.

The College of Commissioners decides by majority vote which proposals for legislation to send to the Council of Ministers and the European Parliament. The College can also decide to take antitrust action (without the approval of the Council of Ministers) and can argue cases before the European Court of Justice.

The Commission's bureaucracy, although very small in comparison to national bureaucracies, is the most important administrative component of the entire Community and is key to the Commission's ability to promote the process of integration. Sometimes known as Eurocrats, officials who work for the Commission are multilingual and highly educated, and they typically receive their position after passing a competitive examination. They do the initial drafting of the legislation (which is then approved by the College) and are present at the negotiations within the Council of Ministers on all proposals from the College of Commissioners. Commission officials are emphatically not the functional equivalents of international civil servants, those who work for global international organizations such as the United Nations. Commission officials are viewed as having much more authority when dealing with national officials than are traditional international civil servants.[30]

The operations of its civil servants allow the Commission to play a complex role. Commission officials often operate very effectively behind the scenes. They consult with a wide variety of interest groups and often receive complaints about noncompliance with Community laws from citizens in the member-states.

Fundamentally, the Commission promotes European integration and provides the administrative resources absolutely essential for policymaking in a system as complex as the European Union. Without the Commission, the European Union would not have an administrative apparatus.

Because of its centrality in the definition of problems and the formulation of policy, its access to significant administrative resources, and its links to a variety of groups throughout the Community as well as in Brussels, the Commission plays a key role in the policymaking process. It is at the heart of the European Union.[31] The fact that the European Union has a policymaking body not directly controlled by the member-states and able to wield important influence clearly distinguishes the organization as different from all others. The Commission as an institution symbolizes that supranational dimension within European integration that was so vigorously promoted by Jean Monnet.

The Commission's prestige, influence, and credibility were, however, damaged in 1999 when the Santer Commission was forced to resign due to pressure from the European Parliament. In brief, the Parliament decided in March 1998 to postpone the discharge of the EU's budget for financial year 1996 (the right to discharge the budget is a crucial aspect of the Parliament's oversight powers over the budget). After asking the Commission to address failures in a variety of areas, including the management of monies spent outside the EU, the Parliament in December 1998 decided that the Commission had not sufficiently improved its performance in a variety of areas and refused to discharge the budget. The unprecedented action led to a great deal of confusion within the Parliament, with a Committee of Independent Experts being named under the sponsorship of both the Commission and the Parliament to examine the possibility of fraud and mismanagement of EU funds. The Committee's report, published on March 15, 1999, was so damaging that a cross-party coalition formed which had the votes to sustain a censure motion. At that point, the Santer Commission resigned.[32] Romano Prodi, who as prime minister of Italy had been credited with restructuring Italian public finance so that Italy was unexpectedly able to join EMU, was chosen as the new Commission President. Some members of the Santer Commission were reappointed by their respective national governments to the Prodi Commission. Other members of the Prodi Commission, however, were completely new appointees.

TABLE **11.1**   DISPROPORTIONATE POWER OF SMALL COUNTRIES

Member-State	Number of Commissioners	Number of Votes in Council of Ministers	Number of Citizens per Vote (Millions)	Number Members of European Parliament (MEPs)	Inhabitants Per MEP (1999 Figures)
Germany	2	10	8.22	99	829,000
U.K.	2	10	5.85	87	681,000
France	2	10	5.82	87	678,000
Italy	2	10	5.72	87	663,000
Spain	2	8	4.96	64	616,000
Netherlands	1	5	3.14	31	508,000
Greece	1	5	2.10	25	422,000
Belgium	1	5	2.04	25	409,000
Portugal	1	5	1.96	25	399,000
Sweden	1	4	2.20	22	402,000
Austria	1	4	2.05	21	385,000
Denmark	1	3	1.73	16	332,000
Finland	1	3	1.70	16	323,000
Ireland	1	3	1.20	15	249,000
Luxembourg	1	2	0.20	6	72,000
		87			

Source: Richard Corbett, Francis Jacobs, and Michael Shackleton, *The European Parliament,* 4th ed. (London: John Harper, 2000), p. 12; John McCormick, *The European Union: Politics and Policies,* 2nd ed. (Boulder, CO: Westview, 1999, p. 131.

The Council of Ministers

The *Council of Ministers* is the institution that adopts Community legislation and develops the budget along with the Commission and the Parliament. It is the top decision-making body. Its decisions become Community law. Its members are ministers from national governments and participate in the Council as long as the national government is in power.

The Council of Ministers, as the Union's main legislature, is a more powerful decision maker than either the Commission or the Parliament. Above all, it adopts Community legislation that is then incorporated into national legal codes. It does not, however, participate in the formation of the Commission and cannot dismiss it.

Technically speaking, there are many Councils of Ministers, but the term "Council of Ministers" is applied to each of the numerous sectoral councils. A separate Council of Ministers exists for each policy sector in which the Union has jurisdiction (at present there are over twenty sectoral councils)—for

example, for environmental affairs, finance, education, development, transportation, agriculture, health, and justice and home affairs. Each Council is composed of the relevant ministers from each of the member-state governments (or someone delegated to represent them). Thus the Ministers of the Environment from national governments would attend the meeting of the Council of Environment Ministers, and the Ministers for Transport would attend the Council of Transport Ministers.

Some councils meet more frequently than others, reflecting the fact that the Community is more active in certain policy areas. For example, the foreign ministers (meeting in the so-called General Affairs Council) and the Council of Agriculture Ministers usually meet at least once a month, whereas the Council of Environment Ministers meet once formally and once informally within every three-month period.

All ministers operating within a Council do not carry the same weight as they have unequal voting power. (see Table 11.1). In a similar vein, not all

Councils are equal in significance. The most important is the General Affairs Council (composed of the foreign ministers of the national governments), the key Council for pillar two. Nonetheless, finance ministers are constantly competing with foreign ministers for influence, and in pillar one the Council of Economic and Finance Ministers (especially the Euro-Group) comes next in the hierarchy of influence.[33] The Justice and Home Affairs Council became important after the Maastricht Treaty came into effect and is now a key council in both pillar one and pillar three.

The Council of the European Union, as the Council of Ministers is formally known, is the EU institution in which national interests are represented, defended, and ultimately compromised in the interests of reaching agreement. It is a "club" in the sense that the participants understand that ultimately compromises will have to be made by everyone and in the sense that participants acknowledge that the Council is not a traditional international organization. "Although the Council zealously guards its prerogatives and keeps a close eye on activities to ensure that the Commission does not encroach on the Council's territory, it must be emphasized that the Council is very much an EU institution. While it represents national interests, it does so within the framework of European integration.[34] Member-states, by operating within the framework of the Council, have accepted an institutional framework that leads to a collective—rather than a unilateral—decision. By participating in the Council, national governments give up the maneuverability and autonomy that is implicit in national (unilateral) decision making. It is for that reason that "Euro-skeptics" argue that participation in the Union means giving up sovereignty—defined as the ability to make unilateral decisions.

On the other hand, the power of the Council of Ministers ensures that the Union always adopts legislation that meets with the approval of most or all of the member-state governments. The Community does not impose legislation on national governments—they adopt the legislation themselves in the Council of Ministers (and in many areas in partnership with the European Parliament). Opposition parties in national parliaments, however, do not have access to Council of Ministers meetings so that

the EU does in fact enhance the power of those political parties that have won national elections and are in government.

The Council of Ministers plays a stronger role in pillars two and three than it does in pillar one. In pillar one, the policymaking process gives an important role to both the Commission and the Parliament (the latter, however, is excluded from Justice and Home Affairs even in pillar one) and the European Court of Justice can be central. The Commission plays a smaller role, and the Parliament no role, in the policymaking process within pillars two and three.

It is important to highlight that the culture of the Council is based on negotiation and is predisposed toward finding agreement:

> The whole system depends on a crucial assumption that there is give and take between the positions of the member-states and that, whatever the starting positions of the members, there is *both* scope for those positions to evolve *and* a predisposition to find agreement. Thus atmospherics, mutual confidence and trust are important ingredients.[35]

The member governments, acting within the Council of Ministers, are engaged in an institutional process that is unlike that of any other legislative body in the world. Multinational, bound by Community rather than international law, and (in pillar one) engaged in important relationships with the Commission and the European Parliament, the Council of Ministers "locks" national ministers into an ongoing cooperative venture that includes a shared and enlarging policy agenda. It is that "locking" effect that helps ensure that national officials do not decide to act unilaterally rather than multilaterally.

Although some analysts view the Council as blocking further integration, comparison with other attempts at regional integration throughout the world highlight the importance of having national ministers involved in the nitty-gritty of policymaking at the European level. The Council of Ministers, in essence, is the guarantor of European integration in that national governments must participate in it and cannot ignore it. Without the Council, the actions of the Commission and the Parliament could conceivably be ignored by national governments, but their membership in the Council helps ensure that national governments address the issues proposed by the Commission.

The European Council

The key strategic institution within the Union is clearly the *European Council*. Strictly speaking, it does not form part of the Council of Ministers hierarchy, but it is closely linked to it. The European Council does not adopt legislation, leaving that to the Council of Ministers. It does, however, set out the key guidelines for action and future development. The European Council is attended by prime ministers (the president in the case of France and Finland), foreign ministers, the Commission President and another designated Commissioner. The foreign ministers provide the institutional continuity between the Council of Ministers and the European Council.

The Council meets formally every six months in "summits" designated by the name of the city in which they are held (the Dublin Summit, the Amsterdam Summit, for example). These meetings receive far more publicity than do meetings of the various sectoral Councils and may well symbolize the European Union for the average citizen.

The European Council usually operates through unanimity. It chooses the Commission President and is responsible for monitoring work in all three pillars. The European Council now "occupies a position at the apex of the EU's institutional system, overseeing the work of each of the three pillars, and the specialized sectoral Councils which operate therein. It monitors their work, sets framework principles to guide their future deliberations, takes or clears major political decisions, and frequently engages in trouble-shooting."[36] It is the European Council, for example, that will decide key issues such as when enlargement to Eastern Europe will occur.

The European Council as well as the Council of Ministers is chaired by representatives of the member-state government holding the *Presidency of the European Council and the Council of Ministers*. Every six months the Presidency of the European Union rotates, so that each member government exercises the powers of the Presidency in both the European Council and the Council of Ministers for a six-month period. The Presidency represents the Union exter-

nally: at summit meetings between the president of the United States and the Union (which take place every six months), the Union is represented by the Commission President and the foreign minister of the country holding the Presidency of the Union at that point. Most burdensome perhaps is the fact that officials representing the member-state government holding the Presidency will chair all of the hundreds of meetings that go on in the Council of Ministers.

Finally, it is the European Council that controls the agenda and negotiations of the Intergovernmental Conference (IGC) which is called to revise treaties. The most difficult compromises made at the IGC which led to the Single European Act, the Maastricht Treaty, and the Treaty of Amsterdam were all made at the end of the negotiations by the European Council. It is only prime ministers (accompanied by their foreign ministers) who have the political power necessary to make concessions which are very difficult for national governments to accept but which are critical for the success of negotiations.

The European Parliament

The *European Parliament* is the only supranational assembly in the world whose members are chosen by voters rather than by governments. Its 626 members serve five-year terms congruent with the Commissioners' five-year terms. *Members of the European Parliament* (*MEPs*) are elected at the same time across the Community, but each country uses its own electoral system. (A uniform European Community electoral system does not yet exist.) Because of the disproportionate influence of small countries (discussed later) in the Community, members represent constituencies vastly different in size. (see Table 11.1). Turnover is very high after each Parliamentary election—after the 1999 Parliamentary election, over half of all the MEPS were new rather than returning incumbents. Some MEPs go on to have distinguished careers in national politics, especially in France (where 10 of the 16 prime ministers and 4 of the 6 presidents in the Fifth Republic have served as MEPs). In fact, except for Greece, the UK, and Ireland, all of the member-states (excluding the three which just recently joined) have had at least one prime minister who had been an MEP at one time. In reverse, six former prime ministers were elected as MEPs in the 1999 elections, and over 10 percent of MEPs have been ministers in national governments. Roughly 30 percent of the MEPs are women, with the highest proportion in the Finnish delegation and the lowest in the Italian.[37]

Arguing that it is the only directly elected European institution (it became directly elected in 1979) and is therefore closer to the citizens of Europe than either the Commission or the Council, the Parliament has pressured, coaxed, threatened, and in general become an important presence on the political scene. It is not yet an equal partner with the other institutions across the board, but since the Treaty of Amsterdam went into effect in 1999, its influence is very strong on most legislation falling under pillar one. Although the Parliament can only ask the Commission to draft proposals rather than initiating its own draft proposals, the Parliament is able to offer amendments which can substantially change the proposal offered by the Commission. The fact that in the year after Amsterdam went into effect, the Parliament had 81 percent of its amendments accepted by the Council of Ministers indicates that it is effective in shaping legislation.[38]

The Parliament has control (within limits) of so-called "noncompulsory" spending—that is, spending not directed toward agricultural support (the largest single portion of the budget) or based on international agreements with third countries. Over time, the proportion of noncompulsory spending as a percentage of the total budget has increased. Currently, it is over 50 percent and in 1999, the Parliament and the Council of Ministers agreed that 10 percent of spending in agriculture traditionally classified as compulsory would be reclassified as noncompulsory.[39] In fact, the granting of budgetary authority to the Parliament in 1975 could be seen as a key step that has undergirded the subsequent increases in the parliamentary power.

The Parliament's formal powers were strengthened by the Treaty of Maastricht and strengthened still further by Amsterdam which extended the use of the co-decision procedure in the adoption of legislation.[1] The Parliament's power of co-decision allows it to stop legislation which it does not want even if the Council of Ministers unanimously supports it. In cases in which the Parliament and Council approve different versions of a piece of legisla-

tion, conciliation talks are held to try to agree on a compromise. If such talks fail, the legislation dies. Now that co-decision is so frequently used within pillar one, the Council and the Parliament have begun to contact each other early in the legislative process so that conciliation talks will not be necessary. Between November 1993 and April 1999, 165 directives requiring co-decision were dealt with and 40 percent required conciliation talks (three of the proposed directives considered were killed as no agreement could be reached). However, in the year after Amsterdam, 65 pieces of legislation were addressed and only 25 percent required conciliation talks.[40]

Parliament also exercises the right to approve the President of the Commission as well as givng a formal vote of approval of the College of Commissioners as a whole. Finally, it also approves the President of the European Central Bank. The Parliament must also assent to certain international agreements, including accession treaties and association agreements.

Most of the Parliament's work is done in committee. Each committee can decide whether its work will be done in public view or whether it will be carried out in closed session. Whereas committees in most national parliaments work in closed session, most European parliamentary committees now work in public. Each MEP is a full member of at least one committee. Final parliamentary approval however has to be granted in plenary sessions, and at times committee recommendations are overridden in the plenary.

The European Court of Justice

The *European Court of Justice*, located in Luxembourg, is a powerful "supranational" institution making what is in effect judicial law. The Court is composed of one judge from each member-state (chosen by the national government) plus one other. Judges serve a six-year term of office that can be renewed. They elect one of the sitting judges as president. The ECJ established the Court of First Instance, which has been operating since November 1989. That court has a more limited jurisdiction and cannot hear what might be termed constitutionally important cases.

The European Court of Justice is often the arbiter in disputes between an individual member-state and the Commission. It also handles interinstitutional disputes—for example, between the

Commission and the Council of Ministers. Individual citizens can bring cases before the Courts only if, for example, a Community action has directly harmed them. It is typically easier for a firm to argue such harm than a noneconomic actor. Nongovernmental groups such as environmental organizations do not have easy access to the Court. The Court has jurisdiction over issues areas falling within pillar one as well as very limited jurisdiction in pillar three.

Most of the Court's cases come from national courts asking for a preliminary ruling. The national court then takes the ECJ's preliminary ruling and delivers it as its own opinion. National judges therefore have been an important factor in developing the effectiveness of the Community's legal order.

Initially established as an international court operating under the constraints of international law, the Court rather quickly began to represent the "European interest" in its own right. After the Treaty of Rome went into effect, the Court "constitutionalized" that international law under which it had been operating. Rather than simply becoming an international court with limited impact, it gradually evolved into a powerful body resembling, in some striking albeit limited ways, the U.S. Supreme Court. Its influence in the policymaking process is such that one scholar has concluded that "for many areas of European and national policy, knowing the position of the ECJ is as important as knowing the position of the member-states and national interest groups."[41] The Court performs an important role in the policy making process as we discuss later.

The Single Currency and the European Central Bank

Although Economic and Monetary Union (EMU) had been discussed since the late 1960s, it was not until the Maastricht Treaty that a timetable was established and a serious commitment made to move ahead to that milestone of integration. A *single currency* and a European Central Bank were established in 1999, although citizens would not actually use the common currency until 2002.

The political dynamics behind EMU were clear to political elites but difficult to explain to the general public. Under the previous European Monetary System (EMS), the system established in 1979 by which currencies were allowed to fluctuate only within an agreed-upon range, the German Bundesbank had become the dominant decision maker. The German currency, the deutsche mark, became the "anchor currency." That is, when the Bundesbank raised interest rates, the other EMS members were forced to do so as well in order to keep their currencies within the range to which they had agreed. When such a need arose during a recession, the impacts on national economies were harmful. The high interest rates in a recession exacerbated high unemployment and therefore were very painful.

The high cost of German unification led the German Bundesbank to raise interest rates while many other EMS members were indeed in a recession. The French and the Italians in particular realized that they needed to gain a voice in European monetary policy. To do so, they would have to give up their own monetary sovereignty (largely illusory in any case because of the dynamics of the EMS) and convince the Germans to give up their own monetary sovereignty within the framework of a European Central Bank in which each central bank would have equal representation.

Although the Bundesbank was reluctant to embrace EMU, Chancellor Kohl, anxious to show that unification was not leading Germany away from the European Community, agreed to economic and monetary union. The decision over EMU fell within the "Chancellor's perogative."[42] That is, the ultimate decision about EMU was the Chancellor's. The Maastricht Treaty embodied that agreement. The German government, however, insisted on certain conditions in order to ensure that the new *Euro-currency* would be as "strong" a currency as the deutsche mark that the Germans were to give up. In particular, the European Central Bank was to have price stability (rather than, for example, low unemployment or high rates of economic growth) as its primary objective, and countries would not be allowed to join EMU unless their deficits were at 3 percent of GDP or lower.

Years of brutal budget-cutting were required for many countries (such as Italy) to qualify. In 1999, 11 countries joined what became known as the euro-zone; Britain, Sweden, and Denmark stayed out. Greece was allowed to join in 2001.

The European Central Bank, established in Frankfurt, is composed of the governors of the national central banks and is extremely independent of all the other EU institutions as well as of the member-state governments. It is arguably the most independent central bank in the world. In fact, that independence has been criticized, but the ECB believes it is necessary to convince the financial markets that it will not pursue a monetary policy which would allow inflation. Price stability is its policy mantra.

National Governments as Actors

As already indicated in our discussion of the Community's institutions, national governments play a key role in the Community's policymaking process. Their influence is felt directly in the Council of Ministers and through the power of appointment in the Commission and the European Court of Justice. Typically, the focus on understanding how and why national governments operate as they do within the European Union highlights the role of ruling parties and bureaucracies, for national governments are able to defend their national interest in all the Union's institutions in one fashion or another. The opportunity to defend one's national interest has lubricated the path of integration for the member-states.

The need to prepare the Union's institutions for enlargement, however, highlighted the disproportionate power of the small member-states, a feature of the Union which had not been the subject of controversy since the Treaty of Rome. As the negotiations proceeded for the Treaty of Nice, that same feature became the object of intense political conflict among the current member-states. Simply put, the negotiations for the Treaty of Nice forced the question of *which* governments would be able to adequately defend their national interests in the future. In addition to wielding disproportionate power within the EU as indicated by Table 11.1, small countries are given a status equal to that of the large countries in the European Court of Justice, the European Council, and the governing council of the European Central Bank. Given that many new small countries will join the EU once enlargement occurs, the large member-states in 2000 sought to redress the balance in the negotiations leading to the Treaty of Nice (agreed to in December 2000).

The small states, however, fear being "pushed around" by the large states and rejected many of the demands made by the five large states (France, Germany, Italy, the UK, and Spain). The last half of 2000 was filled with acrimony as the small states accused the large of trying to weaken the Commission (which the small states view as an ally) in the name of efficient decision making, of trying to make the EU more intergovernmental so that the large states would have more influence, and of generally being insensitive to the national interests of the small states. The large states, for their part, were adamant that they needed more power within the Council of Ministers and were likely to want more representation in the European Parliament; furthermore, they viewed their proposals for the Commission as strengthening it by making it more effective. In brief, the large states want to ensure that the next enlargement does not privilege small countries even further, while the current small member-states worry that if the large member-states are allowed to gain too much power, the EU will become more like an international organization (in which small countries fare very badly) and less like a federation (in which small subfederal units exercise disproportionate power as they do in the United States). The small countries want the policy making process to respect their wishes as it has since the Treaty of Rome.

Political Parties

Political parties do not play the same role in European Union politics as they do in the national politics of the European countries described in this book. On the one hand, political parties in Europe generally do not offer alternative policies and analyses at the European level. In almost every member-state the focus of party competition throughout the development of the EU has continued to be domestic politics.[43] Thus, while national elections may determine which party controls the government that chooses representatives to the Commission and the Council of Ministers, the electoral debate has seldom focused on the policies of those representatives. Even direct elections to the European Parliament have tended to operate primarily as referenda on the domestic achievements and promises of the competing parties. On the other hand, this inattention is encouraged by the fact that election outcomes do not directly determine the control of the EU's governing institutions.

Politics in the European Union revolves around broad territorial (national) divisions rather than the socioeconomic divisions that characterize politics at the national level. The "left-right" division so pivotal in structuring political party positions and alternatives at the national level manifests itself less often and in different ways in Brussels. Political conflict at the European Union level is characterized by "the dominance of national cultural and territorial differences over socio-economic divisions."[44] Whereas differences related to class have shaped political conflict in Europe throughout the postwar period, those differences have been muted in Brussels where national differences are more significant. "It is, therefore, essentially via governments that political parties influence European affairs."[45]

The histories of national political parties are not rooted in conflicts over European integration as such. Until voters in some member-states became concerned with the impact of integration, parties had not needed to address policy issues dealt with in Brussels. Even when integration became more politicized, major parties did not take clear positions on the issues they would face in the Council of Ministers. On the contrary, they cloaked their actions in the garb of national interest:

> Instead of defending their participation in European regulatory decision-making on the grounds of fulfilling an electoral mandate, ruling parties have consistently defended such actions on the grounds that they have done their best to protect national interests, thus casting European politics as a zero-sum game between the member-states.[46]

In spite of not offering European-level policy alternatives, parties have nonetheless begun to organize a bit more extensively on the European level than they have in the past. In 1992 and 1993, all the major transnational party federations institutionalized themselves to a greater degree. Furthermore, the transnational federations have begun meeting right before the European Council meetings, so that prime ministers and other leading politicians as well as members of the European Parliament and Commissioners from each of the leading political families gather to discuss EU issues.[47] Whether and how quickly transnational parties will evolve, however, is still an open question.

The issues with which the Community deals typically have a strong economic component that often manifests itself in technical issues not usually the subject of political discourse. That economic component is shaped by the Treaty of Rome and the Single European Act, both of which embodied a certain model of economics. Expanding cross-border trade and competition as well as opening rather than protecting economies and markets are the economic objectives of the Community. That model does not easily lend itself to addressing problems in the way that parties have traditionally done so in national contexts. Finally, much national party competition revolves around issues related to the welfare state. The Community does not directly legislate on welfare state issues, which means that a central element of national political party conflict is not even on the Community agenda.[48]

Parliamentary Elections

Elections to the European Parliament differ from national parliamentary elections in a variety of ways. Most centrally, they do not set in motion a process of government formation in the same way as do national elections in the member-states. Turnout is higher in national (and sometimes even in subnational) elections, and the big parties typically do better in national elections while small parties do better in elections to the European Parliament. Worrisome for those concerned about the "democratic deficit" (discussed later in this chapter) is the fact that in most countries the turnout for parliamentary elections has declined since the elections of 1979, as shown in Table 11.2.

European elections have been analyzed as "pale reflections of national elections."[49] The elec-

TABLE 11.2   Turnout in the European Parliament Elections, 1979–1999

	1979	1981	1984	1987	1989	1994	1995	1996	1999
EU	**63.0**	—	**61.0**	—	**58.5**	**56.8**	—	—	**49.4**
Belgium	91.6	—	92.2	—	90.7	90.7	—	—	90.0
Luxembourg	88.9	—	87.0	—	87.4	88.5	—	—	85.8
Italy	85.5	—	83.9	—	81.5	74.8	—	—	70.8
Greece	—	78.6	77.2	—	79.9	71.2	—	—	70.2
Spain	—	—	—	68.9	54.8	59.1	—	—	64.4
Ireland	63.6	—	47.6	—	68.3	44.0	—	—	50.5
Denmark	47.1	—	52.3	—	46.1	52.9	—	—	50.4
Austria	—	—	—	—	—	—	—	67.7	49.0
France	60.7	—	56.7	—	48.7	52.7	—	—	47.0
Germany	65.7	—	56.8	—	62.4	60.0	—	—	45.2
Portugal	—	—	—	72.2	51.1	35.5	—	—	40.4
Sweden	—	—	—	—	—	—	41.6	—	38.3
Finland	—	—	—	—	—	—	—	60.3	30.1
Netherlands	57.8	—	50.5	—	47.2	35.7	—	—	29.9
United Kingdom	31.6	—	32.6	—	36.2	36.4	—	—	24.0

Source: Francis Jacobs, Richard Corbett, and Michael Shackleton, *The European Parliament,* 4th Ed. (London: John Harper 2000), p. 25.

toral campaign does not highlight choices that will be made at the European level, but rather emphasizes the kinds of issues typically debated within the voters' "habitual national party context."[50]

While national elections are often viewed as "first-order" elections, elections to the European Parliament are "second order" elections because no actual executive power is at stake. Rather than being focused on European issues, elections to the Parliament provide a forum for voters to express their support of, or discontent with, national parties. National cues, rather than the specific policies of the European Union, are paramount in shaping how voters cast their ballots.[51]

Parties in the European Parliament

Within the Community's institutions, political parties are most visible in the European Parliament. Europe's extraordinary cultural and political diversity is demonstrated by the fact that over 140 parties are represented in the European Parliament. These in turn are combined in Political Groups which are the centers of power within the Parliament (see Table 11.3). After the 1999 parliamentary elections, seven Political Groups emerged; each Group includes MEPs with a political affinity and from at least two member-states. The Groups set the parliamentary agenda and de facto choose the president and 14 vice-presidents of the Parliament as well as the chairs, vice-chairs, and rapporteurs of the various parliamentary committees. The Groups each have staffs.

Political Groups in the European Parliament do not perform the same role as do parties in national parliaments. The appointment of the executive—that is the Commission—is not determined by any of the Political Groups within the Parliament. Neither do they influence the portfolios that the individual Commissioners receive. The Groups do not have any influence on the partisan coloring of the ministers in the Council of Ministers. National governments choose both the Commissioners and the ministers in the Council of Ministers. To understand the difference between a party in a national parliament and a Political Group in the European Parliament, it is important to remember that "European elections do not initiate a process of government formation, as they do in most parliamentary democracies."[52]

The Political Groups provide an important channel of information for national parties, and

TABLE 11.3 Political Groups in the European Parliament (1999-2004)

Group	Number of Political Parties in Group	Number of Member-States Represented	Number of Seats (626 Total)
European People's Party (Christian Democrats) and European Democrats (EPP-ED)	33	15	233
Party of European Socialists (PES/PSE)	21	15	180
European Liberal Democratic and Reformist Group (ELDR)	16	10	51
Greens/European Free Alliance	19	12	48
Confederal Group of the European United Left/Nordic Green Left	15	10	41
Europe of Nations	5	5	30
Europe of Democracies and Diversities	5	4	16
Nonattached	9	6	26

Source: Richard Corbett, Frances Jacobs, and Michael Shackleton, *The European Parliament,* 4th ed. (London: John Harper, 2000), pp. 67–80.

they are also important in organizing meetings, typically held before European Council meetings, in which heads of government and Commissioners from that particular party, party leaders, and the Chair of the Political Group meet to try to achieve a consensus on certain key issues affecting European integration.

The two largest Political Groups have been the European People's Party (previously named the Christian Democrats) and the Socialist Group. Until the parliamentary elections of 1999, the Socialists had obtained the most seats and were the dominant party within the Parliament. However, in 1999, much to the shock of the Socialists, the European People's Party (EPP) won 233 seats while the Socialists won only 180. Whereas previously the Socialists and the EPP had engaged in a kind of "grand coalition" and shared the committee chairmanships and the Presidency of the Parliament amongst themselves, the EPP decided to pursue a different strategy. It concluded an informal alliance with the third largest party, the Liberals (with 51 seats) and agreed to share the Presidency of the Parliament with the Liberals rather than with the Socialists.

Most importantly, however, it began to stress the left-right division within the Parliament and the Commission. The Parliament became more "politicized," for rather than subordinating partisan conflict to the desire to increase the Parliament's power vis à vis the Commission and the Council of Ministers, the EPP began to highlight the policy differences which exist between the Socialists and the center-right parties. The EPP tends to view government intervention in the market less favorably than do the Socialists. In fact, the Parliament began to vote in ways which were more pro-business and less environmentally friendly than had been the case in the past.

It is important to note, however, that the party families (especially the EPP and the Socialists) still often cooperate with one another. The EPP, the Socialists, and the Liberals need to cooperate because neither alone can mobilize the majorities needed under parliamentary procedures. Given the necessity to cooperate, the Parliament is not the forum for the kinds of partisan clashes found in the British House of Commons.[53] Nonetheless, it is true that a greater degree of adversarialism is now present in the Parliament. Partisanship which divides tends to dilute the Parliament's power when dealing with the other institutions. For example, when the partisan divisions between right and left are highlighted on an issue, the Parliament is in a weaker position when entering conciliation talks with the Council than when such divisions are subordinated to a unitary parliamentary position. In general politics within the Parliament is now less predictable and more fluid than had been the case with other parliaments. The fact that the EPP is itself divided in that its members include both Christian Democrats who have traditionally been very strongly in favor of European integration and 36 anti-euro British Conservatives means that the political dynamics of the Parliament are very complex. They are less structured than in the past. At times partisanship is subordinated so that the Parliament is able to act in a unified manner vis à vis the other institutions. At other times, however, partisanship is so strong that the Parliament is internally divided and therefore weakened when dealing with the Council or the Commission.[54]

Interest Groups

As the Community has expanded the range of policies about which it can legislate, a "seemingly endless increase in interest group mobilization at the European level" has taken place.[55] The growth in their number has been so great and so rapid that scholars better understand the role of interest groups in national systems than in the Community. Research is still trying to catch up with the growth and activity of groups. What is clear is that the system of policymaking within the Union is so open that interest groups are able to participate at some point in the process of making public policy.

Interest groups interact with the Community's institutions in relatively unpredictable ways and at different points in the policy process. They lobby the Parliament for favorable amendments to Commission proposals as well as the relevant Commission officials. They have become an integral part of the policy process in Brussels much as they are in Britain, Germany, Holland, Denmark, and Sweden. Although groups representing a variety of interests are becom-

ing ever more numerous in Brussels, the structure of interest group interaction is not "corporatist," as it is in several European nations (see Chapter 3). That is, business and labor groups do not work with government officials in a structured way to make policy.

Interest groups have become so numerous in fact that both the Commission and the Parliament have felt the need to regularize their activities in some fashion. The Parliament in 1993 began to require lobbyists to register. The Commission, for its part, developed some guidelines to help guide Commission officials in their dealings with representatives of interest groups.[56] The Commission, which is the object of most of the lobbying, has found it particularly difficult to maintain access to its relatively small staff while not being overwhelmed by the demands on its time and attention.

Given the fact that political parties are not the key actors in Brussels that they are in national political systems and given the absence of a "government" in the traditional sense, the Commission is the key target of interest groups. The Commission for its part encourages European-level groups, which it sees as a way to support further integration. Such groups are transnational actors—that is, they bring together national associations so as to form a European group. Transnational groups have not, however, been as important as many had assumed, at least partially because national associations often find it difficult to agree on a common position. Many such groups are much weaker than are their national counterparts. National organizations rather than the European federations of such organizations often possess the information that is the interest group's chief asset and the resource most valuable to the Commission as it attempts to formulate policy. Thus the Commission "unwittingly undermine[s] the development of effective European-level groups by frequently consulting directly with national groups and individual firms."[57]

Although it is difficult to gauge with precision the relative power and influence of diverse groups, many analysts argue that business interests have the most access and are the most influential.[58] Trade unions, although members of the European Trade Union Conference, have been unable to organize as effectively, and in general labor representatives are less visible in policy debates. Environmental and consumer groups, although nurtured and supported by the Commission, are still much weaker in general than are business groups.

In spite of the number of interest groups operating in Brussels and their varied activities, it is important not to overestimate their influence. As indicated earlier, the Economic and Monetary Union represents a historic milestone for European integration. The new European Central Bank and the Euro are key changes in the economic landscape of the Union. Yet interest groups were not involved at key decision-making points. Business groups, labor representatives, and associations representing banks were all excluded. Heads of state and government and finance ministers along with their advisers and civil servants were the key actors in negotiations about EMU, not interest groups. The same general argument can be made about the decision in the Treaty of Amsterdam to Europeanize pillar three—interest groups were not relevant.

Although interest groups are not necessarily included in the "historic" decisions, they are typically woven into the Community's policy process. In particular, sophisticated groups lobby at both the national and European level. They lobby the Commission when it is drafting the legislation, the Parliament for favorable amendments, and national officials who will be involved when the issue reaches the Council of Ministers. The European Union has many access points for groups or individual actors, and they are increasingly taking advantage of all of them. A large business firm's lobbying effort may therefore use its national association—which has an office in the national capital as well as an office in Brussels, a Euro-association that brings together national associations, and the firm's own office in Brussels. It can thus lobby a variety of officials using a variety of venues and strategies.

Public Opinion— Does It Matter?

The European Community is different from the national systems which constitute it in that mass politics plays a different role. It is also an ambiguous

role, and scholars are still in the process of delineating how public opinion intersects with the Community's policymaking process. In the Community, the wishes of voters are transmitted primarily through national governments whereas in national systems the voters directly choose those in power. Because the Community does involve negotiations among governments, similar in that sense to international relations, governments can pursue policies somewhat independently from the wishes of voters.

Governments, once in power, have more discretion on issues related to integration than they do on national issues centrally identified with their political party. The question of "Europe" is not clearly positioned within national political systems; it tends to divide political parties internally rather than to distinguish one party from another. A prime minister therefore tends to be able to exercise considerable discretion when deciding broad issues of European integration. In countries where referenda are common (Denmark and Sweden, for example), voters are able to express their views more directly and have them be more binding than can voters in countries without referenda (such as Germany). In some cases, where referenda are possible but infrequent (France), the results can be surprising as was evident when President Mitterrand, assuming that the French would support the Maastricht Treaty, called for a referendum only to see the Treaty supported by the thinnest of margins. Even when referenda are used, the substantive results can be somewhat surprising. Although Norwegian voters rejected membership in the Community (having rejected it already once before) in a 1995 referendum, Norwegian governments have tried to pass legislation and pursue economic policies compatible with those being adopted by the European Union. If one examines selected aspects of Norwegian public policy, it would not be immediately obvious that Norway is not a member of the Union.

That discretion has implications for the role of public opinion, which emerges as a factor that does not constrain political leaders as directly as it does in national, strictly domestic, politics. That is not to say that it does not constrain them at all. However, the type of constraint exercised is more subtle and diffuse. Public opinion as expressed in the elections to the European Parliament is again diluted as the Parliament does not form the government.

Although compromise is a normal part of the democratic process, especially in systems with coalition governments, national politicians do not feel comfortable explaining the policy positions they take in Brussels to their mass electorate. While political elites understand the necessity for compromise, the Community's decision-making process is often presented to mass publics as one in which countries lose or win. Depending on the circumstances, ministers either claim to have "won" (when carrying out popular policies) or to have been "forced" by the Community to take an (unpopular) action.

When taking unpopular actions, it is quite likely that the national government voted in favor of the unpopular action, but the government conveniently does not mention that fact. The process of "scapegoating" Brussels is made easier by the fact that legislation approved by the Council of Ministers often does not actually take effect until several years later. Only the most sophisticated newspaper reporter is likely to track the legislative history of an EU law which, when it goes into effect, is criticized by national politicians.

The lack of a direct transmission belt between public opinion and voting and the EU executive has led many to argue that a "democratic deficit" exists. Some argue that a much stronger European Parliament is necessary for the deficit to be remedied while others argue that national parliaments need to be given a stronger role in the Community policy process. Yet neither of these two positions confronts the fact that the Union is not a state. As long as the policy process involves bargaining among legally constituted national governments, the influence of public opinion and the electorate will face many of the same constraints they have faced in the making of foreign policy. Multilateral decision making that requires bargaining with foreigners is not the same as decision making within national systems in which foreigners do not play a role, and that difference raises difficult issues in trying to remedy the democratic deficit.

The Council of Ministers operates in a great deal of secrecy, and that secrecy helps political leaders operate in Brussels with less scrutiny than they receive in their national capitals. That is, minutes of Council meetings are not accessible to the public, and the deals made between ministers are often not revealed to the press. Each minister may well claim "victory" for his or her position, but what is typically not revealed is what concessions were made by that same minister. Even though the Council could not reach a decision without each national government being willing to compromise, ministers do not publicize their role in reaching a compromise.

The secrecy accompanying Council of Ministers decision making has led many critics to identify such secrecy as a contributor to the democratic deficit. The fact that citizens do not know what kinds of concessions their national government made in negotiations or even how their government voted on a particular piece of legislation leads to a lack of "transparency" in the Community's operations which is seen by many as intrinsically undemocratic.

Again, secrecy in decision making is more characteristic of international relations than of domestic politics. Many international "deals" are made away from public scrutiny. The making of foreign policy is one of the least transparent policy arenas within national systems. International diplomacy has historically been rooted in secrecy, partially so that negotiators can protect their negotiating flexibility and thereby arrive at a compromise. Negotiations with foreign states differ in important ways from negotiations carried on by domestic actors within a national system. Although the European Union exhibits a great deal of integration, and negotiations within the Council of Ministers differ in significant ways from those in other international forums, such negotiations are nonetheless different from their domestic counterparts.[59] The Union is composed of states that still regard each other as foreign. That basic fact affects the dynamics of negotiation and raises difficult questions about whether such a system can be democratized without paralyzing its decision-making capacity.

However, as Brussels has come to penetrate more and more deeply into domestic political systems and as it has come to wield greater power in policy areas traditionally seen as domestic, the lack of openness in its decision making has become increasingly problematic. Given the lack of strong European transnational parties that could claim some legitimacy in the tradition of "party government," and given the lack of oversight by national parliaments of Cabinet ministers when operating within the framework of EU's executive levels, the Council of Ministers is open to the charge that it is "undemocratic." But can multilateral decision making involving foreign governments be democratic in the same way in which national systems are? Can public opinion be as influential?

The current policy process does not allow public opinion, defined either ideologically or nationally, to be directly transmitted into decision making. The relative absence of transnational political parties and the discretion exercised by national ministers both dilute the impact of public opinion. It is therefore difficult to predict the position a national government will take by looking at the state of public opinion. Chancellor Helmut Kohl, for example, strongly supported the drive for a single currency even though at times a majority of Germans opposed it. While elections that bring in new political parties can certainly change a government's position on integration, such change is not automatic.

In spite of the relative insulation policymaking has enjoyed, public opinion became far more important during the ratification of the Maastricht Treaty.[60] That ratification process politicized the issue of European integration, so much so that elites negotiating the Treaty of Amsterdam in 1997 had to keep public opinion in the forefront of their calculations. (That is particularly true for political leaders in countries that use referenda for ratification.) Such politicization did not, however, lead to a political debate in any country about the desirability of the common currency in the campaign for the 1994 European Parliament elections, most probably because the issue would have divided political parties internally and therefore was kept off the agenda by those same parties.[61]

Although it can be argued that the main consequence of adverse public opinion has been to slow down the progress of integration rather than to change its orientation in any strategic or fundamental way, there is no doubt that political leaders now take it into account tactically if not strategically. On the other hand, outside of a referendum, public opinion becomes most influential when it is mobilized by political parties. European political parties are divided by religion, the proper role of government in the economy, and the limits of social welfare rather than by issues linked to European integration. Thus they have not been able to capitalize on different opinions about integration within the mass electorate, and they have not engaged in a sustained debate about the policy choices presented by integration. Consequently, public opinion has less impact on the European arena than it does on the national.

Cross-National Differences

Support for European integration varies cross-nationally most of the time. It is important to remember that there is no "European" public opinion; there is instead only public opinion within 15 different national political discourses. Such segmentation is reinforced by the lack of a "European" media; nationally based newspapers and television reporting strengthen the notion of national opinion, national electorates, and national victories and losses within the Community. In a similar vein, the notion of a "European identity" gains more support in some member-states than others but is secondary to national identity.

In general, the citizens of the founding six members have been more supportive of European integration than have the citizens of Britain and Denmark. The latter show far more ambivalence than do others, although the citizens of the most recent new members (Sweden, Finland, and Austria) seem to share such ambivalence.[62] Public support for "Europe" kept rising until 1989, went into decline subsequently, and in late 1994 began to stabilize at a lower level of support than had been found in the pre–1989 period.[63] Cross-national support of EU membership varies widely. In mid-2000, only 6 percent of the Irish, Luxembourg, Dutch, and Spaniards thought EU membership was a bad thing while 24 percent of the Danes, 38 percent of the Swedes, 25 percent of the Austrians and 24 percent of the British judged membership negatively. If we examine only the original big member-states, we find that in mid-2000 only 9 percent of the Italians, 14 percent of the French, and 15 percent of the Ger-

Box 11.3   Who Is "Pro European"?

- Has Had Some Higher Education
- Relatively Young

- Manager or White-Collar Worker
- Interested in Politics

mans thought EU membership was a "bad thing."[64] (See box 11.3.)

Support for the Euro has also been volatile and has generally been lower than has support for EU membership. Support was at its peak (64 percent in favor) in autumn 1998, and then fell after it was introduced as a "virtual" currency on January 1, 1999. Support varies cross-nationally however. In mid-2000, only 14 percent of Italians opposed the Euro while 29 percent of the French and 39 percent of Germans did so and 61 percent of the British. In September 2000, 53 percent of Danes voting in a referendum on the Euro voted against Danish membership in the euro-zone.

The citizens of states that joined in 1981 and 1986 (Greece, Spain, and Portugal) have consistently been favorable, far more favorable than the attitudes of the Danes and the British. For members such as the Irish, the Spanish, and the Portuguese, favorable attitudes may be rooted in the view that the modernization of the economic and political system is inextricably entangled with admission to the Union. Modern Spain or modern Ireland are viewed as intrinsically "European" while the traditional Spain was outside of the European mainstream. In general, attitudes in Greece, Spain, Portugal, and Ireland are now as favorable toward integration as are attitudes in the original Six.[66]

Public opinion became especially salient during the process of ratifying the Maastricht Treaty. Given the broad consensus among all the key political parties in the member-states, the leaders meeting in Maastricht in December 1991 to conclude the final shape of the treaty expected no trouble during ratification. Much to the surprise of political elites, however, the Danish electorate voted "no" on Maastricht on June 1992, and only voted yes in May 1993 after the Danish government had obtained key "opt-outs" from central provisions of Maastricht. Even more troubling was the French reaction to Maastricht. In October 1992, the French barely approved the ratification of Maastricht. The shock waves from the Danish and French results obscured the fact that the Irish electorate approved the treaty by a substantial margin. Denmark and France become the symbols of a troubled European integration whereas the Irish results were largely discounted.

Most analysts interpreted the referenda results as a warning light that mass electorates were either hostile to or deeply skeptical about further European integration. Within the Commission itself, a new sense of caution and circumspection emerged. National politicians clearly interpreted the referenda as a vote on integration, and the importance of public opinion in setting the parameters for elite action increased

In sum, the role of public opinion concerning integration is still ambiguous. How to mobilize public opinion in a system of multilateral decision making involving foreigners is still an open question. The issues linked to European integration, although nearly fifty years old, have not yet found their place on the national political agenda as shaped by national political parties.

The Policymaking Process

Given the institutional complexity of the European Union—its unusual institutions, its differing decision-making procedures across pillars—the policymaking process is more variegated, segmented, and less uniform than in traditional nation-states. The system itself is in flux while the cast of political characters is often unpredictable. Nonetheless, certain key characteristics of the Community will help make that process more understandable.

The first is the fact that small states wield a surprising amount of power within the Union

TABLE 11.4 Member States' Shares in EU financing and in EU$_{15}$ GNP (percent of total, data for 1997), including UK

Country	Share in EU GNP	Share in the Financing of EU Budget
Austria	2.6	2.8
Belgium	3.1	3.9
Denmark	1.9	2.0
Finland	1.4	1.4
France	17.2	17.5
Germany	26.0	28.2
Greece	1.5	1.6
Ireland	0.8	0.9
Italy	14.2	11.5
Luxembourg	0.2	0.2
Netherlands	4.5	6.4
Portugal	1.2	1.4
Spain	6.6	7.1
Sweden	2.7	3.1
UK	16.1	11.9

Source: European Commission, *Agenda 2000: Financing the European Union* (1998).

In Bridge Laffan and Michael Shackleton, "The Budget," *Policy-Making in the European Union,* Helen Wallace and William Wallace, eds. (Oxford, England: Oxford University Press, 2000), Ch. 8, p. 234.

(see Table 11.1). While the large countries have more administrative resources to bring to bear in the Union's policymaking process, small member-state national governments typically focus on issues of particular concern to them and do extraordinarily well in defending their national interests in those specific policy arenas. Especially in pillar one, where the small member-states tend to view the Commission as an ally that can help protect them from overly aggressive big country pressure, officials representing small member-state governments can be quite important in the policymaking process.

Second, the net financial contributions to the Union are disproportionately paid by Germany, as Table 11.4 indicates. If Germany refuses to support a new initiative which would require new expenditure, its opposition is particularly important because of Germany's role as paymaster.

As it stands, the Union's budget is very small compared with that of the member-states. In 1997

the Community spent under 1.2 percent of the Community's gross national product. The lack of money encourages the Union to use regulation rather than expenditure as an instrument of policy. While expenditure is comparatively small, however, it is very important for the smaller, poorer countries: Community funds (known as structural funds) in the period between 1994 and 1999 accounted for 3.67 percent of Greek GDP, 2.8 percent of Irish GDP, 4 percent of Portuguese GDP, and 1.7 percent of Spanish GDP.[67]

Third, questions about expenditure and financial resources invariably run up into the compulsory expenditure for the Common Agricultural Policy (CAP), which has dominated the Community's budget. Although such spending has declined significantly—from roughly 70 percent of its budget in 1984 to under 45 percent—it still represents the single largest expenditure. Designed as a key element of the European postwar welfare state, it maintains the incomes of farmers by keeping food prices high and cheaper agricultural products out of the European Community's market. It has consistently been criticized internationally (by the United States especially) as well as by some member-states, the United Kingdom in particular. The GATT Agreement on Agriculture and reforms which the Commission had been successful in promoting in 1992 helped to reduce the budgetary burden of agriculture, but a great deal more change needs to be made if the accession of the post-communist applicant countries with their large agricultural sectors are not to intolerably strain the Union's finances. Although the Commission had hoped for more reform, the Berlin European Council meeting of 1999, operating under the pressures of the Kosovo crisis and the uncertainty of the forced resignation of the Santer Commission, agreed on only relatively modest changes. In essence, Germany, facing very strong French resistance to major changes in the financing of the CAP, agreed to continue its role as paymaster of the Union. Even though Germany is the largest contributor because it pays (in 1997 figures) 28.2 percent of the total EU budget, it agreed to receive only 14.2 percent of CAP monies while France receives 22.5 percent of the CAP while only contributing 17.5 percent of the EU's budget.[68] (See Table 11.4.)

Fourth, the policy process is rooted in a culture in which consensus building is highly valued. Even when qualified majority voting is permissible, the Commission as well as member-states will try to arrive at a piece of legislation that is acceptable to all 15 member-states. The consensual style of decision making reflects the style in many of the member-states but is clearly different from the more adversarial political cultures found in Britain and France.

Finally, the Community is characterized by such diversity of interests, administrative and political cultures, and regulatory arrangements that the policy outcomes tend to show the influence of several models. No national government is able to impose its own framework on others, and no national government is consistently forced to accept models alien to its own traditions. In the field of regulation, the outcome has been described as a "patchwork" that incorporates aspects of varied traditions.[69] In a similar vein, no national government consistently loses in terms of policy outcomes.

Policy Initiation

The European Commission formally initiates all policy in pillar one and in the process of following its proposals through the policy process it interacts closely with both the Council of Ministers and the European Parliament. The Commission can be viewed as the spoke in the wheel, with constant and routine contacts with both the Parliament and the Council. The Commission is the focal point of attention in the policymaking system because it is instrumental in shaping the agenda of the other institutions. The Commission's "work in progress" is an excellent predictor of the issues that the Council and the Parliament will be debating in the future.

The Commission is represented at all meetings within the Council of Ministers and the Parliament but neither the Council nor the Parliament is represented at Commission meetings. The role of the Commission in the Council is in fact so visible that it is sometimes referred to as the "sixteenth member state." The Commission plays such a powerful role in various stages of the policymaking process that it can be described as a "co-player" with the Council of Ministers: "neither institution can act without the other."[70]

THE COMMISSION PRESIDENT The *President of the Commission* plays a critical role in the policy process because of the visibility and the intensely political nature of the position. He is appointed as a Commissioner by his home country, but he is chosen as president by unanimous consent of all the national governments. Jacques Delors, the president from 1985 to 1995, was a Commissioner from France (having served as the French Minister of Finance) who served five two-year terms, making him the longest-serving Commission President in the Community's history. He was followed by Jacques Santer, appointed in 1995, who had been the prime minister of Luxembourg and who was forced to resign, along with the entire Commission in March 1999. Romano Prodi, the former prime minister of Italy, was chosen as his successor.

Choosing a President of the Commission is a delicate, intensely political task carried out by the chief executives of the member governments when meeting in European Council. Delors was chosen because another Frenchman, Claude Cheysson, was opposed by British Prime Minister Margaret Thatcher and German Chancellor Helmut Kohl. His successor, Jacques Santer of Luxembourg, was chosen because the choice of the French and Germans, Jean-Luc Dehaene (the prime minister of Belgium), was vetoed by John Major (the British prime minister). Santer then became the candidate who could receive unanimous support.

Jacques Delors was especially important in increasing the prestige and political weight of the Commission, both within the Community and in the international arena. Described by his admirers as strategic, brilliant, intellectual, and visionary, he was, critics argued, arrogant and too much of a centralizer, and did not give enough consideration to the wishes of national governments or the other Commissioners. Both his critics and admirers would agree, however, that under his leadership the Community made some of its most important steps toward further integration. His advocacy and implementation of the *1992 Project*, the initiative to create a single market, will undoubtedly give him a firm place in the history of European integration. It is in fact possible that future histories of the Community will identify Monnet and Delors as the two most important individuals associated with the project of European integration in the twentieth century.

CIVIL SERVICE The Commission's civil service is organized by Directorate-General (DG) rather than by ministry, as in national executives. The Commission's Secretary-General plays an important albeit discreet role in coordinating the work of the various directorate-generals. He is responsible for the relations between the Commission and the Parliament and the Council of Ministers and is the only non-Commissioner who sits with the Commissioners when the College meets.

NATIONAL GOVERNMENTS The relationship between the Commission and the national governments is critical. Delors's success in Brussels made him a potential candidate for the French presidency, which in fact strengthened his political power in Brussels.[71] His close friendship with Helmut Kohl, the German Chancellor throughout Delors's tenure, was also an important political resource. When Romano Prodi faced problems during his first year, the fact he was not receiving support from the Italian government added to his travails. Thus are the politics of Brussels and the politics of key national capitals entangled. Power in a national political system, especially within the French or German system, is a tremendous asset when operating within the Community's policymaking system.

The Commission is in constant contact with national executives during the routine of policy initiation. The Commissioners have political contacts at the highest national level while Commission officials have frequent contact with their national counterparts. In fact, the Commission often introduces proposals at the behest of a national government.

The national governments must be dealt with by the Commission President as soon as the appointments process begins in national capitals. Although Prodi was in a stronger position to bargain with the national governments because of the increased powers given to the president by the Treaty of Amsterdam, there were definitely limits to his ability to persuade the national governments to appoint the people he would have preferred. After negotiations between the Commission President and national governments, each Commissioner is given

a portfolio—a specific policy area for which he or she is primarily responsible. For example, one Commissioner would be put in charge of environmental policy while another would be given the internal market and still another would be responsible for transportation programs. As in a national cabinet, some portfolios are more attractive and prestigious than others. Those dealing with external relations are always desirable, as are those dealing with economic matters. At the beginning of each new term, the president assigns portfolios with an eye to seniority, national government pressure, expertise, and political clout back home.

The policy initiation process, broadly defined, is complex because Commissioners must deal with their national governments, other national governments in the areas of their policy responsibilities, and with the institutions of the Community. Given that the Commission is involved in nearly all phases of the policy process, officials are in contact with an innumerable range of actors as a proposal is drafted, refined, accepted by the College of Commissioners, and then shepherded through the Community's institutional process.

Although Commissioners are required formally to represent the European interest, they need to keep their prime ministers at home happy if they want to be reappointed. In general, Commissioners try to represent both the European and the national interest within certain boundaries. While they do not accept instructions from their government, they typically do put forth policy positions (especially in areas such as industrial, competition [antitrust], and environmental policy) which are recognizable as "national" positions.

Keeping a political master minimally satisfied without sacrificing one's European credentials can be a difficult tightrope to walk. Typically, an effective Commissioner will be able to inform his colleagues in Brussels when a proposed piece of legislation will run into severe political trouble with his national government. Conversely, he will be able to keep his capital well informed about developments within the Commission so that the national capital is not surprised. Finally, he will be able to mobilize his colleagues in the College of Commissioners to support the positions he advocates, positions that his national government is likely to support.

Legislating Policy

Once the College of Commissioners approves draft legislation by majority vote, it goes to the Council of Ministers and often the Parliament. In the Council, the draft legislation is usually amended, with input from both the Commission and the Parliament, depending on the case, until the Council of Ministers passes it (a process that can take years if the Council has difficulty in arriving at a consensus). If the legislation falls under the co-decision procedure, the Parliament and the Council of Ministers need to agree on the legislation.

The Commission does not have the political clout in relation to the Council of Ministers that, say, the German chancellor or the U.S. president has in relation to the Bundesrat or the Senate. The Commission's leverage over the collectivity of national governments comes more from the power that accompanies the setting of the policy agenda and the definition of problems than from the formal powers typically associated with a cabinet or executive branch.

COREPER   When ministers fly into Brussels for Council of Ministers meetings, they consider only the most difficult issues, those that need compromise at the high political level of a minister. Most of the other issues have already been negotiated by the *Committee of Permanent Representatives* (known as *COREPER*, its French acronym).

COREPER is critical to the successful functioning of the Council of Ministers as an institution. It has been viewed by some as "the contemporary battlefield on which the nations of Europe settle their differences."[72] It is this group, made up of the ambassadors to the European Union from each of the member-states, that resolves all but the most politically sensitive issues embedded in the legislation passed by the Council of Ministers. The group meets every Thursday morning, with the Commission and the Secretariat of the Council of Ministers both represented. At least once a month, they have a very private lunch at which time no interpreters and no note takers are present; English and French are the only languages spoken. That kind of privacy

allows the real deals to be made, as both the Commission representatives and the ambassadors can select what they report back to their superiors. In the words of one participant, "It's very simple, there are no spies."[73]

COREPER represents the views of national capitals in Brussels and gives officials in those same capitals a sense of which arguments are likely to be accepted by the other national governments within the Council of Ministers. COREPER officials play a key role in the entanglement of the "European" and the "national." They are taken seriously by both national and Community officials.[74] COREPER operates in pillar one while the Political Committee plays a similar function in pillar two and the so-called K-4 Committee (named after Article K.4 (1) of the Maastricht Treaty, which called for the creation of such a committee) is its equivalent in pillar three (see Figure 11.5).

The Parliament has become a much more important legislative actor in many policy arenas. The triangular relationship between the Commission, the Council, and the Parliament is one in which the Commission and the Parliament have typically been allies. Increasingly, the Council and the Parliament are participating in direct relations as the co-decision procedure forces the Council to take the Parliament seriously. Given the Parliament's significant budgetary powers, the three institutions are inextricably linked when fashioning budgetary policy.[75]

Policy Implementation

While the Commission is the "motor" of European integration, it is not the implementor of Community legislation. That function falls to the member-states. The Commission's civil service is too small to carry out the duties of monitoring that a national bureaucracy naturally assumes. Furthermore, the Commission does not have all the enforcement powers of a national bureaucracy.

The Commission is largely restricted to the use of legal instruments in its efforts to oversee implementation. In particular, it can bring a member-state government before the European Court of Justice if a directive passed by the Council of Ministers has not been appropriately "transposed" into national law. It can also bring a member-state before the Court if the implementation in actual practice of a Community directive is not being properly pursued. Such an action is difficult, however, as the Commission does not have the power physically to enter a member-state to gather the kind of evidence it would need to persuade the judges of the European Court of Justice. Nongovernmental groups (NGOs) and private citizens do, however, write to the Commission with complaints of infringements of Community law, and the Commission often uses informal pressure on a national government to improve the execution of directives on the ground.

Judicial Review

The European Court of Justice has evolved in a way that the member-states did not expect. Established to ensure that the Commission did not overstep its authority, the Court, however, expanded the scope of Community authority in several ways. Most importantly, it declared that Community law was supreme—that is, superior to member-state law.[76] It also ruled that the Community gained powers in external relations in those areas in which it approved intra-Community legislation, thereby giving the Community a much greater international profile than had been anticipated.

The sweep and direction of the Court's decisions have been so important that the Court has been viewed by some as the "motor" of European integration at times when national governments were reluctant to move integration forward. Although its power is limited by the constraints that affect all courts, it has also gradually obtained the unique legitimacy enjoyed by courts. The process of integration would have proceeded much more slowly, and in some areas might not have proceeded at all, without the Court's activism. Martin Shapiro offers this explanation:

> The European Court of Justice has played a crucial role in shaping the European Community. In a sense, the Court created the present-day Community; it declared the Treaty of Rome to be not just a treaty but a constitutional instrument that obliged individual citizens and national government officials to abide by those provisions that were enforceable through their normal judicial processes.[77]

The Court has been helped in its integrationist project by several factors. The first is that the use of legal reasoning and argument seems apolitical. In that sense, the very language and procedures of the judiciary and the legal profession help "mask" the political consequences of legal decisions.[78] Second, it has been very difficult for the member-states to agree among themselves to pass legislation overriding Court decisions. In fact, the supranational institutions in general benefit from the fact that each one typically has allies on any issue among at least several states. Dissenting states therefore find it difficult to reverse "integrationist" decisions or processes once they are established.[79]

Third, the Court has benefited from the use of national courts (through what is known as the preliminary ruling system) in implementing Community law. Once national judges accepted the legitimacy of the rulings of the European Court of Justice, the maneuverability available to national governments that disagreed with the Court's decisions narrowed considerably. It is difficult for national governments to ignore the decisions of their own national courts so the Court's use of national judges has given the Court powerful allies within the member-states themselves. The Court has been a powerful instrument of integration. Until very recently, it typically promoted further integration through its decisions and has been viewed as a powerful ally of the Commission as well as of the Parliament. In policy terms, it set the stage for the single market with ground-breaking decisions, granted the Commission external power in those areas in which the Community was allowed to legislate internally, decided the boundaries within which environmental protection could act as a nontariff barrier, and promoted gender equality in the workplace.

In general, the Court has "constitutionalized" the treaties that underpin the Community and have evolved into "a vertically integrated legal regime conferring judicially enforceable rights and obligations on all legal persons and entities, public and private, within EC territory."[80] The Court therefore has provided the Community with a legal order in which EC law is supreme to national law, a supremacy accepted by national judges. The Court, in the words of one of its distinguished judges, has sought "to fashion a constitutional framework for a quasi-federal structure in Europe."[81]

External Relations

The powers of the Commission in the field of external relations have been growing. The Treaty of Rome specifically identified the Commission as representing the Community in organizations such as the Organization for Economic Cooperation and Development (OECD) and the United Nations Economic Commission for Europe (UNECE): the Commission was thus granted an external role very early. Furthermore, the fact that the Commission was the sole negotiator for the Community in the various rounds of the General Agreement on Tariffs and Trade (GATT) enhanced the Community's presence in the field of international economic relations. It, along with the member-states, became a contracting party to the World Trade Organization.

The EU (whether represented by the Commission or the Commission and the Presidency of the Council of Ministers) has had to struggle, however, to be granted recognition in the United Nations. While it has the status of an observer, it has to negotiate very hard to be treated as an equal negotiating partner in, for example, international environmental negotiations. In the case of global agreements (such as the Montreal Protocol limiting CFCs), for example, the Commission bargained hard and long to be recognized as a signatory.[82] Generally, outside of the trade area (trade in goods specifically), the member-states regard treaties as "mixed" agreements in which the Commission signs on behalf of the Community and the member-states sign as well.

Entanglement of the "National" and the "European"

The coexistence of "intergovernmental" and "supranational" elements within the Community makes the Community clearly distinct from any of the nation-states that belong to the Community. The institutions can be thought of as being in a delicate balance. Some (the Council of Ministers) are intended to ensure that the views of national governments are respected and that integration does not proceed further than that permitted by the "permissive consensus" within which national governments have operated. The functions of other institutions (the Commission, the European Court of Justice, and the Parliament) are to push the goal of integration, to set the agenda, raise issues, and keep the pressure on to further integrate. These institutions might be thought of as testing the boundaries of the "permissive consensus." They project a broad strategic "European" perspective that does not match the views of any of the national governments per se but can be argued to represent the interest of the collectivity rather than that of any specific member government. They are the "supranational" component of the Community. Proponents of a more "federal" Europe see the Court, the Parliament, and the Commission as the institutions that should be given more power, while the proponents of an "intergovernmental" Europe wish to increase the power of the Council of Ministers and the European Council.

Because political parties have much less power than they do at the national level and because the key institutions are not directly elected, the Community's institutions *qua* institutions are more important than at the national level. The Union is above all its institutions, for there is not a European Union political culture, media, party system, electoral system, welfare state, or society. National diversity in all those areas is so great that the Union is identified more by its institutions than by those societal and cultural factors so important in shaping national polities.[83] In brief, there is no European Union "public" or "culture" as such.

Given the delicate balance between institutions and the still evolving nature of the European Union, it is not surprising that much of the "politics" observed in Brussels involves the various institutions jockeying for institutional power. The Council of Ministers, the Commission, and the Parliament are constantly engaged in trying to maximize their institutional reach and influence as they collectively struggle to construct a consensus on proposed legislation. The Commission tries to protect itself from encroachments from both the Parliament and the Council of Ministers, and the Council and the Parliament eye each other warily. Rather than being based on some kind of balance of power between the executive and the legislative branches as in the United States, the Community's political system is based on a balance between the representation of national interests and of "European" interests. That is, the (national) governmental interest and the supranational interest coexist but are in constant tension. In that sense, the Community is more recognizable to students of federal systems than of unitary systems, for in federal systems the states and the federal government are typically struggling to maximize their own power.

In a parallel vein, those institutions representing national governments are "Europeanized" so that national governments when operating within them are enmeshed in a decision-making machinery that is significantly different from that of a traditional international organization and from decision making at the national level. A national government operating within the Council of Ministers is a "co-decision maker," rather than a "decision maker," as it is when operating unilaterally at the national level.[84]

The member governments of the Community collectively work together so that each individual national government has submitted to the "European" collectivity in the foregoing of unilateral decision making. A national government operates within the boundaries of the Community's institutional structure in a qualitatively different manner from the way it operates unilaterally in other international forums or at home. In brief, France in the European Union acts differently from France in the rest of the world, as does Paris acting as the sole decision maker in French national politics.

The *supranational* and the *intergovernmental* institutions are both integral to the project of European integration. The Council of Ministers, the main intergovernmental body, is there to bring the member-states to a collective view in contrast to the unilateral national decision making that would take place if the European Union did not exist. National government acting within the Council of Ministers is not acting unilaterally. The Union's institutions, whether representing national governments or the "European" interest, all implicitly reject the exercise of unilateral national power.

It is that rejection of unilateral national power across a broad range of issues that makes the European Union so distinctive when viewed from the outside. Even when the member-states decide to cooperate within the Council of Ministers, downgrade the Commission's role, and exclude the European Court of Justice, the degree of integration that they accept is far greater than that found in other parts of the world. Even when an arrangement is considered to be "intergovernmental" by Europeans, it would be considered far too integrationist for a country such as the United States to accept. The debate between the "intergovernmental" states (such as the United Kingdom and Denmark) and the "federalist" states (such as the Benelux states, Germany, and Italy) takes place within a context in which the rejection of the exercise of unilateral national decision making is much more commonly accepted than it is anywhere else in the world. In brief, an "intergovernmental" posture within the European Union would typically be considered as radically "integrationist" or "federalist" in Asia, North America, or Latin America.[85]

Policy Performance

National governments provide social services; the European Union makes laws, but it does not engage, with a few exceptions (in the field of agriculture and regional policy) in activities that involve large public expenditure. The Union's comparatively small budget keeps it from engaging in the kinds of activities traditionally the province of national governments.

The Union does engage in regulation, for the costs of regulation are borne by the objects of regulation rather than the regulators.[86] Two examples are illustrative of the importance of regulation. The first has to do with the single-market program and with the removal of national regulations, the second with environmental protection and with the imposition of Community regulations, in many cases where none existed in most national systems.

The Single-Market Program

As already mentioned, the Single European Act allowed the member-states to create a true single market. The single-market program involved the removal of nontariff barriers from the Community's economy. That is, regulatory barriers which protected national markets from competition as well as from goods and services produced in other EU countries have been largely dismantled. The 1992 Project as it was known (the goal was to approve nearly 300 pieces of single-market legislation in Brussels by 1992, a goal largely achieved) was the foundation stone of the more integrated European economy with which Europe entered the twenty-first century. Its effects in both the economic and the political spheres were huge. Once firms no longer benefited from protected national markets, they realized they had to become global rather than simply European players to survive the competition from American firms which were attracted to the single market, invested huge sums in building production facilities in Europe, and bought promising European firms. European firms therefore entered the American market in a sustained fashion, set up production facilities in the United States, and bought promising American firms. Interestingly, the relationship became quite symmetrical—the number of Americans working for European firms roughly equaled the number of Europeans working for American firms.[87]

Although there are still a few areas in which agreement has not been reached, the Community's legislative program for the single market is largely finished. Whereas in 1980, a citizen from one EU country was stopped when crossing the border into another EU state, by 2001 the frontiers within the EU were usually crossed without any interruption. Capital can now move freely without capital controls being imposed by national government. Firms based in one country have been able to acquire firms in other member-states, and banks have been able to set up offices outside their home country. Airlines have begun competing with one another. The telecommunications sector is now open to fierce competition whereas previously it had been a monopoly run by the state. As a result of the competitive forces unleashed by the single market, nationalized industries have increasingly been privatized throughout the member-states so that the European economy has been transformed. The single-market program was such a pivotal program for the process of European integration that the proponents of the single currency argued that a single market required a single currency—"one market, one currency."

Environmental Protection

The EU has been involved in environmental protection since 1973. After the Single European Act of 1987, it became increasingly aggressive in establishing EU legislation in nearly every issue area. Most of those areas involve the regulation of economic activity resulting in pollution, but major legislation in habitat and species protection has also been adopted by Brussels.

In fact, so much environmental legislation has been adopted since 1973 that a reaction has set in. Although the various treaties have each given the EU institutions more power in this area, the political salience of environmental protection declined in the 1990s. German unification was so difficult for Germany's economy that Germany no longer consistently plays the "leader" role which it did in the 1980s (when it supported stringent legislation) while the high levels of unemployment found in many EU member-states during the 1990s also made environmental protection seem too costly for many of its former supporters. The gap between the former "leader" countries (Germany, Netherlands, and Denmark) and the "laggards" closed during the 1990s as Gemany became less supportive of stringent environmental regulations and other countries became more accepting of the necessity for environmental protection.

In spite of the change in Germany's stance, Brussels did adopt several major pieces of legislation. In those instances, the major argument concerned the instruments which should be used to achieve environmental protection. Should the traditional legalistic "command and control" approach, supported by Germany, be the dominant approach? Or should new policy instruments, such as allowing environmental groups access to environmental information, be used? Whereas the British government, traditionally a "laggard" in the area of most environmental protection policies, became the champion of the new policy instruments (which it had adopted in its own national legislation), Germany supported the more traditional use of detailed and legally enforceable regulations.

During the 1990s, the EU became a leader in global environmental negotiations, especially in the area of climate change. It was a key actor in the negotiations, which led to the Kyoto Protocol (which was agreed in December 1997), and in November 2000 during a follow-up meeting, the EU forcefully challenged the American position concerning the most appropriate instruments for cutting greenhouse emissions.[88] The EU is now a major presence in global environmental politics whereas previously it had been a major actor only in the politics of global trade through its key role in the GATT (now the World Trade Organization).[89]

Does the European Union Make a Difference?

The European Union now affects a great many people, some of them more directly than others. It makes the most difference for the farmer whose prices and subsidies are largely dependent on the decisions made by the Council of Agricultural Ministers and the Commission; fishermen whose catches and allotments are significantly influenced by Brussels; business people affected by the provisions of the single market (especially the mobility of capital and the liberalization of numerous once-protected markets), the move to the Euro, the robust antitrust policy implemented by the Commission (and coordinated with the antitrust policy of the United States in relevant cases), and the Union's environmental policy; bankers and investors who are affected by the policies of the European Central Bank and the move to a common currency; environmentalists who want to increase environmental protection; consumers worried about the safety of the food they eat; soccer players who now enjoy "free agency" because of the EU; women seeking equal pay for equal work; airline passengers benefiting from airline deregulation; retirees who decide to live in another member-state; regional government officials who receive funds from Brussels to help their region develop roads and jobs; patients benefiting from more rapid approval of new medicinal drugs now that they fall under the jurisdiction of the EU, and telephone users who have benefited enormously in terms of both price and level of service from the deregulation of the telecommunications sector pushed through by the Commission. In 2002, everyone living in the member-states which have accepted the Euro will need to become accustomed to paying their bills by using a new currency and relinquishing their old familiar national currency.

By contrast, in areas such as the provision of health care, education, urban policies, social security, and unemployment compensation, national governments have retained the right to unilaterally make policy. These policy areas are only indirectly affected by the European Union. The "welfare state" is largely still under the unilateral control of national policymakers (although its financing is affected by the policies of the European Central Bank). It is in those areas that are related to economic activity and social regulation (consumer and environmental protection for example) rather than social services that the European Union is particularly relevant. Thus the European Union does not legislate as to the health benefits that any citizen of any member-state is entitled to enjoy. However, the fact that the doctor chosen by a patient may be of a different nationality from the patient will be because of EU regulations allowing medical degrees to be recognized across borders. The drugs that the doctor prescribes will have come under EU regulations if they are new to the market, and the competition among firms selling that drug will also have been shaped by EU rules.

Countries outside of the EU are also particularly aware of the European Union. The United States must bargain with the Union in important global forums such as the World Trade Organization, poor developing world countries are given preferential access to EU markets as institutionalized in the Cotonou Agreement, and countries such as Turkey and Israel and in Central and Eastern Europe have negotiated special trade agreements with the Union.[90] Although at this point in time the EU may exercise "civilian" rather than "military" power, its economic reach and power make it an important international actor.

From the beginning, the external economic role that "Europe" would be able to play if organized into a relatively integrated unit has been an important consideration for European policymakers. In the field of agriculture, for example, the Common Agricultural Policy allowed the Community to ward off strong American pressure to open up the European agricultural market.[91] This external role was particularly important given that the states initially involved in European integration were not "self-confident" states; their capacities were not in any way similar to those enjoyed by the United States, a superpower with enormous resources and global power.[92] European integration allowed these states to have much greater influence in the international environment than they would have had if exercising traditional sovereignty. Public opinion attitudes among mass electorates, in fact, show high

---

Box 11.4 Candidate Countries for Membership in the European Union as of 2000

Countries seeking to enter the EU must first be officially accepted as candidate countries by the current 15 member-states. The second stage in the process of accession involves entering into complex negotiations during which the candidate countries must demonstrate that they satisfy criteria laid down by the EU. Once negotiations are completed both the European Parliament and all 15 national parliaments must approve the accession of the candidate countries.

Negotiations Began 1998
    Czech Republic
    Estonia
    Hungary
    Poland
    Slovenia
    Cyprus

Negotiations Began 2000
    Bulgaria
    Latvia
    Lithuania
    Romania
    Slovakia
    Malta

No Ongoing Negotiations
    Turkey

---

degrees of support for Union activity regarding the international environment in all policy arenas, not simply those having to do with economics. "European elites may emphasize the difficulties of coordinating foreign and defense policies among the European states, but European publics see this as a natural area of joint action."[93] In fact, as we shall see later, the leaders of the EU member-states have begun to follow the lead of public opinion in that they have begun to cooperate more extensively in the field of foreign and security policy. However, they are in the position of trying to lead public opinion when it comes to the issue of enlarging the Union so as to include the countries recently referred to as "Eastern" Europe, a term based on the divisions of the Cold War.

Policy Challenges

The European Union faces three key challenges in the years ahead—all extremely difficult. How to incorporate the former communist states of Eastern and Central Europe without undermining the process of integration is one. The second involves developing a European identity in the field of for-

eign and security policy while maintaining Europe's important transatlantic ties. The third requires creating a balance between integration and the protection of cultural diversity so that ordinary citizens of very diverse member-states do not feel they are being culturally "homogenized" and blame European integration for that threat to their identity.

The Challenge of Enlargement

How can the European Union incorporate the Central and Eastern European countries that began asking for a "return to Europe" as soon as the Berlin Wall fell in November 1989? At the end of 2000, 13 countries had been accepted as candidates for admission, with 10 of them belonging to the post-communist group (see Box 11.4). The leaders of these 10, however, were expressing impatience with the slowness of negotiations and the fact that while they had hoped to be members by 2000, the conventional wisdom in 2000 was that enlargement might well not take place until 2004.

Why is it so difficult for the European Union to accept these 10 countries as members? Economics, politics, and public opinion is the short answer.

The new entrants from the East are primarily small states with large agricultural populations and will all be net gainers under present distributive policies within the Union. Funds which have heretofore helped the poorer member-states—Spain, Portugal, Ireland, and Greece—will either need to be expanded, eliminated, or redirected toward the new entrants and away from the traditional recipients. In 1999, for example, even Slovenia, the wealthiest of the ten, had a per capita GDP which was only 70 percent of the EU average; the Czech Republic and Hungary had 57 percent and 50 percent respectively. Bulgaria, the poorest, had a per capita GDP which was only 24 percent of the EU's GDP per capita. At 1999 levels of wealth, the EU after the accession of the ten would have a total population which would be a third larger but an economy (Gross Domestic Product) that would be less than 10 percent larger.

Perhaps the key question, however, has to do with how to restructure the policymaking institutions of the European Union. Should each member-state be allowed one Commissioner or should there be a rotation of countries with a Commissioner? If the latter option is chosen, would the Commission have the legitimacy required to offend the big member-states? How should votes in the Council of Ministers be allocated? Small countries are by far the majority of the ten states, with only Poland (with a population of 39 million) and Romania (with 22.5 million) having a population of more than 10 million. At present, 71 percent of the votes (62 votes out of 87) are needed to approve legislation which requires only qualified majority voting; 26 votes are needed to block legislation. Enlargement would change the dynamics of coalitions within the Council, especially if the use of qualified majority voting expands so as to avoid decision-making paralysis. The big member-states do not want the disproportionate power of small countries to be reinforced, but the current small member-states are determined to protect their role in current decision-making process. In December 2000, some of these issues were addressed in the negotiations for the Treaty of Nice, which incorporated very difficult compromises.

Finally, the process of enlargement faces the problem that while political and economic elites accept its necessity, the general public does not. In mid-2000, only 26 percent of the French public favored enlargement while 34 percent were in favor in Germany and 41 percent in Italy. Only 38 percent of the EU public taken as a whole favored allowing the 13 applicants to join the Union.[94] Public fears center around the possibility of immigration from the newly admitted countries, with consequent negative impacts on local job markets. The fact that several of the candidate countries share long land frontiers with Russia, Belarus, and Ukraine helps reinforce fears that illegal immigrants from those countries will make their way into the newly admitted countries, Poland especially, and then move into the current member-states. Political elites face an important challenge in mobilizing public opinion in favor of an enlarged European Union, but they do not need to worry about referenda as previous enlargements have not required a referendum in any member-state.

The Central and Eastern European countries view admission to the Union as a necessary component of their road toward democratization, a market economy, and a "return to Europe" (that Europe of which they were a part before the Cold War). From the point of view of the member-states of the European Union, admitting the countries of Central and Eastern Europe involves a whole series of decisions with profound implications for the future governance of the Union. Whereas Germany favors enlargement and thinks that such a process will necessarily lead to more majority voting and greater powers for the European Parliament, that federalist perspective is countered by the United Kingdom, which also favors enlargement but thinks it will lead toward a more "intergovernmental" Community with fewer inroads on national sovereignty. For the poor countries—Greece, Spain, Portugal, and Ireland—the Eastern applicants are potential competitors for funds that have been invaluable in accelerating the economic modernization of these four countries.[95]

As the Union faces eastward, therefore, it has to answer questions about where its final external frontier will be. Will it be the eastern border of Poland? Or beyond? It has to answer questions about whether it will become more integrated or less integrated, as the current stage of integration is likely to lead to paralysis if extended to a Union with many more countries. It will have to consider whether it must become more integrated in the area of foreign and security policy. Or does the fact that NATO has enlarged to admit some Central European countries imply that those countries, once admitted to the EU, will be less likely to favor the further development of a European (rather than transatlantic) defense identity even if the present EU members would desire it?

As Europe enters the next century, it is striking that an organization rooted in the geopolitics of the past is the arbiter of "the challenge of continental order."[96] The European Union has succeeded to such an extent that it now has the responsibility of drawing the political and economic map of Europe. Yet the average man in the street is not certain that he wants to accept that responsibility.

European Security and Defense Policy

The collapse of the Soviet Union has led both to the pressure for enlargement and the Balkan crises which galvanized the member-states to develop a European rather than solely a transatlantic identity in the field of defense. The desire to develop a Common Foreign and Security Policy (CFSP) was evident in the Maastricht Treaty. The European role in the various Balkan crises, including the bombing campaign of Serbia, was viewed by many political leaders as inadequate, and the Treaty of Amsterdam strengthened the commitment of the member-states to CFSP. However, CFSP became a fast moving area of Union policy after the December 1998 St. Malo declaration issued after a British-French Summit in Saint-Malo, France. Essentially, the UK, a key player in European defense, agreed to cooperate with European efforts to develop a European capability in security and defense policy while the French agreed that such efforts should not weaken NATO. A common defense policy would be developed within the framework of the CFSP through summit meetings among the fifteen (the European Council), meetings of the fifteen's foreign ministers (General Af-

fairs Council) and meetings of defense ministers. For the first time, defense ministers, who previously had operated solely within NATO, would be brought under the EU's umbrella.

Once the British-French bargain had been struck—the UK willing to become more European in its defense policy in return for the French accepting NATO's crucial role in Europe's collective defense—movement came quickly. The Helsinki European Council in December 1999 agreed to develop by 2003 a collective European capability to deploy a rapid-reaction force of 60,000 troops for crisis management operations. These troops would be capable of being deployed at 60 days' notice and remain operational for one year. They would intervene in humanitarian and rescue tasks as well as in peace-keeping and crisis management. In March 2000 an Interim Political and Security Committee began to meet weekly to develop the organizational structures necessary for crisis management, and a military staff has been established to provide the Council of Ministers with military expertise. In November 2000 each member-state specified the assets that it will contribute to the rapid-reaction force. National sensitivities in this area are very tender. The British Defence Minister, in advance of the November meeting, sought to reassure skeptics by pointing out that the British contingent (10-20,000 men) in the rapid-reaction force will not be placed under the EU flag nor will they even wear EU cap badges.

Since the goal of the European Security and Defence Policy (ESDP), the rubric which refers to the security and defense components of the CFSP, is not to create a European army, EU-NATO relations are critical. Yet these two organizations have had no relationship with each other throughout the entire post war period (see Box 11.5). Although France initially wanted to keep NATO at arm's length from the ESDP, it reversed its position in April 2000 and at the Feira European Council Summit in June 2000 agreed to the establishment of four ad-hoc EU/NATO working groups. In September 2000, for the first time, the Interim Political and Security Committee and NATO's Permanent Council met—the first formal high-level contact between the EU and NATO. The two organizations which have been central to postwar European affairs finally met.

Box 11.5 European Integration and Transatlantic Security Meet At Last

Since 1949 responsibility for European defense policy has been in the hands of individual governments and the North Atlantic Treaty Organization, an intergovernmental body involving (and relying heavily upon) the United States. In 1999 the member-states of the European Union finally agreed to take important steps in the direction of more integrated defense and security policies, but cooperating with NATO, rather than replacing it.

	EU	Nato
Membership:	European Member-States Only	Transatlantic Membership (Most EU States, Norway, Turkey, U.S., and Canada)
Main Objective:	Political & Economic Integration	Collective Defense
Key Officials:	Foreign Ministers and, after 1999, Defense Ministers and the High Representative for Common Foreign and Security Policy	Foreign and Defense Ministers
Headquarters:	Headquartered in Brussels	Headquartered in Brussels
Type of Organization:	Supranational Organization	Intergovernmental Organization
Role of U.S.:	U.S. does not have a "seat at the table"	U.S. has the most important "seat at the table"
EU-NATO Relationship:	No relationship with NATO until 2000	No relationship with EU until 2000

Cultural Diversity

As of 2001, the European Union was composed of 15 member-states, including most of Scandinavia and key Mediterranean countries. The Union's gross national product and population were larger than that of the United States, and today it is the largest market in the industrialized world. As the Union has expanded, what has become more striking is its cultural diversity. As the economies of the fifteen have become more intertwined and as more policy areas have become included in an integrated Europe's policy portfolio, questions of national identity have become more salient. Diverse European cultures have emerged out of many centuries of disparate historical experiences, and the current economic convergence is proceeding far more quickly than is any type of cultural (or linguistic) convergence. Although the EU is firmly committed to protecting cultural diversity, the tension between culture, economics, policy, and identity is becoming more pronounced now that the European Union includes nearly all of Western Europe while facing enlargement to the East. How far will the average person accept being made into a "European" in political and economic terms without feeling that his or her identity is being fundamentally threatened? That question has not yet been answered.

KEY TERMS

Council of Ministers
    (Council of the
    European Union)
Committee of
    Permanent
    Representatives
    (COREPER)
Economic and
    Monetary Union
    (EMU)
European Central Bank
European Commission

European Council
European Court of
    Justice
European Economic
    Community (EEC)
European Free Trade
    Association (EFTA)
European Parliament
European Union (EU)
Intergovernmental
Justice and Home
    Affairs (JHA)

Maastricht Treaty
    (Treaty of
    European Union)
Marshall Plan
Members of the
    European
    Parliament (MEPs)
North Atlantic Treaty
    Organization
    (NATO)
Presidency of the
    European Council

and the Council of
    Ministers
President of the
    Commission
Schuman Plan
single currency (Euro)
Single European Act
    (SEA)
supranational
Treaty of Amsterdam
Treaty of Rome
1992 Project

SUGGESTED READINGS

Corbett, Richard, Francis Jacobs, and Michael Shackleton. *The European Parliament*, 4th ed. London: John Harper, 2000.

Cowles, Maria, Thomas Risse, and James Caporaso, eds. *Transforming Europe*. Cornell University Press, 2001.

Dinan, Desmond. *Ever Closer Union? An Introduction to the European Community*, 2nd ed. Boulder, CO: Lynne Rienner, 1999.

Dinan, Desmond, ed. *Encyclopedia of the European Union*. Boulder, CO: Lynne Rienner, 1998.

Hayes-Renshaw, Fiona, and Helen Wallace. *The Council of Ministers*. London: Macmillan, 1997.

Keohane, Robert O., and Stanley Hoffmann, eds. *The New European Community: Decisionmaking and Institutional Change*. Boulder, CO: Westview, 1991.

McCormick, John. *European Union: Politics and Policies*, 2nd ed. Boulder, CO: Westview Press, 1999, p. 207.

Moravcsik, Andrew. The Choice for Europe: Social Purpose & State Power from Messina to Maastricht. Ithaca, NY: Cornell University Press, 1998.

Ross, George. *Jacques Delors and European Integration*. Oxford, England: Oxford University Press, 1995.

Sbragia, Alberta M. *Euro-Politics: Institutions and Policy-Making in the "New" European Community*. Washington: Brookings Institution, 1992.

Wallace, Helen, and William Wallace, eds. *Policy-Making in the European Union*, 4th ed. Oxford, England: Oxford University Press, 2000.

Winand, Pascaline. *Eisenhower, Kennedy, and the United States of Europe*. New York: St. Martin's, 1993.

ENDNOTES

1. Giandomenico Majone, "The Rise of Statutory Regulation in Europe," in Giandomenico Majone, ed., *Regulating Europe* (New York: Routledge, 1996), p. 57.
2. Beate Kohler-Koch, "Catching Up with Change: The Transformation of Governance in the European Union," *Journal of European Public Policy* 3, No. 3 (September 1996): 359–80.
3. Jack Hayward, "Populist Challenge to Elitist Democracy in Europe," in Jack Hayward, ed., *Elitism, Populism, and European Politics* (Oxford, England: Clarendon, 1996), p. 29.
4. Wolfgang Wessels, "The EC Council: The Community's Decisionmaking Center," *The New European Community: Decisionmaking and Institutional Change*, Robert O. Keohane and Stanley Hoffman, eds. (Boulder, CO: Westview, 1991), p. 136.

5. Many scholars have debated whether national governments are the only real decision makers in the Union, with the Community institutions which do not represent state interests being in fact agents of the national governments, or whether national governments share their decisionmaking power with those other "non-state-centric" institutions. For example, see Andrew Moravcsik, *The Choice for Europe* (Ithaca, NY: Cornell University Press, 1998); Gary Marks, Liesbet Hooghe, and Kermit Blank, "European Integration from the 1980s: State-Centric v. Multi-Level Governance," *Journal of Common Market Studies* 34, No. 3 (September 1996): 341–78; James A. Caporaso and John T. S. Keeler, "The European Union and Regional Integration Theory," in Carolyn Rhodes and Sonia Mazey, ed., *Building*

a European Polity? (Boulder, CO: Lynne Rienner, 1995), pp. 29–62.

6. Alberta M. Sbragia, "Introduction," in Alberta M. Sbragia, ed., *Euro-Politics: Institutions and Policymaking in the "New" European Community* (Washington: Brookings Institution, 1992), pp. 1–22.

7. Cited in Edmund Dell, *The Schuman Plan and the British Abdication of Leadership in Europe* (New York: Oxford University Press, 1995), p. 22.

8. John Gillingham, *Coal, Steel, and the Rebirth of Europe, 1945–1955: The Germans and French from Ruhr Conflict to Economic Community* (Cambridge, England: Cambridge University Press, 1991), p. xi.

9. George Ross, *Jacques Delors and European Integration* (New York: Oxford University Press, 1995), p. 1.

10. F. Roy Willis, "Schuman Breaks the Deadlock," in F. Roy Willis, ed., *European Integration* (New York: New Viewpoints, 1975), p. 27.

11. For a sophisticated study of Kurt Schumacher and his attitude toward France and European integration, see Lewis J. Edinger, *Kurt Schumacher: A Study in Personality and Political Behavior* (Stanford, CA: Stanford University Press, 1965), pp. 144–89.

12. Albert Kersten, "A Welcome Surprise? The Netherlands and the Schuman Plan Negotiations," in Klaus Schwabe, ed., *Die Anfange des Schuman-Plans 1950/51; The Beginnings of the Schuman Plan*, Contributions to the Symposium in Aachen, May 28–30, 1986 (Baden-Baden, Germany: Nomosverlag, 1988), p. 287.

13. See F. Roy Willis, *Italy Chooses Europe* (New York: Oxford University Press, 1971), pp. 1–52.

14. Dell, *The Schuman Plan and the British Abdication of Leadership in Europe*, p. 4.

15. Stephen D. Krasner, "United States Commercial and Monetary Policy: Unraveling the Paradox of External Strength and Internal Weakness," in Peter Katzenstein, ed., *Between Power and Plenty: Foreign Economic Policies of Advanced Industrial States* (Madison: University of Wisconsin Press, 1978), p. 52.

16. Derek W. Urwin, *The Community of Europe: A History of European Integration since 1945*, 2nd ed. (New York: Longman, 1995), p. 21.

17. Pascaline Winand, *Eisenhower, Kennedy, and the United States of Europe* (New York: St. Martin's, 1993).

18. Miles Kahler, "The Survival of the State in European International Relations," in Charles Maier, ed., *Changing Boundaries of the Political* (Cambridge, England: Cambridge University Press, 1987), p. 289.

19. William Wallace, *Regional Integration: The West European Experience* (Washington: Brookings Institution, 1994), p. 11. See also David Armstrong, Lorna Lloyd, and John Redmond, *From Versailles to Maastricht: International Organization in the Twentieth Century* (New York: St. Martin's, 1996), p. 148.

20. Peter Ludlow, "The European Commission," in Keohane and Hoffman, eds., *The New European Community*, p. 111.

21. I have drawn heavily from Winand, *Eisenhower, Kennedy, and the United States of Europe*, pp. 24–73.

22. Cited in Desmond Dinan, *Ever Closer Union? An Introduction to the European Community* (Boulder, CO: Lynne Rienner, 1994), p. 34.

23. David Armstrong, Lorna Lloyd, and John Redmond, *From Versailles to Maastricht: International Organization in the Twentieth Century* (New York: St. Martin's, 1996), p. 159.

24. Wolfgang Wessels, "Institutions of the EU System: Models of Explanation," in Dietrich Rometsch and Wolfgang Wessels, eds., *The European Union and Member States: Towards Institutional Fusion?* (New York: Manchester University Press, 1996), pp. 20–36.

25. Graham T. Allison and Kalypso Nicolaidis, eds., *The Greek Paradox: Promise vs. Performance* (Cambridge, MA: MIT Press, 1997).

26. Cited in Charles Grant, *Delors: Inside the House that Jacques Built* (London: Nicholas Brealey, 1994), p. 70.

27. David Allen, "Competition Policy: Policing the Single Market," in Helen Wallace and William Wallace, eds., *Policy-Making in the European Union*, 3rd ed. (Oxford, England: Oxford University Press, 1996), pp. 157–84.

28. Giandomenico Majone, "The Rise of the Regulatory State in Europe," *West European Politics* 17, No. 3 (July 1994): 77–101; see also Majone, *Regulating Europe*.

29. Damian Chalmers and Erika Szysczak, *European Union Law: Towards a European Polity?* Volume II, Brookfield, VT: Ashgate, 1998, 146-47.

30. Wallace, *Regional Integration: The West European Experience*, p. 34.

31. Neill Nugent, ed., *At the Heart of the Union: Studies of the European Commission*, 2nd ed. (New York: St. Martin's Press, 2000); Alberta Sbragia, "The European Union as Coxswain: Governance by Steering," *Debating Governance: Authority,, Steering, and Democracy*, Jon Pierre, ed. (Oxford: Oxford University Press, 2000), pp. 219–40.

32. David Judge and David Earnshaw, "The European Parliament and the Commission Crisis: A New Assertiveness?" *Governance*, forthcoming.

33. Dinan, *Ever Closer Union*, pp. 247–49; Hayes-Renshaw and Wallace, *The Council of Ministers*, pp. 7, 29–32.

34. Alberta Sbragia, "The Community: A Balancing Act," *Publius* 23 (Summer 1993): 23–38; Wolfgang Wessels, "The EC Council: The Community's Decisionmaking Center," in Keohane and Hoffmann, eds., *The New European Community* (Boulder, CO: Westview, 1991), pp. 133–54.

35. Hayes-Renshaw and Wallace, *The Council of Ministers*, p. 18.

36. Hayes-Renshaw and Wallace, *The Council of Ministers*, p. 163.

37. Richard Corbett, Francis Jacobs, and Michael Shackleton, *The European Parliament*, 4th ed. (London: John Harper, 2000), pp. 49–54.

38. Rory Watson, "MEPs win 81% of tussles over new EU laws," *European Voice*, 19–25 (October 2000): p. 5.

39. Richard Corbett, Francis Jacobs, and Michael Shackleton, *The European Parliament*, 4th ed. (London: John Harper, 2000), p. 226.

40. Rory Watson, "MEPs win 81% of tussles over new EU laws," *European Voice*, 19–25 October 2000), p. 5; Michael

Shackleton, "The Politics of Codecision," *Journal of Common Market Studies* 38 (June 2000): 327.

41. Karen J. Alter, "The European Court's Political Power," *West European Politics* 19, No. 3 (July 1996): 458.

42. Beate Kohler-Koch, "Germany: Fragmented but Strong Lobbying," in M.P.C.M. van Schendelen, ed., *National Public and Private EC Lobbying* (Brookfield, England: Dartmouth, 1993), p. 32.

43. Denmark is an exception: the People's Movement against the European Community competes in European parliamentary elections—but not in domestic elections—on an anti-integration platform. Vernon Bogdanor, "The European Union, the Political Class, and the People," in Jack Hayward, ed., *Elitism, Populism, and European Politics* (Oxford, England: Clarendon, 1996), p. 110.

44. Simon Hix, "Parties at the European Level and the Legitimacy of EU Socio-Economic Policy," *Journal of Common Market Studies* 33, No. 4 (December 1995): 534.

45. John Gaffney, "Introduction: Political Parties and the European Union," in John Gaffney, ed., *Political Parties and the European Union* (London: Routledge, 1996), p. 13.

46. Mark Franklin and Cees van der Eijk, "The Problem: Representation and Democracy in the European Union," in Cees van der Eijk and Mark N. Franklin, eds., *Choosing Europe? The European Electorate and National Politics in the Face of Union* (Ann Arbor: University of Michigan Press, 1996), p. 8.

47. Simon Hix, "Parties at the European Level and the Legitimacy of EU Socio-Economic Policy," *Journal of Common Market Studies* 33, No. 4 (December 1995): 545; Robert Ladrech, "Partisanship and Party Formation in European Union Politics," *Comparative Politics* (January 1997): 176.

48. For an analysis of how the Community's policies indirectly affect various aspects of welfare state provision, see Stephen Leibried and Paul Pierson, eds., *European Social Policy: Between Fragmentation and Integration* (Washington: Brookings Institution, 1995).

49. Mark Franklin, "European Elections and the European Voter," in Jeremy J. Richardson, ed., *European Union: Power and Policymaking* (London: Routledge, 1996), p. 187.

50. Michael Marsh and Mark Franklin, "The Foundations: Unanswered Questions from the Study of European Elections, 1979–1994," in Cees van der Eijk and Mark N. Franklin, ed., *Choosing Europe? The European Electorate and National Politics in the Face of Union* (Ann Arbor: University of Michigan Press, 1996), p. 11.

51. Cees van der Eijk and Mark Franklin, "The Research: Studying the Elections of 1989 and 1994," in van der Eijk and Franklin, *Choosing Europe*, p. 42.

52. Mark Franklin and Cees van der Eijk, "The Problem: Representation and Democracy in the European Union," in van der Eijk and Franklin, *Choosing Europe*, p. 5.

53. For a good description of the differences between the British House of Commons and the European Parliament, see Bogdanor, "Britain," pp. 211–15.

54. Gareth Harding, "Winds of change blow through Parliament," *European Voice*, 8–14 (June 2000): p. 18; "Breaking new ground in Euro-politics," *European Voice*, 10–17 (November 1999): 22.

55. Sonia Mazey and Jeremy Richardson, "The Logic of Organization," in Jeremy J. Richardson, ed., *European Union: Power and Policy-making* (London: Routledge, 1996), p. 204.

56. Sonia Mazey and Jeremy Richardson, "Promiscuous Policymaking: The European Policy Style?" in Carolyn Rhodes and Sonia Mazey, eds., *Building a European Polity? The State of the European Union*, Vol. 3 (Boulder, CO: Lynne Rienner, 1995), p. 342; Andrew M. McLaughlin and Justin Greenwood, "The Management of Interest Representation in the European Union," *Journal of Common Market Studies* 33, No. 1 (March 1995): 143–56.

57. Mazey and Richardson, "Promiscuous Policymaking," p. 350.

58. For a discussion of a powerful business group, see Maria Green Cowles, "Setting the Agenda for a New Europe: The ERT and EC 1992," *Journal of Common Market Studies* 33 (December 1995): 501–26.

59. For a sophisticated discussion of how bargaining and negotiations proceed within the Council of Ministers, see Hayes-Renshaw and Wallace, *The Council of Ministers*, pp. 244–73.

60. Russell J. Dalton and Richard Eichenberg, "Citizen Support for Policy Integration," in Wayne Sandholtz and Alec Stone Sweet, eds., *European Integration and Supranational Governance* (Oxford: Oxford University Press, 1998), pp. 250–82.

61. Mark Franklin, Cees van der Eijk, and Michael Marsh, "Conclusions: The Electoral Connection and the Democratic Deficit," in van der Eijk and Franklin, *Choosing Europe*, p. 370.

62. Richard C. Eichenberg and Russell J. Dalton, "Europeans and the European Community: The Dynamics of Public Support for European Integration," *International Organization* (Autumn 1993): 507–34; European Commission, *Eurobarometer: Public Opinion in the European Union* 53 (October 2000): 8.

63. European Commission, *Eurobarometer* 43 (Autumn 1995): xi.

64. European Commission, Eurobarometer: Public Opinion in the European Union 53: October 2000, p. 8.

65. European Commission, Eurobarometer: Public Opinion in the European Union. 53: October 2000, p. 46.

66. Oskar Niedermayer, "Trends and Contrasts," in Oskar Niedermayer and Richard Sinnott, eds., *Public Opinion and Internationalized Governance* (Oxford: Oxford University Press, 1995), pp. 59–62; Christopher Anderson, "Economic Uncertainty and European Solidarity Revisited: Trends in Public Support for European Integration," in Rhodes and Mazey, eds., *Building a European Polity*, pp. 111–133.

67. Brigid Laffan and Michael Shackleton, "The Budget: Who Gets What, When, and How" in *Policy-Making in the European Union*, 4th ed. (Oxford, England: Oxford University Press, 2000), pp. 213–14.

68. Elmar Rieger, "The Common Agricultural Policy: Politics Against Markets," in Helen Wallace and William Wallace, eds., *Policy-Making in the European Union*, 4th ed. (Oxford: Oxford University Press, 2000), pp. 202-203.

69. A. Heritier, "The Accommodation of Diversity in European Policy-Making and Its Outcomes: Regulatory Policy as a Patchwork," *Journal of European Public Policy* 3, 2 (1996): 149–67.

70. Dietrich Rometsch and Wolfgang Wessels, "The Commission and the Council of Ministers," in Geoffrey Edwards and David Spence, eds., *The European Commission* (Essex: Longman, 1994), p. 221.

71. He was widely considered a major presidential contender, and in November 1994 the Socialist Party Conference announced that it would support Delors if he decided to run for the French presidency. However, on December 11, 1994, Delors announced that he would not be a candidate after all. Colete Ysmal, "France," *European Journal of Political Research* 28, No. 3, 4, (December 1995): 337.

72. Lionel Barber, "The Men Who Run Europe," *Financial Times*, March 11–12, 1995, sect. 2, p. I.

73. Barber, "The Men Who Run Europe," p. II.

74. Hayes-Renshaw and Wallace, *The Council of Ministers*, p. 76.

75. Martin Westlake, *The Commission and the Parliament: Partners and Rivals in the European Policy-making Process* (London: Butterworths, 1994), p. 10; Brigid Laffan, *The Finances of the European Union* (New York: St. Martin's, 1997).

76. See Joseph Weiler, "The Transformation of Europe," *Yale Law Journal* 100 (1991): 2403–83 and "A Quiet Revolution: the European Court of Justice and Its Interlocutors," *Comparative Political Studies* 26 (1994): Vol. 26, No. 4, January 1994, pp. 510–534; Eric Stein, "Lawyers, Judges and the Making of a Transnational Constitution," *American Journal of International Law* 75/1 (1981); Anne-Marie Slaughter Burley and Walter Mattli, "Europe before the Court: A Political Theory of Legal Integration," *International Organization* 47 (1993): 41–76; Martin Shapiro, "The European Court of Justice," in Sbragia, *Euro-Politics*, pp. 123–56; Alter, "The European Court's Political Power," pp. 458–87.

77. Shapiro, "The European Court of Justice," p. 123.

78. Burley and Mattli, "Europe Before the Court," pp. 72–73.

79. Karen Alter, "Who are the 'Masters of the Treaty'? European Governments and the European Court of Justice," *International Organization* 52, No. 1 (Winter 1998): 121–48; Alec Stone Sweet and Thomas L. Brunell, "Constructing a Supranational Constitution: Dispute Resolution and Governance in the European Community," *American Political Science Review*, 92, No. 1 (March 1998): 63–81.

80. Alec Stone Sweet and Thomas L. Brunell, "Constructing a Supranational Constitution: Dispute Resolution and Governance in the European Community," *American Political Science Review*, 92, No. 1 (March 1998): 63–82.

81. C. Federico Mancini, "The Making of a Constitution for Europe," in Keohand and Hoffmann, *The New European Community*, p. 178.

82. Alberta Sbragia, "Institution-Building from Above and from Below: The European Community in Global Envi-

ronmental Politics," in Wayne Sandholtz and Alec Stone, eds., *European Integration and Supranational Governance.*

83. For instance, even the imported titles on best-seller book lists differ in the various member-states. In a similar vein, even though the inhabitants of Freiburg, Germany, and of Strasbourg, France, are close geographically, they do not buy each other's newspapers. Ralf Dahrendorf, "Mediocre Elites Elected by Mediocre Peoples," in Jack Hayward, ed., *Elitism, Populism, and European Politics* (Oxford, England: Clarendon, 1996), p. 7.

84. Wolfgang Wessels, "The EC Council," p. 136.

85. For example, see Miles Kahler, *Regional Futures and Transatlantic Economic Relations* (New York: Council on Foreign Relations Press, 1995).

86. Majone, *Regulating Europe.*

87. Alberta Sbragia, "The Transatlantic Relationship: A Case of Deepening and Broadening," Carolyn Rhodes, ed., *The European Union in the World Community* (Boulder, CO: Lynne Rienner, 1998), pp. 147–164.

88. Alberta M. Sbragia, "Environmental Policy: Economic Constraints and External Pressures," Wallace and Wallace, *Policy-Making in the European Union*, 4th ed., pp. 293–316; Sbragia with Chad Damro (1999), "The Changing Role of the European Union in International Environmental Politics: Institution Building and the Politics of Climate Change," *Environment and Planning C: Government and Policy* 17 (February): 53–68.

89. Alberta M. Sbragia, "Institution-Building from Below and Above: The European Community in Global Environmental Politics," *European Integration and Supranational Governance*, Wayne Sandholtz and Alec Stone Sweet, eds. (Oxford: Oxford University Press, 1998), pp. 283–303

90. To get a sense of the policy areas in which the Union is most important, see Wallace and Wallace, *Policy-Making in the European Union*, 4th ed; Calingaert, *European Integration Revisited*; Dinan, *Ever Closer Union*, 2nd ed. part III.

91. Elmar Rieger, "The Common Agricultural Policy: External and Internal Dimensions," in Wallace and Wallace, *Policy-Making in the European Union*, 3rd ed. pp. 102–106.

92. William Wallace, "Government Without Statehood: The Unstable Equilibrium," in Wallace and Wallace, *Policy-Making in the European Union*, 3rd ed., p. 453.

93. Dalton and Eichenberg, "Citizen Support for Policy Integration," p. 260.

94. European Commission, *Eurobarometer: Public Opinion in the European Union* 53: October 2000.

95. Anna Michalski and Helen Wallace, *The European Community: The Challenge of Enlargement* (London: Royal Institute of International Affairs, 1992), p. 55.

96. Brigid Laffan, "The Intergovernmental Conference and the Challenge of Governance in the European Union," European Community Studies Association Conference, Brock University, Ontario Canada, May 31–June 2, 1996, p. 29.

APPENDIX

A GUIDE TO COMPARING NATIONS

Topics	Ch. 1–3	England	France	Germany	Spain	Russia	Poland	Hungary	EU
History	3–7	87–90	140–141	199–205	254–257	308–311	357–363	411–418	455–466
Social Conditions	7–11, 14–23	90–94	141–143, 148–151	205–208	257–259	321	359, 365–366	418–421	463–466
Executive	54–59	95–103	177–179	210–212	259–261, 263–266	313–314	370–373	424–425	469–474
Parliament	54–59	103–104	179–184	209–210	261–263	314–316	370–371	422–424	474–475
Judiciary	59	—	146	240	266–268	343–348	373	426–427	467–469
Provincial Government	59–60	90–93	184–187	207–209	268–269	318–320	—	427–433	—
Political Culture	29–42	109–110	146–151	212–217	269–271	320–322	374–375	427–430	482–485
Political Socialization	—	110–113	151–155	217–220	271–273	321	378–381	—	—
Recruitment/ Participation	42–50	113–120	155–162	220–223	—	322–325	381–384	430–432	—
Interest Groups	47–49, 72–74	116–118	162–167	224–227	273–278	325–329	384–388	434–437	481–482
Parties and Elections	60–69	120–125	167–177	227–236	278–287	330–338	389–397	442–448	477–481
Policy Process	70–72	125–133	177–184	236–240	263	315–316	397–399	448–449	485–492
Outputs and Outcomes	11–17	133–134	187–189	240–248	291–300	338–343	399–403	449–450	492–498
International Relations	7	94–95	189–191	247–248	300–301	348	403–404	450–451	491

INDEX